THE BOOK ®

Peugeot & Citroën timing belt renewal manual

Ian Barnes BSc

(3568-304)

D1439022

ABCDE
FGHIJ
KLMNO
PQRST

Printed by **J H Haynes & Co Ltd, Sparkford, Nr Yeovil, Somerset BA22 7JJ, England**

Haynes Publishing
Sparkford, Nr Yeovil, Somerset BA22 7JJ, England

Haynes North America, Inc
861 Lawrence Drive, Newbury Park, California 91320, USA

Editions Haynes S.A.
Tour Aurore - La Défense 2, 18 Place des Reflets,
92975 PARIS LA DEFENSE Cedex, France

Haynes Publishing Nordiska AB
Box 1504, 751 45 UPPSALA, Sweden

© Haynes Publishing 1999

A book in the **Haynes Service and Repair Manual Series**

ISBN 1 85960 568 0

British Library Cataloguing in Publication Data
A catalogue record for this book is available from the British Library.

Contents

Contents

Contents

Contents

Contents

This timing belt renewal manual is aimed at the more experienced mechanic who has some experience of the work involved, and already has most of the specialised tools needed for such work.

Tasks are described and photographed in a clear step-by-step sequence. The illustrations are numbered by the Section number and paragraph number to which they relate - if there is more than one illustration per paragraph, the sequence is denoted alphabetically.

A brief history of timing belts

The timing belt (also known as a camshaft drivebelt) first appeared on mass-produced vehicles in the early 1970s. Traditionally, camshaft drive had been via gears or by sprockets and chains, both of which were adequate for a block-mounted camshaft and pushrod valvegear. The development of overhead camshaft designs, however, implied long chain runs with problems of noise, lubrication, wear and tensioning. By comparison the toothed belt offered the advantages of relatively silent running and much reduced cost and complexity of manufacture and assembly. With a couple of notable exceptions, most manufacturers adopted belt drive with enthusiasm.

At first the timing belt was thought to be everlasting, or at least as long-lived as any other engine component. (To put this optimism in perspective, remember that vehicle manufacturers were still experimenting with novelties such as timing gears made of reinforced cardboard, or timing chain tensioners which caused a catastrophic loss of oil pressure when the chain stretched beyond a certain point. Many drivers accepted the idea that engine rebuilds and overhauls were an inevitable part of the motoring year.) Reality soon intruded, however, and regular inspection became part of the service schedules, followed by regular renewal as mechanics' X-ray vision proved unable to detect incipient belt failure.

Timing belt failure in service would have been no more than an irritant had it not been for other developments in engine design. Higher compression ratios and larger valves meant that in many cases a piston passing TDC would collide with the head of an open valve when the timing belt broke. The resulting damage could range from no more than a bent valve stem and a souvenir scar on the piston crown, to an engine which was effectively a write-off. Most modern engines will suffer serious damage if the timing belt breaks or slips in service. Diesel engines are worst affected because their combustion space is necessarily smaller.

This brings us to the present day. The design and construction of toothed belts has improved considerably, but regular renewal is still required.

Types of belt

Timing belts have a core made of fibreglass strands. The teeth are made of an elastic nylon facing material and are bonded to the core with a flexible rubber compound. The precise characteristics of the various construction materials will vary to meet the vehicle manufacturer's specification.

The belt tooth profile was originally trapezoidal (straight-sided). This was superseded by a semi-circular type which is stronger and longer-wearing. There are numerous variations on these two basic profiles, some of them matched to particular sprocket teeth. For this reason it is essential that belts are only used for their catalogued applications, even if they appear similar to belts used in other applications.

Storage and handling of belts

Like any rubber product, timing belts should be stored in dry temperate conditions and out of direct sunlight. Do not allow them to become contaminated by oil or solvents. Ideally the belts should be stored in their original packaging. Do not bend them tightly, roll them up or hang them on pegs or hooks.

When fitting a new belt, be careful not to bend or kink it sharply. Avoid contamination of the belt by engine fluids and make sure that any fuel, oil or coolant leaks near the belt run are rectified.

Renewal intervals

Manufacturers' specified renewal intervals vary widely and sometimes apparently arbitrarily. In the absence of any specific recommendation to the contrary, an interval of 36 000 to 40 000 miles (60 000 to 65 000 km) is suggested.

Some manufacturers specify a shorter renewal interval for vehicles operating under adverse conditions. 'Adverse conditions' include taxi work, full-time towing, driving on unmade roads and operation in extremes of climate. If in doubt, the only safe course of action is to opt for the shorter interval.

As a general rule, a used timing belt should not be refitted once it has been removed. This is because the tensioning procedure laid down by the manufacturer applies to a new belt; once the old belt has stretched in service it is virtually impossible to regain the correct tension.

Reasons for belt failure

A belt which has been in service for longer than the recommended period can be expected to fail simply as a result of ageing and fatigue. Premature failure can be caused by a number of factors, some of which leave characteristic signs.

The photographs overleaf showing various types of failure have been provided by AE Auto Parts Ltd.

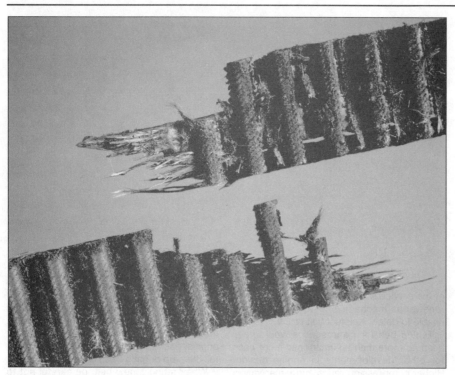

Foreign Body Entrapment

Cause

A foreign body (nut, bolt, washer, etc) has become trapped in the drive and has over-stretched and broken the tensile cords.

Symptom

Belt breakage, in a curved or ragged tear.

Remedy

Attempt to locate and identify foreign body

Ensure belt covers are effective.

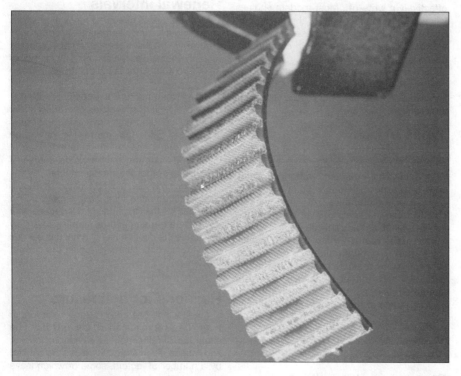

Land Wear

Cause

Excessive tension, causing the belt to wear on the pulley lands.

Rough sprocket(s) abrading the belt.

Symptom

Wear, or polishing, on the lands between the teeth, possibly wearing down to the tension cords; with polishing on the tooth crests of trapezoidal belts.

Remedy

Replace sprocket(s) if required.

Edge Wear

Cause

Damaged sprocket flange, or misaligned sprockets.

Symptom

Excessive wear and damage to the belt edges.

Remedy

Replace damaged sprockets and ensure correct belt alignment.

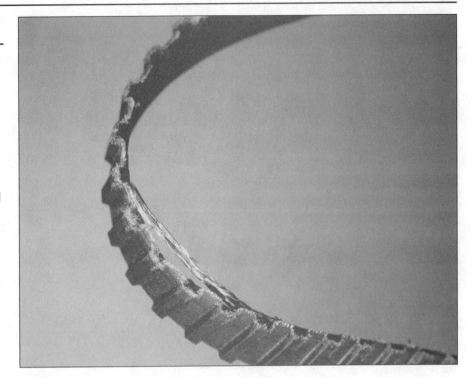

Back Cracks

Cause

The rubber has been over-heated and has degraded, possibly from friction on a siezed idler or water pump. Extreme cold may have the same effect.

Symptom

A series of cracks across the back of the rubber stock.

Remedy

Ensure all spindles driven off the back of the belt, including water pumps, rotate freely.

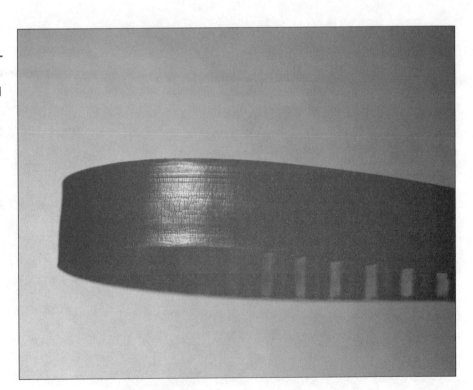

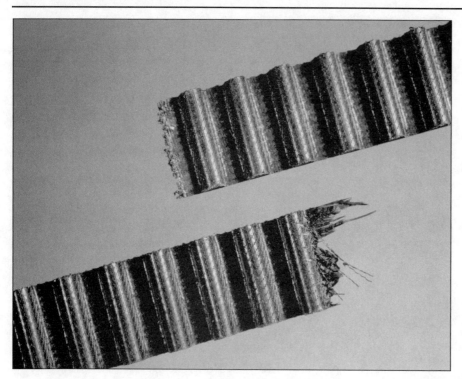

Tensile Failure

Cause

Some of the tensile cord's fibres have broken due to crimping (folding) before or during assembly, creating a weak point.

A belt running over-tensioned may sometimes cause teeth to ride up onto sprocket lands, resulting in vast over-stretching and tensile failure.

Symptom

Tensile breakage, with a straight break between two teeth.

Remedy

Replace belt carefully, without pinching or levering.

Set new belt to correct tension.

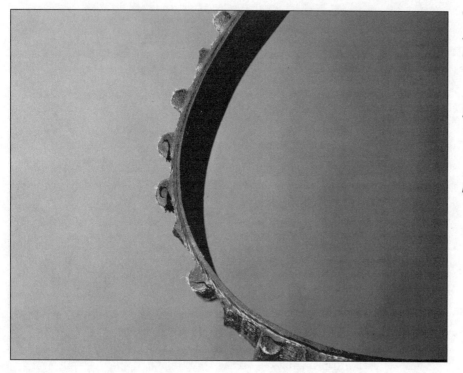

Tooth Peel

Cause

Very low tension allowing the belt to jump teeth.

Symptom

Teeth peeling, emanating from root cracks. Often is present together with tooth shear.

Remedy

Set new belt to correct tension and ensure tensioner mechanism is tight.

Tooth Wear

Cause

Extremely low tension allows the belt to ride out on the sprocket, causing localised wear on edge of the thrust face.

Sometimes excessive tension, pulling the belt up the land, may wear the tooth face, before a tensile failure.

Symptom

Hollows through the facing fabric.

Remedy

Set new belt to correct tension.

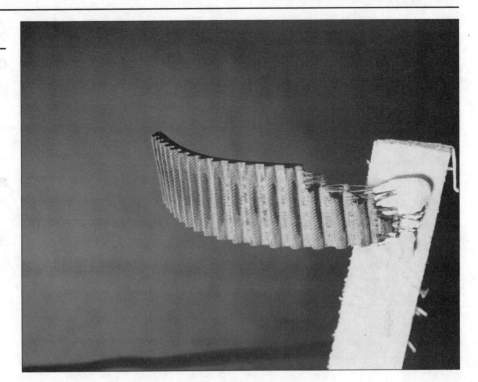

Tooth Shear

Cause

May be due to sudden overload of the drive from the seizure of a driven pump, such as a water pump.

Also may be due to low tension, which allows the belt to ride high on the sprocket, producing excessive bending moments, and deflection of the teeth until cracks form.

Symptom

Six or more teeth missing, often with cracking in roots of a number of teeth.

Remedy

Ensure all driven items rotate freely.

Set new belt to correct tension and ensure tensioner mechanism is tight.

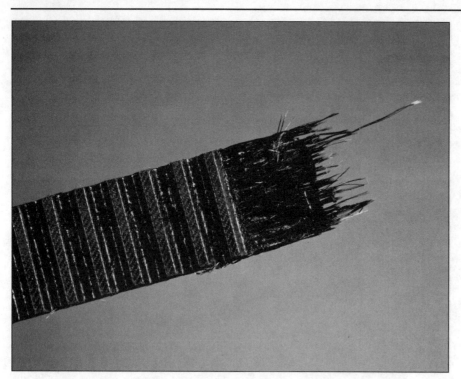

Oil Contamination

Cause

Contamination from a failed oil seal, or an oil or diesel leak, breaks down the adhesion of the rubber. Swelling can also cause mis-meshing leading to other types of failure.

Symptom

Dirty or smelly belt, with a ragged decomposing structure.

Remedy

Ensure oil leak is stopped. Check belt covers and dust shields.

Consequences of timing belt breaking in service

Almost all modern engines will suffer some damage if the timing belt breaks in service. The severity of such damage varies according to the design of the engine, the speed at which it was turning when the belt broke and a certain amount of good or bad luck. Belts often break when the engine is being started or when pulling away - in these cases damage may not be severe.

If engine damage is suspected, the only sure way of checking is by removing the cylinder head and dismantling the valvegear. Some authorities recommend that a compression test be performed before going to the trouble of dismantling, but this will only be possible if a spare timing belt can be fitted. A cylinder leak-down test can be performed instead, rotating the camshaft as necessary to close the appropriate pair of valves, but this will only detect gross damage (holes in pistons, valve heads snapped off).

When faced with an engine on which the belt has broken, the following course of action is suggested:

(a) *Remove the camshaft cover and check for visible damage (broken rocker fingers or valve springs, valves stuck open, etc).*

(b) *Position the pistons at mid-stroke and rotate the camshaft. If the camshaft will not turn, or jams at some point, further investigation is required.*

(c) *If the camshaft turns satisfactorily, position the crankshaft and camshaft in their correct relative positions and fit a timing belt - for preference an old one. Perform a compression test.*

(d) *If the compression test is satisfactory, the engine has probably escaped damage. If the compression on one or more cylinders is low, suspect a bent valve stem or other damage.*

Tensioning gauges and units

On some engines timing belt tension is set automatically by a spring-loaded tensioner. Provided the tensioner is in good condition and the correct procedure is followed, no problems will be encountered and no tensioning gauge will be needed.

More usually, belt tension is set manually and checked using a particular gauge specified by the vehicle manufacturer. The experienced mechanic may rely on the 'feel' of the belt to judge when tension is correct. As a rule of thumb, it should not be possible to twist the belt further than 90° (a quarter of a turn) with the fingers. A further check can be made when the engine is running: a belt which is too tight will often make a characteristic droning or honking noise. However, even in experienced hands it is only possible to achieve an approximately correct setting without a tensioning gauge and in the worst case it is a recipe for disaster.

A universal belt tensioning gauge would be welcomed by many mechanics, but it appears not to exist. Conversion of (often arbitrary and non-linear) units from one make of gauge to another is not always possible, because not only are the gauges calibrated differently, they also work in different ways. Some gauges are also sensitive to belt thickness.

It will be seen, therefore, that the only way to be certain of correctly tensioning manually-adjusted timing belts is to use the manufacturer's specified gauge. Other methods may work, but unless specifically recommended they must be regarded as second best.

Acknowledgements

Thanks are due to AE Auto Parts Ltd, Bradford, West Yorkshire, for the provision of timing belt fault finding information. Thanks are also due to Sykes-Pickavant Limited, who provided some of the workshop tools, and to all those people at Sparkford who helped in the production of this manual, especially Mark Coombs, Spencer Drayton, Bob Jex, Andy Legg and Steve Rendle.

We take great pride in the accuracy of information given in this manual, but vehicle manufacturers make alterations and design changes during the production run of a particular vehicle of which they do not inform us. No liability can be accepted by the authors or publishers for loss, damage or injury caused by errors in, or omissions from, the information given.

Working on your car can be dangerous. This page shows just some of the potential risks and hazards, with the aim of creating a safety-conscious attitude.

General hazards

Scalding

• Don't remove the radiator or expansion tank cap while the engine is hot.
• Engine oil, automatic transmission fluid or power steering fluid may also be dangerously hot if the engine has recently been running.

Burning

• Beware of burns from the exhaust system and from any part of the engine. Brake discs and drums can also be extremely hot immediately after use.

Crushing

• When working under or near a raised vehicle, always supplement the jack with axle stands, or use drive-on ramps. *Never venture under a car which is only supported by a jack.*

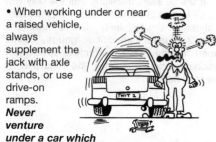

• Take care if loosening or tightening high-torque nuts when the vehicle is on stands. Initial loosening and final tightening should be done with the wheels on the ground.

Fire

• Fuel is highly flammable; fuel vapour is explosive.
• Don't let fuel spill onto a hot engine.
• Do not smoke or allow naked lights (including pilot lights) anywhere near a vehicle being worked on. Also beware of creating sparks (electrically or by use of tools).
• Fuel vapour is heavier than air, so don't work on the fuel system with the vehicle over an inspection pit.
• Another cause of fire is an electrical overload or short-circuit. Take care when repairing or modifying the vehicle wiring.
• Keep a fire extinguisher handy, of a type suitable for use on fuel and electrical fires.

Electric shock

• Ignition HT voltage can be dangerous, especially to people with heart problems or a pacemaker. Don't work on or near the ignition system with the engine running or the ignition switched on.

• Mains voltage is also dangerous. Make sure that any mains-operated equipment is correctly earthed. Mains power points should be protected by a residual current device (RCD) circuit breaker.

Fume or gas intoxication

• Exhaust fumes are poisonous; they often contain carbon monoxide, which is rapidly fatal if inhaled. Never run the engine in a confined space such as a garage with the doors shut.
• Fuel vapour is also poisonous, as are the vapours from some cleaning solvents and paint thinners.

Poisonous or irritant substances

• Avoid skin contact with battery acid and with any fuel, fluid or lubricant, especially antifreeze, brake hydraulic fluid and Diesel fuel. Don't syphon them by mouth. If such a substance is swallowed or gets into the eyes, seek medical advice.
• Prolonged contact with used engine oil can cause skin cancer. Wear gloves or use a barrier cream if necessary. Change out of oil-soaked clothes and do not keep oily rags in your pocket.
• Air conditioning refrigerant forms a poisonous gas if exposed to a naked flame (including a cigarette). It can also cause skin burns on contact.

Asbestos

• Asbestos dust can cause cancer if inhaled or swallowed. Asbestos may be found in gaskets and in brake and clutch linings. When dealing with such components it is safest to assume that they contain asbestos.

Special hazards

Hydrofluoric acid

• This extremely corrosive acid is formed when certain types of synthetic rubber, found in some O-rings, oil seals, fuel hoses etc, are exposed to temperatures above 400°C. The rubber changes into a charred or sticky substance containing the acid. *Once formed, the acid remains dangerous for years. If it gets onto the skin, it may be necessary to amputate the limb concerned.*
• When dealing with a vehicle which has suffered a fire, or with components salvaged from such a vehicle, wear protective gloves and discard them after use.

The battery

• Batteries contain sulphuric acid, which attacks clothing, eyes and skin. Take care when topping-up or carrying the battery.
• The hydrogen gas given off by the battery is highly explosive. Never cause a spark or allow a naked light nearby. Be careful when connecting and disconnecting battery chargers or jump leads.

Air bags

• Air bags can cause injury if they go off accidentally. Take care when removing the steering wheel and/or facia. Special storage instructions may apply.

Diesel injection equipment

• Diesel injection pumps supply fuel at very high pressure. Take care when working on the fuel injectors and fuel pipes.

⚠️ *Warning: Never expose the hands, face or any other part of the body to injector spray; the fuel can penetrate the skin with potentially fatal results.*

Remember...

DO

• Do use eye protection when using power tools, and when working under the vehicle.

• Do wear gloves or use barrier cream to protect your hands when necessary.

• Do get someone to check periodically that all is well when working alone on the vehicle.

• Do keep loose clothing and long hair well out of the way of moving mechanical parts.

• Do remove rings, wristwatch etc, before working on the vehicle – especially the electrical system.

• Do ensure that any lifting or jacking equipment has a safe working load rating adequate for the job.

DON'T

• Don't attempt to lift a heavy component which may be beyond your capability – get assistance.

• Don't rush to finish a job, or take unverified short cuts.

• Don't use ill-fitting tools which may slip and cause injury.

• Don't leave tools or parts lying around where someone can trip over them. Mop up oil and fuel spills at once.

• Don't allow children or pets to play in or near a vehicle being worked on.

Chapter 1A
Citroën AX petrol 1987 to 1994

Contents

Specifications

Timing belt renewal interval . . . . Every 36 000 miles (60 000 km)

Note: *Although the normal interval for timing belt renewal is 72 000 miles (120 000 km), it is strongly recommended that the interval is halved on vehicles which are subjected to intensive use, ie, mainly short journeys or a lot of stop-start driving. The actual belt renewal interval is therefore very much up to the individual owner. That being said, it is highly recommended to err on the side of safety, and renew the belt at this earlier interval, bearing in mind the drastic consequences resulting from belt failure.*

Torque wrench settings	Nm	lbf ft
Camshaft sprocket retaining bolt	80	59
Crankshaft pulley retaining bolts	8	6
Crankshaft sprocket retaining bolt	110	81
Roadwheel bolts	90	66
Timing belt cover bolts	8	6
Timing belt tensioner pulley nut	23	17

1 Auxiliary drivebelt - removal refitting and adjustment

1 Apply the handbrake, then jack up the front of the car and support it on axle stands.
2 Remove the right-hand front roadwheel.
3 Where necessary, undo the retaining nut, and free the coolant hoses from the retaining clip to improve access to the crankshaft sprocket bolt.

Models without air conditioning

Removal

4 Disconnect the battery negative lead.
5 Slacken both the alternator upper and lower mounting bolts, and the bolt securing the adjuster strap to the mounting bracket.
6 Back off the adjuster bolt to relieve the tension in the drivebelt, then slip the drivebelt from the pulleys (see illustrations).

Refitting

7 Fit the belt around the pulleys, ensuring that the belt is of the correct type if it is being renewed, and take up the slack in the belt by tightening the adjuster bolt.
8 Tension the drivebelt as described in the following paragraphs.

Adjustment

9 Correct tensioning of the drivebelt will ensure that it has a long life. Beware, however, of overtightening, as this can cause wear in the alternator bearings.
10 The belt should be tensioned so that, under firm thumb pressure, there is approximately 5.0 mm of free movement at the mid-point between the pulleys, on the longest belt run.
11 To adjust, with the upper mounting bolt just holding the alternator firm, and the lower mounting bolt loosened, turn the adjuster bolt until the correct tension is achieved. Rotate

the crankshaft through two complete turns, then recheck the tension. When the tension is correct, securely tighten both the alternator mounting bolts and, where necessary, the bolt securing the adjuster strap to its mounting bracket.
12 Reconnect the battery negative lead.
13 Clip the coolant hoses in position and secure them with the retaining nut (where removed). Refit the roadwheel, and lower the vehicle to the ground.

Models with air conditioning

Removal

14 Disconnect the battery negative lead.
15 Slacken the two bolts securing the tensioner pulley assembly to the engine, and the lower alternator mounting bolt.
16 Rotate the adjuster bolt to move the tensioner pulley away from the drivebelt, until there is sufficient slack for the drivebelt to be removed from the pulleys.

Refitting

17 Fit the belt around the pulleys, ensuring that the belt is of the correct type if it is being renewed, and take up the slack in the belt by tightening the adjuster bolt.
18 Tension the drivebelt as described in the following paragraphs.

Adjustment

19 Correct tensioning of the drivebelt will ensure that it has a long life. Beware, however, of overtightening, as this can cause wear in the alternator bearings.
20 The belt should be tensioned so that, under firm thumb pressure, there is approximately 5.0 mm of free movement at the mid-point between the pulleys, on the longest belt run.
21 To adjust the tension, with the two tensioner pulley assembly retaining bolts and the lower alternator mounting bolt slackened, rotate the adjuster bolt until the correct tension is achieved. Once the belt is correctly

tensioned, rotate the crankshaft through two complete turns, and recheck the tension.
22 When the belt is correctly tensioned, securely tighten the tensioner pulley assembly retaining bolts, and the lower alternator mounting bolt.
23 Reconnect the battery negative lead.
24 Clip the coolant hoses back in position, and secure with the retaining nut (where removed). Refit the roadwheel, and lower the vehicle to the ground.

2 Top dead centre (TDC) for No 1 piston – locating

Note: *Do not attempt to rotate the engine whilst the crankshaft/camshaft are locked in position. If the engine is to be left in this state for a long period of time, it is a good idea to place warning notices inside the vehicle, and in the engine compartment. This will reduce the possibility of the engine being accidentally cranked on the starter motor, which is likely to cause damage with the locking tools in place.*

1 On all models, timing holes are drilled in the camshaft sprocket and in the flywheel. The holes are used to ensure that the crankshaft and camshaft are correctly positioned when assembling the engine (to prevent the possibility of the valves contacting the pistons when refitting the cylinder head), or when refitting the timing belt. When the timing holes are aligned with access holes in the cylinder head and the front of the cylinder block, suitable diameter tools can be inserted to lock both the camshaft and crankshaft in position, preventing them from rotating. Proceed as follows. **Note:** *With the timing holes aligned, No 1 cylinder is at TDC on its compression stroke. No 1 cylinder is at the transmission end of the cylinder block.*
2 Remove the timing belt upper cover, as described in Section 3.

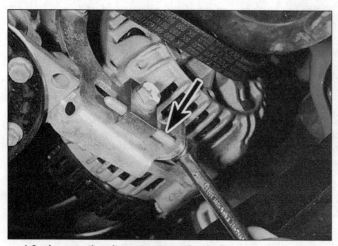

1.6a Loosen the alternator mounting bolts, then slacken the adjuster bolt (arrowed) . . .

1.6b . . . and slip the drivebelt off its pulleys

2.4 Insert a 6 mm bolt (arrowed) through the hole in cylinder block flange and into the timing hole in the flywheel . . .

2.5 . . . then insert a 10 mm bolt through the camshaft sprocket timing hole, and locate it in the cylinder head

3 The crankshaft must now be turned until the timing hole in the camshaft sprocket is aligned with the corresponding hole in the cylinder head. The holes are aligned when the camshaft sprocket hole is in the 2 o'clock position, when viewed from the right-hand end of the engine. The crankshaft can be turned by using a spanner on the crankshaft sprocket bolt, noting that it should always be rotated in a clockwise direction (viewed from the right-hand end of the engine). Turning the crankshaft will be much easier if the spark plugs are removed first.

4 With the camshaft sprocket hole correctly positioned, insert a 6 mm diameter bolt, or drill bit, through the hole in the front, left-hand flange of the cylinder block, and locate it in the timing hole in the flywheel **(see illustration)**. Note that it may be necessary to rotate the crankshaft slightly, to get the holes to align.

5 With the flywheel correctly positioned, insert a 10 mm diameter bolt, or drill bit,

through the timing hole in the camshaft sprocket, and locate it in the hole in the cylinder head **(see illustration)**.

6 The crankshaft and camshaft are now locked in position, preventing unnecessary rotation.

---

3 Timing belt covers -
removal and refitting

Removal

Upper cover

1 Slacken and remove the two retaining bolts (one at the front and one at the rear), and remove the upper timing cover from the cylinder head **(see illustrations)**.

Centre cover

2 Remove the upper cover as described in

paragraph 1, then free the wiring from its retaining clips on the centre cover **(see illustration)**.

3 Slacken and remove the retaining bolts, and manoeuvre the centre cover out

3.1a Undo the two retaining bolts (arrowed) . . .

3.1b . . . and remove the upper timing belt cover

3.2 Free the wiring loom from its retaining clips . . .

3.3 . . . then undo the retaining bolts (locations arrowed) and remove the centre timing belt cover

3.6a Undo the three retaining bolts (arrowed) . . .

from the engine compartment **(see illustration)**.

Lower cover

4 Remove the auxiliary drivebelt as described in Section 1.

5 Remove the upper and centre covers as described in paragraphs 1 to 3.

6 Undo the three crankshaft pulley retaining bolts and remove the pulley, noting which way round it is fitted **(see illustrations)**.

7 Slacken and remove the single retaining bolt, and slide the lower cover off the end of the crankshaft **(see illustration)**.

Refitting

Upper cover

8 Refit the cover, ensuring that it is correctly located with the centre cover, and tighten its retaining bolts.

Centre cover

9 Manoeuvre the centre cover back into position, ensuring it is correctly located with the lower cover, and tighten its retaining bolts.

10 Clip the wiring loom into its retaining clips on the front of the centre cover, then refit the upper cover as described in paragraph 8.

Lower cover

11 Locate the lower cover over the timing belt sprocket, and tighten its retaining bolt.

12 Fit the pulley to the end of the crankshaft, ensuring that it is fitted the correct way round, and tighten its retaining bolts to the specified torque.

13 Refit the centre and upper covers as described above, then refit and tension the auxiliary drivebelt as described in Section 1.

---

4 Timing belt -
removal and refitting

Removal

1 Disconnect the battery negative terminal.

2 Align the engine assembly/valve timing holes as described in Section 2, and lock both the camshaft sprocket and the flywheel in position. *Do not* attempt to rotate the engine whilst the locking tools are in position.

3 Remove the timing belt centre and lower covers as described in Section 3.

4 Loosen the timing belt tensioner pulley retaining nut. Pivot the pulley in a clockwise

direction, using a square-section key fitted to the hole in the pulley hub, then retighten the retaining nut.

5 If the timing belt is to be re-used, use white paint or similar to mark the direction of rotation on the belt (if markings do not already exist) **(see illustration)**. Slip the belt off the sprockets.

6 If signs of oil contamination are found, trace the source of the oil leak, and rectify it. Wash down the engine timing belt area and all related components, to remove all traces of oil.

Refitting

7 Prior to refitting, thoroughly clean the timing belt sprockets. Check that the tensioner pulley rotates freely, without any sign of roughness. If necessary, renew the tensioner pulley as described in Section 5. Make sure that the locking tools are still in place, as described in Section 2.

8 Manoeuvre the timing belt into position, ensuring that the arrows on the belt are pointing in the direction of rotation (clockwise when viewed from the right-hand end of the engine).

9 Do not twist the timing belt sharply while

3.6b . . . and remove the crankshaft pulley

3.7 Undo the retaining bolt and remove the lower timing belt cover

4.5 Mark the direction of rotation on the belt, if it is to be re-used

refitting it. Fit the belt over the crankshaft and camshaft sprockets. Make sure that the front run of the belt is taut - ie, ensure that any slack is on the tensioner pulley side of the belt. Fit the belt over the water pump sprocket and tensioner pulley. Ensure that the belt teeth are seated centrally in the sprockets.

10 Loosen the tensioner pulley retaining nut. Pivot the pulley anti-clockwise to remove all free play from the timing belt, then retighten the nut.

11 Citroën dealers use a special tool to tension the timing belt **(see illustration)**. A similar tool may be fabricated using a suitable square-section bar attached to an arm; a hole should be drilled in the arm at a distance of 80 mm from the centre of the square-section bar. Fit the tool to the hole in the tensioner pulley, keeping the tool arm as close to the horizontal as possible, and hang a 1.5 kg (3.3 lb) weight (aluminium block engine) or 2.0 kg (4.4 lb) weight (cast-iron block engine) from the hole in the tool. In the absence of an object of the specified weight, a spring balance can be used to exert the required force, ensuring that the spring balance is held at 90° to the tool arm. Slacken the pulley retaining nut, allowing the weight or force exerted (as applicable) to push the tensioner pulley against the belt, then retighten the pulley nut.

12 Remove the locking tools from the camshaft sprocket and flywheel.

13 Using a socket and extension bar on the crankshaft sprocket bolt, rotate the crankshaft through four complete rotations in a clockwise direction (viewed from the right-hand end of the engine). *Do not* at any time rotate the crankshaft anti-clockwise.

14 Slacken the tensioner pulley nut, re-tension the belt using one of the methods just described, then tighten the tensioner pulley nut to the specified torque.

15 Rotate the crankshaft through a further two turns clockwise, and check that both the camshaft sprocket and flywheel timing holes are still correctly aligned.

16 If all is well, refit the timing belt covers as described in Section 3, and reconnect the battery negative terminal.

5 Timing belt tensioner and sprockets - removal and refitting

Removal

Note: *This Section describes the removal and refitting of the components concerned as individual operations. If more than one of them is to be removed at the same time, start by removing the timing belt as described in Section 4; remove the actual component as described below, ignoring the preliminary dismantling steps.*

1 Disconnect the battery negative terminal.

2 Position the engine assembly/valve timing holes as described in Section 2, and lock both

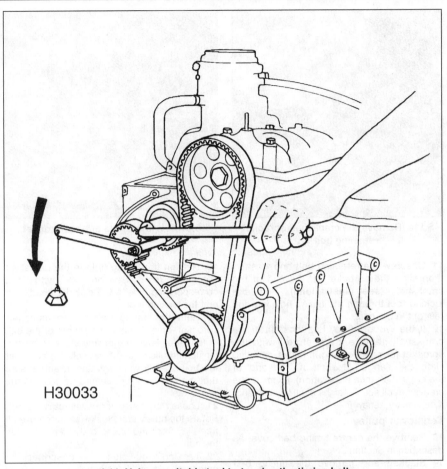

H30033

4.11 Using a suitable tool to tension the timing belt

the camshaft sprocket and flywheel in position. *Do not* attempt to rotate the engine whilst the locking tools are in position.

Camshaft sprocket

3 Remove the upper and centre timing belt covers as described in Section 3. Also, where fitted on cast-iron block engines, remove the electronic control unit.

4 Loosen the timing belt tensioner pulley retaining nut. Rotate the pulley in a clockwise direction, using a square-section key fitted to the hole in the pulley hub, then retighten the retaining nut.

5 Disengage the timing belt from the sprocket, and move the belt clear, taking care not to bend or twist it sharply. Remove the locking tool from the camshaft sprocket.

6 Slacken the camshaft sprocket retaining bolt and remove it, along with its washer. To prevent the camshaft rotating as the bolt is slackened, a sprocket-holding tool will be required. *Do not* attempt to use the locking tool to prevent the sprocket from rotating whilst the bolt is slackened. In the absence of the special Citroën tool to prevent the camshaft rotating, an acceptable substitute can be fabricated as follows. Use two lengths of steel strip (one long, the other short), and

three nuts and bolts; one nut and bolt forms the pivot of a forked tool, with the remaining two nuts and bolts at the tips of the 'forks' to engage with the sprocket spokes **(see illustration 5.18)**.

7 With the retaining bolt removed, slide the sprocket off the end of the camshaft. If the locating peg is a loose fit in the rear of the sprocket, remove it for safe-keeping. Examine the camshaft oil seal for signs of oil leakage and, if necessary, renew it.

Crankshaft sprocket

8 Remove the centre and lower timing belt covers as described in Section 5.

9 Loosen the timing belt tensioner pulley retaining nut. Rotate the pulley in a clockwise direction, using a square-section key fitted to the hole in the pulley hub, then retighten the retaining nut.

10 To prevent crankshaft rotation whilst the sprocket retaining bolt is slackened, select top gear, and have an assistant apply the brakes firmly. *Do not* be tempted to use the locking tool described in Section 2 to prevent the crankshaft from rotating; temporarily remove this tool from the rear of the flywheel prior to slackening the pulley bolt, then refit it once the bolt has been slackened.

1A

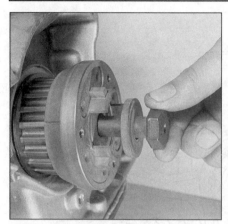

5.11a Remove the crankshaft sprocket retaining bolt . . .

5.11b . . . then slide off the sprocket

11 Unscrew the retaining bolt and washer, then slide the sprocket off the end of the crankshaft (see illustrations). Refit the locking tool through the timing hole into the rear of the flywheel.

12 If the Woodruff key is a loose fit in the crankshaft, remove it and store it with the sprocket for safe-keeping. If necessary, also slide the flanged spacer off the end of the crankshaft (see illustration). Examine the crankshaft oil seal for signs of oil leakage and, if necessary, renew it.

Tensioner pulley

13 Remove the centre timing belt cover as described in Section 3.

14 Slacken and remove the timing belt tensioner pulley retaining nut, and slide the pulley off its mounting stud. Examine the mounting stud for signs of damage and, if necessary, renew it.

Refitting

15 Clean the sprockets thoroughly, and renew any that show signs of wear, damage or cracks.

16 Clean the tensioner assembly, but do not use any strong solvent which may enter the pulley bearing. Check that the pulley rotates freely about its hub, with no sign of stiffness or of free play. Renew the tensioner pulley if there is any doubt about its condition, or if there are any obvious signs of wear or damage.

Camshaft sprocket

17 Refit the locating peg (where removed) to the rear of the sprocket, then locate the sprocket on the end of the camshaft. Ensure that the locating peg is correctly engaged with the cut-out in the camshaft end.

18 Refit the sprocket retaining bolt and washer. Tighten the bolt to the specified torque, whilst retaining the sprocket with the tool used on removal (see illustration).

19 Realign the timing hole in the camshaft sprocket (see Section 2) with the corresponding hole in the cylinder head, and refit the locking tool.

20 Refit the timing belt to the camshaft sprocket. Ensure that the front run of the belt is taut - ie, ensure that any slack is on the tensioner pulley side of the belt. Do not twist the belt sharply while refitting it, and ensure that the belt teeth are seated centrally in the sprockets.

21 Loosen the tensioner pulley retaining nut. Rotate the pulley anti-clockwise to remove all free play from the timing belt, then retighten the nut.

22 Tension the belt as described in paragraphs 11 to 15 of Section 4.

23 Refit the timing belt covers as described in Section 3, and reconnect the battery negative terminal.

Crankshaft sprocket

24 Where removed, locate the Woodruff key in the crankshaft end, then slide on the

5.12 Remove the flanged spacer if necessary

flanged spacer, aligning its slot with the Woodruff key.

25 Align the crankshaft sprocket slot with the Woodruff key, and slide it onto the end of the crankshaft.

26 Temporarily remove the locking tool from the rear of the flywheel, then refit the crankshaft sprocket retaining bolt and washer. Tighten the bolt to the specified torque, whilst preventing crankshaft rotation using the method employed on removal. Refit the locking tool through the timing hole into the rear of the flywheel.

27 Relocate the timing belt on the crankshaft sprocket. Ensure that the front run of the belt is taut - ie, ensure that any slack is on the tensioner pulley side of the belt. Do not twist the belt sharply while refitting it, and ensure that the belt teeth are seated centrally in the sprockets.

28 Loosen the tensioner pulley retaining nut. Rotate the pulley anti-clockwise to remove all free play from the timing belt, then retighten the nut.

29 Tension the belt as described in paragraphs 11 to 15 of Section 4.

30 Refit the timing belt covers as described in Section 3, and reconnect the battery negative terminal.

Tensioner pulley

31 Refit the tensioner pulley to its mounting stud, and fit the retaining nut.

32 Ensure that the front run of the belt is taut - ie, ensure that any slack is on the pulley side of the belt. Check that the belt is centrally located on all its sprockets. Rotate the pulley anti-clockwise to remove all free play from the timing belt, then tighten the pulley retaining nut securely.

33 Tension the belt as described in paragraphs 11 to 15 of Section 4.

34 Refit the timing belt covers as described in Section 3, and reconnect the battery negative terminal.

5.18 Using a home-made tool to hold the camshaft sprocket stationary whilst the retaining bolt is tightened (shown with the cylinder head on the bench)

Chapter 1B
Citroën AX diesel 1987 to 1994

Note: *This Chapter covers the 1360 cc Diesel engine. For information on the 1527cc Diesel engine refer to Chapter 5B*

Contents

Specifications

Timing belt renewal interval . . . . Every 36 000 miles (60 000 km)

Note: *Although the normal interval for timing belt renewal is 72 000 miles (120 000 km), it is strongly recommended that the interval is halved on vehicles which are subjected to intensive use, ie, mainly short journeys or a lot of stop-start driving. The actual belt renewal interval is therefore very much up to the individual owner. That being said, it is highly recommended to err on the side of safety, and renew the belt at this earlier interval, bearing in mind the drastic consequences resulting from belt failure.*

Torque wrench settings	Nm	lbf ft
Camshaft sprocket retaining bolt	80	59
Crankshaft pulley-to-sprocket	16	12
Crankshaft sprocket retaining bolt	110	81
Injection pump sprocket nut	50	37
Roadwheel bolt	90	66
Timing belt cover bolts:		
Except upper cover-to-cylinder head cover	8	6
Upper cover-to-cylinder head cover	5	4
Timing belt tensioner pulley nut	23	17

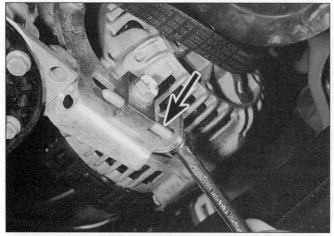

1.6a Loosen the alternator mounting bolts, then slacken the adjuster bolt (arrowed) . . .

1.6b . . . and slip the drivebelt off its pulleys

1 Auxiliary drivebelt - removal refitting and adjustment

1 Apply the handbrake, then jack up the front of the car and support it on axle stands.
2 Remove the right-hand front roadwheel.
3 Where necessary, undo the retaining nut, and free the coolant hoses from the retaining clip to improve access to the crankshaft sprocket bolt.

Models without air conditioning

Removal

4 Disconnect the battery negative lead.
5 Slacken both the alternator upper and lower mounting bolts, and the bolt securing the adjuster strap to the mounting bracket.
6 Back off the adjuster bolt to relieve the tension in the drivebelt, then slip the drivebelt from the pulleys **(see illustrations)**.

Refitting

7 Fit the belt around the pulleys, ensuring that the belt is of the correct type if it is being renewed, and take up the slack in the belt by tightening the adjuster bolt.
8 Tension the drivebelt as described in the following paragraphs.

Adjustment

9 Correct tensioning of the drivebelt will ensure that it has a long life. Beware, however, of overtightening, as this can cause wear in the alternator bearings.
10 The belt should be tensioned so that, under firm thumb pressure, there is approximately 5.0 mm of free movement at the mid-point between the pulleys, on the longest belt run.
11 To adjust, with the upper mounting bolt just holding the alternator firm, and the lower mounting bolt loosened, turn the adjuster bolt until the correct tension is achieved. Rotate

the crankshaft through two complete turns, then recheck the tension. When the tension is correct, securely tighten both the alternator mounting bolts and, where necessary, the bolt securing the adjuster strap to its mounting bracket.
12 Reconnect the battery negative lead.
13 Clip the coolant hoses in position and secure them with the retaining nut (where removed). Refit the roadwheel, and lower the vehicle to the ground.

Models with air conditioning

Removal

14 Disconnect the battery negative lead.
15 Slacken the two bolts securing the tensioner pulley assembly to the engine, and the lower alternator mounting bolt.
16 Rotate the adjuster bolt to move the tensioner pulley away from the drivebelt, until there is sufficient slack for the drivebelt to be removed from the pulleys.

Refitting

17 Fit the belt around the pulleys, ensuring that the belt is of the correct type if it is being renewed, and take up the slack in the belt by tightening the adjuster bolt.
18 Tension the drivebelt as described in the following paragraphs.

Adjustment

19 Correct tensioning of the drivebelt will ensure that it has a long life. Beware, however, of overtightening, as this can cause wear in the alternator bearings.
20 The belt should be tensioned so that, under firm thumb pressure, there is approximately 5.0 mm of free movement at the mid-point between the pulleys, on the longest belt run.
21 To adjust the tension, with the two tensioner pulley assembly retaining bolts and the lower alternator mounting bolt slackened, rotate the adjuster bolt until the correct tension is achieved. Once the belt is correctly

tensioned, rotate the crankshaft through two complete turns, and recheck the tension.
22 When the belt is correctly tensioned, securely tighten the tensioner pulley assembly retaining bolts, and the lower alternator mounting bolt.
23 Reconnect the battery negative lead.
24 Clip the coolant hoses back in position, and secure with the retaining nut (where removed). Refit the roadwheel, and lower the vehicle to the ground.

2 Top dead centre (TDC) for No 4 piston – locating

Note: *This engine is timed on No 4 cylinder. Three 8 mm diameter bolts and one 6 mm diameter rod or drill will be required for this procedure. Do not attempt to rotate the engine whilst the crankshaft, camshaft or injection pump are locked in position. If the engine is to be left in this state for a long period of time, it is a good idea to place warning notices inside the vehicle, and in the engine compartment. This will reduce the possibility of the engine being accidentally cranked on the starter motor, which is likely to cause damage with the locking tools in place.*
1 Top dead centre (TDC) is the highest point in the cylinder that each piston reaches as the crankshaft turns. Each piston reaches TDC at the end of the compression stroke, and again at the end of the exhaust stroke. For the purpose of timing this engine, TDC refers to the position of No 4 piston at the end of its compression stroke. On this engine, No 1 piston is at the flywheel end of the engine, therefore No 4 piston is at the timing belt end of the engine.
2 Remove the upper and centre timing belt covers as described in Section 3.
3 The crankshaft must now be turned until

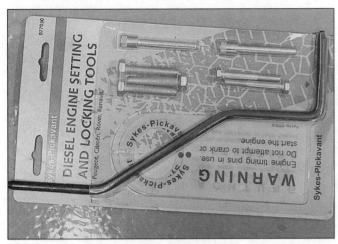

2.4a Suitable tools available for locking engine with No 4 piston at TDC

2.4b Insert a 6 mm bolt (arrowed) through the hole in the cylinder block flange and into the timing hole in the flywheel

the three bolt holes in the camshaft and injection pump sprockets (one hole in the camshaft sprocket, two holes in the injection pump sprocket) are aligned with the corresponding holes in the cylinder head and injection pump mounting bracket. The crankshaft can be turned by using a spanner on the pulley bolt (remove the glow plugs to make it easier to turn the engine). Improved access to the pulley bolt can be obtained by jacking up the front right-hand corner of the vehicle and removing the roadwheel and the wheel arch covers (secured by plastic clips).

4 Insert the 6 mm diameter rod or drill through the hole in the left-hand flange of the cylinder block (just above the TDC sensor position); if necessary, carefully turn the crankshaft either way until the rod enters the TDC hole in the flywheel **(see illustrations)**.

5 Insert three M8 bolts through the holes in the camshaft and fuel injection pump sprockets, and screw them into the engine finger-tight **(see illustrations)**.

6 The crankshaft, camshaft and injection pump are now locked in position with No 4 piston at TDC.

7 If the engine is to be left in this state for a long period of time, it is a good idea to place suitable warning notices inside the vehicle, and in the engine compartment **(see illustration)**. This will reduce the possibility of the engine being accidentally cranked on the starter motor, which is likely to cause damage with the locking tools in place.

3 Timing belt covers - removal and refitting

Removal
Upper cover

1 Slacken and remove the retaining bolts,

2.5a Insert an 8 mm bolt (arrowed) through the camshaft sprocket timing hole, and screw it into the cylinder head . . .

2.5b . . . then insert two 8 mm bolts (arrowed) into the injection pump sprocket holes, and screw them into the mounting bracket

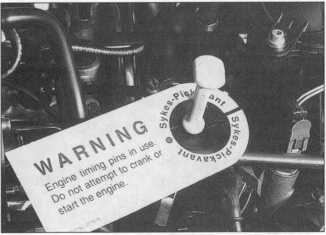

2.7 Warning notice in place in (typical) engine compartment

1B

3.1 Removing the timing belt upper cover

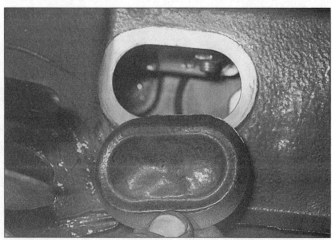

3.3a Remove the rubber plug from the right-hand wing valance . . .

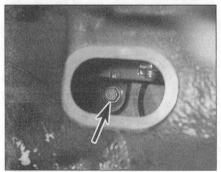

3.3b . . . to gain access to the timing belt centre cover bolt (arrowed)

3.4 Unscrew the remaining bolt (location arrowed) and remove the centre cover

3.7a Undo the retaining bolts (arrowed) . . .

and remove the upper timing cover from the cylinder head **(see illustration)**.

Centre cover

2 Remove the upper cover as described in paragraph 1.
3 Turn the wheels onto full right-hand lock, then prise out the rubber plug from underneath the right-hand front wheel arch.

Unscrew the timing belt cover bolt which is accessible through the hole in the wing valance **(see illustrations)**.
4 Unscrew the other retaining bolt from the centre of the cover, then manoeuvre the cover out of position **(see illustration)**.

Lower cover

5 Remove the auxiliary drivebelt as described in Section 1.

6 Remove the upper and centre covers as described in paragraphs 1 to 4.
7 Undo the crankshaft pulley retaining bolts and remove the pulley, noting which way round it is fitted **(see illustrations)**.
8 Slacken and remove the retaining bolts, and withdraw the lower cover over the crankshaft sprocket outer flange **(see illustration)**.

3.7b . . . and remove the crankshaft pulley from the engine

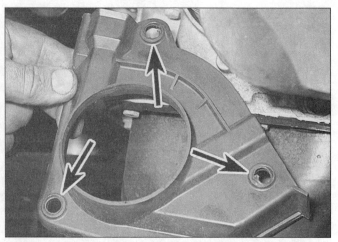

3.8 Undo the retaining bolts (locations arrowed) and remove the lower cover

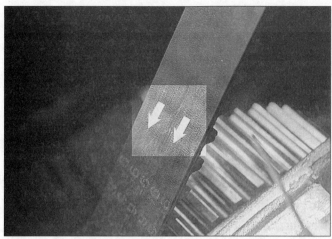

4.5 Mark the direction of rotation on the belt if it is to be re-used

4.10 Engage the timing belt with the sprockets as described in text

Refitting

Upper cover

9 Refit the cover, ensuring it is correctly located with the centre cover, and tighten its retaining bolts.

Centre cover

10 Manoeuvre the centre cover back into position, ensuring that it is correctly located with the cut-out in the lower cover, then tighten its retaining bolts. Refit the rubber plug to the wing valance.
11 Refit the upper cover as described above.

Lower cover

12 Locate the lower cover over the crankshaft sprocket outer flange, and tighten its retaining bolts.
13 Fit the pulley onto the crankshaft sprocket flange, ensuring that it is fitted the correct way round, and tighten its retaining bolts to the specified torque.
14 Refit the centre and upper covers as described above, then refit and tension the auxiliary drivebelt as described in Section 1.

4 Timing belt - removal and refitting

Removal

1 Disconnect the battery negative terminal. For improved access, remove the right-hand headlight as described in Section 6.
2 Set No 4 piston to TDC, then lock the crankshaft, and the camshaft and fuel injection pump sprockets, in position as described in Section 2. *Do not* attempt to rotate the engine whilst the locking tools are in position.
3 Remove the timing belt covers as described in Section 3.
4 Loosen the timing belt tensioner pulley retaining nut. Pivot the pulley in a clockwise direction, using a square-section key fitted to

the hole in the pulley hub, then retighten the retaining nut.
5 If the timing belt is to be re-used, use white paint or similar to mark the direction of rotation on the belt (if markings do not already exist) **(see illustration)**.
6 Slip the belt off the sprockets, idler and tensioner.
7 If signs of oil contamination are found, trace the source of the oil leak, and rectify it. Wash down the engine timing belt area and all related components, to remove all traces of oil.

Refitting

8 Prior to refitting, thoroughly clean the timing belt sprockets. Check that the tensioner pulley rotates freely, without any sign of roughness. If necessary, renew the tensioner pulley as described in Section 5. Make sure that the locking tools are still in place, as described in Section 2.
9 Manoeuvre the timing belt into position, ensuring that the arrows on the belt are pointing in the direction of rotation (clockwise when viewed from the right-hand end of the engine).
10 Do not twist the timing belt sharply while refitting it. First locate the belt over the crankshaft sprocket, then feed it over the

4.11 Remove all free play from the belt, then securely tighten the tensioner pulley retaining nut

coolant pump sprocket, idler and injection pump sprocket, making sure that it is kept taut **(see illustration)**. Locate the back of the belt under the tensioner roller, then engage it with the camshaft sprocket. Ensure that the belt teeth are seated centrally in the sprockets.
11 Loosen the tensioner pulley retaining nut. Pivot the pulley anti-clockwise to remove all free play from the timing belt, then retighten the nut **(see illustration)**.
12 Citroën dealers use one of two special tools to tension the timing belt - one of these tools is fitted on the timing belt between the injection pump and camshaft sprockets - the belt is tensioned until the tool reads 25 units. The other tool consists of a bar and weight applied to the tensioner pulley **(see illustration)**.

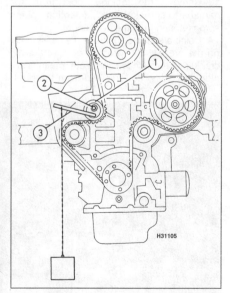

4.12a Using one of the methods to tension the timing belt

1 Tensioner roller
2 Pulley retaining nut
3 Special tool fitted to tensioner roller

4.12b Using a home-made special tool and spring balance to tension the timing belt

A similar tool may be fabricated using a suitable square-section bar attached to an arm; a hole should be drilled in the arm at a distance of 80 mm from the centre of the square-section bar. Fit the tool to the hole in the tensioner pulley, keeping the tool arm as close to the horizontal as possible, and hang a 2.0 kg (4.4 lb) weight from the hole in the tool. In the absence of an object of the specified weight, a spring balance can be used to exert the required force, ensuring that the spring balance is held at 90° to the tool arm **(see illustration)**. Slacken the pulley retaining nut, allowing the weight or force exerted (as applicable) to push the tensioner pulley against the belt, then retighten the pulley nut.

13 Remove the locking tools from the camshaft sprocket and injection pump sprocket, and from the flywheel.

14 Using a suitable socket and extension bar on the crankshaft sprocket bolt, rotate the crankshaft through ten complete rotations in a clockwise direction (viewed from the right-hand end of the engine). *Do not* at any time rotate the crankshaft anti-clockwise.

15 Slacken the tensioner pulley nut, re-tension the belt using the method just described, then tighten the tensioner pulley nut to the specified torque.

16 Rotate the crankshaft through a further two turns clockwise, and check that both the camshaft sprocket and flywheel timing holes are correctly aligned once more.

17 If all is well, refit the timing belt covers as described in Section 3, and reconnect the battery negative terminal. If removed, refit the right-hand headlight.

5 Timing belt tensioner and sprockets - removal and refitting

Removal

Note: *This Section describes the removal and refitting of the components concerned as individual operations. If more than one of them is to be removed at the same time, start by removing the timing belt as described in Section 4; remove the actual component as described below, ignoring the preliminary dismantling steps.*

1 Disconnect the battery negative terminal.

2 Position the engine at top dead centre (TDC on No 4 cylinder) as described in Section 2, and lock the camshaft sprocket, injection pump sprocket and flywheel in position. *Do not* attempt to rotate the engine whilst the locking tools are in position.

Camshaft sprocket

3 Remove the upper and centre timing belt covers as described in Section 3.

4 Loosen the timing belt tensioner pulley retaining nut. Rotate the pulley in a clockwise direction, using a suitable square-section key

fitted to the hole in the pulley hub, then retighten the retaining nut.

5 Disengage the timing belt from the sprocket, and move the belt clear, taking care not to bend or twist it sharply. Remove the locking tool from the camshaft sprocket.

6 Slacken the camshaft sprocket retaining bolt and remove it, along with its washer. To prevent the camshaft rotating as the bolt is slackened, a sprocket-holding tool will be required. In the absence of the special Citroën tool, an acceptable substitute can be fabricated as follows. Use two lengths of steel strip (one long, the other short), and three nuts and bolts; one nut and bolt forms the pivot of a forked tool, with the remaining two nuts and bolts at the tips of the 'forks' to engage with the sprocket spokes **(see illustrations)**. Do not attempt to use the sprocket locking tool (Section 2) to prevent the sprocket from rotating whilst the retaining bolt is slackened.

7 With the retaining bolt removed, slide the sprocket off the end of the camshaft. Note that the tab on the rear of the sprocket engages with a cut-out on the end of the camshaft. Examine the camshaft oil seal for signs of oil leakage and, if necessary, renew it.

Crankshaft sprocket

8 Remove all of the timing belt covers as described in Section 3.

9 Loosen the timing belt tensioner pulley retaining nut. Rotate the pulley in a clockwise direction, using a suitable square-section key fitted to the hole in the pulley hub, then retighten the retaining nut.

10 Disengage the timing belt from the crankshaft sprocket, and move the belt clear, taking care not to bend or twist it sharply.

11 To prevent crankshaft rotation whilst the sprocket retaining bolt is slackened, select top gear, and have an assistant apply the brakes firmly. Note that Citroën technicians use a special tool inserted through the TDC sensor hole, which is located near the locking

5.6a Prevent the camshaft rotating with a sprocket-holding tool

5.6b Remove the retaining bolt and washer, then remove the camshaft sprocket

1B

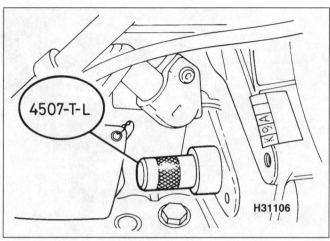

5.11 The Citroën flywheel-locking tool inserted in the TDC sensor hole

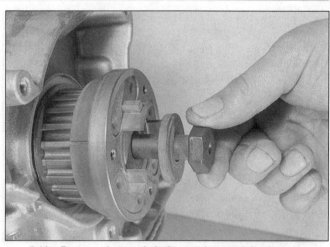

5.12a Remove the crankshaft sprocket retaining bolt . . .

tool hole in the cylinder block rear flange **(see illustration)** - if possible, obtain and use this tool. *Do not* be tempted to use the locking tool described in Section 2 to prevent the crankshaft from rotating; temporarily remove this tool from the rear of the flywheel prior to slackening the pulley bolt, then refit it once the bolt has been slackened.

12 Unscrew the retaining bolt and washer, then slide the sprocket off the end of the crankshaft **(see illustrations)**. Refit the locking tool through the timing hole into the rear of the flywheel.

13 If the Woodruff key is a loose fit in the crankshaft, remove it and store it with the sprocket for safe-keeping. If necessary, also slide the flanged spacer off the end of the crankshaft **(see illustration)**. Examine the crankshaft oil seal for signs of oil leakage and, if necessary, renew it

Fuel injection pump sprocket

14 Remove the upper and centre timing belt covers as described in Section 3.

15 Make alignment marks on the fuel

injection pump sprocket and the timing belt, to ensure that the sprocket and timing belt are correctly aligned on refitting.

16 Loosen the timing belt tensioner pulley retaining nut. Rotate the pulley in a clockwise direction, using a suitable square-section key fitted to the hole in the pulley hub, then retighten the retaining nut.

17 Disengage the timing belt from the injection pump sprocket, and move the belt clear, taking care not to bend or twist it sharply.

18 Remove the locking tools securing the fuel injection pump sprocket in the TDC position.

19 On some engines, the sprocket may be fitted with a flanged nut over which the Citroën puller may be fitted. The puller consists of a plate which is bolted to the sprocket; when the nut is unscrewed, the sprocket is pulled off the injection pump shaft. On other engines, the sprocket is retained by a normal nut and washer, which must be removed before the Citroën puller and special flanged nut is attached. If necessary, a suitable puller can be made up using a short length of bar, and two M7 bolts screwed into the holes provided in

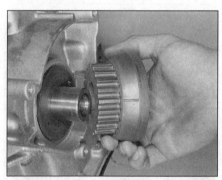

5.12b . . . then slide off the sprocket

the sprocket. The bolts must be approximately 40 mm in length, and the holes in the bar 45 mm apart.

20 The fuel injection pump shaft must be prevented from turning as the sprocket nut is unscrewed, and this can be achieved using a tool similar to that shown. Use the tool to hold the sprocket stationary by means of the holes in the sprocket **(see illustration)**.

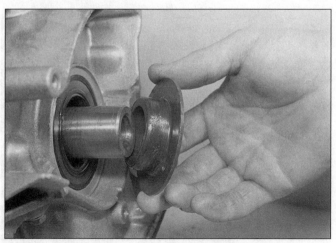

5.13 Remove the flanged spacer if necessary

5.20 Using a home-made tool to hold the injection pump sprocket stationary whilst the retaining bolt is slackened - viewed through headlight aperture

5.22a Home-made injection pump sprocket removal tool in position on the sprocket

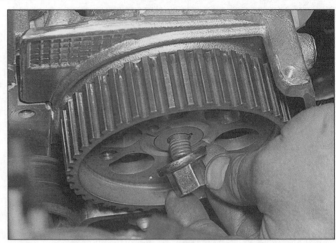

5.22b Unscrew the retaining nut, then remove the sprocket . . .

5.22c . . . and recover the Woodruff key (arrowed) from the injection pump shaft

21 On engines with a flanged securing nut, bolt the puller to the sprocket, then unscrew the sprocket securing nut until the sprocket is freed from the taper on the pump shaft. Recover the Woodruff key from the end of the pump shaft, if it is loose. Unbolt the puller assembly from the sprocket by removing the two securing screws and washers.

22 On engines fitted with a normal nut and washer, first remove the nut and washer, then attach the puller tool and bolt it to the sprocket. Remove the sprocket as described in the previous paragraph. If an improvised puller is being used, partially unscrew the sprocket securing nut, then fit the puller, and tighten the two bolts (forcing the bar against the sprocket nut), until the sprocket is freed from the taper on the pump shaft. Withdraw the sprocket, and recover the Woodruff key from the end of the pump shaft if it is loose (see illustrations). Remove the puller from the sprocket.

Tensioner pulley

23 Remove the timing belt upper and centre covers as described in Section 3.
24 Slacken and remove the timing belt tensioner pulley retaining nut, and slide the pulley off its mounting stud (see illustration). Carefully tie the timing belt down so that it is kept in full engagement with the sprockets. Examine the mounting stud for signs of

damage and, if necessary, renew it - it is removed by unscrewing it from the cylinder block.

Idler

25 Remove the timing belt upper and centre covers as described in Section 3.
26 Loosen the timing belt tensioner pulley retaining nut. Rotate the pulley in a clockwise direction, using a suitable square-section key fitted to the hole in the pulley hub, then retighten the retaining nut. In order to provide some slack in the timing belt between the crankshaft and injection pump sprockets, it will be necessary to remove the locking tool from the flywheel, and rotate the crankshaft slightly anti-clockwise. Make sure, however, that the timing belt remains in full contact with the crankshaft sprocket.
27 Unscrew the bolt retaining the idler to the cylinder block, and withdraw the idler (see illustration). Carefully tie the timing belt up, so that it is kept in full engagement with all of the sprockets.

5.24 Timing belt tensioner pulley retaining nut (arrowed)

5.27 Timing belt idler pulley retaining bolt (arrowed)

5.30 On refitting, ensure that the camshaft sprocket key and camshaft slot are correctly aligned (arrowed)

5.31 Tighten the camshaft sprocket retaining bolt to the specified torque setting

1B

Refitting

28 Clean the sprockets thoroughly, and renew any that show signs of wear, damage or cracks.

29 Clean the tensioner pulley and idler, but do not use any strong solvent which may enter the bearings. Check that each roller rotates freely about its hub, with no sign of stiffness or of free play. Renew the tensioner pulley or idler if there is any doubt about its condition, or if there are any obvious signs of wear or damage.

Camshaft sprocket

30 Locate the sprocket on the end of the camshaft. Ensure that the locating tab is correctly engaged with the cut-out in the camshaft end **(see illustration)**.

31 Refit the sprocket retaining bolt and washer. Tighten the bolt to the specified torque, retaining the sprocket with the tool used on removal **(see illustration)**.

32 Realign the timing hole in the camshaft sprocket (see Section 2) with the corresponding hole in the cylinder head, and refit the locking tool.

33 Refit the timing belt to the camshaft sprocket. Ensure that the front run of the belt is taut around the injection pump sprocket - ie, ensure that any slack is on the tensioner pulley side of the belt. Do not twist the belt sharply while refitting it, and ensure that the belt teeth are seated centrally in the sprockets.

34 Loosen the tensioner pulley retaining nut. Rotate the pulley anti-clockwise to remove all free play from the timing belt, then retighten the nut.

35 Tension the belt as described in paragraphs 12 to 16 of Section 4.

36 Refit the timing belt covers as described in Section 3.

37 Reconnect the battery negative terminal.

Crankshaft sprocket

38 Where removed, locate the Woodruff key

in the crankshaft end, then slide on the flanged spacer, aligning its slot with the Woodruff key.

39 Align the crankshaft sprocket slot with the Woodruff key, and slide it onto the end of the crankshaft.

40 Temporarily remove the locking tool from the rear of the flywheel, then refit the crankshaft sprocket retaining bolt and washer. Tighten the bolt to the specified torque, preventing crankshaft rotation using the method employed on removal. Refit the locking tool to the rear of the flywheel.

41 Relocate the timing belt on the crankshaft sprocket. Ensure that the belt is taut between the crankshaft, injection pump and camshaft sprockets, and over the idler roller - ie, ensure that any slack is on the tensioner pulley side of the belt. Do not twist the belt sharply while refitting it, and ensure that the belt teeth are seated centrally in the sprockets.

42 Loosen the tensioner pulley retaining nut. Rotate the pulley anti-clockwise to remove all free play from the timing belt, then retighten the nut.

5.46 Align the sprocket groove (arrowed) with the Woodruff key when refitting the injection pump sprocket

43 Tension the belt as described in paragraphs 12 to 16 of Section 4.

44 Refit the timing belt covers as described in Section 3.

Fuel injection pump sprocket

45 Where applicable, refit the Woodruff key to the pump shaft, ensuring that it is correctly located in its groove.

46 Locate the sprocket on the injection pump shaft, and engage it with the key **(see illustration)**.

47 Tighten the securing nut to the specified torque, preventing the pump shaft from turning as during removal.

48 Make sure that the locking tools are fitted to the camshaft and fuel injection pump sprockets, and to the TDC hole in the flywheel.

49 Fit the timing belt around the fuel injection pump sprocket, ensuring that the marks made on the belt and sprocket before removal are aligned.

50 Tension the belt as described in paragraphs 12 to 16 of Section 4.

51 Refit the upper and centre timing belt covers as described in Section 3.

Tensioner pulley

52 Check that the mounting stud is tightened in the cylinder block.

53 While holding the timing belt down, locate the tensioner pulley on the stud and refit the retaining nut. Make sure that the rest of the timing belt is not displaced from the other sprockets.

54 Tension the belt as described in paragraphs 12 to 16 of Section 4.

55 Refit the upper and centre timing belt covers as described in Section 3.

Idler

56 While holding the timing belt up, locate the idler on the cylinder block, and refit the retaining bolt. Tighten the bolt securely.

57 Carefully turn the crankshaft clockwise

until the locking tool can be inserted into the flywheel.

58 Tension the belt as described in paragraphs 12 to 16 of Section 4.

59 Refit the upper and centre timing belt covers as described in Section 3.

6 Headlight - removal and refitting

Removal

1 To remove a headlight unit, grip and pull the unit outwards from the front to disengage it from the two inboard adjusters, then pull it towards the centre to disengage it from the single outer adjuster **(see illustration)**. Where applicable, also disconnect it from the headlight level adjustment unit.

2 Remove the rear cover (where applicable), then detach the wiring connectors and remove the unit.

3 If desired, the balljoint and adjuster units (and the electric adjuster motor, where applicable) can be removed from the body after twisting the unit itself (or the locking collar, as applicable) to release the unit from the aperture in the body.

Refitting

4 Refitting is a reversal of removal, ensuring that the headlight balljoints are correctly engaged. Have the beam alignment checked at the earliest opportunity.

6.1 Headlight unit removal

Chapter 2A
Citroën BX petrol 1983 to 1994

Contents

Specifications

Timing belt renewal interval .... Every 36 000 miles (60 000 km)

Ignition timing
BX 14 models .... 6 to 10° BTDC
All other models .... 10° BTDC

Torque wrench settings	Nm	lbf ft
All except BX 14 models		
Camshaft sprocket	80	59
Crankshaft pulley	110	81
Timing belt tensioner lock cam (interlock plunger)	15	11
Timing belt tensioner	16	12
Timing covers	8	6
BX 14 models		
Camshaft sprocket	82	61
Crankshaft pulley	102	75
Timing belt tensioner	21	15
Timing cover	6	4

1.2 Alternator drivebelt and adjustment strap - BX 16

1.5 Checking alternator drivebelt tension

1 Alternator drivebelt - removal, refitting and adjustment

Removal

1 On BX and BX 14 engines, remove the HP pump drivebelt.
2 Loosen the alternator adjustment and pivot bolts, swivel the alternator towards the engine and remove the drivebelt from the pulley (see illustration).

Refitting

3 Refitting is a reversal of removal but drivebelt adjustment must be made before fully tightening the mounting/adjustment bolts.

Adjustment

4 To adjust drivebelt tension, first check that it is correctly located in both pulleys then, with the mounting and adjustment strap bolts loosened, pivot the alternator outwards to tighten the drivebelt. You can use a lever to help achieve this but it must be a wooden one

and it must be used only at the pulley end of the alternator. Levering on the case or at the end opposite to the drive pulley can easily cause expensive damage.
5 Tighten the belt as much as possible (but without over stretching it) to take up any play in the belt at its mid point on the longest run between the pulleys. Whilst a taut tension is required the belt must not be overtightened (see illustration). Tighten the alternator mounting and adjuster strap bolts to set the tension.
6 If a new belt has been fitted, recheck its tension after a nominal mileage has been covered.

2 High pressure (HP) pump drivebelt - removal, refitting and adjustment

Removal

1 On BX 16 and BX 19 models, remove the alternator drivebelt.
2 Loosen the HP pump drivebelt jockey

wheel mounting and adjuster bolts then pivot the jockey wheel inwards towards the engine to release the drivebelt tension (see illustration).
3 Remove the drivebelt from the HP pump and associate pulleys.

Refitting

4 Refit in the reverse order to removal.

Adjustment

5 With the belt fitted on the pulleys, set the tension by pivoting the jockey pulley outwards as much as possible by hand to take up any play in the belt on its longest run between pulleys. If any form of leverage is employed to achieve this tension great care must be taken not to damage any fittings. Tighten the jockey pulley mounting/adjuster bolt to set the tension.
6 With the jockey wheel position set, the belt tension must be felt to be taut under a reasonable thumb pressure at the midway point between the pulleys on its longest run. Recheck the tension of a new belt after a nominal mileage has been covered.

3 Timing belt - removal and refitting

BX 16 and BX 19 models prior to January 1992

Removal

1 Disconnect the battery earth lead.
2 Remove the alternator drivebelt and HP pump drivebelt (Sections 1 and 2).
3 Unbolt and remove the camshaft sprocket cover (see illustration).
4 Turn the crankshaft until the dowel hole in the pulley is at approximately 12 o'clock and the hole in the camshaft sprocket is at approximately 7 o'clock. In this position a

2.2 HP pump drivebelt jockey wheel mounting and adjuster bolts (arrowed) - BX 16

3.3 Camshaft sprocket cover removal

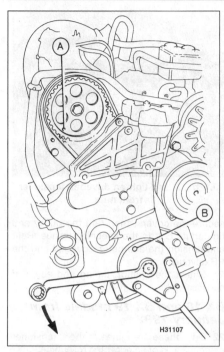

3.4a Set crankshaft pulley and camshaft sprocket dowel holes to positions 'A' and 'B'

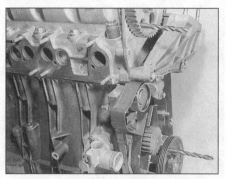

3.4b Timing dowels (drills) in position

10 mm dowel should pass through each hole and into the timing recess behind (see illustrations). Verify this and then remove the dowels.

5 Remove the clutch/torque converter bottom shield. Have an assistant jam the starter ring gear while the crankshaft pulley bolt is undone. This bolt is very tight. Do not jam the pulley by means of the timing dowel as damage will result. Remove the bolts and washer.

6 Refit the 10 mm dowels into the timing holes. Adjust the crankshaft position if

necessary by means of the starter ring gear. Remove the crankshaft pulley, retrieving the Woodruff key if it is loose.

7 Remove the timing belt covers from the front of the timing belt. Note that from May 1987, a simplified three-piece timing belt cover has been fitted. This simplified cover can be fitted to earlier vehicles but will require the purchase of an additional nut and screw.

8 Slacken the two nuts on the front of the drivebelt tensioner and the single nut at the rear. Use a spanner on the square end of the tensioner cam spindle to turn the cam to the horizontal position and so compress the tensioner spring. Tighten the cam locknut (see illustrations).

9 Remove the timing belt, taking care not to kink it or contaminate it with oil if it is to be re-used.

Refitting

10 Commence refitting by positioning the belt on the crankshaft sprocket, then refitting the pulley and verifying the correct position of the crankshaft by means of the dowel. Observe the arrows on the belt showing the direction of rotation, and the timing lines which align with marks on the crankshaft and camshaft sprockets (see illustrations). The

2A

3.8a Central timing cover removed for access to tensioner

3.8b Tensioner cam spindle (square end) and locknut

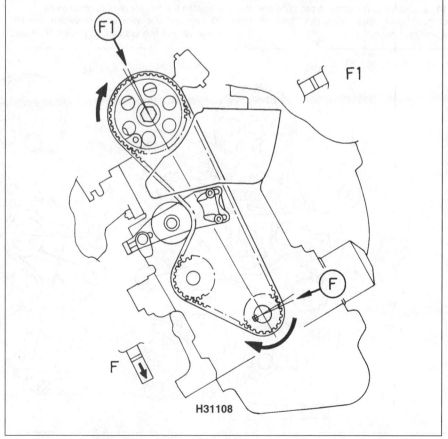

3.10a Timing belt-to-sprockets alignment. Arrow indicates normal direction of belt rotation

3.10b Line on belt aligns with mark on camshaft sprocket

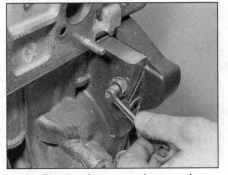

3.12a Turn tensioner cam downwards . . .

3.12b . . . and tighten drivebelt tensioner front nuts

drivebelt used with the type of tensioner mechanism fitted to these engines should have 113 teeth and white markings.

11 Fit the belt to the camshaft sprocket, around the tensioner and to the coolant pump sprocket.

12 Release the tensioner cam locknut and turn the cam downwards to release the spring. Tighten the locknut and the tensioner front nuts **(see illustrations)**.

13 Remove the timing dowels and turn the crankshaft through two full turns in the normal direction of rotation. Turn the crankshaft further to bring No 1 piston to TDC on the firing stroke (flywheel index mark aligned with the O-mark).

14 Slacken the tensioner front nuts and the cam locknut, then retighten them to the specified torque.

15 Turn the crankshaft further and make sure that the timing dowels can still be inserted. If not, remove the drivebelt and start again.

16 If a new belt has been fitted, it must be run in and retensioned as follows.

17 Tighten the crankshaft pulley bolt to the specified torque, then refit and tension the alternator drivebelt and the HP drivebelt. Temporarily refit the camshaft sprocket cover.

18 Run the engine up to operating temperature (indicated by the cooling fan operating) then stop it and allow it to cool for at least two hours.

19 Rotate the crankshaft to the TDC position, No 1 cylinder firing, then slacken and retighten the tensioner nuts once more.

20 Remove the alternator drivebelt, the HP drivebelt and the crankshaft pulley. Refit and

secure the covers, then refit the pulley and tighten its bolt to the specified torque. Refit and tension the alternator drivebelt and the HP drivebelt.

21 Check the ignition timing and adjust if necessary.

BX 16 and BX 19 models from January 1992

22 On these engines, the tensioner mechanism is of an eccentric roller type.

23 To accommodate this revised mechanism, a number of the surrounding engine components have been changed from those fitted to engines manufactured before January 1992 **(see illustration)**. They are as follows:

a) *Tensioner assembly*

b) *Timing belt*

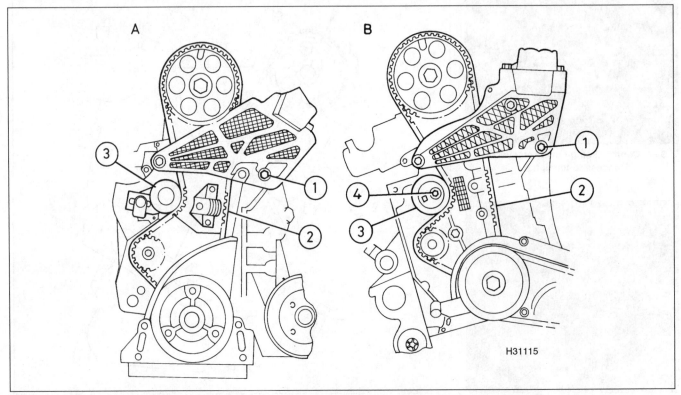

3.23 Spring-loaded timing belt tensioner (A) and eccentric roller type tensioner (B)

1 Right-hand engine mounting   *2 Timing belt*   *3 Tensioner assembly*   *4 Tensioner roller bolt*

c) Front crankshaft oil seal carrier plate
d) Coolant pump
e) Right-hand engine mounting
f) Cylinder block (has an extra threaded hole for tensioner centre bolt)
g) Timing belt covers

24 Note that the type of timing belt fitted to these engines should have 114 teeth and yellow/orange markings. If the drivebelt is to be renewed, ensure that the correct type of replacement drivebelt is obtained.

Removal

Note: *Citroën specify the use of a special tool (SEEM belt tension measuring equipment) to correctly set the belt tension*

25 Proceed as described in paragraphs 1 to 7, noting that the crankshaft pulley timing dowel must be of 10 mm diameter, stepped down to 8 mm at one end to engage with the smaller hole in the timing recess.

26 With the timing belt covers removed, slacken the tensioner roller bolt to relieve the belt tension, then withdraw the belt, noting the direction of fitting and the markings.

Refitting

27 Commence refitting by slipping the belt over the camshaft sprocket, followed by the crankshaft sprocket, the coolant pump sprocket, and finally over the tensioner roller. Observe the arrows on the belt indicating the direction of rotation and the timing lines which align with corresponding marks on the crankshaft and camshaft sprockets.

28 With the camshaft timing dowel fitted, rotate the tensioner roller anti-clockwise by hand as far as possible to take up any slack in the belt, then tighten the tensioner roller bolt sufficiently to hold the roller in position. The special belt tension measuring equipment should be fitted to the front run of the belt and the tensioner roller should be moved to give a reading of 30 SEEM units. Tighten the roller bolt to the specified torque, taking care not to move the roller as the bolt is tightened.

29 Check that the crankshaft and camshaft are still positioned correctly by temporarily refitting the crankshaft pulley and reinserting the timing dowel.

30 Remove the timing dowels, temporarily refit the crankshaft pulley and turn the crankshaft through two full turns in the normal direction of rotation. Check that both timing dowels can still be inserted. If not, remove the

timing belt and start again. Never turn the crankshaft backwards during this procedure.

31 If all is well, remove the dowels and turn the crankshaft through two further turns in the normal direction of rotation.

32 Refit the camshaft timing dowel and then check the tension measuring equipment reading is between 42 and 46 units.

33 If the tension is not as specified, repeat the tensioning operation.

34 On completion, refit all disturbed components, tightening the crankshaft pulley bolt to the specified torque. Tension the alternator drivebelt and HP pump drivebelt.

BX 14 models

Removal

35 Disconnect the battery earth lead.

36 Remove the hydraulic pump and the alternator drivebelts (Sections 1 and 2).

37 Remove the rocker cover and remove the rubber gasket from the cover **(see illustrations)**.

38 Remove the two spacers and baffle plate from the studs **(see illustrations)**.

39 Unbolt the upper timing cover, followed

3.37a Removing a rocker cover nut

3.37b Removing rocker cover gasket

3.38a Remove rocker cover spacers (arrowed) . . .

3.38b . . . and baffle plate

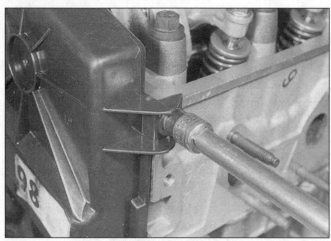

3.39a Unbolting upper timing cover

3.39b Removing upper timing cover

3.39c Removing intermediate timing cover

3.39d Removing lower timing cover

by the intermediate cover and lower cover **(see illustrations)**.

40 Turn the engine clockwise, using a socket on the crankshaft sprocket bolt, until the small hole in the camshaft sprocket is aligned with the corresponding hole in the cylinder head. Insert the shank of a close-fitting twist drill into the holes **(see illustration)**.

41 Align the TDC holes in the flywheel and cylinder block rear flange, then insert a further twist drill or long bolt **(see illustration)**.

42 Loosen the timing belt tensioner roller nut **(see illustration)**, turn the tensioner clockwise using a screwdriver or square drive in the special hole, then re-tighten the nut.

43 Mark the normal direction of rotation on

the timing belt, then remove it from the camshaft, coolant pump, and crankshaft sprockets.

Refitting

Caution: Take care not to kink or contaminate the timing belt with oil

44 Engage the timing belt with the crankshaft

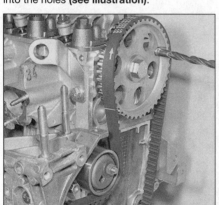

3.40 Camshaft sprocket held at TDC

3.41 Using long bolt (arrowed) to align TDC holes in flywheel and cylinder block

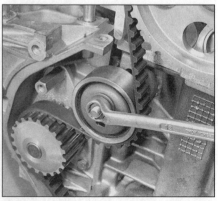

3.42 Loosening timing belt tensioner roller nut

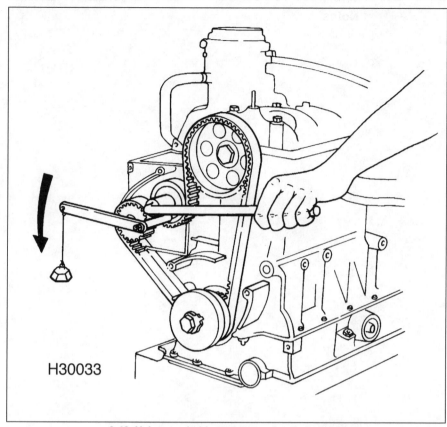

3.46 Using a suitable tool to tension timing belt

3.47 Timing cover correctly refitted

long arm and a 1.5 kg (3.3 lb) weight. The torque applied to the roller will approximate 12 kgf (10.5 lbf in). Pre-tension the timing belt with the tool and tighten the nut, then remove the timing pins and rotate the crankshaft through two complete turns. Loosen the nut and allow the roller to re-position itself. Tighten the nut.

47 Refit the lower, intermediate, and upper timing covers, then tighten the bolts **(see illustration)**.

48 Refit the baffle plate with its edges pointing downwards, followed by the two spacers.

49 Fit the rubber gasket to the rocker cover, locate the cover in position and tighten the nuts.

50 Refit and tension the hydraulic pump and the alternator drivebelts.

51 Reconnect the battery earth lead.

sprocket then, keeping it taut, feed it onto the camshaft sprocket, around the tensioner pulley, and onto the coolant pump sprocket.

45 Loosen the nut and turn the tensioner roller anti-clockwise by hand. Tighten the nut.

46 Citroën dealers use a special tool **(see illustration)** to tension the timing belt. A similar tool may be fabricated using an 8.0 cm

Notes

Chapter 2B
Citroën BX diesel 1983 to 1994

Contents

Specifications

Timing belt renewal interval . . . .   Every 36 000 miles (60 000 km)

Note: *Although the normal interval for timing belt renewal is 48 000 miles (80 000 km), it is strongly recommended that the interval is reduced on vehicles which are subjected to intensive use, ie, mainly short journeys or a lot of stop-start driving. The actual belt renewal interval is therefore very much up to the individual owner. That being said, it is highly recommended to err on the side of safety, and renew the belt at this earlier interval, bearing in mind the drastic consequences resulting from belt failure.*

Torque wrench settings	Nm	lbf ft
Alternator mountings	35	26
Camshaft sprocket	35	26
Crankshaft pulley bolt:		
Stage 1	40	30
Stage 2	plus 60° or to 150	plus 60° or to 111
Engine mounting bracket, right-hand lower	18	13
Engine mounting bracket, right-hand upper:		
To engine	35	26
To mounting rubber	28	21
Engine mounting, left-hand:		
Centre nut	35	26
Centre stud to transmission	50	37
Small nuts	18	13
Timing belt intermediate roller	18	13
Timing belt tensioner	18	13
Timing cover, lower	12	9

1.1a Alternator pivot bolt

1.1b Alternator adjustment locknut (1) and adjustment bolt (2)

1 Auxiliary belt – removal, refitting and adjustment

Removal and refitting

1 To remove the belt, loosen the pivot bolt and adjustment locknut **(see illustrations)**.
2 Unscrew the adjustment bolt to release the tension. The drivebelt can now be removed from the pulleys.
3 Refitting is a reversal of removal.

Adjustment

4 To adjust the tension, first check that the belt is correctly fitted over the pulleys. With the alternator mountings loose, tighten the adjustment bolt to tension the belt. The belt should be able to move by approximately 6.0 mm, with moderate thumb pressure midway between the pulleys **(see illustration)**. Tighten the mounting bolts to the correct torque.

1.4 Checking tension of alternator drivebelt

Later models with air conditioning

5 During 1988, the three-pulley drivebelt system previously used was replaced by a five-pulley system, as shown **(see illustration)**.
6 With the new system, drivebelt tension is adjusted by movement of the bottom idler wheel. Tension is checked at the longest belt run, ie between the alternator and compressor pulleys.

2 Timing belt - removal, refitting and tensioning

Removal

1 Chock the rear wheels and release the handbrake, as the handbrake operates on the front wheels.

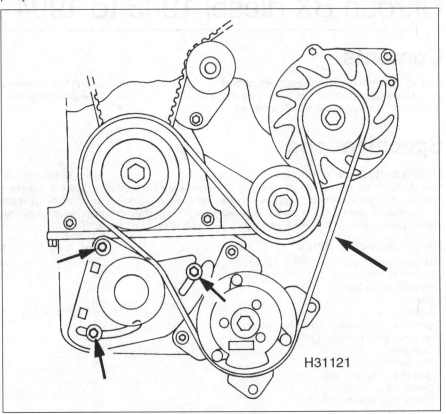

1.5 Drivebelt run - later models with air conditioning
Arrow shows tension checking point
Smaller arrows indicate idler wheel securing bolts

2.9 Right-hand engine mounting bracket

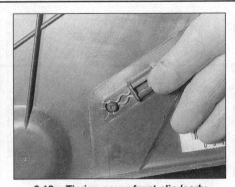

2.10a Timing cover front clip (early models) . . .

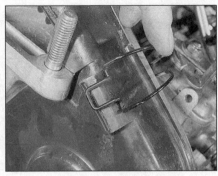

2.10b . . . and spring clips

2 On manual transmission models jack up the front right-hand corner of the vehicle until the wheel is just clear of the ground. Support the vehicle on an axle stand and engage 4th or 5th gear. This will enable the engine to be turned easily by turning the right-hand wheel. On automatic transmission models use an open-ended spanner on the crankshaft pulley bolt.

3 Remove the engine splash guard from under the right-hand front wheel arch.

4 Disconnect the battery negative lead.

5 Loosen the alternator pivot and adjustment bolts then unscrew the tension bolt until it is possible to slip the drivebelt from the pulleys.

6 With 4th or 5th gear selected on manual transmission models have an assistant depress the footbrake pedal, then unscrew the crankshaft pulley bolt. The handbrake may be applied instead of the footbrake pedal to hold the crankshaft stationary. On automatic transmission models unbolt the transmission cover and lock the starter ring gear. Note that the bolt is extremely tight.

7 Slide the pulley from the front of the crankshaft. Unbolt the bottom timing cover.

8 Support the weight of the engine using a hoist or trolley jack.

9 Unscrew the nuts and remove the right-hand engine mounting bracket **(see illustration)**.

10 Pull up the front clip (early models), release the spring clips, and withdraw the two

timing cover sections **(see illustrations)**. Note that the spring clip is not fitted to later models, which have a modified cover and fastenings.

11 Turn the engine by means of the front right-hand wheel or crankshaft pulley bolt until the three bolt holes in the camshaft and injection pump sprockets are aligned with the corresponding holes in the engine front plate.

12 Insert an 8.0 mm diameter metal dowel rod or drill through the special hole in the left-hand rear flange of the cylinder block by

the starter motor. Then carefully turn the engine either way until the rod enters the TDC hole in the flywheel **(see illustration)**.

13 Insert three M8 bolts through the holes in the camshaft and injection pump sprockets and screw them into the engine front plate finger-tight **(see illustration)**.

14 Loosen the timing belt tensioner pivot nut and adjustment bolt, then turn the bracket anti-clockwise to release the tension and retighten the adjustment bolt to hold the tensioner in the released position. If available

2.12 Using a twist drill to enter the TDC hole in the flywheel

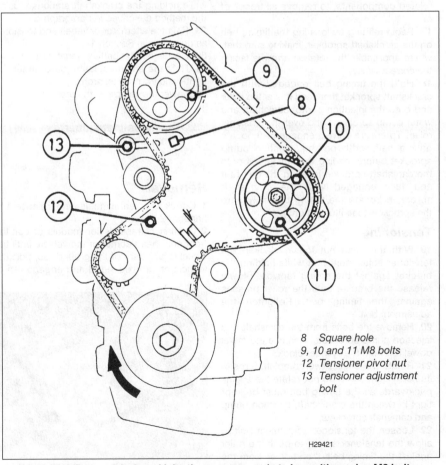

8   Square hole
9, 10 and 11 M8 bolts
12 Tensioner pivot nut
13 Tensioner adjustment bolt

H29421

2.13 Holding camshaft and injection pump sprockets in position using M8 bolts

2B

2.18a Fitting the timing belt over the injection pump sprocket . . .

2.18b . . . the camshaft sprocket . . .

2.18c . . . and the water pump sprocket

use a 3/8 inch square drive extension in the hole provided to turn the bracket against the spring tension.

15 Mark the timing belt with an arrow to indicate its normal direction of turning then remove it from the camshaft, injection pump, water pump and crankshaft sprockets.

Refitting

16 If signs of oil contamination are found, trace the source of the oil leak, and rectify it. Wash down the engine timing belt area and all related components, to remove all traces of oil.

17 Begin refitting by locating the timing belt on the crankshaft sprocket, making sure that, where applicable, the rotation arrow is facing the correct way.

18 Hold the timing belt engaged with the crankshaft sprocket then feed it over the roller and onto the injection pump, camshaft, and water pump sprockets and over the tensioner roller. To ensure correct engagement, locate only a half width on the injection pump sprocket before feeding the timing belt onto the camshaft sprocket keeping the belt taut and fully engaged with the crankshaft sprocket. Locate the timing belt fully onto the sprockets **(see illustrations)**.

Tensioning

19 With the pivot nut loose, slacken the tensioner adjustment bolt while holding the bracket against the spring tension. Slowly release the bracket until the roller presses against the timing belt. Retighten the adjustment bolt.

20 Remove the bolts from the camshaft and injection pump sprockets. Remove the metal dowel rod from the cylinder block.

21 Rotate the engine two complete turns in its normal direction. Do not rotate the engine backwards as the timing belt must be kept tight between the crankshaft, injection pump and camshaft sprockets.

22 Loosen the tensioner adjustment bolt to allow the tensioner spring to push the roller against the timing belt, then tighten both the adjustment bolt and pivot nut.

23 Recheck the engine timing as described

in paragraphs 11 and 12 then remove the metal dowel rod.

24 Refit the three timing cover sections and secure with the special clip and spring clips.

25 Refit the right-hand engine mounting bracket and tighten the nuts.

26 Remove the trolley jack or hoist.

27 Slide the pulley onto the front of the crankshaft.

28 Apply three drops of locking fluid on the threads of the crankshaft pulley bolt then insert it and tighten to the specified torque while holding the crankshaft stationary using the method described in paragraph 6.

29 Refit the alternator drivebelt and tension it as described in Section 1.

30 Reconnect the battery negative lead.

31 Refit the engine splash-guard under the right-hand front wheel arch.

32 Lower the vehicle to the ground.

---

3 Timing belt tensioner - removal and refitting

Removal

1 Chock the rear wheels and release the handbrake.

2 On manual transmission models jack up the front right-hand corner of the vehicle until the wheel is just clear of the ground. Support the vehicle on an axle stand and engage 4th or

3.10 Home-made tool for holding the tensioner plunger

5th gear so that the engine may be rotated by turning the right-hand wheel. On automatic transmission models use an open-ended spanner on the crankshaft pulley bolt.

3 Support the weight of the engine using a hoist or trolley jack.

4 Unscrew the nuts and remove the right-hand engine mounting bracket.

5 Pull up the special clip, release the spring clips and withdraw the two timing cover sections.

6 Turn the engine by means of the front right-hand wheel or crankshaft pulley bolt until the three bolt holes in the camshaft and injection pump sprockets are aligned with the corresponding holes in the engine front plate.

7 Insert an 8.0 mm diameter metal dowel rod or drill through the special hole in the left-hand rear flange of the cylinder block by the starter motor. Then carefully turn the engine either way until the rod enters the TDC hole in the flywheel.

8 Insert three M8 bolts through the holes in the camshaft and injection pump sprockets and screw them into the engine front plate finger-tight.

9 Loosen the timing belt tensioner pivot nut and adjustment bolt, then turn the bracket anti-clockwise until the adjustment bolt is in the middle of the slot and retighten the bolt. If available use a 3/8 inch square drive extension in the hole provided to turn the bracket against the spring tension.

10 A tool must now be obtained to hold the tensioner plunger in the mounting bracket. Citroën tool 7009-T1 is designed to slide in the two lower bolt holes of the mounting bracket and it is quite easy to fabricate a similar tool out of sheet metal using long bolts instead of metal dowel rods **(see illustration)**.

11 Unscrew the two lower bolts then fit the special tool. Grease the inner surface of the tool to prevent any damage to the end of the tensioner plunger.

12 Unscrew the pivot nut and adjustment bolt and withdraw the tensioner bracket, complete with roller.

13 Unbolt the engine mounting bracket noting that the uppermost bolt is on the inside face of the engine front plate.

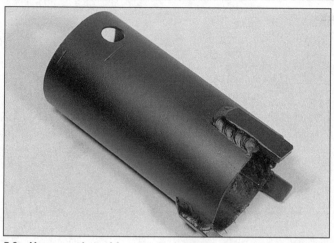

5.2a Home-made tool for unscrewing the engine mounting rubber

5.2b Engine mounting rubber showing slots

2B

14 Compress the tensioner plunger into the mounting bracket, remove the special tool then withdraw the plunger and spring.

Refitting

15 Refitting is a reversal of removal, but refer to Section 2, paragraphs 19 to 23 for details of the timing belt adjustment procedure.

4 Timing belt intermediate roller - removal and refitting

Removal

1 Follow the procedure given in paragraphs 1 to 9 of Section 3.
2 Remove the engine splash guard from under the right-hand front wheel arch.
3 Disconnect the battery negative lead.
4 Loosen the alternator pivot and adjustment bolts then unscrew the tension bolt until it is possible to slip the drivebelt from the pulleys.
5 With 4th or 5th gear selected on manual transmission models have an assistant depress the footbrake pedal, then unscrew the crankshaft pulley bolt. The handbrake may be applied instead of the footbrake pedal to hold the crankshaft stationary. On automatic transmission models unbolt the transmission cover and lock the starter ring gear.
6 Slide the pulley from the front of the crankshaft.

7 Unbolt the lower timing cover.
8 Remove the spacer from the stud for the upper timing cover sections. Note the position of the stud then unscrew and remove it.
9 Unscrew the remaining bolts securing the intermediate roller bracket to the cylinder block noting that the upper bolt also secures the engine mounting bracket.
10 Slightly loosen the remaining engine mounting bracket bolts then slide out the intermediate roller and bracket.

Refitting

11 Refitting is a reversal of removal, but note the following additional points:
a) *Tighten all bolts to the specified torque*
b) *Apply three drops of locking fluid to the threads of the crankshaft pulley bolt before inserting it*
c) *Tension the alternator drivebelt as described in Section 1*
d) *Adjust the timing belt as described in Section 2, paragraphs 19 to 23*

5 Engine right-hand mounting - removal and refitting

Removal

1 Support the engine with a hoist or with a trolley jack and block of wood beneath the sump.

5.3 Right-hand engine mounting bracket

2 Make up a tool similar to that shown, to engage with the slots in the rim of the rubber **(see illustrations)**. Unscrew the old rubber from the body using the tool.
3 Unscrew the nuts and remove the right-hand mounting bracket, noting the location of any shims **(see illustration)**.

Refitting

4 Refitting is a reversal of removal. Tighten the rubber firmly to the body using the tool, to the specified torque. With the weight of the engine on the mounting, the clearance between the mounting bracket and each rubber stop should be 1.0 ± 0.7 mm. If necessary adjust the clearance by means of shims positioned under the stops.

Notes

Chapter 3A
Citroën XM petrol 1989 to 1998

Contents

Specifications

Timing belt renewal interval . . . .   Every 36 000 miles (60 000 km)

Note: *Although the normal interval for timing belt renewal is 72 000 miles (120 000 km), it is strongly recommended that the interval is halved on vehicles which are subjected to intensive use, ie, mainly short journeys or a lot of stop-start driving. The actual belt renewal interval is therefore very much up to the individual owner. That being said, it is highly recommended to err on the side of safety, and renew the belt at this earlier interval, bearing in mind the drastic consequences resulting from belt failure.*

Torque wrench settings	Nm	lbf ft
Camshaft sprocket retaining bolt	35	26
Crankshaft pulley retaining bolt	110	81
Cylinder head cover nuts/bolts	10	7
Roadwheel bolts	90	66
Timing belt cover bolts	8	6
Timing belt tensioner pulley bolt	20	15

1 Auxiliary drivebelt – adjustment, removal and refitting

Adjustment

1 The belt(s) should be tensioned to that, under firm thumb pressure, there is approximately 5.0 mm of free movement at the mid-point between the pulleys on the longest belt run.

2 If adjustment is necessary, loosen the alternator pivot bolt first, then loosen the adjustment bolt(s). Alternatively, on models equipped with a separate belt tensioner/ adjuster mechanism, loosen the tensioner bolt(s) and move or turn the tensioner (as applicable) to relieve the tension in the belt (see illustrations).

3 To apply tension to the belt on models without a separate belt tensioner/adjuster mechanism, turn the adjuster screw as necessary, and move the alternator to tension the belt. Tighten the adjustment bolt(s) and the pivot bolt.

4 To apply tension to the belt on models with a separate belt tensioner/adjuster mechanism, turn or reposition the tensioner (as applicable) to achieve the correct belt tension. Tighten the tensioner bolt(s) securely on completion.

5 Run the engine for about 5 minutes, then recheck the tension.

Removal and refitting

6 To remove a belt, slacken the belt tension fully as described previously. Slip the belt off the pulleys, noting its routing to aid refitting, then fit the new belt ensuring that it is routed correctly. Note that on models with two drivebelts, it will be necessary to remove the front drivebelt for access to the rear belt.

7 With the belt in position, adjust the tension as previously described.

2 Engine assembly/valve timing holes – general information and usage

Note: Do not attempt to rotate the engine whilst the crankshaft/camshaft are locked in position. If the engine is to be left in this state for a long period of time, it is a good idea to place suitable warning notices inside the vehicle, and in the engine compartment. This will reduce the possibility of the engine being accidentally cranked on the starter motor, which is likely to cause damage with the locking pins in place.

1 On all models, timing holes are drilled in the camshaft sprocket and crankshaft pulley. The holes are used to align the crankshaft and camshaft, to prevent the possibility of the valves contacting the pistons when refitting the cylinder head, or when refitting the timing belt. When the holes are aligned with their corresponding holes in the cylinder head and cylinder block (as appropriate), suitable diameter pins can be inserted to lock both the camshaft and crankshaft in position. Proceed as follows:

2 Jack up the front of the car and support it on axle stands. Remove the right-hand front roadwheel.

3 From underneath the front of the car, unscrew the bolts and prise out the clips securing the plastic cover to the inner wing valance. Remove the cover to gain access to the crankshaft pulley bolt. The crankshaft can then be turned using a suitable socket and extension bar fitted to the pulley bolt. Note that the crankshaft must always be turned in a clockwise direction (viewed from the right-hand side of vehicle).

4 Remove the timing belt upper cover with reference to Section 4.

5 Rotate the crankshaft pulley until the timing hole in the camshaft sprocket is aligned with its corresponding hole in the cylinder head. Note that the holes are aligned when the sprocket hole is in the 8 o'clock position, when viewed from the right-hand end of the engine.

6 With the camshaft sprocket timing hole correctly positioned, insert an 8 mm diameter bolt or drill through the timing (8 mm diameter) hole in the crankshaft pulley, and locate it in the corresponding hole in the end of the

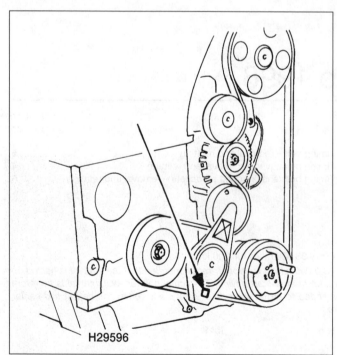

1.2a Auxiliary drivebelt arrangement – later turbo models with air conditioning

Insert a square-drive extension into the hole (arrowed) and lever to release the belt tension

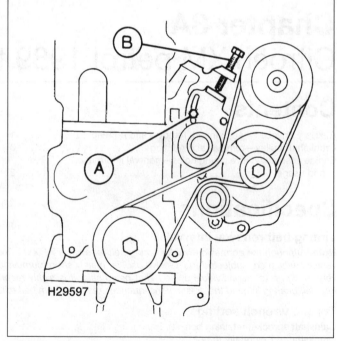

1.2b Auxiliary drivebelt arrangement – later turbo models without air conditioning

Slacken the bolt (A) and turn the bolt (B) to adjust the tension

2.6 8 mm diameter drill inserted through the crankshaft pulley timing hole

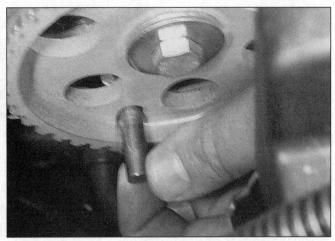

2.7 9.5 mm diameter drill inserted through the camshaft pulley timing hole

cylinder block **(see illustration)**. Note that it may be necessary to rotate the crankshaft slightly, to get the holes to align.

7 Once the crankshaft pulley is locked in position, insert an 9.5 mm diameter bolt or drill through the camshaft sprocket hole and locate it in the cylinder head **(see illustration)**.

8 The crankshaft and camshaft are now locked in position, preventing rotation.

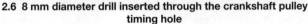

3 Crankshaft pulley –
removal and refitting

Removal

1 Remove the auxiliary drivebelt (Section 1).

2 To prevent the crankshaft turning whilst the pulley retaining bolt is being slackened, select 4th gear and have an assistant apply the brakes firmly. *Do not* attempt to lock the pulley by inserting a bolt/drill through the

timing hole. If the locking pin is in position, temporarily remove it prior to slackening the pulley bolt, then refit it once the bolt has been slackened.

3 Unscrew the retaining bolt and washer, then slide the pulley off the end of the crankshaft **(see illustrations)**. If the pulley locating roll pin or Woodruff key (as applicable) is a loose fit, remove it and store it with the pulley for safe-keeping. If the pulley is tight fit, it can be drawn off the crankshaft using a suitable puller.

Refitting

4 Ensure the Woodruff key is correctly located in its crankshaft groove, or that the roll pin is in position (as applicable). Refit the pulley to the end of the crankshaft, aligning its locating groove or hole with the Woodruff key or pin.

5 Thoroughly clean the threads of the pulley retaining bolt, then apply a coat of locking compound to the bolt threads. Citroën

recommend Loctite (available from your Citroën dealer); in the absence of this, any good-quality locking compound may be used.

6 Refit the crankshaft pulley retaining bolt and washer. Tighten the bolt to the specified torque (see *Specifications*), preventing the crankshaft from turning using the method employed on removal.

7 Refit and tension the auxiliary drivebelt as described in Section 1.

4 Timing belt covers –
removal and refitting

Removal

Upper cover

1 Release the retaining clip, and free the fuel hoses from the top of the timing belt cover.

2 Slacken and remove the two cover retaining bolts, then lift the upper cover upwards and

3A

3.3a Removing the crankshaft pulley retaining bolt

3.3b Removing the crankshaft pulley from the end of the crankshaft

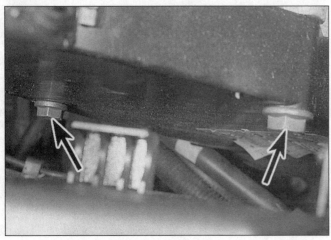

4.2a Upper timing belt cover retaining bolts (arrowed)

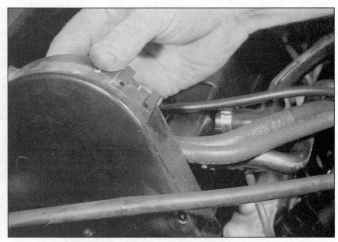

4.2b Removing the upper timing belt cover

out of the engine compartment **(see illustrations).**

Lower cover

3 Remove the crankshaft pulley (Section 3).
4 Slacken and remove the three retaining bolts, then remove the lower timing belt cover from the engine. Note that on some models it

4.4a Removing the auxiliary drivebelt tensioner assembly

may be necessary to unbolt the auxiliary drivebelt tensioner assembly and remove it from the engine in order to allow the cover to be removed **(see illustrations).**

Refitting

5 Refitting is a reversal of the relevant removal procedure, ensuring that each cover section is correctly located, and that the cover retaining nuts and/or bolts are securely tightened to the specified torque, where given (see *Specifications*).

---

5 Timing belt –
removal and refitting

Note: *Citroën specify the use of a special electronic tool (SEEM 4122-T) to correctly set the timing belt tension.*

Removal

1 Disconnect the battery negative terminal.

2 Jack up the front of the vehicle and support it on axle stands. Remove the right-hand front wheel.
3 Prise out the clips and unbolt the inner splash guard.
4 Remove the auxiliary drivebelt as described in Section 1. Also unbolt and remove the auxiliary drivebelt tensioner, if fitted.
5 Unbolt and remove the upper timing belt cover as described in Section 4.
6 Align the engine assembly/valve timing holes as described in Section 2, and lock the camshaft sprocket and crankshaft pulley in position. *Do not* attempt to rotate the engine whilst the pins are in position.
7 Remove the crankshaft pulley as described in Section 3.
8 Unbolt and remove the lower timing belt cover (refer to Section 4 if necessary).
9 Loosen the timing belt tensioner pulley retaining bolt. Pivot the pulley in a clockwise direction, using a suitable square-section key fitted to the hole in the pulley hub, then securely retighten the retaining bolt.

4.4b Unscrew the retaining bolts . . .

4.4c . . . and remove the lower timing cover

5.10 Removing the timing belt from the water pump sprocket

6.6 Using a home-made tool to retain the camshaft sprocket

10 If the timing belt is to be re-used, use white paint or chalk to mark the direction of rotation on the belt (if markings do not already exist), then slip the belt off the sprockets **(see illustration)**. Note that the crankshaft must not be rotated whilst the belt is removed.

11 If signs of oil contamination are found, trace the source of the oil leak and rectify it. Wash down the engine timing belt area and all related components, to remove all traces of oil.

Refitting

12 Before refitting, thoroughly clean the timing belt sprockets. Check that the tensioner pulley rotates freely, without any sign of roughness. If necessary, renew the tensioner pulley as described in Section 6.

13 Ensure that the camshaft sprocket locking pin is still in position. Temporarily refit the crankshaft pulley, and insert the locking pin through the pulley timing hole to ensure that the crankshaft is still correctly positioned.

14 Remove the crankshaft pulley. Manoeuvre the timing belt into position, ensuring that any arrows on the belt are pointing in the direction of rotation (clockwise when viewed from the right-hand end of the engine).

15 Do not twist the timing belt sharply while refitting it. Fit the belt over the crankshaft and camshaft sprockets. Ensure that the belt front run is taut - ie, any slack should be on the tensioner pulley side of the belt. Fit the belt over the water pump sprocket and tensioner pulley. Ensure that the belt teeth are seated centrally in the sprockets.

16 Temporarily refit the crankshaft pulley at this stage and tighten the bolt moderately, then refit the locking pin. **Note:** *The timing belt is tensioned with the timing covers removed, then the pulley is removed to fit the covers and finally refitted.*

17 Loosen the tensioner pulley retaining bolt. Using the square-section key, pivot the pulley anti-clockwise to remove all free play from the timing belt.

18 The special belt tension measuring equipment is fitted to the front run of the timing belt. The tensioner roller should be adjusted so that the initial belt tension is 16 ± 2 units .

19 Remove the locking pins, then rotate the crankshaft through two complete rotations in a clockwise direction (viewed from the right-hand end of the engine). Realign the camshaft and crankshaft engine assembly/valve timing holes (see Section 2). *Do not* at any time rotate the crankshaft anti-clockwise. Both camshaft and crankshaft timing holes should be aligned so that the locking pins can be easily inserted. This indicates that the valve timing is correct. If all is well, remove the pins.

20 If the timing holes are not correctly positioned, repeat the fitting procedure so far.

21 Rotate the crankshaft two more turns without turning backwards and refit the camshaft locking pin, then check that the final belt tension on the taut front run of the belt is 44 ± 2 units. If not, repeat the complete fitting procedure.

22 With the belt tension correctly set remove the camshaft locking pin, then remove the crankshaft pulley and refit the timing cover(s).

23 Refit the crankshaft pulley but this time apply locking fluid to the threads of the bolt before inserting it. Tighten the bolt to the specified torque (see *Specifications*) and refer to Section 3 if necessary.

24 Refit the auxiliary drivebelt tensioner then refit and tension the drivebelt with reference to Section 1.

25 Refit the inner splash guard and front right-hand wheel, then lower the vehicle to the ground.

26 Reconnect the battery negative terminal.

---

6 Timing belt tensioner and sprockets – removal and refitting

Note: *This Section describes the removal and refitting of the components concerned as individual operations – if more than one is to*

be removed at the same time, start by removing the timing belt as described in Section 5; remove the actual component as described below, ignoring the preliminary dismantling steps.

Removal

1 Disconnect the battery negative lead.

2 Align the engine assembly/valve timing holes as described in Section 2, locking the camshaft sprocket and the crankshaft pulley in position, and proceed as described under the relevant sub-heading. *Do not* attempt to rotate the engine whilst the pins are in position.

Camshaft sprocket

3 Remove the upper timing belt cover as described in Section 4.

4 Loosen the timing belt tensioner pulley retaining bolt. Rotate the pulley in a clockwise direction, using a suitable square-section key fitted to the hole in the pulley hub, then retighten the retaining bolt.

5 Remove the locking pin from the camshaft sprocket. Disengage the timing belt from the sprocket and position it clear, taking care not to bend or twist the belt sharply.

6 Slacken the camshaft sprocket retaining bolt and remove it, along with its washer. To prevent the camshaft rotating as the bolt is slackened, a sprocket holding tool will be required. In the absence of the special Citroën tool, an acceptable substitute can be fabricated from two lengths of steel strip (one long, the other short) and three nuts and bolts, as follows. One nut and bolt form the pivot of a forked tool, with the remaining two nuts and bolts at the tips of the 'forks' to engage with the sprocket spokes **(see illustration)**. *Do not* attempt to use the sprocket locking pin to prevent the sprocket from rotating whilst the bolt is slackened.

7 With the retaining bolt removed, slide the sprocket off the end of the camshaft. If the locating peg is a loose fit in the rear of the sprocket, remove it for safe-keeping. Examine

3A

the camshaft oil seal for signs of oil leakage and, if necessary, renew it.

Crankshaft sprocket

8 Remove the upper, centre and/or lower timing belt cover(s) (as applicable) as described in Section 4.

9 Loosen the timing belt tensioner pulley retaining bolt. Rotate the pulley in a clockwise direction, using a suitable square-section key fitted to the hole in the pulley hub, then retighten the retaining bolt.

10 Disengage the timing belt from the crankshaft sprocket, and slide the sprocket off the end of the crankshaft. Remove the Woodruff key from the crankshaft, and store it with the sprocket for safe-keeping. Where necessary, also slide the spacer (where fitted) off the end of the crankshaft.

11 Examine the crankshaft oil seal for signs of oil leakage and, if necessary, renew it.

Tensioner pulley

12 Remove the upper and where necessary the centre timing belt covers (see Section 4).

13 Slacken and remove the timing belt tensioner pulley retaining bolt, and slide the pulley off its mounting stud. Examine the mounting stud for signs of damage and if necessary, renew it.

Refitting

14 Clean the camshaft/crankshaft sprockets thoroughly, and renew any that show signs of wear, damage or cracks.

15 Clean the tensioner assembly, but do not use any strong solvent which may enter the pulley bearing. Check that the pulley rotates freely on the backplate, with no sign of stiffness or free play. Renew the assembly if there is any doubt about its condition, or if there are any signs of wear or damage.

Camshaft sprocket

16 Refit the locating peg (where removed) to the rear of the sprocket. Locate the sprocket on the end of the camshaft, ensuring that the locating peg is correctly engaged with the cutout in the camshaft end.

17 Refit the sprocket retaining bolt and washer, and tighten it to the specified torque (see *Specifications*). Retain the sprocket with the tool used on removal **(see illustration 6.6)**.

18 Realign the hole in the camshaft sprocket with the corresponding hole in the cylinder head, and refit the locking pin. Check that the crankshaft pulley locking pin is still in position.

19 Refit the timing belt to the camshaft sprocket. Ensure that the front run of the belt is taut – ie, that any slack is on the tensioner pulley side of the belt. Do not twist the belt sharply while refitting it, and ensure that the belt teeth are seated centrally in the sprockets.

20 With the timing belt correctly engaged on the sprockets, tension the belt (see Section 5).

21 Once the belt is correctly tensioned, refit the timing belt covers (refer to Section 4).

Crankshaft sprocket

22 Slide the spacer (where fitted) into position, taking great care not to damage the crankshaft oil seal, and refit the Woodruff key to its slot in the crankshaft end.

23 Slide on the crankshaft sprocket, aligning its slot with the Woodruff key.

24 Ensure that the camshaft sprocket locking pin is still in position. Temporarily refit the crankshaft pulley, and insert the locking pin through the pulley timing hole, to ensure that the crankshaft is still correctly positioned.

25 Remove the crankshaft pulley. Engage the timing belt with the crankshaft sprocket. Ensure the belt front run is taut – ie, that any slack is on the tensioner pulley side of the belt. Fit the belt over the water pump sprocket and tensioner pulley. Do not twist the belt sharply while refitting it, and ensure the belt teeth are seated centrally in the sprockets.

26 Tension the timing belt (see Section 5).

27 Remove the crankshaft pulley, then refit the timing belt cover(s) (refer to Section 4).

28 Refit the crankshaft pulley as described in Section 3, and reconnect the battery negative terminal.

Tensioner pulley

29 Refit the tensioner pulley to its mounting stud, and fit the retaining bolt.

30 Ensure that the front run of the belt is taut – ie, that any slack is on the pulley side of the belt. Check that the belt is centrally located on all its sprockets. Rotate the pulley anti-clockwise to remove all free play from the timing belt, and securely tighten the pulley retaining nut.

31 Tension the belt (see Section 5).

32 Once the belt is correctly tensioned, refit the timing belt covers (refer to Section 4).

Chapter 3B
Citroën XM diesel 1989 to 1998

Contents

Specifications

Timing belt renewal interval . . . . Every 36 000 miles (60 000 km)

Note: *Although the normal interval for timing belt renewal is 48 000 miles (80 000 km) on models up to 1984, and 72 000 miles (120 000 km) on models from 1984, it is strongly recommended that the interval is reduced on vehicles which are subjected to intensive use, ie, mainly short journeys or a lot of stop-start driving. The actual belt renewal interval is therefore very much up to the individual owner. That being said, it is highly recommended to err on the side of safety, and renew the belt at this earlier interval, bearing in mind the drastic consequences resulting from belt failure.*

Camshaft timing belt
Belt tension (2.5 litre engine only)*:
  New belt:
    Pre-tension . . . . 800 N (107 SEEM units)
    Final tension . . . . 300 N (58 SEEM units)
  Used belt:
    Pre-tension . . . . 500 N (80 SEEM units)
    Final tension . . . . 250 N (51 SEEM units)
On 2.1 litre engines, the camshaft timing belt tension is set by the automatic tensioner.

Balance shaft timing belt
Belt tension:
  New belt
    Pre-tension . . . . 400 N (70 SEEM units)
    Final tension . . . . 120 N (31 SEEM units)
  Used belt:
    Pre-tension . . . . 250 N (51 SEEM units)
    Final tension . . . . 90 N (26 SEEM units)

Torque wrench settings

	Nm	lbf ft
2.1 litre engines*		
Camshaft sprocket bolt	50	37
Crankshaft pulley bolt:		
Stage 1	40	30
Stage 2	Tighten through a further 60°	
Injection pump sprocket puller retaining screws	10	7
Injection pump sprocket nut	50	37
Left-hand engine/transmission mounting:		
Mounting bracket-to-body	30	22
Rubber mounting-to-bracket bolts	30	22
Mounting stud-to-transmission	60	44
Centre nut	65	48
Lower engine movement limiter-to-driveshaft intermediate bearing		
housing	50	37
Lower engine movement limiter-to-subframe	85	63
Right-hand engine/transmission mounting:		
Mounting bracket-to-engine nuts	45	33
Mounting bracket-to-rubber mounting nut	45	33
Rubber mounting-to-body nut	40	30
Upper engine movement limiter bolts	50	37
Roadwheel bolts	90	66
Timing belt idler pulley	37	27
Timing belt tensioner nut/bolt	10	7
2.5 litre engines		
Auxiliary drivebelt tensioner pulley	43	32
Balance shaft drivebelt tensioner centre nut	45	33
Balance shaft drivebelt idler pulley centre nut	45	33
Camshaft sprocket bolts:		
Stage 1	10	7
Stage 2	25	18
Camshaft sprocket centre nut	43	32
Crankshaft pulley bolts	20	15
Crankshaft sprocket bolt:		
Stage 1	70	52
Stage 2	Angle tighten through 51°	
Left-hand engine/transmission mounting:		
Centre nut	65	48
Mounting bracket-to-body	30	22
Mounting stud-to-transmission	50	37
Rubber mounting-to-bracket bolts	20	15
Lower torque control mechanism:		
Pushrod mounting bolts	110	81
Torque arm mounting bracket-to-chassis bolts	50	37
Torque arm-to-mounting bracket bolts (front)	110	81
Torque arm-to-mounting bracket bolts (rear)	60	44
Rear engine mounting/torque control mechanism:		
Mounting bracket to engine	55	41
Torque arm to mounting bracket	50	37
Right hand engine mounting:		
Mounting bracket-to-chassis bolts	50	37
Through-bolt	90	66
Roadwheel bolts	90	66
Timing belt tensioner centre nut	45	33

*Note: *At the time of writing, a definitive set of torque figures was not available for the 2.1 litre engine. The above settings are given for guidance only.*

1 Electronic control unit (ECU) – removal and refitting

Note: *The ECU is fragile. Take care not to drop it or subject it to any other kind of impact, and do not subject it to extremes of temperature, or allow it to get wet. Once disconnected from its wiring harness, do not touch the exposed ECU connector pins, as stray static electricity can easily damage the internal components.*

1 The ECU is located in a plastic casing, which is mounted in the right-hand front corner of the engine compartment.

2 Lift off the ECU module box lid.

3 Release the wiring connector by lifting the locking lever on top of the connector upwards. Lift the connector at the rear, disengage the tag at the front and carefully withdraw the connector from the ECU pins.

4 Lift the ECU upwards and remove it from its location.

5 To remove the ECU module box, turn the injection pump wiring connector on the top of the box clockwise, disengage the retaining lug

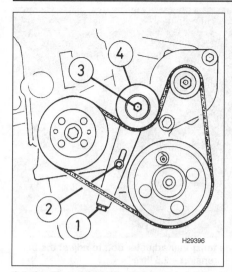

2.4 Auxiliary drivebelt adjustment details – 2.1 litre

1 *Adjuster bolt*
2 *Tensioner pulley assembly – lower securing bolt*
3 *Tensioner pulley assembly – upper securing bolt*
4 *Tensioner pulley*

using a screwdriver, then turn the connector anti-clockwise and lift off.

6 Undo the two screws securing the wiring connector base to the module box and lift off the connector base.

7 Undo the internal and external retaining bolts and remove the module box.

8 Refitting is a reversal of removal.

---

2 Auxiliary drivebelt – removal, refitting and adjustment

Note: *Depending on model and equipment fitted, access to the auxiliary drivebelt can be*

extremely limited. Where necessary, greater working clearance can be gained by removing the diesel injection electronic control unit (ECU) and its mounting box as described Section 1. If working on the 2.1 litre model, the help of an assistant will also be beneficial.

2.1 litre models without air conditioning

Removal

1 Apply the handbrake, then jack up the front of the car and support it on axle stands. Remove the right-hand front roadwheel.

2 Release the screws and clips and remove the wheel arch liner from under the right-hand front wing for access to the crankshaft pulley bolt. Where fitted, also remove the splash guard from under the front of the engine.

3 Disconnect the battery negative lead.

4 Slacken the two bolts securing the tensioning pulley assembly to the engine (see illustration).

5 Rotate the adjuster bolt to move the tensioner pulley away from the drivebelt until there is sufficient slack for the drivebelt to be removed from the pulleys.

Refitting

6 Fit the drivebelt around the pulleys in the following order:
a) *Power steering pump.*
b) *Crankshaft.*
c) *Alternator.*
d) *Tensioner pulley.*

7 Ensure that the ribs on the belt are correctly engaged with the grooves in the pulleys, and that the drivebelt is correctly routed. Take all the slack out of the belt by turning the tensioner pulley adjuster bolt. Tension the belt as follows.

Adjustment

8 If not already done, proceed as described in paragraphs 1 and 2.

9 The belt should be tensioned so that, under firm thumb pressure, there is approximately 5.0 mm of free movement at the mid-point between the pulleys on the longest belt run.

10 To adjust the tension, with the tensioner pulley assembly retaining bolts slackened, rotate the adjuster bolt until the correct tension is achieved.

11 Once the belt is correctly tensioned, rotate the crankshaft four complete revolutions in the normal direction of rotation and recheck the tension.

12 When the belt is correctly tensioned, tighten the tensioner pulley assembly retaining bolts, then reconnect the battery negative lead.

13 Refit the wheel arch liner and, where fitted, the engine splash guard. Refit the roadwheel, and lower the vehicle to the ground.

2.5 litre models without air conditioning

Removal

14 If not already done, proceed as described in paragraphs 1 and 2.

15 Disconnect the battery negative lead.

16 Relieve all tension from the drivebelt tensioner by slackening the tensioner adjuster bolt (see illustration).

17 Reach through the right-hand wheel arch and release the belt from the tensioner pulley. Slide the belt from the alternator, hydraulic pump and crankshaft pulleys and remove it from the vehicle (see illustration).

Refitting and adjustment

18 Fit the drivebelt around the pulleys in the following order:
a) *Crankshaft.*
b) *Hydraulic pump*
c) *Alternator*
d) *Tensioner pulley.*

19 Adjust the drivebelt tension by tightening

3B

2.16 Slackening the auxiliary drivebelt tensioner pulley bolt – 2.5 litre

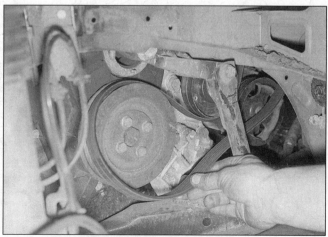

2.17 Removing the auxiliary drivebelt via the right-hand wheel arch (2.5 litre without air conditioning)

2.19a Slacken the tensioner locknut (arrowed) . . .

2.19b . . . then turn the tensioner adjuster bolt to adjust the belt tension – 2.5 litre

the adjuster bolt **(see illustrations)**. The belt should be tensioned so that, under firm thumb pressure, there is approximately 5.0 mm of free movement at the mid-point between the pulleys on the longest belt run.

20 Once the belt is correctly tensioned, rotate the crankshaft four complete revolutions in the normal direction of rotation and recheck the tension.

21 When the belt is correctly tensioned, reconnect the battery negative lead, refit the wheel arch liner and, where fitted, the engine splash guard/undertray. Refit the roadwheel, and lower the vehicle to the ground.

2.5 litre models with air conditioning

Removal

22 If not already done, proceed as described in paragraphs 1 and 2.

23 Disconnect the battery negative lead.

24 Working under the wheel arch, slacken the retaining bolt located in the centre of the eccentric tensioner pulley **(see illustration)**.

25 Insert a cranked, square section bar (a quarter inch square drive socket bar for example) into the square hole on the front face of the eccentric tensioner pulley.

26 Using the bar, turn the eccentric tensioner pulley until the hole in the arm of the automatic tensioner pulley is aligned with the hole in the mounting bracket behind. When the holes are aligned, slide a suitable setting tool (a bolt, or cranked length of rod of approximately 8.0 mm diameter) through the hole in the arm and into the mounting bracket.

27 With the automatic tensioner locked, turn the eccentric tensioner pulley until the drivebelt tension is released sufficiently to enable the belt to be removed.

Refitting and adjustment

28 Fit the drivebelt around the pulleys in the following order:
a) *Air conditioning compressor.*
b) *Crankshaft.*
c) *Automatic tensioner pulley.*
d) *Hydraulic pump/power steering pump.*
e) *Alternator.*
f) *Eccentric tensioner pulley.*

29 Ensure that the ribs on the belt are correctly engaged with the grooves in the pulleys.

30 Turn the eccentric tensioner pulley to apply tension to the drivebelt, until the load is released from the setting bolt. Without altering the position of the eccentric tensioner pulley, tighten its retaining bolt to the specified torque.

31 Remove the setting bolt from the automatic tensioner arm, then rotate the crankshaft four complete revolutions in the normal direction of rotation.

32 Check that the holes in the automatic adjuster arm and the mounting bracket are still aligned by re-inserting the setting bolt. If the bolt will not slide in easily, repeat the tensioning procedure from paragraph 30 onward.

33 On completion, reconnect the battery negative lead, refit the wheel arch liner and, where fitted, the engine splash guard. Refit the roadwheel, and lower the vehicle to the ground.

---

3 Engine assembly and valve timing holes – general information and usage

Note: *Do not attempt to rotate the engine whilst the crankshaft/camshaft/injection pump are locked in position. If the engine is to be left in this state for a long period of time, it is a good idea to place suitable warning notices inside the vehicle, and in the engine compartment. This will reduce the possibility*

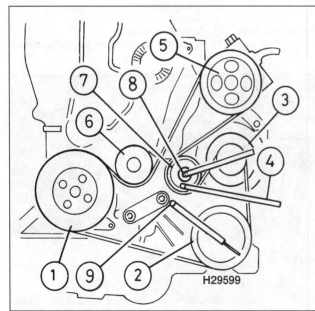

1 Crankshaft pulley
2 Air con compressor pulley
3 Alternator pulley
4 Cranked, square section bar
5 Hydraulic pump pulley
6 Automatic tensioner pulley
7 Eccentric tensioner pulley
8 Eccentric tensioner pulley retaining bolt (with socket and wrench attached)
9 Setting tool inserted in 8 mm hole in arm of automatic tensioner pulley

2.24 Auxiliary drivebelt tensioning details – 2.5 litre with air conditioning

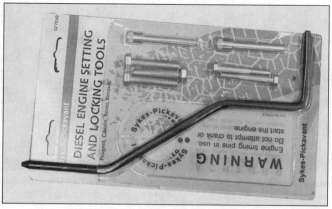

3.1 Typical kit of engine locking tools

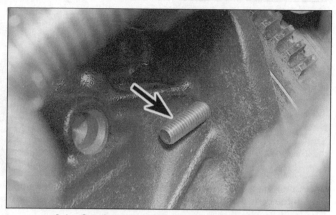

3.4a Crankshaft locking tool in place – 2.1 litre

of the engine being accidentally cranked on the starter motor, which is likely to cause damage with the locking pins in place.

1 On all models, timing holes are provided in the camshaft sprocket, injection pump sprocket and flywheel. The holes are used to align the crankshaft, camshaft and injection pump and to prevent the possibility of the valves contacting the pistons when refitting the cylinder head, or when refitting the timing belt. When the holes are aligned with their corresponding holes in the cylinder head and cylinder block (as appropriate), suitable diameter bolts/pins can be inserted to lock both the camshaft, injection pump and crankshaft in position, preventing them from rotating unnecessarily **(see illustration)**. Proceed as follows. **Note:** *With the timing holes aligned, No 4 cylinder is at TDC on its compression stroke.*

2 Remove the upper timing belt covers as described in Section 4.

3 The crankshaft must now be turned until the bolt holes in the camshaft and injection pump sprockets (one hole in the camshaft sprocket, one or two holes in the injection pump sprocket) are aligned with the corresponding holes in the engine front plate. The crankshaft can be turned by using a spanner on the pulley bolt. To gain access to the pulley bolt, from underneath the front of the car, prise out the retaining clips and remove the screws, then withdraw the plastic

3.4b Crankshaft locking tool in place – 2.5 litre

wheel arch liner from the wing valance, to gain access to the crankshaft pulley bolt. Where necessary, unclip the coolant hoses from the bracket, to improve access further. The crankshaft can then be turned using a suitable spanner or socket and extension bar fitted to the pulley bolt. Note that the crankshaft must always be turned in a clockwise direction (viewed from the right-hand side of the vehicle).

4 Insert a cranked rod of approximately 8 mm in diameter (or a long bolt of the same diameter) through the hole in the left-hand flange of the cylinder block by the starter motor. Access is very restricted, and it may be easier to remove the starter motor to be able

3.4c Crankshaft locking tool in place (alternative hole at rear of engine block) – 2.5 litre

to locate the hole. On 2.5 litre models, there is an alternative hole at the rear of the engine (accessible from underneath the car), drilled into the mating surface between the cylinder block and the transmission bellhousing **(see illustrations)**

5 Insert one 8 mm bolt through the guides at the base of the camshaft sprocket hub, and another through the guides at the base of the fuel injection pump sprocket hub. Screw the bolts into the engine by hand to ensure that they can't fall out **(see illustrations)**.

3B

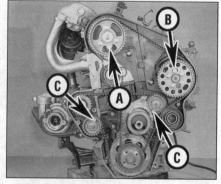

3.5c Complete set of sprocket locking tools in use – 2.5 litre

A *Camshaft sprocket locking tool*
B *Fuel injection pump sprocket locking tool*
C *Balance shaft sprocket locking tools*

3.5a Camshaft sprocket locking tool in use – 2.1 litre

3.5b Fuel injection pump sprocket locking tool in use – 2.1 litre

4.1 Undo the single retaining bolt, located in the centre of the cover – 2.1 litre

4.2 Turn the upper fastener a quarter of a turn clockwise to release the locking peg – 2.1 litre

4.5 Remove the centre cover from the front of the injection pump – 2.1 litre

6 The crankshaft, camshaft and injection pump are now locked in position, preventing unwanted rotation.

7 Note that on 2.5 litre engines, there are also timing holes that allow the balance shaft sprockets to be locked in position. Refer to Section 7 for details.

4 Timing belt outer covers – removal and refitting

2.1 litre engine upper cover - removal

1 Undo the single retaining bolt, located in the centre of the cover (see illustration).

2 Turn the upper fastener a quarter of a turn clockwise to release the locking peg (see illustration).

3 Manipulate the cover up and off the front of the engine.

2.1 litre engine centre cover - removal

4 Remove the auxiliary drivebelt as described in Section 2.

5 Undo the two bolts and remove the centre cover from the front of the injection pump (see illustration).

2.1 litre engine lower cover - removal

6 Remove the crankshaft pulley.

7 Remove the right-hand engine mounting assembly as described in Section 8.

8 Remove both upper covers as described previously.

9 Slacken and remove the retaining bolts, and remove the lower cover (see illustration).

2.5 litre engine upper cover - removal

10 Disconnect the battery negative cable.

11 Withdraw each of the ECUs from the casing at the front right-hand corner of the engine compartment. Unbolt the casing and remove it from the engine compartment.

12 Disconnect the plastic housing from the side of the upper cover.

13 Remove the auxiliary drivebelt as described in Section 2.

14 Unbolt the auxiliary drivebelt tensioner mechanism and remove it from the engine.

15 Undo the securing screws and lift off the upper cover (see illustration).

4.9 Removing the timing belt lower cover – 2.1 litre

2.5 litre engine lower cover - removal

16 Remove the upper cover as described in the previous sub-Section.

17 Remove the four bolts which secure the crankshaft pulley, followed by the pulley itself. There is no need to remove the centre bolt.

18 Undo the securing screws and lift off the lower cover (see illustration).

Refitting - all engines

19 Refitting is a reversal of the relevant removal procedure, ensuring that each cover section is correctly located.

4.15 Removing the upper timing belt cover – 2.5 litre

4.18 Removing the lower timing belt cover – 2.5 litre

5.4 On 2.1 litre models, slacken the timing belt tensioner locking bolt using a 5 mm Allen key

5.5a Timing belt tensioner pulley retaining nut (A) and locking bolt (B) – 2.1 litre

5.5b Timing belt tensioner arrangement on 2.1 litre models showing tensioner 10 mm shaft (arrowed)

5 Timing belt –
removal and refitting

Removal

2.1 litre engines

1 Remove the timing belt covers as described in Section 4.

2 Align the engine assembly/valve timing holes as described in Section 3, and lock the camshaft sprocket, injection pump sprocket and flywheel in position. *Do not* attempt to rotate the engine whilst the pins are in position. Disconnect the battery negative terminal.

3 Slacken the timing belt tensioner pulley retaining nut, situated just to the left of the engine mounting carrier bracket.

4 Using a 5 mm Allen key inserted through the hole in the engine mounting carrier bracket, slacken the timing belt tensioner locking bolt **(see illustration)**.

5 Using a 10 mm socket or box spanner inserted through the same hole, retract the

tensioner by turning its shaft clockwise to the extent of its travel **(see illustrations)**.

6 Mark the timing belt with an arrow to indicate its running direction, if it is to be re-used. Remove the belt from the sprockets **(see illustration)**.

2.5 litre engines

7 Jack up the front of the car and support it securely on axle stands. Remove the front right-hand roadwheel.

8 Remove the fixings and detach the front section of the right-hand wheel arch inner liner.

9 Remove the timing belt covers as described in Section 4.

10 Refer to Section 3 and lock the engine at TDC on cylinder No 4 using the appropriate locking tools at the flywheel, camshaft sprocket and fuel injection pump sprocket.

11 Slacken the timing belt tensioner pulley retaining nut, to relieve the tension on the timing belt.

12 Support the engine at the lifting eyelet, using a lifting beam or a engine crane.

13 Working via the right-hand wheel arch and with reference to Section 8, unbolt the right-

hand lower engine mounting from the chassis, together with its tie-rod. Note that there is no need to remove the large centre bolt from the cylinder block engine mounting.

14 Lower the engine slightly, using the crane or lifting beam, until there is a gap of about 20-30 mm between the chassis and the right-hand engine mounting **(see illustration)**.

15 Mark the timing belt with an arrow to indicate its running direction, if it is to be re-used. Remove the belt from the crankshaft sprocket, pass it between the right-hand engine mounting and the chassis and then remove it from the camshaft and fuel injection pump sprockets.

Refitting

16 If signs of oil contamination are found, trace the source of the oil leak and rectify it.

17 Wash down the engine timing belt area and all related components, to remove all traces of oil. Check that the tensioner and idler pulleys rotate freely, without any sign of roughness.

2.1 litre models

18 Commence refitting by ensuring that the locking tools are still fitted to the camshaft

3B

5.6 Removing the timing belt from the sprockets

5.14 Lower the engine slightly, using the crane or lifting beam, until there is a gap of about 20 to 30 mm between the chassis and the right-hand engine mounting

and fuel injection pump sprockets, and that the rod/drill is positioned in the timing hole in the flywheel.

19 Ensure that the timing belt tensioner is still retracted, then tighten the tensioner pulley retaining nut. Using the 10 mm socket or box spanner, release the tensioner by turning it anti-clockwise to the extent of its travel.

21 Locate the timing belt on the crankshaft sprocket, making sure that, where applicable, the direction of rotation arrow is facing the correct way.

21 Engage the timing belt with the crankshaft sprocket, hold it in position, then feed the belt over the remaining sprockets in the following order:

a) *Idler roller.*
b) *Fuel injection pump.*
c) *Camshaft.*
d) *Coolant pump.*
e) *Tensioner roller.*

22 Be careful not to kink or twist the belt. To ensure correct engagement, locate only a half-width on the injection pump sprocket before feeding the timing belt onto the camshaft sprocket, keeping the belt taut and fully engaged with the crankshaft sprocket. Locate the timing belt fully onto the sprockets.

23 Slacken the tensioner pulley retaining nut to allow the tensioner to tension the belt.

24 Unscrew and remove the bolts from the camshaft and fuel injection pump sprockets and remove the rod/drill from the timing hole in the flywheel.

25 Rotate the crankshaft through two complete turns in the normal running direction (clockwise). **Do not** rotate the crankshaft backwards, as the timing belt must be kept tight between the crankshaft, fuel injection pump and camshaft sprockets.

26 Tighten the tensioner pulley retaining nut, then rotate the crankshaft through a further two complete turns in the normal running direction, stopping at the timing setting position.

27 Slacken the tensioner pulley retaining nut one turn to allow the tensioner to finally tension the belt. Tighten the tensioner pulley retaining nut and the timing belt tensioner locking bolt to the specified torque.

28 Check that the timing holes are all

5.31a Rotate the camshaft sprocket fully clockwise, so that the securing bolts reach the end of their slotted mounting holes – 2.5 litre (arrowed bolt is slackened to show positioning)

correctly positioned by reinserting the sprocket locking bolts and the rod/drill in the flywheel timing hole, as described in Section 3. If the timing holes are not correctly positioned, the timing belt has been incorrectly fitted (possibly one tooth out on one of the sprockets) - in this case, repeat the refitting procedure from the beginning.

29 The remaining refitting procedure is a reversal of removal.

2.5 litre models

Note: *The tension of the timing belt must be set using a dedicated Citroën electronic tester.*

30 Check that the engine locking tools are still in place at the flywheel, camshaft sprocket and fuel injection pump sprocket (see Section 3).

31 With reference to Section 6, slacken off the camshaft sprocket securing bolts. Re-tighten them by hand, so that the sprocket is only just held in position. Repeat this procedure at the fuel injection pump sprocket. Rotate both sprockets fully clockwise, so that the securing bolts reach the ends of the slotted mounting holes **(see illustrations)**.

32 Locate the timing belt on the crankshaft sprocket, making sure that, where applicable, the direction of rotation arrow is facing the correct way.

5.31b Fuel injection pump sprocket rotated fully clockwise, so that the securing bolts reach the end of their slotted mounting holes – 2.5 litre

A   *Securing bolt (slackened to show positioning)*
B   *Locking tool inserted through sprocket timing hole*

33 Engage the timing belt with the crankshaft sprocket, hold it in position, then feed the belt over the remaining sprockets in the following order (be careful not to kink or twist the belt) **(see illustrations)**:

a) *Idler roller.*
b) *Fuel injection pump.*
c) *Camshaft.*
d) *Tensioner roller.*

34 Adjust the position of the camshaft and fuel injection pump sprockets by rotating them anti-clockwise as necessary, until the teeth of the timing belt engage with those on the sprockets. The rotation needed to engage the belt with the sprockets should not exceed the width of one sprocket tooth. After fitting the belt, the sprocket bolts should now be positioned near the centre of their slotted mounting holes **(see illustration)**.

35 Fit the dedicated electronic tester to the mid-point of the longest belt run(between the camshaft and injection pump sprockets). Tension the belt by fitting a wrench to the square hole in the side of the tensioner pulley. Turn the pulley with the wrench until the correct **pre-tension** value for a new or used

5.33a Fitting the camshaft timing belt – 2.5 litre

5.33b Correctly fitted camshaft timing belt – 2.5 litre

5.34 After fitting the belt, the sprocket bolts should now be positioned near the centre of their slotted mounting holes (arrowed) – 2.5 litre

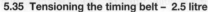

5.35 Tensioning the timing belt – 2.5 litre

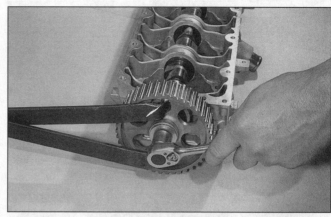

6.2 A sprocket holding tool can be made from two lengths of steel strip bolted together to form a forked end. Bend the ends of the strip through 90º to form the fork 'prongs'

belt (as applicable) is attained. Keep the tensioner pulley in this position, and use a second wrench to tighten the tensioner centre nut to the specified torque **(see illustration)**.

36 Remove the engine locking tools from the flywheel, camshaft and fuel injection pump sprockets, and the tension tester from the belt.

37 Using a socket and bar on the crankshaft sprocket, turn the engine **in its normal direction of rotation** through at least ten revolutions.

38 Refit the flywheel locking tool, as described in Section 3.

39 Slacken the tensioner pulley centre nut, so that the tension on the belt is completely removed. Slacken off the camshaft and fuel injection pump sprocket securing bolts again, then refit the engine locking tools to both sprockets.

40 Refit the dedicated tester, then tension the belt by fitting a wrench to the square hole in the side of the tensioner pulley. Turn the pulley with the wrench until the correct **final-tension** value for a new or used belt (as applicable) is attained. Keep the tensioner pulley in this position, and use a second wrench to tighten the tensioner centre nut to the specified torque. Remove the tension tester.

41 Tighten the camshaft and fuel injection pump securing bolts, as described in Section 6.

42 Using a socket and bar on the crankshaft sprocket, turn the engine **in its normal direction of rotation** through two revolutions.

43 Check that the timing holes are all correctly positioned by reinserting the engine locking tools in the flywheel, and the camshaft and fuel injection pump sprockets, as described in Section 3. If the timing holes are not correctly positioned, the timing belt has been incorrectly fitted (possibly one tooth out on one of the sprockets) - in this case, repeat the refitting procedure from the beginning.

44 The remaining refitting procedure is a reversal of removal.

6 Timing belt sprockets – removal and refitting

Camshaft sprocket (2.1 litre models)

Removal

1 Remove the timing belt (see Section 5).

2 Slacken the camshaft sprocket retaining bolt and remove it, along with its washer. To prevent the camshaft rotating as the bolt is slackened, a sprocket holding tool will be required **(see illustration)**. Do not attempt to use the sprocket locking pin to prevent the sprocket from rotating whilst the bolt is slackened.

3 Remove the camshaft sprocket retaining bolt and washer.

4 Unscrew and remove the locking bolt from the camshaft sprocket.

5 With the retaining bolt removed, slide the sprocket off the end of the camshaft **(see illustration)**. Recover the Woodruff key from the end of the camshaft if it is loose. Examine the camshaft oil seal for signs of oil leakage and, if necessary, renew it.

Refitting

6 Refit the Woodruff key to the end of the camshaft, then refit the camshaft sprocket.

Note that the sprocket will only fit one way round (with the protruding centre boss against the camshaft), as the end of the camshaft is tapered.

7 Refit the sprocket retaining bolt and washer. Tighten the bolt to the specified torque, preventing the camshaft from turning as during removal.

8 Where applicable, refit the cylinder head cover.

9 Align the holes in the camshaft sprocket and the engine front plate, and refit the 8 mm bolt to lock the camshaft in position.

10 Refit the timing belt as described in Section 5.

11 Refit the timing belt covers as described in Section 4.

Crankshaft sprocket (2.1 litre models)

Note: On vehicles built before build code 6176, a new version of the crankshaft sprocket Woodruff key must be retro-fitted; refer to your Citroën dealer for details.

Removal

12 Remove the timing belt (see Section 5).

13 Slide the sprocket off the end of the crankshaft **(see illustration)**.

14 Remove the Woodruff key from the crankshaft, and store it with the sprocket for safe-keeping.

6.5 Removing the camshaft sprocket – 2.1 litre

6.13 Removing the crankshaft sprocket – 2.1 litre

6.21 Using a home made tool to prevent the fuel injection pump sprocket from turning – 2.1 litre

6.23 Home-made puller fitted to the fuel injection pump sprocket – 2.1 litre

15 Examine the crankshaft oil seal for signs of oil leakage and, if necessary, renew it.

Refitting

16 Refit the Woodruff key to the end of the crankshaft, then refit the crankshaft sprocket (with the flange nearest the cylinder block).

17 Refit the timing belt as described in Section 5.

Fuel injection pump sprocket (2.1 litre models)

Removal

18 Remove the timing belt as described in Section 5.

19 Remove the locking bolt securing the fuel injection pump sprocket in the TDC position (See Section 3).

20 On certain models, the sprocket may be fitted with a built-in puller, which consists of a plate bolted to the sprocket. The plate contains a captive nut (the sprocket securing nut), which is screwed onto the fuel injection pump shaft. On models not fitted with the built-in puller, a suitable puller can be made up using a short length of bar, and two M7 bolts screwed into the holes provided in the sprocket.

21 The fuel injection pump shaft must be prevented from turning as the sprocket nut is unscrewed, and this can be achieved using a tool similar to that shown **(see illustration)**. Use the tool to hold the sprocket stationary by means of the holes in the sprocket.

22 On models with a built-in puller, unscrew the sprocket securing nut until the sprocket is freed from the taper on the pump shaft, then withdraw the sprocket. Recover the Woodruff key from the end of the pump shaft if it is loose. If desired, the puller assembly can be removed from the sprocket by removing the two securing screws and washers.

23 On models not fitted with a built-in puller, partially unscrew the sprocket securing nut, then fit the improvised puller, and tighten the two bolts (forcing the bar against the sprocket

nut), until the sprocket is freed from the taper on the pump shaft **(see illustration)**. Withdraw the sprocket and recover the Woodruff key from the end of the pump shaft if it is loose. Remove the puller from the sprocket.

Refitting

24 Refit the Woodruff key to the pump shaft, ensuring that it is correctly located in its groove.

25 Where applicable, if the built-in puller assembly has been removed from the sprocket, refit it, and tighten the two securing screws securely ensuring that the washers are in place.

26 Refit the sprocket, then tighten the securing nut to the specified torque, preventing the pump shaft from turning as during removal.

27 Make sure that the 8 mm locking bolts are fitted to the camshaft and fuel injection pump sprockets, and that the rod/drill is positioned in the flywheel timing hole.

28 Fit the timing belt around the fuel injection pump sprocket, ensuring that the marks made on the belt and sprocket before removal are aligned.

6.36 Offer the camshaft sprocket up to its mounting flange, then insert the sprocket securing bolts and tighten them by hand – 2.5 litre

29 Tension the timing belt as described in Section 5.

30 Refit the upper timing belt covers as described in Section 4.

Camshaft sprocket (2.5 litre engine)

Note: *If the camshaft sprocket is being removed to allow the removal of the camshaft, the timing belt can be secured to the sprocket with cable ties, so that the valve timing is preserved.*

Removal

31 Remove the timing belt cover as described in Section 4, then set the engine to TDC on cylinder No 4 and lock it in this position, using the information given in Section 3.

32 With reference to Section 5, relieve the tension on the timing belt, then slide the belt off the camshaft sprocket.

33 Slacken and remove the three camshaft sprocket retaining bolts. To prevent the camshaft rotating as the nut/bolts are slackened, a sprocket holding tool will be required **(see illustration 6.2)**. *Do not* attempt to use the sprocket locking pin to prevent the sprocket from rotating whilst the bolt is slackened.

34 Remove the sprocket from its mounting flange.

Refitting

35 Ensure that the flywheel and fuel injection pump locking tools are still in position before proceeding.

36 Offer the camshaft sprocket up to its mounting flange at the end of the camshaft **(see illustration)**. At the same time, engage the camshaft sprocket locking tool with the timing hole at the bottom of the sprocket hub.

37 Insert the sprocket securing bolts and tighten them by hand.

38 With reference to Section 5, refit and tension the timing belt. On completion, tighten the sprocket securing bolts to the specified torque remove the engine locking tools.

6.47 Refit the fuel injection pump sprocket, then insert the sprocket securing bolts and tighten them by hand – 2.5 litre

6.53 Remove the crankshaft sprocket securing bolt – 2.5 litre

39 Using a socket and bar of the crankshaft pulley, rotate the engine in its normal direction of rotation through two crankshaft revolutions. **40** Re-check the engine valve timing by fitting the engine locking tools, as described in Section 3. If the valve timing holes do not line up, the fuel injection pump sprocket has been refitted incorrectly - it will be necessary to remove the timing belt and set the valve timing from scratch - refer to Section 5 for details.
41 On completion, refit the timing outer cover.

Fuel injection pump sprocket (2.5 litre engine)

Note: *If the fuel injection pump sprocket is being removed to allow the removal of the fuel injection pump, the timing belt can (if required) be secured to the sprocket with cable ties, so that the valve/pump timing is preserved.*

Removal

42 Remove the timing belt cover as described in Section 4, then set the engine to TDC on cylinder No 4 and lock it in this position, using the information given in Section 3.
43 With reference to Section 5, relieve the tension on the timing belt and slide it from the fuel injection pump sprocket.
44 Unscrew and remove the three fuel injection pump sprocket retaining bolts. To prevent the pump shaft rotating as the nut/bolts are slackened, a sprocket holding tool will be required **(see illustration 6.2)**. *Do not* attempt to use the sprocket locking pin to prevent the sprocket from rotating whilst the bolt is slackened.
45 Remove the sprocket from the pump shaft.

Refitting

46 Ensure that the flywheel and camshaft sprocket locking tools are still in position before proceeding.
47 Offer the fuel injection pump sprocket up to the end of the pump shaft. At the same time, engage the sprocket locking tool with the timing hole in the sprocket hub **(see illustration)**.
48 Insert the sprocket securing bolts and hand tighten them.
49 With reference to Section 5, refit and tension the timing belt. On completion, tighten the sprocket securing bolts and remove the engine locking tools.
50 Using a socket and bar of the crankshaft pulley, rotate the engine in its normal direction

of rotation through two crankshaft revolutions. Re-check the engine valve timing by fitting the engine locking tools, as described in Section 3. If the valve timing holes so not line up, the fuel injection pump sprocket has been refitted incorrectly - it will be necessary to remove the timing belt and set the valve timing from scratch - refer to Section 5 for details.
51 On completion, refit the timing belt outer covers.

Crankshaft sprocket (2.5 litre engine)

Removal

52 Remove the timing belt (see Section 5).
53 Remove the sprocket securing bolt then slide the sprocket off the end of the crankshaft **(see illustration)**.
54 Remove the Woodruff key from the crankshaft, and store it with the sprocket for safe-keeping.
55 Examine the crankshaft oil seal for signs of oil leakage and, if necessary, renew it.

Refitting

56 Refit the Woodruff key to the end of the crankshaft, then refit the crankshaft sprocket, ensuring that the sprocket cut-out engages with the woodruff key . Fit a new sprocket retaining bolt and tighten it to the specified stage 1 and 2 torque settings **(see illustrations)**.
57 Refit the timing belt as described in Section 5.

7   Balance shaft drivebelt (2.5 litre engine) – removal and refitting

Removal

1 Disconnect the negative cable from the battery terminal.
2 Raise the front of the car and support it securely on axle stands. Remove the front right-hand roadwheel.

6.56a Ensure that the crankshaft sprocket cut-out engages with the Woodruff key – 2.5 litre

6.56b Angle tightening the crankshaft sprocket securing bolt

7.7 Remove the camshaft timing belt guide roller and its mountings from the engine bracket

7.10 Balance shaft sprocket locking tools (arrowed) in place

3 Extract the fixings and remove the engine bay undertray. Remove the screws and lift off the wheel arch inner plastic liner.

4 Refer to Section 2 and remove the auxiliary drivebelt.

5 Refer to Section 5 and remove the timing belt. Unbolt the timing belt guide roller assembly from the engine.

6 Lock the balance shafts in position by inserting a suitable bolt through the timing hole in each balance shaft sprocket. Thread the bolts into the holes in the cylinder block, behind the balance shaft sprockets, to prevent them from falling out.

7 Slacken and withdraw the securing bolts(s), then remove the guide roller and its mountings from the engine (see illustration).

8 Slacken the tensioner roller centre nut to release the tension on the balance shaft belt.

9 Remove the balance shaft belt from the sprockets.

Refitting

Caution: Do not try to fit the balance shaft

drivebelt without the sprocket locking tools in place. Incorrect balance shaft timing will result in severe engine vibration that may lead to damage.

Note: *The final tension of the balance shaft belt must be checked using a dedicated Citroën electronic tester.*

10 Check that the balance shaft sprocket locking tools are still in place before proceeding (see illustration).

11 Pass the drivebelt over the sprockets, tensioner roller and guide roller and ensure that it seats correctly.

12 Fit the dedicated electronic tester to the mid-point of the longest belt run. Tension the belt by fitting a wrench to the square hole in the side of the tensioner pulley. Turn the pulley with the wrench until the correct **pre-tension** value for a new or used belt (as applicable) is attained. Keep the tensioner pulley in this position, and use a second wrench to tighten the tensioner centre nut to the specified torque (see illustration). Remove the tension tester.

13 Refer to Section 5 and refit the timing belt; ensure that the two stage tensioning procedure is carried out correctly.

14 Slacken the balance shaft belt tensioner pulley centre nut, so that the tension on the balance shaft belt is completely removed.

15 Refit the dedicated tester, then tension the belt by fitting a wrench to the square hole in the side of the tensioner pulley. Turn the pulley with the wrench until the correct **final-tension** value for a new or used belt (as applicable) is attained. Keep the tensioner pulley in this position, and use a second wrench to tighten the tensioner centre nut to the specified torque.

16 Using a socket and bar on the crankshaft sprocket, turn the engine **in its normal direction of rotation** through two revolutions. Bring the engine around to TDC on cylinder No 4 and lock it in position again, using the engine locking tools as described in Section 3. Re-insert the balance shaft sprocket locking tools (as described in *Removal*) (see illustration).

17 If all the timing holes are all correctly

7.12 Tensioning the balance shaft belt

7.16 Correctly fitted balance shaft belt, with sprocket locking tools in place

positioned, it should be possible to fit the engine locking tools in the flywheel, and the camshaft, fuel injection pump and balance shaft sprockets without difficulty or misalignment. If the timing holes are not correctly positioned, the balance shaft belt has been incorrectly fitted (possibly one tooth out on one of the sprockets) - in this case, repeat the refitting procedure from the beginning.

18 The remaining refitting procedure is a reversal of removal.

8 Engine right-hand mounting – removal and refitting

2.1 litre engines

1 Disconnect the battery negative lead. Release all the relevant hoses and wiring from their retaining clips. Place the hoses/wiring clear of the mounting so that the removal procedure is not hindered.

2 Place a jack beneath the engine, with a block of wood on the jack head. Raise the jack until it is supporting the weight of the engine.

3 Undo the two bolts securing the curved mounting retaining plate to the body. Lift off the plate, and withdraw the rubber damper from the top of the mounting bracket.

4 Slacken and remove the two nuts and two bolts securing the right-hand engine/transmission mounting bracket to the engine. Remove the single nut securing the bracket to the mounting rubber, and lift off the bracket.

5 Lift the rubber buffer plate off the mounting rubber stud, then unscrew the mounting rubber from the body and remove it from the vehicle. If necessary, the mounting bracket can be unbolted and removed from the front of the cylinder block.

6 On reassembly, screw the mounting rubber into the vehicle body, and tighten it securely. Where removed, refit the mounting bracket to the front of the cylinder head, and securely tighten its retaining bolts.

7 Refit the rubber buffer plate to the mounting

8.15 Extract the flexible rubber coupling from the bodywork socket and remove it from the engine bay

rubber stud, and install the mounting bracket.

8 Tighten the mounting bracket retaining nuts to the specified torque setting (see *Specifications*), and remove the jack from underneath the engine.

9 Refit the rubber damper to the top of the mounting bracket, and refit the curved retaining plate. Tighten the retaining plate bolts to the specified torque (see *Specifications*), and reconnect the battery.

2.5 litre engines

10 If not already done, chock the rear wheels, then jack up the front of the vehicle and support it securely on axle stands.

11 Remove the right-hand front roadwheel, then extract the fixings and remove the centre section of the inner wheel arch liner.

12 Place a jack beneath the engine, with a block of wood on the jack head. Raise the jack until it is supporting the weight of the engine. Do not jack under the sump.

13 Where applicable, remove the screws and lift the EGR solenoid valve from the end of the inlet manifold. Unclip the fuel supply and return hoses from the support bracket at top end of the timing belt casing.

14 Remove the three bolts that secure the flexible rubber coupling to the cylinder head bracket.

15 Extract the flexible rubber coupling from the bodywork socket and remove it from the engine bay **(see illustration)**

8.16 Slacken and withdraw the bolts (arrowed) at either end of the torque control mechanism pushrod

16 Slacken and withdraw the bolts at either end of the torque control mechanism pushrod **(see illustration)**. Remove the pushrod from the engine mounting.

17 Unbolt the front torque mechanism from the subframe **(see illustration)** and extract the coupling shaft together with its rubber buffer from the circular housing bracket mounted on the engine. Note that the front torque mechanism bolt holes are slotted to allow adjustment on refitting.

18 Slacken and withdraw the first of the two bolts that secure the right-hand engine mounting bracket to the chassis. Obtain a section of threaded rod of the same diameter as the bolt just removed, approximately 200 mm long. Fit three nuts and a large washer to the rod and screw it in place of the engine mounting bolt, until the end of the rod protrudes through the bottom of the mounting. Lock two of the nuts together and use them to adjust the protrusion of the rod. Repeat this procedure on the second engine mounting bolt **(see illustration)**.

19 Lower the engine slightly using the jack, until the head of the right-hand engine mounting through-bolt can be seen. Ensure that the washers and nuts at the top of the threaded rods are now resting on the chassis **(see illustration)**.

20 The next step is to slacken and withdraw the through-bolt, to separate the right-hand engine mounting from the engine. The

8.17 Unbolt the front torque mechanism from the subframe

8.18 Using improvised tools (arrowed) to support the right-hand engine mounting

8.19 Lower the engine using the jack, until the head of the right-hand engine mounting through-bolt (arrowed) can be seen

3B

8.20 Slacken and withdraw the right-hand engine mounting through-bolt

8.21 Removing the right-hand engine mounting

8.22 The rear torque mechanism bolt holes (arrowed) are slotted to allow adjustment

threaded rods will brace the engine mounting as you do this, to avoid stressing the rubber material at the centre (see illustration).

21 Slacken and withdraw the through bolt from the right-hand engine mounting, then remove the temporarily-fitted threaded rods and remove the right-hand engine mounting from the engine bay (see illustration).

22 Refitting is a reversal of removal, but note that the right-hand engine mounting must be braced (as described during removal), to avoid stressing the rubber components, when the through bolt is refitted and tightened to its specified torque. Note also that the right-hand engine mounting is dowelled to ensure correct positioning on the chassis member (see illustration).

Chapter 4A
Citroën ZX petrol 1991 to 1994

Contents

Specifications

Engine codes

1124 cc and 1360 cc . . . . TU
1580 cc, 1761cc, 1905 cc and 1998 cc . . . . XU

Timing belt renewal interval . . . . Every 48 000 miles (80 000 km)

Note: *Although the normal interval for timing belt renewal is 48 000 miles (80 000 km) for all except the 1998 cc engine, and 72 000 miles (120 000 km) for the 1998 cc engine, it is strongly recommended that the interval is reduced on vehicles which are subjected to intensive use, ie, mainly short journeys or a lot of stop-start driving. The actual belt renewal interval is therefore very much up to the individual owner. That being said, it is highly recommended to err on the side of safety, and renew the belt at this earlier interval, bearing in mind the drastic consequences resulting from belt failure.*

Torque wrench settings

	Nm	lbf ft
1124 cc and 1360 cc engines		
Camshaft sprocket retaining bolt	80	59
Crankshaft pulley retaining bolts	8	6
Crankshaft sprocket retaining bolt	110	81
Roadwheel bolts	90	66
Timing belt cover bolts	8	6
Timing belt tensioner pulley nut	23	17
1580 cc, 1761 cc and 1905 cc engines		
Camshaft sprocket retaining bolt	35	26
Crankshaft pulley retaining bolt	110	81
Crankshaft sprocket retaining bolt	110	81
Roadwheel bolts	90	66
Timing belt cover bolts	8	6
Timing belt tensioner:		
Manually-adjusted tensioner pulley bolt	20	15
Semi-automatic timing belt tensioner:		
Cam spindle locknut	13	10
Retaining nuts	16	12
1998 cc engines		
Camshaft sprocket retaining bolt:		
8-valve engine	35	26
16-valve engine	45	33
Crankshaft pulley retaining bolt(s):		
8-valve engine	110	81
16-valve engine	27	20
Crankshaft sprocket retaining bolt - 16-valve engine	110	81
Engine/transmission left-hand mounting:		
Centre nut	80	59
Mounting bracket-to-body bolts	25	18
Mounting stud	50	37
Engine/transmission rear mounting:		
Mounting assembly-to-block bolts	45	33
Mounting bracket-to-mounting bolt	50	37
Mounting bracket-to-subframe bolt	50	37
Engine/transmission right-hand mounting:		
Curved retaining plate	20	15
Mounting bracket retaining nuts/bolts	45	33
Roadwheel bolts	90	66
Timing belt cover bolts	8	6
Timing belt tensioner:		
8-valve engine	20	15
16-valve engine (both pulley bolt and backplate bolts)	20	15

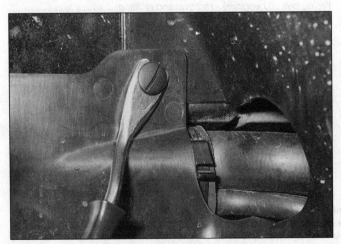

1.2a Prise out the retaining clips ...

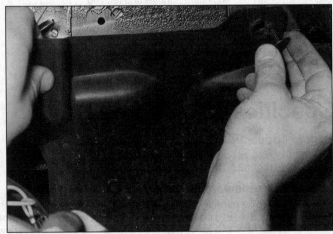

1.2b ... and remove the plastic cover from underneath the wheel arch ...

1.2c Where necessary, unclip the coolant hoses to improve access to the crankshaft pulley/sprocket bolt

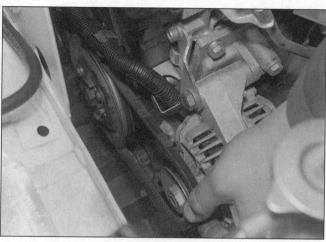

1.6 Removing the drivebelt - 1360 cc models

1 Auxiliary drivebelt - removal, refitting and adjustment

1 Apply the handbrake, then jack up the front of the car and support it on axle stands. Remove the right-hand front roadwheel.
2 From underneath the front of the car, prise out the two retaining clips, and remove the plastic cover from the wing valance to gain access to the crankshaft sprocket/pulley bolt. Where necessary, unclip the coolant hoses from the bracket to improve access further (see illustrations).

Models with manual adjuster on the alternator lower mounting point

Removal

3 On 1580 cc and 1905 cc models with air conditioning, remove the air conditioning drivebelt as described in paragraphs 41 to 42.
4 Disconnect the battery negative lead.

5 Slacken both the alternator upper and lower mounting nuts/bolts (as applicable).
6 Back off the adjuster bolt(s) to relieve the tension in the drivebelt, then slip the drivebelt from the pulleys (see illustration).

Refitting

7 Fit the belt around the pulleys, and take up the slack in the belt by tightening the adjuster bolt.
8 Tension the drivebelt as described in the following paragraphs. On 1580 cc and 1905 cc models, where necessary, refit the air conditioning compressor drivebelt as described in paragraphs 33 to 37.

Adjustment

9 The belt should be tensioned so that, under firm thumb pressure, there is approximately 5.0 mm of free movement at the mid-point between the pulleys on the longest belt run.
10 To adjust, with the upper mounting nut/bolt just holding the alternator firm, and the lower mounting nut/bolt loosened, turn the adjuster bolt until the correct tension is

achieved (see illustration). Rotate the crankshaft a couple of times, recheck the tension, then securely tighten both the alternator mounting nuts/bolts. Where applicable, also tighten the bolt securing the adjuster strap to its mounting bracket.
11 Reconnect the battery negative lead.
12 Clip the coolant hoses into position (where necessary), then refit the plastic cover to the wing valance. Refit the roadwheel, and lower the vehicle to the ground.

Models with a manually-adjusted tensioning pulley

Note: For information on the air conditioning compressor drivebelt on 1580 cc and 1905 cc models, refer to paragraphs 31 to 37.

Removal

13 Disconnect the battery negative lead.
14 Slacken the two screws securing the tensioning pulley assembly to the engine (see illustration).
15 Rotate the adjuster bolt to move the tensioner pulley away from the drivebelt until

4A

1.10 Adjusting the drivebelt tension - drivebelt adjuster on lower alternator mounting point (1905 cc model shown)

1.14 On models with a manually-adjusted tensioner pulley, slacken the two pulley retaining screws (arrowed) . . .

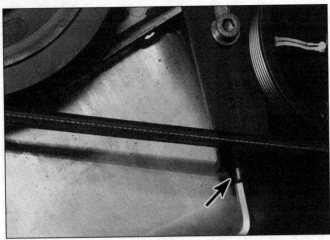

1.15a . . . then slacken the pulley adjuster bolt . . .

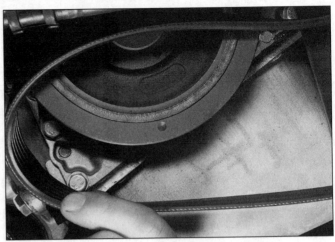

1.15b . . . and slip the drivebelt off its pulleys

there is sufficient slack for the drivebelt to be removed from the pulleys **(see illustrations)**.

Refitting

16 Fit the drivebelt around the pulleys in the following order:
(a) Power steering pump and/or air conditioning compressor.
(b) Crankshaft.
(c) Alternator.
(d) Tensioner roller.

17 Ensure that the ribs on the belt are correctly engaged with the grooves in the pulleys, and that the drivebelt is correctly routed. Take all the slack out of the belt by turning the tensioner pulley adjuster bolt. Tension the belt as follows.

Adjustment

18 The belt should be tensioned so that, under firm thumb pressure, there is approximately 5.0 mm of free movement at the mid-point between the pulleys on the longest belt run.
19 To adjust the tension, with the two tensioner pulley assembly retaining screws slackened, rotate the adjuster bolt until the correct tension is achieved. Once the belt is correctly tensioned, rotate the crankshaft a couple of times and recheck the tension.
20 When the belt is correctly tensioned, securely tighten the tensioner pulley assembly retaining screws, then reconnect the battery negative lead.
21 Clip the coolant hoses into position, then refit the plastic cover to the wing valance. Refit the roadwheel, and lower the vehicle to the ground.

Models with an automatic spring-loaded tensioner pulley

Removal

22 Disconnect the battery negative lead.
23 Where necessary, remove the retaining screws from the power steering pump pulley

shield, and remove the shield to gain access to the top of the drivebelt.
24 Move the tensioner pulley away from the drivebelt, using a ratchet handle or extension bar with the same size square-section end as the hole in the base of the automatic tensioner arm. Disengage the drivebelt from all the pulleys, noting its correct routing. Remove the drivebelt from the engine, noting that in some cases, it may be necessary to slacken the automatic tensioner mounting bolts to disengage the belt from behind the tensioner pulley.

Refitting and adjustment

25 Fit the drivebelt around the pulleys in the following order:
(a) Automatic tensioner pulley.
(b) Crankshaft.
(c) Air conditioning compressor.
(d) Power steering pump.
(e) Idler pulley
(f) Alternator.
26 Where necessary, securely tighten the automatic tensioner mounting bolts.
27 Whilst holding the tensioner arm away from the belt, ensure that the ribs on the belt are correctly engaged with the grooves in the pulleys. Release the tensioner arm; the tensioner is spring-loaded, removing the need to manually adjust the belt tension.
28 Refit the power steering pump pulley shield (where removed), and securely tighten its retaining screws.
29 Reconnect the battery negative lead.
30 Clip the coolant hoses into position, then refit the plastic cover to the wing valance. Refit the roadwheel, and lower the vehicle to the ground.

Air conditioning compressor drivebelt (1580 cc and 1905 cc models)

Removal

31 Disconnect the battery negative lead.
32 Slacken the three bolts securing the

tensioner pulley to the sump, to release the drivebelt tension, and unhook the drivebelt from the pulleys.

Refitting

33 Fit the new drivebelt around the pulleys, ensuring that its ribs are correctly located in the pulley grooves.
34 Obtain a suitable ratchet handle or extension bar with the same size square-section end as one of the holes in the tensioner arm. Using this, force the tensioner pulley against the drivebelt to remove the drivebelt slack. Tension the belt as follows.

Adjustment

35 The belt should be tensioned so that, under firm thumb pressure, there is approximately 5.0 mm of free movement at the mid-point between the pulleys on the top belt run.
36 To adjust the tension, first slacken the three tensioner pulley assembly retaining bolts. Using the ratchet handle or extension bar described in paragraph 34, force the tensioner pulley against the drivebelt until the correct drivebelt tension is obtained. Hold the pulley in this position, and securely tighten its three retaining bolts. Rotate the crankshaft a couple of times, and recheck the tension.
37 When the belt is correctly tensioned, clip the coolant hoses into position, then refit the plastic cover to the wing valance. Refit the roadwheel, and lower the vehicle to the ground.

2 Engine assembly/valve timing holes (TU engines) - general information and usage

Note: Do not attempt to rotate the engine whilst the crankshaft/camshaft are locked in position. If the engine is to be left in this state for a long period of time, it is a good idea to place warning notices inside the vehicle, and in the engine compartment. This will reduce

2.4 Insert a 6 mm bolt (arrowed) through hole in cylinder block flange and into timing hole in the flywheel . . .

2.5 . . . then insert a 10 mm bolt through the cam sprocket timing hole, and locate it in the cylinder head

the possibility of the engine being accidentally cranked on the starter motor, which is likely to cause damage with the locking pins in place.

1 On all models, timing holes are drilled in the camshaft sprocket and in the rear of the flywheel. The holes are used to ensure that the crankshaft and camshaft are correctly positioned when assembling the engine (to prevent the possibility of the valves contacting the pistons when refitting the cylinder head), or refitting the timing belt. When the timing holes are aligned with access holes in the cylinder head and the front of the cylinder block, suitable diameter pins can be inserted to lock both the camshaft and crankshaft in position, preventing them from rotating. Proceed as follows.

2 Remove the timing belt upper cover as described in Section 6.

3 The crankshaft must now be turned until the timing hole in the camshaft sprocket is aligned with the corresponding hole in the cylinder head. The holes are aligned when the camshaft sprocket hole is in the 2 o'clock position, when viewed from the right-hand end of the engine. The crankshaft can be turned by using a spanner on the crankshaft sprocket bolt, noting that it should always be rotated in a clockwise direction (viewed from the right-hand end of the engine).

4 With the camshaft sprocket hole correctly positioned, insert a 6 mm diameter bolt or drill through the hole in the front, left-hand flange of the cylinder block, and locate it in the timing hole in the rear of the flywheel **(see illustration)**. Note that it may be necessary to rotate the crankshaft slightly, to get the holes to align.

5 With the flywheel correctly positioned, insert a 10 mm diameter bolt or a drill through the timing hole in the camshaft sprocket, and locate it in the hole in the cylinder head **(see illustration)**.

6 The crankshaft and camshaft are now locked in position, preventing unnecessary rotation.

3 Engine assembly/valve timing holes (XU engines) - general information and usage

Note: Do not attempt to rotate the engine whilst the crankshaft/camshaft are locked in position. If the engine is to be left in this state for a long period of time, it is a good idea to place suitable warning notices inside the vehicle, and in the engine compartment. This will reduce the possibility of the engine being accidentally cranked on the starter motor, which is likely to cause damage with the locking pins in place.

1 On all models, timing holes are drilled in the camshaft sprocket(s) and crankshaft pulley. The holes are used to align the crankshaft and camshaft(s), to prevent the possibility of the valves contacting the pistons when refitting the cylinder head, or when refitting the timing belt. When the holes are aligned with their corresponding holes in the cylinder head and cylinder block (as appropriate), suitable diameter pins can be inserted to lock both the camshaft and crankshaft in position, preventing them rotating unnecessarily. Proceed as follows.

2 Remove the timing belt upper cover as described in Section 6.

3 Apply the handbrake, jack up the front of the car and support it on axle stands. Remove the right-hand front roadwheel.

4 From underneath the front of the car, prise out the two retaining clips and remove the plastic cover from the wing valance, to gain access to the crankshaft pulley bolt. Where necessary, unclip the coolant hoses from the bracket, to improve access further. The crankshaft can then be turned using a suitable socket and extension bar fitted to the pulley bolt. Note that the crankshaft must always be turned in a clockwise direction (viewed from the right-hand side of vehicle).

1998 cc 16-valve models

5 Rotate the crankshaft pulley until the timing

holes in both camshafts are aligned with their corresponding holes in the cylinder head. The holes are aligned when the inlet camshaft sprocket hole is in the 8 o'clock position, and the exhaust camshaft sprocket is in the 6 o'clock position, when viewed from the right-hand end of the engine.

6 With the camshaft sprocket holes correctly positioned, insert a 6 mm diameter bolt (or a drill of suitable size), through the timing hole in the crankshaft pulley, and locate it in the corresponding hole in the end of the cylinder block. Note that it may be necessary to rotate the crankshaft slightly, to get the holes to align.

7 With the crankshaft pulley locked in position, insert a 6 mm diameter bolt (or a drill) through the timing hole in each camshaft sprocket, and locate it in the cylinder head head **(see illustration)**. Note that the special Citroën locking pins are actually 8 mm in diameter, with only their ends stepped down to 6 mm to locate in the cylinder. To simulate this, wrap insulation tape around the outer end of the bolt or drill, to build it up until it is a snug fit in the camshaft hole.

8 The crankshaft and camshafts are now locked in position, preventing unnecessary rotation.

3.7 Camshaft sprocket locking pins in position (arrowed) - 1998 cc 16-valve models

4A

3.13 Camshaft sprocket and crankshaft pulley locking pins in position (1580 cc model shown)

All other models

9 Rotate the crankshaft pulley until the timing hole in the camshaft sprocket is aligned with its corresponding hole in the cylinder head. Note that the hole is aligned when the sprocket hole is in the 8 o'clock position, when viewed from the right-hand end of the engine.

10 On early 1580 cc and 1905 cc models having a semi-automatic timing belt tensioner, a 10 mm diameter bolt (or a drill of suitable size) will be required to lock the crankshaft pulley in position.

11 On later 1580 cc and 1905 cc models, and all 1761 and 1998 cc 8-valve models (which have a manually-adjusted timing belt tensioner pulley) the pulley can be locked in position with an 8 mm diameter bolt or drill. The special Citroën locking pin is actually 10 mm in diameter, with only its end stepped down to 8 mm to locate in the cylinder block. To simulate this, wrap insulation tape around the outer end of the bolt/drill, to build it up until it is a snug fit in the pulley hole.

12 With the camshaft sprocket holes correctly positioned, insert the required bolt or drill through the timing hole in the crankshaft pulley, and locate it in the corresponding hole in the end of the cylinder block. Note that it may be necessary to rotate the crankshaft slightly, to get the holes to align.

13 With the crankshaft pulley locked in position, insert the appropriate bolt or drill through the timing hole in the camshaft sprocket and locate it in the cylinder head **(see illustration)**.

14 The crankshaft and camshaft are now locked in position, preventing unnecessary rotation.

4 Crankshaft pulley (XU engines) - removal and refitting

Removal

1 Remove the auxiliary drivebelt as described in Section 1.

1998 cc 16-valve models

2 Undo the four pulley retaining bolts and remove the pulley from the end of the crankshaft, noting which way around it is fitted. If the pulley locating roll pin is a loose fit, remove it and store it with the pulley for safe-keeping. If necessary, the pulley can be prevented from rotating as described in paragraph 3.

All other models

3 To prevent crankshaft turning whilst the pulley retaining bolt is being slackened, select top gear and have an assistant apply the brakes firmly. *Do not* attempt to lock the pulley by inserting a bolt/drill through the pulley timing hole.

4 Unscrew the retaining bolt and washer, then slide the pulley off the end of the crankshaft. If the pulley locating roll pin or Woodruff key (as applicable) is a loose fit, remove it and store it with the pulley for safe-keeping.

Refitting

1998 cc 16-valve models

5 Ensure that the locating roll pin is in position in the crankshaft. Offer up the pulley, ensuring that it is the correct way around. Locate the pulley on the roll pin, then refit the retaining bolts and tighten them to the specified torque. If necessary, prevent the pulley from rotating as described in paragraph 3.

6 Refit and tension the auxiliary drivebelt as described in Section 1.

All other models

7 Ensure that the Woodruff key is correctly located in its crankshaft groove, or that the roll pin is in position (as applicable). Refit the pulley to the end of the crankshaft, aligning its locating groove or hole with the Woodruff key or pin.

8 Thoroughly clean the threads of the pulley retaining bolt, then apply a coat of locking compound to the bolt threads. Citroën recommend the use of Frenbloc E6 (available from your Citroën dealer); in the absence of this, any good-quality locking compound may be used.

9 Refit the crankshaft pulley retaining bolt and washer. Tighten the bolt to the specified torque, preventing the crankshaft from turning using the method employed on removal.

10 Refit and tension the auxiliary drivebelt as described in Section 1.

5 Timing belt covers (TU engines) - removal and refitting

Removal

Upper cover

1 Slacken and remove the two retaining bolts (one at the front and one at the rear), and remove the upper timing cover from the cylinder head **(see illustrations)**.

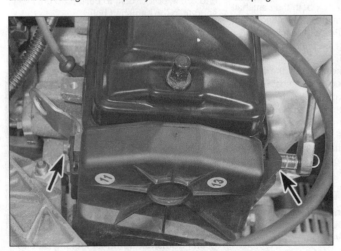

5.1a Undo the two retaining bolts (arrowed) . . .

5.1b . . . and remove the upper timing belt cover

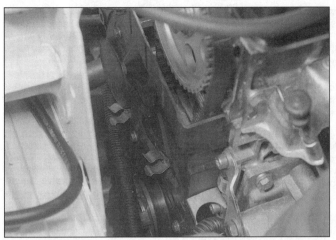

5.2 Free the wiring loom from its retaining clip . . .

5.3 . . . then undo the three retaining bolts (locations arrowed) and remove the centre timing belt cover

Centre cover

2 Remove the upper cover as described in paragraph 1, then free the wiring from its retaining clips on the centre cover **(see illustration)**.

3 Slacken and remove the three retaining bolts (one at the rear of the cover, beneath the engine mounting plate, and two directly above the crankshaft pulley), and manoeuvre the centre cover out from the engine compartment **(see illustration)**.

Lower cover

4 Remove the auxiliary drivebelt as described in Section 1.

5 Remove the upper and centre covers as described in paragraphs 1 to 3.

6 Undo the three crankshaft pulley retaining bolts and remove the pulley, noting which way round it is fitted **(see illustrations)**.

7 Slacken and remove the single retaining bolt, and slide the lower cover off the end of the crankshaft **(see illustration)**.

Refitting

Upper cover

8 Refit the cover, ensuring it is correctly located with the centre cover, and tighten its retaining bolts.

Centre cover

9 Manoeuvre the centre cover back into position, ensuring it is correctly located with the lower cover, and tighten its retaining bolts.

10 Clip the wiring loom into its retaining clips on the front of the centre cover, then refit the upper cover as described in paragraph 8.

Lower cover

10 Locate the lower cover over the timing belt sprocket, and tighten its retaining bolt.

11 Fit the pulley to the end of the crankshaft, ensuring it is fitted the correct way round, and tighten its retaining bolts to the specified torque.

12 Refit the centre and upper covers as described above, then refit and tension the auxiliary drivebelt as described in Section 1.

5.6a Undo the three retaining bolts (arrowed) . . .

4A

5.6b . . . and remove the crankshaft pulley

5.7 Undo the retaining bolt and remove the lower timing belt cover

6 Timing belt covers (XU engines) - removal and refitting

1580 cc and 1905 cc models

Upper cover

1 Release the retaining clips, and free the fuel hoses from the top of the cover.
2 Undo the two cover retaining bolts (situated at the base of the cover), and remove the cover from the engine compartment.

Centre cover - early (pre-1992) models with a semi-automatic belt tensioner

3 Slacken and remove the four cover retaining nuts and bolts (two directly below the mounting bracket, and two at the base of the cover), then manoeuvre the cover upwards out of the engine compartment.

Centre cover - later (1992-on) models with a manually-adjusted belt tensioner pulley

4 Slacken and remove the two cover retaining bolts (located directly beneath the mounting bracket). Move the cover upwards to free it from the two locating pins situated at the base of the cover, and remove it from the engine compartment.

Lower cover

5 Remove the crankshaft pulley as described in Section 4.
6 Remove the centre cover as described above.
7 On early models, undo the three lower cover retaining bolts and remove the cover from the engine.
8 On later models, undo the two cover retaining bolts and remove the cover from the engine.

Lower (inner) cover - early (pre-1992) models with a semi-automatic belt tensioner

9 Remove the timing belt as described in Section 8.
10 Slacken and remove the remaining bolts, noting their correct fitted positions, and remove the cover from the end of the cylinder block.

1761 cc models

Upper cover

11 Proceed as described in paragraphs 1 and 2.

Centre cover

12 Proceed as described in paragraph 4.

Lower cover

13 Remove the crankshaft pulley as described in Section 4.
14 Remove the centre cover as described in paragraph 4.
15 Undo the two cover retaining bolts, and remove the cover from the engine.

1998 cc 8-valve models

Upper cover

16 Release the retaining clip, and free the fuel hoses from the top of the timing belt cover.
17 Slacken and remove the two cover retaining bolts, then lift the upper cover upwards and out of the engine compartment.

Lower cover

18 Remove the crankshaft pulley as described in Section 4.
19 Slacken and remove the three retaining bolts, then remove the lower timing belt cover from the engine.

1998 cc 16-valve models

Upper (outer) cover

20 Undo the two upper retaining bolts securing the outer cover to the inner cover. Slide the cover retaining clip upwards to release it from its fasteners (see illustration).
21 Ease the outer cover away from the engine. Lift it upwards, freeing it from its locating bolts at the base of the cover, and out of the engine compartment.

Lower cover

22 Remove the crankshaft pulley as described in Section 4.
23 Remove the upper (outer) cover as described above.
24 Slacken and remove the two upper cover lower locating bolts, along with their spacers. Undo the two lower cover retaining bolts, and remove the cover from the engine.

Upper (inner) cover

25 Remove the timing belt as described in Section 8.
26 Remove both camshaft sprockets as described in Section 10.
27 Undo the six bolts securing the cover to the side of the cylinder head, and remove the cover from the engine.

Refitting

28 Refitting is a reversal of the relevant removal procedure, ensuring that each cover section is correctly located, and that the cover retaining nuts and/or bolts are securely tightened (to the specified torque, where given).

7 Timing belt (TU engines) - removal and refitting

Removal

1 Disconnect the battery negative terminal.
2 Align the engine assembly/valve timing holes as described in Section 3, and lock both the camshaft sprocket and the flywheel in position. Do not attempt to rotate the engine whilst the locking pins are in position.
3 Remove the timing belt centre and lower covers as described in Section 5.
4 Loosen the timing belt tensioner pulley retaining nut. Pivot the pulley in a clockwise direction, using a square-section key fitted to the hole in the pulley hub, then retighten the retaining nut.
5 If the timing belt is to be re-used, use white paint or similar to mark the direction of rotation on the belt (if markings do not already exist) (see illustration). Slip the belt off the sprockets.
6 If signs of oil contamination are found, trace the source of the oil leak, and rectify it. Wash down the engine timing belt area and all related components, to remove all traces of oil.

Refitting

7 Prior to refitting, thoroughly clean the timing belt sprockets. Check that the tensioner pulley rotates freely, without any sign of roughness. If necessary, renew the tensioner pulley as described in Section 9. Make sure that the locking pins are still in place, as described in Section 2.
8 Manoeuvre the timing belt into position, ensuring that the arrows on the belt are pointing in the direction of rotation (clockwise when viewed from the right-hand end of the engine).

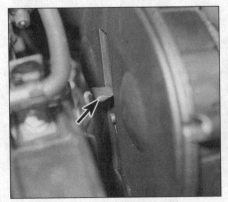

6.20 Timing belt upper (outer) cover retaining clip (arrowed) - 1998 cc 16-valve models

7.5 Mark the direction of rotation on the belt, if it is to be re-used

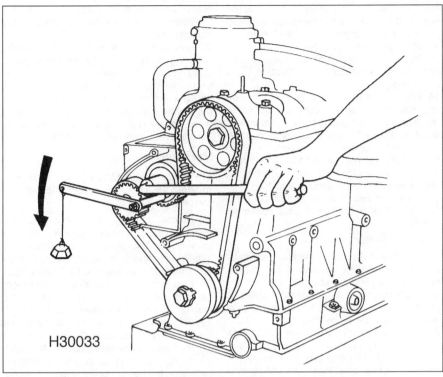

7.11 Using a suitable tool to tension the timing belt

H30033

12 Remove the locking pins from the camshaft sprocket and flywheel.

13 Using a suitable socket and extension bar on the crankshaft sprocket bolt, rotate the crankshaft through four complete rotations in a clockwise direction (viewed from the right-hand end of the engine). *Do not* at any time rotate the crankshaft anti-clockwise.

14 Slacken the tensioner pulley nut, re-tension the belt, then tighten the tensioner pulley nut to the specified torque.

15 Rotate the crankshaft through a further two turns clockwise, and check that both the camshaft sprocket and flywheel timing holes are still correctly aligned.

16 If all is well, refit the timing belt covers as described in Section 5, and reconnect the battery negative terminal.

8 Timing belt (XU engines) - removal and refitting

Removal

Early (pre-1992) 1580 cc and 1905 cc models with a semi-automatic belt tensioner

1 Disconnect the battery negative terminal.

2 Align the engine assembly/valve timing holes as described in Section 3, and lock the camshaft sprocket and crankshaft pulley in position. *Do not* attempt to rotate the engine whilst the pins are in position.

3 Remove the centre and lower timing belt covers as described in Section 6.

4 Slacken (but do not remove) the two nuts securing the tensioner assembly to the end of the cylinder block (see illustration).

5 Loosen the tensioner cam spindle locknut, located on the rear of cylinder block flange.

6 Using a suitable open-ended spanner on the square-section end of the tensioner cam spindle, rotate the cam until the tensioner spring is fully compressed and the belt tension is relieved (see illustration).

9 Do not twist the timing belt sharply while refitting it. Fit the belt over the crankshaft and camshaft sprockets. Make sure that the front run of the belt is taut - ie, ensure that any slack is on the tensioner pulley side of the belt. Fit the belt over the water pump sprocket and tensioner pulley. Ensure that the belt teeth are seated centrally in the sprockets.

10 Loosen the tensioner pulley retaining nut. Pivot the pulley anti-clockwise to remove all free play from the timing belt, then retighten the nut.

11 Citroën dealers use a special tool to tension the timing belt (see illustration). A similar tool may be fabricated using a suitable square-section bar attached to an arm; a hole should be drilled in the arm at a distance of 80 mm from the centre of the square-section bar. Fit the tool to the hole in the tensioner pulley, keeping the tool arm as close to the horizontal as possible, and hang a 1.5 kg (3.3 lb) weight from the hole in the tool. In the absence of an object of the specified weight, a spring balance can be used to exert the required force, ensuring that the spring balance is held at 90° to the tool arm. Slacken the pulley retaining nut, allowing the weight or force exerted (as applicable) to push the tensioner pulley against the belt, then retighten the pulley nut.

8.4 On early 1580 cc and 1905 cc models, slacken the tensioner assembly retaining nuts . . .

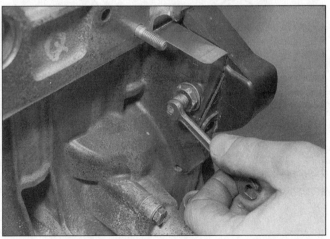

8.6 . . . and the spindle locknut, then release the belt tension by turning the tensioner cam spindle using an open-ended spanner

4A

7 Hold the cam in this position, and securely tighten the locknut.

8 Place a jack beneath the engine, with a block of wood on the jack head. Raise the jack until it is supporting the weight of the engine.

9 Slacken and remove the three nuts securing the engine/transmission right-hand mounting bracket to the engine bracket. Remove the single nut securing the bracket to the mounting rubber, and lift off the bracket.

10 Undo the three bolts securing the engine bracket to the end of the cylinder head/block, and remove the bracket.

11 If the timing belt is to be re-used, use white paint or chalk to mark the direction of rotation on the belt (if markings do not already exist), then slip the belt off the sprockets. Note that the crankshaft must not be rotated whilst the belt is removed.

12 If signs of oil contamination are found, trace the source of the oil leak and rectify it. Wash down the engine timing belt area and all related components, to remove all traces of oil.

Later (1992-on) 1580 cc and 1905 cc models with a manually-adjusted belt tensioner pulley, and all 1761 cc and 1998 cc 8-valve models

13 Disconnect the battery negative terminal.

14 Align the engine assembly/valve timing

holes as described in Section 3, and lock the camshaft sprocket and crankshaft pulley in position. *Do not* attempt to rotate the engine whilst the pins are in position.

15 Remove the centre and/or lower timing belt cover(s) as described in Section 6 (as applicable).

16 Loosen the timing belt tensioner pulley retaining bolt. Pivot the pulley in a clockwise direction, using a suitable square-section key fitted to the hole in the pulley hub, then securely retighten the retaining bolt.

17 On 1580 cc, 1761 cc and 1905 cc models, dismantle the engine right-hand mounting as described above in paragraphs 8 to 10.

18 On all models, remove and inspect the timing belt as described in paragraphs 11 and 12.

1998 cc 16-valve models

19 Disconnect the battery negative terminal.

20 Align the engine assembly/valve timing holes as described in Section 3, and lock the camshaft sprockets and crankshaft pulley in position. *Do not* attempt to rotate the engine whilst the pins are in position.

21 Remove the timing belt lower cover as described in Section 6.

22 Loosen the timing belt rear tensioner pulley retaining bolt. Pivot the pulley in a clockwise direction, using a suitable square-

section key fitted to the hole in the pulley hub, then securely retighten the retaining bolt **(see illustration)**.

23 Loosen the two front tensioner assembly retaining bolts. Move the tensioner pulley away from the belt, using the same square-section key on the pulley backplate.

24 Check that the camshaft sprocket and crankshaft locking pins are still in position, then remove and inspect the timing belt as described in paragraphs 11 and 12.

Refitting

Early (pre-1992) 1580 cc and 1905 cc models with a semi-automatic belt tensioner

25 Before refitting, thoroughly clean the timing belt sprockets. Check that the tensioner pulley rotates freely, without any sign of roughness. If necessary, renew the tensioner pulley as described in Section 10.

26 Ensure that the camshaft sprocket locking pin is still in position. Temporarily refit the crankshaft pulley, and insert the locking pin through the pulley timing hole to ensure that the crankshaft is still correctly positioned.

27 Remove the crankshaft pulley. Manoeuvre the timing belt into position, ensuring that any arrows on the belt are pointing in the direction of rotation (clockwise when viewed from the right-hand end of the engine).

28 Do not twist the timing belt sharply while refitting it. Fit the belt over the crankshaft and camshaft sprockets. Ensure that the belt front run is taut - ie, any slack should be on the tensioner pulley side of the belt. Fit the belt over the water pump sprocket and tensioner pulley. Ensure that the belt teeth are seated centrally in the sprockets.

29 Slacken the tensioner cam spindle locknut, and check that the tensioner pulley is forced against the timing belt by spring pressure.

30 Refit the crankshaft pulley, tightening its retaining bolt by hand only.

31 Rotate the crankshaft through at least two complete rotations in a clockwise direction (viewed from the right-hand end of the engine). Realign the camshaft and crankshaft engine assembly/valve timing holes (see Section 3). *Do not* at any time rotate the crankshaft anti-clockwise. Both camshaft and crankshaft timing holes should be aligned so that the locking pins can be easily inserted. This indicates that the valve timing is correct.

32 If the timing holes are not correctly positioned, release the tensioner assembly as described in paragraph 6, and disengage the belt from the camshaft sprocket. Rotate the camshaft and crankshaft slightly as required until both locking pins are in position. Relocate the timing belt on the camshaft sprocket. Ensure that the belt front run is taut - ie, that any slack is on the tensioner pulley side of the belt. Slacken the tensioner locknut, then remove the locking pins and repeat the procedure described in paragraph 31.

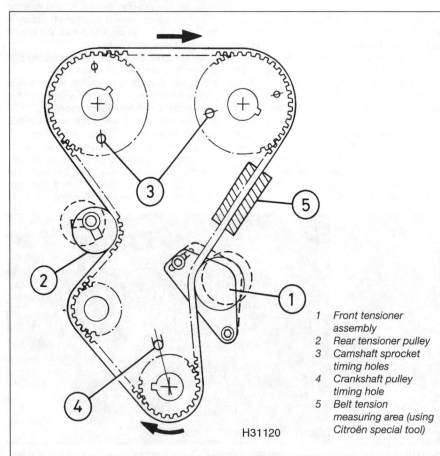

1 Front tensioner assembly
2 Rear tensioner pulley
3 Camshaft sprocket timing holes
4 Crankshaft pulley timing hole
5 Belt tension measuring area (using Citroën special tool)

H31120

8.22 Timing belt arrangement - 1998 cc 16-valve models

33 Once both timing holes are correctly aligned, tighten the two tensioner assembly retaining nuts to the specified torque. Tighten the tensioner cam spindle locknut to its specified torque.

34 With the belt correctly installed and tensioned, refit the engine bracket to the side of the cylinder head/block, and securely tighten its retaining bolts. Refit the right-hand mounting bracket, and tighten its retaining nuts to the specified torque. The jack can then be removed from underneath the engine.

35 Remove the crankshaft pulley, then refit the timing belt covers as described in Section 6.

36 Install the crankshaft pulley as described in Section 4, and reconnect the battery negative terminal.

Later (1992-on) 1580 cc and 1905 cc models with a manually-adjusted belt tensioner pulley, and all 1761 cc and 1998 cc 8-valve models

Note: *Citroën specify the use of a special electronic tool (SEEM belt tension measuring tool) to correctly set the timing belt tension.*

37 Install the timing belt as described above in paragraphs 25 to 28.

38 Loosen the tensioner pulley retaining bolt. Using the square-section key, pivot the pulley anti-clockwise to remove all free play from the timing belt.

39 The special belt tension measuring equipment should be fitted to the front run of the timing belt. The tensioner roller should be adjusted so that the initial belt tension is 16 ± 2 units on 1998 cc 8-valve models, and 30 ± 2 units on all other models.

40 Tighten the pulley retaining bolt to the specified torque. Refit the crankshaft pulley again, tightening its retaining bolt by hand only.

41 Carry out the operations described in paragraph 31 (and where necessary, paragraph 32, ignoring the information about the tensioner) to ensure that both timing holes are correctly aligned and the valve timing is correct.

42 Using the special measuring tool, the belt tension on the front run of the belt on all models should be 44 ± 2 units. Readjust the tensioner pulley position as required, then retighten the retaining bolt to the specified torque.

43 Rotate the crankshaft through a further two rotations clockwise, and recheck the tension. Repeat this procedure as necessary until the correct tension reading is obtained after rotating the crankshaft.

44 With the belt tension correctly set, on 1580 cc, 1761 cc and 1905 cc models, refit the engine bracket to the side of the cylinder head/block, and securely tighten its retaining bolts. Refit the right-hand engine mounting bracket, and tighten its retaining nuts to the specified torque. The jack can then be removed from underneath the engine.

45 On all models, remove the crankshaft

pulley, then refit the timing belt cover(s) as described in Section 6.

46 Refit the crankshaft pulley as described in Section 4, and reconnect the battery negative terminal.

1998 cc 16-valve models

Note: *Citroën specify the use of a special electronic tool (SEEM belt tension measuring tool) to correctly set the timing belt tension.*

47 Before refitting, thoroughly clean the timing belt sprockets. Check that each tensioner pulley rotates freely, without any sign of roughness. If necessary, renew the tensioner pulley(s) as described in Section 10.

48 Ensure that the camshaft and crankshaft sprocket locking pins are still in position. Slacken both tensioner mounting bolts so that they are free to pivot easily.

49 Manoeuvre the timing belt into position, ensuring that any arrows on the belt are pointing in the direction of rotation (clockwise when viewed from the right-hand end of the engine).

50 Note that there are also timing marks on the belt, in the form of yellow lines, to ensure it is correctly positioned on both camshaft sprockets and the crankshaft sprocket. The two single-line timing marks should be aligned with the timing dot (directly opposite the sprocket timing hole) on each camshaft sprocket. The double-line timing mark should be aligned with the crankshaft sprocket, where it will be directly opposite the sprocket Woodruff key slot. Citroën state that the use of these timing marks is optional, but they are useful in helping to ensure that the valve timing is correctly set at the first attempt.

51 With the three locking pins in position, move both the front and rear tensioner pulleys towards the timing belt until both pulleys are contacting the belt. Securely tighten the rear tensioner retaining bolt.

52 The special belt tension measuring equipment should be fitted to the front run of the timing belt, between the front tensioner and the camshaft sprocket. Move the tensioner pulley backplate so that the belt is initially over-tensioned to a setting of 45 units, then back the tensioner off until the belt tension is 22 ± 2 units.

53 Hold the backplate in this position, and tighten both the tensioner pulley retaining bolts to the specified torque.

54 Slacken the rear tensioner pulley retaining bolt. Using the square-section key, pivot the pulley anti-clockwise until all free play is removed from the belt. Set the tensioner pulley so that the belt tension on the front run is 32 ± 2 units. Hold the tensioner in position, and tighten its retaining bolt to the specified torque setting.

55 Remove the locking pins from the camshaft and crankshaft sprockets and, where fitted, the tensioning measuring device from the belt.

56 Rotate the crankshaft through at least two complete rotations in a clockwise direction

(viewed from the right-hand end of the engine). Realign the camshaft and crankshaft engine assembly/valve timing holes (see Section 3). *Do not* at any time rotate the crankshaft anti-clockwise. Both camshaft timing holes and the crankshaft timing hole should be correctly positioned so that the locking pins can be easily inserted, indicating that the valve timing is correct.

57 If the timing holes are not correctly positioned, slacken the tensioner assembly retaining bolts, and disengage the belt from the camshaft sprockets. Rotate the camshafts and crankshaft slightly as required until all locking pins are in position, then relocate the timing belt on the camshaft sprocket. Ensure that the belt top run and front run are taut - ie, ensure that any slack is on the rear tensioner pulley and water pump side of the belt. Repeat the tensioning procedure described in paragraphs 51 to 56 until the valve timing is correct.

58 Once the valve timing is correctly set, remove the locking pins and recheck the belt tension.

59 The final belt tension on the front run of the belt, between the camshaft sprocket and tensioner pulley, should be 53 ± 2 units. Readjust the rear tensioner pulley position as required, then retighten the retaining bolt to the specified torque. Rotate the crankshaft through a further two rotations clockwise, and recheck the tension. Repeat this procedure as necessary, until the correct tension reading is obtained after the crankshaft has been rotated.

60 Once the belt tension is correctly set, refit the timing belt covers as described in Section 6. Refit the crankshaft pulley as described in Section 4, and reconnect the battery negative terminal

4A

---

9 Timing belt tensioner and sprockets (TU engines) - removal, inspection and refitting

Note: *This Section describes the removal and refitting of the components concerned as individual operations. If more than one of them is to be removed at the same time, start by removing the timing belt as described in Section 7; remove the actual component as described below, ignoring the preliminary dismantling steps.*

Removal

1 Disconnect the battery negative terminal.

2 Position the engine assembly/valve timing holes as described in Section 2, and lock both the camshaft sprocket and flywheel in position. *Do not* attempt to rotate the engine whilst the pins are in position.

Camshaft sprocket

3 Remove the centre timing belt cover as described in Section 5.

4 Loosen the timing belt tensioner pulley

9.6 To prevent the camshaft sprocket from rotating, use two lengths of steel strip (one long, the other short), and three nuts and bolts; one nut and bolt forms the pivot of a forked tool, with the remaining two nuts and bolts at the tips of the 'forks' to engage with the sprocket spokes

9.11a Remove the crankshaft sprocket retaining bolt . . .

retaining nut. Rotate the pulley in a clockwise direction, using a suitable square-section key fitted to the hole in the pulley hub, then retighten the retaining nut.

5 Disengage the timing belt from the sprocket, and move the belt clear, taking care not to bend or twist it sharply. Remove the locking pin from the camshaft sprocket.

6 Slacken the camshaft sprocket retaining bolt and remove it, along with its washer. To prevent the camshaft rotating as the bolt is slackened, a sprocket-holding tool will be required (see illustration). Do not attempt to use the sprocket locking pin to prevent the sprocket from rotating whilst the bolt is slackened.

7 With the retaining bolt removed, slide the sprocket off the end of the camshaft. If the locating peg is a loose fit in the rear of the sprocket, remove it for safe-keeping. Examine

the camshaft oil seal for signs of oil leakage and, if necessary, renew it.

Crankshaft sprocket

8 Remove the centre and lower timing belt covers as described in Section 5.

9 Loosen the timing belt tensioner pulley retaining nut. Rotate the pulley in a clockwise direction, using a suitable square-section key fitted to the hole in the pulley hub, then retighten the retaining nut.

10 To prevent crankshaft rotation whilst the sprocket retaining bolt is slackened, select top gear, and have an assistant apply the brakes firmly. Do not be tempted to use the flywheel locking pin to prevent the crankshaft from rotating; temporarily remove the locking pin from the rear of the flywheel prior to slackening the pulley bolt, then refit it once the bolt has been slackened. Disengage the

timing belt from the sprocket, and move the belt clear, taking care not to bend or twist it sharply.

11 Unscrew the retaining bolt and washer, then slide the sprocket off the end of the crankshaft (see illustrations). Refit the locating pin to the rear of the timing hole in the rear of the flywheel.

12 If the Woodruff key is a loose fit in the crankshaft, remove it and store it with the sprocket for safe-keeping. If necessary, also slide the flanged spacer off the end of the crankshaft (see illustration). Examine the crankshaft oil seal for signs of oil leakage and, if necessary, renew.

Tensioner pulley

13 Remove the centre timing belt cover as described in Section 5.

14 Slacken and remove the timing belt

9.11b . . . then slide off the sprocket

9.12 Remove the flanged spacer if necessary

tensioner pulley retaining nut, and slide the pulley off its mounting stud. Examine the mounting stud for signs of damage and, if necessary, renew it.

Refitting

15 Clean the sprockets thoroughly, and renew any that show signs of wear, damage or cracks.
16 Clean the tensioner assembly, but do not use any strong solvent which may enter the pulley bearing. Check that the pulley rotates freely about its hub, with no sign of stiffness or of free play. Renew the tensioner pulley if there is any doubt about its condition, or if there are any obvious signs of wear or damage.

Camshaft sprocket

17 Refit the locating peg (where removed) to the rear of the sprocket, then locate the sprocket on the end of the camshaft. Ensure that the locating peg is correctly engaged with the cutout in the camshaft end.
18 Refit the sprocket retaining bolt and washer. Tighten the bolt to the specified torque, whilst retaining the sprocket with the tool used on removal.
19 Realign the timing hole in the camshaft sprocket (see Section 3) with the corresponding hole in the cylinder head, and refit the locking pin.
20 Refit the timing belt to the camshaft sprocket. Ensure that the front run of the belt is taut - ie, ensure that any slack is on the tensioner pulley side of the belt. Do not twist the belt sharply while refitting it, and ensure that the belt teeth are seated centrally in the sprockets.
21 Loosen the tensioner pulley retaining nut. Rotate the pulley anti-clockwise to remove all free play from the timing belt, then retighten the nut.
22 Tension the belt as described in Section 7.
23 Refit the timing belt covers as described in Section 5.

Crankshaft sprocket

24 Where removed, locate the Woodruff key in the crankshaft end, then slide on the flanged spacer, aligning its slot with the Woodruff key.
25 Align the crankshaft sprocket slot with the Woodruff key, and slide it onto the end of the crankshaft.
26 Temporarily remove the locking pin from the rear of the flywheel, then refit the crankshaft sprocket retaining bolt and washer. Tighten the bolt to the specified torque, whilst preventing crankshaft rotation using the method employed on removal. Refit the locking pin to the rear of the flywheel.
27 Relocate the timing belt on the crankshaft sprocket. Ensure that the front run of the belt is taut - ie, ensure that any slack is on the tensioner pulley side of the belt. Do not twist the belt sharply while refitting it, and ensure that the belt teeth are seated centrally in the sprockets.
28 Loosen the tensioner pulley retaining nut. Rotate the pulley anti-clockwise to remove all free play from the timing belt, then retighten the nut.
29 Tension the belt as described in Section 7.
30 Refit the timing belt covers as described in Section 5.

Tensioner pulley

31 Refit the tensioner pulley to its mounting stud, and fit the retaining nut.
32 Ensure that the front run of the belt is taut - ie, ensure that any slack is on the pulley side of the belt. Check that the belt is centrally located on all its sprockets. Rotate the pulley anti-clockwise to remove all free play from the timing belt, then tighten the pulley retaining nut securely.
33 Tension the belt as described in Section 7.
34 Refit the timing belt covers as described in Section 5.

10 Timing belt tensioner and sprockets (XU engines) - removal and refitting

Note: *This Section describes the removal and refitting of the components concerned as individual operations - if more than one is to be removed at the same time, start by removing the timing belt as described in Section 8; remove the actual component as described below, ignoring the preliminary dismantling steps.*

Removal

1 Disconnect the battery negative lead.
2 Align the engine assembly/valve timing holes as described in Section 3, locking the camshaft sprocket(s) and the crankshaft pulley in position, and proceed as described under the relevant sub-heading. *Do not attempt to rotate the engine whilst the pins are in position.*

Camshaft sprocket - early (pre-1992) 1580 cc and 1905 cc models with a semi-automatic belt tensioner

3 Remove the centre timing belt cover as described in Section 6.
4 Slacken (but do not remove) the two nuts securing the tensioner assembly to the end of the cylinder block. Loosen the tensioner cam spindle locknut, located on the rear of cylinder block flange.
5 Using a suitable open-ended spanner on the square-section end of the tensioner cam spindle, rotate the cam until the tensioner spring is fully compressed and the belt tension is relieved. Hold the cam in this position, and securely tighten the locknut.
6 Remove the locking pin from the camshaft sprocket. Disengage the timing belt from the

sprocket and position it clear, taking care not to bend or twist the belt sharply.
7 Slacken the camshaft sprocket retaining bolt and remove it, along with its washer. To prevent the camshaft rotating as the bolt is slackened, a sprocket holding tool will be required **(see illustration 9.6)**. *Do not* attempt to use the sprocket locking pin to prevent the sprocket from rotating whilst the bolt is slackened
8 With the retaining bolt removed, slide the sprocket off the end of the camshaft. If the locating peg is a loose fit in the rear of the sprocket, remove it for safe-keeping. Examine the camshaft oil seal for signs of oil leakage and, if necessary, renew it.

Camshaft sprocket - later (1992-on) 1580 cc and 1905 cc models with a manually-adjusted belt tensioner pulley, and all 1761 cc and 1998 cc 8-valve models

9 On all except 1998 cc 8-valve models, remove the centre timing belt cover as described in Section 6.
10 Loosen the timing belt tensioner pulley retaining bolt. Rotate the pulley in a clockwise direction, using a suitable square-section key fitted to the hole in the pulley hub, then retighten the retaining bolt.
11 Remove the camshaft sprocket as described above in paragraphs 6 to 8.

Camshaft sprocket(s) - 1998 cc 16-valve models

12 Loosen the timing belt rear tensioner pulley retaining bolt. Pivot the pulley in a clockwise direction, using a suitable square-section key fitted to the hole in the pulley hub, then securely retighten the retaining bolt.
13 Loosen the two front tensioner assembly retaining bolts. Move the tensioner pulley away from the belt, using the same square-section key on the pulley backplate.
14 Remove the camshaft sprocket retaining bolt as described above in paragraphs 6 and 7.
15 Slide the sprocket off the end of the camshaft. If the Woodruff key is a loose fit in the camshaft, remove it and store it with the sprocket for safe-keeping. Examine the camshaft oil seal for signs of oil leakage and, if necessary, renew it.

Crankshaft sprocket - 1580 cc, 1761 cc, 1905 cc and 1998 cc 8-valve models

16 Remove the centre and/or lower timing belt cover(s) (as applicable) as described in Section 6.
17 On early (pre-1992) 1580 cc and 1905 cc models with a semi-automatic belt tensioner, release the timing belt tensioner as described above in paragraphs 4 and 5.
18 On later (1992-on) 1580 cc and 1905 cc models with a manually-adjusted belt tensioner pulley, and all 1761 cc and 1998 cc 8-valve models, release the timing belt tensioner as described in paragraph 10.
19 Disengage the timing belt from the

4A

crankshaft sprocket, and slide the sprocket off the end of the crankshaft. Remove the Woodruff key from the crankshaft, and store it with the sprocket for safe-keeping. Where necessary, also slide the flanged spacer (where fitted) off the end of the crankshaft.

20 Examine the crankshaft oil seal for signs of oil leakage and, if necessary, renew it.

Crankshaft sprocket - 1998 cc 16-valve models

21 Remove the lower timing belt cover as described in Section 6.

22 Release the timing belt tensioners as described above in paragraphs 12 and 13. Disengage the timing belt from the crankshaft sprocket, and remove the locking pin.

23 To prevent the crankshaft turning whilst the sprocket retaining bolt is being slackened, select top gear, and have an assistant apply the brakes firmly. *Do not* be tempted to use the locking pin to prevent the crankshaft from rotating.

24 Unscrew the retaining bolt and washer, then slide the sprocket off the end of the crankshaft. If the Woodruff key is a loose fit in the crankshaft, remove it and store it with the sprocket for safe-keeping.

25 Where necessary, slide the flanged spacer (where fitted) off the end of the crankshaft.

26 Examine the crankshaft oil seal for signs of oil leakage and, if necessary, renew it.

Tensioner assembly - early (pre-1992) 1580 cc and 1905 cc models with a semi-automatic belt tensioner

27 Remove the centre timing belt cover as described in Section 6.

28 Slacken and remove the two nuts and washers securing the tensioner assembly to the end of the cylinder block. Carefully ease the spring cover off its studs, taking care not to allow the spring to fly out as the cover is withdrawn. Remove the spring and cover from the engine **(see illustration)**.

29 Slacken and remove the tensioner cam spindle locknut and washer, located on the rear of cylinder block flange, and withdraw the cam spindle.

30 The tensioner pulley and backplate

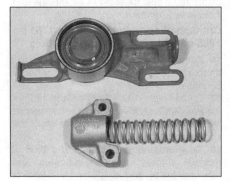

10.28 Timing belt tensioner assembly components - early 1580 cc and 1905 cc models

assembly can then be manoeuvred out from behind the timing belt.

Tensioner pulley - later (1992-on) 1580 cc and 1905 cc models with a manually-adjusted belt tensioner pulley, and all 1761 cc and 1998 cc 8-valve models

31 On all except 1998 cc 8-valve models, remove the centre timing belt cover as described in Section 6.

32 Slacken and remove the timing belt tensioner pulley retaining bolt, and slide the pulley off its mounting stud. Examine the mounting stud for signs of damage and if necessary, renew it.

Tensioner pulleys - 1998 cc 16-valve models

33 The rear tensioner pulley is removed as described above in paragraph 32.

34 To remove the front tensioner pulley, slacken and remove the two bolts securing the pulley backplate to the cylinder block, and remove the assembly from the engine unit.

Refitting

35 Clean the camshaft/crankshaft sprockets thoroughly, and renew any that show signs of wear, damage or cracks.

36 Clean the tensioner assembly, but do not use any strong solvent which may enter the pulley bearing. Check that the pulley rotates freely on the backplate, with no sign of stiffness or free play. Renew the assembly if there is any doubt about its condition, or if there are any obvious signs of wear or damage.

37 On early 1580 cc and 1905 cc models, the tensioner spring should also be carefully checked, as its condition is critical for the correct tensioning of the timing belt. The only way of checking the spring tension is to compare it with a new one; if there is any doubt as to its condition, the spring should be renewed.

Camshaft sprocket - early (pre-1992) 1580 cc and 1905 cc models with a semi-automatic belt tensioner

38 Refit the locating peg (where removed) to the rear of the sprocket. Locate the sprocket on the end of the camshaft, ensuring that the locating peg is correctly engaged with the cutout in the camshaft end.

39 Refit the sprocket retaining bolt and washer, and tighten it to the specified torque. Retain the sprocket with the tool used on removal **(see illustration 9.6)**.

40 Realign the hole in the camshaft sprocket with the corresponding hole in the cylinder head, and refit the locking pin. Check that the crankshaft pulley locking pin is still in position.

41 Refit the timing belt to the camshaft sprocket. Ensure that the front run of the belt is taut - ie, that any slack is on the tensioner pulley side of the belt. Do not twist the belt sharply while refitting it, and ensure that the belt teeth are seated centrally in the sprockets.

42 Release the tensioner cam spindle locknut, and check that the tensioner pulley is forced against the timing belt under spring pressure.

43 Tension the timing belt as described in paragraphs 31 to 33 of Section 8.

44 With the belt correctly tensioned, and the tensioner retaining nuts and locknut tightened to the specified torque setting, refit the timing belt covers as described in Section 6. Reconnect the battery on completion.

Camshaft sprocket - later (1992-on) 1580 cc and 1905 cc models with a manually-adjusted belt tensioner pulley, and all 1761 cc and 1998 cc 8-valve models

45 Refit the camshaft sprocket as described above in paragraphs 38 to 41.

46 With the timing belt correctly engaged on the sprockets, tension the belt as described in paragraphs 38 to 43 of Section 8.

47 Once the belt is correctly tensioned, refit the timing belt covers as described in Section 6.

Camshaft sprocket(s) - 1998 cc 16-valve models

48 Refit the Woodruff key to its slot in the camshaft end. Slide on the sprocket, aligning its slot with the Woodruff key.

49 Refit the sprocket retaining bolt and washer. Tighten the bolt to the specified torque, whilst retaining the sprocket with the tool used on removal.

50 Realign the hole in the camshaft sprocket with the corresponding hole in the cylinder head, and refit the locking pin.

51 Relocate the timing belt on the camshaft sprocket(s), and tension the timing belt as described in paragraphs 50 to 59 of Section 7.

52 Once the belt is correctly tensioned, refit the timing belt cover as described in Section 6.

Crankshaft sprocket - 1580 cc, 1761 cc, 1905 cc and 1998 cc 8-valve models

53 Slide on the flanged spacer (where fitted), and refit the Woodruff key to its slot in the crankshaft end.

54 Slide on the crankshaft sprocket, aligning its slot with the Woodruff key.

55 Ensure that the camshaft sprocket locking pin is still in position. Temporarily refit the crankshaft pulley, and insert the locking pin through the pulley timing hole, to ensure that the crankshaft is still correctly positioned.

56 Remove the crankshaft pulley. Engage the timing belt with the crankshaft sprocket. Ensure that the belt front run is taut - ie, that any slack is on the tensioner pulley side of the belt. Fit the belt over the water pump sprocket and tensioner pulley. Do not twist the belt sharply while refitting it, and ensure that the belt teeth are seated centrally in the sprockets.

57 On early (pre-1992) 1580 cc and 1905 cc models with a semi-automatic tensioner,

release the tensioner cam spindle locknut, checking that the tensioner pulley is forced against the timing belt under spring pressure. Tension the timing belt as described in paragraphs 30 to 33 of Section 8.

58 On later (1992-on) 1580 cc and 1905 cc models with a manually-adjusted belt tensioner pulley, and all 1761 cc and 1998 cc 8-valve models, tension the timing belt as described in paragraphs 38 to 42 of Section 8.

59 On all models, remove the crankshaft pulley, then refit the timing belt cover(s) as described in Section 6.

60 Refit the crankshaft pulley as described in Section 4, and reconnect the battery negative terminal.

Crankshaft sprocket - 1998 cc 16-valve models

61 Slide on the flanged spacer (where fitted), and refit the Woodruff key to its slot in the crankshaft end.

62 Slide on the crankshaft sprocket, aligning its slot with the Woodruff key.

63 Thoroughly clean the threads of the sprocket retaining bolt, then apply a coat of locking compound to the threads of the bolt. Citroën recommend the use of Frenbloc E6 (available from your Citroën dealer); in the absence of this, any good-quality locking compound may be used.

64 Refit the crankshaft sprocket retaining bolt and washer. Tighten the bolt to the specified torque, whilst preventing crankshaft rotation using the method employed on removal.

65 Refit the locking pin to the crankshaft sprocket, and check that both the camshaft sprocket locking pins are still in position.

66 Relocate the timing belt on the crankshaft sprocket, and tension the timing belt as described in paragraphs 50 to 59 of Section 8.

67 Once the belt is correctly tensioned, refit the timing belt cover as described in Section 6.

Tensioner assembly - early (pre-1992) 1580 cc and 1905 cc models with a semi-automatic belt tensioner

68 Manoeuvre the tensioner pulley and backplate assembly into position behind the timing belt, and locate it on the mounting studs.

69 Insert the tensioner cam spindle through the backplate from the front of the block, and refit its washer and locknut, tightening it by hand only at this stage.

70 Fit the spring to the inside of the spring cover. Compress the spring, and slide the spring cover onto the two mounting studs, ensuring that the spring end is correctly located behind the backplate tang.

71 Refit the tensioner mounting nuts and washers, tightening them by hand only. Check that the tensioner is forced against the timing belt by spring pressure, and is free to move smoothly and easily.

72 Ensure that the front run of the belt is taut - ie, that any slack is on the pulley side of the belt. Check that the belt is centrally located on all its sprockets, then release the tensioner assembly and allow it to tension the belt.

73 Tension the timing belt, and check the valve timing as described in paragraphs 31 to 33 of Section 8.

74 With the belt correctly tensioned, and the tensioner retaining nuts and locknut tightened to the specified torque setting, refit the timing belt covers as described in Section 6. Reconnect the battery on completion.

Tensioner pulley - later (1992-on) 1580 cc and 1905 cc models with a manually-adjusted belt tensioner pulley, and all 1761 cc and 1998 cc 8-valve models

75 Refit the tensioner pulley to its mounting stud, and fit the retaining bolt.

76 Ensure that the front run of the belt is taut - ie, that any slack is on the pulley side of the belt. Check that the belt is centrally located on all its sprockets. Rotate the pulley anti-clockwise to remove all free play from the timing belt, and securely tighten the pulley retaining nut.

77 Tension the belt as described in 38 to 42 of Section 8.

78 Once the belt is correctly tensioned, refit the timing belt covers as described in Section 6.

Tensioner pulleys - 1998 cc 16-valve models

79 Refit the rear tensioner pulley to its mounting stud, and fit the retaining bolt. Align

the front pulley backplate with its holes, and refit both its retaining bolts. Tighten all retaining bolts finger-tight only, so that both tensioners are free to pivot.

80 Tension the timing belt as described in paragraphs 51 to 59 of Section 8.

81 Once the belt is correctly tensioned, refit the timing belt cover as described in Section 6.

11 Engine right-hand mounting (1580 cc, 1761 cc and 1905 cc models) - removal and refitting

1 Disconnect the battery negative lead. Release all the relevant hoses and wiring from their retaining clips, and position clear of the mounting so that they do not hinder the removal procedure.

2 Place a jack beneath the engine, with a block of wood on the jack head. Raise the jack until it is supporting the weight of the engine.

3 Slacken and remove the three nuts securing the right-hand mounting bracket to the engine unit. Remove the single nut securing the bracket to the mounting rubber, and lift off the bracket.

4 Lift the rubber buffer plate off the mounting rubber stud, then unscrew the mounting rubber from the body and remove it from the vehicle. If necessary, the mounting bracket can be unbolted and removed from the side of the cylinder head.

5 Check all components carefully for signs of wear or damage, and renew them where necessary.

6 On reassembly, screw the mounting rubber into the vehicle body, and tighten it securely. Where removed, refit the mounting bracket to the side of the cylinder head, and securely tighten its retaining bolts.

7 Refit the rubber buffer plate to the mounting rubber stud, and install the mounting bracket.

8 Tighten the mounting bracket retaining nuts to the specified torque setting.

9 Remove the jack from underneath the engine, and reconnect the battery negative terminal.

4A

Notes

Chapter 4B
Citroën ZX diesel 1991 to 1993

Contents

Specifications

Timing belt renewal interval .... Every 36 000 miles (60 000 km)

Note: *Although the normal interval for timing belt renewal is 48 000 miles (80 000 km), it is strongly recommended that the interval is reduced on vehicles which are subjected to intensive use, ie, mainly short journeys or a lot of stop-start driving. The actual belt renewal interval is therefore very much up to the individual owner. That being said, it is highly recommended to err on the side of safety, and renew the belt at this earlier interval, bearing in mind the drastic consequences resulting from belt failure.*

Torque wrench settings	Nm	lbf ft
Camshaft cover bolts	20	15
Camshaft sprocket bolt	35	26
Crankshaft pulley bolt*:		
Stage 1	40	30
Stage 2	Tighten through a further 50°	
Engine right-hand mounting-to-body nut	40	30
Engine right-hand mounting-to-engine mounting bracket nuts	45	33
Engine right-hand mounting bracket-to-engine bolts	18	13
Engine/transmission lower mounting horizontal bracket nuts and bolts ..	50	37
Fuel injection pump sprocket puller nut	50	37
Fuel injection pump sprocket puller securing screws	10	7
Roadwheel bolts	90	66
Timing belt cover bolts	8	6
Timing belt tensioner adjustment bolt	18	13
Timing belt tensioner pivot nut	18	13

* A new bolt must be used on refitting

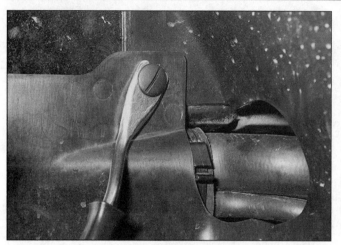

1.3a Release the securing clips . . .

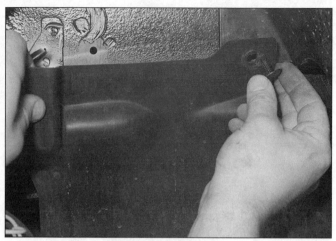

1.3b . . . and remove the lower wheelarch cover . . .

1.3c . . . then unclip the coolant hoses

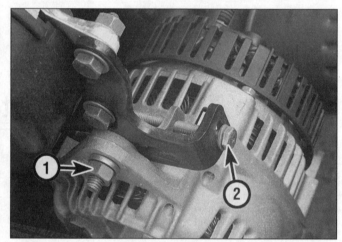

1.5 Alternator upper mounting nut (1) and adjuster bolt (2)

1 Auxiliary drivebelt - removal, refitting and adjustment

1 Apply the handbrake. Jack up the right-hand front corner of the vehicle, and support securely on an axle stand.

2 Remove the roadwheel.

3 Remove the lower wheelarch liner (see Section 13), then unclip the coolant hoses from the wing panel **(see illustrations)**. Lower the coolant hoses clear of the pulleys.

Models without power steering or air conditioning

Removal

4 Disconnect the battery negative lead.

5 Working at the upper end of the alternator, slacken the upper alternator mounting nut **(see illustration)**.

6 Back off the adjuster bolt to relieve the tension in the drivebelt, then slip the drivebelt from the pulleys.

Refitting and adjustment

7 Fit the belt around the pulleys, ensuring that the belt is of the correct type if it is being renewed, and take up the slack in the belt by tightening the adjuster bolt.

8 The belt should be tensioned so that there is approximately 5.0 mm of movement under firm thumb pressure at the mid-point of the belt run between the pulleys.

9 With the upper mounting nut just holding the alternator firm, and the adjuster bolt loosened, turn the adjuster bolt until the correct tension is achieved, then tighten the upper mounting nut.

10 Reconnect the battery negative lead.

11 Clip the coolant hoses into position, refit the wheelarch liner and roadwheel, then lower the vehicle to the ground.

Models with power steering or air conditioning

Removal

12 Disconnect the battery negative lead.

13 Slacken the two lockscrews securing the tensioner roller assembly **(see illustration)**.

1.13 Slacken the two tensioner roller lockscrews (arrowed)

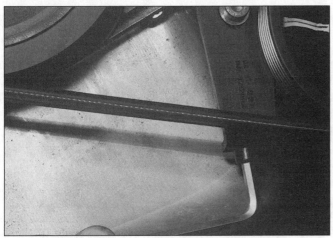

1.14a Turn the tensioner roller adjuster bolt . . .

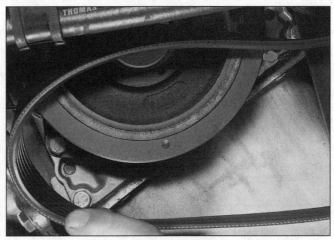

1.14b . . . until the belt can be removed from the pulleys

14 Turn the tensioner roller adjuster bolt to move the tensioner roller assembly until the drivebelt can be removed from the pulleys **(see illustrations)**.

Refitting and adjustment

15 Fit the drivebelt around the pulleys in the following order.
a) *Power steering pump/air conditioning compressor.*
b) *Crankshaft.*
c) *Alternator.*
d) *Tensioner roller.*
16 Ensure that the ribs on the belt are correctly engaged with the grooves in the pulleys.
17 Tension the drivebelt by turning the tensioner roller adjuster screw until the belt can be twisted through approximately 90° under firm thumb and finger pressure at the mid-point of the belt run between the power steering pump/air conditioning compressor and crankshaft pulleys **(see illustration)**.
18 Tighten the two lockscrews securing the tensioner roller.
19 Reconnect the battery negative lead.
20 Clip the coolant hoses into position, refit the wheelarch liner and roadwheel, then lower the vehicle to the ground.

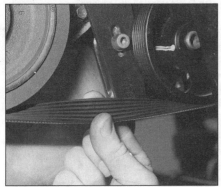

1.17 It should be possible to twist the belt through 90°

Models with power steering and air conditioning

Removal

21 Disconnect the battery negative lead.
22 Remove the upper securing screw from

the power steering pump pulley shield. Push the shield to one side, to allow access to the drivebelt.
23 Slacken the two lockscrews securing the manual tensioner roller **(see illustration)**.
24 Tighten the manual tensioner roller

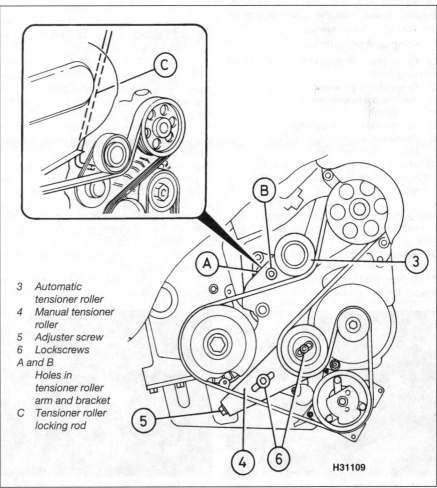

3   *Automatic tensioner roller*
4   *Manual tensioner roller*
5   *Adjuster screw*
6   *Lockscrews*
A and B
    Holes in tensioner roller arm and bracket
C   *Tensioner roller locking rod*

H31109

1.23 Auxiliary drivebelt arrangement on models with power steering and air conditioning

4B

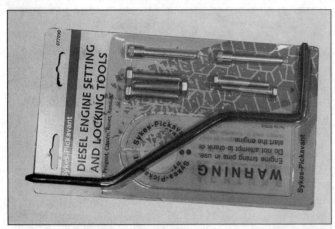

2.4a Suitable tools available for locking engine with No 1 piston at TDC

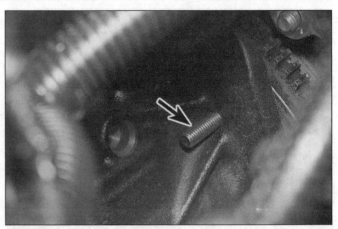

2.4b Rod (arrowed) inserted through cylinder block into TDC hole in flywheel

adjuster screw until the holes in the automatic tensioner roller bracket and the power steering pump bracket are aligned.

25 Lock the automatic tensioner roller in position by inserting a suitable rod (such as a twist drill) through the holes in the automatic tensioner roller arm and the bracket.

26 Slacken the manual tensioner roller adjuster screw until the drivebelt can be removed from the pulleys.

Refitting and adjustment

27 Fit the drivebelt around the pulleys in the following order.
a) Power steering pump.
b) Automatic tensioner roller.
c) Crankshaft.
d) Air conditioning compressor.
e) Alternator.
f) Manual tensioner roller.

28 Ensure that the ribs on the belt are correctly engaged with the grooves in the pulleys.

29 Tension the drivebelt, by turning the manual tensioner roller adjuster screw, until the rod inserted in paragraph 25 begins to slide.

30 Remove the rod from the holes in the automatic tensioner roller arm and the bracket.

31 Tighten the two lockscrews securing the manual tensioner roller.

32 Move the power steering pump pulley shield back into position, and refit the upper securing screw.

33 Reconnect the battery negative lead.

34 Clip the coolant hoses into position, refit the wheelarch liner and roadwheel, then lower the vehicle to the ground.

---

2 Top dead centre (TDC) for No 1 piston - locating

Note: *Three 8 mm diameter bolts and one 8 mm diameter rod or drill will be required for this procedure.*

1 Top dead centre (TDC) is the highest point in the cylinder that each piston reaches as the crankshaft turns. Each piston reaches TDC at the end of the compression stroke, and again at the end of the exhaust stroke. For the purpose of timing the engine, TDC refers to the position of No 1 piston at the end of its compression stroke. On all engines in this manual, No 1 piston is at the flywheel/driveplate end of the engine.

2 Remove the upper timing belt covers as described in Section 5.

3 The crankshaft must now be turned until the three bolt holes in the camshaft and

injection pump sprockets (one hole in the camshaft sprocket, two holes in the injection pump sprocket) are aligned with the corresponding holes in the engine front plate. The crankshaft can be turned by using a spanner on the pulley bolt. Improved access to the pulley bolt can be obtained by jacking up the front right-hand corner of the vehicle and removing the roadwheel and the lower wheelarch cover (secured by plastic clips).

4 Insert an 8 mm diameter rod or drill through the hole in the left-hand flange of the cylinder block by the starter motor; if necessary, carefully turn the crankshaft either way until the rod enters the TDC hole in the flywheel **(see illustrations)**.

5 Insert three M8 bolts through the holes in the camshaft and fuel injection pump sprockets, and screw them into the engine finger-tight **(see illustrations)**.

6 The crankshaft, camshaft and injection pump are now locked in position with No 1 piston at TDC.

7 If the engine is to be left in this state for a long period of time, it is a good idea to place suitable warning notices inside the vehicle, and in the engine compartment **(see illustration)**. This will reduce the possibility of the engine being accidentally cranked on the starter motor, which is likely to cause damage with the locking tools in place.

2.5a M8 bolt (arrowed) inserted through TDC hole in camshaft sprocket

2.5b M8 bolts (arrowed) inserted through TDC holes in fuel injection pump sprocket

2.7 Warning notice in place in engine compartment

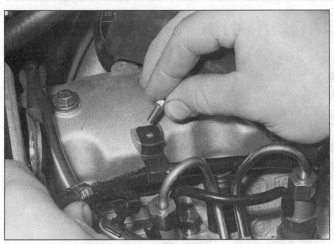

3.3 Removing the fuel hose bracket from the camshaft cover

3.4 Remove the securing bolts and washers . . .

3 Camshaft cover - removal and refitting

Note: *A new camshaft cover gasket must be used on refitting.*

Removal

1 Remove the intercooler (turbo models) or the air distribution housing (XUD9A/D9B engine) where applicable, as described in Sections 10 and 11.

2 Disconnect the breather hose from the front of the camshaft cover and, where applicable, disconnect the air hose from the top of the inlet manifold.

3 Unscrew the securing bolt and remove the fuel hose bracket from the right-hand end of the camshaft cover **(see illustration)**.

4 Note the locations of any brackets secured by the three camshaft cover securing bolts, then unscrew the bolts. Recover the metal and fibre washers under each bolt **(see illustration)**.

5 Carefully move any hoses clear of the camshaft cover.

6 Lift off the camshaft cover, and recover the rubber gasket **(see illustration)**.

Refitting

7 Refitting is a reversal of removal, bearing in mind the following points:

a) *Use a new camshaft cover gasket.*

b) *Refit any brackets in their original positions noted before removal.*

c) *Where applicable, refit the intercooler or the air distribution housing.*

4 Crankshaft pulley - removal and refitting

Note: *A new crankshaft pulley bolt will be required on refitting.*

Removal

1 Remove the auxiliary drivebelt, as described in Section 1.

2 To prevent the crankshaft from turning as the pulley bolt is unscrewed, remove the starter motor (see Section 12) and lock the flywheel using a suitable notched tool engaged in the ring gear teeth **(see illustrations)**.

3 Unscrew and remove the crankshaft pulley bolt. Note that the bolt is extremely tight. Recover the thrustwasher **(see illustration)**.

4 Remove the pulley from the end of the

3.6 . . . and lift off the camshaft cover

crankshaft, and recover the Woodruff key if it is loose. If the pulley is tight on the crankshaft, it can be removed using a puller as follows.

5 Refit the pulley bolt without the thrustwasher, but do not screw it fully home.

6 Improvise a suitable puller, using a short length of metal bar, two M6 bolts, and a large nut and bolt.

7 Pass the two M6 bolts through the bar, and screw them into the tapped holes in the pulley.

8 Tighten the large bolt, forcing it against the head of the pulley bolt while counterholding the nut, to force the pulley from the crankshaft.

4.2a Suitable tool . . .

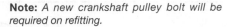

4.2b . . . positioned on ring gear teeth to lock flywheel

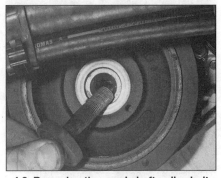

4.3 Removing the crankshaft pulley bolt and thrustwasher

4B

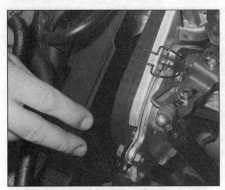

5.3 Removing the right-hand timing belt cover

Refitting

9 Where applicable, refit the Woodruff key to the end of the crankshaft, then refit the pulley.
10 Prevent the crankshaft from turning as during removal, then fit a new pulley securing bolt. Ensure that the thrustwasher is in place under the bolt head.
11 Tighten the bolt to the specified torque, and then through the specified angle (see Specifications).
12 Remove the locking tool from the flywheel ring gear, and refit the starter motor.
13 Refit and tension the auxiliary drivebelt as described in Section 1.

5 Timing belt covers - removal and refitting

Right-hand cover

Removal

1 Remove the right-hand engine mounting-to-body bracket as described in Section 8. This will greatly improve access.
2 Release the upper spring clip from the cover.
3 Release the lower securing lug using a screwdriver, then lift the cover upwards from the engine (see illustration).

Refitting

5.10 Lower timing belt cover securing bolts (arrowed)

5.6 Removing the left-hand timing belt cover

4 Refitting is a reversal of removal, but refit and tension the auxiliary drivebelt as described in Section 1.

Left-hand cover

Removal

5 Remove the right-hand outer cover as described previously.
6 Release the two securing clips, manipulate the cover over the studs on the front of the engine, then withdraw the cover upwards (see illustration).

Refitting

7 Refitting is a reversal of removal, noting that if the engine mounting bracket has been removed, it should be refitted with reference to Section 8.

8 On completion, refit and tension the auxiliary drivebelt as described in Section 1.

Lower cover

Removal

9 Remove the crankshaft pulley as described in Section 4.
10 Unscrew the two securing bolts and remove the cover (see illustration).

Refitting

11 Refitting is a reversal of removal.

6 Timing belt - removal and refitting

Removal

1 Set No 1 piston to TDC, then lock the crankshaft, and the camshaft and fuel injection pump sprockets, in position as described in Section 2.
2 Remove the crankshaft pulley as described in Section 4.
3 Remove the right-hand engine mounting-to-body bracket as described in Section 8.
4 Loosen the timing belt tensioner pivot nut and adjustment bolt, then turn the tensioner bracket anti-clockwise to release the tension. Retighten the adjustment bolt to hold the tensioner in the released position. If available, use a 10 mm square drive extension in the hole provided to turn the tensioner bracket against the spring tension (see illustration).

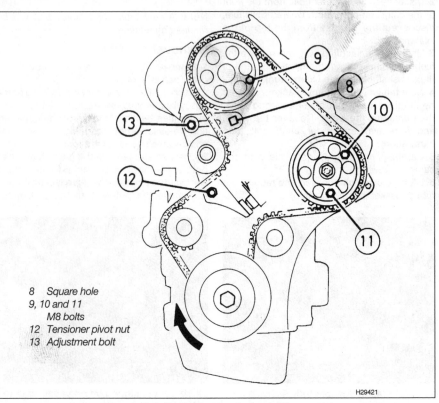

8   Square hole
9, 10 and 11
    M8 bolts
12 Tensioner pivot nut
13 Adjustment bolt

6.4 Removing the timing belt

6.5a Mark the timing belt with an arrow to indicate its running direction

6.5b Removing the timing belt

5 Mark the timing belt with an arrow to indicate its running direction, if it is to be re-used. Remove the belt from the sprockets **(see illustrations)**.

6 If signs of oil contamination are found, trace the source of the oil leak and rectify it. Wash down the engine timing belt area and all related components, to remove all traces of oil.

Refitting

7 Commence refitting by ensuring that the M8 bolts are still fitted to the camshaft and fuel injection pump sprockets, and that the rod or drill is positioned in the TDC hole in the flywheel.

8 Locate the timing belt on the crankshaft sprocket, making sure that, where applicable, the direction of rotation arrow is facing the correct way.

9 Engage the timing belt with the crankshaft sprocket, hold it in position, then feed the belt over the remaining sprockets in the following order:
a) Idler roller.
b) Fuel injection pump.
c) Camshaft.
d) Tensioner roller.
e) Coolant pump.

10 Be careful not to kink or twist the belt. To ensure correct engagement, locate only a

half-width on the injection pump sprocket before feeding the timing belt onto the camshaft sprocket, keeping the belt taut and fully engaged with the crankshaft sprocket. Locate the timing belt fully onto the sprockets **(see illustration)**.

11 Remove the bolts from the camshaft and fuel injection pump sprockets. Remove the rod or drill from the TDC hole in the flywheel.

12 With the pivot nut loose, slacken the tensioner adjustment bolt while holding the bracket against the spring tension. Slowly release the bracket until the roller presses against the timing belt. Retighten the adjustment bolt and the pivot nut.

13 Rotate the crankshaft through two complete turns in the normal running direction (clockwise). Do not rotate the crankshaft backwards, as the timing belt must be kept tight between the crankshaft, fuel injection pump and camshaft sprockets.

14 Loosen the tensioner adjustment bolt and the pivot nut to allow the tensioner spring to push the roller against the timing belt, then tighten both the adjustment bolt and pivot nut to the specified torque.

15 Check that No 1 piston is at TDC by reinserting the sprocket locking bolts and the rod or drill in the flywheel TDC hole, as

described in Section 2. If No 1 piston is not at TDC as described, the timing belt has been incorrectly fitted (possibly one tooth out on one of the sprockets) - in this case, repeat the refitting procedure from the beginning.

16 Refit the upper timing belt covers as described in Section 5, but do not lower the vehicle to the ground until the engine mounting-to-body bracket has been refitted.

17 Refit the right-hand engine mounting-to-body bracket, with reference to Section 8.

18 Refit the crankshaft pulley as described in Section 4.

4B

---

7 Timing belt sprockets - removal and refitting

Camshaft sprocket

Removal

1 Remove the upper timing belt covers as described in Section 5.

2 The camshaft sprocket bolt should now be loosened. The camshaft must be prevented from turning as the sprocket bolt is unscrewed, and this can be achieved in one of two ways, as follows **(see illustrations)**. Do

6.10 Half-width of timing belt correctly engaged with camshaft sprocket

7.2a Using an improvised tool to prevent the camshaft sprocket from turning

7.2b Holding the camshaft using a spanner on the lug between Nos 3 and 4 lobes

7.7 Withdrawing the camshaft sprocket

not remove the camshaft sprocket bolt at this stage.
a) *Make up a tool similar to that shown, and use it to hold the sprocket stationary by means of the holes in the sprocket.*
b) *Remove the camshaft cover as described in Section 3. Prevent the camshaft from turning by holding it with a suitable spanner on the lug between Nos 3 and 4 camshaft lobes.*

3 Set No 1 piston to TDC, then lock the crankshaft, and the camshaft and fuel injection pump sprockets, in position as described in Section 2.

4 Loosen the timing belt tensioner pivot nut and adjustment bolt, then turn the tensioner bracket anti-clockwise to release the tension, and retighten the adjustment bolt to hold the tensioner in the released position. If available, use a 10 mm square drive extension in the hole provided to turn the tensioner bracket against the spring tension.

5 Unscrew the camshaft sprocket bolt and recover the thrustwasher.

6 Withdraw the TDC locking bolt from the camshaft sprocket.

7 Withdraw the sprocket, manipulating the timing belt from it as it is withdrawn **(see illustration)**. Recover the Woodruff key from the end of the camshaft if it is loose. **Do not** allow the camshaft to rotate, otherwise the valves will strike the pistons of Nos 1 and 4 cylinders. If necessary, remove the rod or drill from the TDC hole in the flywheel, and turn the crankshaft one quarter-turn to position all the pistons halfway down the cylinders in order to prevent any damage, but release the timing belt from the injection pump sprocket first.

Refitting

8 Where applicable, refit the Woodruff key to the end of the camshaft, then refit the camshaft sprocket. Note that the sprocket will only fit one way round (with the protruding centre boss against the camshaft), as the end of the camshaft is tapered.

9 Refit the sprocket securing bolt, ensuring that the thrustwasher is in place. Tighten the bolt to the specified torque, preventing the camshaft from turning as during removal. Do not allow the camshaft to rotate, unless the crankshaft has been positioned as described in paragraph 7.

10 Where applicable, refit the camshaft cover as described in Section 3.

11 Align the holes in the camshaft sprocket and the engine front plate, and refit the M8 bolt to lock the camshaft in the TDC position.

12 If the crankshaft was turned a quarter-turn from TDC in paragraph 7, turn it back by the same amount so that pistons 1 and 4 are again at TDC. Do not turn the crankshaft more than a quarter-turn, otherwise pistons 2 and 3 will pass their TDC positions, and will strike valves 4 and 6.

13 Where applicable, refit the rod or drill to the TDC hole in the flywheel.

14 Fit the timing belt around the fuel injection pump sprocket (where applicable) and the

camshaft sprocket, and tension the timing belt as described in Section 6.

15 Refit the upper timing belt covers as described in Section 5.

Crankshaft sprocket

Removal

16 Remove the crankshaft pulley as described in Section 4.

17 Proceed as described in paragraphs 1, 3 and 4.

18 Withdraw the sprocket, manipulating the timing belt from it as it is withdrawn. Recover the Woodruff key from the end of the crankshaft if it is loose **(see illustrations)**. **Do not** allow the crankshaft to rotate, otherwise the valves may strike the pistons. If necessary, remove the rod or drill from the TDC hole in the flywheel, remove the flywheel locking tool, then turn the crankshaft one quarter-turn. This will position all the pistons halfway down the cylinders, in order to prevent any damage.

Refitting

19 Where applicable, refit the Woodruff key to the end of the crankshaft, then refit the crankshaft sprocket (with the flange nearest the cylinder block).

20 If the crankshaft was turned a quarter-turn from TDC in paragraph 18, turn it back by the same amount so that pistons 1 and 4 are again at TDC. Do not turn the crankshaft more than a quarter-turn, otherwise pistons 2 and 3 will pass their TDC positions, and may strike the valves.

21 Where applicable, refit the rod or drill to the TDC hole in the flywheel.

22 Fit the timing belt around the crankshaft sprocket, and tension the timing belt as described in Section 6.

23 Refit the crankshaft pulley as described in Section 4.

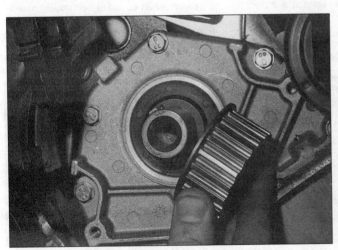

7.18a Withdrawing the crankshaft sprocket

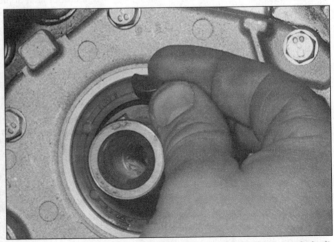

7.18b Removing the Woodruff key from the end of the crankshaft

7.28 Using an improvised tool to prevent the fuel injection pump sprocket from turning

7.30 Improvised puller fitted to fuel injection pump sprocket

4B

Fuel injection pump sprocket

Removal

24 Proceed as described in paragraphs 1, 3 and 4.

25 Make alignment marks on the fuel injection pump sprocket and the timing belt, to ensure that the sprocket and timing belt are correctly aligned on refitting.

26 Remove the M8 bolts securing the fuel injection pump sprocket in the TDC position.

27 On certain models, the sprocket may be fitted with a built-in puller, which consists of a plate bolted to the sprocket. The plate contains a captive nut (the sprocket securing nut), which is screwed onto the fuel injection pump shaft. On models not fitted with the built-in puller, a suitable puller can be made up using a short length of bar, and two M7 bolts screwed into the holes provided in the sprocket.

28 The fuel injection pump shaft must be prevented from turning as the sprocket nut is unscrewed, and this can be achieved using a tool similar to that shown **(see illustration)**. Use the tool to hold the sprocket stationary by means of the holes in the sprocket.

29 On models with a built-in puller, unscrew the sprocket securing nut until the sprocket is freed from the taper on the pump shaft, then withdraw the sprocket. Recover the Woodruff key from the end of the pump shaft if it is loose. If desired, the puller assembly can be removed from the sprocket by removing the two securing screws and washers.

30 On models not fitted with a built-in puller, partially unscrew the sprocket securing nut, then fit the improvised puller, and tighten the two bolts (forcing the bar against the sprocket nut), until the sprocket is freed from the taper on the pump shaft **(see illustration)**. Withdraw the sprocket and recover the Woodruff key from the end of the pump shaft

if it is loose. Remove the puller from the sprocket.

Refitting

31 Where applicable, refit the Woodruff key to the pump shaft, ensuring that it is correctly located in its groove.

32 Where applicable, if the built-in puller assembly has been removed from the sprocket, refit it, and tighten the two securing screws to the specified torque, ensuring that the washers are in place.

33 Refit the sprocket, then tighten the securing nut to the specified torque, preventing the pump shaft from turning as during removal.

34 Make sure that the M8 TDC bolts are fitted to the camshaft and fuel injection pump sprockets, and that the rod or drill is positioned in the TDC hole in the flywheel.

35 Fit the timing belt around the fuel injection pump sprocket, ensuring that the marks made on the belt and sprocket before removal are aligned.

36 Tension the timing belt as described in Section 6.

37 Refit the upper timing belt covers as described in Section 5.

Coolant pump sprocket

38 The coolant pump sprocket is integral with the pump, and cannot be removed.

---

8   Timing belt tensioner - removal and refitting

General

1 The timing belt tensioner is operated by a spring and plunger housed in the right-hand

engine mounting bracket, which is bolted to the end face of the engine. The engine mounting is attached to the mounting on the body via the engine mounting-to-body bracket.

Right-hand engine mounting-to-body bracket

Removal

2 Before removing the bracket, the engine must be supported, preferably using a suitable hoist and lifting tackle attached to the lifting bracket at the right-hand end of the engine. Alternatively, the engine can be supported using a trolley jack and interposed block of wood beneath the sump, in which case, be prepared for the engine to tilt backwards when the bracket is removed.

3 Release the fuel hose and the fuel priming bulb from the clips attached to the engine mounting assembly and suspension top mounting, and move the hose and bulb to one side **(see illustration)**.

4 Where applicable, unscrew the two securing bolts, and remove the plate covering the engine mounting on the body. Note that

8.3 Releasing the fuel hose and the fuel priming bulb from their support clips

8.4a Removing the engine mounting cover plate rear securing bolt and fuel priming bulb bracket

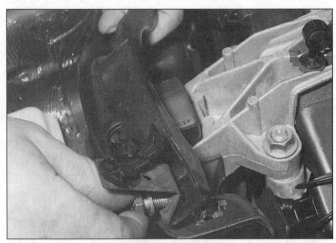

8.4b Removing the engine mounting cover plate

the bolts also secure the fuel priming bulb and hose mounting brackets **(see illustrations)**.

5 Where applicable, lift out the rubber buffer to expose the engine mounting bracket-to-body securing nut **(see illustration)**.

6 Unscrew the three nuts securing the bracket to the engine mounting, and the

8.5 Lifting the rubber buffer from the engine mounting

single nut securing the bracket to the body, then lift off the bracket **(see illustration)**.

Refitting

7 Refitting is a reversal of removal. Tighten the bracket securing nuts to the specified torque.

Timing belt tensioner and right-hand engine mounting bracket

Note: *A suitable tool will be required to retain the timing belt tensioner plunger during this operation.*

Removal

8 Remove the engine mounting-to-body bracket as described previously in this Section, and remove the auxiliary drivebelt as described in Section 1.

9 If not already done, support the engine with a trolley jack and interposed block of wood beneath the sump.

10 To prevent the engine from tilting, make a bracket from a length of stout rod, and fit the bracket between the upper alternator mounting and the body front panel (see

illustration). Ensure that the bracket is strong enough to support the load imposed by the engine, and wrap a rag around the body panel to prevent damage to the finish.

11 Where applicable, disconnect the hoist and lifting tackle supporting the engine from the right-hand lifting bracket (this is necessary because the lifting bracket is attached to the engine mounting bracket, and must be removed).

12 Unscrew the two securing bolts and remove the engine lifting bracket.

13 Set No 1 piston to TDC, then lock the crankshaft, and the camshaft and fuel injection pump sprockets, in position as described in Section 2.

14 Loosen the timing belt tensioner pivot nut and adjustment bolt, then turn the tensioner bracket anti-clockwise until the adjustment bolt is in the middle of the slot, and retighten the adjustment bolt. If available, use a 10 mm square drive extension in the hole provided to turn the tensioner bracket against the spring tension.

8.6 Removing the engine mounting-to-body bracket

8.10 Bracket fitted between alternator mounting and body front panel to support engine

8.16 Fabricated tool for holding tensioner plunger in engine mounting bracket

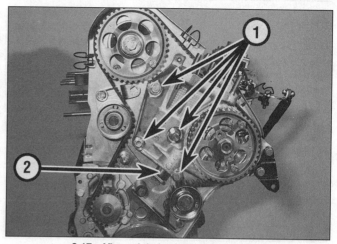

8.17a View of timing belt end of engine

1   Engine mounting bracket securing bolts
2   Timing belt tensioner plunger

15 Mark the timing belt with an arrow to indicate its running direction, if it is to be re-used. Remove the belt from the sprockets.

16 A tool must now be obtained in order to hold the tensioner plunger in the engine mounting bracket. The Citroën tool is designed to slide in the two lower bolt holes of the mounting bracket. It should be straightforward to fabricate a similar tool out of sheet metal, and using M10 bolts and nuts instead of metal dowel rods **(see illustration)**.

17 Unscrew the two lower engine mounting bracket bolts, then fit the special tool. Grease the inner surface of the tool, to prevent any damage to the end of the tensioner plunger **(see illustrations)**. Unscrew the pivot nut and adjustment bolt, and withdraw the tensioner assembly.

18 Remove the two remaining engine mounting bracket bolts, and withdraw the bracket **(see illustration)**.

19 Compress the tensioner plunger into the engine mounting bracket, remove the special tool, then withdraw the plunger and spring.

Refitting

20 Refitting is a reversal of removal, bearing in mind the following points:
a) *Tighten all fixings to the specified torque.*
b) *Refit and tension the timing belt as described in Section 6.*
c) *Refit and tighten the auxiliary drivebelt as described in Section 1.*

9   Timing belt idler roller - removal and refitting

Removal

1 Remove the auxiliary drivebelt as described in Section 1.

2 Set No 1 piston to TDC, then lock the crankshaft, and the camshaft and fuel injection pump sprockets, in position as described in Section 2.

3 Loosen the timing belt tensioner pivot nut and adjustment bolt, then turn the tensioner bracket anti-clockwise to release the tension, and retighten the adjustment bolt to hold the tensioner in the released position. If available, use a 10 mm square drive extension in the hole provided to turn the tensioner bracket against the spring tension.

4 Unscrew the two bolts and the stud securing the idler roller assembly to the cylinder block, noting that the upper bolt also secures the engine mounting bracket.

5 Slightly loosen the remaining four engine mounting bolts, noting that the uppermost bolt is on the inside face of the engine front plate, and also secures the engine lifting bracket. Slide out the idler roller assembly.

Refitting

6 Refitting is a reversal of removal, bearing in mind the following points:

4B

8.17b Tool in place to hold tensioner plunger in engine mounting bracket - timing belt removed for clarity

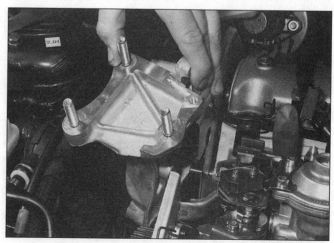

8.18 Removing the right-hand engine mounting bracket

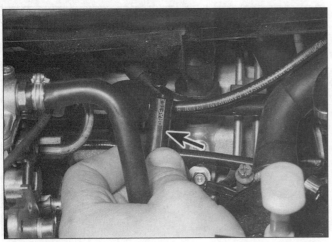

10.1a Disconnect the hose (arrowed) from the front edge of the intercooler

10.1b Disconnect the two hoses (arrowed) from the valve on the left-hand side of the intercooler

10.1c Disconnect the hose from the right-hand end of the intercooler

10.1d Lift the surround from the top of the intercooler

10.1e Unscrew the three upper securing bolts (arrowed) . . .

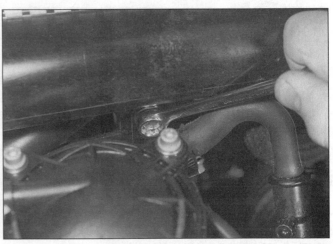

10.1f . . . and the two front securing bolts . . .

10.1g . . . and remove the intercooler

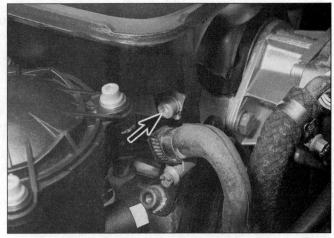

11.2 Front air distribution housing securing bolt (arrowed)

a) Tighten all fixings to the specified torque.
b) Tension the timing belt as described in Section 6.
c) Refit and tension the auxiliary drivebelt as described in Section 1.

10 Intercooler -
removal and refitting

Removal

1 To remove the intercooler, follow the procedure shown in the accompanying sequence of photographs (see illustrations).

Refitting

2 Refitting is a reversal of removal.

11 Air distribution housing (XUD9A/D9B engine) -
removal and refitting

Removal

1 Disconnect the air hose and the crankcase breather hose from the front of the air distribution housing.
2 Unscrew the two bolts securing the housing to the front mounting brackets (see illustration). Recover the spacer plates.
3 Unscrew the four bolts securing the housing to the inlet manifold. Recover the washers (see illustration).
4 Lift the housing from the inlet manifold, and recover the four O-ring seals.

Refitting

5 Refitting is a reversal of removal, but examine the condition of the O-ring seals, and renew if necessary.

12 Starter motor -
removal and refitting

Removal

1 Disconnect the battery negative lead.
2 Unscrew the two securing nuts, and disconnect the wiring from the rear of the starter motor. Recover the washers under the nuts (see illustration).

11.3 Air distribution housing-to-inlet manifold bolts (arrowed)

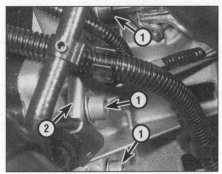

12.3 Unscrew the starter motor securing bolts (1). Note the location of the bracket (2)

3 Working at the rear of the starter motor, unscrew the three securing bolts, supporting the motor as the bolts are withdrawn. Recover the washers under the bolt heads, and note the locations of any wiring or hose brackets secured by the bolts (see illustration). Note that the top securing bolt may foul the clutch release mechanism as it is withdrawn, but there is no need to withdraw it completely to remove the starter motor.
4 Withdraw the starter motor from the engine (see illustration).

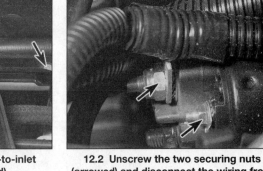

12.2 Unscrew the two securing nuts (arrowed) and disconnect the wiring from the rear of the starter motor

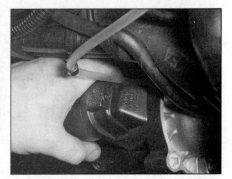

12.4 Withdrawing the starter motor

4B

Refitting

5 Refitting is a reversal of removal, ensuring that any wiring or hose brackets are in place under the bolt heads, as noted before removal.

13 Wheelarch liners -
removal and refitting

Removal

1 The various plastic covers fitted to the underside of the vehicle are secured in position by a mixture of screws and retaining clips, and removal will be fairly obvious on inspection. Work methodically around the panel, removing its retaining screws and releasing its retaining clips until the panel is free and can be removed from the underside of the vehicle.

Refitting

2 On refitting, renew any retaining clips that may have been broken on removal, and ensure that the panel is securely retained by all the relevant clips and screws.

Chapter 5A
Citroën Saxo petrol 1996 to 1998

Contents

Specifications

Timing belt renewal interval . . . . Every 36 000 miles (60 000 km)

Note: *Although the normal interval for timing belt renewal is 72 000 miles (120 000 km), it is strongly recommended that the interval is halved on vehicles which are subjected to intensive use, ie, mainly short journeys or a lot of stop-start driving. The actual belt renewal interval is therefore very much up to the individual owner. That being said, it is highly recommended to err on the side of safety, and renew the belt at this earlier interval, bearing in mind the drastic consequences resulting from belt failure.*

5A

Idle speed
Models without air conditioning . . . . 850 ± 50 rpm
Models with air conditioning . . . . 900 ± 50 rpm

Torque wrench settings

	Nm	lbf ft
Auxiliary drivebelt tensioner assembly retaining bolts	25	18
Camshaft sprocket retaining bolt (SOHC engines)	80	59
Camshaft sprocket hub-to-camshaft bolt (DOHC engines)	80	59
Camshaft sprocket-to-hub bolts (DOHC engines)	10	7
Crankshaft pulley retaining bolts	10	7
Crankshaft sprocket retaining bolt	100	74
Engine left-hand mounting:		
Centre nut	65	48
Mounting bracket-to-body bolts	30	22
Mounting bracket-to-transmission nuts	25	18
Engine rear mounting:		
Mounting link-to-body bolt:		
SOHC engine	70	52
DOHC engine	55	41
Mounting link-to-transmission bracket bolt	50	37
Transmission bracket-to-transmission casing bolts	85	63
Engine right-hand mounting:		
Mounting bracket-to-body nut(s)	30	22
Mounting bracket-to-engine nuts	45	33
Roadwheel bolts	85	63
Spark plugs	25	18
Timing belt cover bolts	5	4
Timing belt idler pulley nut (DOHC engines)	20	15
Timing belt tensioner pulley nut	20	15

1.4a Slacken the alternator upper mounting bolt (1.1 litre models shown) . . .

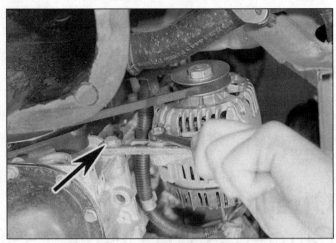

1.4b . . . and the alternator lower mounting bolt. On models where the adjustment strut is located underneath the alternator, also slacken the bolt (arrowed) securing the strut to its mounting bracket

1 Auxiliary drivebelt – removal, refitting and adjustment

1 Apply the handbrake, jack up the front of the car and support it on axle stands, then remove the right-hand front roadwheel.

2 Undo the securing screws and remove the plastic liner from the wheel arch. Where necessary, undo the retaining nut, and free the coolant hoses from the retaining clip to improve access to the crankshaft sprocket bolt

Models without air conditioning (excluding 16-valve models)

Removal

3 Disconnect the battery negative cable and position it away from the terminal.

4 Slacken both the alternator upper and lower mounting bolts. On models where the adjustment strut is located underneath the alternator, also slacken the bolt securing the strut to its mounting bracket **(see illustrations)**.

5 Turn the adjuster bolt to relieve the tension in the drivebelt, then slip the drivebelt from the pulleys **(see illustrations)**.

Refitting

6 Fit the belt around the pulleys, ensuring that the belt is of the correct type if it is being renewed, and take up the slack in the belt by tightening the adjuster bolt.

7 Tension the drivebelt as described in the following paragraphs.

Adjustment

8 The belt should be tensioned so that, under firm thumb pressure, there is approximately 5.0 mm of free movement at the mid-point between the pulleys, on the longest belt run.

9 To adjust, with the upper mounting bolt just holding the alternator firm, and the lower mounting bolt loosened, turn the adjuster bolt until the correct tension is achieved. Rotate the crankshaft through two complete turns, then recheck the tension. When the tension is correct, tighten the alternator mounting bolts and, where necessary, tighten securely the bolt securing the adjuster strap to its mounting bracket.

10 Reconnect the battery negative lead.

11 Clip the coolant hoses in position and secure them with the retaining nut (where removed). Refit the wheel arch liner, then refit the roadwheel, and lower the vehicle to the ground. Tighten the roadwheel bolts to the specified torque.

Models with air conditioning and all 16-valve models

Removal

12 Disconnect the battery negative lead.

13 Slacken the two bolts securing the tensioner pulley assembly to the engine.

14 Rotate the adjuster bolt to move the tensioner pulley away from the drivebelt, until there is sufficient slack for the drivebelt to be removed from the pulleys.

Refitting

15 Fit the belt around the pulleys, ensuring that the belt is of the correct type if it is being renewed, and take up the slack in the belt by tightening the adjuster bolt.

16 Tension the drivebelt as described in the following paragraphs.

Adjustment

17 The belt should be tensioned so that, under

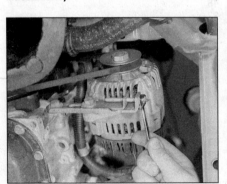

1.5a Turn the adjuster bolt to relieve the tension in the drivebelt . . .

1.5b . . .then slip the drivebelt from the pulleys (1.1 litre model shown)

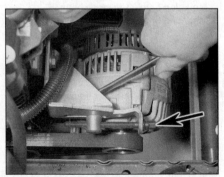

1.5c Auxiliary drivebelt adjuster bolt (arrowed, 1.6 litre 8-valve model shown)

2.1 Removing the expansion tank filler cap

2.2 Radiator drain plug (arrowed)

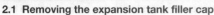

firm thumb pressure, there is approximately 5.0 mm of free movement at the mid-point of the longest belt run between two pulleys.

18 To adjust the tension, with the two tensioner pulley assembly retaining bolts slackened, rotate the adjuster bolt until the correct tension is achieved. Once the belt is correctly tensioned, rotate the crankshaft through two complete turns, and recheck the tension.

19 When the belt is correctly tensioned, tighten the tensioner pulley assembly retaining bolts to the specified torque.

20 Reconnect the battery negative lead.

21 Clip the coolant hoses back in position, and secure with the retaining nut (where removed). Refit the wheel arch liner and roadwheel, then lower the vehicle to the ground. Tighten the roadwheel bolts to the specified torque.

2 Coolant –
draining and refilling

Draining

Warning: Wait until the engine is cold before starting this procedure. Do not allow antifreeze to come in contact with your skin, or with the painted surfaces of the vehicle. Rinse off spills immediately with plenty of water. Never leave antifreeze lying around in an open container, or in a puddle in the driveway or on the garage floor. Children and pets are attracted by its sweet smell, but antifreeze can be fatal if ingested.

1 With the engine completely cold, remove the expansion tank filler cap (see illustration). Turn the cap anti-clockwise until it reaches the first stop. Wait until any pressure remaining in the system is released, then push the cap down, turn it anti-clockwise to the second stop, and lift it off.

2 Position a suitable container beneath the coolant drain outlet at the lower left-hand side of the radiator (see illustration).

3 Loosen the drain plug (there is no need to remove it completely) and allow the coolant to drain into the container.

4 To assist draining, open the cooling system bleed screws. These are located in the coolant gallery/heater hose (as applicable) at the right-hand side of the engine compartment, in the thermostat housing, and in the top left-hand side of the radiator (see illustrations).

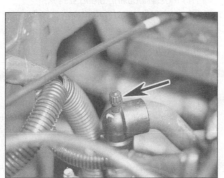

2.4a Cooling system bleed screws located in the heater hose at the right-hand side of the engine compartment . . .

2.4c . . . and the thermostat housing

Caution: When refilling the engine with coolant, it's important to make sure that all the trapped air is allowed to escape, by bleeding , as described in the text. Air trapped in the cooling system could cause overheating problems later, which will quickly lead to expensive engine damage.

5 When the flow of coolant stops, reposition the container below the cylinder block drain plug, located at the front left-hand corner of the cylinder block (see illustration).

2.4b . . . the radiator . . .

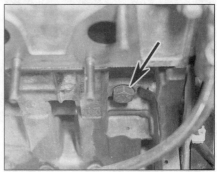

2.5 Cylinder block drain plug (arrowed) - 1.1 litre model shown with inlet manifold removed for clarity

5A

2.10 Opening the thermostat housing bleed screw

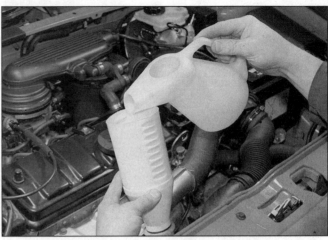

2.12 Fill the cooling system using a home-made header tank (see text)

6 Remove the drain plug, and allow the coolant to drain into the container.

7 Refit the radiator and cylinder block drain plugs on completion of draining.

Filling

8 Before attempting to fill the cooling system, make sure that all hoses and clips are in good condition, and that the clips are tight.

9 Remove the expansion tank filler cap.

10 Open all the cooling system bleed screws (see paragraph 4) **(see illustration)**.

11 Some of the cooling system hoses are positioned at a higher level than the top of the radiator expansion tank. It is therefore necessary to use a 'header tank' when refilling the cooling system, to reduce the possibility of air being trapped in the system. Although Citroën dealers use a special header tank, the same effect can be achieved by using a suitable bottle, with a rubber water-tight seal between the bottle and the expansion tank neck.

12 Fit the header tank to the expansion tank, then slowly fill the cooling system **(see illustration)**. Coolant will emerge from each of

the bleed screws in turn, starting with the lowest screw. As soon as coolant free from air bubbles emerges from the lowest screw, tighten that screw, and watch the next bleed screw in the system. Repeat the procedure until the coolant is emerging from the highest bleed screw in the cooling system and all bleed screws are securely tightened. Note that the bleed screws should be tightened in the following order:

a) Radiator bleed screw.
b) Thermostat housing bleed screw.
c) Coolant gallery or heater hose bleed screw.

13 Ensure that the header tank is full (at least 0.5 litres of coolant). Start the engine, and run it at a fast idle speed (do not exceed 2000 rpm) until the cooling fan cuts in and out again three times. Stop the engine.

14 Remove the header tank, taking great care not to scald yourself with the hot coolant, then fit the expansion tank cap **(see illustration)**.

15 Allow the engine to cool, then check the coolant level. Top-up the level if necessary.

2.14 Refit the cooling system filler cap securely

3 Engine assembly/valve timing holes - general information and usage

Note: *Do not attempt to rotate the engine whilst the crankshaft/camshaft are locked in position. If the engine is to be left in this state for a long period of time, it is a good idea to place warning notices inside the vehicle, and in the engine compartment. This will reduce the possibility of the engine being accidentally cranked on the starter motor, which is likely to cause damage with the locking tools in place.*

1 On all models, timing holes are drilled in the camshaft sprocket(s) and in the flywheel. The holes are used to ensure that the crankshaft and camshaft(s) are correctly positioned when assembling the engine (to prevent the possibility of the valves contacting the pistons

when refitting the cylinder head). They also ensure that the correct valve timing is preserved, when removing/refitting the timing belt. When the timing holes are aligned with access holes in the cylinder head and the front of the cylinder block, suitable-diameter pins or bolts can be inserted to lock the camshaft(s) and crankshaft in position, preventing them from rotating. Proceed as follows. **Note:** *With the timing holes aligned, No 4 cylinder is at TDC on its compression stroke.*

2 On DOHC engines, raise the front of the vehicle and rest it securely on axle stands with the front roadwheels clear of the ground. Unbolt and remove the engine management system ECU splash shield, then remove the ECU, together with its support bracket, with reference to the relevant part of Section 8. Slacken and withdraw the securing bolts, then remove the exhaust manifold heat shield.

3 Remove the timing belt cover as described in Section 4. Note that on SOHC engines, only the upper section of the cover need be removed.

4 The crankshaft must now be turned until the timing hole in the camshaft sprocket(s) is aligned with the corresponding hole in the cylinder head. On SOHC engines, the holes are aligned when the camshaft sprocket hole is in the 2 o'clock position, when viewed from the right-hand end of the engine. On DOHC engines, the holes are aligned when the inlet camshaft sprocket is in the 5 o'clock position, and the exhaust camshaft is in the 7 o'clock position. The crankshaft can be turned by using a spanner on the crankshaft sprocket bolt, noting that it should always be rotated in a clockwise direction (viewed from the right-hand end of the engine). Turning the engine will be much easier if the spark plugs are removed first.

5 With the camshaft sprocket hole(s) correctly positioned, insert a 6 mm diameter bolt or drill bit through the hole in the front left-hand flange of the cylinder block, and

3.5 Crankshaft locking tool in position

3.6a Camshaft locking tool in position - SOHC engine

locate it in the timing hole in the flywheel **(see illustration)**. Note that it may be necessary to rotate the crankshaft slightly, to get the holes to align.

6 With the flywheel locked in position, insert a 10 mm diameter bolt or drill bit through the timing hole in the camshaft sprocket (one for each sprocket on DOHC engines), and locate

it in the hole in the cylinder head **(see illustrations)**.

7 The crankshaft and camshaft(s) are now locked in the TDC on cylinder No 1 position, preventing unwanted rotation.

4 Timing belt covers - emoval and refitting

Removal - SOHC models

Upper cover

1 Unclip the hose from the top of the upper cover. Slacken and remove the two retaining bolts (one at the front and one at the rear), and remove the timing belt upper cover from the cylinder head **(see illustrations)**.

Centre cover

2 Remove the upper cover as described in paragraph 1, then free the wiring from its

3.6b Camshaft locking tools in position - DOHC engine

5A

4.1a Unclip the hose from the top of the upper cover

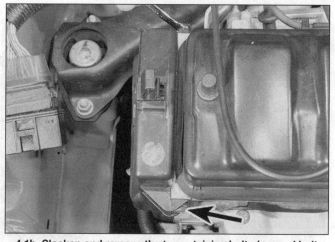

4.1b Slacken and remove the two retaining bolts (second bolt arrowed) . . .

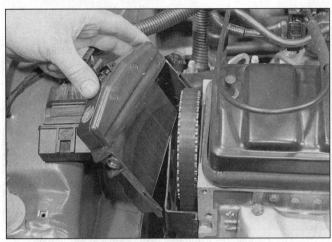

4.1c . . . and remove the timing belt upper cover from the cylinder head

4.2 Free the wiring from its retaining clips on the centre cover

retaining clips on the centre cover **(see illustration)**.

3 On some models, the centre timing belt cover cannot be withdrawn from the engine without first removing the left-hand engine mounting bracket; see Section 7 for engine mounting removal and refitting details.

4 Slacken and remove the retaining bolts, and manoeuvre the centre cover out from the engine compartment **(see illustration)**.

Lower cover
Note: *On some later models, the lower and centre covers are combined.*
5 Remove the auxiliary drivebelt as described in Section 1.

6 Remove the upper and centre covers as described in paragraphs 1 to 3.
7 Undo the three crankshaft pulley retaining bolts and remove the pulley, noting which way round it is fitted **(see illustrations)**.
8 Slacken and remove the retaining bolt(s), and slide the lower cover off the end of the crankshaft **(see illustrations)**.

4.4 Remove the retaining bolts and withdraw the centre cover

4.7a Undo the three retaining bolts . . .

4.7b . . . and remove the crankshaft pulley

4.8a Slacken and remove the retaining bolts . . .

4.8b . . . and slide the lower cover off the end of the crankshaft

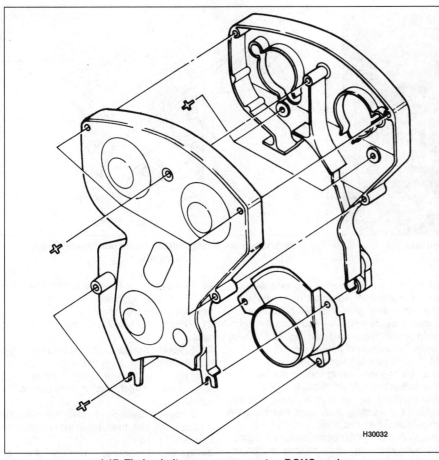

4.17 Timing belt cover components - DOHC engine

Refitting - SOHC models

Upper cover

9 Refit the cover, ensuring that it is correctly located with the centre cover, and tighten its retaining bolts.

Centre cover

10 Manoeuvre the centre cover back into position, ensuring that it is correctly located with the lower cover, and tighten its retaining bolts.

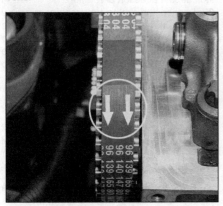

5.3 Manufacturers markings indicating direction of rotation

11 Clip the wiring loom into its retaining clips on the front of the centre cover, then refit the upper cover as described in paragraph 9.

Lower cover

12 Locate the lower cover over the timing belt sprocket, and tighten its retaining bolt(s).
13 Fit the pulley to the end of the crankshaft, ensuring that it is fitted the correct way round, and tighten its retaining bolts to the specified torque.
14 Refit the centre and upper covers as

5.4 Loosen the timing belt tensioner pulley retaining nut

described above, then refit and tension the auxiliary drivebelt as described in Section 1.

Removal - DOHC models

Upper cover

15 Disconnect the battery negative cable and position it away from the terminal.
16 Remove the screws and lift the cover away from the engine management system ECU. Unscrew the bolts and remove the ECU, together with its mounting bracket, from the inner wing.
17 Work around the edge of the upper timing cover, slackening and withdrawing the retaining bolts, then manoeuvre the cover out from the engine compartment **(see illustration)**.

Lower cover

18 Remove the auxiliary drivebelt as described in Section 1.
19 Remove the upper covers a described in the previous sub-Section.
20 Undo the crankshaft pulley retaining bolt(s) and remove the pulley, noting which way round it is fitted.
21 Slacken and remove the remaining retaining bolt(s), and slide the lower cover off the end of the crankshaft.

Refitting - DOHC models

22 Refitting is a reversal of removal. Ensure that the groove at the base of the upper cover engages correctly with the upper edge of the lower cover.

5 Timing belt - removal, refitting and tensioning

5A

Note: *Citroën specify the use of a special electronic tool (SEEM belt tensioning measuring tool) to correctly set the timing belt tension.*

SOHC models

Removal

1 Disconnect the battery negative cable and position it away from the terminal.
2 Align the engine assembly/valve timing holes as described in Section 3, and lock the camshaft sprocket(s) and the flywheel in position. *Do not* attempt to rotate the engine whilst the locking tools are in position.
3 Remove the timing belt centre and lower covers as described in Section 4. If the timing belt is to be re-used, and there are no manufacturers markings visible on the timing belt, mark an arrow in chalk on the surface of the belt to indicate the direction of rotation **(see illustration)**.
4 Loosen the timing belt tensioner pulley retaining nut **(see illustration)**. Allow the pulley to pivot in a clockwise direction, to relieve the tension from the timing belt.

5.5 Slip the timing belt off the sprockets

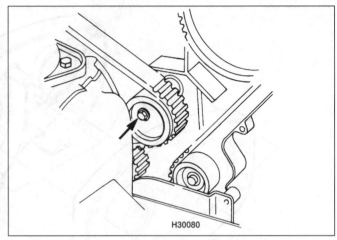

5.29 Loosen the timing belt tensioner pulley retaining nut (arrowed)

Retighten the tensioner pulley retaining nut to secure it in the slackened position.

5 Slip the timing belt off the sprockets **(see illustration)**.

6 If signs of oil contamination are found, trace the source of the oil leak, and rectify it. Wash down the engine timing belt area and all related components, to remove all traces of oil.

Refitting

7 Prior to refitting, thoroughly clean the timing belt sprockets. Check that the tensioner pulley rotates freely, without any sign of roughness. If necessary, renew the tensioner pulley as described in Section 6. Make sure that the locking tools are still in place, as described in Section 3.

8 Manoeuvre the timing belt into position, ensuring that the arrows indicating the belt's direction of rotation are pointing in the right direction (clockwise, when viewed from the right-hand end of the engine).

9 Do not twist or kink the timing belt while refitting it. Fit the belt over the crankshaft and camshaft sprockets. Make sure that the front run of the belt is taut - ie, ensure that any slack is on the tensioner pulley side of the belt. Fit the belt over the coolant pump sprocket and tensioner pulley. Ensure that the belt teeth are seated centrally in the sprockets.

10 Loosen the tensioner pulley retaining nut. Pivot the pulley anti-clockwise to remove all freeplay from the timing belt, then retighten the nut.

11 Fit the special belt tensioning measuring equipment to the front run of the timing belt, approximately midway between the camshaft and crankshaft sprockets. Fit an 8mm square key to the hole in the front face of the tensioner pulley. Turn the tensioner so that the timing belt is tensioned to a setting of 45 units, then retighten its retaining nut.

12 Remove the locking tools from the camshaft sprocket and flywheel, and remove the measuring tool from the belt.

13 Using a suitable socket and extension bar on the crankshaft sprocket bolt, rotate the crankshaft through four complete rotations in a clockwise direction (viewed from the right-hand end of the engine). Do not at any time rotate the crankshaft anti-clockwise.

14 Slacken the tensioner pulley retaining nut, and refit the measuring tool to the belt. If a new belt is being fitted, tension it to a setting of 40 units. If an old belt is being re-used, tighten it to a setting of 36 units. **Note:** Citroën state that a belt becomes old after 1 hour's use. With the belt correctly tensioned, tighten the pulley retaining nut to the specified torque.

15 Remove the measuring tool from the belt, then rotate the crankshaft through another two complete rotations in a clockwise direction, so that both the camshaft sprocket and flywheel timing holes are realigned. Do not at any time rotate the crankshaft anti-clockwise. Fit the measuring tool to the belt, and check the belt tension. A new belt should give a reading of 51 ± 3 units; an old belt should be 45 ± 3 units.

16 If the belt tension is incorrect, repeat the procedures in paragraphs 14 and 15.

17 With the belt tension correctly set, refit the timing belt covers as described in Section 4, and reconnect the battery negative terminal.

DOHC models

 Warning: It is recommended that the special Citroën belt tensioning tool is hired or borrowed for this operation; attempting to set the belt tension by approximation is unlikely to be successful and could lead to belt slippage or failure, resulting in extensive and engine damage.

Removal

18 Refer to Section 9 and remove the air cleaner housing and resonator.

19 Remove the cover panel from the engine management system ECU, then refer to Section 8 and remove the ECU, together with its mounting bracket.

20 Remove the relay casing from the bodywork and position it to one side, away from the timing belt cover.

21 Refer to Section 2 and drain the cooling system.

22 Slacken the clip and disconnect the radiator top hose from the engine. Slacken and withdraw the securing screws, then remove the air inlet ducting from behind the radiator.

23 Refer to Section 1 and remove the auxiliary drivebelt, then unbolt and remove the crankshaft pulley.

24 Where applicable, release the air conditioning refrigerant pipe from its securing clips and move it to one side, to give greater access to the timing belt cover.

25 Refer to Section 4 and remove the timing belt upper cover.

26 Unbolt the heat shield from the exhaust manifold, then refer to Section 3 and lock the crankshaft and camshafts in the TDC position using bolts or rods of suitable diameter.

27 Remove the securing screws and lift off the lower timing belt cover.

28 If the timing belt is to be re-used, mark an arrow, in chalk, on the surface of the belt to indicate the direction of rotation.

29 Loosen the timing belt tensioner pulley retaining nut **(see illustration)**. Pivot the pulley in a clockwise direction, using a square-section key fitted to the hole in the pulley hub, then retighten the retaining nut to secure the pulley in the slackened position.

30 Slip the timing belt off the sprockets.

31 If signs of oil contamination are found, trace the source of the oil leak, and rectify it. Wash down the engine timing belt area and all related components, to remove all traces of oil.

Refitting

32 Prior to refitting, thoroughly clean the timing belt sprockets. Check that the tensioner pulley rotates freely, without any sign of roughness. If necessary, renew the

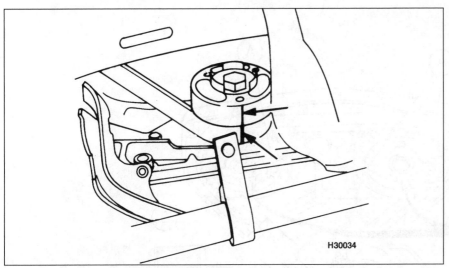

5.34a Ensure that the timing belt mark lines up with the marking on the lower edge of the crankshaft pulley hub

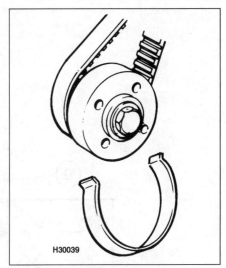

5.34b Secure the belt in position over the sprocket using a W-shaped tool board clip or similar

tensioner pulley as described in Section 5. Make sure that the locking tools are still in place, as described in Section 3.

33 The timing belt has three line markings on its flat outer surface. When the belt is correctly fitted, these markings must line up with corresponding markings on the crankshaft and camshaft pulleys. Note that the markings are not evenly spaced around the belt; the first marking must line up with the bottom of the crankshaft pulley, the second and third markings line up with the top of the inlet camshaft and exhaust camshaft sprockets respectively. Identify the markings and then hold the belt up the sprockets, to be sure of its correct orientation, before attempting to refit it.

34 Fit the belt underneath the crankshaft sprocket, ensuring that the first belt mark lines up with the marking on the lower edge of the crankshaft pulley hub. Secure the belt in position over the sprocket using a Ω-shaped toolboard clip or similar, to ensure that the belt cannot disengage from the sprocket teeth (**see illustrations**).

35 Ensure that both camshaft sprockets are still locked in the TDC position, then with reference to Section 6, slacken the bolts securing both camshaft sprockets to their respective hubs (three bolts on each sprocket). *Do not* remove the bolts completely, but slacken them just enough to allow the sprockets to be rotated by hand. Do not slacken the centre bolts that secure the sprocket hubs to the ends of the camshafts. Turn both sprockets fully clockwise, so that the sprocket securing bolts are positioned at the ends of their slots.

36 Pass the timing belt over the inlet and exhaust camshaft sprockets, so that the two remaining marks on the timing belt line up with the marks on the edges of the sprockets (**see illustration**). Ensure that the section of the belt that runs between the exhaust camshaft and crankshaft sprockets passes over the idler pulley and remains taught at all times.

37 Keep the belt engaged with the camshaft sprockets, then pass it over the coolant pump sprocket and the tensioner pulley. It may be necessary to remove the crankshaft sprocket clip at this point, as the slack in the belt is taken up, but ensure that the belt-to-sprocket alignment is not lost.

38 Attach the belt tensioning tool to the timing belt, at a point mid-way along the section of the belt that runs between the exhaust camshaft and crankshaft sprockets.

39 Fit a square-section adapter to the hole in the front face of the tensioner pulley and using a wrench, pivot the tensioner pulley anti-clockwise until the tensioning tool reads 63 SEEM units. Tighten the tensioner pulley centre nut to secure it in this position.

40 Check that the belt markings are still aligned with those on the camshaft and crankshaft sprockets. Also check that the camshaft sprocket securing bolts are now

5A

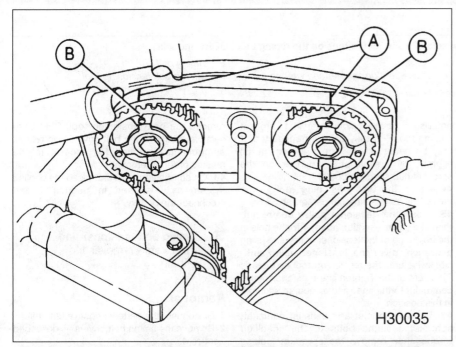

5.36 Pass the timing belt over the inlet and exhaust camshaft sprockets, so that the two marks on the belt (A) line up with the marks on the edges of the sprockets (B)

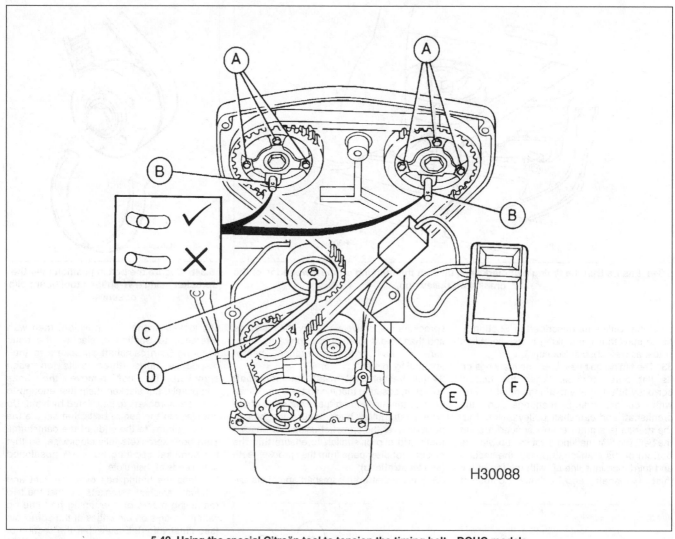

5.40 Using the special Citroën tool to tension the timing belt - DOHC models

A Camshaft sprocket securing bolts
B Sprocket locking tools

C Tensioner
D Square section adapter and wrench

E Timing belt
F Citroën belt tensioning tool

positioned part-way along their slots **(see illustration)**. If the belt and sprocket marks are not aligned, or if the sprocket securing bolts are positioned hard against the end of their slots, the belt may be positioned one tooth out - remove the belt and start again from paragraph 32.

41 Remove the belt tensioning tool, then tighten the inlet and exhaust camshaft sprocket securing bolts to the specified torque.

42 Remove the flywheel and camshaft locking tools. Using a ring spanner on the pulley hub bolt, turn the crankshaft in its normal direction of rotation through four revolutions. Bring the engine to TDC as before, then re-insert the flywheel locking tool.

43 Slacken the six exhaust and inlet camshaft sprocket securing bolts slightly, and allow the sprockets to rotate slightly to

equalise the belt tension. Insert the sprocket locking tools - if they cannot be inserted, it may be necessary to turn the camshaft(s) slightly, by means of a spanner on the sprocket hub securing bolt(s).

44 Attach the belt tensioning tool to the timing belt as described in paragraph 38.

45 Loosen the tensioner pulley centre nut, then fit a square-section adapter to the hole in the front face of the tensioner pulley and using a wrench, pivot the tensioner pulley anti-clockwise until the tensioning tool now reads 37 SEEM units. Tighten the tensioner pulley centre nut to the specified torque, to secure it in this position.

46 Tighten the inlet and exhaust camshaft sprocket securing bolts to the specified torque, then remove the sprocket locking tools.

47 Remove the flywheel locking tool, then

remove the belt tensioning tool. Refit both sections of the timing belt cover, then refit all components removed for access, in the reverse order of removal.

48 On completion, refill and bleed the cooling system as described in Section 1 and reconnect the battery.

6 Timing belt tensioner and sprockets - removal and refitting

Removal

1 Disconnect the battery negative terminal.

2 Remove the timing belt covers as described Section 4.

3 Refer to Section 5 and remove the timing belt.

6.5a Slacken the retaining bolt and washer . . .

6.5b . . . then remove the camshaft sprocket

Camshaft sprocket

4 Temporarily remove the locking pin from the camshaft sprocket.

5 On SOHC models, slacken the camshaft sprocket retaining bolt and remove it, along with its washer **(see illustrations)**. *Do not* attempt to use the sprocket TDC locking pin to prevent the sprocket from rotating whilst the bolt is slackened **(see illustration)**.

6 On DOHC models, the sprockets are of two-piece construction. Slacken and withdraw the centre sprocket hub-to-camshaft bolt, but *do not* attempt to use the sprocket hub locking pin to prevent the sprocket from rotating whilst the bolt is slackened.

7 With the retaining bolt removed, slide the sprocket off the end of the camshaft. If the locating peg is a loose fit in the rear of the sprocket, remove it for safe-keeping. Examine the camshaft oil seal for signs of oil leakage and, if necessary, renew it.

Crankshaft sprocket

8 To prevent crankshaft rotation whilst the crankshaft sprocket bolt is slackened, select top gear, and have an assistant apply the brakes firmly. *Do not* be tempted to use the flywheel locking pin to prevent the crankshaft from rotating; temporarily remove the locking pin from the rear of the flywheel prior to slackening the sprocket bolt, then refit it once the bolt has been slackened.

9 Unscrew the retaining bolt and washer, then slide the sprocket off the end of the crankshaft **(see illustrations)**. Refit the locating pin through the timing hole into the rear of the flywheel.

10 If the Woodruff key is a loose fit in the crankshaft, remove it and store it with the sprocket for safe-keeping. If necessary, also slide the flanged spacer off the end of the crankshaft **(see illustration)**. Examine the crankshaft oil seal for signs of oil leakage and, if necessary, renew it.

Tensioner/idler pulley

11 Slacken and remove the timing belt tensioner pulley retaining nut, and slide the pulley off its mounting stud. Examine the mounting stud for signs of damage and, if necessary, renew it.

12 On DOHC models, an idler pulley is also fitted; its removal is as described for the tensioner pulley.

6.5c To make a camshaft sprocket holding tool, obtain two lengths of steel strip about 6 mm thick by 30 mm wide or similar, one 600 mm long, the other 200 mm long (all dimensions approximate). Bolt the two strips together to form a forked end, leaving the bolt slack so that the shorter strip can pivot freely. At the end of each 'prong' of the fork, secure a bolt with a nut and a locknut, to act as the fulcrums; these will engage with the cut-outs in the sprocket, and should protrude by about 30 mm

5A

6.9a Unscrew the retaining bolt and washer . . .

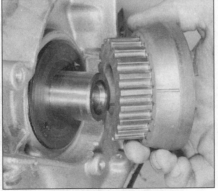

6.9b . . . then slide the sprocket off the end of the crankshaft

6.10 Recover the flanged spacer (where fitted)

7.1 Battery support tray securing nuts (arrowed)

7.3a Slacken and remove the mounting rubber centre nut and washer . . .

Refitting

13 Clean the sprockets thoroughly, and renew any that show signs of wear, damage or cracks.

14 Clean the tensioner assembly, but do not use any strong solvent which may enter the pulley bearing. Check that the pulley rotates freely about its hub, with no sign of stiffness or of free play. Renew the tensioner pulley if there is any doubt about its condition, or if there are any obvious signs of wear or damage.

Camshaft sprocket

15 On SOHC models, refit the locating peg (where applicable) to the rear of the sprocket, then locate the sprocket on the end of the camshaft. Ensure that the locating peg is correctly engaged with the cut-out in the end of the camshaft.

16 On DOHC models, ensure that the peg on the rear surface of the sprocket hub locates correctly in the cut-out in the end of the camshaft.

17 Refit the sprocket retaining bolt and washer. Tighten the bolt to the specified torque, whilst retaining the sprocket with the tool used on removal.

18 Realign the timing hole in the camshaft sprocket (see Section 3) with the corresponding hole in the cylinder head, and refit the locking pin.

19 Refit and tension the timing belt as described in Section 5.

20 Refit the timing belt covers (followed by the crankshaft pulley and auxiliary drivebelt, where applicable) as described in Section 4.

Crankshaft sprocket

21 Where removed, locate the Woodruff key in the crankshaft end, then slide on the flanged spacer, aligning its slot with the Woodruff key.

22 Align the crankshaft sprocket slot with the Woodruff key, and slide it onto the end of the crankshaft.

23 Temporarily remove the locking pin from the rear of the flywheel, then refit the crankshaft sprocket retaining bolt and washer. Tighten the bolt to the specified torque, whilst preventing crankshaft rotation using the method employed on removal. Refit the locking pin to the rear of the flywheel.

24 Refit and tension the timing belt as described in Section 5.

25 Refit the timing belt covers (followed by the crankshaft pulley and auxiliary drivebelt, where applicable) as described in Section 4.

Tensioner/idler pulley

26 Refit the tensioner pulley to its mounting stud, and fit the retaining nut.

27 Refit and tension the timing belt as described in Section 5.

28 Refit the timing belt covers (followed by the crankshaft pulley and auxiliary drivebelt, where applicable) as described in Section 4.

7 Engine left-hand mounting – removal and refitting

1 Remove the battery as described in Section 10, then unbolt and remove the battery support tray (see illustration).

2 Place a jack beneath the transmission, with a block of wood on the jack head. Raise the jack until it is supporting the weight of the transmission.

3 Slacken and remove the mounting rubber centre nut and washer, then unscrew the two bolts securing the bracket to the body. Remove the mounting rubber, and slide the spacer off the mounting bracket stud (see illustrations).

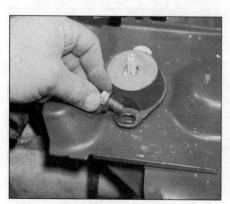

7.3b . . . then unscrew the two securing bolts . . .

7.3c . . . and remove the mounting rubber from the body

7.3d Slide the spacer off the mounting bracket stud

8.3a Release the purge valve vacuum hose from the side of the ECU plastic cover

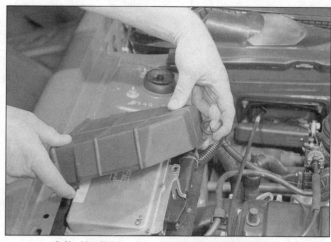

8.3b Unclip the cover from the mounting plate

4 Where necessary, unscrew the nuts and remove the bracket from the transmission.

5 Refit the bracket to the transmission, tightening its mounting nuts to the specified torque.

6 Refit the spacer, then fit the mounting to the body, and tighten its retaining bolts to the specified torque.

7 Refit the mounting centre nut, and tighten it to the specified torque.

8 Remove the jack from underneath the transmission, then refit the battery as described in Section 10.

8 Electronic control unit (ECU) – removal and refitting

Single-point fuel injection models

1 The ECU is located on the right-hand side of the engine compartment, underneath a large plastic cover.

2 To remove the ECU, first disconnect the battery negative cable and position it away from the terminal.

3 Unfasten the securing clips and release the purge valve vacuum hose from the side of the ECU plastic cover. Unclip the cover from the mounting plate, then lift the retaining clip and disconnect the wiring connector from the ECU. Slacken and remove the ECU retaining bolts, and remove it from the vehicle. Alternatively, unbolt the mounting bracket from the bodywork and remove it complete with the ECU (see illustrations).

4 Refitting is a reverse of the removal procedure, ensuring that the wiring connector is securely reconnected.

Multi-point fuel injection models

5 The ECU is located on the right-hand side of the engine compartment. On some models,

a large plastic cover is mounted over the ECU.

6 To remove the ECU, first disconnect the battery negative lead.

7 Unclip the cover from the mounting plate, then lift the retaining clip and disconnect the wiring connector from the ECU. Slacken and remove the ECU retaining bolts, and remove it from the vehicle (refer to the illustrations for single-point fuel injection models for greater detail).

8 Refitting is a reverse of the removal procedure, ensuring that the wiring connector is securely reconnected by pushing the retaining clip firmly home.

9 Air cleaner assembly - removal and refitting

1 Release the securing screws and lift off the air cleaner cover. Slacken the hose clips and detach the air ducting from the air cleaner cover and throttle body. Release the clips and disconnect the breather hose from the side of the air cleaner cover.

2 Lift out the air filter element, then slacken and withdraw screws securing the air cleaner housing to its mounting bracket.

3 Slacken the hose clip and detach the inlet air hose from the underside of the air cleaner housing. Lift the housing from the engine compartment - recover the mounting rubbers if they are loose.

4 Release the hose clip and disconnect the inlet duct assembly from the air inlet scoop. Undo the securing screws and lift the duct assembly, together with the resonator, from the engine compartment.

Refitting

5 Refitting is a reversal of removal. Ensure that the cylinder head breather hose is correctly reconnected and that all hose clips are securely tightened

8.3c Unbolt the mounting bracket from the bodywork and remove it complete with the ECU

10 Battery - removal and refitting

Note 1: *On models with a Citroën anti-theft alarm system, disable the alarm before disconnecting the battery.*

Note 2: *After reconnecting the battery on 1.6 litre petrol-engined models with multi-point fuel injection, the sequence described in the last paragraph of this Section must be observed, to ensure that the idle speed actuator valve is correctly reset.*

Removal

1 The battery is located on the left-hand side of the engine compartment.

2 Disconnect the lead(s) at the negative (earth) terminal. There are two possible types of battery terminal fixings fitted on these models. With the first type, the leads are secured to a stud on the top of the terminal by means of a plastic-capped nut **(see**

5A

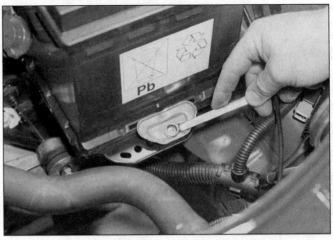

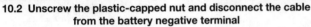

10.2 Unscrew the plastic-capped nut and disconnect the cable from the battery negative terminal

10.4 Removing the battery retaining clamp

illustration), on the second, a conventional fitting is used, secured in position by a clamp bolt and nut.

3 Remove the insulation cover (where fitted) and disconnect the positive terminal lead(s) in the same way.

4 Unscrew the nut/bolt (as applicable) and remove the battery retaining clamp **(see illustration)**.

5 Lift the battery out of the engine compartment and, where necessary, remove the insulation plate(s).

6 If required for access, the battery support tray may be unbolted and removed from the bodywork **(see illustration)**.

Refitting

7 Refitting is a reversal of removal, but smear petroleum jelly on the terminals when reconnecting the leads, and always reconnect the positive lead first, and the negative lead last.

8 On 1.6 litre petrol models with multi-point fuel injection, carry out the following steps, to reset the position of the idle speed actuator valve:

1   *Switch off the ignition.*
2   *Wait at least 10 seconds.*
3   *Switch on the ignition.*
4   *Wait at least 10 seconds.*
5   *Start the engine and allow it to idle; check that the idle speed stabilises at the figure specified. Introduce loads by switching on the headlights and/or air conditioning, and turn the steering from lock to lock (models with PAS only) - check that the idle speed remains stable.*

10.6 If required for access, the battery support tray may be unbolted and removed from the bodywork

Chapter 5B
Citroën Saxo diesel 1996 to 1998

Contents

Specifications

Timing belt renewal interval . . . . Every 36 000 miles (60 000 km)

Note: *Although the normal interval for timing belt renewal is 72 000 miles (120 000 km), it is strongly recommended that the interval is halved on vehicles which are subjected to intensive use, ie, mainly short journeys or a lot of stop-start driving. The actual belt renewal interval is therefore very much up to the individual owner. That being said, it is highly recommended to err on the side of safety, and renew the belt at this earlier interval, bearing in mind the drastic consequences resulting from belt failure.*

Timing belt tension
Using Citroën tension measuring tool:
    Stage 1 . . . . 100 SEEM units
    Stage 2 . . . . 55 ± 5 SEEM units

Torque wrench settings	Nm	lbf ft
Auxiliary drivebelt tensioner assembly retaining bolts	25	18
Camshaft sprocket hub-to-camshaft bolt:		
Engines up to 31/12/98	80	59
Engines built after 1/1/99:		
Stage 1	40	30
Stage 2	Angle-tighten a further 20°	
Camshaft sprocket-to-hub bolts	23	17
Crankshaft pulley bolts	15	11
Crankshaft sprocket retaining bolt:		
Engines up to 31/12/98	110	81
Engines built after 1/1/99:		
Stage 1	70	52
Stage 2	Angle-tighten a further 45°	
Injection pump sprocket fastener(s):		
Injection pump sprocket-to-hub bolts	23	17
Injection pump sprocket hub retaining nut	Not available	
Roadwheel bolts	85	63
Timing belt cover bolts	7	5
Timing belt idler pulley bolt	20	15
Timing belt tensioner pulley nut	25	18

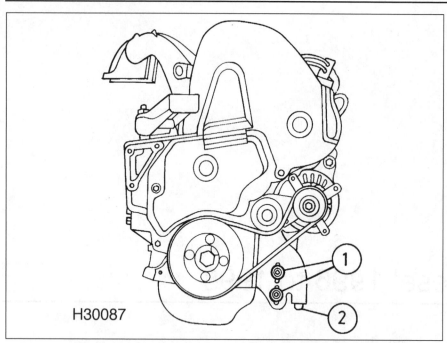

1.4 Auxiliary drivebelt tensioner securing bolts (1) and adjustment bolt (2)

1 Auxiliary drivebelt - removal, refitting and adjustment

Removal

1 Apply the handbrake, jack up the front of the car and support it on axle stands, then remove the right-hand front roadwheel.

2 Undo the securing screws and remove the plastic liner from the wheel arch. Where necessary, undo the retaining nut, and free the coolant hoses from the retaining clip to improve access to the crankshaft sprocket bolt.

3 Disconnect the battery negative lead.

4 Slacken the two bolts securing the tensioner pulley assembly to the engine **(see illustration)**.

5 Rotate the (vertical) adjuster bolt on the underside of the tensioner pulley assembly to move the pulley away from the drivebelt. When there is sufficient slack, remove the drivebelt from the pulleys.

Refitting

6 Fit the belt around the pulleys, ensuring that the belt is of the correct type if it is being renewed, and take up the slack in the belt by tightening the adjuster bolt.

Adjustment

7 The belt should be tensioned so that, under firm thumb pressure, the belt can be displaced by approximately 5.0 mm, at the mid-point of the longest belt run between two pulleys.

8 To adjust the tension, with the two tensioner pulley assembly retaining bolts slackened, rotate the adjuster bolt until the correct belt tension is achieved. Once the belt is correctly tensioned, rotate the crankshaft through two complete turns, and recheck the tension.

9 When the belt is correctly tensioned, securely tighten the tensioner pulley assembly retaining bolts.

10 Reconnect the battery negative lead.

11 Clip the coolant hoses back in position, and secure with the retaining nut (where removed). Refit the wheel arch liner and roadwheel, then lower the vehicle to the ground and tighten the roadwheel bolts to the specified torque.

2 Engine assembly/valve timing holes - general information and usage

Caution: Do not attempt to rotate the engine whilst the crankshaft, camshaft or injection pump are locked in position. If the engine is to be left in this state for a long period of time, it is a good idea to place warning notices inside the vehicle, and in the engine compartment. This will reduce the possibility of the engine being accidentally cranked on the starter motor, which is likely to cause damage with the locking tools in place.

1 Timing holes are drilled in the camshaft sprocket and fuel injection pump sprocket hubs and in the flywheel. The holes are used to ensure that the crankshaft, camshaft and injection pump are correctly positioned when assembling the engine (to prevent the possibility of the valves contacting the pistons when refitting the cylinder head), or refitting the timing belt. When the timing holes are aligned with access holes, suitable-diameter pins or bolts can be inserted to position the camshaft, injection pump sprocket and crankshaft. Proceed as follows. **Note:** *With the timing holes aligned, No 4 cylinder is at TDC on its compression stroke.*

2 Remove the upper and centre timing belt covers as described in Section 3.

3 The crankshaft must now be turned until the timing holes in the camshaft sprocket and injection pump sprocket hubs are aligned with the corresponding holes in the cylinder head and pump body. The holes are aligned when the camshaft sprocket hub hole is in the 4 o'clock position, when viewed from the right-hand end of the engine. The crankshaft can be turned by using a spanner on the crankshaft sprocket bolt, noting that it should always be rotated in a clockwise direction (viewed from the right-hand end of the engine). If necessary, firmly apply the handbrake then jack up the front of the car, support it on axle stands and remove the right-hand roadwheel to improve access to the crankshaft pulley. Turning the engine will be much easier if the glow plugs are removed first.

4 With the camshaft sprocket hub hole correctly positioned, insert a 6 mm diameter bolt or drill bit through the hole in the front left-hand flange of the cylinder block, and locate it in the timing hole in the flywheel **(see illustration)**. Note that it may be necessary to rotate the crankshaft slightly, to get the holes to align.

5 With the flywheel correctly positioned, insert an 8 mm diameter bolt through the elongated hole in the camshaft sprocket, through the slot in the hub, and screw it into the cylinder head. Also insert a 6 mm diameter pin or drill bit through the elongated hole on the injection pump sprocket, through the slot

2.4 Insert a 6 mm bolt through the hole in the cylinder block flange and into the timing hole in the flywheel

in the hub and insert it into the hole in the pump body. **(see illustration)**.
6 The crankshaft, camshaft and injection pump are now accurately positioned.

3 Timing belt covers - removal and refitting

Removal

Upper cover

1 Disconnect the battery negative cable and position it away from the terminal.
2 Remove the securing screw and detach the glow plug controller from the side of the cooling system expansion tank **(see illustration)**.
3 Disconnect the wiring from the underside of the glow plug control module **(see illustration)**.
4 Remove the expansion tank securing screws. Move the expansion tank to one side to gain greater access to the timing belt cover; there is no need to disconnect the cooling hoses.
5 Slacken and remove the three upper cover retaining screws; two are located at the front of the cover - above and below the injection pump sprocket - and the third is located at the rear of the cover. Disengage the upper timing cover from the lower cover and then remove it from the cylinder head **(see illustration)**.

Lower cover

6 Remove the upper cover as described in paragraph 1.
7 Turn the wheels onto full right-hand lock, then prise out the rubber plug from underneath the right-hand front wheel arch. Unscrew the timing belt cover bolt which is accessible through the hole in the wheel arch liner **(see illustrations)**.
8 Remove the auxiliary drivebelt as described in Section 1.
9 Undo the crankshaft pulley retaining bolts

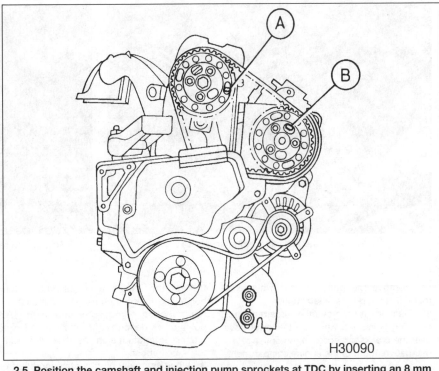

2.5 Position the camshaft and injection pump sprockets at TDC by inserting an 8 mm bolt (A) and a 6 mm pin (B) as described in the text

3.2 Unscrew the retaining bolt securing the control module to the coolant expansion tank

3.3 Unplug the wiring connector from the base of the module

3.5 Removing the timing belt upper cover

3.7a Remove the rubber plug from the right-hand wing valance . . .

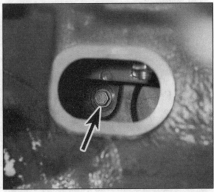

3.7b . . . to gain access to the timing belt centre cover bolt (arrowed)

5B

3.9a Undo the retaining bolts (arrowed) . . .

3.9b . . . and remove the crankshaft pulley from the engine

and remove the pulley, noting which way round it is fitted **(see illustrations)**.

10 Slacken and remove the three remaining retaining bolts, and withdraw the lower cover over the crankshaft sprocket outer flange and manoeuvre it out of the engine compartment.

Refitting

11 Refitting is a reversal of removal. When refitting the upper cover ensure that the inner edge engages with the lug on the side of the cylinder head cover **(see illustration)**.

4 Timing belt -
removal and refitting

Removal

1 Disconnect the battery negative cable and position it away from the terminal.

2 Align the engine assembly/valve timing holes, and lock the crankshaft, camshaft and fuel injection pump sprockets in the TDC position as described in Section 2. *Do not* attempt to rotate the engine whilst the locking tools are in position.

3 Unbolt the glow plug control module from the side of the coolant expansion tank and position it to one side.

4 Remove the upper and lower timing belt covers as described in Section 3. If the belt is to be re-used and there are no manufacturer's direction of rotation markings on the belt's surface, make your own using chalk or similar **(see illustration)**. The crankshaft rotates clockwise, as viewed from the right hand end of the engine.

5 Loosen the timing belt tensioner pulley retaining nut. Rotate the pulley in a clockwise direction, using a suitable square-section key fitted to the hole in the pulley. Retighten the retaining

nut, with the pulley in the slackened position.

6 Slip the timing belt off the sprockets, idler and tensioner pulleys, and remove it from the engine.

7 If signs of oil contamination are found, trace the source of the oil leak, and rectify it. Wash down the engine timing belt area and all related components, to remove all traces of oil.

Refitting

8 Prior to refitting, thoroughly clean the timing belt sprockets. Check that both the tensioner and idler pulleys rotate freely, without any sign of roughness. If necessary, renew damaged pulley(s) as described in Section 5. Make sure that the sprocket and flywheel TDC locking tools are still in place, as described in Section 2.

9 Slacken the three camshaft sprocket hub bolts. Similarly, slacken the three injection

3.11 Ensure that the inner edge engages with the lug (arrowed) on the side of the cylinder head cover

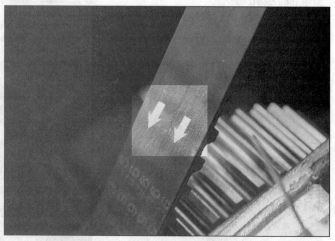

4.4 If the timing belt is to be re-used, use white paint or similar to mark the direction of rotation on the belt (if markings do not already exist)

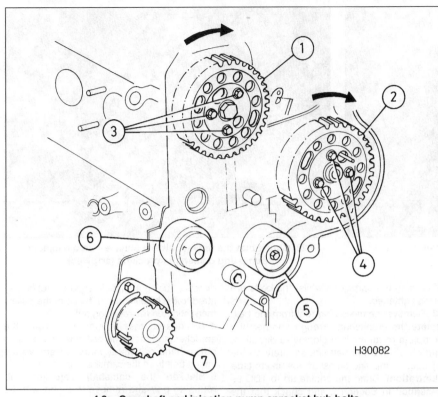

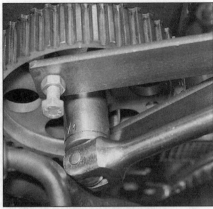

4.9b To prevent the camshaft rotating as the bolt is slackened, a sprocket-holding tool will be required. Use two lengths of steel strip (one long, the other short), and three nuts and bolts; one nut and bolt forms the pivot of a forked tool, with the remaining two nuts and bolts at the tips of the 'forks' to engage with the sprocket spokes

4.9a Camshaft and injection pump sprocket hub bolts

1	Camshaft sprocket	5	Tensioner
2	Injection pump sprocket	6	Idler roller
3	Camshaft sprocket hub bolts	7	Coolant pump sprocket
4	Injection pump sprocket hub bolts		

pump sprocket hub bolts **(see illustration)**. Do not be tempted to use the TDC locking tools as a means of bracing the sprockets, whilst the bolts are being slackened **(see illustration)**. Ensure that both sprockets move freely on their hubs (as far as the sprockets' slotted bolt holes will allow). Now finger-tighten all the sprocket hub bolts, so that it is just possible to turn the sprockets by hand.

10 Turn the camshaft and injection pump sprockets fully clockwise, so that the sprocket mounting bolts are positioned against the end of their slotted holes.

11 Pass the timing belt under the crankshaft sprocket, then over the idler pulley (nearest to the injection pump), paying attention to the direction of rotation markings on the belt where applicable. Pass the belt around the injection pump sprocket, ensuring that the belt does not jump on the crankshaft sprocket. If

necessary, move the injection pump sprocket anti-clockwise - by no more than *one* tooth - to enable the belt to seat properly. Ensure that the belt remains taught at all times.

12 Fit the belt on the camshaft sprocket in the same way. If necessary, move the camshaft sprocket anti-clockwise (again, by no more than *one* tooth) to enable the belt to seat properly **(see illustration)**. Ensure that the belt remains taught at all times.

13 Feed the belt around the tensioner pulley and finally around the coolant pump sprocket. Pretension the belt (see paragraph 16) until all its runs are slightly tightened.

14 Ensure that the camshaft and injection sprocket hub bolts are positioned in the centre of their slotted holes **(see illustration)**. If they are hard against either end of their slotted holes, the belt has been probably been incorrectly fitted - remove the belt and start the refitting procedure again.

5B

4.12 Engage the timing belt with the camshaft sprocket as described in text

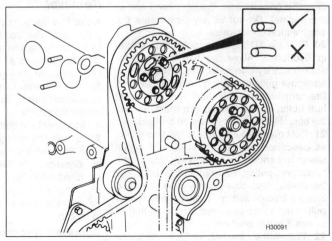

4.14 Correct location of camshaft and injection pump sprocket hub bolts

4.16 Tightening the tensioner pulley retaining nut

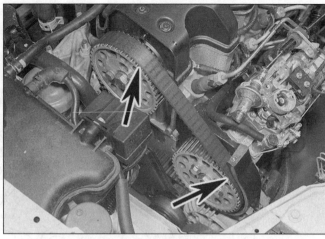

4.23 Check that the timing belt sits squarely on the injection pump and camshaft sprockets (arrowed)

15 Ensure that the fuel injection pump and camshaft sprocket hub bolts are still only hand-tight, then fit the belt tension measuring tool to the front run of the timing belt, midway between the camshaft and injection pump sprockets.

16 Fit a square-section key to the hole in the front face of the tensioner pulley and pivot the tensioner pulley anti-clockwise until the tensioning tool displays the specified Stage 1 tension setting. Tighten the tensioner pulley nut to secure it in this position (see illustration).

17 Fully tighten the injection pump and camshaft sprocket hub bolts to their specified torque settings. Do not use the TDC tools as a means of bracing the sprockets whilst the bolts are being tightened.

18 Remove the locking tools from the camshaft sprocket, injection pump sprocket and flywheel, and remove the measuring tool from the belt.

19 Using a socket and extension bar on the crankshaft sprocket bolt, rotate the crankshaft through ten complete rotations in a clockwise direction (viewed from the right-hand end of the engine). Do not at any time rotate the crankshaft anti-clockwise.

20 Refit the TDC locking tools as described in Section 2. Allow the belt to stand for approximately one minute then slacken the tensioner pulley retaining nut. Fully slacken the camshaft and injection pump sprocket hub bolts, then finger-tighten them, so that the sprockets can just be turned by hand.

21 Refit the measuring tool to the timing belt, as described earlier in this Section. Again using a square-section key, pivot the tensioner pulley anti-clockwise until the tensioning tool now displays the specified Stage 2 tension setting. Tighten the tensioner pulley nut to its specified torque setting to secure it in this position.

22 Tighten the camshaft and injection pump hub sprocket bolts to their specified torque settings. Do not use the TDC tools as a means

of bracing the sprockets whilst the bolts are being tightened.

23 Remove the measuring tool from the belt. Rotate the crankshaft through another two complete rotations in a clockwise direction, and check that the belt sits squarely on the injection pump and camshaft sprockets (see illustration). Bring the engine up to TDC as described in Section 2 and check that the locking tools can still be inserted through the camshaft sprocket, injection pump sprocket and flywheel alignment holes. If this is not the case, the timing belt has been fitted incorrectly and it will be necessary to remove the belt and start the refitting procedure again.

24 With the belt tension correctly set, remove locking tools, and refit the timing belt covers as described in Section 3.

5 Timing belt tensioner and sprockets - removal and refitting

Removal

Note: This Section describes the removal and refitting of the components concerned as individual operations. If more than one of them is to be removed at the same time, start by removing the timing belt as described in Section 4; remove the actual component as described below, ignoring the preliminary dismantling steps.

1 Disconnect the battery negative terminal.

2 Remove the timing belt upper cover, then align the engine assembly/valve timing holes as described in Section 2 and lock the camshaft sprocket, injection pump sprocket and flywheel in position. Do not attempt to rotate the engine whilst the locking tools are in position.

Camshaft sprocket

3 Loosen the timing belt tensioner pulley retaining nut. Rotate the pulley in a clockwise

direction, using a suitable square-section key fitted to the hole in the front face of the pulley, then retighten the retaining nut.

4 Disengage the timing belt from the sprocket, and move the belt clear, taking care not to bend or twist it sharply. Remove the timing bolt from the camshaft sprocket.

5 Slacken the camshaft sprocket hub retaining bolt and remove it, along with its washer (see illustration).

Caution: Do not attempt to use the sprocket timing bolt to prevent the sprocket from rotating whilst the retaining bolt is slackened (see illustration 4.9b).

6 With the retaining bolt removed, slide the sprocket off the end of the camshaft. Note the key on the rear of the sprocket hub, which engages with a cut-out on the end of the camshaft. Examine the camshaft oil seal for signs of oil leakage and, if necessary, renew it.

Crankshaft sprocket

7 Remove the lower timing belt cover as described in Section 3.

8 Loosen the timing belt tensioner pulley retaining nut. Rotate the pulley in a clockwise direction, using a suitable square-section key fitted to the hole in the

5.5 Remove the retaining bolt and washer, then remove the camshaft sprocket

5.16 Fuel injection pump sprocket-to-hub retaining screws (arrowed)

5.18 Timing belt tensioner pulley retaining nut (arrowed)

front face of the pulley, then retighten the retaining nut.

9 Disengage the timing belt from the crankshaft sprocket, and move the belt clear, taking care not to bend or twist it sharply.

10 To prevent crankshaft rotation whilst the sprocket retaining bolt is slackened, select top gear, and have an assistant apply the brakes firmly. *Do not* be tempted to use the flywheel TDC locking pin to prevent the crankshaft from rotating; temporarily remove the pin from the rear of the flywheel prior to slackening the pulley bolt, then refit it once the bolt has been slackened.

11 Unscrew the retaining bolt and washer, then slide the sprocket off the end of the crankshaft. Refit the locking pin/bolt through the timing hole into the rear of the flywheel.

12 If the Woodruff key is a loose fit in the crankshaft, remove it and store it with the sprocket for safe-keeping. If necessary, also slide the flanged spacer off the end of the crankshaft. Examine the crankshaft oil seal for signs of oil leakage and, if necessary, renew it.

Fuel injection pump sprocket

13 Loosen the timing belt tensioner pulley retaining nut. Rotate the pulley in a clockwise direction, using a suitable square-section key fitted to the hole in the pulley, then retighten the retaining nut.

14 Disengage the timing belt from the injection pump sprocket, and move the belt clear, taking care not to bend or twist it sharply. If necessary, remove the right-hand headlight unit as described in Section 7 to improve access to the sprocket.

15 Remove the timing pin or bolt from the pump body.

16 Slacken the injection pump sprocket-to-hub retaining screws **(see illustration)**. Undo and remove the screws.

Caution: Do not attempt to use the timing pin or bolt to prevent the sprocket from rotating whilst the retaining bolts are slackened (see illustration 4.9b).

17 Remove the sprocket from the injection pump sprocket hub.

Tensioner pulley

18 Slacken and remove the timing belt tensioner pulley retaining nut, and slide the pulley off its mounting stud **(see illustration)**. Examine the mounting stud for signs of damage and, if necessary, renew it - it is removed by unscrewing it from the cylinder block. Carefully tie the timing belt up so that it is kept in full engagement with all of the sprockets.

Idler pulley

19 Loosen the timing belt tensioner pulley retaining nut. Rotate the pulley in a clockwise direction, using a suitable square-section key fitted to the hole in the pulley, then retighten the retaining nut. In order to provide some slack in the timing belt between the crankshaft and injection pump sprockets, it will be necessary to remove the locking tool from the flywheel and rotate the crankshaft slightly anti-clockwise.

20 Unscrew the bolt retaining the idler to the cylinder block **(see illustration)**, and withdraw the idler pulley. Carefully tie the timing belt up so that it is kept in full engagement with all of the sprockets.

Refitting

21 Clean the sprockets thoroughly, and renew any that show signs of wear, damage or cracks.

22 Clean the tensioner pulley and idler, but do not use any strong solvent which may enter the bearings. Check that each roller rotates freely about its hub, with no sign of stiffness or free play. Renew the tensioner pulley or idler if there is any doubt about its condition, or if there are any obvious signs of wear or damage.

Camshaft sprocket

23 Locate the sprocket and hub on the end of the camshaft. Ensure that the locating key

at the rear of the sprocket hub is correctly engaged with the cut-out at the end of the camshaft.

24 Coat the threads of the sprocket hub bolt with locking compound. Refit the sprocket and hub then insert the bolt, together with the washer (where applicable). Tighten the bolt to the specified torque, whilst retaining the sprocket with the tool used during removal.

25 Realign the timing hole in the camshaft sprocket hub (see Section 2) with the corresponding hole in the cylinder head, and refit the timing bolt.

26 With the crankshaft, injection pump and camshaft locked in position, refit the timing belt to the camshaft sprocket, as described in Section 4. Do not twist the belt sharply while refitting it, and ensure that the belt teeth are seated centrally in the sprockets.

27 Ensure that the belt is taut around the crankshaft sprocket, idler pulley and injection pump sprocket, so that any slack is on the tensioner pulley side of the belt. Tension the timing belt as described at the end of Section 4.

28 Remove the TDC locking tools, then verify that the timing belt has been refitted correctly

5.20 Timing belt idler pulley retaining bolt (arrowed)

5B

by rotating the engine through two revolutions, then checking that the TDC locking tools can be reinserted.

29 Refit the timing belt covers as described in Section 3.

30 Reconnect the battery negative terminal.

Crankshaft sprocket

31 Coat the rear surface of the spacer and the Woodruff key with a suitable sealant. Locate the Woodruff key in the crankshaft end, then slide on the flanged spacer, aligning its slot with the Woodruff key.

32 Align the crankshaft sprocket slot with the Woodruff key, and slide it onto the end of the crankshaft.

33 Temporarily remove the locking pin from the rear of the flywheel, then refit the crankshaft sprocket retaining bolt and washer. Tighten the bolt to the specified torque, whilst preventing crankshaft rotation using the method employed on removal. Refit the locking pin to the rear of the flywheel.

Caution: Ensure that there are no traces of adhesive on the crankshaft sprocket teeth.

34 With the crankshaft, injection pump and camshaft locked in position, refit the timing belt to the crankshaft sprocket. Ensure that the belt is taut between the crankshaft, idler pulley, injection pump and camshaft sprockets, so that any slack is on the tensioner pulley side of the belt. Do not twist the belt sharply while refitting it, and ensure that the belt teeth are seated centrally in the sprockets.

35 Loosen the tensioner pulley retaining nut. Rotate the pulley anti-clockwise to remove all free play from the timing belt, then retighten the nut.

36 Tension the belt as described in Section 4.

37 Refit the timing belt covers as described in Section 3.

Fuel injection pump sprocket

38 Thoroughly clean the mating surfaces of the fuel injection pump shaft hub and the rear of the sprocket.

39 Locate the sprocket on the injection pump sprocket hub.

40 Tighten the sprocket retaining screws to the specified torque, preventing the pump shaft from turning using the method employed during removal. Align the sprocket hub timing hole, and refit the timing pin.

41 With the crankshaft, injection pump and camshaft locked in position, refit the timing belt to the injection pump sprocket, as described in Section 4. Do not twist the belt excessively while refitting it, and ensure that the belt teeth are seated centrally in the sprockets.

42 Ensure that the belt is taut around the crankshaft sprocket, idler pulley and camshaft sprocket, so that any slack is on the tensioner pulley side of the belt. Tension the timing belt as described at the end of Section 4.

43 Remove the TDC locking tools, then verify that the timing belt has been refitted correctly by rotating the engine through two revolutions, then checking that the TDC locking tools can be reinserted.

44 Refit the timing belt covers as described in Section 3.

Tensioner pulley

45 Check that the mounting stud is tightened in the cylinder block.

46 Locate the tensioner pulley on the stud, and lightly tighten its retaining nut.

47 With the crankshaft, injection pump and camshaft locked in position, ensure that the belt is taut between the crankshaft, idler pulley, injection pump and camshaft sprockets, so that any slack is on the tensioner pulley side of the belt.

48 Loosen the tensioner pulley retaining nut. Rotate the pulley anti-clockwise to remove all free play from the timing belt, then retighten the nut.

49 Tension the belt as described in Section 4.

50 Refit the timing belt covers as described in Section 3.

Idler pulley

51 Refit the idler pulley to the cylinder block, and tighten its retaining bolt securely.

52 Carefully turn the crankshaft clockwise until the locking tool can be inserted into the flywheel.

53 With the crankshaft, injection pump and camshaft locked in position, ensure that the belt is taut between the crankshaft, idler pulley, injection pump and camshaft sprockets, so that any slack is on the tensioner pulley side of the belt.

54 Loosen the tensioner pulley retaining nut. Rotate the pulley anti-clockwise to remove all free play from the belt, then retighten the nut.

55 Tension the belt as described in Section 4.

56 Refit the timing belt covers as described in Section 3.

6 Front direction indicator - removal and refitting

Removal

1 Open the bonnet, and working between the direction indicator light and the headlight, release the indicator light unit retaining clip by pressing it down gently with a flat-bladed screwdriver **(see illustration)**.

2 Withdraw the light unit forwards from the front wing **(see illustration)**.

3 Twist the bulbholder anti-clockwise to release it from the rear of the light unit.

Refitting

4 Refitting is a reversal of removal, bearing in mind the following points:
a) *Ensure that the bulbholder sealing ring is in good condition.*
b) *When refitting the light unit, ensure that the light unit retaining clip and slide engage correctly, and that the light unit wiring does not get trapped.*

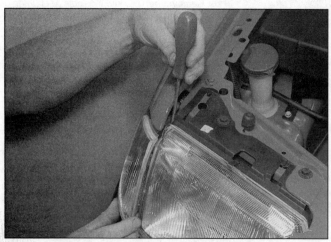

6.1 Using a screwdriver to release the indicator locating clip . . .

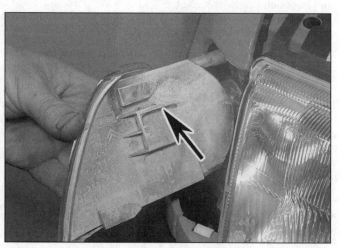

6.2 . . . which can more easily be seen (arrowed) with the unit removed

7.2 Disconnecting the headlight adjuster motor wiring plug

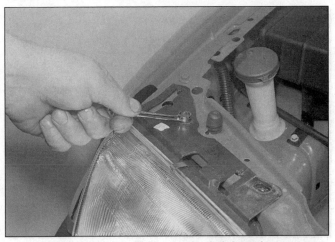

7.3a Remove the headlight mounting bolt from the top . . .

7 Headlight -
removal and refitting

Removal

1 Remove the radiator grille/headlight surround as described in Section 8.
2 Working at the rear of the headlight assembly, disconnect the main wiring plug from the headlight bulb. Twist the sidelight bulbholder through a quarter-turn, and withdraw it from the rear of the headlight. Where applicable, disconnect the wiring plug from the headlight adjustment motor **(see illustration)**.
3 Remove the retaining bolt from the top and bottom of the headlight unit **(see illustrations)**.
4 Using a flat-bladed screwdriver, prise up the plastic flap at the rear of the headlight, to release the two retaining lugs from the body **(see illustration)**.

5 Pull the headlight unit forwards to release the L-shaped clip at the base of the unit **(see illustration)**, and withdraw it from the car.

Refitting

6 Refitting is a reversal of removal.
7 We had difficulty aligning the L-shaped clip at the base of the headlight unit, and found it could only be achieved if an assistant guided the clip and the slot in the light unit together, using a screwdriver through the direction indicator light aperture.
8 Refit the radiator grille/headlight surround as described in Section 8.

8 Radiator grille/headlight
surround -
removal and refitting

Removal

1 Remove both front direction indicator light units as described in Section 6.

7.3b . . . and from below the headlight

2 Using a small flat-bladed screwdriver, prise up and remove the U-shaped plastic retaining

7.4 Pull up the plastic flap to release the two retaining lugs (arrowed)

7.5 Showing the L-shaped headlight retaining clip, and the slot on the base of the headlight in which it fits

5B

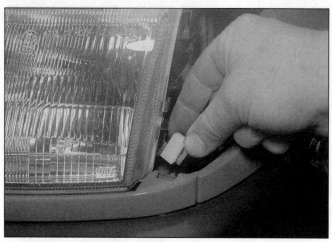

8.2 Remove the U-shaped clip from the direction indicator aperture

8.3 Prise the end of the surround forwards to disengage the locating peg

clips at the base of each direction indicator light aperture **(see illustration)**.

3 Again using a screwdriver, gently prise each end of the headlight surround forwards to release the peg from the hole in the body **(see illustration)**.

4 Remove the three retaining bolts along the top of the radiator grille **(see illustrations)**.

5 Pull the grille/headlight surround gently forwards to release the two slotted clips under each headlight unit, and remove it from the car **(see illustration)**. Care must be taken, as the clips (and the section of the panel under each headlight) are rather fragile.

Refitting

6 Refitting is a reversal of removal. Make sure that the clips under each headlight are lined up with their respective slots before pushing the panel back into place. Refit the direction indicator light units as described in Section 6.

8.4a Radiator grille/headlight surround retaining bolts (arrowed)

8.4b Removing one of the grille/surround bolts

8.5 Pull the grille/surround forwards, releasing the two clips each side

Chapter 6A
Citroën Visa petrol 1985 to 1988

Contents

Specifications

Timing belt renewal interval . . . .   Every 36 000 miles (60 000 km)

Ignition timing

Static and at idle speed (vacuum advance disconnected) . . . .   10° BTDC
At 3000 rpm (vacuum advance disconnected) . . . .   30° BTDC

Torque wrench settings

	Nm	lbf ft
Alternator pivot bolt	39	29
Alternator adjustment bolt	20	15
Camshaft sprocket bolt	78	58
Crankshaft pulley bolt	109	80
Spark plugs	18	13
Starter motor bolts	34	25
Timing belt tensioner nuts	15	11
Wheel nuts:		
Aluminium rims	75	55
Steel rims	60	44

1.2a Alternator mounting/adjustment bolt (arrowed)
A Adjustment screw

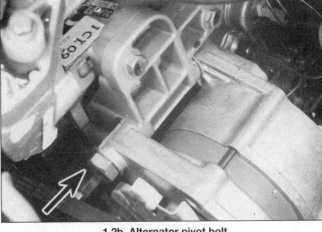

1.2b Alternator pivot bolt

1 Alternator drivebelt - removal, refitting and adjustment

Removal and refitting

1 Disconnect the battery negative lead.
2 Loosen the pivot and adjustment bolts, swivel the alternator towards the engine. then remove the drivebelt **(see illustrations)**.
3 Refitting is a reversal of removal.

Adjustment

4 Check the belt adjustment by applying thumb pressure midway between the pulleys. It should deflect by approximately 6.0 mm. If the adjustment is incorrect, loosen the pivot and adjustment bolts, reposition the alternator by turning the special adjustment screw as required, then retighten the bolts.

2 Timing belt - removal and refitting

Removal

1 Disconnect the battery earth lead.
2 Remove the alternator drivebelt (Section 1).
3 Remove the inner shield from the right-hand wheel arch **(see illustration)**, and wedge the radiator bottom hose under the sump.
4 Remove the shield from the camshaft sprocket.
5 Turn the crankshaft until the dowel hole in the pulley is at about 12 o'clock and the hole in the camshaft sprocket is at about 7 o'clock. In this position a 10 mm dowel should pass through each hole and into the timing recess behind. Verify this and then remove the dowels **(see illustration)**.
6 Remove the clutch bottom shield **(see illustration)**. Have an assistant jam the starter

ring gear while the crankshaft pulley bolt is undone. This bolt is very tight. **Do not** jam the pulley by means of the timing dowel, damage will result. Remove the bolt and washer.
7 Check that the 10 mm dowels will still enter the timing holes; adjust the crankshaft position if necessary by means of the starter

2.3 Inner shield removal from right-hand wheel arch. Prise clips free as shown

2.5 Timing dowels in position – engine removal for clarity

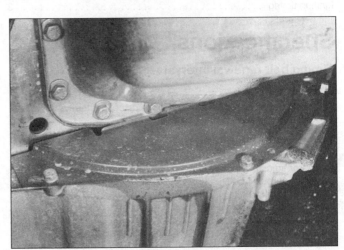

2.6 Unbolt and remove the clutch bottom shield

2.9 Turning the tensioner cam spindle

2.11 Line on belt aligns with mark on sprocket

ring gear. Remove the crankshaft pulley, retrieving the Woodruff key if it is loose.

8 Remove the plastic covers from the front of the timing belt. Note the location of the various bolts.

9 Slacken the two nuts on the front of the belt tensioner and the single nut at the rear. Use a spanner on the square end of the tensioner cam spindle to turn the cam to the horizontal position and so compress the tensioner spring **(see illustration)**. Tighten the cam locknut.

10 Remove the timing belt, taking care not to kink it or contaminate it with oil if it is to be re-used.

Refitting

11 Commence refitting by positioning the belt on the crankshaft sprocket, then refitting the pulley and verifying the correct position of the crankshaft by means of the dowel. (Observe the arrows on the belt showing the direction of rotation, and the timing lines which align with marks on the crankshaft and camshaft sprockets) **(see illustration)**.

12 Fit the belt to the camshaft sprocket, round the tensioner and to the coolant pump sprocket.

13 Release the tensioner cam locknut and turn the cam downwards to release the spring. Tighten the locknut and the tensioner front nuts **(see illustration)**.

14 Remove the timing dowels and turn the crankshaft through two full turns in the normal direction of rotation. Turn the crankshaft further to bring No 1 piston to TDC on the firing stroke.

15 Slacken the tensioner front nuts and the cam locknut, then retighten them.

16 Turn the crankshaft further and make sure that the timing dowels can still be inserted. If not, remove the belt and start again.

17 If a new belt has been fitted, it must be run in and retensioned, as follows.

18 Tighten the crankshaft pulley bolt to the specified torque, then refit and tension the alternator drivebelt (Section 1). Temporarily refit the camshaft sprocket cover.

19 Run the engine up to operating temperature. indicated by the cooling fan operating, then stop it and allow it to cool for at least two hours.

20 Rotate the crankshaft to the TDC position, No 1 cylinder firing, then slacken and retighten the tensioner nuts once more.

21 Remove the alternator drivebelt and the crankshaft pulley. Refit and secure the plastic covers, then refit the pulley and tighten its bolt

to the specified torque. Refit and tension the alternator drivebelt.

22 Check the ignition timing and adjust if necessary (Section 3).

3 Ignition timing

1 Run the engine to normal operating temperature. then stop it and connect a tachometer to it.

2 Disconnect and plug the vacuum pipe at the distributor vacuum advance unit.

3 Disconnect and remove the air cleaner inlet duct. then connect a stroboscopic timing light to the engine using the HT pick-up lead connected to No 1 spark plug HT lead.

4 Run the engine at 3000 rpm and point the timing light into the timing aperture in the clutch housing/gearbox casing. The double mark on the flywheel should be aligned with the TDC mark on the timing plate; indicating that the ignition is advanced by 30° **(see illustrations)**.

2.13 Drivebelt tensioner front nuts

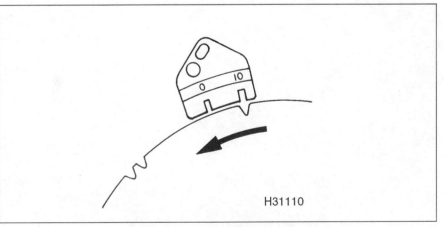

H31110

3.4a Static and idle speed ignition timing
Arrow indicates normal rotational direction of flywheel
Flywheel single mark aligns with 10° BTDC mark on timing plate

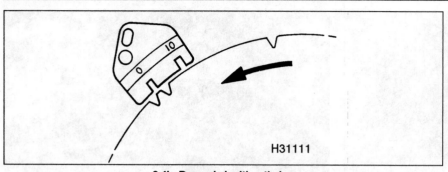

3.4b Dynamic ignition timing
Double mark on flywheel aligns with TDC mark on timing plate

5 If adjustment is necessary, loosen the distributor mounting nuts and rotate the distributor body as required. Tighten the nuts on completion.

7 Stop the engine, disconnect the tachometer and timing light and reconnect the vacuum pipe. Refit the timing aperture cover.

Chapter 6B
Citroën Visa diesel 1984 to 1988

Contents

6B

Specifications

Timing belt renewal interval . . . . Every 36 000 miles (60 000 km)

Note: *Although the normal interval for timing belt renewal is 48 000 miles (80 000 km), it is strongly recommended that the interval is reduced on vehicles which are subjected to intensive use, ie, mainly short journeys or a lot of stop-start driving. The actual belt renewal interval is therefore very much up to the individual owner. That being said, it is highly recommended to err on the side of safety, and renew the belt at this earlier interval, bearing in mind the drastic consequences resulting from belt failure.*

Torque wrench settings	Nm	lbf ft
Alternator mountings	35	26
Camshaft sprocket	35	26
Crankshaft pulley bolt:		
Stage 1	40	30
Stage 2	plus 60° or to 150	plus 60° or to 111
Engine mounting bracket, right-hand lower	18	13
Engine mounting bracket, right-hand upper:		
To engine	35	26
To mounting rubber	28	21
Engine mounting, left-hand:		
Centre nut	35	26
Centre stud to transmission	50	37
Small nuts	18	13
Timing belt intermediate roller	18	13
Timing belt tensioner	18	13
Timing cover, lower	12	9

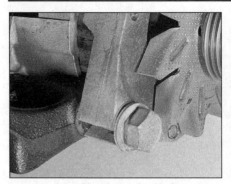

1.1a Alternator pivot bolt

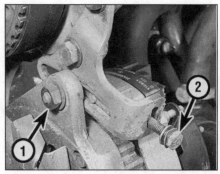

1.1b Alternator adjustment locknut (1) and adjustment bolt (2)

1.4 Checking tension of alternator drivebelt

1 Auxiliary belt – removal, refitting and adjustment

Removal and refitting

1 To remove the belt, loosen the pivot bolt and adjustment locknut **(see illustrations)**.
2 Unscrew the adjustment bolt to release the tension. The drivebelt can now be removed from the pulleys.
3 Refitting is a reversal of removal.

Adjustment

4 To adjust the tension, first check that the belt is correctly fitted over the pulleys. With the alternator mountings loose, tighten the adjustment bolt to tension the belt. The belt should be able to move by approximately 6.0 mm, with moderate thumb pressure midway between the pulleys **(see illustration)**. Tighten the mounting bolts to the correct torque.

Later models with air conditioning

5 During 1988, the three-pulley drivebelt system previously used was replaced by a five-pulley system, as shown **(see illustration)**.
6 With the new system, drivebelt tension is adjusted by movement of the bottom idler wheel. Tension is checked at the longest belt run, ie between the alternator and compressor pulleys.

2 Timing belt - removal, refitting and tensioning

Removal

1 Apply the handbrake.
2 On manual transmission models jack up the front right-hand corner of the vehicle until the wheel is just clear of the ground. Support the vehicle on an axle stand and engage 4th or 5th gear. This will enable the engine to be turned easily by turning the right-hand wheel. On automatic transmission models use an open-ended spanner on the crankshaft pulley bolt.
3 Remove the engine splash guard from under the right-hand front wheel arch.
4 Disconnect the battery negative lead.
5 Loosen the alternator pivot and adjustment bolts then unscrew the tension bolt until it is possible to slip the drivebelt from the pulleys.
6 With 4th or 5th gear selected on manual transmission models have an assistant depress the footbrake pedal, then unscrew the crankshaft pulley bolt. On automatic transmission models unbolt the transmission cover and lock the starter ring gear. Note that the bolt is extremely tight.
7 Slide the pulley from the front of the crankshaft. Unbolt the bottom timing cover.
8 Support the weight of the engine using a hoist or trolley jack.
9 Unscrew the nuts and remove the right-hand engine mounting bracket **(see illustration)**.

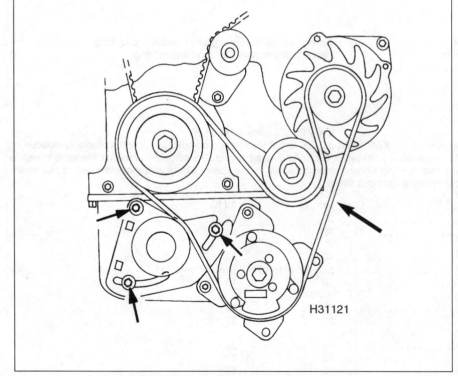

1.5 Drivebelt run - later models with air conditioning
Arrow shows tension checking point
Smaller arrows indicate idler wheel securing bolts

2.9 Right-hand engine mounting bracket

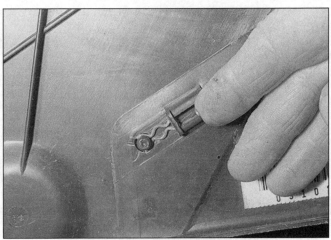

2.10a Timing cover front clip (early models) . . .

2.10b . . . and spring clips

10 Pull up the front clip (early models), release the spring clips, and withdraw the two timing cover sections **(see illustrations)**. Note that the spring clip is not fitted to later models, which have a modified cover and fastenings.

11 Turn the engine by means of the front right-hand wheel or crankshaft pulley bolt until the three bolt holes in the camshaft and injection pump sprockets are aligned with the corresponding holes in the engine front plate.

12 Insert an 8.0 mm diameter metal dowel rod or drill through the special hole in the left-hand rear flange of the cylinder block by the starter motor. Then carefully turn the engine either way until the rod enters the TDC hole in the flywheel **(see illustration)**.

13 Insert three M8 bolts through the holes in the camshaft and injection pump sprockets and screw them into the engine front plate finger-tight **(see illustration)**.

14 Loosen the timing belt tensioner pivot nut and adjustment bolt, then turn the bracket anti-clockwise to release the tension and retighten the adjustment bolt to hold the tensioner in the released position. If available use a 3/8 inch square drive extension in the hole provided to turn the bracket against the spring tension.

15 Mark the timing belt with an arrow to indicate its normal direction of turning then remove it from the camshaft, injection pump, water pump and crankshaft sprockets.

Refitting

16 If signs of oil contamination are found, trace the source of the oil leak, and rectify it. Wash down the engine timing belt area and all related components, to remove all traces of oil.

17 Begin refitting by locating the timing belt on the crankshaft sprocket, making sure that, where applicable, the rotation arrow is facing the correct way.

18 Hold the timing belt engaged with the crankshaft sprocket then feed it over the roller and onto the injection pump, camshaft, and

2.12 Using a twist drill to enter the TDC hole in the flywheel

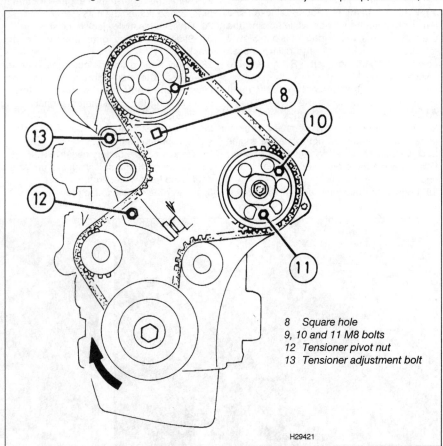

8   Square hole
9, 10 and 11 M8 bolts
12   Tensioner pivot nut
13   Tensioner adjustment bolt

2.13 Holding camshaft and injection pump sprockets in position using M8 bolts

6B

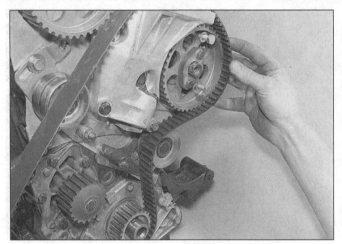

2.18a Fitting the timing belt over the injection pump sprocket . . .

2.18b . . . the camshaft sprocket . . .

water pump sprockets and over the tensioner roller. To ensure correct engagement, locate only a half width on the injection pump sprocket before feeding the timing belt onto the camshaft sprocket keeping the belt taut and fully engaged with the crankshaft sprocket. Locate the timing belt fully onto the sprockets (see illustrations).

Tensioning

19 With the pivot nut loose, slacken the tensioner adjustment bolt while holding the bracket against the spring tension. Slowly release the bracket until the roller presses against the timing belt. Retighten the adjustment bolt.
20 Remove the bolts from the camshaft and injection pump sprockets. Remove the metal dowel rod from the cylinder block.
21 Rotate the engine two complete turns in its normal direction. Do not rotate the engine backwards as the timing belt must be kept tight between the crankshaft, injection pump and camshaft sprockets.
22 Loosen the tensioner adjustment bolt to

allow the tensioner spring to push the roller against the timing belt, then tighten both the adjustment bolt and pivot nut.
23 Recheck the engine timing as described in paragraphs 11 and 12 then remove the metal dowel rod.
24 Refit the three timing cover sections and secure with the special clip and spring clips.
25 Refit the right-hand engine mounting bracket and tighten the nuts.
26 Remove the trolley jack or hoist.
27 Slide the pulley onto the front of the crankshaft.
28 Apply three drops of locking fluid on the threads of the crankshaft pulley bolt then insert it and tighten to the specified torque while holding the crankshaft stationary using the method described in paragraph 6.
29 Refit the alternator drivebelt and tension it as described in Section 1.
30 Reconnect the battery negative lead.
31 Refit the engine splash-guard under the right-hand front wheel arch.
32 Lower the vehicle to the ground.

3 Timing belt tensioner - removal and refitting

Removal

1 Apply the handbrake.
2 On manual transmission models jack up the front right-hand corner of the vehicle until the wheel is just clear of the ground. Support the vehicle on an axle stand and engage 4th or 5th gear so that the engine may be rotated by turning the right-hand wheel. On automatic transmission models use an open-ended spanner on the crankshaft pulley bolt.
3 Support the weight of the engine using a hoist or trolley jack.
4 Unscrew the nuts and remove the right-hand engine mounting bracket.
5 Remove the battery and the tray, then unbolt the support bracket (see illustration).
6 Unscrew the nut from the left-hand engine mounting and remove the rubber mounting.

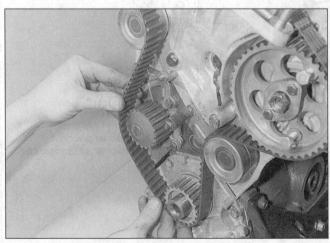

2.18c . . . and the water pump sprocket

3.5 Battery support bracket, also showing left-hand engine/transmission mounting

3.13 Home-made tool for holding the tensioner plunger

7 Move the engine and transmission to the left as far as possible and support it in this position.

8 Pull up the special clip, release the spring clips and withdraw the two timing cover sections.

9 Turn the engine by means of the front right-hand wheel or crankshaft pulley bolt until the three bolt holes in the camshaft and injection pump sprockets are aligned with the corresponding holes in the engine front plate.

10 Insert an 8.0 mm diameter metal dowel rod or drill through the special hole in the left-hand rear flange of the cylinder block by the starter motor. Then carefully turn the engine either way until the rod enters the TDC hole in the flywheel.

11 Insert three M8 bolts through the holes in the camshaft and injection pump sprockets and screw them into the engine front plate finger-tight.

12 Loosen the timing belt tensioner pivot nut and adjustment bolt, then turn the bracket anti-clockwise until the adjustment bolt is in the middle of the slot and retighten the bolt. If available use a 3/8 inch square drive extension in the hole provided to turn the bracket against the spring tension.

13 A tool must now be obtained to hold the tensioner plunger in the mounting bracket. Citroën tool 7009-T1 is designed to slide in

the two lower bolt holes of the mounting bracket and it is quite easy to fabricate a similar tool out of sheet metal using long bolts instead of metal dowel rods **(see illustration)**.

14 Unscrew the two lower bolts then fit the special tool. Grease the inner surface of the tool to prevent any damage to the end of the tensioner plunger.

15 Unscrew the pivot nut and adjustment bolt and withdraw the tensioner bracket, complete with roller.

16 Unbolt the engine mounting bracket noting that the uppermost bolt is on the inside face of the engine front plate.

17 Compress the tensioner plunger into the mounting bracket, remove the special tool then withdraw the plunger and spring.

Refitting

18 Refitting is a reversal of removal, but refer to Section 2, paragraphs 19 to 23 for details of the timing belt adjustment procedure.

4 Timing belt intermediate roller - removal and refitting

Removal

1 Follow the procedure given in paragraphs 1 to 12 of Section 3.

2 Remove the engine splash guard from under the right-hand front wheel arch.

3 Loosen the alternator pivot and adjustment bolts then unscrew the tension bolt until it is possible to slip the drivebelt from the pulleys.

4 With 4th or 5th gear selected on manual transmission models have an assistant depress the footbrake pedal, then unscrew the crankshaft pulley bolt. On automatic transmission models unbolt the transmission cover and lock the starter ring gear.

5 Slide the pulley from the front of the crankshaft.

6 Unbolt the lower timing cover.

7 Remove the spacer from the stud for the upper timing cover sections. Note the position

of the stud then unscrew and remove it.

8 Unscrew the remaining bolts securing the intermediate roller bracket to the cylinder block noting that the upper bolt also secures the engine mounting bracket.

9 Slightly loosen the remaining engine mounting bracket bolts then slide out the intermediate roller and bracket.

Refitting

10 Refitting is a reversal of removal, but note the following additional points:

a) Tighten all bolts to the specified torque

b) Apply three drops of locking fluid to the threads of the crankshaft pulley bolt before inserting it

c) Tension the alternator drivebelt as described in Section 1

d) Adjust the timing belt as described in Section 2, paragraphs 19 to 23

5 Engine right-hand mounting - removal and refitting

Removal

1 Support the engine with a hoist or with a trolley jack and block of wood beneath the sump.

2 Make up a tool similar to that shown, to engage with the slots in the rim of the rubber **(see illustrations)**. Unscrew the old rubber from the body using the tool.

3 Unscrew the nuts and remove the right-hand mounting bracket, noting the location of any shims.

Refitting

4 Refitting is a reversal of removal. Tighten the rubber firmly to the body using the tool, to the specified torque. With the weight of the engine on the mounting, the clearance between the mounting bracket and each rubber stop should be 1.0 ± 0.7 mm. If necessary adjust the clearance by means of shims positioned under the stops.

6B

5.2a Home-made tool for unscrewing the engine mounting rubber

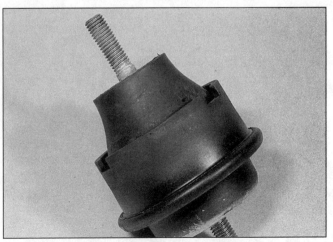

5.2b Engine mounting rubber showing slots

Notes

Chapter 7A
Citroën Xantia petrol 1993 to 1998

Contents

Specifications

Timing belt renewal interval . . . . Every 36 000 miles (60 000 km)

Note: *Although the normal interval for timing belt renewal is 72 000 miles (120 000 km), it is strongly recommended that the interval is halved on vehicles which are subjected to intensive use, ie, mainly short journeys or a lot of stop-start driving. The actual belt renewal interval is therefore very much up to the individual owner. That being said, it is highly recommended to err on the side of safety, and renew the belt at this earlier interval, bearing in mind the drastic consequences resulting from belt failure.*

Torque wrench settings	Nm	lbf ft
Auxiliary drivebelt tensioner bracket mounting bolts	22	16
Roadwheel bolts	90	66
8-valve engines		
Alternator bracket bolts	22	16
Camshaft sprocket retaining bolt:		
M10 bolt	35	26
M12 bolt	80	59
Crankshaft pulley retaining bolt*	130	96
Engine/transmission left-hand mounting:		
1.6 and 1.8 litre engines:		
Centre nut	80	59
Mounting bracket-to-body bolts	25	18
Mounting stud	50	37
2.0 litre engines:		
Centre nut	65	48
Mounting rubber-to-body bolts	20	15
Mounting stud	50	37
Engine/transmission rear mounting:		
1.6 and 1.8 litre engines:		
Mounting assembly-to-block bolts	45	33
Mounting bracket-to-mounting bolt	50	37
Mounting bracket-to-subframe bolt	50	37
2.0 litre engines:		
Mounting assembly-to-block bolts	45	33
Mounting link-to-mounting bolt	50	37
Mounting link-to-subframe bolt	70	52
Engine/transmission right-hand mounting:		
1.6 and 1.8 litre engines:		
Bracket-to-engine bolts*	45	33
Mounting bracket retaining nuts	45	33
2.0 litre engines:		
Curved retaining plate	20	15
Mounting bracket retaining nuts	45	33
Timing belt cover bolts	8	6
Timing belt tensioner pulley bolt:		
1.6 and 1.8 litre engines	21	15
2.0 litre engines*	17	13

* Use locking fluid

Torque wrench settings (continued)

	Nm	lbf ft
16-valve engines		
Camshaft sprocket-to-hub retaining bolts	10	7
Camshaft sprocket hub-to-camshaft retaining bolts	75	55
Crankshaft pulley retaining bolt*	130	96
Engine/transmission left-hand mounting:		
Centre nut	65	48
Mounting bracket-to-body	30	22
Mounting stud bracket-to-transmission	60	44
Mounting stud-to-transmission	60	44
Rubber mounting-to-bracket bolts	30	22
Engine/transmission right-hand mounting:		
1.8 litre engines:		
Mounting bracket-to-engine bolts	60	44
Mounting bracket-to-engine nuts	45	33
Mounting bracket-to-rubber mounting nut	45	33
Rubber mounting-to-body nut	40	30
2.0 litre engines:		
Mounting bracket-to-engine nuts/bolts	80	59
Mounting bracket-to-rubber mounting nut	45	33
Rubber mounting-to-body nut	40	30
Timing belt cover bolts	8	6
Timing belt idler pulley bolt	37	27
Timing belt tensioner pulley bolt	21	15

*Use locking fluid

1 Auxiliary drivebelt - removal, refitting and adjustment

1 Chock the rear wheels, then jack up the front of the car and support it on axle stands. Remove the right-hand front roadwheel.

2 To gain access to the right-hand end of the engine, the wheelarch plastic liner must be removed. The liner is secured by a bolt to the front subframe, and by various screws and clips under the wheelarch. Release all the fasteners, and remove liner from under the front wing **(see illustrations)**.

1.2a The wheelarch liner is secured by a bolt to the front subframe . . .

1.2b . . . and by various screws . . .

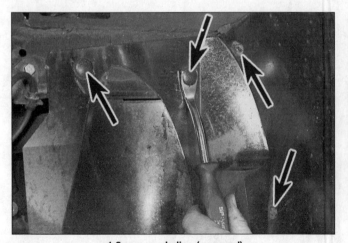

1.2c . . . and clips (arrowed)

1.2d Removing the wheelarch liner from under the front wing

1.4a Removing the tensioner pulley bracket upper mounting bolt . . .

1.4b . . . and lower mounting bolt

Manual adjuster

Removal

3 Disconnect the battery negative lead.
4 Slacken the tensioner pulley bracket adjustment/mounting bolts (one located in the middle of the pulley and the other located below on the bracket) (see illustrations).
5 Fully tighten the adjustment bolt to its stop, then slip the drivebelt from the pulleys (see illustrations).
6 Check that the tensioner pulley turns freely without any sign of roughness.

Refitting and adjustment

7 Fit the belt around the pulleys, and take up the slack in the belt by tightening the adjuster bolt.
8 The belt should be tensioned so that, under firm thumb pressure, there is approximately 5.0 mm of free movement at the mid-point between the pulleys on the longest belt run.
9 To adjust, unscrew the adjustment bolt until the tension is correct, then rotate the crankshaft a couple of times, and recheck the tension. Securely tighten the tensioner pulley bracket adjustment/mounting bolts.

10 Reconnect the battery negative lead.
11 Refit the wheelarch liner. Refit the roadwheel, and lower the vehicle to the ground.

Automatic adjuster

Removal

12 Disconnect the battery negative lead.
13 Using a square drive key in the square hole in the bottom of the automatic adjuster bracket, turn the bracket anticlockwise to release the tension on the belt. Hold the bracket in this position by inserting a 4.0 mm Allen key or drill bit through the special hole.
14 Unscrew the mounting bolts and remove the tensioner roller, then slip the auxiliary drivebelt from the pulleys.
15 Check that the tensioner pulleys turn freely without any sign of roughness.

Refitting

16 Fit the belt around the pulleys, making sure that it is engaged with the correct grooves in the pulleys.
17 Refit the tensioner roller and tighten the mounting bolts.
18 Using the square drive key hold the

automatic adjuster, then release the Allen key or drill bit, and slowly allow the tensioner to tighten the belt. Check again that the belt is correctly located in the pulley grooves.
19 Reconnect the battery negative lead.
20 Refit the wheelarch liner. Refit the roadwheel, and lower the vehicle to the ground.

2 Engine assembly/valve timing holes - general information and usage

Note: Do not attempt to rotate the engine whilst the crankshaft/camshaft are locked in position. If the engine is to be left in this state for a long period of time, it is a good idea to place suitable warning notices inside the vehicle, and in the engine compartment. This will reduce the possibility of the engine being accidentally cranked on the starter motor, which is likely to cause damage with the locking pins in place.

1 On all models, timing holes are drilled in the camshaft sprocket(s) and crankshaft pulley. The holes are used to align the crankshaft and

7A

1.5a Tighten the drivebelt tension adjustment bolt to its stop . . .

1.5b . . . and remove the drivebelt from the pulleys

2.6 8 mm diameter drill inserted through the crankshaft pulley timing hole

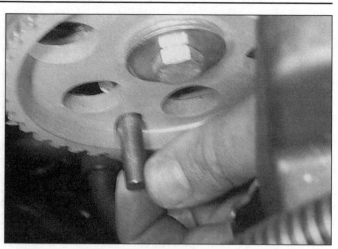

2.7 9.5 mm diameter drill inserted through the camshaft pulley timing hole

camshaft, to prevent the possibility of the valves contacting the pistons when refitting the timing belt. When the holes are aligned with their corresponding holes in the cylinder head and cylinder block (as appropriate), suitable diameter pins can be inserted to lock both the camshaft and crankshaft in position. Proceed as follows:

2 Remove the timing belt upper (outer) cover with reference to Section 4.

3 Jack up the front of the car and support it on axle stands. Remove the right-hand front roadwheel.

4 From underneath the front of the car, unscrew the bolts and prise out the clips securing the plastic cover to the inner wing valance. Remove the cover to gain access to the crankshaft pulley bolt. The crankshaft can then be turned using a suitable socket and extension bar fitted to the pulley bolt. Note that the crankshaft must always be turned in a clockwise direction (viewed from the right-hand side of vehicle).

8-valve engine models

5 Rotate the crankshaft pulley until the timing

hole in the camshaft sprocket is aligned with its corresponding hole in the cylinder head. Note that the holes are aligned when the sprocket hole is in the 8 o'clock position, when viewed from the right-hand end of the engine.

6 With the camshaft sprocket timing hole correctly positioned, insert an 8 mm diameter bolt or drill through the timing (8 mm diameter) hole in the crankshaft pulley, and locate it in the corresponding hole in the end of the cylinder block **(see illustration)**. Note that it may be necessary to rotate the crankshaft slightly to get the holes to align.

7 Once the crankshaft pulley is locked in position, insert an 9.5 mm diameter bolt or drill through the camshaft sprocket hole and locate it in the cylinder head **(see illustration)**.

8 The crankshaft and camshaft are now locked in position, preventing rotation.

16-valve engine models

9 Rotate the crankshaft pulley until the timing holes in both camshafts are aligned with their

corresponding holes in the cylinder head. The holes are aligned when the inlet camshaft sprocket hole is in approximately the 5 o'clock position and the exhaust camshaft sprocket hole is in approximately the 7 o'clock position, when viewed from the right-hand end of the engine.

10 With the camshaft sprocket holes correctly positioned, insert a 6 mm diameter bolt or drill through the timing hole in the crankshaft pulley, and locate it in the corresponding hole in the end of the engine **(see illustration)**. Note that the hole size may vary according to the type of pulley fitted and auxiliary drivebelt arrangement. If the bolt or drill is not a snug fit, try a larger size until a good fit is achieved in both the pulley and cylinder block.

11 With the crankshaft locked in position, insert a suitable bolt or drill through the timing hole in each camshaft sprocket and locate it in the cylinder head **(see illustration)**.

12 The crankshaft and camshafts are now locked in position, preventing rotation.

2.10 Drill bit (arrowed) inserted through crankshaft pulley

2.11 Bolts (arrowed) inserted through timing holes in each camshaft sprocket

3.3a Removing the crankshaft pulley retaining bolt

3.3b Removing the crankshaft pulley from the end of the crankshaft

3 Crankshaft pulley - removal and refitting

Removal

1 Remove the auxiliary drivebelt (Section 1).
2 To prevent the crankshaft turning whilst the pulley retaining bolt is being slackened, select 4th gear and have an assistant apply the brakes firmly. *Do not* attempt to lock the pulley by inserting a bolt/drill through the timing hole. If the locking pin is in position, temporarily remove it prior to slackening the pulley bolt, then refit it once the bolt has been slackened.
3 Unscrew the retaining bolt and washer, then slide the pulley off the end of the crankshaft **(see illustrations)**. If the pulley locating roll pin or Woodruff key (as applicable) is a loose fit, remove it and store it with the pulley for safe-keeping. If the pulley is tight fit, it can be drawn off the crankshaft using a suitable puller.

Refitting

4 Ensure the Woodruff key is correctly located in its crankshaft groove, or that the roll pin is in position (as applicable). Refit the pulley to the end of the crankshaft, aligning its locating groove or hole with the Woodruff key or pin.
5 Thoroughly clean the threads of the pulley retaining bolt, then apply a coat of locking compound to the bolt threads. Citroën recommend Loctite (available from your Citroën dealer); in the absence of this, any good-quality locking compound may be used.
6 Refit the crankshaft pulley retaining bolt and washer. Tighten the bolt to the specified torque, preventing the crankshaft from turning using the method employed on removal.
7 Refit and tension the auxiliary drivebelt as described in Section 1.

4 Timing belt covers - removal and refitting

1.6 and 1.8 litre 8-valve models

Upper cover

1 Release the retaining clips, and free the fuel hoses from the top of the cover.
2 Undo the two cover retaining bolts (situated at the base of the cover), and remove the cover from the engine compartment.

Centre cover

3 Slacken and remove the two cover retaining bolts (located directly beneath the mounting bracket). Move the cover upwards to free it from the two locating pins situated at the base of the cover, and remove it from the engine compartment.

Lower cover

4 Remove the crankshaft pulley (Section 3).
5 Remove the centre cover (paragraph 3).
6 Undo the two cover retaining bolts, and remove the cover from the engine. Note that

on some models it may be necessary to unbolt the auxiliary drivebelt tensioner assembly and remove it from the engine in order to allow the cover to be removed.
7 Refitting is a reversal of the relevant removal procedure, ensuring that each cover section is correctly located, and that the cover retaining nuts and/or bolts are securely tightened to the specified torque, where given.

2.0 litre 8-valve models

Upper cover

8 Release the retaining clip, and free the fuel hoses from the top of the timing belt cover. Slacken and remove the two cover retaining bolts, then lift the upper cover upwards and out of the engine compartment **(see illustrations)**.

Lower cover

9 Remove the crankshaft pulley (Section 3).
10 Slacken and remove the three retaining bolts, then remove the lower timing belt cover from the engine. Note that on some models it may be necessary to unbolt the auxiliary drivebelt tensioner assembly and remove it

7A

4.8a Upper timing belt cover retaining bolts (arrowed)

4.8b Removing the upper timing belt cover

4.10a Removing the auxiliary drivebelt tensioner assembly

4.10b Unscrew the retaining bolts . . .

4.10c . . . and remove the lower timing cover

from the engine in order to allow the cover to be removed (see illustrations).

Refitting

11 Refitting is a reversal of the relevant removal procedure, ensuring that each cover section is correctly located, and that the cover retaining nuts and/or bolts are securely tightened to the specified torque, where given.

1.8 and 2.0 litre 16-valve models

Upper (outer) cover

12 Unclip the wiring harness from its location in the shaped top of the engine right-hand mounting, and from the inlet manifold bracket (see illustrations). Where applicable, release the air conditioning hose which runs between the timing belt cover and the engine mounting. Move the hose and wiring harness to one side (do NOT attempt to disconnect the air conditioning hose).

13 Prise out the clips and remove the trim cover from the top of the engine right-hand mounting (see illustrations).

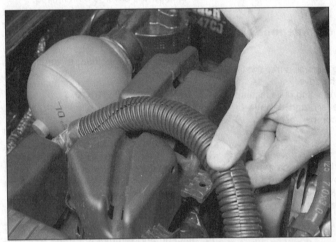

4.12a Unclip the wiring harness from the engine mounting . . .

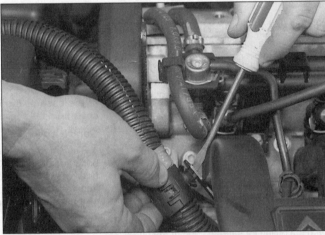

4.12b . . . and from the inlet manifold bracket

4.13a Using a suitable tool, release the retaining clips . . .

4.13b . . . and remove the trim cover from the top of the engine mounting

4.14 Lift up the locking tab in the centre of the cover

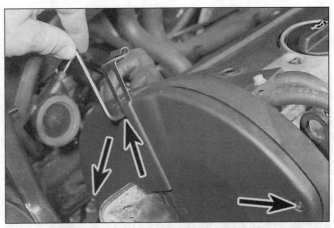

4.15a Remove the Allen screws (arrowed) . . .

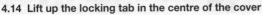

14 On models up to 1998, lift the tab provided in the centre of the timing belt cover upwards to release the centre locating pegs **(see illustration)**.

15 Unscrew and remove the three upper retaining screws, and withdraw the timing belt cover **(see illustrations)**. Recover the rubber pads from the centre locating pegs, where applicable.

Lower cover

16 Remove the crankshaft pulley (Section 3).

17 Slacken and remove the retaining bolts, then remove the lower timing belt cover from the engine. Note that on some models it may be necessary to unbolt the auxiliary drivebelt tensioner assembly and remove it from the engine in order to allow the cover to be removed.

Upper (inner) cover

18 Remove the timing belt as described in Section 5.

19 Remove both camshaft sprockets as described in Section 6.

20 Remove the six bolts securing the cover to the side of the cylinder head, and remove the cover from the engine.

Refitting

21 Refitting is a reversal of removal. When

refitting the upper (outer) cover with the locating tab, ensure that the rubber pads are in place on the centre locating pegs, where applicable. Locate the cover in place over the centre and lower pegs, then press the centre of the cover inwards to engage the locating pegs, and secure by lowering the plastic tab. Refit and locate all other components securely.

---

5 Timing belt -
removal and refitting

Note: *Citroën specify the use of a special electronic tool (SEEM 4122-T) to correctly set the timing belt tension.*

Removal

1 Disconnect the battery negative terminal.

2 Jack up the front of the vehicle and support it on axle stands. Remove the right-hand front wheel.

3 To improve access, refer to Section 7 and remove the engine right-hand mounting. This is not essential, but it does make several of

the timing belt components much easier to remove with the engine in the car.

4 Where applicable, prise out the clips and unbolt the inner splash guard.

5 Remove the auxiliary drivebelt as described in Section 1. Where applicable, unbolt and remove the auxiliary drivebelt tensioner.

6 Remove the timing belt upper (outer) cover with reference to Section 4.

7 Align the engine assembly/valve timing holes as described in Section 2, and lock the camshaft sprocket(s) in position. *Do not attempt to rotate the engine whilst the pins are in position.*

8 Remove the crankshaft pulley as described in Section 3.

9 On 1.6 and 1.8 litre 8-valve models, remove the centre and lower timing belt covers as described in Section 4. On all other models, unbolt and remove the timing belt lower cover (refer to Section 4 if necessary).

10 Refit the crankshaft pulley, and tighten the bolt moderately, holding the engine against rotation as for removal. Fit the locking tool through the crankshaft pulley, to prevent rotation.

11 Loosen the timing belt tensioner pulley retaining bolt **(see illustration)**. Pivot the

7A

4.15b . . . and lift away the upper cover

5.11 Release the belt tensioner retaining bolt

5.12 Lift the timing belt off the sprockets

5.17 Fit the timing belt over the water pump sprocket

pulley in a clockwise direction, using a suitable square-section key fitted to the hole in the pulley hub, then securely retighten the retaining bolt.

12 If the timing belt is to be re-used, use white paint or chalk to mark the direction of rotation on the belt (if markings do not already exist), then slip the belt off the sprockets **(see illustration)**. Note that the crankshaft must not be rotated whilst the belt is removed.

13 If signs of oil contamination are found, trace the source of the oil leak and rectify it. Wash down the engine timing belt area and all related components, to remove all traces of oil.

Refitting

8-valve engine models

14 Before refitting, thoroughly clean the timing belt sprockets. Check that the tensioner pulley rotates freely, without any sign of roughness. If necessary, renew the tensioner pulley as described in Section 6.

15 Ensure that the camshaft sprocket and crankshaft pulley locking pins are still in position.

16 Manoeuvre the timing belt into position, ensuring that any arrows on the belt are pointing in the direction of rotation (clockwise when viewed from the right-hand end of the engine).

17 Do not twist the timing belt sharply while refitting it. Fit the belt over the crankshaft and camshaft sprockets (if preferred, the crankshaft pulley can be removed for this stage, but ensure that the crankshaft is not moved from its reference position). Ensure that the belt front run is taut - ie, any slack should be on the tensioner pulley side of the belt. Fit the belt over the water pump sprocket and tensioner pulley **(see illustration)**. Ensure that the belt teeth are seated centrally in the sprockets.

18 If removed, refit the crankshaft pulley at this stage and tighten the bolt moderately,

then refit the locking pin. **Note:** *The timing belt is tensioned with the timing covers removed, then the crankshaft pulley is removed again to fit the belt lower cover, before being finally refitted.*

19 Loosen the tensioner pulley retaining bolt. Using the square-section key, pivot the pulley anti-clockwise to remove all free play from the timing belt.

20 Fit the special belt tension measuring equipment to the front run of the timing belt. The tensioner roller should be adjusted so that the initial belt tension is 16 ± 2 units on 2.0 litre models, and 30 ± 2 units on 1.6 and 1.8 litre models.

21 Remove the locking pins, then rotate the crankshaft through two complete rotations in a clockwise direction (viewed from the right-hand end of the engine). Realign the camshaft and crankshaft engine assembly/valve timing holes (see Section 2). *Do not* at any time rotate the crankshaft anti-clockwise. Both camshaft and crankshaft timing holes should be aligned so that the locking pins can be easily inserted. This indicates that the valve timing is correct. If all is well, remove the pins.

22 If the timing holes are not correctly positioned, repeat the fitting procedure so far.

23 Rotate the crankshaft two more turns without turning backwards and refit the camshaft locking pin, then check that the final belt tension on the taut front run of the belt is 44 ± 2 units. If not, repeat the complete fitting procedure.

24 With the belt tension correctly set remove the camshaft locking pin, then remove the crankshaft pulley and refit the timing cover(s).

25 Refit the crankshaft pulley but this time apply locking fluid to the threads of the bolt before inserting it. Tighten the bolt to the specified torque and refer to Section 3 if necessary.

16-valve engine models

26 Before refitting, thoroughly clean the timing belt sprockets. Check that the

tensioner and idler pulleys rotate freely, without any sign of roughness. If necessary, renew the pulleys as described in Section 6.

27 Ensure that the camshaft sprocket locking pins are still in position. Temporarily refit the crankshaft pulley (if removed), and insert the locking pin through the pulley timing hole to ensure that the crankshaft is still correctly positioned.

28 Without removing the locking pins, on models up to 1998, slacken the camshaft sprocket retaining bolts (three on each sprocket). On models after 1998, only the single bolt securing each camshaft sprocket need be slackened. Check that both sprockets are free to turn within the limits of their elongated bolt holes, or that the protruding lug on single-bolt sprockets can move within its limits **(see illustrations)**.

29 Tighten the camshaft sprocket retaining bolts finger-tight, then slacken them all by one sixth of a turn.

30 Again without removing the locking pins, turn each camshaft sprocket clockwise to the

5.28a Slacken the camshaft sprocket retaining bolts (arrowed)

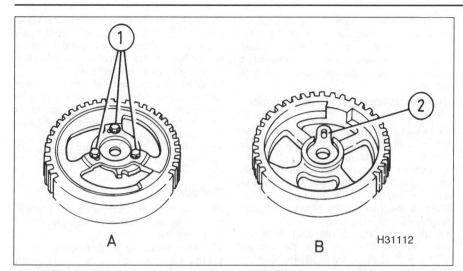

5.28b Camshaft sprocket details - models up to 1998 (A) have three retaining bolts (1) in elongated slots, while models after 1998 have a single bolt and a protruding lug (2)

ends of their retaining bolt slots, or until the protruding lug reaches the end of its travel.

31 Remove the crankshaft pulley. Manoeuvre the timing belt into position on the crankshaft sprocket, ensuring that any arrows on the belt are pointing in the direction of rotation (clockwise when viewed from the right-hand end of the engine).

32 Refit the timing belt lower cover and the crankshaft pulley (Sections 4 and 3).

33 With the timing belt engaged with the crankshaft sprocket, keep it tight on its right-hand run and engage it with the front idler pulley then up and into engagement with the inlet camshaft sprocket.

34 Keeping the belt tight and rotating the inlet camshaft sprocket anti-clockwise as necessary, feed the belt over the exhaust camshaft sprocket, taking care not to let the belt jump a tooth on the crankshaft sprocket as it is being fitted.

35 While still keeping the belt tight, feed it over the rear tensioner pulley and finally around the coolant pump.

36 If the special belt tension measuring equipment is available, it should be fitted to the front run of the timing belt.

37 The tensioner pulley should be adjusted, by turning it anti-clockwise to give a belt pre-tensioning setting of 45 units. Hold the tensioner pulley in this position and tighten the retaining bolt to the specified torque.

38 Check that the sprockets have not been turned so far that the retaining bolts are at the end of their slots, or that the protruding lug on single-bolt sprockets is at the end of its travel. If either condition is evident, repeat the refitting operation. If all is satisfactory, tighten the sprocket retaining bolts to the specified torque.

39 Remove the locking pins, then rotate the crankshaft through two complete rotations in a clockwise direction (viewed from the right-hand end of the engine). Realign the

crankshaft engine assembly/valve timing hole and refit the locking pin to the crankshaft pulley.

40 Slacken the camshaft sprocket retaining bolts, retighten them finger-tight, then slacken them all by one sixth of a turn.

41 Refit the camshaft sprocket locking pins, then slacken the tensioner pulley retaining bolt once more. Refit the belt tension measuring equipment to the front run of the belt, and turn the tensioner pulley to give a final setting of 26 units (models with three bolts per camshaft sprocket) or 32 units (single-bolt sprocket models) on the tensioning gauge. Hold the tensioner pulley in this position and tighten the retaining bolt to the specified torque.

42 Retighten all sprocket retaining bolts to the specified torque.

43 The belt tension must now be checked as follows. Remove the locking pins, then rotate the crankshaft once again through two complete rotations in a clockwise direction. Realign the crankshaft engine assembly/valve timing hole, and refit the locking pin to the crankshaft pulley.

44 Slacken the camshaft sprocket retaining bolts, retighten them finger-tight, then slacken them all by one sixth of a turn.

45 Refit the camshaft sprocket locking pins, turning the sprockets slightly if required. Tighten the camshaft sprocket retaining bolts to the specified torque.

46 Remove the camshaft and crankshaft locking tools. Turn the crankshaft approximately one quarter of a turn in the normal direction of rotation, until the locking tool hole in the crankshaft pulley is aligned with the timing belt lower cover front retaining bolt. It is important that this position is achieved ONLY by turning the belt forwards - if the belt is turned back at all to achieve alignment, the belt tension check will not be valid.

47 In this position, refit the tension measuring

equipment to the front run of the belt, and check that the reading is between 32 and 40 units. If not, the entire belt tensioning procedure must be repeated from the start.

48 Once the belt tension has been correctly set, refit the engine right-hand mounting components as described in Section 7.

49 Refit the timing belt upper, centre and lower covers (as applicable) as described in Section 4.

50 Refit the auxiliary drivebelt tensioner then refit and tension the drivebelt with reference to Section 1.

51 Refit the inner splash guard and front right-hand wheel, then lower the vehicle to the ground.

52 Reconnect the battery negative terminal.

---

6 Timing belt tensioner and sprockets - removal and refitting

Note: *This Section describes the removal and refitting of the components concerned as individual operations - if more than one is to be removed at the same time, start by removing the timing belt as described in Section 5; remove the actual component as described below, ignoring the preliminary dismantling steps.*

Removal

1 Disconnect the battery negative terminal.

2 Align the engine assembly/valve timing holes as described in Section 2, locking the camshaft sprocket(s) and the crankshaft pulley in position, and proceed as described under the relevant sub-heading. *Do not attempt to rotate the engine whilst the pins are in position. Once the sprockets have been removed, their shafts should not be turned.*

Camshaft sprocket - 8-valve engine models

3 Remove the timing belt upper cover as described in Section 4.

4 Loosen the timing belt tensioner pulley retaining bolt. Rotate the pulley in a clockwise direction, using a suitable square-section key fitted to the hole in the pulley hub, then retighten the retaining bolt.

5 Remove the locking pin from the camshaft sprocket. Disengage the timing belt from the sprocket and position it clear, taking care not to bend or twist the belt sharply.

6 Slacken the camshaft sprocket retaining bolt and remove it, along with its washer. To prevent the camshaft rotating as the bolt is slackened, a sprocket holding tool will be required. In the absence of the special Citroën tool, an acceptable substitute can be

7A

6.6 Using a home-made tool to retain the camshaft sprocket whilst the sprocket retaining bolt is tightened

fabricated at home **(see illustration)**. *Do not attempt to use the sprocket locking pin to prevent the sprocket from rotating whilst the bolt is slackened.*

7 With the retaining bolt removed, slide the sprocket off the end of the camshaft. If the locating peg is a loose fit in the rear of the sprocket, remove it for safe-keeping. Examine the camshaft oil seal for signs of oil leakage and, if necessary, renew it.

Camshaft sprockets - 16-valve engine models

8 Remove the timing belt upper (outer) and lower covers as described in Section 4.

9 For improved access, support the engine on a jack, and remove the right-hand engine mounting components as described in Section 7.

10 Loosen the timing belt tensioner pulley retaining bolt and pivot the pulley in a clockwise direction, using a suitable square-section key fitted to the hole in the pulley hub, then retighten the retaining bolt.

11 Check that the camshaft sprocket locking pins are still in position, then disengage the timing belt from the camshaft sprockets and position it clear, taking care not to bend or twist the belt sharply.

12 If the early-type sprockets are to be removed without their hubs, undo the three retaining bolts and remove the relevant sprocket. Suitably mark the sprockets inlet and/or exhaust as they are removed (although in fact the sprockets are identical).

13 If both the sprockets and the hubs are to be removed, remove the sprocket locking pins, then slacken the sprocket hub centre retaining bolt. To prevent the sprockets rotating as the bolt is slackened, a sprocket holding tool will be required. In the absence of the special Peugeot tool, an acceptable substitute can be fabricated at home **(see illustration 6.6)**. *Do not* attempt to use the sprocket locking pin to prevent the sprocket from rotating whilst the bolt is slackened.

14 Undo the retaining bolt(s) and remove the relevant sprocket. Remove the previously-slackened hub retaining bolt, and withdraw the hub from the end of the camshaft. Note that the hubs are marked for identification

with a single digit on their front face. On 1.8 litre models, the inlet hub is marked 1 and the exhaust hub is marked 2. On 2.0 litre models, the inlet hub is marked 3 and the exhaust hub is marked 4. Make your own markings if none are visible.

Crankshaft sprocket - 8-valve engine models

15 Remove the upper, centre and/or lower timing belt cover(s) (as applicable) as described in Section 4.

16 Loosen the timing belt tensioner pulley retaining bolt. Rotate the pulley in a clockwise direction, using a suitable square-section key fitted to the hole in the pulley hub, then retighten the retaining bolt.

17 Disengage the timing belt from the crankshaft sprocket, and slide the sprocket off the end of the crankshaft. Remove the Woodruff key from the crankshaft, and store it with the sprocket for safe-keeping. Where necessary, also slide the spacer (where fitted) off the end of the crankshaft.

18 Examine the crankshaft oil seal for signs of oil leakage and, if necessary, renew it.

Crankshaft sprocket - 16-valve engine models

19 Remove the timing belt upper (outer) and lower covers as described in Section 4.

20 For improved access, support the engine on a jack, and remove the right-hand engine mounting components as described in Section 18.

21 Loosen the timing belt tensioner pulley retaining bolt, and pivot the pulley in a clockwise direction, using a suitable square-section key fitted to the hole in the pulley hub, then retighten the retaining bolt.

22 Check that the camshaft sprocket locking pins are still in position, then disengage the timing belt from the crankshaft sprocket, and slide the sprocket off the end of the crankshaft. Remove the Woodruff key from the crankshaft, and store it with the sprocket for safe-keeping.

23 Examine the crankshaft oil seal for signs of oil leakage and, if necessary, renew it.

Tensioner pulley - 8-valve engine models

24 Remove the upper and where necessary the centre timing belt covers as described in Section 4.

25 Slacken and remove the timing belt tensioner pulley retaining bolt, and slide the pulley off its mounting stud. Examine the mounting stud for signs of damage and if necessary, renew it.

Tensioner and idler pulleys - 16-valve engine models

26 Remove the timing belt upper (outer) and lower covers as described in Section 4.

27 For improved access, support the engine on a jack, and remove the right-hand engine mounting components as described in Section 7.

28 Loosen the timing belt tensioner pulley retaining bolt, and pivot the pulley in a clockwise direction, using a suitable square-section key fitted to the hole in the pulley hub, then retighten the retaining bolt.

29 Check that the camshaft sprocket locking pins are still in position, then disengage the timing belt from the camshaft sprockets and position it clear, taking care not to bend or twist the belt sharply.

30 Undo the tensioner and idler pulley retaining bolts, and remove the pulleys from the engine.

Refitting

31 Clean the camshaft/crankshaft sprockets thoroughly, and renew any that show signs of wear, damage or cracks.

32 Clean the tensioner/idler pulleys, but do not use any strong solvent, as it may enter the pulley bearings. Check that the pulleys rotate freely, with no sign of stiffness or free play. Renew them if there is any doubt about their condition, or if there are any obvious signs of wear or damage.

Camshaft sprocket - 8-valve engine models

33 Refit the locating peg (where removed) to the rear of the sprocket. Locate the sprocket on the end of the camshaft, ensuring that the locating peg is correctly engaged with the cut-out in the camshaft end.

34 Refit the sprocket retaining bolt and washer, and tighten it to the specified torque. Retain the sprocket with the tool used on removal.

35 Realign the hole in the camshaft sprocket with the corresponding hole in the cylinder head, and refit the locking pin. Check that the crankshaft pulley locking pin is still in position.

36 Refit the timing belt to the camshaft sprocket. Ensure that the front run of the belt is taut - ie, that any slack is on the tensioner pulley side of the belt. Do not twist the belt sharply while refitting it, and ensure that the belt teeth are seated centrally in the sprockets.

37 With the timing belt correctly engaged on the sprockets, tension the belt as described in Section 5.

38 Once the belt is correctly tensioned, refit the timing belt covers (see Section 4).

Camshaft sprockets - 16-valve engine models

39 If both the sprockets and the hubs have been removed, engage the sprocket hub with the camshaft. Ensure that the correct hub is fitted to the relevant camshaft by observing the hub identification markings described in paragraph 14.

40 Refit the sprocket retaining bolt and washer, and tighten it to the specified torque. On models with the early-type three-bolt sprockets, temporarily refit the sprockets, to allow the hub to be held stationary with the tool as the bolt is tightened.

41 Turn the hub so that the locking pin can be engaged.

42 If the three-bolt sprockets have been removed, leaving the hubs in place, position the sprocket on its hub, and refit the three bolts finger-tight only at this stage. Ensure that the correct sprocket is fitted to the relevant camshaft according to the identification made on removal (see paragraph 12).

43 Relocate and tension the timing belt as described in Section 5. If removed, refit the engine right-hand mounting as described in Section 7.

Crankshaft sprocket - 8-valve engine models

44 Slide the spacer (where fitted) into position, taking great care not to damage the crankshaft oil, and refit the Woodruff key to its slot in the crankshaft end.

45 Slide on the crankshaft sprocket, aligning its slot with the Woodruff key.

46 Ensure that the camshaft sprocket locking pin is still in position. Temporarily refit the crankshaft pulley, and insert the locking pin through the pulley timing hole, to ensure that the crankshaft is still correctly positioned.

47 Remove the crankshaft pulley. Engage the timing belt with the crankshaft sprocket. Ensure that the belt front run is taut - ie, that any slack is on the tensioner pulley side of the belt. Fit the belt over the water pump sprocket and tensioner pulley. Do not twist the belt sharply while refitting it, and ensure that the belt teeth are seated centrally in the sprockets.

48 Tension the timing belt as described in Section 5.

49 Remove the crankshaft pulley, then refit the timing belt cover(s) as described in Section 4.

50 Refit the crankshaft pulley as described in Section 3, and reconnect the battery negative terminal.

Crankshaft sprocket - 16-valve engine models

51 Refit the Woodruff key to its slot in the crankshaft end.

52 Slide on the crankshaft sprocket, aligning its slot with the Woodruff key.

53 Relocate and tension the timing belt as described in Section 5. If removed, refit the engine right-hand mounting as described in Section 7.

Tensioner pulley - 8-valve engine models

54 Refit the tensioner pulley to its mounting stud, and fit the retaining bolt.

55 Ensure that the front run of the belt is taut - ie, that any slack is on the pulley side of the belt. Check that the belt is centrally located on all its sprockets. Rotate the pulley anti-clockwise to remove all free play from the timing belt, and securely tighten the pulley retaining nut.

56 Tension the belt as described in Section 5.

57 Once the belt is correctly tensioned, refit the timing belt covers as described in Section 4.

Tensioner and idler pulleys - 16-valve engine models

58 Refit the tensioner and idler pulleys and secure with the retaining bolts.

59 Relocate and tension the timing belt as described in Section 5. If removed, refit the engine right-hand mounting as described in Section 7.

7 Engine right-hand mounting - removal and refitting

1.6 and 1.8 litre models

1 Disconnect the battery negative lead. Release all the relevant hoses and wiring from their retaining clips, and position clear of the mounting so that they do not hinder the removal procedure.

2 Place a jack beneath the engine, with a block of wood on the jack head. Raise the jack until it is supporting the weight of the engine.

3 Slacken and remove the three nuts securing the right-hand mounting bracket to the engine. Release the securing clips and remove the plastic cover from the engine mounting on the inner wing. Remove the single nut securing the bracket to the mounting rubber, and lift off the bracket.

4 Lift the rubber buffer plate off the mounting rubber stud, then unscrew the mounting rubber from the body and remove it from the vehicle. If necessary, the mounting bracket can be unbolted and removed from the side of the cylinder head.

5 Check all components carefully for signs of wear or damage, and renew them where necessary.

6 On reassembly, screw the mounting rubber into the vehicle body, and tighten it securely. Where removed, refit the mounting bracket to the side of the cylinder head, apply a drop of locking compound to the retaining bolts and tighten them to the specified torque.

7 Refit the rubber buffer plate to the mounting rubber stud, and install the mounting bracket.

8 Tighten the mounting bracket retaining nuts to the specified torque setting. Refit the plastic cover over the engine mounting, and secure with the clips.

9 Remove the jack from below the engine, and reconnect the battery negative terminal.

2.0 litre models

10 Disconnect the battery negative lead. Release all the relevant hoses and wiring from their retaining clips. Place the hoses/wiring clear of the mounting so that the removal procedure is not hindered.

11 Place a jack beneath the engine, with a block of wood on the jack head. Raise the jack until it is supporting the weight of the engine.

12 Release the securing clips and remove the plastic cover from the engine mounting on the inner wing. Undo the two bolts securing the curved mounting retaining plate to the body. Lift off the plate, and withdraw the rubber damper from the top of the mounting bracket.

13 Slacken and remove the two nuts and two bolts securing the right-hand engine/transmission mounting bracket to the engine. Remove the single nut securing the bracket to the mounting rubber, and lift off the bracket.

14 Lift the rubber buffer plate off the mounting rubber stud, then unscrew the mounting rubber from the body and remove it from the vehicle. If necessary, the mounting bracket can be unbolted and removed from the front of the cylinder block.

15 Check all components carefully for signs of wear or damage, and renew as necessary.

16 On reassembly, screw the mounting rubber into the vehicle body, and tighten it securely. Where removed, refit the mounting bracket to the front of the cylinder head, and securely tighten its retaining bolts.

17 Refit the rubber buffer plate to the mounting rubber stud, and install the mounting bracket.

18 Tighten the mounting bracket retaining nuts to the specified torque setting, and remove the jack from underneath the engine.

19 Refit the rubber damper to the top of the mounting bracket, and refit the curved retaining plate. Tighten the retaining plate bolts to the specified torque, and reconnect the battery. Refit the plastic cover over the engine mounting, and secure with the clips.

7A

Notes

Chapter 7B
Citroën Xantia diesel 1993 to 1998

Contents

Specifications

Timing belt renewal interval . . . . Every 36 000 miles (60 000 km)

Note: *Although the normal interval for timing belt renewal is 72 000 miles (120 000 km), it is strongly recommended that the interval is halved on vehicles which are subjected to intensive use, ie, mainly short journeys or a lot of stop-start driving. The actual belt renewal interval is therefore very much up to the individual owner. That being said, it is highly recommended to err on the side of safety, and renew the belt at this earlier interval, bearing in mind the drastic consequences resulting from belt failure.*

Torque wrench settings	Nm	lbf ft
Auxiliary drivebelt eccentric roller securing bolt	50	37
Auxiliary drivebelt tensioner bracket mounting bolts	22	16
Roadwheel bolts	90	66
1.9 litre engines		
Camshaft sprocket bolt	45	33
Crankshaft front oil seal housing bolts	16	12
Crankshaft pulley bolt:		
Stage 1	40	30
Stage 2	Tighten through a further 60°	
Camshaft cover bolts	20	15
Engine/transmission left-hand mounting:		
Mounting rubber-to-body bolts	20	15
Mounting stud	50	37
Centre nut	65	48
Engine/transmission rear mounting:		
Mounting assembly-to-block bolts	45	33
Mounting link-to-mounting bolt	50	37
Mounting link-to-subframe bolt	70	52

Torque wrench settings (continued)

	Nm	lbf ft
1.9 litre engines (continued)		
Engine/transmission right-hand mounting:		
Engine (tensioner assembly) bracket bolts	18	13
Mounting bracket retaining nuts	45	33
Curved retaining plate bolts	20	15
Fuel injection pump sprocket nut	50	37
Fuel injection pump sprocket puller retaining screws	10	7
Timing belt cover bolts	8	6
Timing belt tensioner adjustment bolt	18	13
Timing belt tensioner pivot nut	18	13
2.1 litre engines		
Camshaft sprocket bolt	50	37
Crankshaft pulley bolt:		
Stage 1	40	30
Stage 2	Tighten through a further 60°	
Camshaft cover bolts	8	6
Engine/transmission left-hand mounting:		
Mounting rubber-to-body bolts	20	15
Mounting stud	50	37
Centre nut	65	48
Engine/transmission rear mounting:		
Mounting assembly-to-block bolts	45	33
Mounting link-to-mounting bolt	50	37
Mounting link-to-subframe bolt	70	52
Engine/transmission right-hand mounting:		
Mounting bracket-to-engine nuts/bolts	27	20
Rubber mounting-to-body bolts	27	20
Torque link through-bolt and nut	50	37
Upper half retaining nuts	45	33
Fuel injection pump sprocket nut	50	37
Fuel injection pump sprocket puller retaining screws	10	7
Timing belt idler pulley	37	27
Timing belt tensioner nut and lockbolt	10	7

---

1 Auxiliary drivebelt - removal, refitting and adjustment

1 Chock the rear wheels, then jack up the front of the car and support It on axle stands. Remove the right-hand front roadwheel.

2 From underneath the right-hand front wing, remove the plastic cover from the wing valance to gain access to the right-hand end of the engine **(see illustrations)**. Where applicable, access to the belt can be improved by releasing the fasteners and moving the ECU case to one side.

Manual adjuster

Removal

3 Disconnect the battery negative lead.
4 Slacken the tensioner pulley bracket adjustment/mounting bolts (one located in the middle of the pulley and the other located below on the bracket) **(see illustrations)**.

1.2a Prise out the clips . . .

1.2b . . . and remove the plastic cover from the wing valance

1.4a Tensioner pulley bracket lower mounting bolt . . .

1.4b . . . and upper mounting bolt

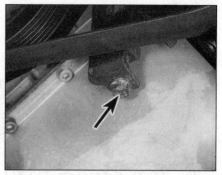

1.5 Auxiliary drivebelt tension adjustment bolt

5 Fully tighten the adjustment bolt to its stop, then slip the drivebelt from the pulleys (see illustration).

6 Check that the tensioner pulley turns freely without any sign of roughness.

Refitting and adjustment

7 Fit the belt around the pulleys, and take up the slack in the belt by tightening the adjuster bolt.

8 The belt should be tensioned so that, under firm thumb pressure, there is about 5.0 mm of free movement at the mid-point between the pulleys on the longest belt run.

9 To adjust, unscrew the adjustment bolt until the tension is correct, then rotate the crankshaft a couple of times, and recheck the tension. Securely tighten the tensioner pulley bracket adjustment/mounting bolts.

10 Refit the inner wing cover (and ECU case, where removed), then refit the wheel and lower the car to the ground.

11 Reconnect the battery negative lead.

1.9 litre engines with automatic adjuster

Removal

12 Disconnect the battery negative lead.

13 Slacken the tensioner pulley bracket adjustment/mounting bolts (one located in the middle of the pulley and the other located below on the bracket).

14 Unscrew the adjustment bolt until it is possible to insert a rod through the special hole in the back of the automatic adjustment roller bracket (see illustration). The rod should be made from a metal rod bent at

right-angles at one end. The rod will hold the automatic adjuster roller while the auxiliary drivebelt is removed and the new one fitted.

15 Fully tighten the manual adjustment bolt to its stop.

16 Unscrew the bolt from the bottom of the air conditioning compressor and push the plastic cover to one side.

17 Slip the auxiliary drivebelt from the pulleys (see illustration).

18 Check that the two tensioner pulleys turn freely without any sign of roughness.

Refitting

19 Locate the new drivebelt on the pulleys making sure that it is correctly engaged with the grooves.

20 Unscrew the manual adjustment bolt so that the drivebelt is just tensioned enough to

7B

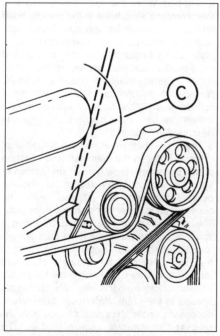

1.14 Inserting the rod (c) through the special hole in the back of the automatic tensioner roller bracket

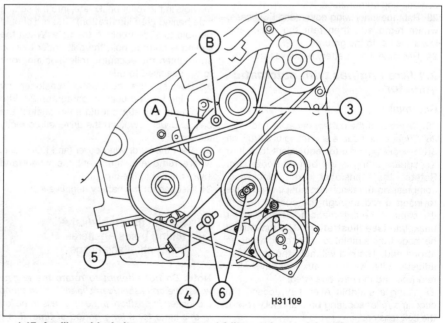

H31109

1.17 Auxiliary drivebelt arrangement on 1.9 litre engine models with air conditioning

3	Automatically adjusted roller	5	Adjusting bolt
4	Manually adjusted roller	6	Manually adjusted roller bracket mounting bolts

A and B
Special holes for rod to hold the roller bracket

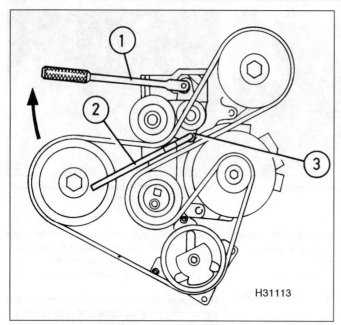

1.26 Relieving drivebelt tension for belt removal - 2.1 litre engine models with air conditioning

1   *Socket handle (or equivalent)*   3   *Hole in tensioner backplate*
2   *Rod*

1.31 Setting the manually-adjusted eccentric roller - 2.1 litre engine models with air conditioning

1   *Tool engaged in square hole*   3   *Eccentric roller securing bolt*
2   *Rod*

remove the rod from the back of the bracket. The automatic adjuster will now keep the drivebelt correctly tensioned.
21 Tighten the tensioner pulley bracket adjustment/mounting bolts including the one located in the middle of the pulley.
22 Refit and tighten the bolt securing the plastic cover to the bottom of the air conditioning compressor.
23 Refit the inner wing cover (and ECU case, where removed), then refit the wheel and lower the car to the ground.
24 Reconnect the battery negative lead.

2.1 litre engines with automatic adjuster

Removal

25 Disconnect the battery negative lead.
26 Engage the square end fitting of a 3/8 inch drive socket handle (or equivalent tool) into the square fitting in the belt tensioner arm. Rotate the tensioner arm clockwise, compressing the tensioner, until it is possible to insert a rod through the special hole in the back of the automatic adjustment roller backplate **(see illustration)**. The rod should be made from a metal rod bent at right-angles at one end. The rod will hold the automatic adjuster roller while the auxiliary drivebelt is removed and the new one fitted.
27 Using a suitable Allen key, loosen the eccentric roller securing bolt, and fully relieve the belt tension.
28 Slip the auxiliary drivebelt from the pulleys.
29 Check that the two tensioner pulleys turn freely without any sign of roughness.

Refitting

30 Locate the new drivebelt on the pulleys, making sure that it is correctly engaged with the grooves.
31 Insert a suitable tool in the square hole provided in the front face of the eccentric roller. Pivot the roller so that the drivebelt is just tensioned enough to slide a rod through the hole in the roller backplate, into the setting hole behind **(see illustration)**. The rod should be able to slide freely in the hole. When the setting is correct, hold the belt under tension and tighten the eccentric roller securing bolt to the specified torque.
32 Release the automatic tensioner by removing the rod used in paragraph 26. The automatic adjuster should snap against the belt, and will now keep the drivebelt correctly tensioned.
33 Refit the inner wing cover (and ECU case, where removed), then refit the wheel and lower the car to the ground.
34 Reconnect the battery negative lead.

2   Engine assembly/valve timing holes - general information and usage

Note: *Do not attempt to rotate the engine whilst the crankshaft/camshaft/injection pump are locked in position. If the engine is to be left in this state for a long period of time, it is a good idea to place suitable warning notices inside the vehicle, and in the engine compartment. This will reduce the possibility of the engine being accidentally cranked on*

the starter motor, which is likely to cause damage with the locking pins in place.
1 On all models, timing holes are drilled in the camshaft sprocket, injection pump sprocket and flywheel. The holes are used to align the crankshaft, camshaft and injection pump and to prevent the possibility of the valves contacting the pistons when refitting the timing belt. When the holes are aligned with their corresponding holes in the cylinder head and cylinder block (as appropriate), suitable diameter bolts/pins can be inserted to lock both the camshaft, injection pump and crankshaft in position, preventing them from rotating unnecessarily. Proceed as follows.
Note: *With the timing holes aligned, No 4 cylinder is at TDC on its compression stroke.*
2 Remove the upper timing belt covers as described in Section 5.
3 The crankshaft must now be turned until the bolt holes in the camshaft and injection pump sprockets (one hole in the camshaft sprocket, one or two holes in the injection pump sprocket) are aligned with the corresponding holes in the engine front plate. The crankshaft can be turned by using a spanner on the pulley bolt. To gain access to the pulley bolt, from underneath the front of the car, prise out the retaining clips and remove the screws, then withdraw the plastic wheelarch liner from the wing valance, to gain access to the crankshaft pulley bolt. Where necessary, unclip the coolant hoses from the bracket, to improve access further. The crankshaft can then be turned using a suitable socket and extension bar fitted to the pulley bolt. Note that the crankshaft must always be

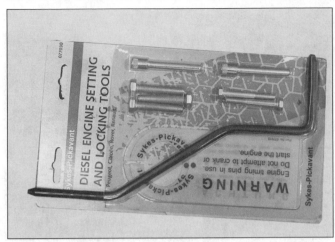

2.4a Suitable tools available for locking engine in position

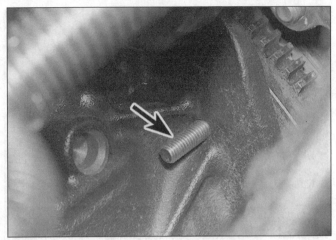

2.4b Rod (arrowed) inserted through cylinder block into timing hole in flywheel/driveplate

2.5a Bolt (arrowed) inserted through timing hole in camshaft sprocket

2.5b Bolts (arrowed) inserted through timing holes in fuel injection pump sprocket

7B

turned in a clockwise direction (viewed from the right-hand side of the vehicle).

4 Insert an 8 mm diameter rod or drill through the hole in the left-hand flange of the cylinder block by the starter motor; if necessary, carefully turn the crankshaft either way until the rod enters the timing hole in the flywheel/driveplate **(see illustrations)**. On 2.1 litre models, access is very restricted, and it may be easier to remove the starter motor to be able to locate the hole.

5 Insert one 8 mm bolt through the hole in the camshaft sprocket, and two (1.9 litre models) or one (2.1 litre models) bolt(s) through the fuel injection pump sprocket, and screw them into the engine finger-tight **(see illustrations)**.

6 The crankshaft, camshaft and injection pump are now locked in position, preventing unnecessary rotation.

3 Camshaft cover - removal and refitting

Removal

1.9 litre engines

1 Remove the air distribution housing as described in Section 12.

2 Disconnect the breather hose from the front of the camshaft cover and, where necessary, remove the intake duct from the inlet manifold.

3 Unscrew the securing bolt and remove the fuel hose bracket from the right-hand end of the camshaft cover **(see illustration)**.

4 Note the locations of any brackets held by the three camshaft cover bolts, then unscrew the bolts. Recover the metal and fibre washers under each bolt **(see illustration)**.

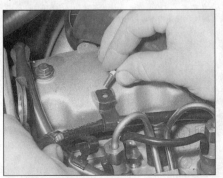

3.3 Removing the fuel hose bracket from the cylinder head cover

3.4 Remove the retaining bolts and washers . . .

3.6 . . . and lift off the cylinder head cover - 1.9 litre engine

3.12 Lifting off the cylinder head cover - 2.1 litre engine

5 Carefully move any hoses clear of the camshaft cover.

6 Lift off the cover, and recover the rubber seal **(see illustration)**. Examine the seal for signs of damage and deterioration, and if necessary, renew it.

2.1 litre models

7 Remove the timing belt upper cover as described in Section 5.

8 Remove the inlet manifold upper part as described in Section 11.

9 Disconnect the breather hose from the front of the cylinder head cover.

10 Note the locations of any brackets secured by the cylinder head cover retaining bolts, then unscrew the eleven bolts in a progressive spiral sequence.

11 Carefully move any hoses clear of the cylinder head cover.

12 Lift off the cover, and recover the rubber seal **(see illustration)**. Examine the seal for signs of damage and deterioration, and if necessary, renew it.

Refitting

1.9 litre models

13 Refitting is a reversal of removal, bearing in mind the following points:
a) *Refit any brackets in their original positions noted before removal.*
b) *Refit the air distribution housing, as described in Section 12.*

2.1 litre models

14 Refitting is a reversal of removal, bearing in mind the following points:
a) *Refit any brackets in their original positions noted before removal.*
b) *Refit the inlet manifold and air inlet ducts described in Section 11.*

4 Crankshaft pulley - removal and refitting

Note: *Although not strictly necessary, due to its tightening sequence (see Specifications) it*

is recommended that the bolt is renewed whenever it is disturbed.

Removal

1 Remove the auxiliary drivebelt (Section 1).

2 To prevent the crankshaft turning whilst the pulley retaining bolt is being slackened, select 4th gear and have an assistant apply the brakes firmly. *Do not* attempt to lock the pulley by inserting a bolt/drill through the timing hole. If the locking pin is in position, temporarily remove it prior to slackening the pulley bolt, then refit it once the bolt has been slackened.

3 Unscrew the retaining bolt and washer, then slide the pulley off the end of the crankshaft **(see illustrations)**. If the pulley locating roll pin or Woodruff key (as applicable) is a loose fit, remove it and store it with the pulley for safe-keeping. If the pulley is tight fit, it can be drawn off the crankshaft using a suitable puller.

Refitting

4 Ensure the Woodruff key is correctly located in its crankshaft groove, or that the roll pin is in

4.3a Removing the crankshaft pulley retaining bolt

4.3b Removing the crankshaft pulley from the end of the crankshaft

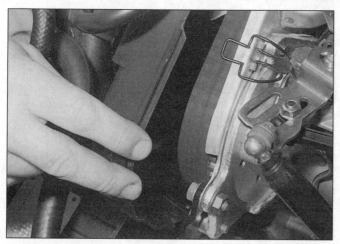

5.3 Removing the upper-front timing belt cover - early models

5.5 Removing the upper-rear timing belt cover - early models

position (as applicable). Refit the pulley to the end of the crankshaft, aligning its locating groove or hole with the Woodruff key or pin.

5 Thoroughly clean the threads of the pulley retaining bolt, then apply a coat of locking compound to the bolt threads. Citroën recommend Loctite (available from your Citroën dealer); in the absence of this, any good-quality locking compound may be used.

6 Refit the crankshaft pulley retaining bolt and washer. Tighten the bolt to the specified torque, preventing the crankshaft from turning using the method employed on removal.

7 Refit and tension the auxiliary drivebelt as described in Section 1.

5 Timing belt covers - removal and refitting

Removal - 1.9 litre models

Upper front cover - early models

1 If procedures are to be carried out which involve removal of the timing belt, remove the right-hand engine mounting-to-body bracket as described in Section 8. This will greatly improve access.

2 Release the upper spring clip from the cover.

3 Release the lower securing lug using a screwdriver, then lift the cover upwards from the engine (see illustration).

Upper rear cover - early models

4 Remove the upper front cover as described previously.

5 Release the two securing clips, manipulate the cover over the studs on the front of the engine, then withdraw the cover upwards (see illustration). Clearance is limited, and if desired, access can be improved by removing the engine mounting bracket (see Section 8).

Upper front cover - later models

6 Slacken and remove the retaining screw and nut, and remove the cover from the engine.

Upper rear cover - later models

7 Remove the front cover as described in paragraph 6, then undo the retaining bolts and remove the rear cover from the engine.

Lower cover - early models

8 Remove the crankshaft pulley (Section 4).

9 Unscrew the two securing bolts and remove the cover (see illustration).

Lower cover - later models

10 Remove the crankshaft pulley (Section 4).

11 Remove both upper covers as described previously.

12 Slacken and remove the retaining nuts and bolts, and remove the lower cover.

Removal - 2.1 litre models

Upper cover

13 Undo the single retaining bolt, located in the centre of the cover (see illustration).

14 Turn the upper fastener a quarter of a turn

7B

5.9 Lower timing belt cover securing bolts (arrowed)

5.13 Undo the single retaining bolt (arrowed), located in the centre of the upper cover on 2.1 litre models

5.14 On 2.1 litre models, turn the fastener clockwise to release the cover locking peg

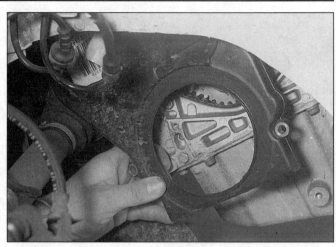

5.21 Removing the lower timing belt cover on 2.1 litre models

clockwise to release the locking peg **(see illustration)**.

15 Manipulate the cover up and off the front of the engine.

Centre cover

16 Remove the auxiliary drivebelt as described in Section 1.

17 Undo the two bolts and remove the centre cover from the front of the injection pump.

Lower cover

18 Remove the crankshaft pulley as described in Section 4.

19 Remove the right-hand engine mounting assembly as described in Section 10.

20 Remove both upper covers as described previously.

21 Slacken and remove the retaining bolts, and remove the lower cover **(see illustration)**.

Refitting

22 Refitting is a reversal of the relevant removal procedure, ensuring that each cover section is correctly located, and that the cover retaining nuts and/or bolts are tightened to the specified torque.

---

6 Timing belt - removal and refitting

Removal

1.9 litre models

Note: *On models with Hydractive suspension, the system will first have to be depressurised with the engine running (Section 13).*

1 Align the engine assembly/valve timing holes (see Section 2), and lock the camshaft sprocket, injection pump sprocket and flywheel in position. *Do not* attempt to rotate the engine whilst the pins are in position. Disconnect the battery negative lead.

2 Remove the timing belt covers (Section 5).

3 Remove the sphere from the main accumulator (Section 14), and unbolt the lower cover from the transmission. Have an assistant lock the starter ring gear with a wide-bladed screwdriver, then unscrew the crankshaft pulley bolt. Remove the crankshaft pulley.

4 Remove the right-hand engine mounting metal plate and mounting bracket (Section 8), then loosen the timing belt tensioner pivot nut and adjustment bolt, then turn the tensioner bracket anti-clockwise to release the tension. Retighten the adjustment bolt to hold the tensioner in the released position. If available, use a 10 mm square drive extension in the hole provided, to turn the tensioner bracket against the spring tension **(see illustration)**.

5 Mark the timing belt with an arrow to indicate its running direction, if it is to be re-

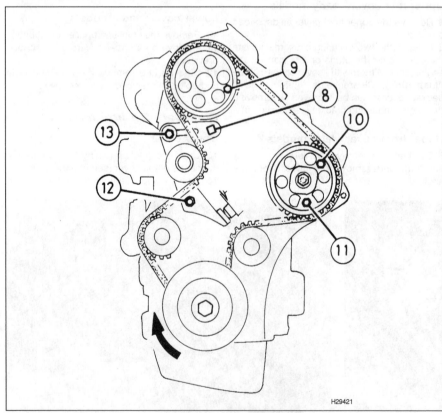

6.4 Removing the timing belt

8   *Square hole*
9 to 11 *Bolts*
12 *Tensioner pivot nut*
13 *Adjustment bolt*

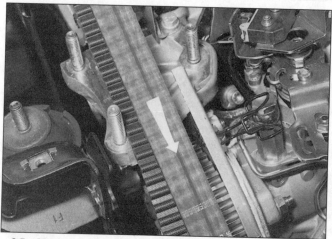

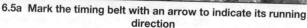

6.5a Mark the timing belt with an arrow to indicate its running direction

6.5b Removing the timing belt

used. Remove the belt from the sprockets **(see illustrations)**.

2.1 litre models

6 Align the engine assembly/valve timing holes as described in Section 2, and lock the camshaft sprocket, injection pump sprocket and flywheel in position. *Do not* attempt to rotate the engine whilst the locking bolts/pins are in position. Disconnect the battery negative terminal.

7 Remove the remaining timing belt covers as described in Section 5.

8 Remove the top part of the engine right-hand mounting as described in Section 10.

9 Slacken the timing belt tensioner pulley retaining nut.

10 Using a 5 mm Allen key inserted through the hole in the engine mounting carrier bracket, slacken the timing belt tensioner locking bolt. If preferred, the carrier bracket can be unbolted from the engine for easier access.

11 Using a 10 mm socket or box spanner

inserted through the same hole, retract the tensioner by turning its shaft clockwise to the extent of its travel **(see illustrations)**. Retighten the tensioner pulley retaining nut.

12 Mark the timing belt with an arrow to indicate its running direction, if it is to be re-used. Remove the belt from the sprockets **(see illustration)**.

Refitting

13 If signs of oil contamination are found, trace the source of the oil leak and rectify it. Wash down the engine timing belt area and all related components, to remove all traces of oil. Check that the tensioner and idler pulley rotates freely, without roughness. If necessary, renew as described in Sections 8 and 9 (as applicable).

1.9 litre models

14 Commence refitting by ensuring that the 8 mm bolts are still fitted to the camshaft and fuel injection pump sprockets, and that the rod/drill is positioned in the timing hole in the flywheel.

15 Locate the timing belt on the crankshaft sprocket, making sure that, where applicable, the direction of rotation arrow is facing the correct way.

6.11a Timing belt tensioner pulley retaining nut (A) and locking bolt (B) on 2.1 litre models

6.11b Timing belt tensioner arrangement on 2.1 litre models showing tensioner 10 mm shaft (arrowed)

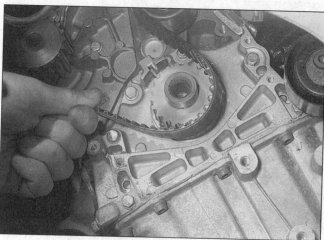

6.12 Removing the timing belt

16 Engage the timing belt with the crankshaft sprocket, hold it in position, then feed the belt over the remaining sprockets in the following order:
a) *Idler roller.*
b) *Fuel injection pump.*
c) *Camshaft.*
d) *Tensioner roller.*
e) *Coolant pump.*

17 Be careful not to kink or twist the belt. To ensure correct engagement, locate only a half-width on the injection pump sprocket before feeding the timing belt onto the camshaft sprocket, keeping the belt taut and fully engaged with the crankshaft sprocket. Locate the timing belt fully onto the sprockets **(see illustration)**.

18 Unscrew and remove the bolts from the camshaft and fuel injection pump sprockets and remove the rod/drill from the timing hole in the flywheel.

19 With the pivot nut loose, slacken the tensioner adjustment bolt while holding the bracket against the spring tension. Slowly release the bracket until the roller presses against the timing belt. Retighten the adjustment bolt and the pivot nut.

20 Rotate the crankshaft through two complete turns in the normal running direction (clockwise). **Do not** rotate the crankshaft backwards, as the timing belt must be kept tight between the crankshaft, fuel injection pump and camshaft sprockets.

21 Loosen the tensioner adjustment bolt and the pivot nut to allow the tensioner spring to push the roller against the timing belt, then tighten both the adjustment bolt and pivot nut to the specified torque.

22 Check that the timing holes are all correctly positioned by reinserting the sprocket locking bolts and the rod/drill in the flywheel timing hole, as described in Section 2. If the timing holes are not correctly positioned, the timing belt has been incorrectly fitted (possibly one tooth out on one of the sprockets) - in this case, repeat the refitting procedure from the beginning.

23 The remaining refitting procedure is a reversal of removal.

2.1 litre models

24 Commence refitting by ensuring that the 8 mm bolts are still fitted to the camshaft and fuel injection pump sprockets, and that the rod/drill is positioned in the timing hole in the flywheel.

25 Ensure that the timing belt tensioner is still retracted, then tighten the tensioner pulley retaining nut. Using the 10 mm socket or box spanner, release the tensioner by turning it anti-clockwise to the extent of its travel.

26 Locate the timing belt on the crankshaft sprocket, making sure that, where applicable, the direction of rotation arrow is facing the correct way.

27 Engage the timing belt with the injection pump sprocket, hold it in position, then feed the belt over the remaining sprockets in the following order:
a) *Idler roller.*
b) *Crankshaft.*
c) *Coolant pump.*
d) *Camshaft.*
e) *Tensioner roller.*

28 Be careful not to kink or twist the belt. To ensure correct engagement, locate only a half-width on the idler roller before feeding the timing belt onto the camshaft sprocket, keeping the belt taut and fully engaged with the crankshaft sprocket. Locate the timing belt fully onto the sprockets.

29 Slacken the tensioner pulley retaining nut to allow the tensioner to tension the belt.

30 Remove the locking bolts from the camshaft and fuel injection pump sprockets, and remove the rod/drill from the timing hole in the flywheel.

31 Rotate the crankshaft through two complete turns in the normal running direction (clockwise). **Do not** rotate the crankshaft backwards, as the timing belt must be kept tight between the crankshaft, fuel injection pump and camshaft sprockets.

32 Check that the locking bolts can be inserted into the sprockets and into the flywheel timing hole.

33 Tighten the tensioner pulley retaining nut, then rotate the crankshaft through a further two complete turns in the normal running direction, stopping at the timing setting position.

34 Check that the locking bolts can be inserted into the sprockets and into the flywheel timing hole.

35 Slacken the tensioner pulley retaining nut one turn to allow the tensioner to finally tension the belt. Tighten the tensioner pulley retaining nut and the timing belt tensioner lockbolt to the specified torque.

36 Check that the timing holes are all correctly positioned by reinserting the sprocket locking bolts and the rod/drill in the flywheel timing hole, as described in Section 2. If the timing holes are not correctly positioned, the timing belt has been incorrectly fitted (possibly one tooth out on one of the sprockets) - in this case, repeat the refitting procedure from the beginning.

37 The remaining refitting procedure is a reversal of removal.

7 Timing belt sprockets - removal and refitting

Camshaft sprocket

Removal

1 Remove the timing belt (see Section 6).
2 The camshaft sprocket retaining bolt must now be loosened. To prevent the camshaft rotating as the bolt is slackened, a sprocket holding tool will be required **(see illustration)**.

6.17 Locate the timing belt on the sprockets as described in text

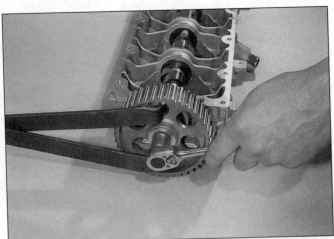

7.2a A sprocket holding tool can be made from two lengths of steel strip bolted together to form a forked end. Bend the ends of the strip through 90° to form the fork 'prongs'

7.2b Holding the camshaft using a spanner on the lug between Nos 3 and 4 lobes

7.5 Withdrawing the camshaft sprocket

Do not attempt to use the sprocket locking pin to prevent the sprocket from rotating whilst the bolt is slackened. Alternatively on 1.9 litre models, remove the camshaft cover as described in Section 3. Prevent the camshaft from turning by holding it with a suitable spanner on the lug between Nos 3 and 4 camshaft lobes **(see illustration)**.

3 Remove the camshaft sprocket retaining bolt and washer.

4 Remove the locking bolt from the camshaft sprocket.

5 With the retaining bolt removed, slide the sprocket off the end of the camshaft **(see illustration)**. Recover the Woodruff key from the end of the camshaft if it is loose. Examine the camshaft oil seal for signs of oil leakage and, if necessary, renew it.

Refitting

6 Refit the Woodruff key to the end of the camshaft, then refit the camshaft sprocket. Note that the sprocket will only fit one way

round (with the protruding centre boss against the camshaft), as the end of the camshaft is tapered.

7 Refit the sprocket retaining bolt and washer. Tighten the bolt to the specified torque, preventing the camshaft from turning as during removal.

8 Where applicable, refit the camshaft cover as described in Section 3.

9 Align the holes in the camshaft sprocket and the engine front plate, and refit the 8 mm bolt to lock the camshaft in position.

10 Refit the timing belt as described in Section 6.

Crankshaft sprocket

Removal

11 Remove the timing belt (see Section 6).

12 Slide the sprocket off the end of the crankshaft **(see illustration)**.

13 Remove the Woodruff key from the crankshaft, and store it with the sprocket for safe-keeping **(see illustration)**.

14 Examine the crankshaft oil seal for signs of oil leakage and, if necessary, renew it.

Refitting

15 Refit the Woodruff key to the end of the crankshaft, then refit the crankshaft sprocket (with the flange nearest the cylinder block).

16 Refit the timing belt as described in Section 6.

Fuel injection pump sprocket

Removal

17 Remove the timing belt covers as described in Section 5.

18 Make alignment marks on the fuel injection pump sprocket and the timing belt, to ensure that the sprocket and timing belt are correctly aligned on refitting.

19 Remove the timing belt as described in Section 6.

20 Remove the 8 mm bolt(s) securing the fuel injection pump sprocket in the TDC position.

21 On certain models, the sprocket may be fitted with a built-in puller, which consists of a

7B

7.12 Withdrawing the crankshaft sprocket

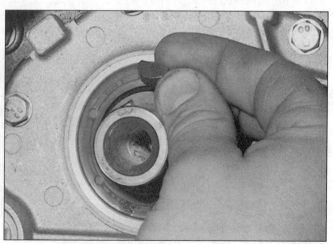

7.13 Removing the Woodruff key from the end of the crankshaft

7.22 Using a home-made tool to prevent the injection pump sprocket from turning

7.24 Home-made puller fitted to fuel injection pump sprocket

plate bolted to the sprocket. The plate contains a captive nut (the sprocket securing nut), which is screwed onto the fuel injection pump shaft. On models not fitted with the built-in puller, a suitable puller can be made up using a short length of bar, and two M7 bolts screwed into the holes provided in the sprocket.

22 The fuel injection pump shaft must be prevented from turning as the sprocket nut is unscrewed, and this can be achieved using a tool to hold the sprocket stationary by means of the holes in the sprocket **(see illustration)**.

23 On models with a built-in puller, unscrew the sprocket securing nut until the sprocket is freed from the taper on the pump shaft, then withdraw the sprocket. Recover the Woodruff key from the end of the pump shaft if it is loose. If desired, the puller assembly can be removed from the sprocket by removing the two securing screws and washers.

24 On models not fitted with a built-in puller, partially unscrew the sprocket securing nut, then fit the improvised puller, and tighten the two bolts (forcing the bar against the sprocket nut), until the sprocket is freed from the taper on the pump shaft **(see illustration)**. Withdraw the sprocket and recover the Woodruff key from the end of the pump shaft if it is loose. Remove the puller from the sprocket.

Refitting

25 Refit the Woodruff key to the pump shaft, ensuring that it is correctly located in its groove.

26 Where applicable, if the built-in puller assembly has been removed from the sprocket, refit it, and tighten the two securing screws securely ensuring that the washers are in place.

27 Refit the sprocket, then tighten the securing nut to the specified torque, preventing the pump shaft from turning as during removal.

28 Make sure that the 8 mm bolts are fitted to the camshaft and fuel injection pump sprockets, and that the rod/drill is positioned in the flywheel timing hole.

29 Fit the timing belt around the fuel injection pump sprocket, ensuring that the marks made on the belt and sprocket before removal are aligned.

30 Fit and tension the timing belt as described in Section 6.

Coolant pump sprocket

31 The coolant pump sprocket is integral with the pump, and cannot be removed.

---

8 Timing belt tensioner (1.9 litre models) - removal and refitting

General

1 The timing belt tensioner is operated by a spring and plunger housed in the right-hand engine mounting bracket, which is bolted to the end face of the engine. The engine mounting is attached to the mounting on the

body via the engine mounting-to-body bracket.

Right-hand engine mounting-to-body bracket

Removal

2 Before removing the bracket, the engine must be supported, preferably using a suitable hoist and lifting tackle attached to the lifting bracket at the right-hand end of the engine. Alternatively, the engine can be supported using a trolley jack and interposed block of wood beneath the sump. In which case, be prepared for the engine to tilt backwards when the bracket is removed.

3 Release the retaining clips and position all the relevant hoses and cables clear of the engine mounting assembly and suspension top mounting.

4 Unscrew the two retaining bolts and remove the curved retaining plate from the top of the mounting **(see illustration)**.

5 Lift out the rubber buffer to expose the engine mounting bracket-to-body securing nut **(see illustration)**.

6 Unscrew the three nuts securing the bracket to the engine mounting, and the

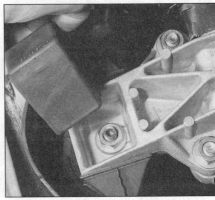

8.4 Remove the curved retaining plate . . .

8.5 . . . and lift the rubber buffer out from the engine mounting

8.6 Removing the engine mounting-to-body bracket

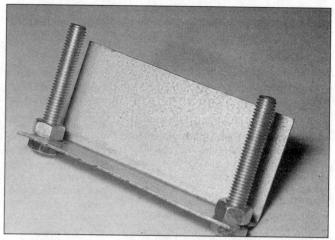

8.16 Fabricated tool for holding tensioner plunger in engine mounting bracket

single nut securing the bracket to the body, then lift off the bracket (see illustration).

Refitting

7 Refitting is a reversal of removal. Tighten the retaining nuts and bolts to the specified torque.

Timing belt tensioner and right-hand engine mounting bracket

Note: *A suitable tool will be required to retain the timing belt tensioner plunger during this operation.*

Removal

8 Remove the engine mounting-to-body bracket as described previously in this Section, and remove the auxiliary drivebelt as described in Section 1.
9 If not already done, support the engine with a trolley jack and interposed block of wood beneath the sump.
10 Where applicable, disconnect the hoist

and lifting tackle supporting the engine from the right-hand lifting bracket (this is necessary because the lifting bracket is attached to the engine mounting bracket, and must be removed).
11 Unscrew the two retaining bolts and remove the engine lifting bracket.
12 Align the engine assembly/valve timing holes (see Section 2), and lock the camshaft sprocket, injection pump sprocket and flywheel in position. Do *not* attempt to rotate the engine whilst the pins are in position.
13 Loosen the timing belt tensioner pivot nut and adjustment bolt, then turn the tensioner bracket anti-clockwise until the adjustment bolt is in the middle of the slot, and retighten the adjustment bolt. If available, use a 10 mm square drive extension in the hole provided, to turn the tensioner bracket against the spring tension.
14 Mark the timing belt with an arrow to indicate its running direction, if it is to be re-used. Remove the belt from the sprockets.

15 A tool must now be obtained in order to hold the tensioner plunger in the engine mounting bracket.
16 The Citroën tool is designed to slide in the two lower bolt holes of the mounting bracket. It should be straightforward to fabricate a similar tool out of sheet metal, and using 10 mm bolts and nuts instead of metal dowel rods (see illustration).
17 Unscrew the two lower engine mounting bracket bolts, then fit the special tool. Grease the inner surface of the tool, to prevent any damage to the end of the tensioner plunger (see illustrations). Unscrew the pivot nut and adjustment bolt, and withdraw the tensioner assembly.
18 Remove the two remaining engine mounting bracket bolts, and withdraw the bracket.
19 Compress the tensioner plunger into the engine mounting bracket, remove the special tool, then withdraw the plunger and spring.

7B

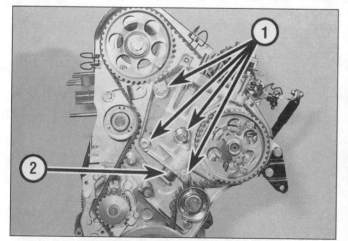

8.17a View of timing belt end of engine

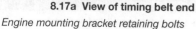
1 Engine mounting bracket retaining bolts
2 Timing belt tensioner plunger

8.17b Tool in place to hold tensioner plunger in engine mounting bracket - timing belt removed for clarity

Refitting

20 Refitting is a reversal of removal, bearing in mind the following points:
a) *Tighten all fixings to the specified torque.*
b) *Refit and tension the timing belt as described in Section 6.*
c) *Refit and tighten the auxiliary drivebelt as described in Section 1.*

9 Timing belt idler roller - removal and refitting

Removal

1.9 litre models

1 Remove the auxiliary drivebelt (Section 1).
2 Align the engine assembly/valve timing holes as described in Section 2, and lock the camshaft sprocket, injection pump sprocket and flywheel in position. *Do not* attempt to rotate the engine whilst the pins are in position.

11.1 Slacken the retaining clip and disconnect the air intake duct from the inlet manifold upper part

3 Loosen the timing belt tensioner pivot nut and adjustment bolt, then turn the tensioner bracket anti-clockwise to release the tension, and retighten the adjustment bolt to hold the tensioner in the released position. If available, use a 10 mm square drive extension in the hole provided, to turn the tensioner bracket against the spring tension.
4 Unscrew the two bolts and the stud securing the idler roller assembly to the cylinder block, noting that the upper bolt also secures the engine mounting bracket.
5 Slightly loosen the remaining four engine mounting bolts, noting that the uppermost bolt is on the inside face of the engine front plate, and also secures the engine lifting bracket. Slide out the idler roller assembly.

2.1 litre models

6 Remove the timing belt as described in Section 6.
7 Unscrew the idler roller centre bolt and remove it from the engine.

Refitting

8 Refitting is a reversal of removal, bearing in mind the following points:
a) *Tighten all fixings to the specified torque.*
b) *Refit and/or tension the timing belt as described in Section 6.*
c) *Refit and tension the auxiliary drivebelt as described in Section 1.*

10 Engine right-hand mounting - removal and refitting

1.9 litre models

1 Refer to Section 8.

2.1 litre models

2 Disconnect the battery negative lead. Release all the relevant hoses and wiring from

their retaining clips. Place the hoses/wiring clear of the mounting so that the removal procedure is not hindered.
3 Place a jack beneath the engine, with a block of wood on the jack head. Raise the jack until it is supporting the weight of the engine.
4 Remove the nut and through-bolt from the torque link to the rear of the main mounting, and release the link from its bracket.
5 Remove the four nuts from the top of the main mounting, and lift off the top half.
6 If required, the rubber mounting on the inner wing can now be unbolted and removed.
7 The right-hand mounting bracket can be removed from the engine by removing the two nuts and two bolts. Withdraw the bracket over the timing belt tensioner lockbolt.
8 Refit in the reverse order of removal, tightening all fittings to the specified torque.

11 Inlet manifold upper part (2.1 litre models) - removal and refitting

Removal

1 Slacken the retaining clip and disconnect the air intake duct from the manifold upper part **(see illustration)**.
2 Remove the clip securing the flexible portion of the EGR pipe to the manifold. If the original crimped clip is still in place, cut it off; new clips are supplied by Citroën parts stockists with a screw clamp fixing **(see illustration)**. If a screw clamp type clip is fitted, undo the screw and manipulate the clip off the pipe.
3 Undo the four retaining bolts and lift off the manifold upper part. Recover the four rubber connecting tubes from the lower part **(see illustrations)**.

11.2 Remove the clip securing the flexible portion of the EGR pipe to the manifold

11.3a Undo the four retaining bolts (arrowed) . . .

11.3b . . . lift off the manifold upper part . . .

11.3c . . . and recover the four rubber connecting tubes

Refitting

4 Refitting is a reversal of removal, bearing in mind the following points:

a) *Renew the four rubber connecting tubes as a set if any one shows signs of deterioration.*

b) *Tighten all fixings to the specified torques, where applicable.*

c) *Secure the EGR pipe with a new screw clamp type clip, if a crimped type was initially fitted (see illustration).*

12 Air cleaner and associated components - removal and refitting

Removal

Air cleaner - non-turbo models

1 Slacken the retaining clips securing the air cleaner to manifold duct in position and, where necessary, remove the duct mounting

bolt. Disconnect the duct and remove it from the engine. Recover the seal from the air distribution housing.

2 Slacken and remove the bolt securing the inlet duct to the crossmember then unclip the duct from the side of the air cleaner and remove it from the vehicle.

3 Slacken and remove the bolts securing the air cleaner and mounting bracket in position, and remove both items as an assembly.

Air cleaner - turbo models

4 Slacken the retaining clips securing the air cleaner-to-turbocharger duct in position (see illustration), and undo the duct mounting bolt. Manoeuvre the duct assembly out from the engine compartment. Recover the seal fitted to each end of the duct.

5 On 2.1 litre models, release the coolant hose and the oil separator from their locations on the air filter housing lid (see illustration).

6 Undo the screws securing the lid to the air cleaner housing body. Lift off the lid and take out the filter element.

11.4 Secure the EGR pipe with a screw clamp type clip (arrowed) when refitting

7 Slacken and remove the retaining bolts and remove the air cleaner from the engine compartment. Lift the housing body upward to disengage it from the lower locating lugs.

8 Slacken and remove the bolt securing the cold-air inlet duct to the crossmember, then unclip the duct and remove it from the vehicle.

7B

12.4 Air cleaner-to-turbocharger duct retaining clip (arrowed)

12.5 Lift the coolant expansion tank hose from the air cleaner clip - oil separator (arrowed) also lifts out of its retaining bracket

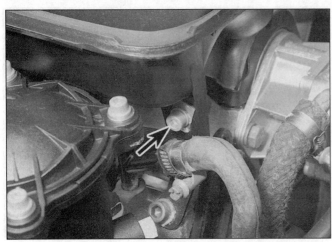

12.10 Front air distribution housing securing bolt (arrowed)

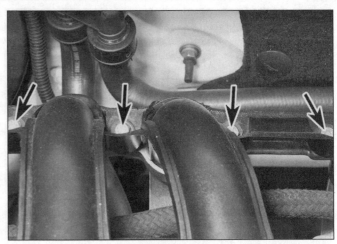

12.11 Air distribution housing-to-inlet manifold bolts (arrowed)

Air distribution housing - non-turbo models

9 Disconnect the air hose and the crankcase breather hose from the front of the air distribution housing.

10 Unscrew the two bolts securing the housing to the front mounting brackets **(see illustration)**. Recover the spacer plates.

11 Unscrew the four bolts securing the housing to the inlet manifold. Recover the washers **(see illustration)**.

12 Lift the housing from the inlet manifold, and recover the seal(s).

Intake ducts

13 Particularly on turbo engines, the intake ducting is a complex arrangement of flexible hoses and rigid ducts connecting the air cleaner assembly, intercooler and turbocharger, as applicable.

14 Cold air enters the base of the air cleaner through a duct attached to the front crossmember. The filtered air then passes directly to the inlet manifold on non-turbo models; on turbo models, the filtered air

passes to the turbocharger, where it is compressed. This compressed air is fed into the inlet manifold (after passing through the intercooler, on models so equipped).

15 The intake ducts pass over the top and rear of the engine and, on 2.1 litre models, also along the underside of the engine between the transmission bellhousing and the sump. To remove the underside ducts, it will be necessary to jack up the front of the car and support it on axle stands, then remove the engine splash guard.

16 To remove a section of intake ducting, slacken the retaining clips at each end and undo the bolts securing the relevant duct to its mounting bracket or support. On 2.1 litre models, when removing the intercooler-to-manifold duct over the engine, it will be necessary to disconnect the inlet air temperature sensor wiring connector **(see illustration)**.

17 Release the ends of the duct, then work it from its location.

Refitting

18 Refitting is the reverse of the relevant

removal procedure. Examine the seal(s) (where fitted) and renew if necessary.

---

13 Hydraulic system - depressurising, pressurising and priming

Depressurising

Early models without Hydractive suspension

Note: *This procedure applies only to early models which were not fitted with a suspension circuit isolator valve to maintain the vehicle ride height with the engine stopped. Such vehicles will sink when the engine is stopped.*

1 The main accumulator and the front brakes are depressurised using the pressure regulator release screw. The screw is located on the main accumulator assembly mounted at the front of the engine **(see illustration)**.

2 Unscrew the release screw by one turn. A

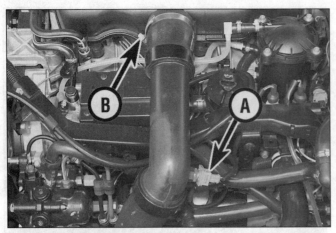

12.16 Intercooler-to-manifold air intake duct on 2.1 litre engine, showing air temperature sensor wiring connector (A) and duct retaining clip (B)

13.1 Hydraulic pressure regulator release screw (arrowed) - viewed from above engine compartment

whistling sound should be heard, which indicates that hydraulic fluid under pressure is flowing and returning to the reservoir.

Caution: Do not remove the release screw, as the sealing ball beneath the screw is easily lost.

3 The suspension and rear brakes can be depressurised using the suspension height control lever as follows (the main accumulator should already have been depressurised as described previously).

4 Move the height control lever to the Minimum position, and allow the vehicle suspension to sink down.

Later models and all models with Hydractive suspension

Note: *The following operation must be carried out with the engine running. The system can be depressurised with the engine stopped, but special equipment is required, and the operation should therefore be entrusted to a Citroën dealer.*

5 Ensure that the pressure regulator release screw is fully closed (see paragraph 1).

6 With the engine running, set the suspension height lever to the Minimum position.

7 With the engine running, allow the vehicle suspension to sink down. **Do not** move the steering wheel.

8 When the suspension has stopped sinking, stop the engine, then unscrew the pressure regulator release screw by one turn (see paragraph 2).

Pressurising

9 On completion of work, to pressurise the system, tighten the pressure regulator release screw, then move the suspension height control lever to the Maximum position.

10 Start the engine, and allow the vehicle suspension to rise to its maximum height. Operate the height control lever through its full range of movement several times to check the operation of the hydraulic system.

Priming

11 Normally, the system will prime automatically when the engine is started, but sometimes it may be necessary to assist priming of the high-pressure pump as follows.

12 Ensure that the pressure regulator release screw is slackened (see paragraph 1).

13 Disconnect the high-pressure fluid hose from the top of the reservoir **(see illustration)**.

14 Pour LHM hydraulic fluid directly into the hose.

15 Start the engine.

16 Reconnect the hose as soon as the fluid level in the hose falls.

17 Once the pump has been primed, loosen and then tighten the pressure regulator

release screw several times to bleed the air from the system.

18 Move the suspension height control lever to the Maximum position, then top up the level in the fluid reservoir.

14 Suspension spheres - removal and refitting

Removal

Note: *A strap wrench will be required for this operation. A new seal will be required on refitting.*

1 Depressurise the hydraulic system as described in Section 13.

2 Using a strap wrench, loosen the sphere, then unscrew the sphere from the relevant hydraulic unit **(see illustration)**. Note that the spheres are self-sealing, but be prepared for fluid spillage from the hydraulic unit. Plug the open end of the hydraulic unit to prevent dirt ingress.

Refitting

3 Grease the contact face of the sphere, and refit the sphere using a new seal. Tighten the sphere by hand only.

4 Check and if necessary top up the hydraulic fluid level.

7B

13.13 Fluid reservoir high-pressure hose (arrowed)

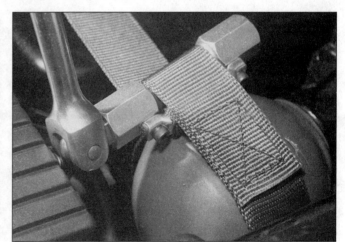

14.2 Using a strap wrench to unscrew a front suspension sphere

Notes

Chapter 8A
Peugeot 106 petrol 1991 to 1996

Contents

Specifications

Timing belt renewal interval . . . . Every 36 000 miles (60 000 km)

Note: *Although the normal interval for timing belt renewal is 72 000 miles (120 000 km), it is strongly recommended that the interval is halved on vehicles which are subjected to intensive use, ie, mainly short journeys or a lot of stop-start driving. The actual belt renewal interval is therefore very much up to the individual owner. That being said, it is highly recommended to err on the side of safety, and renew the belt at this earlier interval, bearing in mind the drastic consequences resulting from belt failure.*

Torque wrench settings	Nm	lbf ft
Camshaft sprocket retaining bolt	80	59
Crankshaft pulley retaining bolts	8	6
Crankshaft sprocket retaining bolt	110	81
Roadwheel bolts	85	63
Timing belt cover bolts	8	6
Timing belt tensioner pulley nut	23	17

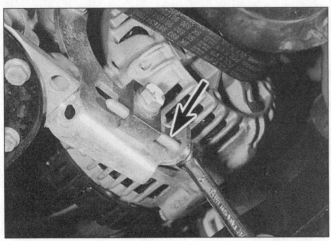

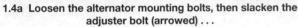

1.4a Loosen the alternator mounting bolts, then slacken the adjuster bolt (arrowed) . . .

1.4b . . . and slip the drivebelt off its pulleys

1 Auxiliary drivebelt – removal, refitting and adjustment

1 Apply the handbrake, then jack up the front of the car and support it on axle stands. Remove the right-hand front roadwheel. Where necessary, undo the retaining nut, and free the coolant hoses from the retaining clip to improve access to the crankshaft sprocket bolt.

Models without air conditioning

Removal

2 Disconnect the battery negative lead.
3 Slacken both the alternator upper and lower mounting bolts, and the bolt securing the adjuster strap to the mounting bracket.
4 Back off the adjuster bolt to relieve the tension in the drivebelt, then slip the drivebelt from the pulleys (see illustrations).

Refitting

5 Fit the belt around the pulleys, ensuring that the belt is of the correct type if it is being renewed, and take up the slack in the belt by tightening the adjuster bolt.
6 Tension the drivebelt as described in the following paragraphs.

Adjustment

7 The belt should be tensioned so that, under firm thumb pressure, there is approximately 5.0 mm of free movement at the mid-point between the pulleys, on the longest belt run.
8 To adjust, with the upper mounting bolt just holding the alternator firm, and the lower mounting bolt loosened, turn the adjuster bolt until the correct tension is achieved. Rotate the crankshaft through two complete turns, then recheck the tension. When the tension is correct, securely tighten both the alternator mounting bolts and, where necessary, the bolt securing the adjuster strap to its mounting bracket.

9 Reconnect the battery negative lead.
10 Clip the coolant hoses in position and secure them with the retaining nut (where removed). Refit the roadwheel, and lower the vehicle to the ground.

Models with air conditioning

Removal

11 Disconnect the battery negative lead.
12 Slacken the two bolts securing the tensioner pulley assembly to the engine, and the lower alternator mounting bolt.
13 Rotate the adjuster bolt to move the tensioner pulley away from the drivebelt, until there is sufficient slack for the drivebelt to be removed from the pulleys.

Refitting

14 Fit the belt around the pulleys, ensuring that the belt is of the correct type if it is being renewed, and take up the slack in the belt by tightening the adjuster bolt.
15 Tension the drivebelt as described in the following paragraphs.

Adjustment

16 The belt should be tensioned so that, under firm thumb pressure, there is approximately 5.0 mm of free movement at the mid-point between the pulleys, on the longest belt run.
17 To adjust the tension, with the two tensioner pulley assembly retaining bolts and the lower alternator mounting bolt slackened, rotate the adjuster bolt until the correct tension is achieved. Once the belt is correctly tensioned, rotate the crankshaft through two complete turns, and recheck the tension.
18 When the belt is correctly tensioned, securely tighten the tensioner pulley assembly retaining bolts, and the lower alternator mounting bolt.
19 Reconnect the battery negative lead.
20 Clip the coolant hoses back in position, and secure with the retaining nut (where removed). Refit the roadwheel, and lower the vehicle to the ground.

2 Engine assembly/valve timing holes - general information and usage

Note: Do not attempt to rotate the engine whilst the crankshaft/camshaft are locked in position. If the engine is to be left in this state for a long period of time, it is a good idea to place warning notices inside the vehicle, and in the engine compartment. This will reduce the possibility of the engine being accidentally cranked on the starter motor, which is likely to cause damage with the locking tools in place.

1 On all models, timing holes are drilled in the camshaft sprocket and in the flywheel. The holes are used to ensure that the crankshaft and camshaft are correctly positioned when assembling the engine (to prevent the possibility of the valves contacting the pistons when refitting the cylinder head), or refitting the timing belt. When the timing holes are aligned with access holes in the cylinder head and the front of the cylinder block, suitable-diameter pins or bolts can be inserted to lock both the camshaft and crankshaft in position, preventing them from rotating. Proceed as follows. Note: With the timing holes aligned, No 1 cylinder is at TDC on its compression stroke.
2 Remove the timing belt upper cover as described in Section 3.
3 The crankshaft must now be turned until the timing hole in the camshaft sprocket is aligned with the corresponding hole in the cylinder head. The holes are aligned when the camshaft sprocket hole is in the 2 o'clock position, when viewed from the right-hand end of the engine. The crankshaft can be turned by using a spanner on the crankshaft sprocket bolt, noting that it should always be rotated in a clockwise direction (viewed from the right-hand end of the engine). Turning the engine will be much easier if the spark plugs are removed first .

2.4 Insert a 6 mm bolt (arrowed) through hole in cylinder block flange and into timing hole in the flywheel . . .

2.5 . . . then insert a 10 mm bolt through the cam sprocket timing hole, and locate it in the cylinder head

4 With the camshaft sprocket hole correctly positioned, insert a 6 mm diameter bolt or drill bit through the hole in the front left-hand flange of the cylinder block, and locate it in the timing hole in the flywheel **(see illustration)**. Note that it may be necessary to rotate the crankshaft slightly, to get the holes to align.

5 With the flywheel correctly positioned, insert a 10 mm diameter bolt or drill bit through the timing hole in the camshaft sprocket, and locate it in the hole in the cylinder head **(see illustration)**.

6 The crankshaft and camshaft are now locked in position, preventing unnecessary rotation.

3 Timing belt covers -
removal and refitting

Removal
Upper cover

1 Slacken and remove the two retaining bolts (one at the front and one at the rear), and remove the timing belt upper cover from the cylinder head **(see illustrations)**.

Centre cover

2 Remove the upper cover as described in paragraph 1, then free the wiring from its retaining clips on the centre cover **(see illustration)**.

3 Slacken and remove the retaining bolts, and manoeuvre the centre cover out from the engine compartment **(see illustration)**.

Lower cover

4 Remove the auxiliary drivebelt as described in Section 1.

3.1a Undo the two retaining bolts (arrowed) . . .

3.1b . . . and remove the timing belt upper cover

8A

3.2 Free the wiring loom from its retaining clip . . .

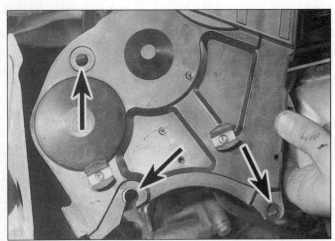

3.3 . . . then undo the three retaining bolts (locations arrowed) and remove the timing belt centre cover

3.6a Undo the three retaining bolts (arrowed) . . .

3.6b . . . and remove the crankshaft pulley

5 Remove the upper and centre covers as described in paragraphs 1 to 3.

6 Undo the three crankshaft pulley retaining bolts and remove the pulley, noting which way round it is fitted **(see illustrations)**.

7 Slacken and remove the remaining retaining bolt(s), and slide the lower cover off the end of the crankshaft **(see illustration)**.

Refitting

Upper cover

8 Refit the cover, ensuring that it is correctly located with the centre cover, and tighten its retaining bolts.

Centre cover

9 Manoeuvre the centre cover back into position, ensuring that it is correctly located with the lower cover, and tighten its retaining bolts.

10 Clip the wiring loom into its retaining clips on the front of the centre cover, then refit the upper cover as described in paragraph 8.

Lower cover

11 Locate the lower cover over the timing belt sprocket, and tighten its retaining bolt(s).

12 Fit the pulley to the end of the crankshaft, ensuring that it is fitted the correct way round, and tighten its retaining bolts to the specified torque.

13 Refit the centre and upper covers as described above, then refit and tension the auxiliary drivebelt as described in Section 1.

---

4 Timing belt -
removal and refitting

Note: *Peugeot specify the use of a special electronic tool (SEEM belt tensioning measuring tool) to correctly set the timing belt tension*

Removal

1 Disconnect the battery negative terminal.

2 Align the engine assembly/valve timing

holes as described in Section 2, and lock both the camshaft sprocket and the flywheel in position. *Do not* attempt to rotate the engine whilst the locking tools are in position.

3 Remove the timing belt centre and lower covers as described in Section 3.

4 Loosen the timing belt tensioner pulley retaining nut. Pivot the pulley in a clockwise direction, using a square-section key fitted to the hole in the pulley hub, then retighten the retaining nut.

5 Slip the belt off the sprockets. If the timing belt is to be re-used, use white paint or similar to mark the direction of rotation on the belt (if markings do not already exist) **(see illustration)**.

6 If signs of oil contamination are found, trace the source of the oil leak, and rectify it. Wash down the engine timing belt area and all related components, to remove all traces of oil.

Refitting

7 Prior to refitting, thoroughly clean the timing belt sprockets. Check that the tensioner

3.7 Undo the retaining bolt and remove the timing belt lower cover

4.5 Mark the timing belt direction of rotation

pulley rotates freely, without any sign of roughness. If necessary, renew the tensioner pulley as described in Section 5. Make sure that the locking tools are still in place, as described in Section 2.

8 Manoeuvre the timing belt into position, ensuring that the arrows on the belt are pointing in the direction of rotation (clockwise, when viewed from the right-hand end of the engine).

9 Do not twist the timing belt sharply while refitting it. Fit the belt over the crankshaft and camshaft sprockets. Make sure that the front run of the belt is taut - ie, ensure that any slack is on the tensioner pulley side of the belt. Fit the belt over the coolant pump sprocket and tensioner pulley. Ensure that the belt teeth are seated centrally in the sprockets.

10 Loosen the tensioner pulley retaining nut. Pivot the pulley anti-clockwise to remove all free play from the timing belt, then retighten the nut.

11 Fit the special belt tensioning measuring equipment to the front run of the timing belt, approximately midway between the camshaft and crankshaft sprockets. Position the tensioner pulley so that the belt is tensioned to a setting of 45 units, then retighten its retaining nut.

12 Remove the locking tools from the camshaft sprocket and flywheel, and remove the measuring tool from the belt.

13 Using a suitable socket and extension bar on the crankshaft sprocket bolt, rotate the crankshaft through four complete rotations in a clockwise direction (viewed from the right-hand end of the engine). *Do not at any time rotate the crankshaft anti-clockwise.*

14 Slacken the tensioner pulley retaining nut, and refit the measuring tool to the belt. If a new belt is being fitted, tension it to a setting of 40 units. If an old belt is being re-used, tighten it to a setting of 36 units. **Note:** *Peugeot state that a belt becomes old after 1 hour's use.* With the belt correctly tensioned, tighten the pulley retaining nut to the specified torque.

15 Remove the measuring tool from the belt, then rotate the crankshaft through another two complete rotations in a clockwise direction, so that both the camshaft sprocket and flywheel timing holes are realigned. *Do not at any time rotate the crankshaft anti-clockwise.* Fit the measuring tool to the belt, and check the belt tension. A new belt should give a reading of 51 ± 3 units; an old belt should be 45 ± 3 units.

16 If the belt tension is incorrect, repeat the procedures in paragraphs 14 and 15.

17 With the belt tension correctly set, refit the timing belt covers as described in Section 3, and reconnect the battery negative terminal.

5.6 To prevent the camshaft rotating as the bolt is slackened, a sprocket-holding tool will be required. Use two lengths of steel strip (one long, the other short), and three nuts and bolts; one nut and bolt forms the pivot of a forked tool, with the remaining two nuts and bolts at the tips of the 'forks' to engage with the sprocket spokes

5 Timing belt tensioner and sprockets - removal and refitting

Removal

Note: *This Section describes the removal and refitting of the components concerned as individual operations. If more than one of them is to be removed at the same time, start by removing the timing belt as described in Section 4; remove the actual component as described below, ignoring the preliminary dismantling steps.*

1 Disconnect the battery negative terminal.

2 Position the engine assembly/valve timing holes as described in Section 2, and lock both the camshaft sprocket and flywheel in position. *Do not attempt to rotate the engine whilst the tools are in position.*

Camshaft sprocket

3 Remove the upper and centre timing belt covers as described in Section 3.

4 Loosen the timing belt tensioner pulley retaining nut. Rotate the pulley in a clockwise direction, using a suitable square-section key fitted to the hole in the pulley hub, then retighten the retaining nut.

5 Disengage the timing belt from the sprocket, and move the belt clear, taking care not to bend or twist it sharply. Remove

the locking pin from the camshaft sprocket.

6 Slacken the camshaft sprocket retaining bolt and remove it, along with its washer. *Do not attempt to use the sprocket locking pin to prevent the sprocket from rotating whilst the bolt is slackened* **(see illustration)**.

7 With the retaining bolt removed, slide the sprocket off the end of the camshaft. If the locating peg is a loose fit in the rear of the sprocket, remove it for safe-keeping. Examine the camshaft oil seal for signs of oil leakage and, if necessary, renew it.

Crankshaft sprocket

8 Remove the centre and lower timing belt covers as described in Section 3.

9 Loosen the timing belt tensioner pulley retaining nut. Rotate the pulley in a clockwise direction, using a suitable square-section key fitted to the hole in the pulley hub, then retighten the retaining nut.

10 To prevent crankshaft rotation whilst the sprocket retaining bolt is slackened, select top gear, and have an assistant apply the brakes firmly. *Do not be tempted to use the flywheel locking pin to prevent the crankshaft from rotating;* temporarily remove the locking pin from the rear of the flywheel prior to slackening the pulley bolt, then refit it once the bolt has been slackened.

11 Unscrew the retaining bolt and washer, then slide the sprocket off the end of the crankshaft **(see illustrations)**. Refit the

5.11a Remove the crankshaft sprocket retaining bolt . . .

5.11b . . . then slide off the sprocket . . .

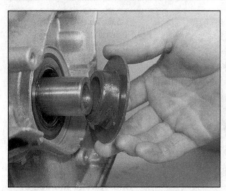

5.12 . . . and remove the flanged spacer

locating pin through the timing hole into the rear of the flywheel.

12 If the Woodruff key is a loose fit in the crankshaft, remove it and store it with the sprocket for safe-keeping. If necessary, also slide the flanged spacer off the end of the crankshaft **(see illustration)**. Examine the crankshaft oil seal for signs of oil leakage and, if necessary, renew it.

Tensioner pulley

13 Remove the centre timing belt cover as described in Section 3.
14 Slacken and remove the timing belt tensioner pulley retaining nut, and slide the pulley off its mounting stud. Examine the mounting stud for signs of damage and, if necessary, renew it.

Refitting

15 Clean the sprockets thoroughly, and renew any that show signs of wear, damage or cracks.
16 Clean the tensioner assembly, but do not

use any strong solvent which may enter the pulley bearing. Check that the pulley rotates freely about its hub, with no sign of stiffness or of free play. Renew the tensioner pulley if there is any doubt about its condition, or if there are any obvious signs of wear or damage.

Camshaft sprocket

17 Refit the locating peg (where removed) to the rear of the sprocket, then locate the sprocket on the end of the camshaft. Ensure that the locating peg is correctly engaged with the cut-out in the end of the camshaft.
18 Refit the sprocket retaining bolt and washer. Tighten the bolt to the specified torque, whilst retaining the sprocket with the tool used on removal **(see illustration 5.6)**.
19 Realign the timing hole in the camshaft sprocket (see Section 2) with the corresponding hole in the cylinder head, and refit the locking pin.
20 Refit the timing belt to the camshaft sprocket. Ensure that the front run of the belt is taut - ie, ensure that any slack is on the tensioner pulley side of the belt. Do not twist the belt sharply while refitting it, and ensure that the belt teeth are seated centrally in the sprockets.
21 Loosen the tensioner pulley retaining nut. Rotate the pulley anti-clockwise to remove all free play from the timing belt, then retighten the nut.
22 Tension the belt as described in Section 4.
23 Refit the timing belt covers as described in Section 3.

Crankshaft sprocket

24 Where removed, locate the Woodruff key in the crankshaft end, then slide on the

flanged spacer, aligning its slot with the Woodruff key.
25 Align the crankshaft sprocket slot with the Woodruff key, and slide it onto the end of the crankshaft.
26 Temporarily remove the locking pin from the rear of the flywheel, then refit the crankshaft sprocket retaining bolt and washer. Tighten the bolt to the specified torque, whilst preventing crankshaft rotation using the method employed on removal. Refit the locking pin to the rear of the flywheel.
27 Relocate the timing belt on the crankshaft sprocket. Ensure that the front run of the belt is taut - ie, ensure that any slack is on the tensioner pulley side of the belt. Do not twist the belt sharply while refitting it, and ensure that the belt teeth are seated centrally in the sprockets.
28 Loosen the tensioner pulley retaining nut. Rotate the pulley anti-clockwise to remove all free play from the timing belt, then retighten the nut.
29 Tension the belt as described in Section 4.
30 Refit the timing belt covers as described in Section 3.

Tensioner pulley

31 Refit the tensioner pulley to its mounting stud, and fit the retaining nut.
32 Ensure that the front run of the belt is taut - ie, ensure that any slack is on the tensioner pulley side of the belt. Check that the belt is centrally located on all its sprockets. Rotate the tensioner pulley anti-clockwise to remove all free play from the timing belt, then tighten the pulley retaining nut securely.
33 Tension the belt as described in Section 4.
34 Refit the timing belt covers as described in Section 3.

Chapter 8B
Peugeot 106 diesel 1991 to 1996

Contents

Specifications

Timing belt renewal interval . . . . Every 36 000 miles (60 000 km)

Note: *Although the normal interval for timing belt renewal is 72 000 miles (120 000 km), it is strongly recommended that the interval is halved on vehicles which are subjected to intensive use, ie, mainly short journeys or a lot of stop-start driving. The actual belt renewal interval is therefore very much up to the individual owner. That being said, it is highly recommended to err on the side of safety, and renew the belt at this earlier interval, bearing in mind the drastic consequences resulting from belt failure.*

Engine codes
1360 cc . . . . TUD 3
1527 cc . . . . TUD 5

Timing belt tension
TUD 3:
   Stage 1 . . . . 50 units
   Stage 2 . . . . 39 units
   Final stage . . . . 51 ± 3 units
TUD 5:
   New belt:
      Stage 1 . . . . 98 units
      Stage 2 . . . . 54 units
      Final stage . . . . 54 ± 3 units
   Used belt:
      Stage 1 . . . . 75 units
      Stage 2 . . . . 44 units
      Final stage . . . . 44 ± 3 units

Torque wrench settings

	Nm	lbf ft
Camshaft sprocket fastener(s):		
Camshaft sprocket retaining bolt - TUD 3 engines	80	59
Camshaft sprocket-to-hub bolts - TUD 5 engines	25	18
Camshaft sprocket hub retaining bolt - TUD 5 engines:		
Engines up to 31/12/98	80	59
Engines built after 1/1/99:		
Stage 1	40	30
Stage 2	Angle-tighten a further 20°	
Crankshaft pulley bolts	15	11
Crankshaft sprocket retaining bolt:		
TUD 3 engines, and TUD 5 engines up to 31/12/98	110	81
TUD 5 engines built after 1/1/99:		
Stage 1	70	52
Stage 2	Angle-tighten a further 45°	
Injection pump sprocket fastener(s):		
Injection pump sprocket retaining nut - TUD 3 engines	50	37
Injection pump sprocket-to-hub bolts - TUD 5 engines	25	18
Injection pump sprocket hub retaining nut - TUD 5 engines	Not available	
Roadwheel bolts	85	63
Timing belt cover bolts:		
TUD 3 engine:		
Centre and lower covers	8	6
Upper cover	5	4
TUD 5 engines (all)	10	7
Timing belt tensioner pulley nut:		
TUD 3	15	11
TUD 5	20	15

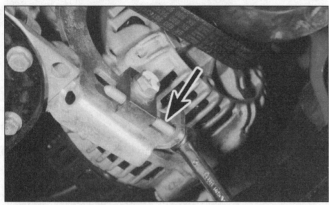

1.4a Loosen the alternator mounting bolts, then slacken the adjuster bolt (arrowed) . . .

1.4b . . . and slip the drivebelt off its pulleys

1 Auxiliary drivebelt – removal, refitting and adjustment

1 Apply the handbrake, then jack up the front of the car and support it on axle stands. Remove the right-hand front roadwheel. Where necessary, undo the retaining nut, and free the coolant hoses from the retaining clip to improve access to the crankshaft sprocket bolt.

Models without air conditioning

Removal

2 Disconnect the battery negative lead.
3 Slacken both the alternator upper and lower mounting bolts, and the bolt securing the adjuster strap to the mounting bracket.
4 Back off the adjuster bolt to relieve the tension in the drivebelt, then slip the drivebelt from the pulleys **(see illustrations)**.

Refitting

5 Fit the belt around the pulleys, ensuring that the belt is of the correct type if it is being renewed, and take up the slack in the belt by tightening the adjuster bolt.
6 Tension the drivebelt as described in the following paragraphs.

Adjustment

7 The belt should be tensioned so that, under firm thumb pressure, there is approximately 5.0 mm of free movement at the mid-point between the pulleys, on the longest belt run.
8 To adjust, with the upper mounting bolt just holding the alternator firm, and the lower mounting bolt loosened, turn the adjuster bolt until the correct tension is achieved. Rotate the crankshaft through two complete turns, then recheck the tension. When the tension is correct, securely tighten both the alternator mounting bolts and, where necessary, the bolt securing the adjuster strap to its mounting bracket.
9 Reconnect the battery negative lead.
10 Clip the coolant hoses in position and secure them with the retaining nut (where removed). Refit the roadwheel, and lower the vehicle to the ground.

Models with air conditioning

Removal

11 Disconnect the battery negative lead.
12 Slacken the two bolts securing the tensioner pulley assembly to the engine, and the lower alternator mounting bolt.
13 Rotate the adjuster bolt to move the tensioner pulley away from the drivebelt, until there is sufficient slack for the drivebelt to be removed from the pulleys.

Refitting

14 Fit the belt around the pulleys, ensuring that the belt is of the correct type if it is being renewed, and take up the slack in the belt by tightening the adjuster bolt.
15 Tension the drivebelt as described in the following paragraphs.

Adjustment

16 The belt should be tensioned so that, under firm thumb pressure, there is approximately 5.0 mm of free movement at the mid-point between the pulleys, on the longest belt run.
17 To adjust the tension, with the two tensioner pulley assembly retaining bolts and the lower alternator mounting bolt slackened, rotate the adjuster bolt until the correct tension is achieved. Once the belt is correctly tensioned, rotate the crankshaft through two complete turns, and recheck the tension.
18 When the belt is correctly tensioned, securely tighten the tensioner pulley assembly retaining bolts, and the lower alternator mounting bolt.
19 Reconnect the battery negative lead.
20 Clip the coolant hoses back in position, and secure with the retaining nut (where removed). Refit the roadwheel, and lower the vehicle to the ground.

2 Engine assembly/valve timing holes - general information and usage

Caution: Do not attempt to rotate the engine whilst the crankshaft, camshaft or injection pump are locked in position. If the engine is to be left in this state for a
long period of time, it is a good idea to place warning notices inside the vehicle, and in the engine compartment. This will reduce the possibility of the engine being accidentally cranked on the starter motor, which is likely to cause damage with the locking tools in place.
Note: *The following text refers only to the TUD 3 engines. The procedure for TUD 5 engines is essentially the same, especially as far as the flywheel and camshaft sprocket timing pins are concerned (except that in the latter case the timing bolt is inserted through one of the elongated holes towards the centre of the sprocket, down a closely-fitting groove in the sprocket hub, to be screwed into the cylinder head). However the injection pump sprocket position is set by inserting a single 6 mm rod or drill bit through one of the elongated holes towards the centre of the sprocket, down a closely-fitting groove in the sprocket hub and into the pump body itself.*

1 Timing holes are drilled in the camshaft sprocket, injection pump sprocket and in the flywheel. The holes are used to ensure that the crankshaft, camshaft and injection pump are correctly positioned when assembling the engine (to prevent the possibility of the valves contacting the pistons when refitting the cylinder head), or refitting the timing belt. When the timing holes are aligned with access holes, suitable-diameter pins or bolts can be inserted to position the camshaft, injection pump sprocket and crankshaft. Proceed as follows.
Note: *With the timing holes aligned, No 4 cylinder is at TDC on its compression stroke.*
2 Remove the upper and centre timing belt covers as described in Section 3.
3 The crankshaft must now be turned until the timing holes in the camshaft sprocket and injection pump sprocket are aligned with the corresponding holes in the cylinder head and pump mounting bracket. The holes are aligned when the camshaft sprocket hole is in the 4 o'clock position, when viewed from the right-hand end of the engine. The crankshaft can be turned by using a spanner on the crankshaft sprocket bolt, noting that it should always be rotated in a clockwise direction (viewed from

2.4 Insert a 6 mm bolt (arrowed) through hole in cylinder block flange and into timing hole in the flywheel

2.5a Insert an 8 mm bolt (arrowed) through the camshaft sprocket timing hole, and screw it into the cylinder head . . .

2.5b . . . then insert two 8 mm bolts (arrowed) into the injection pump sprocket holes, and screw them into the mounting bracket

3.1 Removing the timing belt upper cover

the right-hand end of the engine). If necessary, firmly apply the handbrake then jack up the front of the car, support it on axle stands and remove the right-hand roadwheel to improve access to the crankshaft pulley. Turning the engine will be much easier if the glow plugs are removed first.

4 With the camshaft sprocket hole correctly positioned, insert a 6 mm diameter bolt or drill bit through the hole in the front left-hand flange of the cylinder block, and locate it in the timing hole in the flywheel (see illustration). Note that it may be necessary to rotate the crankshaft slightly, to get the holes to align.

5 With the flywheel correctly positioned, insert an 8 mm diameter bolt through the timing hole in the camshaft sprocket, and screw it into the cylinder head. Also insert an 8 mm diameter bolt through each of the two timing holes on the injection pump sprocket, and screw them into the holes in the mounting bracket (see illustrations).

6 The crankshaft, camshaft and injection pump are now accurately positioned.

3 Timing belt covers - removal and refitting

Removal
Upper cover

1 Slacken and remove the three retaining screws, and remove the upper timing cover from the cylinder head (see illustration).

Centre cover

2 Remove the upper cover as described in paragraph 1.

3 Turn the wheels onto full right-hand lock, then prise out the rubber plug from underneath the right-hand front wheel arch. Unscrew the timing belt cover bolt which is accessible through the hole in the wing valance (see illustrations).

8B

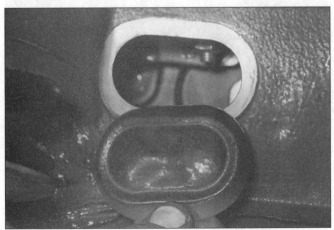

3.3a Remove the rubber plug from the right-hand wing valance . . .

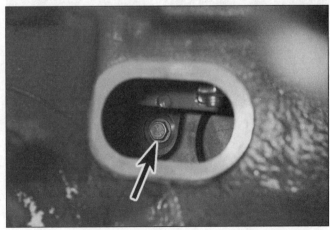

3.3b . . . to gain access to the timing belt centre cover bolt (arrowed)

3.4 Unscrew the remaining bolt (location arrowed) and remove the centre cover

3.7a Undo the retaining bolts (arrowed) . . .

4 Unscrew the remaining bolt from the centre of the cover, then manoeuvre the cover out of position **(see illustration)**.

Lower cover

5 Remove the auxiliary drivebelt as described in Section 1.
6 Remove the upper and centre covers as described above.
7 Undo the crankshaft pulley retaining bolts and remove the pulley, noting which way round it is fitted **(see illustrations)**.
8 Slacken and remove the three retaining bolts, and withdraw the lower cover over the crankshaft sprocket outer flange **(see illustration)**.

Refitting

Upper cover

9 Refit the cover, ensuring that it is correctly located with the centre cover, and tighten its retaining screws.

Centre cover

10 Manoeuvre the centre cover back into position, ensuring that it is correctly located with the lower cover, then tighten its retaining bolts. Refit the rubber plug to the wing valance.
11 Refit the upper cover as described above.

Lower cover

12 Locate the lower cover over the crankshaft sprocket outer flange, and tighten its retaining bolts.
13 Fit the pulley onto the crankshaft sprocket flange, ensuring that it is fitted the correct way round, and tighten its retaining bolts to the specified torque.
14 Refit the centre and upper covers as described above, then refit and tension the auxiliary drivebelt as described in Section 1.

4 Timing belt -
removal and refitting

Note: *Peugeot specify the use of a special electronic tool (SEEM belt tensioning measuring tool) to correctly set the timing belt tension.*

Removal

1 Disconnect the battery negative terminal.
2 Align the engine assembly/valve timing holes, then lock the crankshaft, camshaft and fuel injection pump sprockets in position as described in Section 2. *Do not* attempt to rotate the engine whilst the locking tools are in position.
3 Remove the lower timing belt cover as described in Section 3.
4 Remove the right-hand headlight unit as described in Section 7.

3.7b . . . and remove the crankshaft pulley from the engine

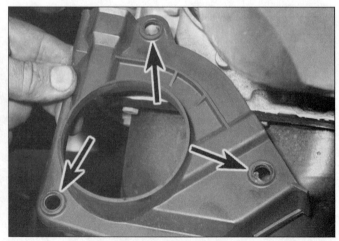

3.8 Undo the retaining bolts (locations arrowed) and remove the lower cover

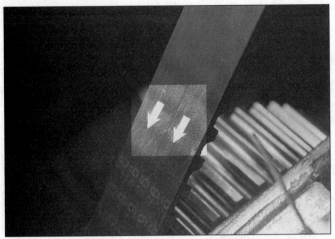

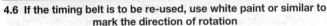

4.6 If the timing belt is to be re-used, use white paint or similar to mark the direction of rotation

4.10 Engage the timing belt with the sprockets as described in text

5 Loosen the timing belt tensioner pulley retaining nut. Pivot the pulley in a clockwise direction, using a square-section key fitted to the hole in the pulley, then retighten the retaining nut.

6 Slip the belt off the sprockets, idler and tensioner, and remove it from the engine. If the timing belt is to be re-used, use white paint or similar to mark the direction of rotation on the belt (if markings do not already exist) **(see illustration)**.

7 If signs of oil contamination are found, trace the source of the oil leak, and rectify it. Wash down the engine timing belt area and all related components, to remove all traces of oil.

Refitting

8 Prior to refitting, thoroughly clean the timing belt sprockets. Check that both the tensioner and idler pulleys rotate freely, without any sign of roughness. If necessary, renew the damaged pulley(s) as described in Section 5. Make sure that the locking tools are still in place, as described in Section 2.

TUD 3 engines

9 Manoeuvre the timing belt into position, ensuring that the arrows on the belt are

pointing in the direction of rotation (clockwise when viewed from the right-hand end of the engine). Do not twist the timing belt sharply while refitting it.

10 First locate the belt over the crankshaft sprocket then, keeping the belt taut, feed it over the idler pulley, around the injection pump sprocket, and over the camshaft sprocket **(see illustration)**. Locate the belt over the tensioner pulley, then finally over the coolant pump sprocket. Ensure that the belt teeth are seated centrally in the sprockets, and that any slack is in the section of the belt between the camshaft and coolant pump sprockets.

11 Loosen the tensioner pulley retaining nut. Pivot the pulley anti-clockwise to remove all

free play from the timing belt, then retighten the nut **(see illustration)**.

TUD 5 engines

12 Slacken the six (three on each) camshaft and injection pump hub bolts **(see illustration)**. Ensure that the sprockets move freely on their hubs. Finger tighten the six sprocket hub bolts, then slacken them all by just under a quarter of a turn.

13 Move the camshaft and injection pump sprockets to the ends of their slots, by turning them in the direction of engine rotation (clockwise).

14 Locate the timing belt, fully taut, firstly on the crankshaft sprocket, then on the tension roller nearest to the injection pump. Wrap the belt around the injection pump sprocket,

4.11 Remove all freeplay from the belt, then securely tighten the tensioner pulley retaining nut

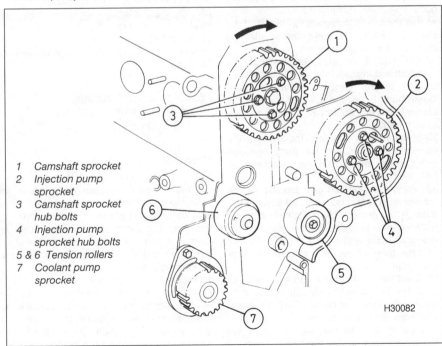

1 Camshaft sprocket
2 Injection pump sprocket
3 Camshaft sprocket hub bolts
4 Injection pump sprocket hub bolts
5 & 6 Tension rollers
7 Coolant pump sprocket

H30082

8B

4.12 Camshaft and injection pump sprocket hub bolts (TUD 5 engines)

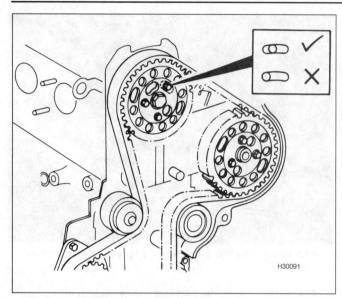

4.17 Correct location of camshaft and injection pump sprocket hub bolts (TUD 5 engines)

5.5a To prevent the camshaft rotating as the bolt is slackened, a sprocket-holding tool will be required. Use two lengths of steel strip (one long, the other short), and three nuts and bolts; one nut and bolt forms the pivot of a forked tool, with the remaining two nuts and bolts at the tips of the 'forks' to engage with the sprocket spokes.

ensuring that the belt does not jump on the crankshaft sprocket. If necessary move the injection pump sprocket, anti-clockwise by no more than one tooth to enable the belt to seat properly.

15 Fit the belt on the camshaft sprocket in the same way. Feed the belt around the remaining tension roller and on around the coolant pump sprocket.

Tensioning

16 Fit the special belt tensioning measuring equipment to the front run of the timing belt, midway between the camshaft and injection pump sprockets. Position the tensioner pulley so that the belt is tensioned to Stage 1 of the specified setting, then retighten its retaining nut without moving the tensioner.

17 On TUD 5 engines, ensure that the camshaft and injection sprocket hub bolts are located in the centre of the slot **(see illustration)**. If they are at either end, refit the timing belt. Fully tighten all six bolts to their correct torque.

18 Remove the locking tools from the camshaft sprocket, injection pump sprocket and flywheel, and remove the measuring tool from the belt.

19 Using a socket and extension bar on the crankshaft sprocket bolt, rotate the crankshaft through four (ten on TUD 5 engines) complete rotations in a clockwise direction (viewed from the right-hand end of the engine). *Do not at any time rotate the crankshaft anti-clockwise.*

20 Refit the locking tools and allow the belt to stand for approximately one minute, then slacken the tensioner pulley retaining nut (and six sprocket hub bolts), and refit the measuring tool to the belt. Position the tensioner pulley so that the belt is tensioned to the Stage 2 setting, then tighten the pulley

retaining nut to the specified torque setting. On TUD 5 engines tighten the six camshaft and injection pump hub sprockets bolts.

21 Remove the measuring tool from the belt. Rotate the crankshaft through another two complete rotations in a clockwise direction, so that the camshaft and injection pump sprocket and flywheel timing holes are realigned. *Do not* at any time rotate the crankshaft anti-clockwise. Refit the measuring tool to the belt and check that the belt tension is as specified at the Final stage.

22 If the belt tension is incorrect, repeat the procedures in paragraphs 20 and 21.

23 With the belt tension correctly set, remove locking tools and refit the timing belt covers as described in Section 3, and refit the headlight (if applicable) as described in Section 7.

---

5 Timing belt tensioner and sprockets - removal and refitting

Removal

Note: *This Section describes the removal and refitting of the components concerned as individual operations. If more than one of them is to be removed at the same time, start by removing the timing belt as described in Section 4; remove the actual component as described below, ignoring the preliminary dismantling steps.*

1 Disconnect the battery negative terminal.

2 Align the engine assembly/valve timing holes as described in Section 2, and lock the camshaft sprocket, injection pump sprocket and flywheel in position. *Do not* attempt to rotate the engine whilst the locking tools are in position.

Camshaft sprocket

3 Loosen the timing belt tensioner pulley retaining nut. Rotate the pulley in a clockwise direction, using a suitable square-section key fitted to the hole in the pulley, then retighten the retaining nut.

4 Disengage the timing belt from the sprocket, and move the belt clear, taking care not to bend or twist it sharply. Remove the locking tool from the camshaft sprocket.

5 Slacken the camshaft sprocket retaining bolt and remove it, along with its washer **(see illustrations). Note:** *On TUD 5 engines, unscrew the larger bolt at the centre of the sprocket, then remove the sprocket and its hub as a single component. Do not attempt to use the sprocket locking tool to prevent the sprocket from rotating whilst the retaining bolt is slackened.*

6 With the retaining bolt removed, slide the sprocket off the end of the camshaft. Note

5.5b Remove the retaining bolt and washer, then remove the camshaft sprocket

5.16 Using a home-made tool to hold the injection pump sprocket stationary whilst the retaining bolt is slackened - viewed through headlight aperture

5.17 Home-made injection pump sprocket removal tool in position on the sprocket

that the key on the rear of the sprocket engages with a cut-out on the end of the camshaft. Examine the camshaft oil seal for signs of oil leakage and, if necessary, renew it.

Crankshaft sprocket

7 Remove the lower timing belt cover as described in Section 3.

8 Loosen the timing belt tensioner pulley retaining nut. Rotate the pulley in a clockwise direction, using a suitable square-section key fitted to the hole in the pulley, then retighten the retaining nut.

9 Disengage the timing belt from the crankshaft sprocket, and move the belt clear, taking care not to bend or twist it sharply.

10 To prevent crankshaft rotation whilst the sprocket retaining bolt is slackened, select top gear, and have an assistant apply the brakes firmly. *Do not* be tempted to use the flywheel locking pin/bolt to prevent the crankshaft from rotating; temporarily remove the pin/bolt from the rear of the flywheel prior to slackening the pulley bolt, then refit it once the bolt has been slackened.

11 Unscrew the retaining bolt and washer, then slide the sprocket off the end of the

crankshaft. Refit the locking pin/bolt through the timing hole into the rear of the flywheel.

12 If the Woodruff key is a loose fit in the crankshaft, remove it and store it with the sprocket for safe-keeping. If necessary, also slide the flanged spacer off the end of the crankshaft. Examine the crankshaft oil seal for signs of oil leakage and, if necessary, renew it.

Fuel injection pump sprocket

13 Loosen the timing belt tensioner pulley retaining nut. Rotate the pulley in a clockwise direction, using a suitable square-section key fitted to the hole in the pulley, then retighten the retaining nut.

14 Disengage the timing belt from the injection pump sprocket, and move the belt clear, taking care not to bend or twist it sharply. If necessary, remove the right-hand headlight unit as described in Section 7 to improve access to the sprocket.

15 Unscrew the locking bolts from the pump sprocket or remove the timing pin, as applicable.

16 On TUD 3 engines, slacken the injection pump sprocket retaining nut whilst holding the sprocket stationary with a suitable peg spanner which engages with the sprocket

holes, similar to that described in paragraph 5 **(see illustration)**. Unscrew the nut slightly so that it is clear of the sprocket. On TUD 5 engines, unscrew the three sprocket-to-hub bolts and remove the sprocket.

17 On TUD 3 engines, a suitable tool will now be needed to free the sprocket from its taper on the pump shaft. In the absence of the special Peugeot clamp (No. 0157H), a suitable home-made alternative can be made out of a stout piece of steel strip and two 7 x 1 mm bolts which are approximately 40 mm in length. Drill two 8 mm holes in the strip, with their centres 45 mm apart. Align the holes in the strip with the two threaded holes in the sprocket, then screw in the bolts, tightening them evenly and progressively, until the sprocket is freed from the pump shaft taper **(see illustration)**. **Do not** be tempted to strike the pump with a hammer in an attempt to free the sprocket, as the pump internals will almost certainly be damaged.

18 Remove the bolts and the strip, then remove the sprocket retaining nut, and slide off the sprocket. If the Woodruff key is a loose fit in the pump shaft, remove it and store it with the sprocket for safe-keeping **(see illustrations)**.

8B

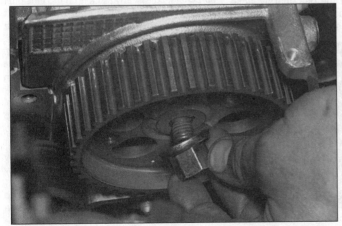

5.18a Unscrew the retaining nut, then remove the sprocket . . .

5.18b . . . and recover the Woodruff key (arrowed) from the injection pump shaft

5.19 Timing belt tensioner pulley retaining nut (arrowed)

5.21 Timing belt idler pulley retaining bolt (arrowed)

Tensioner pulley

19 Slacken and remove the timing belt tensioner pulley retaining nut, and slide the pulley off its mounting stud (see illustration). Examine the mounting stud for signs of damage and, if necessary, renew it - it is removed by unscrewing it from the cylinder block.

Idler pulley

20 Loosen the timing belt tensioner pulley retaining nut. Rotate the pulley in a clockwise direction, using a suitable square-section key fitted to the hole in the pulley, then retighten the retaining nut. In order to provide some slack in the timing belt between the crankshaft and injection pump sprockets, it will be necessary to remove the locking tool from the flywheel and rotate the crankshaft slightly anti-clockwise.

21 Unscrew the bolt retaining the idler to the cylinder block (see illustration), and withdraw the idler pulley. Carefully tie the timing belt up so that it is kept in full engagement with all of the sprockets.

Refitting

22 Clean the sprockets thoroughly, and renew any that show signs of wear, damage or cracks.

23 Clean the tensioner pulley and idler, but do not use any strong solvent which may enter the bearings. Check that each roller rotates freely about its hub, with no sign of stiffness or free play. Renew the tensioner pulley or idler if there is any doubt about its condition, or if there are any obvious signs of wear or damage.

Camshaft sprocket

24 Locate the sprocket on the end of the camshaft. Ensure that the locating key is correctly engaged with the cut-out in the camshaft end (see illustration).

25 Refit the sprocket retaining bolt and washer (on TUD 5 engines, coat the bolt with a suitable thread-locking compound). Tighten the bolt to the specified torque, whilst retaining the sprocket with the tool used on removal.

26 Realign the timing hole in the camshaft sprocket (see Section 2) with the corresponding hole in the cylinder head, and refit the timing bolt.

27 With the crankshaft, injection pump and camshaft locked in position, refit the timing belt to the camshaft sprocket. Ensure that the belt is taut around the crankshaft sprocket, idler pulley and injection pump sprocket, so that any slack is on the tensioner pulley side of the belt. Do not twist the belt sharply while refitting it, and ensure that the belt teeth are seated centrally in the sprockets.

28 Loosen the tensioner pulley retaining nut. Rotate the pulley anti-clockwise to remove all free play from the timing belt, then retighten the nut.

29 Tension the belt as described in Section 4.

30 Refit the timing belt covers as described in Section 3.

31 Reconnect the battery negative terminal.

Crankshaft sprocket

32 Where removed, locate the Woodruff key in the crankshaft end, then slide on the flanged spacer, aligning its slot with the Woodruff key.

33 Align the crankshaft sprocket slot with the Woodruff key, and slide it onto the end of the crankshaft.

34 Temporarily remove the locking pin from the rear of the flywheel, then refit the crankshaft sprocket retaining bolt and washer. Tighten the bolt to the specified torque, whilst preventing crankshaft rotation using the method employed on removal. Refit the locking pin to the rear of the flywheel.

35 With the crankshaft, injection pump and camshaft locked in position, refit the timing belt to the crankshaft sprocket. Ensure that the belt is taut between the crankshaft, idler pulley, injection pump and camshaft sprockets, so that any slack is on the tensioner pulley side of the belt. Do not twist the belt sharply while refitting it, and ensure that the belt teeth are seated centrally in the sprockets.

36 Loosen the tensioner pulley retaining nut. Rotate the pulley anti-clockwise to remove all free play from the timing belt, then retighten the nut.

37 Tension the belt as described in Section 4.

38 Refit the timing belt covers as described in Section 3.

Fuel injection pump sprocket

39 Where applicable, refit the Woodruff key to the pump shaft, ensuring that it is correctly located in its groove.

40 Locate the sprocket on the injection pump shaft, and engage it with the key (see illustration). On TUD 5 engines, refit the sprocket and tighten by hand only the three sprocket-to-hub bolts.

5.24 When refitting, ensure that the camshaft sprocket key and camshaft slot are correctly aligned (arrowed)

5.40 Align the sprocket groove (arrowed) with the Woodruff key when refitting the injection pump sprocket - TUD 3 engines

41 On TUD 3 engines, tighten the sprocket retaining nut to the specified torque, preventing the pump shaft from turning as during removal. Align the sprocket timing holes, and refit the locking tools.

42 With the crankshaft, injection pump and camshaft locked in position, refit the timing belt to the pump sprocket. Ensure that the belt is taut between the crankshaft, idler pulley, injection pump and camshaft sprockets, so that any slack is on the tensioner pulley side of the belt. Do not twist the belt sharply while refitting it, and ensure that the belt teeth are seated centrally in the sprockets.

43 Loosen the tensioner pulley retaining nut. Rotate the pulley anti-clockwise to remove all free play from the timing belt, then retighten the nut.

44 Tension the belt as described in Section 4.

45 Refit the timing belt covers as described in Section 3 and, where necessary, refit the headlight unit as described in Section 7.

Tensioner pulley

46 Check that the mounting stud is tightened in the cylinder block.

47 Locate the tensioner pulley on the stud, and lightly tighten its retaining nut.

48 With the crankshaft, injection pump and camshaft locked in position, ensure that the belt is taut between the crankshaft, idler pulley, injection pump and camshaft sprockets, so that any slack is on the tensioner pulley side of the belt.

49 Loosen the tensioner pulley retaining nut. Rotate the pulley anti-clockwise to remove all free play from the timing belt, then retighten the nut.

50 Tension the belt as described in Section 4.

51 Refit the timing belt covers as described in Section 3.

Idler pulley

52 Refit the idler pulley to the cylinder block, and tighten its retaining bolt securely.

6.1 Release the front direction indicator light unit retaining spring . . .

53 Carefully turn the crankshaft clockwise until the locking tool can be inserted into the flywheel.

54 With the crankshaft, injection pump and camshaft locked in position, ensure that the belt is taut between the crankshaft, idler pulley, injection pump and camshaft sprockets, so that any slack is on the tensioner pulley side of the belt.

55 Loosen the tensioner pulley retaining nut. Rotate the pulley anti-clockwise to remove all free play from the belt, then retighten the nut.

56 Tension the belt as described in Section 4.

57 Refit the timing belt covers as described in Section 3.

6 Front direction indicator – removal and refitting

1 Open the bonnet, and working at the front wing behind the direction indicator light, release the light unit retaining spring from the hole in the body panel (**see illustration**).

2 Withdraw the light unit forwards from the front wing (**see illustration**).

3 Twist the bulbholder anti-clockwise to release it from the rear of the light unit (**see illustration**).

4 Refitting is a reversal of removal, bearing in mind the following points:

(a) *Ensure that the bulbholder sealing ring is in good condition.*

(b) *When refitting the light unit, ensure that the lugs on the rear of the unit engage with the corresponding holes in the body panel.*

(c) *Ensure that the light unit retaining spring is correctly located in the hole in the body panel.*

7 Headlight – removal and refitting

1 Remove the front direction indicator light as described in Section 6.

2 Working at the rear of the headlight assembly, release the securing clip, and lift up the headlight rear cover.

8B

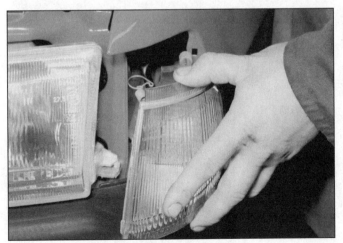

6.2 . . . withdraw the light unit . . .

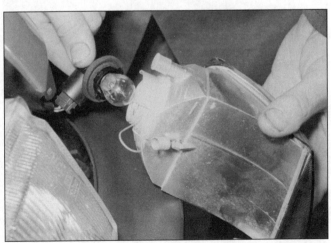

6.3 . . . and remove the bulbholder

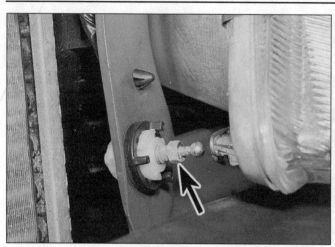

7.4a Pull the corners of the headlight unit from the balljoints (arrowed) . . .

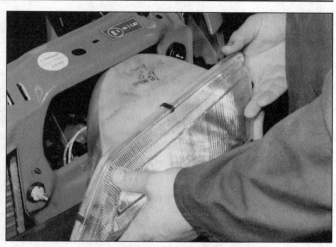

7.4b . . . then withdraw the headlight

3 Pull the wiring plugs from the rear of the bulbs in the headlight unit.
4 Carefully pull the corners of the headlight unit forwards to release the three balljoints, and withdraw the headlight (see illustrations).
5 Refitting is a reversal of removal, ensuring that the headlight balljoints are correctly engaged. Refit the direction indicator light as described in Section 6.

Chapter 9A
Peugeot 205 petrol 1983 to 1995

Contents

Specifications

Timing belt renewal interval . . . . Every 36 000 miles (60 000 km) or 3 years, whichever comes first

Note: *Although the normal interval for timing belt renewal is 72 000 miles (120 000 km), it is strongly recommended that the interval is halved on vehicles which are subjected to intensive use, ie, mainly short journeys or a lot of stop-start driving. The actual belt renewal interval is therefore very much up to the individual owner. That being said, it is highly recommended to err on the side of safety, and renew the belt at this earlier interval, bearing in mind the drastic consequences resulting from belt failure.*

Engine codes

954 cc	TU9
1124 cc	TU1
1360 cc	TU3
1580 cc	XU5
1905 cc	XU9

Ignition timing (vacuum hose disconnected)

XU5J engines (up to VIN 5520364)	30° BTDC at 3500 rpm or 6° BTDC at 700 rpm
XU5J engines (from VIN 5520364)	10° BTDC at 850 ± 50 rpm
XU5JA and XU5JA/K engines	10° BTDC at 900 rpm
XU51C and XU51C/K engines	10° BTDC at 750 rpm
XU5M2/Z, XU5M3/Z and XU5M3/L engines	Not adjustable, controlled by MMFD Mono-point G5/6 engine management system
XU9JA and XU9JA/K engines	5° BTDC at 700 rpm
XU9JA/Z and XU9JA/L engines	Not adjustable, controlled by Motronic M1.3 engine management system
XU9J1/Z and XU9J1/L engines	10° BTDC at 900 rpm

Torque wrench settings

	Nm	lbf ft
XU series engines		
Camshaft sprocket bolt (M10)	40	30
Camshaft sprocket bolt (M12)	80	59
Crankshaft pulley bolt	109	80
Roadwheel bolts	85	63
Timing belt tensioner nuts (spring-loaded type tensioner)	15	11
Timing belt tensioner roller bolt (eccentric roller type tensioner)	20	15
TU series engines		
Camshaft sprocket retaining bolt	80	59
Camshaft thrust fork retaining bolt	16	12
Crankshaft pulley retaining bolts	8	6
Crankshaft sprocket retaining bolt	110	81
Roadwheel bolts	85	63
Timing belt cover bolts	8	6
Timing belt tensioner pulley nut	23	17

9A

1 Auxiliary drivebelt - removal, refitting and adjustment

1 Apply the handbrake, then jack up the front of the car and support it on axle stands. Remove the right-hand front roadwheel.

Removal

2 Disconnect the battery negative lead.
3 Slacken both the alternator upper and lower mounting nuts/bolts (as applicable).
4 Push the alternator toward the engine until the belt is slack then slip the drivebelt from the pulleys. Where an adjuster bolt is fitted, back off the adjuster to relieve the tension in the drivebelt, then slip off the belt **(see illustration)**.

Refitting

5 Fit the belt around the pulleys, and take up the slack in the belt by moving the alternator by hand, or tightening the adjuster bolt.
6 Tension the drivebelt as described in the following paragraphs.

Adjustment

7 Correct tensioning of the drivebelt will ensure that it has a long life. A belt which is too slack will slip and perhaps squeal. Beware, however, of overtightening, as this can cause wear in the alternator bearings.
8 The belt should be tensioned so that, under firm thumb pressure, there is approximately 5.0 mm of free movement at the mid-point between the pulleys on the longest belt run.
9 To adjust, with the upper mounting nut/bolt just holding the alternator firm, and the lower mounting nut/bolt loosened, lever the alternator away from the engine, or turn the adjuster bolt until the correct tension is achieved. Rotate the crankshaft a couple of times, recheck the tension, then securely tighten both the alternator mounting nuts/bolts. Where applicable, also tighten the bolt securing the adjuster strap to its mounting bracket.
10 Reconnect the battery negative lead.

11 Refit the plastic cover to the wing valance. Refit the roadwheel, and lower the vehicle to the ground.

2 Engine assembly/valve timing holes (TU series engines) - general information and usage

Note: *Do not attempt to rotate the engine whilst the crankshaft/camshaft are locked in position. If the engine is to be left in this state for a long period of time, it is a good idea to place warning notices inside the vehicle, and in the engine compartment. This will reduce the possibility of the engine being accidentally cranked on the starter motor, which is likely to cause damage with the locking pins in place.*

1 On all models, timing holes are drilled in the camshaft sprocket and in the rear of the flywheel. The holes are used to ensure that the crankshaft and camshaft are correctly positioned when assembling the engine (to prevent the valves contacting the pistons when refitting the cylinder head), or refitting the timing belt. When the timing holes are aligned with access holes in the cylinder head and the front of the cylinder block, suitable diameter pins can be inserted to lock both the camshaft and crankshaft in position, preventing them from rotating. Proceed as follows.
2 Remove the timing belt upper cover as described in Section 3.
3 The crankshaft must now be turned until the timing hole in the camshaft sprocket is aligned with the corresponding hole in the cylinder head. The holes are aligned when the camshaft sprocket hole is in the 2 o'clock position, when viewed from the right-hand end of the engine. The crankshaft can be turned by using a spanner on the crankshaft sprocket bolt, noting that it should always be rotated in a clockwise direction (viewed from the right-hand end of the engine).
4 With the camshaft sprocket hole correctly positioned, insert a 6 mm diameter bolt or drill

1.4 Slackening the alternator adjuster bolt to release the auxiliary drivebelt

through the hole in the front, left-hand flange of the cylinder block, and locate it in the timing hole in the rear of the flywheel **(see illustration)**. Note that it may be necessary to rotate the crankshaft slightly, to get the holes to align.
5 With the flywheel correctly positioned, insert a 10 mm diameter bolt or a drill through the timing hole in the camshaft sprocket, and locate it in the hole in the cylinder head **(see illustration)**.
6 The crankshaft and camshaft are now locked in position, preventing unnecessary rotation.

3 Timing belt covers (TU series engines) - removal and refitting

Removal
Upper cover

1 Slacken and remove the two retaining bolts (one at the front and one at the rear), and remove the upper timing cover from the cylinder head **(see illustrations)**.

2.4 Insert a 6 mm bolt (arrowed) through hole in cylinder block flange and into timing hole in flywheel . . .

2.5 . . . then insert a 10 mm bolt through the camshaft sprocket timing hole, and locate it in the cylinder head

3.1a Undo the two retaining bolts (arrowed) . . .

3.1b . . . and remove the timing belt upper cover

Centre cover

2 Remove the upper cover as described in paragraph 1, then free the wiring from its retaining clips on the centre cover.
3 Slacken and remove the three retaining bolts (one at the rear of the cover, beneath the engine mounting plate, and two directly above the crankshaft pulley), and manoeuvre the centre cover out from the engine compartment **(see illustration)**.

Lower cover

4 Remove the auxiliary drivebelt as described in Section 1.
5 Remove the upper and centre covers as described in paragraphs 1 to 3.
6 Undo the three crankshaft pulley retaining bolts and remove the pulley, noting which way round it is fitted **(see illustrations)**.
7 Slacken and remove the single retaining bolt, and slide the lower cover off the end of the crankshaft **(see illustration)**.

3.3 . . . then undo the three bolts (locations arrowed) and remove the centre cover

3.6a Undo the three bolts (arrowed) . . .

9A

3.6b . . . and remove the crankshaft pulley

3.7 Undo the retaining bolt and remove the timing belt lower cover

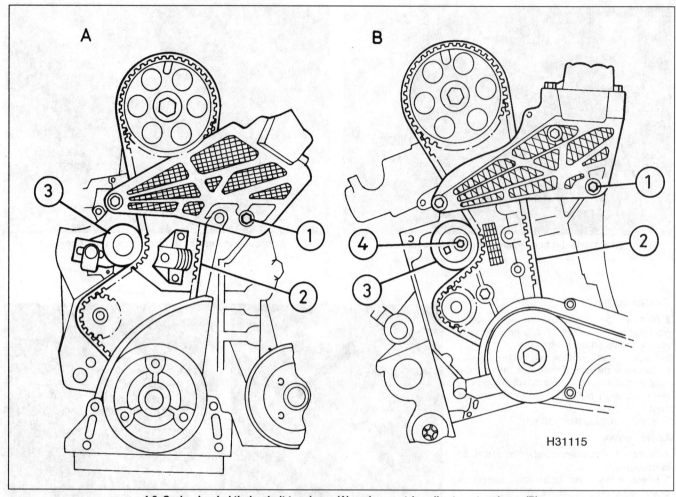

4.6 Spring loaded timing belt tensioner (A) and eccentric roller type tensioner (B)

1 Right-hand engine mounting   2 Timing belt   3 Tensioner roller   4 Tensioner roller nut

Refitting

Upper cover

8 Refit the cover, ensuring it is correctly located with the centre cover, and tighten its retaining bolts.

Centre cover

9 Manoeuvre the centre cover back into position, ensuring it is correctly located with the lower cover, and tighten its retaining bolts.
10 Clip the wiring loom into its retaining clips on the front of the centre cover, then refit the upper cover as described in paragraph 8.

Lower cover

11 Locate the lower cover over the timing belt sprocket, and tighten its retaining bolt.
12 Fit the pulley to the end of the crankshaft, ensuring it is fitted the correct way round, and tighten its retaining bolts to the specified torque.
13 Refit the centre and upper covers as described above, then refit and tension the auxiliary drivebelt as described in Section 1.

4 Timing belt (XU series engines) - removal and refitting

Note: If the timing belt is to be renewed, ensure that the correct belt type is obtained - the timing belt used with the earlier spring-loaded tensioner is not interchangeable with the later type.
Note: Do not attempt to rotate the engine whilst the crankshaft/camshaft are locked in position. If the engine is to be left in this state for a long period of time, it is a good idea to place warning notices inside the vehicle, and in the engine compartment. This will reduce the possibility of the engine being accidentally cranked on the starter motor, which is likely to cause damage with the locking pins in place.

Removal

1 Disconnect the battery negative lead.

2 Remove the auxiliary drivebelt as described in Section 1.
3 Remove the inner shield from the right-hand wheel arch and wedge the radiator bottom hose under the sump.
4 Remove the shield from the camshaft sprocket.
5 Remove the plastic covers from the front of the timing belt. Note the location of the various bolts.
6 Observe the timing belt tensioner assembly and ascertain whether it is of the spring-loaded type or the later eccentric roller type **(see illustration)**. Proceed as follows under the appropriate sub-heading according to type fitted.

Models with spring-loaded tensioner

7 Turn the crankshaft using a spanner on the pulley bolt until the dowel hole in the pulley is at about 12 o'clock and the hole in the camshaft sprocket is at about 7 o'clock. In this position a 10 mm dowel should pass

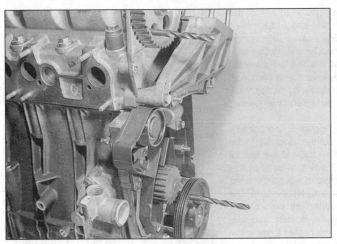

4.7 Crankshaft and camshaft sprockets locked with timing dowels

4.10a Slacken the two nuts at the front of the timing belt tensioner . . .

through each hole and into the timing recess behind. Verify this and then remove the dowels **(see illustration)**.

8 Remove the clutch bottom shield. Have an assistant jam the starter ring gear while the crankshaft pulley bolt is undone. This bolt is very tight. Do not jam the pulley by means of the timing dowel: damage will result. Remove the bolt and washer.

9 Check that the 10 mm dowels will still enter the timing holes: adjust the crankshaft position if necessary by means of the starter ring gear. Remove the crankshaft pulley, retrieving the Woodruff key if it is loose.

10 Slacken the two nuts on the front of the timing belt tensioner and the single nut at the rear. Use a spanner on the square end of the tensioner cam spindle to turn the cam to the horizontal position and so compress the tensioner spring **(see illustrations)**. Tighten the cam locknut.

11 Remove the timing belt, taking care not to kink it or contaminate it with oil if it is to be re-used. Draw an arrow on the belt using

chalk to mark the running direction unless a new belt is to be fitted.

12 If signs of oil contamination are found, trace the source of the oil leak and rectify it. Wash down the engine timing belt area and all related components, to remove all traces of oil.

Models with eccentric roller tensioner

13 Proceed as described in paragraphs 7 to 9, noting that the crankshaft pulley timing dowel must be of 10 mm diameter, stepped down to 8 mm at one end to engage with the smaller hole in the timing recess.

14 Slacken the tensioner roller bolt to relieve the belt tension, then withdraw the belt, noting the direction of fitting and the markings. Take care not to kink it or contaminate it with oil if it is to be re-used. Draw an arrow on the belt using chalk to mark the running direction unless a new belt is to be fitted.

15 If signs of oil contamination are found, trace the source of the oil leak and rectify it. Wash down the engine timing belt area and all

related components, to remove all traces of oil.

Refitting

Models with spring-loaded tensioner

16 Commence refitting by positioning the belt on the crankshaft sprocket, then refitting the pulley and verifying the correct position of the crankshaft by means of the dowel. Observe the arrows on the belt showing the direction of rotation, and the timing lines which align with marks on the crankshaft and camshaft sprockets **(see illustration)**.

17 Fit the belt to the camshaft sprocket, round the tensioner and to the coolant pump sprocket.

18 Release the tensioner cam locknut and turn the cam downwards to release the spring. Tighten the locknut and the tensioner front nuts.

19 Remove the timing dowels and turn the crankshaft through two full turns in the normal direction of rotation. Turn the crankshaft

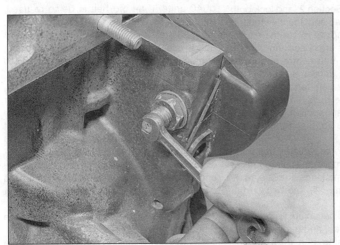

4.10b . . . and turn the tensioner cam spindle to the horizontal position

4.16 Timing line on belt aligned with mark on camshaft sprocket

5.5 Mark the direction of rotation on the belt if it is to be re-used

further to bring No 1 piston to TDC on the firing stroke.

20 Slacken the tensioner front nuts and the cam locknut, then retighten them.

21 Turn the crankshaft further and make sure that the timing dowels can still be inserted. If not, remove the drivebelt and start again.

22 If a new belt has been fitted, it must be run in and retensioned, as follows.

23 Tighten the crankshaft pulley bolt to the specified torque, then refit and tension the auxiliary drivebelt (see Section 1). Temporarily refit the camshaft sprocket cover.

24 Run the engine up to operating temperature, indicated by the cooling fan operating, then stop it and allow it to cool for at least two hours.

25 Rotate the crankshaft to the TDC position, No 1 cylinder firing, then slacken and retighten the tensioner nuts once more.

26 Remove the auxiliary drivebelt and the crankshaft pulley. Refit and secure the plastic covers, then refit the pulley and tighten its bolts to the specified torque. Refit and tension the auxiliary drivebelt.

27 Check the ignition timing and adjust if necessary (Section 8).

Models with eccentric roller tensioner

Note: *Peugeot specify the use of special tool (SEEM C. TRONIC type 105 or 105.5 belt tension measuring equipment) to correctly set the belt tension*

28 Commence refitting by slipping the belt over the camshaft sprocket, followed by the crankshaft sprocket, the coolant pump sprocket, and finally over the tensioner roller. Observe the arrows on the belt indicating the direction of rotation, and the timing lines which align with corresponding marks on the crankshaft and camshaft sprockets.

29 With the camshaft timing dowel fitted, rotate the tensioner roller anti-clockwise by hand as far as possible to take up any slack in the belt, then tighten the tensioner roller bolt sufficiently to hold the roller in position. The special belt tension measuring equipment

should be fitted to the tensioned run of the belt, and the tensioner roller should be moved to give a reading of 30 ± 2 units. Tighten the roller bolt to the specified torque, taking care not to move the roller as the bolt is tightened.

30 Check that the crankshaft and camshaft are still positioned correctly by temporarily refitting the crankshaft pulley and re-inserting the timing dowel.

31 Remove the timing dowels, temporarily refit the crankshaft pulley, and turn the crankshaft through two full turns in the normal direction of rotation. Check that both timing dowels can still be inserted. If not, remove the drivebelt and start again. Never turn the crankshaft backwards during this procedure.

32 If all is well, remove the dowels, and turn the crankshaft through two further turns in the normal direction of rotation.

33 Refit the camshaft timing dowel, and fit the special belt tension measuring to the tensioned run of the belt. The reading should now be between 42 and 46 units.

34 If the tension is not as specified, repeat the tensioning operation.

35 Refit the belt covers and the crankshaft pulley. Apply thread locking compound to the crankshaft pulley bolt threads, and tighten the bolt to the specified torque.

36 On completion, refit all disturbed components, and tension the auxiliary drivebelt, as described in Section 1.

5 Timing belt (TU series engines) - removal and refitting

Note: *Peugeot specify the use of a special electronic tool (SEEM C.TRONIC type 105 belt tensioning measuring tool) to correctly set the timing belt tension.*

Removal

1 Disconnect the battery negative lead.

2 Align the engine assembly/valve timing holes as described in Section 2, and lock both the camshaft sprocket and the flywheel in position. *Do not* attempt to rotate the engine whilst the locking tools are in position.

3 Remove the timing belt centre and lower covers as described in Section 3.

4 Loosen the timing belt tensioner pulley retaining nut. Pivot the pulley in a clockwise direction, using a square-section key fitted to the hole in the pulley hub, then retighten the retaining nut.

5 If the timing belt is to be re-used, use white paint or similar to mark the direction of rotation on the belt (if markings do not already exist) **(see illustration)**. Slip the belt off the sprockets.

6 If signs of oil contamination are found, trace the source of the oil leak, and rectify it. Wash down the engine timing belt area and all related components, to remove all traces of oil.

Refitting

7 Prior to refitting, thoroughly clean the timing belt sprockets. Check that the tensioner pulley rotates freely, without any sign of roughness. If necessary, renew the tensioner pulley as described in Section 7. Make sure that the locking tools are still in place, as described in Section 2.

8 Manoeuvre the timing belt into position, ensuring that the arrows on the belt are pointing in the direction of rotation (clockwise, when viewed from the right-hand end of the engine).

9 Do not twist the timing belt sharply while refitting it. Fit the belt over the crankshaft and camshaft sprockets. Make sure that the front run of the belt is taut - ie, ensure that any slack is on the tensioner pulley side of the belt. Fit the belt over the coolant pump sprocket and tensioner pulley. Ensure that the belt teeth are seated centrally in the sprockets.

10 Loosen the tensioner pulley retaining nut. Pivot the pulley anti-clockwise to remove all free play from the timing belt, then retighten the nut.

11 Fit the special belt tensioning measuring equipment to the front run of the timing belt, approximately midway between the camshaft and crankshaft sprockets. Position the tensioner pulley so that the belt is tensioned to a setting of 45 units, then retighten its retaining nut.

12 Remove the locking tools from the camshaft sprocket and flywheel, and remove the measuring tool from the belt.

13 Using a suitable socket and extension bar on the crankshaft sprocket bolt, rotate the crankshaft through four complete rotations in a clockwise direction (viewed from the right-hand end of the engine). *Do not* at any time rotate the crankshaft anti-clockwise.

14 Slacken the tensioner pulley retaining nut, and refit the measuring tool to the belt. If a new belt is being fitted, tension it to a setting of 40 units. If an old belt is being re-used, tighten it to a setting of 36 units. **Note**: *Peugeot state that a belt becomes old after 1 hour's use.* With the belt correctly tensioned, tighten the pulley retaining nut to the specified torque.

15 Remove the measuring tool from the belt, then rotate the crankshaft through another two complete rotations in a clockwise direction, so that both the camshaft sprocket and flywheel timing holes are realigned. *Do not* at any time rotate the crankshaft anti-clockwise. Fit the measuring tool to the belt, and check the belt tension. A new belt should give a reading of 51 ± 3 units; an old belt should be 45 ± 3 units.

16 If the belt tension is incorrect, repeat the procedures in paragraphs 14 and 15.

17 With the belt tension correctly set, refit the timing belt covers as described in Section 3, and reconnect the battery negative lead.

6.2 To make a camshaft sprocket holding tool, obtain two lengths of steel strip about 6 mm thick by 30 mm wide or similar, one 600 mm long, the other 200 mm long (all dimensions approximate). Bolt the two strips together to form a forked end, leaving the bolt slack so that the shorter strip can pivot freely. At the end of each 'prong' of the fork, secure a bolt with a nut and a locknut, to act as the fulcrums; these will engage with the cut-outs in the sprocket, and should protrude by about 30 mm

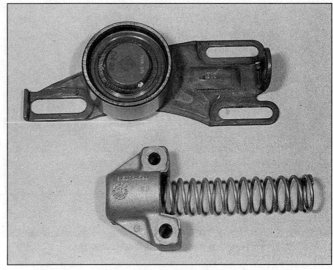

6.12 Spring loaded timing belt tensioner components

6 Timing belt tensioner and sprockets (XU series engines) - removal and refitting

Removal

Camshaft sprocket

1 Remove the timing belt as described in Section 4.

2 Remove the locking pin from the camshaft sprocket, slacken the sprocket retaining bolt and remove it, along with its washer. To prevent the camshaft rotating as the bolt is slackened, restrain the sprocket with a suitable tool through the holes in the sprocket face **(see illustration)**. *Do not* attempt to use the sprocket locking pin to prevent the sprocket from rotating whilst the bolt is slackened.

3 With the retaining bolt removed, slide the sprocket off the end of the camshaft. If the locating peg is a loose fit in the rear of the sprocket, remove it for safe-keeping. Examine the camshaft oil seal for signs of oil leakage and, if necessary, renew it.

Crankshaft sprocket

4 Remove the timing belt as described in Section 4.

5 Slide the sprocket off the end of the crankshaft. Remove the Woodruff key from the crankshaft, and store it with the sprocket for safe-keeping. Where necessary, also slide the spacer (where fitted) off the end of the crankshaft.

6 Examine the crankshaft oil seal for signs of oil leakage and, if necessary, renew it .

Tensioner assembly (models with spring-loaded tensioner)

7 Remove the timing belt as described in Section 4.

8 Undo the two bolts at the front and single nut at the rear and withdraw the spring housing spring and tensioner pulley. Take care to keep the spring under control as the bolts are undone to prevent it flying out.

Tensioner assembly (models with eccentric roller tensioner)

9 Remove the timing belt as described in Section 4.

10 Slacken and remove the timing belt tensioner pulley retaining bolt, and slide the pulley off its mounting stud. Examine the mounting stud for signs of damage and if necessary, renew it.

Refitting

11 Clean the camshaft/crankshaft sprockets thoroughly, and renew any that show signs of wear, damage or cracks.

12 Clean the tensioner assembly, but do not use any strong solvent which may enter the pulley bearing. Check that the pulley rotates freely on the backplate, with no sign of stiffness or free play **(see illustration)**. Renew the assembly if there is any doubt about its condition, or if there are any obvious signs of wear or damage.

Camshaft sprocket

13 Refit the locating peg (where removed) to the rear of the sprocket. Locate the sprocket on the end of the camshaft, ensuring that the locating peg is correctly engaged with the cut-out in the camshaft end.

14 Refit the sprocket retaining bolt and washer, and tighten it to the specified torque. Retain the sprocket with the tool used on removal. Note that on early models the sprocket is secured with an M12 bolt whereas this has been reduced to M10 on later engines. Ensure that the correct torque wrench setting is used according to bolt type.

15 Realign the hole in the camshaft sprocket with the corresponding hole in the cylinder head, and refit the locking pin. Check that the crankshaft pulley locking pin is still in position.

16 Refit the timing belt (Section 4).

Crankshaft sprocket

17 Slide the spacer (where fitted) into position, taking great care not to damage the crankshaft oil seal, and refit the Woodruff key to its slot in the crankshaft end.

18 Slide on the crankshaft sprocket, aligning its slot with the Woodruff key.

19 Refit the timing belt (Section 4).

Tensioner assembly (models with spring-loaded tensioner)

20 Assemble the tensioner spring, spring housing and pulley then locate the assembly on the engine.

21 Fit the front bolts and rear locknut finger tight only. Use a spanner on the square end of the tensioner cam spindle to turn the cam to the horizontal position and so compress the tensioner spring. Tighten the cam locknut.

22 Refit the timing belt (Section 4).

Tensioner assembly (models with eccentric roller tensioner)

23 Refit the tensioner pulley to its mounting stud, and fit the retaining bolt.

24 Refit the timing belt (Section 4).

7 Timing belt tensioner and sprockets (TU series engines) - removal and refitting

Note: *This Section describes the removal and refitting of the components concerned as individual operations. If more than one of them is to be removed at the same time, start by removing the timing belt as described in*

9A

7.11a Remove the crankshaft sprocket bolt . . .

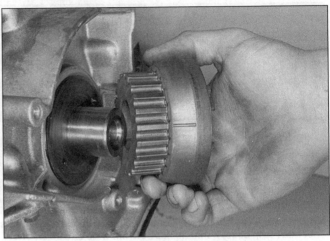

7.11b . . . then slide off the sprocket

Section 5; remove the actual component as described below, ignoring the preliminary dismantling steps.

Removal

1 Disconnect the battery negative lead.
2 Position the engine assembly/valve timing holes as described in Section 2, and lock both the camshaft sprocket and flywheel in position. *Do not* attempt to rotate the engine whilst the pins are in position.

Camshaft sprocket

3 Remove the centre timing belt cover as described in Section 3.
4 Loosen the timing belt tensioner pulley retaining nut. Rotate the pulley in a clockwise direction, using a suitable square-section key fitted to the hole in the pulley hub, then retighten the retaining nut.
5 Disengage the timing belt from the sprocket, and move the belt clear, taking care not to bend or twist it sharply. Remove the locking pin from the camshaft sprocket.
6 Slacken the camshaft sprocket retaining bolt and remove it, along with its washer. To

7.12 Remove the flanged spacer if necessary

prevent the camshaft rotating as the bolt is slackened, restrain the sprocket with a suitable tool through the holes in the sprocket face **(see illustration 6.2)**. *Do not* attempt to use the sprocket locking pin to prevent the sprocket from rotating whilst the bolt is slackened.
7 With the retaining bolt removed, slide the sprocket off the end of the camshaft. If the locating peg is a loose fit in the rear of the sprocket, remove it for safe-keeping. Examine the camshaft oil seal for signs of oil leakage and, if necessary, renew it.

Crankshaft sprocket

8 Remove the centre and lower timing belt covers as described in Section 3.
9 Loosen the timing belt tensioner pulley retaining nut. Rotate the pulley in a clockwise direction, using a suitable square-section key fitted to the hole in the pulley hub, then retighten the retaining nut.
10 To prevent crankshaft rotation whilst the sprocket retaining bolt is slackened, select top gear, and have an assistant apply the brakes firmly. *Do not* be tempted to use the flywheel locking pin to prevent the crankshaft from rotating; temporarily remove the locking pin from the rear of the flywheel prior to slackening the pulley bolt, then refit it once the bolt has been slackened.
11 Unscrew the retaining bolt and washer, then slide the sprocket off the end of the crankshaft **(see illustrations)**. Refit the locating pin to the rear of the timing hole in the rear of the flywheel.
12 If the Woodruff key is a loose fit in the crankshaft, remove it and store it with the sprocket for safe-keeping. If necessary, also slide the flanged spacer off the end of the crankshaft **(see illustration)**. Examine the crankshaft oil seal for signs oil leakage and, if necessary, renew it.

Tensioner pulley

13 Remove the centre timing belt cover as described in Section 3.

14 Slacken and remove the timing belt tensioner pulley retaining nut, and slide the pulley off its mounting stud. Examine the mounting stud for signs of damage and, if necessary, renew it.

Refitting

15 Clean the sprockets thoroughly, and renew any that show signs of wear, damage or cracks.
16 Clean the tensioner assembly, but do not use any strong solvent which may enter the pulley bearing. Check that the pulley rotates freely about its hub, with no sign of stiffness or of free play. Renew the tensioner pulley if there is any doubt about its condition, or if there are any obvious signs of wear or damage.

Camshaft sprocket

17 Refit the locating peg (where removed) to the rear of the sprocket, then locate the sprocket on the end of the camshaft. Ensure that the locating peg is correctly engaged with the cut-out in the camshaft end.
18 Refit the sprocket retaining bolt and washer. Tighten the bolt to the specified torque, whilst retaining the sprocket with the tool used on removal.
19 Realign the timing hole in the camshaft sprocket (see Section 2) with the corresponding hole in the cylinder head, and refit the locking pin.
20 Refit the timing belt to the camshaft sprocket. Ensure that the front run of the belt is taut - ie, ensure that any slack is on the tensioner pulley side of the belt. Do not twist the belt sharply while refitting it, and ensure that the belt teeth are seated centrally in the sprockets.
21 Loosen the tensioner pulley retaining nut. Rotate the pulley anti-clockwise to remove all free play from the timing belt, then retighten the nut.
22 Tension the belt as described in Section 5.

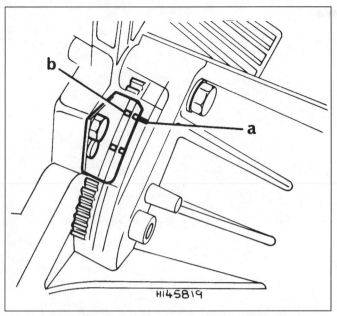

8.2 Initial static ignition timing on XU series engines

a   *Single flywheel mark*
b   *BTDC mark on timing plate*

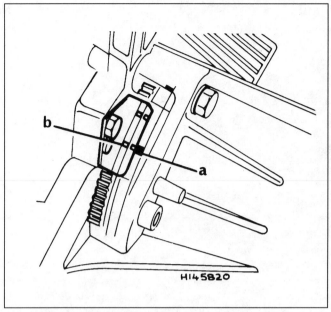

8.8 Dynamic ignition timing on XU series engines

a   *Double flywheel mark*
b   *TDC mark on timing plate*

23 Refit the timing belt covers as described in Section 3.

Crankshaft sprocket

24 Where removed, locate the Woodruff key in the crankshaft end, then slide on the flanged spacer, aligning its slot with the Woodruff key.
25 Align the crankshaft sprocket slot with the Woodruff key, and slide it onto the end of the crankshaft.
26 Temporarily remove the locking pin from the rear of the flywheel, then refit the crankshaft sprocket retaining bolt and washer. Tighten the bolt to the specified torque, whilst preventing crankshaft rotation using the method employed on removal. Refit the locking pin to the rear of the flywheel.
27 Relocate the timing belt on the crankshaft sprocket. Ensure that the front run of the belt is taut - ie, ensure that any slack is on the tensioner pulley side of the belt. Do not twist the belt sharply while refitting it, and ensure that the belt teeth are seated centrally in the sprockets.
28 Loosen the tensioner pulley retaining nut. Rotate the pulley anti-clockwise to remove all free play from the timing belt, then retighten the nut.
29 Tension the belt as described in Section 5.
30 Refit the timing belt covers as described in Section 3.

Tensioner pulley

31 Refit the tensioner pulley to its mounting stud, and fit the retaining nut.
32 Ensure that the front run of the belt is taut

- ie, ensure that any slack is on the pulley side of the belt. Check that the belt is centrally located on all its sprockets. Rotate the pulley anti-clockwise to remove all free play from the timing belt, then tighten the pulley retaining nut securely.
33 Tension the belt as described in Section 5.
34 Refit the timing belt covers as described in Section 3.

<table>
<tr><td>8</td><td>Ignition timing (XU series engines) - checking and adjustment</td></tr>
</table>

Note: *On engines equipped with MMFD Mono-point G5/6 or Motronic M1.3 engine management systems the ignition timing is controlled by the system ECU and cannot be adjusted.*

1 To set the ignition timing statically so that the engine can be started, first remove No 1 spark plug (nearest the flywheel) and turn the engine in the normal rotational direction until pressure is felt - indicating that the piston is commencing the compression stroke. The pressure can be felt using a suitable wooden rod or piece of cork placed over the spark plug hole.
2 While looking into the timing aperture in the clutch housing/transmission casing, continue turning the crankshaft until the single mark on the flywheel is opposite the BTDC mark on the timing plate **(see illustration)**.
3 Check that the distributor rotor arm is facing the No 1 HT lead segment position in

the distributor cap. To do this, remove the cap and mark the outside in line with the segment, then put it back on the distributor noting which way the rotor arm is facing.
4 If necessary, loosen the mounting nuts and turn the distributor body to bring the segment and rotor arm in line, then tighten the nuts. Refit No 1 spark plug.
5 Run the engine to normal operating temperature then stop it and connect a tachometer to it.
6 Disconnect and plug the vacuum pipe at the distributor vacuum advance unit.
7 Disconnect and remove the air cleaner inlet duct then connect a stroboscopic timing light to the engine as described in the timing light manufacturer's instructions, and with the HT pick-up lead connected to No 1 spark plug HT lead.
8 On early models, run the engine at 3500 rpm and point the timing light into the timing aperture. The double mark on the flywheel should be aligned with the TDC mark on the timing plate; indicating that the ignition is advanced by 30° **(see illustration)**. On engines without double timing marks, refer to the *Specifications* for the relevant ignition timing setting and engine speed, then check that the single mark on the flywheel is aligned with the appropriate mark on the timing plate.
9 If adjustment is necessary, loosen the distributor mounting nuts and rotate the distributor body as required. Tighten the nuts on completion.
10 Stop the engine, disconnect the tachometer and timing light then reconnect the vacuum pipe and air cleaner inlet duct.

9A

Notes

Chapter 9B
Peugeot 205 diesel 1983 to 1995

Contents

Specifications

Timing belt renewal interval . . . . Every 36 000 miles (60 000 km)

Note: *Although the normal interval for timing belt renewal is 72 000 miles (120 000 km), it is strongly recommended that the interval is halved on vehicles which are subjected to intensive use, ie, mainly short journeys or a lot of stop-start driving. The actual belt renewal interval is therefore very much up to the individual owner. That being said, it is highly recommended to err on the side of safety, and renew the belt at this earlier interval, bearing in mind the drastic consequences resulting from belt failure.*

Power steering drivebelt tension	Nm	lbf ft
New belt	57	42
Used belt	30	22

Vacuum pump drivebelt tension	Nm	lbf ft
Adjusting pivot (later models)	5	4

Torque wrench settings	Nm	lbf ft
Alternator pivot bolt	39	29
Alternator top mounting bolt and locknut	20	15
Camshaft sprocket	35	26
Crankshaft pulley bolt:		
Stage 1	40	30
Stage 2	Angle tighten by a further 60°	
Engine right-hand mounting bracket:		
Lower bracket	18	13
Upper bracket to engine	35	26
Upper bracket to mounting rubber	28	21
Pump pulley to camshaft	35	26
Timing belt intermediate roller	18	13
Timing belt tensioner	18	13
Timing cover, lower	12	9

9B

---

1 Auxiliary drivebelt - adjustment

Alternator

1 To adjust the tension, first check that the belt is correctly fitted over the pulleys.
2 With the alternator mountings loose, carefully lever the alternator outwards to tighten the drivebelt. Using a wooden lever will minimise the risk of damage to the alternator casing.
3 The belt should be able to move by approximately 6.0 mm, with moderate thumb pressure midway between the pulleys **(see illustration)**.
4 Tighten the mounting bolts to the correct torque.

Power steering pump

5 Adjust the tension by loosening the mounting and adjusting bolts, reposition the pump and retighten the bolts.
6 The deflection should be 5.0 mm.
7 On early models three slotted holes are provided in the bracket and on later models the pump pivots on a single bolt.
8 A torque wrench may be used on the later type to adjust the belt tension using the

1.3 Checking the tension of the alternator drivebelt

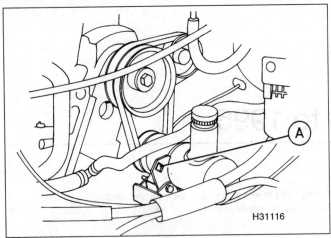

1.8 Square hole (A) for adjusting the belt tension on the later type pump

1.9 Checking the vacuum pump drivebelt tension

12.7 mm (1/2 in) square hole provided (see illustration). With both bolts loose, apply the torque given in the Specifications, then tighten the adjustment bolt, followed by the pivot bolt.

Vacuum pump (early models)

Note: *Later models have a revised mounting arrangement.*

9 On models fitted with a belt-driven brake vacuum pump, it is important to ensure that the drivebelt is correctly tensioned (see illustration).

10 Loosen the mounting bolts and adjust the pump to the correct tension.

11 The deflection should be 5.0 mm.

12 When the drivebelt is at the correct tension, tighten the mounting bolts to the correct torque.

Vacuum pump drivebelt (later models)

13 The following paragraphs describe the adjustment procedure for later models, which have the revised mounting arrangement shown (see illustration).

14 Loosen the pivot and adjustment bolts on the vacuum pump.

15 A welded nut is fitted to the pivot bracket.

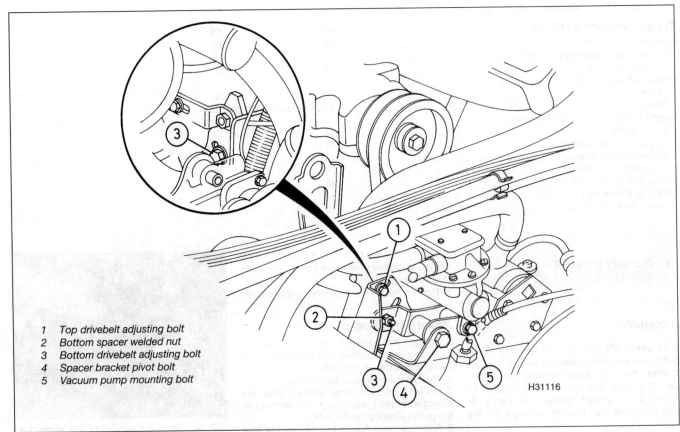

1   Top drivebelt adjusting bolt
2   Bottom spacer welded nut
3   Bottom drivebelt adjusting bolt
4   Spacer bracket pivot bolt
5   Vacuum pump mounting bolt

1.13 Brake vacuum pump drivebelt adjustment on later models

2.6a Bleed screws on the thermostat housing cover (arrowed)

2.6b Bleed screws on the heater hose (arrowed)

Locate a socket and torque wrench on this nut, and apply the correct torque (see Specifications), so that the drivebelt is tensioned.

16 Hold the pivot bracket in this position and tighten the pivot and adjustment bolts. Remove the torque wrench.

2 Coolant – draining and filling

Draining

1 Allow the engine to cool for at least 10 minutes after switching off.
2 Depress the filler cap and slowly turn it anti-clockwise until it can be removed. If the engine is hot cover the cap with a thick cloth before removing it as a precaution against scalding.
3 Position a container beneath the left-hand side of the radiator then unscrew the drain plug and allow the coolant to drain. If there is no drain plug fitted, disconnect the drain pipe on the left-hand side of the radiator or disconnect the bottom hose from the right-hand side.
4 When the radiator is completely drained refit the drain plug, pipe or hose then drain the block by unscrewing the drain plug located on the rear of the engine at the flywheel end. Refit the drain plug on completion.

Filling

5 Make sure that the drain plugs are secure and that all hoses are in good condition and their clips tight.
6 Loosen or remove the bleed screws located on the thermostat housing cover, and where applicable, on the heater hose at the bulkhead (see illustrations).
7 Fill slowly with coolant through the filler neck and at the same time keep an eye on the bleed screw holes. When coolant free of air bubbles emerges refit and tighten the bleed screws.
8 Top up the radiator or expansion tank until it is full to the filler cap seating. There still remains air in the system which must be purged as follows.
9 Start the engine and run at a fast idle speed for several minutes. Stop the engine.
10 Top up the expansion tank to the maximum level. On some models this is marked on the outside of the expansion tank, but on others, a level plate or tube is visible through the filler neck. Both minimum and maximum levels are indicated (see illustration).
11 Fit the filler cap.
12 Start the engine and run to normal operating temperature indicated by the electric cooling fan(s) cutting in then out after a few minutes.
13 Stop the engine and allow to cool for at least 1 hour.
14 Check the coolant level and top-up as necessary (see illustration).

9B

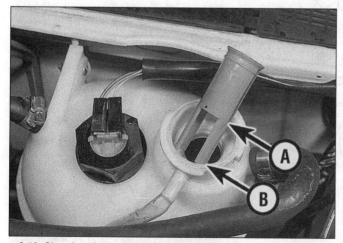

2.10 Showing the level tube removed from the expansion tank

A Maximum level   B Minimum level

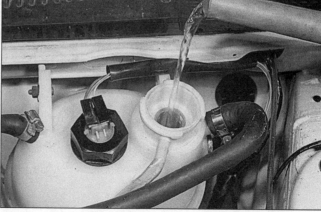

2.14 Filling the cooling system via the expansion tank

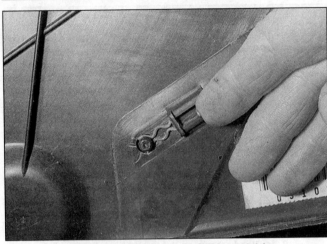

3.10a Timing cover front clip (early models) . . .

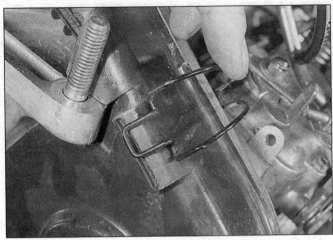

3.10b . . . and spring clips

3 Timing belt - removal, refitting and tensioning

Removal

1 Apply the handbrake, then jack up the front right-hand corner of the vehicle until the wheel is just clear of the ground. Support the vehicle on an axle stand and engage 4th or 5th gear. This will enable the engine to be turned easily by turning the right-hand wheel.

2 Remove the engine splash guard from under the right-hand front wheel arch.

3 For extra working space, drain the cooling system (detailed in Section 2) and disconnect the bottom hose from the water pump inlet. Remove the intermediate metal tube after removing the cross head screws.

4 Disconnect the battery negative lead.

5 Loosen the alternator pivot and adjustment bolts then unscrew the tension bolt until it is possible to slip the drivebelt from the pulleys.

6 With 4th or 5th gear selected on manual transmission models have an assistant depress the footbrake pedal, then unscrew the crankshaft pulley bolt. Alternatively the crankshaft can be locked, by unbolting the transmission cover plate and using a large screwdriver lock the starter ring gear. Note that the crankshaft pulley bolt is extremely tight.

7 Slide the pulley from the front of the crankshaft. Unbolt the bottom timing cover.

8 Support the weight of the engine using a hoist or trolley jack.

9 Unscrew the nuts and remove the right-hand engine mounting bracket.

10 Pull up the front clip (early models), release the spring clips, and withdraw the two timing cover sections. Note that the spring clip is not fitted to later models, which have a modified cover and fastenings (see illustrations).

11 Turn the engine by means of the front right-hand wheel or crankshaft pulley bolt until the three bolt holes in the camshaft and injection pump sprockets are aligned with the corresponding holes in the engine front plate.

12 Insert an 8.0 mm diameter metal dowel rod or drill through the special hole in the left-hand rear flange of the cylinder block by the starter motor. Then carefully turn the engine either way until the rod enters the TDC hole in the flywheel (see illustration).

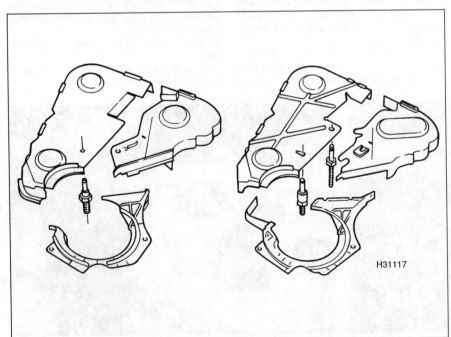

H31117

3.10c Earlier and later type of timing belt covers

3.12 Using a twist drill to enter the TDC hole in the flywheel

13 Insert three M8 bolts through the holes in the camshaft and injection pump sprockets and screw them into the engine front plate finger-tight **(see illustration)**.

14 Loosen the timing belt tensioner pivot nut and adjustment bolt, then turn the bracket anti-clockwise to release the tension and retighten the adjustment bolt to hold the tensioner in the released position. If available use a 3/8 inch square drive extension in the hole provided to turn the bracket against the spring tension.

15 Mark the timing belt with an arrow to indicate its normal direction of turning then remove it from the camshaft, injection pump, water pump and crankshaft sprockets.

Refitting

16 If signs of oil contamination are found, trace the source of the oil leak, and rectify it. Wash down the engine timing belt area and all related components, to remove all traces of oil.

17 Begin refitting by locating the timing belt on the crankshaft sprocket, making sure that, where applicable, the rotation arrow is facing the correct way.

18 Hold the timing belt engaged with the crankshaft roller sprocket then feed it over the roller and onto the injection pump, camshaft, and water pump sprockets and over the tensioner. To ensure correct engagement, locate only a half width on the injection pump sprocket before feeding the timing belt onto the camshaft sprocket keeping the belt taut and fully engaged with the crankshaft sprocket. Locate the timing belt fully onto the sprockets **(see illustrations)**.

Tensioning

19 With the pivot nut loose, slacken the tensioner adjustment bolt while holding the bracket against the spring tension. Slowly release the bracket until the roller presses against the timing belt. Retighten the adjustment bolt.

20 Remove the bolts from the camshaft and injection pump sprockets. Remove the metal dowel rod from the cylinder block.

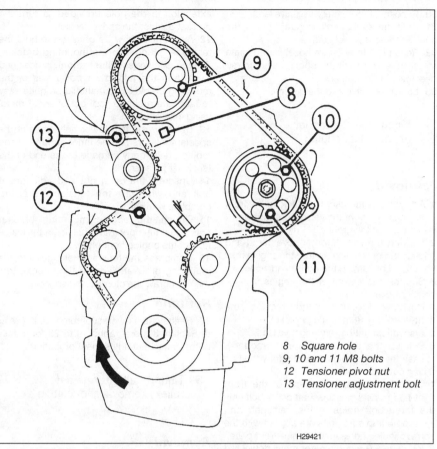

8   Square hole
9, 10 and 11 M8 bolts
12 Tensioner pivot nut
13 Tensioner adjustment bolt

3.13 Holding camshaft and injection pump sprockets in position using M8 bolts

21 Rotate the engine two complete turns in its normal direction. Do not rotate the engine backwards as the timing belt must be kept tight between the crankshaft, injection pump and camshaft sprockets.

22 Loosen the tensioner adjustment bolt to allow the tensioner spring to push the roller against the timing belt, then tighten both the adjustment bolt and pivot nut.

23 Recheck the engine timing as described in paragraphs 12 and 13, then remove the metal dowel rod.

24 Refit the timing cover sections and secure with the special clip and spring clips. as

applicable. Also refit the bottom timing cover and tighten the bolts.

25 Refit the right-hand engine mounting bracket and tighten the nuts.

26 Remove the trolley jack or hoist.

27 Slide the pulley onto the front of the crankshaft.

28 Apply three drops of locking fluid on the threads of the crankshaft pulley bolt then insert it and tighten to the specified torque while holding the crankshaft stationary using the method described in paragraph 6.

29 Refit the alternator drivebelt and tension it as described in Section 1.

9B

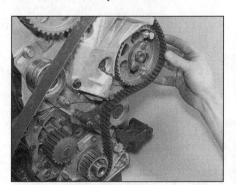

3.18a Fitting the timing belt over the injection pump sprocket . . .

3.18b . . . the camshaft sprocket . . .

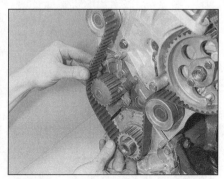

3.18c . . . and the water pump sprocket

30 Reconnect the battery negative lead.
31 Refit the engine splash-guard under the right-hand front wheel arch.
32 Reconnect the bottom hose, intermediate metal tube and refill the cooling system (as described in Section 2).
33 Lower the vehicle to the ground.

4 Timing belt tensioner - removal and refitting

Removal

1 Apply the handbrake, then jack up the front right-hand corner of the vehicle until the wheel is just clear of the ground.
2 Support the vehicle on an axle stand and engage 4th or 5th gear so that the engine may be rotated by turning the right-hand wheel.
3 Support the weight of the engine using a hoist or trolley jack.
4 Unscrew the nuts and remove the right-hand engine mounting bracket.
5 Disconnect the battery negative lead.
6 Pull up the special clip (early models), release the spring clips and withdraw the two timing cover sections.
7 Turn the engine by means of the front right-hand wheel or crankshaft pulley bolt until the three bolt holes in the camshaft and injection pump sprockets are aligned with the corresponding holes in the engine front plate.
8 Insert an 8.0 mm diameter metal dowel rod or drill through the special hole in the left-hand rear flange of the cylinder block by the starter motor.
9 Carefully turn the engine either way until the rod enters the TDC hole in the flywheel.
10 Insert three M8 bolts through the holes in the camshaft and injection pump sprockets and screw them into the engine front plate finger-tight.
11 Loosen the timing belt tensioner pivot nut and adjustment bolt, then turn the bracket anti-clockwise until the adjustment bolt is in the middle of the slot and retighten the bolt. If available use a 3/8 inch square drive

extension in the hole provided to turn the bracket against the spring tension.
12 A tool must now be obtained to hold the tensioner plunger in the mounting bracket. The tool shown **(see illustration)**, is designed to slide in the two lower bolt holes of the mounting bracket and it should be quite easy to fabricate a similar tool out of sheet metal using long bolts.
13 Unscrew the two lower bolts then fit the special tool. Grease the inner surface of the tool to prevent any damage to the end of the tensioner plunger.
14 Unscrew the pivot nut and adjustment bolt and withdraw the tensioner bracket, complete with roller.
15 Unbolt the engine mounting bracket noting that the uppermost bolt is on the inside face of the engine front plate.
16 Compress the tensioner plunger into the mounting bracket, remove the special tool then withdraw the plunger and spring.

Refitting

17 Refitting is a reversal of removal, but refer to Section 3, paragraphs 19 to 23 for details of the timing belt adjustment procedure.

5 Timing belt intermediate roller - removal and refitting

Removal

1 Follow the procedure given in paragraphs 1 to 11 of Section 4.
2 Remove the engine splash guard from under the right-hand front wheel arch. For extra working space, drain the cooling system (Section 2), and disconnect the bottom hose from the water pump inlet. Remove the intermediate metal tube after removing the cross-headed screws.
3 Disconnect the battery negative lead.
4 Loosen the alternator pivot and adjustment bolts then unscrew the tension bolt until it is possible to slip the drivebelt from the pulleys.
5 With 4th or 5th gear selected have an

assistant depress the footbrake pedal, then unscrew the crankshaft pulley bolt. Alternatively, the crankshaft can be locked by unbolting the transmission cover plate and using a wide-bladed screwdriver to lock the starter ring gear.
6 Slide the pulley from the front of the crankshaft.
7 Unbolt the lower timing cover.
8 Remove the spacer from the stud (two studs on later models), for the upper timing cover sections. Note the position of the stud(s), then unscrew and remove it.
9 Unscrew the remaining bolts securing the intermediate roller bracket to the cylinder block noting that the upper bolt also secures the engine mounting bracket.
10 Slightly loosen the remaining engine mounting bracket bolts then slide out the intermediate roller and bracket.

Refitting

11 Refitting is a reversal of removal, but note the following additional points:
a) Tighten all bolts to the specified torque
b) Apply three drops of locking fluid to the threads of the crankshaft pulley bolt before inserting it
c) Tension the alternator drivebelt as described in Section 1
d) Adjust the timing belt as described in Section 3, paragraphs 19 to 23

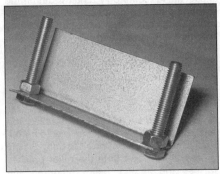

4.12 Home-made tool for holding the tensioner plunger

Chapter 10A
Peugeot 305 petrol 1983 to 1989

Contents

Specifications

Timing belt renewal interval . . . .   Every 36 000 miles (60 000 km)

Alternator drivebelt

Type . . . .   Ribbed
Tension (using Krikit tensioner tool):
  New belt . . . .   60 kg/span*
  Used belt . . . .   40 kg/span*
In the absence of the tensioner tool, adjust belt to give a deflection of 6 mm at centre of longest run

Ignition timing

Static or at idle speed . . . .   10° BTDC

Torque wrench settings	Nm	lbf ft
Alternator mountings:		
Pivot	29	21
Adjustment	15	11
Camshaft sprocket bolt:		
M10	30	22
M12	58	43
Crankshaft pulley bolt	110	81
Timing belt tensioner nuts	11	8
Wheel nuts or bolts	63	46

10A

1.2a Alternator mounting/adjustment bolt (arrowed)

1.2b Alternator pivot bolt

A   Adjustment screw

1 Alternator drivebelt -
removal, refitting and adjustment

Removal and refitting

1 Disconnect the battery negative lead.
2 Loosen the pivot and adjustment bolts, swivel the alternator towards the engine. then remove the drivebelt **(see illustrations)**.
3 Refitting is a reversal of removal.

Adjustment

4 The ribbed drivebelt used on this engine runs under greater tension than the conventional V-belt. For this reason a positive tensioning arrangement is employed **(see illustration)**.
5 Slacken the alternator pivot bolt and the adjusting strap pivot bolt. Screw the adjuster bolt in or out to achieve the desired tension, then tighten the pivot bolts.
6 The correct belt tension is given in the Specifications. In the absence of the proper tensioning gauge, set the belt so that it can be deflected approximately say 6 mm under firm thumb pressure.

2 Timing belt -
removal and refitting

Removal

1 Disconnect the battery earth lead.
2 Remove the alternator drivebelt (Section 1).
3 Remove the inner shield from the right-hand wheel arch and wedge the radiator bottom hose under the sump **(see illustration)**. Move the expansion bottle out of the way without disconnecting it.
4 Remove the shield from the camshaft sprocket.
5 Turn the crankshaft until the dowel hole in the pulley is at about 12 o'clock and the hole in the camshaft sprocket is at about 7 o'clock. In this position a 10 mm rod should pass through each hole and into the timing

1.4 Adjusting the alternator drivebelt tension

recess behind. Verify this and then remove the rods **(see illustration)**.
6 Remove the clutch/torque converter bottom shield. Have an assistant jam the starter ring gear while the crankshaft pulley bolt is

2.3 Removing right-hand wheelarch shield

2.5 Sprocket and pulley aligned using twist drills

2.9 Turning the tensioner cam spindle

2.11 Timing belt and camshaft sprocket marks aligned

undone. This bolt is very tight. **Do not** jam the pulley by means of the timing dowel; damage will result. Remove the bolt and washer.

7 Check that the 10 mm rod will enter the timing holes; adjust the crankshaft position if necessary by means of the starter ring gear. Remove the crankshaft pulley, retrieving the Woodruff key if it is loose.

8 Remove the plastic covers from the front of the timing belt. Note the location of the various bolts.

9 Slacken the two nuts on the front of the drivebelt tensioner and the single nut at the rear. Use a spanner on the square end of the tensioner cam spindle to turn the cam to the horizontal position and so compress the tensioner spring **(see illustration)**. Tighten the cam locknut.

10 Remove the belt, taking care not to kink it or contaminate it with oil if it is to be re-used.

Refitting

11 Commence refitting by positioning the belt on the crankshaft sprocket, then refitting the pulley and verifying the correct position of the crankshaft by means of the rod. Observe the arrows on the belt showing the direction of rotation, and the timing lines which align with marks on the crankshaft and camshaft sprocket(s) **(see illustration)**.

12 Fit the belt to the camshaft sprocket, round the tensioner and to the coolant pump sprocket.

13 Release the tensioner cam locknut and turn the cam downwards to release the spring. Tighten the locknut and the tensioner front nuts **(see illustration)**.

14 Remove the timing rods and turn the crankshaft through two full turns in the normal direction of rotation. Turn the crankshaft further to bring No 1 piston to TDC on the firing stroke.

15 Slacken the tensioner front nuts and the cam locknut, then retighten them.

16 Turn the crankshaft further and make sure that the timing rods can still be inserted. If not, remove the drivebelt and start again.

17 If the old belt has been refitted, proceed to paragraph 21. If a new belt has been fitted, proceed as follows.

18 Tighten the crankshaft pulley bolt to the specified torque, then refit and tension the alternator drivebelt (Section 1). Temporarily refit the camshaft sprocket cover.

19 Run the engine up to operating temperature, indicated by the cooling fan operating, then stop the engine and allow it to cool for at least two hours.

20 Rotate the crankshaft to the TDC position,

No 1 cylinder firing, then slacken and retighten the tensioner nuts once more. Remove the alternator drivebelt.

21 Remove the crankshaft pulley. Refit and secure the plastic covers, then refit the pulley and tighten its bolt to the specified torque. Refit and tension the alternator drivebelt.

22 Check the ignition timing and adjust if necessary (Section 3).

3 Ignition timing

1 Static timing is not possible with electronic ignition. There is a reference mark on the rim of the distributor body corresponding to the rotor tip position when No 1 cylinder is firing - this mark can be used for an initial setting when timing from scratch **(see illustration)**.

2 Dynamic timing is carried out using a strobe connected to No 1 HT lead. The timing marks are on the flywheel rim and flywheel housing; once their location is known they can be viewed without any dismantling **(see illustration)**.

3 Disconnect and plug the vacuum pipe when checking the timing at idle speed.

10A

2.13 Timing belt tensioner front nuts

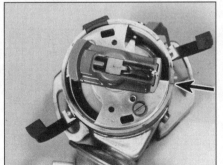

3.1 Tip of rotor arm aligned with rim reference mark (arrowed)

3.2 Timing marks

Notes

Chapter 10B
Peugeot 305 diesel 1983 to 1989

Contents

Specifications

Timing belt renewal interval . . . . Every 36 000 miles (60 000 km)

Note: *Although the normal interval for timing belt renewal is 72 000 miles (120 000 km), it is strongly recommended that the interval is halved on vehicles which are subjected to intensive use, ie, mainly short journeys or a lot of stop-start driving. The actual belt renewal interval is therefore very much up to the individual owner. That being said, it is highly recommended to err on the side of safety, and renew the belt at this earlier interval, bearing in mind the drastic consequences resulting from belt failure.*

Power steering drivebelt tension	**Nm**	**lbf ft**
New belt	57	42
Used belt	30	22

Vacuum pump drivebelt tension	**Nm**	**lbf ft**
Adjusting pivot (later models)	5	4

Torque wrench settings

	Nm	lbf ft
Alternator pivot bolt	39	29
Alternator top mounting bolt and locknut	20	15
Camshaft sprocket	35	26
Crankshaft pulley bolt:		
Stage 1	40	30
Stage 2	Angle tighten by a further 60°	
Engine right-hand mounting bracket:		
Lower bracket	18	13
Upper bracket to engine	35	26
Upper bracket to mounting rubber	28	21
Pump pulley to camshaft	35	26
Timing belt intermediate roller	18	13
Timing belt tensioner	18	13
Timing cover, lower	12	9

---

1 Auxiliary drivebelt - adjustment

Alternator

1 To adjust the tension, first check that the belt is correctly fitted over the pulleys.
2 With the alternator mountings loose,

1.3 Checking the tension of the alternator drivebelt

carefully lever the alternator outwards to tighten the drivebelt. Using a wooden lever will minimise the risk of damage to the alternator casing.
3 The belt should be able to move by approximately 6.0 mm, with moderate thumb pressure midway between the pulleys **(see illustration)**.
4 Tighten the mounting bolts to the correct torque.

Power steering pump

5 Adjust the tension by loosening the mounting and adjusting bolts, reposition the pump and retighten the bolts.
6 The deflection should be 5.0 mm.
7 On early models three slotted holes are provided in the bracket and on later models the pump pivots on a single bolt.
8 A torque wrench may be used on the later type to adjust the belt tension using the 12.7 mm (1/2 in) square hole provided **(see illustration)**. With both bolts loose, apply the torque given in the Specifications, then tighten the adjustment bolt, followed by the pivot bolt.

Vacuum pump (early models)

Note: *Later models have a revised mounting arrangement.*
9 On models fitted with a belt-driven brake vacuum pump, it is important to ensure that the drivebelt is correctly tensioned **(see illustration)**.
10 Loosen the mounting bolts and adjust the pump to the correct tension.
11 The deflection should be 5.0 mm.
12 When the drivebelt is at the correct tension, tighten the mounting bolts to the correct torque.

Vacuum pump drivebelt (later models)

13 The following paragraphs describe the adjustment procedure for later models, which have the revised mounting arrangement shown **(see illustration)**.
14 Loosen the pivot and adjustment bolts on the vacuum pump.
15 A welded nut is fitted to the pivot bracket. Locate a socket and torque wrench on this nut, and apply the correct torque (see

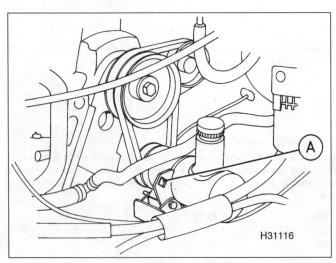

1.8 Square hole (A) for adjusting the belt tension on the later type pump

H31116

1.9 Checking the vacuum pump drivebelt tension

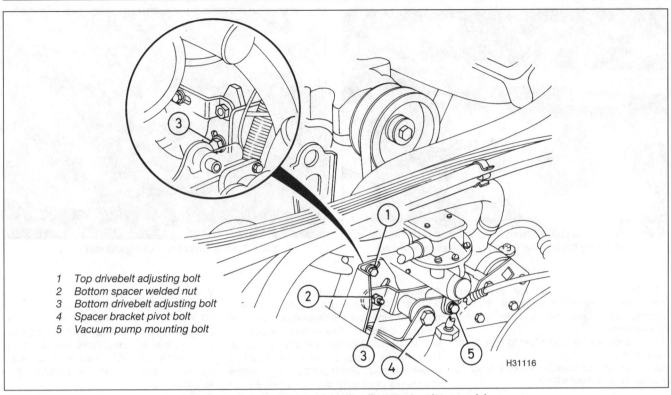

1 Top drivebelt adjusting bolt
2 Bottom spacer welded nut
3 Bottom drivebelt adjusting bolt
4 Spacer bracket pivot bolt
5 Vacuum pump mounting bolt

H31116

1.13 Brake vacuum pump drivebelt adjustment on later models

Specifications), so that the drivebelt is tensioned.

16 Hold the pivot bracket in this position and tighten the pivot and adjustment bolts. Remove the torque wrench.

2 Coolant – draining and filling

Draining

1 Allow the engine to cool for at least 10 minutes after switching off.

2 Depress the filler cap and slowly turn it anti-clockwise until it can be removed. If the engine is hot cover the cap with a thick cloth before removing it as a precaution against scalding.

3 Position a container beneath the left-hand side of the radiator then unscrew the drain plug and allow the coolant to drain. If there is no drain plug fitted, disconnect the drain pipe on the left-hand side of the radiator or disconnect the bottom hose from the right-hand side.

4 When the radiator is completely drained refit the drain plug, pipe or hose then drain the block by unscrewing the drain plug located on the rear of the engine at the flywheel end. Refit the drain plug on completion.

Filling

5 Make sure that the drain plugs are secure and that all hoses are in good condition and their clips tight.

6 Loosen or remove the bleed screws located on the thermostat housing cover, and where applicable, on the heater hose at the bulkhead **(see illustrations)**.

7 Fill slowly with coolant through the filler neck and at the same time keep an eye on the bleed screw holes. When coolant free of air bubbles emerges refit and tighten the bleed screws.

8 Top up the radiator or expansion tank until it is full to the filler cap seating. There still remains air in the system which must be purged as follows.

9 Start the engine and run at a fast idle speed for several minutes. Stop the engine.

10 Top up the expansion tank to the maximum level. On some models this is marked on the outside of the expansion tank, but on others, a level plate or tube is visible through the filler neck. Both minimum and maximum levels are indicated **(see illustration)**.

11 Fit the filler cap.

10B

2.6a Bleed screws on the thermostat housing cover (arrowed)

2.6b Bleed screws on the heater hose (arrowed)

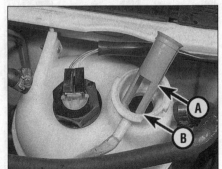

2.10 Showing the level tube removed from the expansion tank

A Maximum level   B Minimum level

2.14 Filling the cooling system via the expansion tank

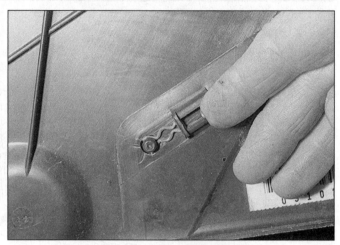

3.10a Timing cover front clip (early models) . . .

12 Start the engine and run to normal operating temperature indicated by the electric cooling fan(s) cutting in then out after a few minutes.

13 Stop the engine and allow to cool for at least 1 hour.

14 Check the coolant level and top-up as necessary **(see illustration)**.

3 Timing belt - removal, refitting and tensioning

Removal

1 Apply the handbrake, then jack up the front right-hand corner of the vehicle until the wheel is just clear of the ground. Support the vehicle on an axle stand and engage 4th or 5th gear. This will enable the engine to be turned easily by turning the right-hand wheel.

2 Remove the engine splash guard from under the right-hand front wheel arch.

3 For extra working space, drain the cooling system (detailed in Section 2) and disconnect the bottom hose from the water pump inlet.

4 Disconnect the battery negative lead.

5 Loosen the alternator pivot and adjustment bolts then unscrew the tension bolt until it is possible to slip the drivebelt from the pulleys.

6 With 4th or 5th gear selected on manual transmission models have an assistant depress the footbrake pedal, then unscrew the crankshaft pulley bolt. Alternatively the crankshaft can be locked, by unbolting the transmission cover plate and using a large screwdriver lock the starter ring gear. Note that the crankshaft pulley bolt is extremely tight.

7 Slide the pulley from the front of the crankshaft. Unbolt the bottom timing cover.

8 Support the weight of the engine using a hoist or trolley jack.

9 Unscrew the nuts and remove the right-hand engine mounting bracket.

10 Pull up the front clip (early models), release the spring clips, and withdraw the two timing cover sections. Note that the spring clip is not fitted to later models, which have a modified cover and fastenings **(see illustrations)**.

11 Turn the engine by means of the front right-hand wheel or crankshaft pulley bolt until the three bolt holes in the camshaft and injection pump sprockets are aligned with the corresponding holes in the engine front plate.

12 Insert an 8.0 mm diameter metal dowel rod or drill through the special hole in the left-hand rear flange of the cylinder block by

3.10b . . . and spring clips

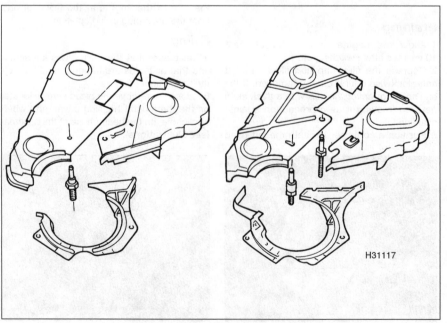

3.10c Earlier and later type of timing belt covers

3.12 Using a twist drill to enter the TDC hole in the flywheel

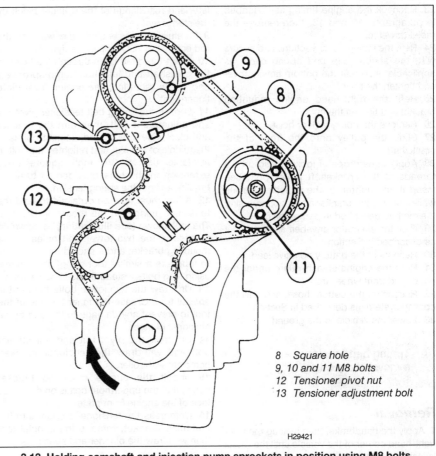

8   Square hole
9, 10 and 11 M8 bolts
12 Tensioner pivot nut
13 Tensioner adjustment bolt

H29421

3.13 Holding camshaft and injection pump sprockets in position using M8 bolts

the starter motor. Then carefully turn the engine either way until the rod enters the TDC hole in the flywheel (see illustration).

13 Insert three M8 bolts through the holes in the camshaft and injection pump sprockets and screw them into the engine front plate finger-tight (see illustration).

14 Loosen the timing belt tensioner pivot nut and adjustment bolt, then turn the bracket anti-clockwise to release the tension and retighten the adjustment bolt to hold the tensioner in the released position. If available use a 3/8 inch square drive extension in the hole provided to turn the bracket against the spring tension.

15 Mark the timing belt with an arrow to indicate its normal direction of turning then remove it from the camshaft, injection pump, water pump and crankshaft sprockets.

Refitting

16 If signs of oil contamination are found, trace the source of the oil leak, and rectify it. Wash down the engine timing belt area and all related components, to remove all traces of oil.

17 Begin refitting by locating the timing belt on the crankshaft sprocket, making sure that, where applicable, the rotation arrow is facing the correct way.

18 Hold the timing belt engaged with the crankshaft roller sprocket then feed it over the roller and onto the injection pump, camshaft,

and water pump sprockets and over the tensioner. To ensure correct engagement, locate only a half width on the injection pump sprocket before feeding the timing belt onto the camshaft sprocket keeping the belt taut and fully engaged with the crankshaft sprocket. Locate the timing belt fully onto the sprockets (see illustrations).

Tensioning

19 With the pivot nut loose, slacken the tensioner adjustment bolt while holding the bracket against the spring tension. Slowly release the bracket until the roller presses

against the timing belt. Retighten the adjustment bolt.

20 Remove the bolts from the camshaft and injection pump sprockets. Remove the metal dowel rod from the cylinder block.

21 Rotate the engine two complete turns in its normal direction. Do not rotate the engine backwards as the timing belt must be kept tight between the crankshaft, injection pump and camshaft sprockets.

22 Loosen the tensioner adjustment bolt to allow the tensioner spring to push the roller against the timing belt, then tighten both the adjustment bolt and pivot nut.

10B

3.18a Fitting the timing belt over the injection pump sprocket . . .

3.18b . . . the camshaft sprocket . . .

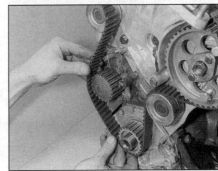

3.18c . . . and the water pump sprocket

23 Recheck the engine timing as described in paragraphs 12 and 13, then remove the metal dowel rod.

24 Refit the timing cover sections and secure with the special clip and spring clips. as applicable. Also refit the bottom timing cover and tighten the bolts.

25 Refit the right-hand engine mounting bracket and tighten the nuts.

26 Remove the trolley jack or hoist.

27 Slide the pulley onto the front of the crankshaft.

28 Apply three drops of locking fluid on the threads of the crankshaft pulley bolt then insert it and tighten to the specified torque while holding the crankshaft stationary using the method described in paragraph 6.

29 Refit the alternator drivebelt and tension it as described in Section 1.

30 Reconnect the battery negative lead.

31 Refit the engine splash-guard under the right-hand front wheel arch.

32 Reconnect the bottom hose, and refill the cooling system (as described in Section 2).

33 Lower the vehicle to the ground.

4 Timing belt tensioner - removal and refitting

Removal

1 Apply the handbrake, then jack up the front right-hand corner of the vehicle until the wheel is just clear of the ground.

2 Support the vehicle on an axle stand and engage 4th or 5th gear so that the engine may be rotated by turning the right-hand wheel.

3 Support the weight of the engine using a hoist or trolley jack.

4 Unscrew the nuts and remove the right-hand engine mounting bracket.

5 Disconnect the battery negative lead.

6 Pull up the special clip (early models), release the spring clips and withdraw the two timing cover sections.

7 Turn the engine by means of the front right-hand wheel or crankshaft pulley bolt until the three bolt holes in the camshaft and injection pump sprockets are aligned with the corresponding holes in the engine front plate.

8 Insert an 8.0 mm diameter metal dowel rod or drill through the special hole in the left-hand rear flange of the cylinder block by the starter motor.

9 Carefully turn the engine either way until the rod enters the TDC hole in the flywheel.

10 Insert three M8 bolts through the holes in the camshaft and injection pump sprockets and screw them into the engine front plate finger-tight.

11 Loosen the timing belt tensioner pivot nut and adjustment bolt, then turn the bracket anti-clockwise until the adjustment bolt is in the middle of the slot and retighten the bolt. If available use a 3/8 inch square drive extension in the hole provided to turn the bracket against the spring tension.

12 A tool must now be obtained to hold the tensioner plunger in the mounting bracket. The tool shown **(see illustration)**, is designed to slide in the two lower bolt holes of the mounting bracket and it should be quite easy to fabricate a similar tool out of sheet metal using long bolts instead of metal dowel rods.

13 Unscrew the two lower bolts then fit the special tool. Grease the inner surface of the tool to prevent any damage to the end of the tensioner plunger.

14 Unscrew the pivot nut and adjustment bolt and withdraw the tensioner bracket, complete with roller.

15 Unbolt the engine mounting bracket noting that the uppermost bolt is on the inside face of the engine front plate.

16 Compress the tensioner plunger into the mounting bracket, remove the special tool then withdraw the plunger and spring.

Refitting

17 Refitting is a reversal of removal, but refer

4.12 Home-made tool for holding the tensioner plunger

to Section 3, paragraphs 19 to 23 for details of the timing belt adjustment procedure.

5 Timing belt intermediate roller - removal and refitting

Removal

1 Follow the procedure given in paragraphs 1 to 11 of Section 4.

2 Remove the engine splash guard from under the right-hand front wheel arch. For extra working space, drain the cooling system (Section 2), and disconnect the bottom hose from the water pump inlet.

3 Disconnect the battery negative lead.

4 Loosen the alternator pivot and adjustment bolts then unscrew the tension bolt until it is possible to slip the drivebelt from the pulleys.

5 With 4th or 5th gear selected have an assistant depress the footbrake pedal, then unscrew the crankshaft pulley bolt. Alternatively, the crankshaft can be locked by unbolting the transmission cover plate and using a wide-bladed screwdriver to lock the starter ring gear.

6 Slide the pulley from the front of the crankshaft.

7 Unbolt the lower timing cover.

8 Remove the spacer from the stud (two studs on later models), for the upper timing cover sections. Note the position of the stud(s), then unscrew and remove it.

9 Unscrew the remaining bolts securing the intermediate roller bracket to the cylinder block noting that the upper bolt also secures the engine mounting bracket.

10 Slightly loosen the remaining engine mounting bracket bolts then slide out the intermediate roller and bracket.

Refitting

11 Refitting is a reversal of removal, but note the following additional points:
a) Tighten all bolts to the specified torque
b) Apply three drops of locking fluid to the threads of the crankshaft pulley bolt before inserting it
c) Tension the alternator drivebelt as described in Section 1
d) Adjust the timing belt as described in Section 3, paragraphs 19 to 23

Chapter 11A
Peugeot 306 petrol 1993 to 1998

Contents

Specifications

Timing belt renewal interval . . . . Every 36 000 miles (60 000 km)

Note: *Although the normal interval for timing belt renewal is 72 000 miles (120 000 km), it is strongly recommended that the interval is halved on vehicles which are subjected to intensive use, ie, mainly short journeys or a lot of stop-start driving. The actual belt renewal interval is therefore very much up to the individual owner. That being said, it is highly recommended to err on the side of safety, and renew the belt at this earlier interval, bearing in mind the drastic consequences resulting from belt failure.*

Engine codes
1.1 litre (1124 cc) engine TU1
1.4 litre (1360 cc) engine TU3
1.6 litre (1587 cc) engine TU5
1.8 litre (1761 cc) engine XU7
2.0 litre (1998 cc) engine XU10

Torque wrench settings

	Nm	lbf ft
Roadwheel bolts	85	63
TU engine		
Camshaft sprocket retaining bolt	80	59
Crankshaft pulley retaining bolts	8	6
Crankshaft sprocket retaining bolt	110	81
Cylinder head cover nuts	16	12
Engine/transmission left-hand mounting:		
Centre nut	65	48
Mounting bracket-to-body bolts	25	18
Mounting bracket-to-transmission nuts	20	15
Mounting rubber nuts	20	15
Engine/transmission rear mounting:		
Mounting link-to-body bolt	50	37
Mounting link-to-mounting bolt	70	52
Mounting-to-cylinder block bolts	40	30
Engine/transmission right-hand mounting bracket nuts	45	33
Timing belt cover bolts	8	6
Timing belt tensioner pulley nut	23	17

11

Torque wrench settings (continued)

	Nm	lbf ft
XU engine - 8-valve		
Camshaft sprocket retaining bolt	35	26
Crankshaft pulley retaining bolt*:		
1761 cc engine	120	89
1998 cc engine	110	81
Engine/transmission left-hand mounting:		
Centre nut	65	48
Mounting bracket-to-body bolts	25	18
Mounting stud:		
1761 cc engine	25	18
1998 cc engine	50	37
Engine/transmission rear mounting:		
Mounting assembly-to-block bolts	45	33
Mounting bracket-to-mounting bolt	50	37
Mounting bracket-to-subframe bolt:		
1761 cc engine	50	37
1998 cc engine	70	52
Engine/transmission right-hand mounting:		
1761 cc engine:		
Bracket-to-engine bolts*	45	33
Mounting bracket retaining nuts	45	33
1998 cc engine:		
Curved retaining plate	20	15
Mounting bracket retaining nuts	45	33
Timing belt cover bolts	8	6
Timing belt tensioner pulley bolt	20	15
XU engine - 16-valve		
Camshaft sprocket-to-hub retaining bolts	10	7
Camshaft sprocket hub-to-camshaft retaining bolts	75	55
Crankshaft pulley retaining bolt*	120	89
Engine/transmission left-hand mounting:		
Centre nut	65	48
Mounting bracket-to-body bolts	25	18
Mounting stud	50	37
Engine lower movement limiter-to-driveshaft intermediate bearing		
Housing	50	37
Engine lower movement limiter-to-subframe:		
1761 cc engine	50	37
1998 cc engine	85	63
Engine/transmission right-hand mounting:		
Engine upper movement limiter bolts	50	37
Mounting bracket-to-engine bolts	50	37
Mounting bracket-to-engine nuts	45	33
Mounting bracket-to-rubber mounting nut	45	33
Rubber mounting-to-body nut	40	30
Timing belt cover bolts	8	6
Timing belt tensioner pulley bolt	20	15

*Use thread-locking compound

---

1 Auxiliary drivebelt - removal, refitting and adjusting

1 Chock the rear wheels then jack up the front of the vehicle and support it on axle stands. Remove the right-hand front roadwheel.

2 From underneath the front of the car, prise out the retaining clips, and remove the plastic cover from the wing valance to gain access to the crankshaft sprocket/pulley bolt. Where necessary, unclip the coolant hoses from the wing to improve access further.

Models with manual adjuster on the alternator lower mounting point

Removal

3 Disconnect the battery negative terminal.
4 Slacken both the alternator upper and lower mounting nuts/bolts (as applicable).
5 Back off the adjuster bolt(s) to relieve the tension in the drivebelt, then slip the drivebelt from the pulleys (see illustrations).

Refitting and adjustment

6 Fit the belt around the pulleys, and take up the slack in the belt by tightening the adjuster bolt.

7 The belt should be tensioned so that, under firm thumb pressure, there is about 5.0 mm of free movement at the mid-point between the pulleys on the longest belt.
8 To adjust, with the upper mounting nut/bolt just holding the alternator firm, and the lower mounting nut/bolt loosened, turn the adjuster bolt until the correct tension is achieved.
9 Rotate the crankshaft a couple of times, recheck the tension, then tighten both the alternator mounting nuts/bolts. Where applicable, also tighten the bolt securing the adjuster strap to its mounting bracket.
10 Reconnect the battery negative terminal.
11 Clip the coolant hoses into position

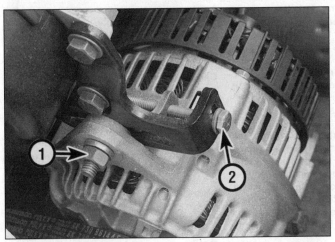

1.5a Alternator upper mounting nut (1) and adjuster bolt (2)

1.5b On TU engines, loosen the alternator mounting bolts, then slacken the adjuster bolt (arrowed)

(where necessary), then refit the plastic cover to the wing valance. Refit the roadwheel, and lower the vehicle to the ground.

Models with a manually-adjusted tensioning pulley

Removal

12 Disconnect the battery negative terminal.
13 Slacken the two screws securing the tensioning pulley assembly to the engine (see illustrations).
14 Rotate the adjuster bolt to move the tensioner pulley away from the drivebelt until there is sufficient slack for the drivebelt to be removed from the pulleys.

Refitting and adjustment

15 Fit the drivebelt around the pulleys in the following order:
a) Power steering pump and/or air conditioning compressor.
b) Crankshaft.
c) Alternator.
d) Tensioner roller.

16 Ensure that the ribs on the belt are correctly engaged with the grooves in the pulleys, and that the drivebelt is correctly routed. Take all the slack out of the belt by turning the tensioner pulley adjuster bolt.
17 The belt should be tensioned so that, under firm thumb pressure, there is approximately 5.0 mm of free movement at the mid-point between the pulleys on the longest belt run.
18 To adjust the tension, with the two tensioner pulley assembly retaining screws slackened, rotate the adjuster bolt until the correct tension is achieved. Once the belt is correctly tensioned, rotate the crankshaft a couple of times and recheck the tension.
19 When the belt is correctly tensioned, securely tighten the tensioner pulley assembly

retaining screws, then reconnect the battery negative terminal.
20 Clip the coolant hoses into position, then refit the plastic cover to the wing valance. Refit the roadwheel, and lower the vehicle to the ground.

Models with an automatic spring-loaded tensioner pulley

Removal

21 Disconnect the battery negative terminal.
22 Where necessary, remove the retaining screws from the power steering pump pulley shield and remove the shield to gain access to the top of the drivebelt.
23 Move the tensioner pulley away from the drivebelt, using a ratchet handle or extension bar with the same size square-section end as the hole in the base of the automatic tensioner arm. Once the tensioner is released, retain it in

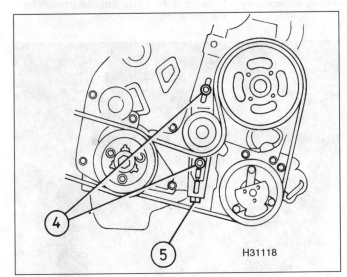

1.13a Tensioning pulley securing screws (4) and adjuster bolt (5) - models with low mounted tensioner

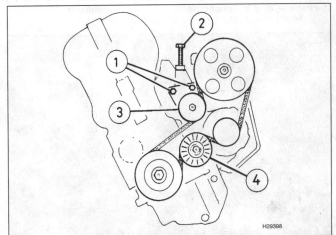

1.13b Tensioning pulley arrangement - models with high mounted tensioner

1 Pulley bracket securing screws	3 Tensioner pulley
2 Adjuster bolt	4 Crankshaft pulley

11

the released position by inserting a 4.0 mm Allen key in the hole provided. Disengage the drivebelt from all the pulleys, noting its correct routing. Remove the drivebelt from the engine, noting that in some cases, it may be necessary to slacken the automatic tensioner mounting bolts to disengage the belt from behind the tensioner pulley.

Refitting and tensioning

24 Fit the drivebelt around the pulleys in the following order:

a) Automatic tensioner pulley.
b) Crankshaft.
c) Air conditioning compressor.
d) Power steering pump.
e) Idler pulley.
f) Alternator.

25 Where necessary, securely tighten the automatic tensioner mounting bolts.

26 Ensure that the ribs on the belt are correctly engaged with the grooves in the pulleys. Take the load off the tensioner arm and remove the Allen key. Release the tensioner arm; the tensioner is spring-loaded, removing the need to manually adjust the belt tension.

27 Refit the power steering pump pulley shield (where removed), and securely tighten its retaining screws.

28 Reconnect the battery negative terminal.

29 Clip the coolant hoses into position, then refit the plastic cover to the wing valance. Refit the roadwheel, and lower the vehicle to the ground.

2 Engine assembly/valve timing holes (TU engines) - general information and usage

Caution: Do not attempt to rotate the engine whilst the crankshaft/camshaft are locked in position. If the engine is to be left in this state for a long period of time, it is a good idea to place warning notices inside the vehicle, and in the engine compartment. This will reduce the possibility of the engine being accidentally cranked on the starter motor, which is likely to cause damage with the locking pins in place.

1 On all models, timing holes are drilled in the camshaft sprocket and in the rear of the flywheel. The holes are used to ensure that the crankshaft and camshaft are correctly positioned to prevent the possibility of the valves contacting the pistons when refitting the timing belt. When the timing holes are aligned with access holes in the cylinder head and the front of the cylinder block, suitable diameter pins can be inserted to lock both the camshaft and crankshaft in position, preventing them from rotating. Proceed as follows.

2 Remove the timing belt upper cover as described in Section 6.

3 The crankshaft must now be turned until the timing hole in the camshaft sprocket is aligned with the corresponding hole in the cylinder head. The holes are aligned when the camshaft sprocket hole is in the 2 o'clock position, when viewed from the right-hand end of the engine. The crankshaft can be turned by using a spanner on the crankshaft sprocket bolt, noting that it should always be rotated in a clockwise direction (viewed from the right-hand end of the engine).

4 With the camshaft sprocket hole correctly positioned, insert a 6 mm diameter bolt or drill through the hole in the front, left-hand flange of the cylinder block, and locate it in the timing hole in the rear of the flywheel **(see illustration)**. Note that it may be necessary to rotate the crankshaft slightly, to get the holes to align.

5 With the flywheel correctly positioned, insert a 10 mm diameter bolt or a drill through the timing hole in the camshaft sprocket, and locate it in the hole in the cylinder head **(see illustration)**.

6 The crankshaft and camshaft are now locked in position, preventing unnecessary rotation.

3 Engine assembly/valve timing holes (XU engines) - general information and usage

Caution: Do not attempt to rotate the engine whilst the crankshaft/camshaft are locked in position. If the engine is to be left in this state for a long period of time, it is a good idea to place suitable warning notices inside the vehicle, and in the engine compartment. This will reduce the possibility of the engine being accidentally cranked on the starter motor, which is likely to cause damage with the locking pins in place.

1 On all models, timing holes are drilled in the camshaft sprocket(s) and crankshaft pulley. The holes are used to align the crankshaft and camshaft(s), to prevent the possibility of the valves contacting the pistons when refitting the timing belt. When the holes are aligned with their corresponding holes in the cylinder head and cylinder block (as appropriate), suitable diameter pins can be inserted to lock both the camshaft(s) and crankshaft in position, preventing them rotating unnecessarily. Proceed as follows.

2 Remove the timing belt upper cover as described in Section 7.

3 Chock the rear wheels then jack up the front of the vehicle and support it on axle stands. Remove the right-hand front roadwheel.

4 From underneath the front of the car, prise out the two retaining clips and remove the plastic cover from the wing valance, to gain access to the crankshaft pulley bolt. Where necessary, unclip the coolant hoses from the bracket, to improve access further. The crankshaft can then be turned using a suitable socket and extension bar fitted to the pulley bolt. Note that the crankshaft must always be turned in a clockwise direction (viewed from the right-hand side of vehicle).

2.4 Insert a 6 mm bolt (arrowed) through hole in cylinder block flange and into timing hole in the flywheel . . .

2.5 . . . then insert a 10 mm bolt through the cam sprocket timing hole, and locate it in the cylinder head

3.6 8.0 mm drill inserted through the crankshaft pulley timing hole
- 8-valve models

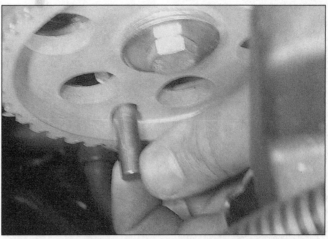

3.7 9.5 mm diameter drill inserted through the camshaft pulley
timing hole - 8-valve models

8-valve models

5 Rotate the crankshaft pulley until the timing hole in the camshaft sprocket is aligned with its corresponding hole in the cylinder head. Note that the holes are aligned when the sprocket hole is in the 8 o'clock position, when viewed from the right-hand end of the engine.

6 With the camshaft sprocket timing hole correctly positioned, insert an 8 mm diameter bolt or an 8 mm drill through the timing hole in the crankshaft pulley, and locate it in the corresponding hole in the end of the cylinder block **(see illustration)**. Note that it may be necessary to rotate the crankshaft slightly, to get the holes to align.

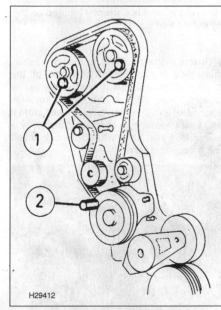

3.11 Camshaft sprocket timing hole (1)
and crankshaft pulley timing hole (2)
locked with suitable timing pins -
16-valve models

7 Once the crankshaft pulley is locked in position, insert a suitable 9.5 mm diameter (approximate) bolt or a drill through the camshaft sprocket hole, and locate it in the cylinder head **(see illustration)**.

8 The crankshaft and camshaft are now locked in position, preventing unnecessary rotation.

16-valve models

9 Rotate the crankshaft pulley until the timing holes in both camshafts are aligned with their corresponding holes in the cylinder head. The holes are aligned when the inlet camshaft sprocket hole is in approximately the 5 o'clock position and the exhaust camshaft sprocket hole is in approximately the 7 o'clock position, when viewed from the right-hand end of the engine.

10 With the camshaft sprocket holes correctly positioned, insert a 6 mm diameter bolt or drill through the timing hole in the crankshaft pulley, and locate it in the corresponding hole in the end of the engine. Note that the hole size may vary according to the type of pulley fitted and auxiliary drivebelt arrangement. If the bolt or drill is not a snug fit, try a larger size until a good fit is achieved in both the pulley and cylinder block.

4.3 Disconnect the breather hose from the
cylinder head cover ...

11 With the crankshaft locked in position, insert a suitable bolt or drill through the timing hole in each camshaft sprocket and locate it in the cylinder head **(see illustration)**.

12 The crankshaft and camshafts are now locked in position, preventing rotation.

4 Cylinder head cover (TU engines) - removal and refitting

Removal

1 Disconnect the battery negative terminal.

2 Where necessary, undo the bolts securing the HT lead retaining clips to the rear of the cylinder head cover, and position the clips clear of the cover.

3 Slacken the retaining clip, and disconnect the breather hose from the left-hand end of the cylinder head cover **(see illustration)**. Where the original crimped-type Peugeot hose clip is still fitted, cut it off and discard it. Use a standard worm-drive clip on refitting.

4 Undo the two retaining nuts, and remove the washer from each of the cylinder head cover studs **(see illustration)**.

4.4 ... then slacken and remove the cover
retaining nuts and washers (arrowed) ...

11

4.5 . . . and lift off the cylinder head cover

4.6a Lift off the spacers (second one arrowed) . . .

4.6b . . . and remove the oil baffle plate

4.8 On refitting, ensure the rubber seal is correctly located on the cylinder head cover

5 Lift off the cylinder head cover, and remove it along with its rubber seal (see illustration). Examine the seal for signs of damage and deterioration, and if necessary, renew it.
6 Remove the spacer from each stud, and lift off the oil baffle plate (see illustrations).

Refitting

7 Carefully clean the cylinder head and cover mating surfaces, and remove all traces of oil.
8 Fit the rubber seal over the edge of the cylinder head cover, ensuring that it is correctly located along its entire length (see illustration).
9 Refit the oil baffle plate to the engine, and locate the spacers in their recesses in the baffle plate.
10 Carefully refit the cylinder head cover to the engine, taking great care not to displace the rubber seal.
11 Check that the seal is correctly located, then refit the washers and cover retaining nuts, and tighten them to the specified torque.
12 Where necessary, refit the HT lead clips to

the rear of the head cover, and securely tighten their retaining bolts.
13 Reconnect the breather hose to the cylinder head cover, securely tightening its retaining clip, and reconnect the battery negative lead.

5 Crankshaft pulley (XU engines) - removal and refitting

Removal

1 Remove the auxiliary drivebelt (Section 1).
2 To prevent crankshaft turning whilst the pulley retaining bolt is being slackened, select top gear and have an assistant apply the brakes firmly. *Do not* attempt to lock the pulley by inserting a bolt/drill through the timing hole. If the locking pin is in position, temporarily remove it prior to slackening the pulley bolt, then refit it once the bolt has been slackened.

3 Unscrew the retaining bolt and washer, then slide the pulley off the end of the crankshaft (see illustrations). If the pulley locating roll pin or Woodruff key (as applicable) is a loose fit, remove it and store it with the pulley for safe-keeping. If the pulley is a tight fit, it can be drawn off the crankshaft using a suitable puller.

5.3a Removing the crankshaft pulley retaining bolt

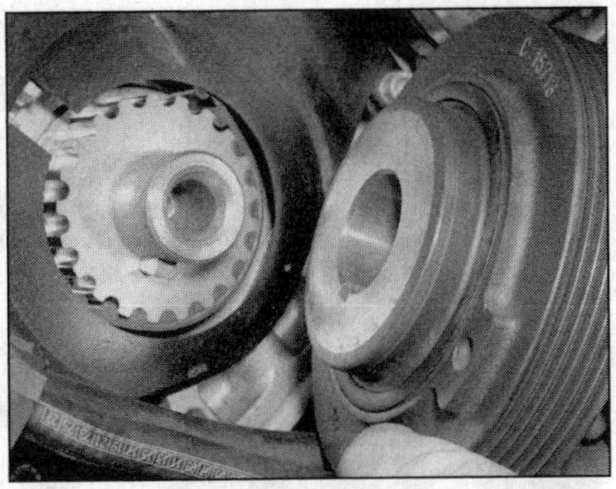

5.3b Removing the crankshaft pulley from the end of the crankshaft

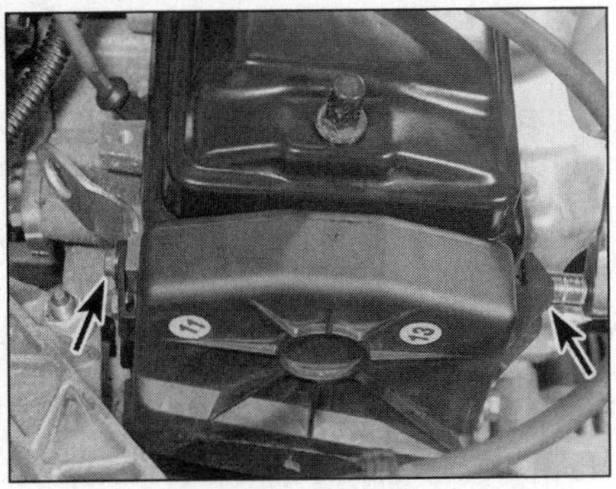

6.1a Undo the two retaining bolts (arrowed) . . .

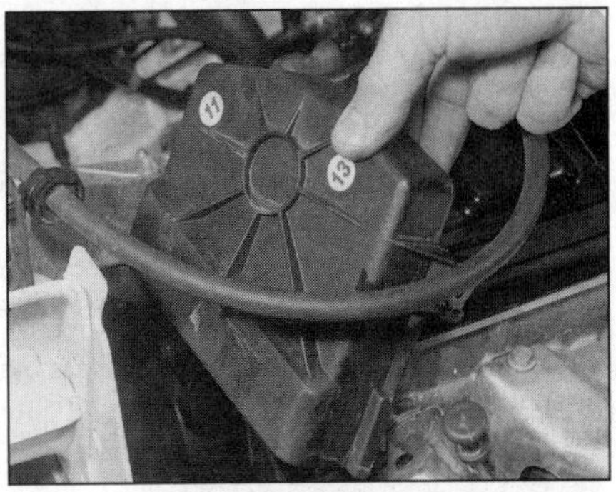

6.1b . . . and remove the timing belt upper cover

Refitting

4 Ensure that the Woodruff key is correctly located in its crankshaft groove, or that the roll pin is in position (as applicable). Refit the pulley to the end of the crankshaft, aligning its locating groove or hole with the Woodruff key or pin.

5 Thoroughly clean the threads of the pulley retaining bolt, then apply a coat of locking compound to the bolt threads. Peugeot recommend the use of Loctite (available from your Peugeot dealer); in the absence of this, any good-quality locking compound may be used.

6 Refit the crankshaft pulley retaining bolt and washer. Tighten the bolt to the specified torque, preventing the crankshaft from turning using the method employed on removal.

7 Refit and tension the auxiliary drivebelt as described in Section 1.

6 Timing belt covers (TU engines) - removal and refitting

Removal

Upper cover

1 Slacken and remove the two retaining bolts (one at the front and one at the rear), and remove the upper timing cover from the cylinder head **(see illustrations)**.

Centre cover

Note: *On later engines the centre cover is combined with the lower cover and is not a separate component.*

2 Remove the upper cover as described in paragraph 1, then free the wiring from its retaining clips on the centre cover **(see illustration)**.

3 Slacken and remove the three retaining bolts (one at the rear of the cover, beneath the engine mounting plate, and two directly above the crankshaft pulley), and manoeuvre the centre cover out from the engine compartment **(see illustration)**.

Lower cover

4 Remove the auxiliary drivebelt as described in Section 1.

5 Remove the upper and, where applicable, the centre covers as described in paragraphs 1 to 3.

6 Undo the three crankshaft pulley retaining bolts and remove the pulley, noting which way round it is fitted **(see illustrations)**.

7 Slacken and remove the single retaining bolt, and slide the lower cover off the end of the crankshaft **(see illustration)**.

Refitting

Upper cover

8 Refit the cover, ensuring it is correctly located with the centre cover, and tighten its retaining bolts.

Centre cover

9 Manoeuvre the centre cover back into position, ensuring it is correctly located with the lower cover, and tighten its retaining bolts.

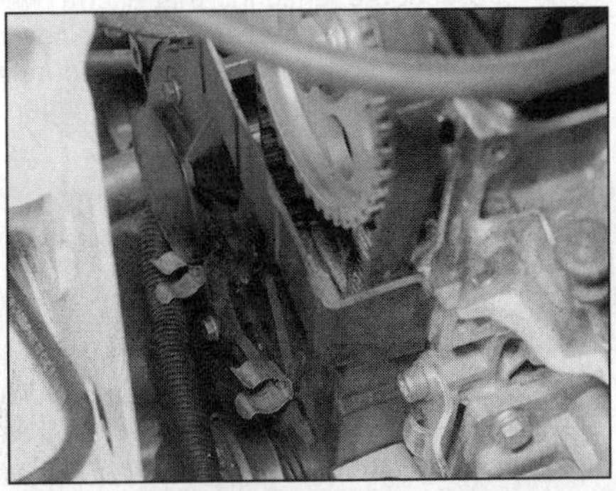

6.2 Free the wiring loom from its clip . . .

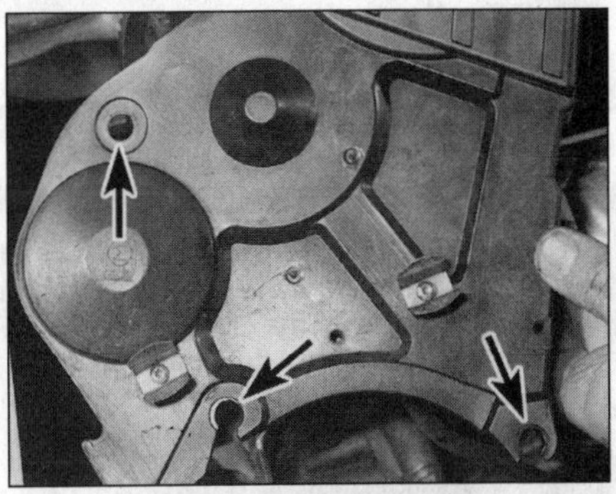

6.3 . . . then undo the three bolts (locations arrowed) and remove the centre cover

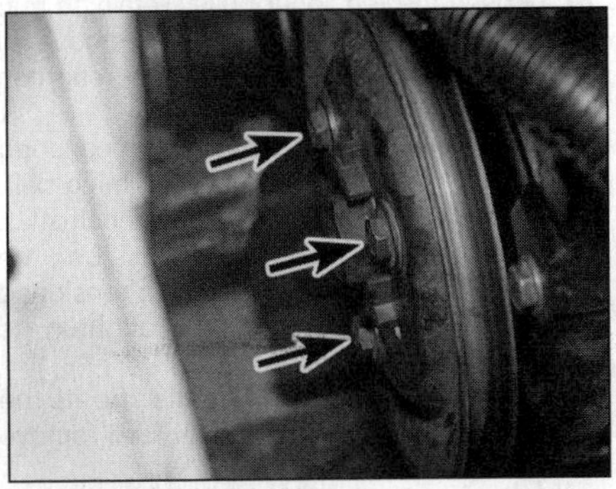

6.6a Undo the three bolts (arrowed) . . .

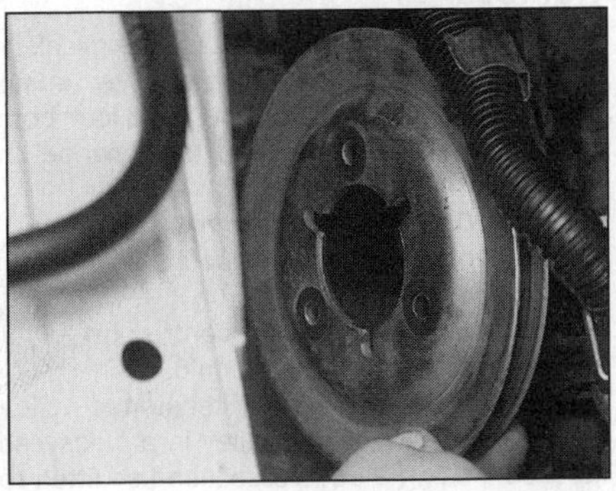

6.6b . . . and remove the crankshaft pulley

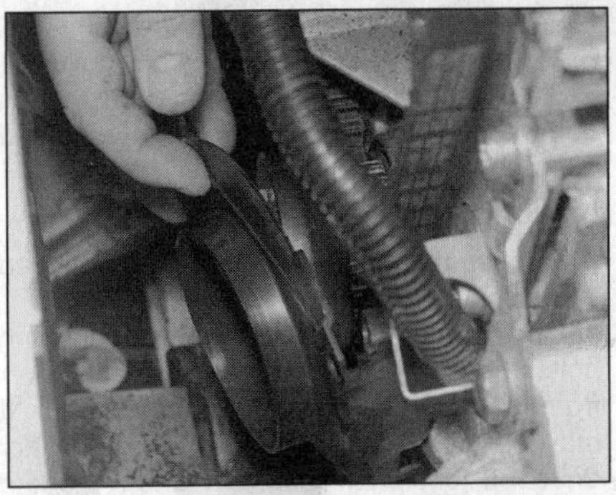

6.7 Undo the retaining bolt and remove the timing belt lower cover

10 Clip the wiring loom into its retaining clips on the front of the centre cover, then refit the upper cover as described in paragraph 8.

Lower cover

11 Locate the lower cover over the timing belt sprocket, and tighten its retaining bolt.
12 Fit the pulley to the end of the crankshaft, ensuring it is fitted the correct way round, and tighten its bolts to the specified torque.
13 Refit the centre and upper covers as described above, then refit and tension the auxiliary drivebelt as described in Section 1.

---

7 Timing belt covers (XU engines) - removal and refitting

1.8 litre 8-valve models

Upper cover

1 Release the retaining clips, and free the fuel hoses from the top of the cover.
2 Undo the two cover retaining bolts (situated at the base of the cover), and remove the cover from the engine compartment.

Centre cover

3 Slacken and remove the two cover retaining bolts (located directly beneath the mounting bracket). Move the cover upwards to free it from the two locating pins situated at the base of the cover, and remove it from the engine compartment.

Lower cover

4 Remove the crankshaft pulley as described in Section 5.
5 Remove the centre cover as described in paragraph 3.
6 Undo the two cover retaining bolts, and remove the cover from the engine. Note that on some models it may be necessary to unbolt the auxiliary drivebelt tensioner assembly and remove it from the engine in order to allow the cover to be removed.

2.0 litre 8-valve models

Upper cover

7 Release the retaining clip, and free the fuel hoses from the top of the timing belt cover.
8 Slacken and remove the two cover retaining bolts, then lift the upper cover upwards and out of the engine compartment.

Lower cover

9 Remove the crankshaft pulley as described in Section 5.
10 Slacken and remove the three retaining bolts, then remove the lower timing belt cover from the engine. Note that on some models it may be necessary to unbolt the auxiliary drivebelt tensioner assembly and remove it from the engine in order to allow the cover to be removed.

1.8 and 2.0 litre 16-valve models

Upper (outer) cover

11 Undo the upper and lower retaining bolts securing the outer cover to the inner cover. Slide the cover retaining clip upwards to release it from its fasteners.
12 Ease the outer cover upwards and away from the engine, freeing it from its lower locations.

Lower cover

13 Remove the crankshaft pulley as described in Section 5.
14 Remove the upper (outer) cover as described above.
15 Slacken and remove the three retaining bolts, then remove the lower timing belt cover from the engine. Note that on some models it may be necessary to unbolt the auxiliary drivebelt tensioner assembly and remove it from the engine in order to allow the cover to be removed.

Upper (inner) cover

16 Remove the timing belt as described in Section 9.
17 Remove both camshaft sprockets as described in Section 11.
18 Remove the six bolts securing the cover to the side of the cylinder head, and remove the cover from the engine.

Refitting

19 Refitting is a reversal of the relevant removal procedure, ensuring that each cover section is correctly located, and that the cover retaining nuts and/or bolts are securely tightened (to the specified torque, where given).

---

8 Timing belt (TU engines) - removal and refitting

Note: *Peugeot specify the use of a special electronic tool (SEEM C.TRONIC type 105 belt tensioning measuring tool, and valve rocker contact plate (-).0132 AE) to correctly set the timing belt tension.*

Removal

1 Disconnect the battery negative terminal.
2 Align the engine assembly/valve timing holes as described in Section 2, and lock both the camshaft sprocket and the flywheel in position.
Caution: Do not attempt to rotate the engine whilst the locking tools are in position.
3 Remove the timing belt centre and lower covers as described in Section 6.
4 Loosen the timing belt tensioner pulley retaining nut. Pivot the pulley in a clockwise direction, using a square-section key fitted to the hole in the pulley hub, then retighten the retaining nut.

8.5 Mark the direction of rotation on the belt, if it is to be re-used

5 If the timing belt is to be re-used, use white paint or similar to mark the direction of rotation on the belt (if markings do not already exist) **(see illustration)**. Slip the belt off the sprockets.
6 If signs of oil contamination are found, trace the source of the oil leak, and rectify it. Wash down the engine timing belt area, and all related components, to remove all traces of oil.

Refitting

7 Prior to refitting, thoroughly clean the timing belt sprockets. Check that the tensioner pulley rotates freely, without any sign of roughness. If necessary, renew the tensioner pulley as described in Section 10. Make sure that the locking tools are still in place, as described in Section 2.
8 Manoeuvre the timing belt into position, ensuring that the arrows on the belt are pointing in the direction of rotation (clockwise, when viewed from the right-hand end of the engine).
9 Do not twist the timing belt sharply while refitting it. Fit the belt over the crankshaft and camshaft sprockets. Make sure that the front run of the belt is taut - ie, ensure that any slack is on the tensioner pulley side of the belt. Fit the belt over the coolant pump sprocket and tensioner pulley. Ensure that the belt teeth are seated centrally in the sprockets.
10 Loosen the tensioner pulley retaining nut. Pivot the pulley anti-clockwise to remove all free play from the timing belt, then retighten the nut.
11 Fit the special belt tensioning measuring equipment to the front run of the timing belt, approximately midway between the camshaft and crankshaft sprockets. Position the tensioner pulley so that the belt is tensioned to a setting of 44 units, then retighten its retaining nut.
12 Remove the locking tools from the camshaft sprocket and flywheel, and remove the measuring tool from the belt.
13 Using a suitable socket and extension bar on the crankshaft sprocket bolt, rotate the

crankshaft through four complete rotations in a clockwise direction (viewed from the right-hand end of the engine). *Do not* at any time rotate the crankshaft anti-clockwise. Refit the locking tool to the flywheel and check that the camshaft sprocket timing hole is aligned.

14 Remove the cylinder head cover. Slacken the eight rocker arm contact bolts in the valve rocker contact plate (special tool (–).0132 AE) and fit the contact plate to the cylinder head, observing the correct fitted direction. Tighten each rocker arm contact bolt until the rockers are just free of the camshaft lobes. Do not over-tighten the contact bolts otherwise the valves will contact the pistons.

15 Refit the measuring tool to the belt, slacken the tensioner pulley retaining nut, and gradually release the tensioner pulley until a setting of between 29 and 33 units is indicated on the measuring tool. Retighten the tensioner pulley retaining nut.

16 Remove the measuring tool from the belt, the valve rocker contact plate from the cylinder head, and the locking tool from the flywheel. Rotate the crankshaft through another two complete rotations in a clockwise direction and check that both the camshaft sprocket and flywheel timing holes are realigned. *Do not* at any time rotate the crankshaft anti-clockwise.

17 With the belt tension correctly set, refit the cylinder head and timing belt covers, and reconnect the battery negative terminal.

9 Timing belt (XU engines) - removal and refitting

Note: *Peugeot specify the use of a special electronic tool (SEEM C.TRONIC type 105 belt tensioning measuring tool) to correctly set the timing belt tension.*

Removal

8-valve models

1 Disconnect the battery negative terminal

2 Align the engine assembly/valve timing holes as described in Section 3, and lock the camshaft sprocket and crankshaft pulley in position. *Do not* attempt to rotate the engine whilst the pins are in position.

3 Remove the centre and/or lower timing belt cover(s) as described in Section 6 (as applicable).

4 Loosen the timing belt tensioner pulley retaining bolt. Pivot the pulley in a clockwise direction, using a suitable square-section key fitted to the hole in the pulley hub, then securely retighten the retaining bolt.

5 On 1.8 litre models, position a jack beneath the engine, with a block of wood on the jack head. Raise the jack until it is supporting the weight of the engine. Slacken and remove the three nuts securing the engine/transmission right-hand mounting bracket to the engine bracket. Remove the single nut securing the

bracket to the mounting rubber, and lift off the bracket. Undo the three bolts securing the engine bracket to the end of the cylinder head/block, and remove the bracket.

6 If the timing belt is to be re-used, use white paint or chalk to mark the direction of rotation on the belt (if markings do not already exist), then slip the belt off the sprockets. Note that the crankshaft must not be rotated whilst the belt is removed.

7 If signs of oil contamination are found, trace the source of the oil leak and rectify it. Wash down the engine timing belt area and all related components, to remove all traces of oil.

16-valve models

8 Disconnect the battery negative terminal

9 Align the engine assembly/valve timing holes as described in Section 3, and lock the camshaft sprockets and crankshaft pulley in position. *Do not* attempt to rotate the engine whilst the pins are in position.

10 Remove the timing belt upper (outer) and lower covers as described in Section 7.

11 Move the engine wiring harness clear of the working area as necessary. This will entail the disconnection of certain connectors, and the removal of the harness from various cable clips and supports. Label any disconnected wiring and components as an aid to refitting.

12 Support the engine on a jack and remove the right-hand engine mounting components as described in Section 12.

13 Loosen the timing belt rear tensioner pulley retaining bolt and pivot the pulley in a clockwise direction, using a suitable square-section key fitted to the hole in the pulley hub, then retighten the retaining bolt.

14 Check that the camshaft sprocket locking pins are still in position, then remove and inspect the belt as described in paragraphs 6 and 7.

Refitting

8-valve models

15 Before refitting, thoroughly clean the timing belt sprockets. Check that the tensioner pulley rotates freely, without any sign of roughness. If necessary, renew the tensioner pulley as described in Section 11.

16 Ensure that the camshaft sprocket locking pin is still in position. Temporarily refit the crankshaft pulley, and insert the locking pin through the pulley timing hole to ensure that the crankshaft is still correctly positioned.

17 Remove the crankshaft pulley. Manoeuvre the timing belt into position, ensuring that any arrows on the belt are pointing in the direction of rotation (clockwise when viewed from the right-hand end of the engine).

18 Do not twist the timing belt sharply while refitting it. Fit the belt over the crankshaft and camshaft sprockets. Ensure that the belt front run is taut - ie, any slack should be on the tensioner pulley side of the belt. Fit the belt over the water pump sprocket and tensioner

pulley. Ensure that the belt teeth are seated centrally in the sprockets.

19 Loosen the tensioner pulley retaining bolt. Using the square-section key, pivot the pulley anti-clockwise to remove all free play from the timing belt.

20 Fit the special belt tension measuring equipment to the front run of the timing belt. The tensioner roller should be adjusted so that the initial belt tension is 16 ± 2 units on 2.0 litre models, and 30 ± 2 units on 1.8 litre models.

21 Tighten the pulley retaining bolt to the specified torque. Refit the crankshaft pulley again, tightening its retaining bolt by hand only.

22 Rotate the crankshaft through at least two complete rotations in a clockwise direction (viewed from the right-hand end of the engine). Realign the camshaft and crankshaft engine assembly/valve timing holes (see Section 3). *Do not* at any time rotate the crankshaft anti-clockwise. Both camshaft and crankshaft timing holes should be aligned so that the locking pins can be easily inserted. This indicates that the valve timing is correct.

23 If the timing holes are not correctly positioned, release the tensioner assembly as described in paragraph 7, and disengage the belt from the camshaft sprocket. Rotate the camshaft and crankshaft slightly as required until both locking pins are in position. Relocate the timing belt on the camshaft sprocket. Ensure that the belt front run is taut - ie, that any slack is on the tensioner pulley side of the belt. Slacken the tensioner locknut, then remove the locking pins and repeat the procedure described in paragraph 22.

24 With the special measuring tool the final belt tension on the front run of the belt on all models should be 44 ± 2 units. Readjust the tensioner pulley position as required, then retighten the retaining bolt to the specified torque. Rotate the crankshaft through a further two rotations clockwise, and recheck the tension. Repeat this procedure as necessary until the correct tension reading is obtained after rotating the crankshaft.

25 With the belt tension correctly set, on 1.8 litre models, refit the mounting bracket to the side of the cylinder head, apply a drop of locking compound to the retaining bolts and tighten them to the specified torque. Refit the right-hand engine mounting bracket, and tighten its retaining nuts to the specified torque. The jack can then be removed from underneath the engine.

26 On all models, remove the crankshaft pulley, then refit the timing belt cover(s) as described in Section 7.

27 Refit the crankshaft pulley as described in Section 5, and reconnect the battery negative terminal.

16-valve models

28 Before refitting, thoroughly clean the timing belt sprockets. Check that the tensioner pulley rotates freely, without any

11

sign of roughness. If necessary, renew the tensioner pulley as described in Section 11.

29 Ensure that the camshaft sprocket locking pin is still in position. Temporarily refit the crankshaft pulley, and insert the locking pin through the pulley timing hole to ensure that the crankshaft is still correctly positioned.

30 Remove the crankshaft pulley. Manoeuvre the timing belt into position on the crankshaft sprocket, ensuring that any arrows on the belt are pointing in the direction of rotation (clockwise when viewed from the right-hand end of the engine).

31 Refit the timing belt lower cover and the crankshaft pulley (Sections 7 and 5).

32 Refit the locking pin to the crankshaft pulley.

33 Without removing the locking pins, slacken the camshaft sprocket retaining bolts (three on each sprocket). Check that both sprockets are free to turn within the limits of their elongated bolt holes.

34 Tighten the camshaft sprocket retaining bolts finger tight, then slacken them all by one sixth of a turn.

35 Turn each sprocket clockwise to the ends of their retaining bolt slots.

36 With the timing belt engaged with the crankshaft sprocket, keep it tight on its right-hand run and engage it with the front idler pulley then up and into engagement with the inlet camshaft sprocket.

37 Keeping the belt tight and rotating the inlet camshaft sprocket anti-clockwise as necessary, feed the belt over the exhaust camshaft sprocket, taking care not to let the belt jump a tooth on the crankshaft sprocket as it is being fitted.

38 While still keeping the belt tight, feed it over the rear tensioner pulley and finally around the coolant pump.

39 Fit the special belt tension measuring equipment to the front run of the timing belt. The tensioner pulley should be adjusted, by turning it anti-clockwise to give a belt pre-tensioning setting of 45 units. Hold the tensioner pulley in this position and tighten the retaining bolt to the specified torque.

40 Remove one retaining bolt from each camshaft sprocket and check that the sprockets are not at the end of their retaining bolt slots. If they are, repeat the refitting operation. If all is satisfactory, refit the two removed bolts, and tighten the sprocket retaining bolts to the specified torque.

41 Remove the locking pins, then rotate the crankshaft through two complete rotations in a clockwise direction (viewed from the right-hand end of the engine). Realign the crankshaft engine assembly/valve timing hole and refit the locking pin to the crankshaft pulley.

42 Slacken the camshaft sprocket retaining bolts, retighten them finger tight, then slacken them all by one sixth of a turn.

43 Refit the camshaft sprocket locking pins, then slacken the tensioner pulley retaining bolt once more. Refit the belt tension

measuring equipment to the front run of the belt and turn the tensioner pulley to give an initial setting of 26 units on the tensioning gauge. Hold the tensioner pulley in this position and tighten the retaining bolt to the specified torque.

44 Retighten the sprocket retaining bolts to the specified torque.

45 Remove the locking pins, then rotate the crankshaft once again through two complete rotations in a clockwise direction. Realign the crankshaft engine assembly/valve timing hole and refit the locking pin to the crankshaft pulley.

46 Slacken the camshaft sprocket retaining bolts, retighten them finger tight, then slacken them all by one sixth of a turn.

47 Refit the camshaft sprocket locking pins, then retighten the sprocket retaining bolts to the specified torque.

48 Remove the locking pins, then slowly turn the crankshaft one quarter turn in a clockwise direction until the timing hole in the crankshaft pulley is aligned with the adjacent bolt on the front of the engine.

49 Refit the belt tension measuring equipment to the front run of the belt and check that a final setting of between 32 and 40 units is indicated on the tensioning gauge. If this is not the case, repeat the tensioning procedure.

50 Once the belt tension has been correctly set, refit the right-hand engine mounting components as described in Section 12, and reconnect all the disconnected engine wiring.

51 Refit the timing belt upper (outer) and lower covers as described in Section 7, and reconnect the battery negative terminal.

10 Timing belt tensioner and sprockets (TU engines) - removal and refitting

Note: *This Section describes the removal and refitting of the components concerned as individual operations. If more than one of them is to be removed at the same time, start by removing the timing belt as described in Section 8; remove the actual component as described below, ignoring the preliminary dismantling steps.*

Removal

1 Disconnect the battery negative terminal.

2 Position the engine assembly/valve timing holes as described in Section 2, and lock both the camshaft sprocket and flywheel in position. *Do not* attempt to rotate the engine whilst the pins are in position.

Camshaft sprocket

3 On engines with a three-piece timing belt cover arrangement, remove the centre cover as described in Section 6. On engines with a two-piece cover, remove the lower cover.

4 Loosen the timing belt tensioner pulley retaining nut. Rotate the pulley in a clockwise

direction, using a suitable square-section key fitted to the hole in the pulley hub, then retighten the retaining nut.

5 Disengage the timing belt from the sprocket, and move the belt clear, taking care not to bend or twist it sharply. Remove the locking pin from the camshaft sprocket.

6 Slacken the camshaft sprocket retaining bolt and remove it, along with its washer. To prevent the camshaft rotating as the bolt is slackened, a sprocket-holding tool will be required. In the absence of the special Peugeot tool, an acceptable substitute can be fabricated as follows. Use two lengths of steel strip (one long, the other short), and three nuts and bolts; one nut and bolt forms the pivot of a forked tool, with the remaining two nuts and bolts at the tips of the 'forks' to engage with the sprocket spokes **(see illustration).**
Caution: Do not attempt to use the sprocket locking pin to prevent the sprocket from rotating whilst the bolt is slackened.

7 With the retaining bolt removed, slide the sprocket off the end of the camshaft. If the locating peg is a loose fit in the rear of the sprocket, remove it for safe-keeping. Examine the camshaft oil seal for signs of oil leakage and, if necessary, renew it.

Crankshaft sprocket

8 Remove the centre (where fitted) and lower timing belt covers as described in Section 6.

9 Loosen the timing belt tensioner pulley retaining nut. Rotate the pulley in a clockwise direction, using a suitable square-section key fitted to the hole in the pulley hub, then retighten the retaining nut.

10 To prevent crankshaft rotation whilst the sprocket retaining bolt is slackened, select top gear, and have an assistant apply the brakes firmly. *Do not* be tempted to use the flywheel locking pin to prevent the crankshaft from rotating; temporarily remove the locking pin from the rear of the flywheel prior to

10.6 Using a home-made tool to hold the camshaft sprocket stationary whilst the bolt is tightened (shown with cylinder head removed)

10.11a Remove the crankshaft sprocket bolt . . .

10.11b . . . then slide off the sprocket

slackening the pulley bolt, then refit it once the bolt has been slackened.

11 Unscrew the retaining bolt and washer, then slide the sprocket off the end of the crankshaft **(see illustrations)**. Refit the locating pin to the rear of the timing hole in the rear of the flywheel.

12 If the Woodruff key is a loose fit in the crankshaft, remove it and store it with the sprocket for safe-keeping. If necessary, also slide the flanged spacer off the end of the crankshaft **(see illustration)**. Examine the crankshaft oil seal for signs of oil leakage and, if necessary, renew it.

Tensioner pulley

13 On engines with a three-piece timing belt cover arrangement, remove the centre cover as described in Section 6. On engines with a two-piece cover, remove the lower cover.

14 Slacken and remove the timing belt tensioner pulley retaining nut, and slide the pulley off its mounting stud. Examine the mounting stud for signs of damage and, if necessary, renew it.

10.12 Remove the flanged spacer if necessary

Refitting

15 Clean the sprockets thoroughly, and renew any that show signs of wear, damage or cracks.

16 Clean the tensioner assembly, but do not use any strong solvent which may enter the pulley bearing. Check that the pulley rotates freely about its hub, with no sign of stiffness or of free play. Renew the tensioner pulley if there is any doubt about its condition, or if there are any obvious signs of wear or damage.

Camshaft sprocket

17 Refit the locating peg (where removed) to the rear of the sprocket, then locate the sprocket on the end of the camshaft. Ensure that the locating peg is correctly engaged with the cut-out in the camshaft end.

18 Refit the sprocket retaining bolt and washer. Tighten the bolt to the specified torque, whilst retaining the sprocket with the tool used on removal.

19 Realign the timing hole in the camshaft sprocket (see Section 2) with the corresponding hole in the cylinder head, and refit the locking pin.

20 Refit the timing belt to the camshaft sprocket. Ensure that the front run of the belt is taut - ie, ensure that any slack is on the tensioner pulley side of the belt. Do not twist the belt sharply while refitting it, and ensure that the belt teeth are seated centrally in the sprockets.

21 Loosen the tensioner pulley retaining nut. Rotate the pulley anti-clockwise to remove all free play from the timing belt, then retighten the nut.

22 Tension the belt as described in paragraphs 11 to 16 of Section 8.

23 Refit the timing belt covers as described in Section 5.

Crankshaft sprocket

24 Where removed, locate the Woodruff key

in the crankshaft end, then slide on the flanged spacer, aligning its slot with the Woodruff key.

25 Align the crankshaft sprocket slot with the Woodruff key, and slide it onto the end of the crankshaft.

26 Temporarily remove the locking pin from the rear of the flywheel, then refit the crankshaft sprocket retaining bolt and washer. Tighten the bolt to the specified torque, whilst preventing crankshaft rotation using the method employed on removal. Refit the locking pin to the rear of the flywheel.

27 Relocate the timing belt on the crankshaft sprocket. Ensure that the front run of the belt is taut - ie, ensure that any slack is on the tensioner pulley side of the belt. Do not twist the belt sharply while refitting it, and ensure that the belt teeth are seated centrally in the sprockets.

28 Loosen the tensioner pulley nut. Turn the pulley anti-clockwise to remove all free play from the timing belt, then retighten the nut.

29 Tension the belt as described in paragraphs 11 to 16 of Section 8.

30 Refit the timing belt covers (see Section 6).

Tensioner pulley

31 Refit the tensioner pulley to its mounting stud, and fit the retaining nut.

32 Ensure that the front run of the belt is taut - ie, ensure that any slack is on the pulley side of the belt. Check that the belt is centrally located on all its sprockets. Rotate the pulley anti-clockwise to remove all free play from the timing belt, then tighten the pulley retaining nut securely.

33 Tension the belt as described in paragraphs 11 to 16 of Section 8.

34 Refit the timing belt covers as described in Section 6.

11

11.6 Using a home-made tool to hold the camshaft sprocket stationary whilst the bolt is tightened (shown with cylinder head removed) (TU engine shown)

11 Timing belt tensioner and sprockets (XU engines) - removal and refitting

Note: *This Section describes the removal and refitting of the components concerned as individual operations - if more than one is to be removed at the same time, start by removing the timing belt as described in Section 9; remove the actual component as described below, ignoring the preliminary dismantling steps.*

Removal

1 Disconnect the battery negative terminal.
2 Align the engine assembly/valve timing holes as described in Section 3, locking the camshaft sprocket and the crankshaft pulley in position, and proceed as described under the relevant sub-heading. *Do not* attempt to rotate the engine whilst the pins are in position.

Camshaft sprocket - 8-valve models

3 On 1.8 litre models, remove the centre timing belt cover as described in Section 7.
4 On all models, loosen the timing belt tensioner pulley retaining bolt. Rotate the pulley in a clockwise direction, using a suitable square-section key fitted to the hole in the pulley hub, then retighten the retaining bolt.
5 Remove the locking pin from the camshaft sprocket. Disengage the timing belt from the sprocket and position it clear, taking care not to bend or twist the belt sharply.
6. Slacken the camshaft sprocket retaining bolt and remove it, along with its washer. To prevent the camshaft rotating as the bolt is slackened, a sprocket holding tool will be required. In the absence of the special Peugeot tool, an acceptable substitute can be fabricated at home **(see illustration)**. *Do not* attempt to use the sprocket locking pin to prevent the sprocket from rotating whilst the bolt is slackened, or the pin may shear off.

7 With the retaining bolt removed, slide the sprocket off the end of the camshaft. If the locating peg is a loose fit in the rear of the sprocket, remove it for safe-keeping. Examine the camshaft oil seal for signs of oil leakage and, if necessary, renew it.

Camshaft sprockets - 16-valve models

8 Remove the timing belt upper (outer) and lower covers as described in Section 7.
9 Move the engine wiring harness clear of the working area as necessary. This will entail the disconnection of certain connectors, and the removal of the harness from various cable clips and supports. Label any disconnected wiring and components as an aid to refitting.
10 Support the engine on a jack and remove the right-hand engine mounting components as described in Section 12.
11 Loosen the timing belt rear tensioner pulley retaining bolt and pivot the pulley in a clockwise direction, using a suitable square-section key fitted to the hole in the pulley hub, then retighten the retaining bolt.
12 Check that the camshaft sprocket locking pins are still in position, then disengage the timing belt from the camshaft sprockets and position it clear, taking care not to bend or twist the belt sharply.
13 If the sprockets are to be removed without their hubs, undo the three retaining bolts and remove the relevant sprocket. Suitably mark the sprockets inlet and/or exhaust as they are removed.
14 If both the sprockets and the hubs are to be removed, remove the sprocket locking pins, then slacken the sprocket hub centre retaining bolt. To prevent the sprockets rotating as the bolt is slackened, a sprocket holding tool will be required. In the absence of the special Peugeot tool, an acceptable substitute can be fabricated at home **(see illustration)**. *Do not* attempt to use the sprocket locking pin to prevent the sprocket from rotating whilst the bolt is slackened.
15 Undo the three retaining bolts and remove the relevant sprocket. Remove the previously slackened hub retaining bolt and withdraw the hub from the end of the camshaft. Note that the hubs are marked for identification with a single digit on their front face. On 1.8 litre models, the inlet hub is marked 1 and the exhaust hub is marked 2. On 2.0 litre models the inlet hub is marked 3 and the exhaust hub is marked 4.

Crankshaft sprocket - 8-valve models

16 Remove the centre and/or lower timing belt cover(s) (as applicable) (see Section 7).
17 Loosen the timing belt tensioner pulley retaining bolt. Rotate the pulley in a clockwise direction, using a suitable square-section key fitted to the hole in the pulley hub, then retighten the retaining bolt.
18 Disengage the timing belt from the crankshaft sprocket, and slide the sprocket off the end of the crankshaft. Remove the Woodruff key from the crankshaft, and store it

with the sprocket for safe-keeping. Where necessary, also slide the spacer (where fitted) off the end of the crankshaft.
19 Examine the crankshaft oil seal for signs of oil leakage and, if necessary, renew it.

Crankshaft sprocket - 16-valve models

20 Remove the timing belt upper (outer) and lower covers as described in Section 7.
21 Move the engine wiring harness clear of the working area as necessary. This will entail the disconnection of certain connectors, and the removal of the harness from various cable clips and supports. Label any disconnected wiring and components as an aid to refitting.
22 Support the engine on a jack and remove the right-hand engine mounting components as described in Section 12.
23 Loosen the timing belt rear tensioner pulley retaining bolt and pivot the pulley in a clockwise direction, using a suitable square-section key fitted to the hole in the pulley hub, then retighten the retaining bolt.
24 Check that the camshaft sprocket locking pins are still in position, then disengage the timing belt from the crankshaft sprocket and slide the sprocket off the end of the crankshaft. Remove the Woodruff key from the crankshaft, and store it with the sprocket for safe-keeping.
25 Examine the crankshaft oil seal for signs of oil leakage and, if necessary, renew it.

Tensioner pulley - 8-valve models

26 On 1.8 litre models, remove the centre timing belt cover as described in Section 7.
27 On all models. slacken and remove the timing belt tensioner pulley retaining bolt, and slide the pulley off its mounting stud. Examine the mounting stud for signs of damage and if necessary, renew it.

Tensioner and idler pulleys - 16-valve models

28 Remove the timing belt upper (outer) and lower covers as described in Section 7.
29 Move the engine wiring harness clear of the working area as necessary. This will entail the disconnection of certain connectors, and the removal of the harness from various cable clips and supports. Label any disconnected wiring and components as an aid to refitting.
30 Support the engine on a jack and remove the right-hand engine mounting components as described in Section 12.
31 Loosen the timing belt rear tensioner pulley retaining bolt and pivot the pulley in a clockwise direction, using a suitable square-section key fitted to the hole in the pulley hub, then retighten the retaining bolt.
32 Check that the camshaft sprocket locking pins are still in position, then disengage the timing belt from the camshaft sprockets and position it clear, taking care not to bend or twist the belt sharply.
33 Undo the tensioner and idler pulley retaining bolts and remove them from the engine.

Refitting

34 Clean the camshaft/crankshaft sprockets thoroughly, and renew any that show signs of wear, damage or cracks.

35 Clean the tensioner/idler pulleys, but do not use any strong solvent which may enter the pulley bearings. Check that the pulleys rotate freely, with no sign of stiffness or free play. Renew them if there is any doubt about their condition, or if there are any obvious signs of wear or damage.

Camshaft sprocket - 8-valve models

36 Refit the locating peg (where removed) to the rear of the sprocket. Locate the sprocket on the end of the camshaft, ensuring that the locating peg is correctly engaged with the cut-out in the camshaft end.

37 Refit the sprocket retaining bolt and washer, and tighten it to the specified torque. Retain the sprocket with the tool used on removal.

38 Realign the hole in the camshaft sprocket with the corresponding hole in the cylinder head, and refit the locking pin. Check that the crankshaft pulley locking pin is still in position.

39 Refit the timing belt to the camshaft sprocket. Ensure that the front run of the belt is taut - ie, that any slack is on the tensioner pulley side of the belt. Do not twist the belt sharply while refitting it, and ensure that the belt teeth are seated centrally in the sprockets.

40 With the timing belt correctly engaged on the sprockets, tension the belt as described in Section 9.

41 Once the belt is correctly tensioned, refit the timing belt covers (see Section 7).

Camshaft sprockets - 16-valve models

42 If both the sprockets and the hubs have been removed, engage the sprocket hub with the camshaft. Ensure that the correct hub is fitted to the relevant camshaft by observing the hub identification markings described in paragraph 15.

43 Refit the sprocket hub retaining bolt and washer, and tighten it to the specified torque. Temporarily refit the sprockets to allow the hub to be held stationary with the tool as the bolt is tightened.

44 Turn the hub so that the locking pin can be engaged.

45 If the sprockets have been removed, leaving the hubs in place, position the sprocket on its hub and refit the three bolts finger tight only at this stage. Ensure that the

correct sprocket is fitted to the relevant camshaft according to the identification made on removal.

46 Relocate and tension the timing belt as described in Section 9.

Crankshaft sprocket - 8-valve models

47 Slide the spacer (where fitted) into position, taking great care not to damage the crankshaft oil seal, and refit the Woodruff key to its slot in the crankshaft end.

48 Slide on the crankshaft sprocket, aligning its slot with the Woodruff key.

49 Ensure that the camshaft sprocket locking pin is still in position. Temporarily refit the crankshaft pulley, and insert the locking pin through the pulley timing hole, to ensure that the crankshaft is still correctly positioned.

50 Remove the crankshaft pulley. Engage the timing belt with the crankshaft sprocket. Ensure that the belt front run is taut - ie, that any slack is on the tensioner pulley side of the belt. Fit the belt over the water pump sprocket and tensioner pulley. Do not twist the belt sharply while refitting it, and ensure that the belt teeth are seated centrally in the sprockets.

51 Tension the timing belt as described in Section 9.

52 On all models, remove the crankshaft pulley, then refit the timing belt cover(s) as described in Section 7.

53 Refit the crankshaft pulley as described in Section 5, and reconnect the battery negative terminal.

Crankshaft sprocket - 16-valve models

54 Refit the Woodruff key to its slot in the crankshaft end.

55 Slide on the crankshaft sprocket, aligning its slot with the Woodruff key.

56 Relocate and tension the timing belt as described in Section 9.

Tensioner pulley - 8-valve models

57 Refit the tensioner pulley to its mounting stud, and fit the retaining bolt.

58 Ensure that the front run of the belt is taut - ie, that any slack is on the pulley side of the belt. Check that the belt is centrally located on all its sprockets. Rotate the pulley anti-clockwise to remove all free play from the timing belt, and securely tighten the pulley retaining nut.

59 Tension the belt as described in Section 9.

60 Once the belt is correctly tensioned, refit the timing belt covers (see Section 7).

Tensioner and idler pulleys - 16-valve models

61 Refit the tensioner and idler pulleys and secure with the retaining bolts.

62 Relocate and tension the timing belt as described in Section 9.

12 Engine right-hand mounting (XU 16-valve models) - removal and refitting

Removal

1 Disconnect the battery negative terminal. Release all the relevant hoses and wiring from their retaining clips. Place the hoses/wiring clear of the mounting so that the removal procedure is not hindered.

2 Place a jack beneath the engine, with a block of wood on the jack head. Raise the jack until it is supporting the weight of the engine.

3 Slacken and remove the two nuts and two bolts securing the right-hand engine/transmission mounting bracket to the engine. Remove the single nut securing the bracket to the mounting rubber.

4 Undo the bolt securing the upper engine movement limiter to the right-hand mounting bracket, and the four bolts securing the movement limiter mounting bracket to the body. Lift away the right-hand mounting bracket and the movement limiter assembly.

5 Lift the rubber buffer plate off the mounting rubber stud, then unscrew the mounting rubber from the body and remove it from the vehicle. If necessary, the mounting bracket can be unbolted and removed from the front of the cylinder block.

Refitting

6 On reassembly, screw the mounting rubber into the vehicle body, and tighten it securely. Refit the mounting bracket to the front of the cylinder head, and securely tighten its retaining bolts.

7 Refit the engine movement limiter assembly to the engine mounting bracket and to the body and tighten the bolts to the specified torque.

8 Refit the rubber buffer plate to the mounting rubber stud, and install the mounting bracket.

9 Tighten the mounting bracket retaining nuts to the specified torque setting. Remove the jack from underneath the engine and reconnect the battery.

11

Notes

Chapter 11B
Peugeot 306 diesel 1993 to 1998

Contents

Specifications

Timing belt renewal interval... Every 36 000 miles (60 000 km)

Note: *Although the normal interval for timing belt renewal is 72 000 miles (120 000 km), it is strongly recommended that the interval is halved on vehicles which are subjected to intensive use, ie, mainly short journeys or a lot of stop-start driving. The actual belt renewal interval is therefore very much up to the individual owner. That being said, it is highly recommended to err on the side of safety, and renew the belt at this earlier interval, bearing in mind the drastic consequences resulting from belt failure.*

Torque wrench settings	Nm	lbf ft
Camshaft sprocket bolt	45	33
Crankshaft pulley bolt*:		
Stage 1	40	30
Stage 2	Tighten through a further 50°	
Left-hand engine/transmission mounting:		
Centre nut	65	48
Mounting bracket-to-body bolts	25	18
Mounting stud	25	18
Engine/transmission rear mounting:		
Mounting assembly-to-block bolts	45	33
Mounting link-to-mounting bolt	50	37
Mounting link-to-subframe bolt	70	52
Engine/transmission right-hand mounting:		
Curved retaining plate bolts	20	15
Engine (tensioner assembly) bracket bolts	18	13
Mounting bracket retaining nuts	45	33
Fuel injection pump sprocket nut	50	37
Fuel injection pump sprocket puller retaining screws	10	7
Roadwheel bolts	85	63
Timing belt cover bolts	8	6
Timing belt tensioner adjustment bolt	18	13
Timing belt tensioner pivot nut	18	13

* Use thread-locking compound

11B

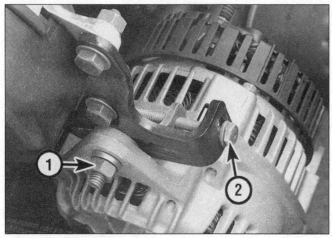

1.5 Alternator upper mounting nut (1) and adjuster bolt (2)

1.13 Slacken the two tensioner roller retaining screws (arrowed) . . .

1 Auxiliary drivebelt - removal, refitting and adjustment

1 Chock the rear wheels then jack up the front of the vehicle and support it on axle stands. Remove the right-hand front roadwheel.

2 From underneath the front of the car, prise out the retaining clips, and remove the plastic cover from the wing valance to gain access to the crankshaft sprocket/pulley bolt. Where necessary, unclip the coolant hoses from the wing to improve access further.

Models with manual adjuster on the alternator lower mounting point

Removal

3 Disconnect the battery negative terminal.
4 Slacken both the alternator upper and lower mounting nuts/bolts (as applicable).
5 Back off the adjuster bolt(s) to relieve the tension in the drivebelt, then slip the drivebelt from the pulleys (see illustration).

Refitting and adjustment

6 Fit the belt around the pulleys, and take up the slack in the belt by tightening the adjuster bolt.
7 The belt should be tensioned so that, under firm thumb pressure, there is about 5.0 mm of free movement at the mid-point between the pulleys on the longest belt run.
8 To adjust, with the upper mounting nut/bolt just holding the alternator firm, and the lower mounting nut/bolt loosened, turn the adjuster bolt until the correct tension is achieved.
9 Rotate the crankshaft a couple of times, recheck the tension, then securely tighten both the alternator mounting nuts/bolts. Where applicable, also tighten the bolt securing the adjuster strap to its mounting bracket.

10 Reconnect the battery negative terminal.
11 Clip the coolant hoses into position (where necessary), then refit the plastic cover to the wing valance. Refit the roadwheel, and lower the vehicle to the ground.

Models with a manually-adjusted tensioning pulley

Removal

12 Disconnect the battery negative terminal.
13 Slacken the two screws securing the tensioning pulley assembly to the engine (see illustration).
14 Rotate the adjuster bolt to move the tensioner pulley away from the drivebelt until there is sufficient slack for the drivebelt to be removed from the pulleys (see illustration).

Refitting and adjustment

15 Fit the drivebelt around the pulleys in the following order:
a) Power steering pump and/or air conditioning compressor.
b) Crankshaft.
c) Alternator.
d) Tensioner roller.
16 Ensure that the ribs on the belt are correctly engaged with the grooves in the pulleys, and that the drivebelt is correctly routed. Take all the slack out of the belt by turning the tensioner pulley adjuster bolt.
26 The belt should be tensioned so that, under firm thumb pressure, there is approximately 5.0 mm of free movement at the mid-point between the pulleys on the longest belt run.
27 To adjust the tension, with the two tensioner pulley assembly retaining screws slackened, rotate the adjuster bolt until the correct tension is achieved. Once the belt is correctly tensioned, rotate the crankshaft a couple of times and recheck the tension.
28 When the belt is correctly tensioned, securely tighten the tensioner pulley assembly

retaining screws, then reconnect the battery negative terminal.
29 Clip the coolant hoses into position, then refit the plastic cover to the wing valance. Refit the roadwheel, and lower the vehicle to the ground.

Early models with an automatic spring-loaded tensioner pulley

Removal

31 Disconnect the battery negative terminal.
32 Where necessary, remove the retaining screws from the power steering pump pulley shield and remove the shield to gain access to the top of the drivebelt.
33 Move the tensioner pulley away from the drivebelt, using a ratchet handle or extension bar with the same size square-section end as the hole in the base of the automatic tensioner arm. Disengage the drivebelt from all the pulleys, noting its correct routing. Remove the drivebelt from the engine, noting that in some cases, it may be necessary to slacken the automatic tensioner mounting bolts to disengage the belt from behind the tensioner pulley.

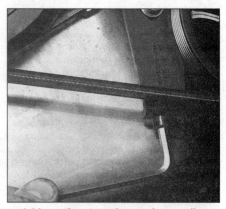

1.14 . . . then turn the tensioner roller adjuster bolt to release the belt tension

Refitting and adjustment

34 Fit the drivebelt around the pulleys in the following order:

a) *Automatic tensioner pulley.*
b) *Crankshaft.*
c) *Air conditioning compressor.*
d) *Power steering pump.*
e) *Idler pulley.*
f) *Alternator.*

35 Where necessary, securely tighten the automatic tensioner mounting bolts.

36 Whilst holding the tensioner arm away from the belt, ensure that the ribs on the belt are correctly engaged with the grooves in the pulleys. Release the tensioner arm; the tensioner is spring-loaded, removing the need to manually adjust the belt tension.

37 Refit the power steering pump pulley shield (where removed), and securely tighten its retaining screws.

38 Reconnect the battery negative terminal.

39 Clip the coolant hoses into position, then refit the plastic cover to the wing valance. Refit the roadwheel, and lower the vehicle to the ground.

Later models with an automatic spring-loaded tensioner pulley

Removal

30 Disconnect the battery negative terminal.

31 Where necessary, remove the retaining screws from the power steering pump pulley shield, and remove the shield to gain access to the top of the drivebelt.

32 Working under the wheelarch, slacken the retaining bolt located in the centre of the eccentric tensioner pulley.

33 Insert a cranked 7.0 mm square section bar (a quarter inch square section drive socket bar for example) into the square hole on the front face of the eccentric tensioner pulley.

34 Using the bar, turn the eccentric tensioner pulley until the hole in the arm of the automatic tensioner pulley is aligned with the hole in the mounting bracket behind. When the holes are aligned, slide a suitable setting tool (a bolt or cranked length of bar of

approximately 8.0 mm diameter) through the hole in the arm and into the mounting bracket.

35 With the automatic tensioner locked, turn the eccentric tensioner pulley until the drivebelt tension is released sufficiently to enable the belt to be removed.

Refitting and adjustment

36 Fit the drivebelt around the pulleys in the following order:

a) *Air conditioning compressor.*
b) *Crankshaft.*
c) *Automatic tensioner pulley.*
d) *Power steering pump.*
e) *Alternator.*
f) *Eccentric tensioner pulley.*

37 Ensure that the ribs on the belt are correctly engaged with the grooves on the pulleys.

38 Turn the eccentric tensioner pulley to apply tension to the drivebelt, until the load is released from the setting bolt. Without altering the position of the eccentric tensioner pulley, tighten its retaining bolt securely.

39 Remove the setting bolt from the automatic tensioner arm, then rotate the crankshaft four complete revolutions in the normal direction of rotation.

40 Check that the holes in the automatic adjuster arm and the mounting bracket are still aligned by re-inserting the setting bolt. If the bolt will not slide in easily, repeat the tensioning procedure from paragraph 38 onward.

41 On completion, reconnect the battery negative lead, and all other disturbed components.

---

2 Engine assembly/valve timing holes - general information and usage

Caution: Do not attempt to rotate the engine whilst the crankshaft/camshaft/injection pump are locked in position. If the engine is to be left in this state for a long period of time, it is a good idea to place suitable warning notices inside the

vehicle, and in the engine compartment. This will reduce the possibility of the engine being accidentally cranked on the starter motor, which is likely to cause damage with the locking pins in place.

1 On all models, timing holes are drilled in the camshaft sprocket, injection pump sprocket and flywheel. The holes are used to align the crankshaft, camshaft and injection pump, and to prevent the possibility of the valves contacting the pistons when refitting the timing belt. When the holes are aligned with their corresponding holes in the cylinder head and cylinder block (as appropriate), suitable diameter bolts/pins can be inserted to lock both the camshaft, injection pump and crankshaft in position, preventing them from rotating unnecessarily. Proceed as follows.

Note: *With the timing holes aligned, No 4 cylinder is at TDC on its compression stroke.*

2 Remove the upper timing belt covers as described in Section 4.

3 The crankshaft must now be turned until the three bolt holes in the camshaft and injection pump sprockets (one hole in the camshaft sprocket, two holes in the injection pump sprocket) are aligned with the corresponding holes in the engine front plate. The crankshaft can be turned by using a socket on the pulley bolt. To gain access to the pulley bolt, from underneath the front of the car, prise out the two retaining clips and remove the plastic cover from the wing valance, to gain access to the crankshaft pulley bolt. Where necessary, unclip the coolant hoses from the bracket, to improve access further. The crankshaft can then be turned using a suitable socket and extension bar fitted to the pulley bolt. Note that the crankshaft must always be turned in a clockwise direction (viewed from the right-hand side of the vehicle).

4 Insert an 8 mm diameter rod or drill through the hole in the left-hand flange of the cylinder block by the starter motor; if necessary, carefully turn the crankshaft either way until the rod enters the timing hole in the flywheel **(see illustrations)**.

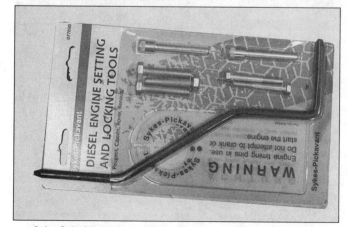

2.4a Suitable tools available for locking engine in position

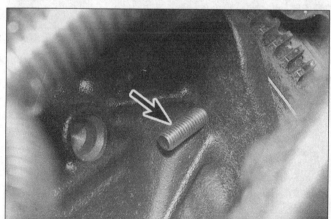

2.4b Rod (arrowed) inserted through cylinder block into timing hole in flywheel

2.5a Bolt (arrowed) inserted through timing hole in camshaft sprocket

2.5b Bolts (arrowed) inserted through timing holes in injection pump sprocket

5 Insert three 8 mm bolts through the holes in the camshaft and fuel injection pump sprockets, and screw them into the engine finger-tight **(see illustrations)**.
6 The crankshaft, camshaft and injection pump are now locked in position, preventing unnecessary rotation.

3.2 Notched tool (arrowed) positioned on ring gear teeth to lock flywheel

3 Crankshaft pulley - removal and refitting

Note: *Although not strictly necessary, it is recommended that the retaining bolt is renewed whenever it is disturbed, due to its tightening sequence (see Specifications).*

Removal

1 Remove the auxiliary drivebelt (Section 1).
2 To prevent crankshaft turning whilst the pulley retaining bolt is being slackened, select top gear and have an assistant apply the brakes firmly. If the engine is in the car and it proves impossible to hold on the brakes, remove the starter motor and use the locking tool shown to retain the flywheel **(see illustration)**. *Do not* attempt to lock the pulley by inserting a bolt/drill through the timing hole. If the locking pin is in position, temporarily remove it prior to slackening the

pulley bolt, then refit it once the bolt has been slackened.
3 Unscrew the retaining bolt and washer, then slide the pulley off the end of the crankshaft **(see illustrations)**. If the pulley locating roll pin or Woodruff key (as applicable) is a loose fit, remove it and store it with the pulley for safe-keeping. If the pulley is a tight fit, it can be drawn off the crankshaft using a suitable puller.

Refitting

4 Ensure that the Woodruff key is correctly located in its crankshaft groove, or that the roll pin is in position (as applicable). Refit the pulley to the end of the crankshaft, aligning its locating groove or hole with the Woodruff key or pin.
5 Thoroughly clean the threads of the pulley retaining bolt, then apply a coat of locking compound to the bolt threads. Peugeot recommend the use of Loctite (available from your Peugeot dealer); in the absence of this, any good-quality locking compound may be used.
6 Refit the crankshaft pulley retaining bolt

3.3a Removing the crankshaft pulley retaining bolt

3.3b Removing the crankshaft pulley from the end of the crankshaft

4.3 Removing the upper front timing belt cover - early models

4.5 Removing the upper rear timing belt cover - early models

4.9 Lower timing belt cover securing bolts (arrowed)

and washer. Tighten the bolt to the specified torque, preventing the crankshaft from turning using the method employed on removal.

7 Refit and tension the auxiliary drivebelt as described in Section 1.

4 Timing belt covers - removal and refitting

Removal

Upper front cover - early models

1 If procedures are to be carried out which involve removal of the timing belt, remove the right-hand engine mounting-to-body bracket as described in Section 7. This will greatly improve access.

2 Release the upper spring clip from the cover.

3 Release the lower securing lug using a screwdriver, then lift the cover upwards from the engine **(see illustration)**.

Upper rear cover - early models

4 Remove the upper front cover as described previously.

5 Release the two securing clips, manipulate the cover over the studs on the front of the engine, then withdraw the cover upwards **(see illustration)**. Clearance is limited, and if desired, access can be improved by removing the engine mounting bracket (see Section 7).

Upper front cover - later models

6 Slacken and remove the retaining screw and nut, and remove the cover from the engine.

Upper rear cover - later models

7 Remove the front cover as described in paragraph 6, then undo the retaining bolts and remove the rear cover from the engine.

Lower cover - early models

8 Remove the crankshaft pulley as described in Section 3.

9 Unscrew the two securing bolts and remove the cover **(see illustration)**.

Lower cover - later models

10 Remove the crankshaft pulley as described in Section 5.

11 Remove both upper covers as described previously.

12 Slacken and remove the retaining nuts and bolts, and remove the lower cover.

Refitting

13 Refitting is a reversal of the relevant removal procedure, ensuring that each cover section is correctly located, and that the cover retaining nuts and/or bolts are tightened to the specified torque.

5 Timing belt - removal and refitting

Removal

1 Align the engine assembly/valve timing holes as described in Section 2, and lock the camshaft sprocket, injection pump sprocket and flywheel in position. *Do not* attempt to rotate the engine whilst the pins are in position.

2 Remove the crankshaft pulley as described in Section 3.

3 Remove the right-hand engine mounting-to-body bracket as described in Section 7.

4 Loosen the timing belt tensioner pivot nut and adjustment bolt, then turn the tensioner bracket anti-clockwise to release the tension. Retighten the adjustment bolt to hold the tensioner in the released position. If available, use a 10 mm square drive extension in the hole provided to turn the tensioner bracket against the spring tension **(see illustration)**.

5 Mark the timing belt with an arrow to indicate its running direction, if it is to be re-

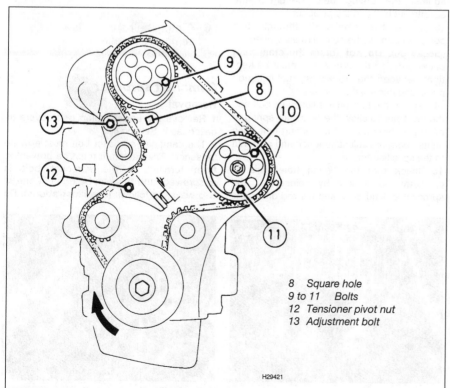

8   Square hole
9 to 11   Bolts
12   Tensioner pivot nut
13   Adjustment bolt

H29421

5.4 Removing the timing belt

11B

5.5a Mark the timing belt with an arrow to indicate its running direction

5.5b Removing the timing belt

used. Remove the belt from the sprockets **(see illustrations)**.

6 If signs of oil contamination are found, trace the source of the oil leak and rectify it. Wash down the engine timing belt area and all related components, to remove all traces of oil. Check that the tensioner and idler pulley rotates freely, without any sign of roughness.

Refitting

7 Commence refitting by ensuring that the 8 mm bolts are still fitted to the camshaft and fuel injection pump sprockets, and that the rod/drill is positioned in the timing hole in the flywheel.

8 Locate the timing belt on the crankshaft sprocket, making sure that, where applicable, the direction of rotation arrow is facing the correct way.

9 Engage the timing belt with the crankshaft sprocket, hold it in position, then feed the belt over the remaining sprockets in the following order:
a) *Idler roller.*
b) *Fuel injection pump.*
c) *Camshaft.*
d) *Tensioner roller.*
e) *Coolant pump.*

10 Be careful not to kink or twist the belt. To ensure correct engagement, locate only a half-

width on the injection pump sprocket before feeding the timing belt onto the camshaft sprocket, keeping the belt taut and fully engaged with the crankshaft sprocket. Locate the timing belt fully onto the sprockets **(see illustration)**.

11 Unscrew and remove the 8 mm locking bolts from the camshaft and fuel injection pump sprockets, and remove the rod/drill from the timing hole in the flywheel.

12 With the pivot nut loose, slacken the tensioner adjustment bolt while holding the bracket against the spring tension. Slowly release the bracket until the roller presses against the timing belt. Retighten the adjustment bolt and the pivot nut.

13 Rotate the crankshaft through two complete turns in the normal running direction (clockwise). **Do not** rotate the crankshaft backwards, as the timing belt must be kept tight between the crankshaft, fuel injection pump and camshaft sprockets.

14 Loosen the tensioner adjustment bolt and the pivot nut to allow the tensioner spring to push the roller against the timing belt, then tighten both the adjustment bolt and pivot nut to the specified torque.

15 Check that the timing holes are all correctly positioned by reinserting the sprocket locking bolts and the rod/drill in the

flywheel timing hole, as described in Section 2. If the timing holes are not correctly positioned, the timing belt has been incorrectly fitted (possibly one tooth out on one of the sprockets) - in this case, repeat the refitting procedure from the beginning.

16 Refit the upper timing belt covers as described in Section 4, but do not lower the vehicle to the ground until the engine mounting-to-body bracket has been refitted.

17 Refit the right-hand engine mounting-to-body bracket, with reference to Section 7.

18 Refit the crankshaft pulley as described in Section 3.

6 Timing belt sprockets - removal and refitting

Camshaft sprocket
Removal

1 Remove the upper timing belt covers as described in Section 4.

2 The camshaft sprocket bolt must now be loosened. The camshaft must be prevented from turning as the sprocket bolt is unscrewed, and this can be done in one of two ways, as follows **(see illustrations)**. Do

5.10 Locate the timing belt on the sprockets as described in text

6.2a Using a home-made tool to prevent the camshaft sprocket from turning

6.2b Holding the camshaft using a spanner on the lug between Nos 3 and 4 lobes

6.7 Withdrawing the camshaft sprocket

6.16 Withdrawing the crankshaft sprocket

not remove the camshaft sprocket bolt at this stage.

a) *Make up a tool similar to that shown, and use it to hold the sprocket stationary by means of the holes in the sprocket.*

b) *Remove the cylinder head cover as described in Section 4. Prevent the camshaft from turning by holding it with a suitable spanner on the lug between Nos 3 and 4 camshaft lobes.*

3 Align the engine assembly/valve timing holes as described in Section 2, and lock the camshaft sprocket, injection pump sprocket and flywheel in position. *Do not* attempt to rotate the engine whilst the pins are in position.

4 Loosen the timing belt tensioner pivot nut and adjustment bolt, then turn the tensioner bracket anti-clockwise to release the tension, and retighten the adjustment bolt to hold the tensioner in the released position. If available, use a 10 mm square drive extension in the hole provided, to turn the tensioner bracket against the spring tension. Slip the timing belt off the sprocket.

5 Slacken and remove the camshaft sprocket retaining bolt and washer.

6 Unscrew and remove the locking bolt from the camshaft sprocket.

7 With the retaining bolt removed, slide the sprocket off the end of the camshaft **(see illustration)**. If the locating peg is a loose fit in the rear of the sprocket, remove it for safe-keeping. Examine the camshaft oil seal for signs of oil leakage and, if necessary, renew it.

Refitting

8 Where applicable, refit the Woodruff key to the end of the camshaft, then refit the camshaft sprocket. Note that the sprocket will only fit one way round (with the protruding centre boss against the camshaft, as the end of the camshaft is tapered.

9 Refit the sprocket retaining bolt and washer. Tighten the bolt to the specified torque, preventing the camshaft from turning as during removal.

10 Where applicable, refit the cylinder head cover.

11 Align the holes in the camshaft sprocket and the engine front plate, and refit the 8 mm bolt to lock the camshaft in position.

12 Fit the timing belt around the fuel injection pump sprocket (where applicable) and the camshaft sprocket, and tension the timing belt as described in Section 5.

13 Refit the upper timing belt covers as described in Section 4.

Crankshaft sprocket

Removal

14 Remove the crankshaft pulley as described in Section 3.

15 Proceed as described in paragraphs 1, 3 and 4.

16 Disengage the timing belt from the crankshaft sprocket, and slide the sprocket off the end of the crankshaft **(see illustration)**.

17 Remove the Woodruff key from the crankshaft, and store it with the sprocket for safe-keeping **(see illustration)**.

18 Examine the crankshaft oil seal for signs of oil leakage and, if necessary, renew it.

Refitting

19 Refit the Woodruff key to the end of the crankshaft, then refit the crankshaft sprocket (with the flange nearest the cylinder block).

20 Fit the timing belt around the crankshaft sprocket, and tension the timing belt as described in Section 5.

21 Refit the crankshaft pulley as described in Section 3.

Fuel injection pump sprocket

Removal

22 Proceed as described in paragraphs 1, 3 and 4.

23 Make alignment marks on the fuel injection pump sprocket and the timing belt, to ensure that the sprocket and timing belt are correctly aligned on refitting.

24 Remove the 8 mm bolts securing the fuel injection pump sprocket in the TDC position.

25 On certain models, the sprocket may be fitted with a built-in puller, which consists of a plate bolted to the sprocket. The plate contains a captive nut (the sprocket securing nut), which is screwed onto the fuel injection pump shaft. On models not fitted with the built-in puller, a suitable puller can be made up using a short length of bar, and two M7 bolts screwed into the holes provided in the sprocket.

26 The fuel injection pump shaft must be prevented from turning as the sprocket nut is unscrewed, and this can be achieved using a tool similar to that shown **(see illustration)**.

11B

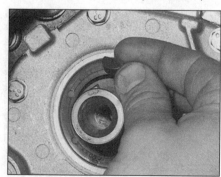

6.17 Removing the Woodruff key from the end of the crankshaft

6.26 Using a home-made tool to prevent the injection pump sprocket from turning

6.28 Home-made puller fitted to fuel injection pump sprocket

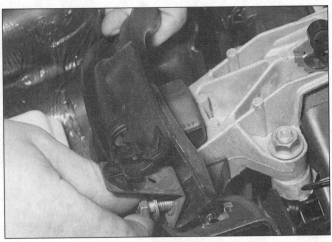

7.4 Remove the curved retaining plate . . .

Use the tool to hold the sprocket stationary by means of the holes in the sprocket.

27 On models with a built-in puller, unscrew the sprocket securing nut until the sprocket is freed from the taper on the pump shaft, then withdraw the sprocket. Recover the Woodruff key from the end of the pump shaft if it is loose. If desired, the puller assembly can be removed from the sprocket by removing the two securing screws and washers.

28 On models not fitted with a built-in puller, partially unscrew the sprocket securing nut, then fit the improvised puller, and tighten the two bolts (forcing the bar against the sprocket nut), until the sprocket is freed from the taper on the pump shaft **(see illustration)**. Withdraw the sprocket, and recover the Woodruff key from the end of the pump shaft if it is loose. Remove the puller from the sprocket.

Refitting

29 Where applicable, refit the Woodruff key to the pump shaft, ensuring that it is correctly located in its groove.

30 Where applicable, if the built-in puller assembly has been removed from the sprocket, refit it, and tighten the two securing screws to the specified torque, ensuring that the washers are in place.

31 Refit the sprocket, then tighten the securing nut to the specified torque, preventing the pump shaft from turning as during removal.

32 Make sure that the 8 mm bolts are fitted to the camshaft and fuel injection pump sprockets, and that the rod/drill is positioned in the flywheel timing hole.

33 Fit the timing belt around the fuel injection pump sprocket, ensuring that the marks made on the belt and sprocket before removal are aligned.

34 Tension the timing belt as described in Section 5.

35 Refit the upper timing belt covers as described in Section 4.

Coolant pump sprocket

36 The coolant pump sprocket is integral with the pump, and cannot be removed.

---

7 Timing belt tensioner - removal and refitting

1 The timing belt tensioner is operated by a spring and plunger housed in the right-hand engine mounting bracket, which is bolted to the end face of the engine. The engine mounting is attached to the mounting on the body via the engine mounting-to-body bracket.

Right-hand engine mounting-to-body bracket

Removal

2 Before removing the bracket, the engine must be supported, preferably using a suitable hoist and lifting tackle attached to the lifting bracket at the right-hand end of the engine. Alternatively, the engine can be supported using a trolley jack and interposed

7.5 . . . and lift the rubber buffer out from the engine mounting

block of wood beneath the sump, in which case, be prepared for the engine to tilt backwards when the bracket is removed.

3 Release the retaining clips, and position all the relevant hoses and cables clear of the engine mounting assembly and suspension top mounting.

4 Unscrew the two retaining bolts, and remove the curved retaining plate from the top of the mounting **(see illustration)**.

5 Lift out the rubber buffer to expose the engine mounting bracket-to-body securing nut **(see illustration)**.

6 Unscrew the three nuts securing the bracket to the engine mounting, and the single nut securing the bracket to the body, then lift off the bracket **(see illustration)**.

Refitting

7 Refitting is a reversal of removal. Tighten the nuts and bolts to the specified torque.

Timing belt tensioner and right-hand engine mounting bracket

Note: *A suitable tool will be required to retain the timing belt tensioner plunger during this operation.*

Removal

8 Remove the engine mounting-to-body

7.6 Removing the engine mounting-to-body bracket

7.16 Fabricated tool for holding tensioner plunger in engine mounting bracket

bracket as described previously in this Section, and remove the auxiliary drivebelt as described in Section 1.

9 If not already done, support the engine with a trolley jack and interposed block of wood beneath the sump.

10 Where applicable, disconnect the hoist and lifting tackle supporting the engine from the right-hand lifting bracket (this is necessary because the lifting bracket is attached to the engine mounting bracket, and must be removed).

11 Unscrew the two retaining bolts and remove the engine lifting bracket.

12 Align the engine assembly/valve timing holes as described in Section 2, and lock the camshaft sprocket, injection pump sprocket and flywheel in position. *Do not* rotate the engine whilst the pins are in position.

13 Loosen the timing belt tensioner pivot nut and adjustment bolt, then turn the tensioner bracket anti-clockwise until the adjustment

bolt is in the middle of the slot, and retighten the adjustment bolt. Use a 10 mm square drive extension in the hole provided, to turn the tensioner bracket against the spring tension.

14 Mark the timing belt with an arrow to indicate its running direction, if it is to be re-used. Remove the belt from the sprockets.

15 A tool must now be obtained in order to hold the tensioner plunger in the engine mounting bracket.

16 The Peugeot tool is designed to slide in the two lower bolt holes of the mounting bracket. It should be easy to fabricate a similar tool out of sheet metal, using 10 mm bolts and nuts instead of metal rods **(see illustration)**.

17 Unscrew the two lower engine mounting bracket bolts, then fit the special tool **(see illustrations)**. Grease the inner surface of the tool, to prevent any damage to the end of the tensioner plunger. Unscrew the pivot nut and adjustment bolt, and withdraw the tensioner assembly.

18 Remove the two remaining engine mounting bracket bolts, and withdraw the bracket.

19 Compress the tensioner plunger into the engine mounting bracket, remove the special tool, then withdraw the plunger and spring.

Refitting

20 Refitting is a reversal of removal, bearing in mind the following points:
a) *Tighten all fixings to the specified torque.*
b) *Refit and tension the timing belt as described in Section 5.*
c) *Refit and tighten the auxiliary drivebelt as described in Section 1.*

8 Timing belt idler roller - removal and refitting

Removal

1 Remove the auxiliary drivebelt as described in Section 1.

2 Align the engine assembly/valve timing holes as described in Section 2, and lock the camshaft sprocket, injection pump sprocket and flywheel in position. *Do not* rotate the engine whilst the pins are in position.

3 Loosen the timing belt tensioner pivot nut and adjustment bolt, then turn the tensioner bracket anti-clockwise to release the tension, and retighten the adjustment bolt to hold the tensioner in the released position. If available, use a 10 mm square drive extension in the hole provided, to turn the tensioner bracket against the spring tension.

4 Unscrew the two bolts and the stud securing the idler roller assembly to the cylinder block, noting that the upper bolt also secures the engine mounting bracket.

5 Slightly loosen the remaining four engine mounting bolts, noting that the uppermost bolt is on the inside face of the engine front plate, and also secures the engine lifting bracket. Slide out the idler roller assembly.

Refitting

6 Refitting is a reversal of removal, bearing in mind the following points:
a) *Tighten all fixings to the specified torque.*
b) *Tension the timing belt as described in Section 5.*
c) *Refit and tension the auxiliary drivebelt as described in Section 1.*

11B

7.17a View of timing belt end of engine

1 *Engine mounting bracket retaining bolts*
2 *Timing belt tensioner plunger*

7.17b Tool in place to hold tensioner plunger in engine mounting bracket - timing belt removed for clarity

Notes

Chapter 12A
Peugeot 309 petrol 1986 to 1993

Contents

Specifications

Timing belt renewal interval . . . . Every 36 000 miles (60 000 km)

Engine codes
1124 cc TU1
1360 cc TU3
1580 cc XU5
1124 cc XU9

Ignition timing (vacuum hose disconnected and plugged)
TU1/K (H1A) . . . . 8° BTDC @ 850 rpm
TU1M/Z (HDZ), TU3M/Z and TU3FM/L (KDY) . . . . 8 ± 1° BTDC @ idle speed
TU3.2/K (K2D) . . . . 8° BTDC @ idle speed
XU52C (B2A), XU52C/K (B2B) . . . . 10° BTDC @ idle speed
XU5M2/Z, XU5M3/Z and XU5M3/L (BDY) . . . . -*
XU5JA/K (B6E) . . . . 10° BTDC @ idle speed
XU9JA/K (D6B) . . . . 5° BTDC @ 700 rpm
XU9JA/Z and XU9JA/L (DKZ) . . . . 10 ± 2° BTDC @ idle speed*
*Nominal value given, where available, for reference only - ignition timing is under control of engine management system ECU, and may vary constantly at idle speed - adjustment is not possible.

Torque wrench settings	Nm	lbf ft
Roadwheel bolts	85	63
XU engine		
Camshaft sprocket bolt:		
M10	40	30
M12	80	59
Crankshaft pulley bolt	110	81
Timing belt eccentric roller-type tensioner bolt	20	15
Timing belt tensioner	15	11
Timing cover bolts	15	11
TU engine		
Crankshaft pulley	100	74
Crankshaft sprocket	80	59
Timing belt tensioner	20	15
Timing cover	6	4

12A

1.4 Alternator drivebelt tension adjuster

1 Auxiliary drivebelt - removal, refitting and adjustment

Removal

1 Disconnect the battery negative lead.
2 Loosen the pivot and adjustment bolts, swivel the alternator towards the engine, and remove the drivebelt.

Refitting and adjustment

3 Refitting is a reversal of removal.
4 To adjust the drivebelt tension, first check that it is correctly located in both pulleys then, with the mounting and adjustment strap bolts loosened, pivot the alternator outwards to tighten the drivebelt. You can use a lever to help achieve this but it must be a wooden one and it must be used only at the pulley end of the alternator. Levering on the case or at the end opposite to the drive pulley can easily cause expensive damage. On some models, adjustment can be made by turning the special adjuster screw as required (see illustration).
5 Tighten the belt to take up any play in the belt at the mid point on the longest run between the pulleys and to give a deflection of 5.0 mm. Whilst a taut tension is required the belt must not be overtightened. Tighten the alternator mounting and adjuster strap bolts to set the tension.

2 Timing belt (XU engine) - removal and refitting

Note: *If the timing belt is to be renewed, ensure that the correct belt type is obtained - the timing belt used with the earlier spring-loaded tensioner is not interchangeable with the later type.*
Note: *Do not attempt to rotate the engine whilst the crankshaft/camshaft are locked in position. If the engine is to be left in this state for a long period of time, it is a good idea to*

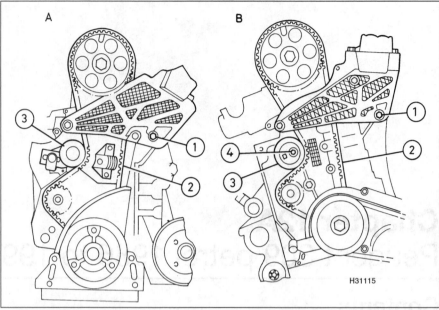

2.6 Spring loaded timing belt tensioner (A) and eccentric roller type tensioner (B)

1 Right-hand engine mounting   2 Timing belt   3 Tensioner roller   4 Tensioner roller nut

place warning notices inside the vehicle, and in the engine compartment. This will reduce the possibility of the engine being accidentally cranked on the starter motor, which is likely to cause damage with the locking pins in place.

Removal

1 Disconnect the battery negative lead.
2 Remove the auxiliary drivebelt as described in Section 1.
3 Remove the inner shield from the right-hand wheelarch and wedge the radiator bottom hose under the sump.
4 Remove the shield from the camshaft sprocket.
5 Remove the plastic covers from the front of the timing belt. Note the location of the various bolts.
6 Observe the timing belt tensioner assembly and ascertain whether it is of the spring-loaded type or the later eccentric roller type

(see illustration). Proceed as follows under the appropriate sub-heading according to type fitted.

Models with spring-loaded tensioner

7 Turn the crankshaft using a spanner on the pulley bolt until the dowel hole in the pulley is at about 12 o'clock and the hole in the camshaft sprocket is at about 7 o'clock. In this position a 10 mm dowel should pass through each hole and into the timing recess behind. Verify this and then remove the dowels (see illustration).
8 Remove the clutch bottom shield. Have an assistant jam the starter ring gear while the crankshaft pulley bolt is undone. This bolt is very tight. Do not jam the pulley by means of the timing dowel: damage will result. Remove the bolt and washer.
9 Check that the 10 mm dowels will still enter the timing holes: adjust the crankshaft

2.7 Timing dowels in position – shown with engine removed for clarity

2.10a Drivebelt tensioner front nuts

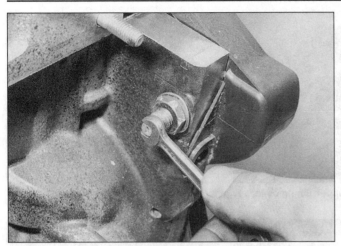

2.10b Turning the tension cam spindle

2.16 Line on belt aligns with mark on sprocket

position if necessary by means of the starter ring gear. Remove the crankshaft pulley, retrieving the Woodruff key if it is loose.

10 Slacken the two nuts on the front of the timing belt tensioner and the single nut at the rear. Use a spanner on the square end of the tensioner cam spindle to turn the cam to the horizontal position and so compress the tensioner spring (see illustrations). Tighten the cam locknut.

11 Remove the timing belt, taking care not to kink it or contaminate it with oil if it is to be re-used. Draw an arrow on the belt using chalk to mark the running direction unless a new belt is to be fitted.

12 If signs of oil contamination are found, trace the source of the oil leak and rectify it. Wash down the engine timing belt area and all related components, to remove all traces of oil.

Models with eccentric roller tensioner

13 Proceed as described in paragraphs 7 to 9, noting that the crankshaft pulley timing dowel must be of 10 mm diameter, stepped down to 8 mm at one end to engage with the smaller hole in the timing recess.

14 Slacken the tensioner roller bolt to relieve the belt tension, then withdraw the belt, noting the direction of fitting and the markings. Take care not to kink it or contaminate it with oil if it is to be re-used. Draw an arrow on the belt using chalk to mark the running direction unless a new belt is to be fitted.

15 If signs of oil contamination are found, trace the source of the oil leak and rectify it. Wash down the engine timing belt area and all related components, to remove all traces of oil.

Refitting

Models with spring-loaded tensioner

16 Commence refitting by positioning the belt on the crankshaft sprocket, then refitting the pulley and verifying the correct position of the crankshaft by means of the dowel.

Observe the arrows on the belt showing the direction of rotation, and the timing lines which align with marks on the crankshaft and camshaft sprockets (see illustration).

17 Fit the belt to the camshaft sprocket, round the tensioner and to the coolant pump sprocket.

18 Release the tensioner cam locknut and turn the cam downwards to release the spring. Tighten the locknut and the tensioner front nuts.

19 Remove the timing dowels and turn the crankshaft through two full turns in the normal direction of rotation. Turn the crankshaft further to bring No 1 piston to TDC on the firing stroke.

20 Slacken the tensioner front nuts and the cam locknut, then retighten them.

21 Turn the crankshaft further and make sure that the timing dowels can still be inserted. If not, remove the drivebelt and start again.

22 If a new belt has been fitted, it must be run in and retensioned, as follows.

23 Tighten the crankshaft pulley bolt to the specified torque, then refit and tension the auxiliary drivebelt (see Section 1). Temporarily refit the camshaft sprocket cover.

24 Run the engine up to operating temperature, indicated by the cooling fan operating, then stop it and allow it to cool for at least two hours.

25 Rotate the crankshaft to the TDC position, No 1 cylinder firing, then slacken and retighten the tensioner nuts once more.

26 Remove the auxiliary drivebelt and the crankshaft pulley. Refit and secure the plastic covers, then refit the pulley and tighten its bolts to the specified torque. Refit and tension the auxiliary drivebelt.

27 Check the ignition timing and adjust if necessary (Section 5).

Models with eccentric roller tensioner

Note: *Peugeot specify the use of special tool (SEEM C. TRONIC type 105 or 105.5 belt tension measuring equipment) to correctly set the belt tension.*

28 Commence refitting by slipping the belt over the camshaft sprocket, followed by the crankshaft sprocket, the coolant pump sprocket, and finally over the tensioner roller. Observe the arrows on the belt indicating the direction of rotation, and the timing lines which align with corresponding marks on the crankshaft and camshaft sprockets.

29 With the camshaft timing dowel fitted, rotate the tensioner roller anti-clockwise by hand as far as possible to take up any slack in the belt, then tighten the tensioner roller bolt sufficiently to hold the roller in position. The special belt tension measuring equipment should be fitted to the tensioned run of the belt, and the tensioner roller should be moved to give a reading of 30 ± 2 units. Tighten the roller bolt to the specified torque, taking care not to move the roller as the bolt is tightened.

30 Check that the crankshaft and camshaft are still positioned correctly by temporarily refitting the crankshaft pulley and re-inserting the timing dowel.

31 Remove the timing dowels, temporarily refit the crankshaft pulley, and turn the crankshaft through two full turns in the normal direction of rotation. Check that both timing dowels can still be inserted. If not, remove the drivebelt and start again. Never turn the crankshaft backwards during this procedure.

32 If all is well, remove the dowels, and turn the crankshaft through two further turns in the normal direction of rotation.

33 Refit the camshaft timing dowel, and fit the special belt tension measuring to the tensioned run of the belt. The reading should now be between 42 and 46 units.

34 If the tension is not as specified, repeat the tensioning operation.

35 Refit the belt covers and the crankshaft pulley. Apply thread locking compound to the crankshaft pulley bolt threads, and tighten the bolt to the specified torque.

36 On completion, refit all disturbed components, and tension the auxiliary drivebelt, as described in Section 1.

12A

3.1a Unscrew the bolts . . .

3.1b . . . remove the upper timing cover . . .

3.1c . . . intermediate cover . . .

3.1d . . . and lower cover

3.2 Camshaft sprocket set to TDC

3.3 Bolt (arrowed) inserted through cylinder block rear flange into the flywheel TDC hole

3 Timing belt (TU engine) - removal and refitting

Removal

1 Unbolt the upper timing cover, followed by the intermediate cover and lower cover **(see illustrations)**.

2 Turn the engine clockwise, using a socket on the crankshaft pulley bolt, until the small hole in the camshaft sprocket is aligned with the corresponding hole in the cylinder head. Insert the shank of a close fitting twist drill (eg a 10 mm drill) into the holes **(see illustration)**.

3 Align the TDC holes in the flywheel and

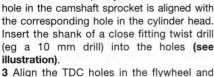

cylinder block rear flange, and insert a further twist drill or long bolt **(see illustration)**.

4 Loosen the timing belt tensioner roller nut **(see illustration)**, turn the tensioner clockwise using a screwdriver or square drive in the special hole, then retighten the nut.

5 Mark the normal direction of rotation on the timing belt, then remove it from the camshaft, water pump, and crankshaft sprockets.

Refitting

6 Engage the timing belt with the crankshaft

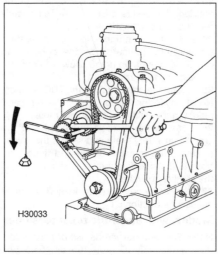

H30033

3.8 Using a suitable tool to tension the timing belt

sprocket then, keeping it taut, feed it onto the camshaft sprocket, around the tensioner pulley, and onto the water pump socket.

7 Loosen the nut, and turn the tensioner roller anti-clockwise by hand. Tighten the nut.

8 Peugeot dealers use a special tool to tension the timing belt. A similar tool may be fabricated using an 8.0 cm long arm and a 1.5 kg weight **(see illustration)**. The torque applied to the roller will approximate 12 kgf cm (10.5 lbf in). Pre-tension the timing belt with the tool and tighten the nut, then remove the timing pins and rotate the crankshaft through two complete turns. Loosen the nut and allow the roller to re-position itself. Tighten the nut.

9 Refit the lower, intermediate, and upper timing covers, and tighten the bolts **(see illustration)**.

3.9 Timing covers refitted

3.4 Loosening the timing belt tensioner roller nut

4 Starter motor -
removal and refitting

Removal

1 Disconnect the battery earth lead.

2 Raise and support the car at the front end, then unclip and remove the engine undershield. This allows the necessary access to the starter motor from underneath the vehicle.

3 Unscrew and remove the oil filter. Allow for oil spillage as it is withdrawn.

4 Detach the crankcase ventilation pipes adjacent to the starter motor.

5 On SRi models, undo the two retaining bolts and remove the inlet manifold support arm.

6 Disconnect the wiring to the starter motor solenoid.

7 Undo the starter motor support bracket bolt from the crankcase (at the rear end).

8 Undo the three retaining bolts to the clutch housing. One of these bolts will require the clutch operating lever pivot arm to be unbolted and moved out of the way so that the bolt can be withdrawn. Remove the starter motor.

Refitting

9 Refitting is a reversal of the removal

5.2 Flywheel timing mark and timing marks on plate

procedure. Ensure that the wiring connections are correctly and securely made. Refit the engine oil filter.

5 Ignition timing -
checking and adjustment

Note: *Where necessary, first remove the air cleaner intake duct to allow access to the timing aperture in the top face of the clutch housing/gearbox casing.*

Static ignition timing

1 To set the ignition timing statically so that the engine can be started, first remove No 1 spark plug (nearest clutch) and turn the engine in the normal rotational direction until pressure is felt indicating that the piston is commencing the compression stroke. The pressure can be felt using a suitable wooden rod or piece of cork placed over the spark plug hole.

2 While looking into the timing aperture in the clutch housing/gearbox casing, continue turning the crankshaft until the single mark on the flywheel is opposite the BTDC mark on the timing plate **(see illustration).**

3 Check that the distributor rotor arm is facing the No 1 HT lead segment position in the distributor cap. To do this, remove the cap and mark the outside in line with the segment, then put it back on the distributor noting which way the rotor arm is facing.

4 If necessary, loosen the mounting nuts and turn the distributor body to bring the segment and rotor arm in line, then tighten the nuts. Refit No 1 spark plug. The ignition timing should now be checked dynamically as described below. For this you will need a stroboscopic timing light. Alternatively the ignition timing may be checked and adjusted using the engine diagnosis socket.

Dynamic ignition timing

5 Because the distributor only gives a timing signal when the shaft is rotating, a stroboscopic timing light must be used with

the engine running at idling speed. The timing light must be suitable for use with electronic ignition systems.

6 First disconnect the vacuum advance pipe from the distributor and connect the timing light between No 1 spark plug (nearest the flywheel end of the engine) and its associated HT lead, or as instructed by the maker of the timing light.

7 Remove the plug from the clutch housing aperture (where fitted). Clean the appropriate flywheel and housing timing marks with a piece of rag and mark them with a spot of white paint. For the correct degree mark, refer to the Specifications at the beginning of this Chapter.

8 Start the engine and adjust the engine idling speed. If a tachometer is not fitted to the car, it will be necessary to obtain a unit that is suitable for use on electronic ignition systems. Some timing lights have a tachometer incorporated.

9 Aim the timing light at the clutch housing aperture and observe the timing marks. They will appear stationary, and if the timing is correct, the mark on the flywheel will be adjacent to the appropriate degree mark on the scale. If this is not the case, slacken the clamp bolt at the base of the distributor and then turn the distributor slowly in the desired direction (clockwise to retard the timing, anti-clockwise to advance it) until the mark on the flywheel is in line with the appropriate mark on the scale. Tighten the clamp bolt and recheck that the marks are still in alignment.

10 To check the centrifugal advance, increase the engine speed and note whether the white mark on the flywheel moves away from the mark on the scale. If it does, the centrifugal advance is functioning.

11 To check the vacuum advance, reconnect the vacuum pipe to the distributor. If the unit is functioning, this should also cause the timing marks to move away from each other slightly.

12 When all checks are completed, readjust the engine idling speed if necessary and then switch off and disconnect the timing light and tachometer (where applicable). Refit the air cleaner intake duct (where applicable).

12A

Notes

Chapter 12B
Peugeot 309 diesel 1986 to 1993

Contents

Specifications

Timing belt renewal interval . . . . Every 36 000 miles (60 000 km)

Note: *Although the normal interval for timing belt renewal is 72 000 miles (120 000 km), it is strongly recommended that the interval is halved on vehicles which are subjected to intensive use, ie, mainly short journeys or a lot of stop-start driving. The actual belt renewal interval is therefore very much up to the individual owner. That being said, it is highly recommended to err on the side of safety, and renew the belt at this earlier interval, bearing in mind the drastic consequences resulting from belt failure.*

Power steering drivebelt tension	**Nm**	**lbf ft**
New belt	57	42
Used belt	30	22

Vacuum pump drivebelt tension	**Nm**	**lbf ft**
Adjusting pivot (later models)	5	4

Torque wrench settings	**Nm**	**lbf ft**
Alternator pivot bolt	39	29
Alternator top mounting bolt and locknut	20	15
Camshaft sprocket	35	26
Crankshaft pulley bolt:		
Stage 1	40	30
Stage 2	Angle tighten by a further 60°	
Engine right-hand mounting bracket:		
Lower bracket	18	13
Upper bracket to engine	35	26
Upper bracket to mounting rubber	28	21
Pump pulley to camshaft	35	26
Timing belt intermediate roller	18	13
Timing belt tensioner	18	13
Timing cover, lower	12	9

12B

1.3 Checking the tension of the alternator drivebelt

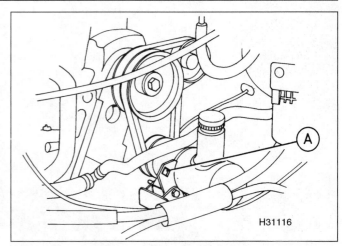

H31116

1.8 Square hole (A) for adjusting the belt tension on the later type pump

1 Auxiliary drivebelt - adjustment

Alternator

1 To adjust the tension, first check that the belt is correctly fitted over the pulleys.

2 With the alternator mountings loose, carefully lever the alternator outwards to tighten the drivebelt. Using a wooden lever will minimise the risk of damage to the alternator casing.

3 The belt should be able to move by approximately 6.0 mm, with moderate thumb pressure midway between the pulleys (see illustration).

4 Tighten the mounting bolts to the correct torque.

Power steering pump

5 Adjust the tension by loosening the mounting and adjusting bolts, reposition the pump and retighten the bolts.

6 The deflection should be 5.0 mm.

7 On early models three slotted holes are provided in the bracket and on later models the pump pivots on a single bolt.

1.9 Checking the vacuum pump drivebelt tension

8 A torque wrench may be used on the later type to adjust the belt tension using the 12.7 mm (1/2 in) square hole provided (see illustration). With both bolts loose, apply the torque given in the Specifications, then tighten the adjustment bolt, followed by the pivot bolt.

Vacuum pump (early models)

Note: *Later models have a revised mounting arrangement.*

9 On models fitted with a belt-driven brake vacuum pump, it is important to ensure that the drivebelt is correctly tensioned (see illustration).

10 Loosen the mounting bolts and adjust the pump to the correct tension.

11 The deflection should be 5.0 mm.

12 When the drivebelt is at the correct tension, tighten the mounting bolts to the correct torque.

Vacuum pump drivebelt (later models)

13 The following paragraphs describe the adjustment procedure for later models, which have the revised mounting arrangement shown (see illustration).

14 Loosen the pivot and adjustment bolts on the vacuum pump.

15 A welded nut is fitted to the pivot bracket. Locate a socket and torque wrench on this nut, and apply the correct torque (see Specifications), so that the drivebelt is tensioned.

16 Hold the pivot bracket in this position and tighten the pivot and adjustment bolts. Remove the torque wrench.

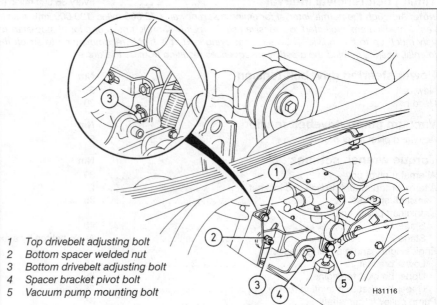

1 Top drivebelt adjusting bolt
2 Bottom spacer welded nut
3 Bottom drivebelt adjusting bolt
4 Spacer bracket pivot bolt
5 Vacuum pump mounting bolt

H31116

1.13 Brake vacuum pump drivebelt adjustment on later models

2.6a Bleed screws on the thermostat housing cover (arrowed)

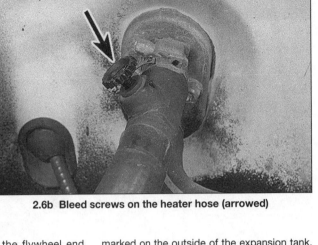

2.6b Bleed screws on the heater hose (arrowed)

2 Coolant – draining and filling

Draining

1 Allow the engine to cool for at least 10 minutes after switching off.
2 Depress the filler cap and slowly turn it anti-clockwise until it can be removed. If the engine is hot cover the cap with a thick cloth before removing it as a precaution against scalding.
3 Position a container beneath the left-hand side of the radiator then unscrew the drain plug and allow the coolant to drain. If there is no drain plug fitted, disconnect the drain pipe on the left-hand side of the radiator or disconnect the bottom hose from the right-hand side.
4 When the radiator is completely drained refit the drain plug, pipe or hose then drain the block by unscrewing the drain plug located on

the rear of the engine at the flywheel end. Refit the drain plug on completion.

Filling

5 Make sure that the drain plugs are secure and that all hoses are in good condition and their clips tight.
6 Loosen or remove the bleed screws located on the thermostat housing cover, and where applicable, on the heater hose at the bulkhead **(see illustrations)**.
7 Fill slowly with coolant through the filler neck and at the same time keep an eye on the bleed screw holes. When coolant free of air bubbles emerges refit and tighten the bleed screws.
8 Top up the radiator or expansion tank until it is full to the filler cap seating. There still remains air in the system which must be purged as follows.
9 Start the engine and run at a fast idle speed for several minutes. Stop the engine.
10 Top up the expansion tank to the maximum level. On some models this is

marked on the outside of the expansion tank, but on others, a level plate or tube is visible through the filler neck. Both minimum and maximum levels are indicated **(see illustration)**.
11 Fit the filler cap.
12 Start the engine and run to normal operating temperature indicated by the electric cooling fan(s) cutting in then out after a few minutes.
13 Stop the engine and allow to cool for at least 1 hour.
14 Check the coolant level and top-up as necessary **(see illustration)**.

3 Timing belt - removal, refitting and tensioning

Removal

1 Apply the handbrake, then jack up the front right-hand corner of the vehicle until the wheel

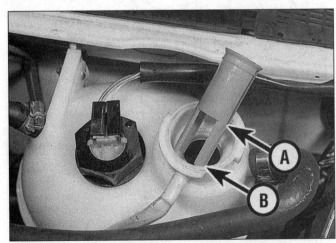

2.10 Showing the level tube removed from the expansion tank

A Maximum level   B Minimum level

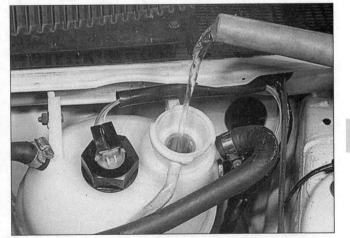

2.14 Filling the cooling system via the expansion tank

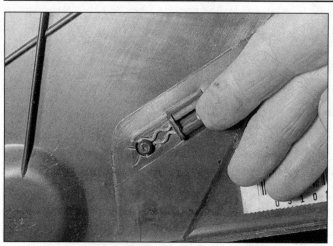

3.10a Timing cover front clip (early models) . . .

3.10b . . . and spring clips

is just clear of the ground. Support the vehicle on an axle stand and engage 4th or 5th gear. This will enable the engine to be turned easily by turning the right-hand wheel.

2 Remove the engine splash guard from under the right-hand front wheel arch.

3 For extra working space, drain the cooling system (detailed in Section 2) and disconnect the bottom hose from the water pump inlet. Remove the intermediate metal tube after removing the cross head screws.

4 Disconnect the battery negative lead.

5 Loosen the alternator pivot and adjustment bolts then unscrew the tension bolt until it

is possible to slip the drivebelt from the pulleys.

6 With 4th or 5th gear selected on manual transmission models have an assistant depress the footbrake pedal, then unscrew the crankshaft pulley bolt. Alternatively the crankshaft can be locked, by unbolting the transmission cover plate and using a large screwdriver lock the starter ring gear. Note that the crankshaft pulley bolt is extremely tight.

7 Slide the pulley from the front of the crankshaft. Unbolt the bottom timing cover.

8 Support the weight of the engine using a hoist or trolley jack.

9 Unscrew the nuts and remove the right-hand engine mounting bracket.

10 Pull up the front clip (early models), release the spring clips, and withdraw the two timing cover sections. Note that the spring clip is not fitted to later models, which have a modified cover and fastenings **(see illustrations)**.

11 Turn the engine by means of the front right-hand wheel or crankshaft pulley bolt until the three bolt holes in the camshaft and injection pump sprockets are aligned with the corresponding holes in the engine front plate.

12 Insert an 8.0 mm diameter metal dowel

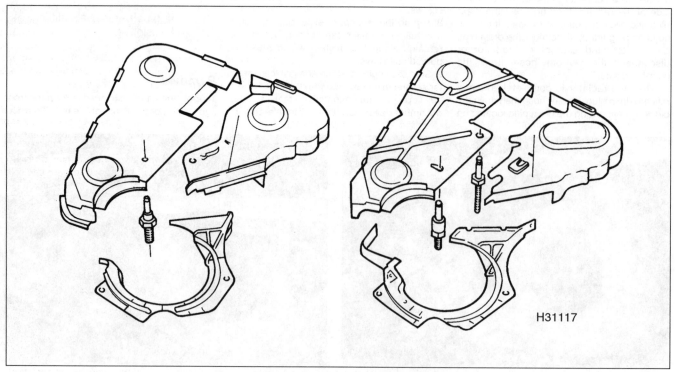

H31117

3.10c Earlier and later type of timing belt covers

3.12 Using a twist drill to enter the TDC hole in the flywheel

rod or drill through the special hole in the left-hand rear flange of the cylinder block by the starter motor. Then carefully turn the engine either way until the rod enters the TDC hole in the flywheel **(see illustration)**.

13 Insert three M8 bolts through the holes in the camshaft and injection pump sprockets and screw them into the engine front plate finger-tight **(see illustration)**.

14 Loosen the timing belt tensioner pivot nut and adjustment bolt, then turn the bracket anti-clockwise to release the tension and retighten the adjustment bolt to hold the tensioner in the released position. If available use a 3/8 inch square drive extension in the hole provided to turn the bracket against the spring tension.

15 Mark the timing belt with an arrow to indicate its normal direction of turning then remove it from the camshaft, injection pump, water pump and crankshaft sprockets.

Refitting

16 If signs of oil contamination are found, trace the source of the oil leak, and rectify it. Wash down the engine timing belt area and all related components, to remove all traces of oil.

17 Begin refitting by locating the timing belt on the crankshaft sprocket, making sure that, where applicable, the rotation arrow is facing the correct way.

18 Hold the timing belt engaged with the

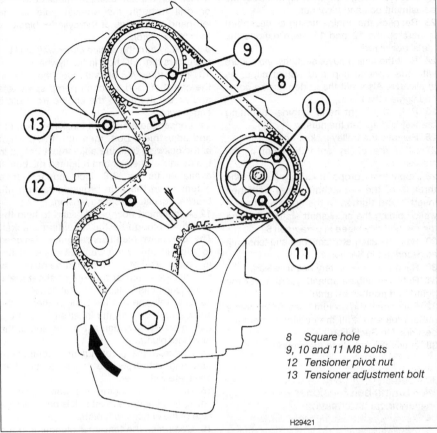

8   Square hole
9, 10 and 11 M8 bolts
12   Tensioner pivot nut
13   Tensioner adjustment bolt

H29421

3.13 Holding camshaft and injection pump sprockets in position using M8 bolts

crankshaft roller sprocket then feed it over the roller and onto the injection pump, camshaft, and water pump sprockets and over the tensioner. To ensure correct engagement, locate only a half width on the injection pump sprocket before feeding the timing belt onto the camshaft sprocket keeping the belt taut and fully engaged with the crankshaft sprocket. Locate the timing belt fully onto the sprockets **(see illustrations)**.

Tensioning

19 With the pivot nut loose, slacken the tensioner adjustment bolt while holding the

bracket against the spring tension. Slowly release the bracket until the roller presses against the timing belt. Retighten the adjustment bolt.

20 Remove the bolts from the camshaft and injection pump sprockets. Remove the metal dowel rod from the cylinder block.

21 Rotate the engine two complete turns in its normal direction. Do not rotate the engine backwards as the timing belt must be kept tight between the crankshaft, injection pump and camshaft sprockets.

22 Loosen the tensioner adjustment bolt to allow the tensioner spring to push the roller

3.18a Fitting the timing belt over the injection pump sprocket . . .

3.18b . . . the camshaft sprocket . . .

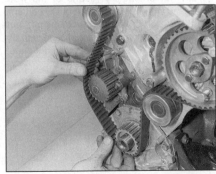

3.18c . . . and the water pump sprocket

12B

against the timing belt, then tighten both the adjustment bolt and pivot nut.

23 Recheck the engine timing as described in paragraphs 12 and 13, then remove the metal dowel rod.

24 Refit the timing cover sections and secure with the special clip and spring clips. as applicable. Also refit the bottom timing cover and tighten the bolts.

25 Refit the right-hand engine mounting bracket and tighten the nuts.

26 Remove the trolley jack or hoist.

27 Slide the pulley onto the front of the crankshaft.

28 Apply three drops of locking fluid on the threads of the crankshaft pulley bolt then insert it and tighten to the specified torque while holding the crankshaft stationary using the method described in paragraph 6.

29 Refit the alternator drivebelt and tension it as described in Section 1.

30 Reconnect the battery negative lead.

31 Refit the engine splash-guard under the right-hand front wheel arch.

32 Reconnect the bottom hose, intermediate metal tube and refill the cooling system (as described in Section 2).

33 Lower the vehicle to the ground.

4 Timing belt tensioner - removal and refitting

Removal

1 Apply the handbrake, then jack up the front right-hand corner of the vehicle until the wheel is just clear of the ground.

2 Support the vehicle on an axle stand and engage 4th or 5th gear so that the engine may be rotated by turning the right-hand wheel.

3 Support the weight of the engine using a hoist or trolley jack.

4 Unscrew the nuts and remove the right-hand engine mounting bracket.

5 Disconnect the battery negative lead.

6 Pull up the special clip (early models), release the spring clips and withdraw the two timing cover sections.

7 Turn the engine by means of the front right-hand wheel or crankshaft pulley bolt until the three bolt holes in the camshaft and injection pump sprockets are aligned with the corresponding holes in the engine front plate.

8 Insert an 8.0 mm diameter metal dowel rod or drill through the special hole in the left-hand rear flange of the cylinder block by the starter motor.

9 Carefully turn the engine either way until the rod enters the TDC hole in the flywheel.

10 Insert three M8 bolts through the holes in the camshaft and injection pump sprockets and screw them into the engine front plate finger-tight.

11 Loosen the timing belt tensioner pivot nut and adjustment bolt, then turn the bracket anti-clockwise until the adjustment bolt is in the middle of the slot and retighten the bolt. If available use a 3/8 inch square drive extension in the hole provided to turn the bracket against the spring tension.

12 A tool must now be obtained to hold the tensioner plunger in the mounting bracket. The tool shown **(see illustration)**, is designed to slide in the two lower bolt holes of the mounting bracket and it should be quite easy to fabricate a similar tool out of sheet metal using long bolts instead of metal dowel rods.

13 Unscrew the two lower bolts then fit the special tool. Grease the inner surface of the tool to prevent any damage to the end of the tensioner plunger.

14 Unscrew the pivot nut and adjustment bolt and withdraw the tensioner bracket, complete with roller.

15 Unbolt the engine mounting bracket noting that the uppermost bolt is on the inside face of the engine front plate.

16 Compress the tensioner plunger into the mounting bracket, remove the special tool then withdraw the plunger and spring.

Refitting

17 Refitting is a reversal of removal, but refer

4.12 Home-made tool for holding the tensioner plunger

to Section 3, paragraphs 19 to 23 for details of the timing belt adjustment procedure.

5 Timing belt intermediate roller - removal and refitting

Removal

1 Follow the procedure given in paragraphs 1 to 11 of Section 4.

2 Remove the engine splash guard from under the right-hand front wheel arch. For extra working space, drain the cooling system (Section 2), and disconnect the bottom hose from the water pump inlet. Remove the intermediate metal tube after removing the cross-headed screws.

3 Disconnect the battery negative lead.

4 Loosen the alternator pivot and adjustment bolts then unscrew the tension bolt until it is possible to slip the drivebelt from the pulleys.

5 With 4th or 5th gear selected have an assistant depress the footbrake pedal, then unscrew the crankshaft pulley bolt. Alternatively, the crankshaft can be locked by unbolting the transmission cover plate and using a wide-bladed screwdriver to lock the starter ring gear.

6 Slide the pulley from the front of the crankshaft.

7 Unbolt the lower timing cover.

8 Remove the spacer from the stud (two studs on later models), for the upper timing cover sections. Note the position of the stud(s), then unscrew and remove it.

9 Unscrew the remaining bolts securing the intermediate roller bracket to the cylinder block noting that the upper bolt also secures the engine mounting bracket.

10 Slightly loosen the remaining engine mounting bracket bolts then slide out the intermediate roller and bracket.

Refitting

11 Refitting is a reversal of removal, but note the following additional points:
a) *Tighten all bolts to the specified torque*
b) *Apply three drops of locking fluid to the threads of the crankshaft pulley bolt before inserting it*
c) *Tension the alternator drivebelt as described in Section 1*
d) *Adjust the timing belt as described in Section 3, paragraphs 19 to 23*

Chapter 13A
Peugeot 405 petrol 1988 to 1996

Contents

Specifications

Timing belt renewal interval . . . . Every 36 000 miles (60 000 km)

Note: *Although the normal interval for timing belt renewal is 72 000 miles (120 000 km), it is strongly recommended that the interval is halved on vehicles which are subjected to intensive use, ie, mainly short journeys or a lot of stop-start driving. The actual belt renewal interval is therefore very much up to the individual owner. That being said, it is highly recommended to err on the side of safety, and renew the belt at this earlier interval, bearing in mind the drastic consequences resulting from belt failure.*

Engine codes
1360 cc	TU3
1580 cc	XU5
1761 cc	XU7
1905 cc	XU9
1998 cc	XU10

Torque wrench settings
	Nm	lbf ft
Roadwheel bolts	85	63
TU engine		
Camshaft sprocket retaining bolt	80	59
Crankshaft pulley retaining bolts	8	6
Crankshaft sprocket retaining bolt	110	81
Cylinder head cover nuts	16	12
Timing belt cover bolts	8	6
Timing belt tensioner pulley nut	23	17
XU5, XU7 and XU9 engines		
Camshaft sprocket retaining bolt	35	26
Crankshaft pulley retaining bolt	120	89
Engine/transmission right-hand mounting:		
Bracket-to-engine bolts	45	33
Mounting bracket retaining nuts	45	33
Timing belt cover bolts	8	6
Timing belt tensioner	20	15
XU10 engine		
Camshaft sprocket retaining bolt	35	26
Crankshaft pulley retaining bolt	110	81
Timing belt cover bolts	8	6
Timing belt tensioner	20	15

1.3 Loosening the alternator adjustment bolts (early models)

1.6 Alternator drivebelt deflection (A)

1 Auxiliary drivebelt - removal, refitting and adjustment

1 Apply the handbrake, then jack up the front of the car and support it on axle stands. Remove the right-hand front roadwheel.
2 Remove the engine undercover and wheelarch cover as applicable.

Early models

Removal

3 Loosen the alternator pivot and link bolts, then unscrew the adjuster bolt to release the drivebelt tension (see illustration).
4 Remove the drivebelt from the alternator, crankshaft and, where necessary, the power steering pulleys.

Refitting and adjustment

5 Locate the drivebelt on the pulleys making sure it is correctly engaged with the grooves.

6 The belt tension must be adjusted so that with moderate thumb pressure applied midway along the belt's longest run, it can be deflected by approximately 6.0 mm. Turn the adjuster bolt in or out to obtain the correct tension, then tighten the pivot and link bolts (see illustration).

Models with a manually-adjusted tensioning pulley

Removal

7 Disconnect the battery negative lead.
8 Slacken the tensioner pulley bracket adjustment/mounting bolts (one located in the middle of the pulley and the other located below on the bracket (see illustration).
9 Fully tighten the adjustment bolt to its stop, then slip the drivebelt from the pulleys (see illustration).

Refitting and adjustment

10 Fit the belt around the pulleys, and take up the slack in the belt by tightening the adjuster bolt. Ensure that the ribs on the belt

are correctly engaged with the grooves in the pulleys.
11 The belt should be tensioned so that, under firm thumb pressure, there is approximately 5.0 mm of free movement at the mid-point between the pulleys on the longest belt run.
12 To adjust, unscrew the adjustment bolt until the tension is correct, then rotate the crankshaft a couple of times, and recheck the tension. Securely tighten the tensioner pulley bracket adjustment/mounting bolts.
13 Reconnect the battery negative lead.
14 Refit the engine undercover and wheelarch cover. Refit the roadwheel, and lower the vehicle to the ground.

Models with an automatic spring-loaded tensioner pulley

Removal

15 Disconnect the battery negative lead.
16 Using a square drive key in the square hole in the bottom of the automatic adjuster

1.8 Tensioner pulley bracket lower mounting bolt (arrowed)

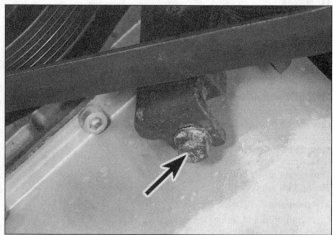

1.9 Auxiliary drivebelt tension adjustment bolt (arrowed)

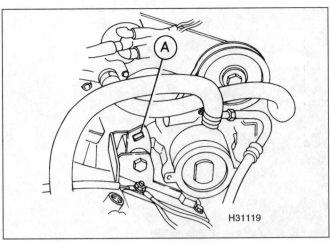

2.2 Square cut-out in power steering pump bracket (A) on XU9J4 16-valve models

3.4 Insert a 6 mm bolt (arrowed) through hole in cylinder block flange and into timing hole in the flywheel . . .

bracket, turn the bracket anticlockwise to release the tension on the belt. Hold the bracket in this position by inserting a 4.0 mm Allen key through the special hole and tightening the peg.

17 Unscrew the mounting bolts and remove the tensioner roller, then slip the auxiliary drivebelt from the pulleys.

18 Check that the tensioner pulleys turn freely without any sign of roughness.

Refitting and adjustment

19 Fit the belt around the pulleys making sure that it is engaged with the correct grooves in the pulleys.

20 Refit the tensioner roller and tighten the mounting bolts.

21 Using the square drive key hold the automatic adjuster, then release the peg and slowly allow the tensioner to tighten the belt. Check again that the belt is correctly located in the pulley grooves.

22 Reconnect the battery negative lead.

23 Refit the engine undercover and wheelarch cover. Refit the roadwheel, and lower the vehicle to the ground.

2 Power steering pump drivebelt - removal, refitting and adjustment

Removal

1 Loosen the pump mounting bolts and remove the drivebelt.

Refitting and adjustment

2 Refit in reverse order, then tension the belt by applying a torque of 55 Nm for a new belt and 30 Nm for a used belt by using the square of a torque wrench in the square cut-out in the pump bracket, tightening the mounting bolts while the torque tension is maintained (see illustration).

3 Engine assembly/valve timing holes (TU engine) - general information and usage

Note: *Do not attempt to rotate the engine whilst the crankshaft/camshaft are locked in position. If the engine is to be left in this state for a long period of time, it is a good idea to place warning notices inside the vehicle, and in the engine compartment. This will reduce the possibility of the engine being accidentally cranked on the starter motor, which is likely to cause damage with the locking pins in place.*

1 On all models, timing holes are drilled in the camshaft sprocket and in the rear of the flywheel. The holes are used to ensure that the crankshaft and camshaft are correctly positioned to prevent the possibility of the valves contacting the pistons when refitting the timing belt. When the timing holes are aligned with the special holes in the cylinder head and the front of the cylinder block, suitable diameter pins can be inserted to lock both the camshaft and crankshaft in position, preventing them from rotating. Proceed as follows.

3.5 . . . then insert a 10 mm bolt through the cam sprocket timing hole, and locate it in the cylinder head

2 Remove the timing belt upper cover as described in Section 6.

3 The crankshaft must now be turned until the timing hole in the camshaft sprocket is aligned with the corresponding hole in the cylinder head. The holes are aligned when the camshaft sprocket hole is in the 2 o'clock position, when viewed from the right-hand end of the engine. The crankshaft can be turned by using a spanner on the crankshaft sprocket bolt, noting that it should always be rotated in a clockwise direction (viewed from the right-hand end of the engine).

4 With the camshaft sprocket hole correctly positioned, insert a 6 mm diameter bolt or drill through the hole in the front, left-hand flange of the cylinder block, and locate it in the timing hole in the rear of the flywheel (see illustration). Note that it may be necessary to rotate the crankshaft slightly, to get the holes to align.

5 With the flywheel correctly positioned, insert a 10 mm diameter bolt or a drill through the timing hole in the camshaft sprocket, and locate it in the hole in the cylinder head (see illustration).

6 The crankshaft and camshaft are now locked in position, preventing unnecessary rotation.

4 Engine assembly/valve timing holes (XU engine) - general information and usage

Note: *Do not attempt to rotate the engine whilst the crankshaft/camshaft are locked in position. If the engine is to be left in this state for a long period of time, it is a good idea to place suitable warning notices inside the vehicle, and in the engine compartment. This will reduce the possibility of the engine being accidentally cranked on the starter motor, which is likely to cause damage with the locking pins in place.*

13A

**4.7 Camshaft sprocket locking pins in position (arrowed) -
1998 cc 16-valve models**

**4.13 Camshaft sprocket and crankshaft pulley locking pins in
position (1580 cc model shown)**

Note: *The introduction of a manually-adjusted timing belt tensioner pulley is 1992.*

1 On all models, timing holes are drilled in the camshaft sprocket(s) and crankshaft pulley. The holes are used to align the crankshaft and camshaft(s), to prevent the possibility of the valves contacting the pistons when refitting the timing belt. When the holes are aligned with their corresponding holes in the cylinder head and cylinder block (as appropriate), suitable diameter pins can be inserted to lock both the camshaft and crankshaft in position, preventing them rotating unnecessarily. Proceed as follows.

2 Remove the timing belt upper cover as described in Section 7.

3 Apply the handbrake, jack up the front of the car and support it on axle stands. Remove the right-hand front roadwheel.

4 From underneath the front of the car, prise out the two retaining clips and remove the plastic cover from the wing valance, to gain access to the crankshaft pulley bolt. Where necessary, unclip the coolant hoses from the bracket, to improve access further. The crankshaft can then be turned using a suitable socket and extension bar fitted to the pulley bolt. Note that the crankshaft must always be turned in a clockwise direction (viewed from the right-hand side of vehicle).

16-valve models

5 Rotate the crankshaft pulley until the timing holes in both camshafts are aligned with their corresponding holes in the cylinder head. The holes are aligned when the inlet camshaft sprocket hole is in the 8 o'clock position, and the exhaust camshaft sprocket is in the 6 o'clock position, when viewed from the right-hand end of the engine.

6 With the camshaft sprocket holes correctly positioned, insert a 6 mm diameter bolt (or a drill of suitable size), through the timing hole in the crankshaft pulley, and locate it in the corresponding hole in the end of the cylinder block. Note that it may be necessary to rotate

the crankshaft slightly, to get the holes to align.

7 With the crankshaft pulley locked in position, insert a 6 mm diameter bolt (or a drill) through the timing hole in each camshaft sprocket, and locate it in the cylinder head. Note that the special Peugeot locking pins are actually 8 mm in diameter, with only their ends stepped down to 6 mm to locate in the cylinder head **(see illustration)**. To simulate this, wrap insulation tape around the outer end of the bolt or drill, to build it up until it is a snug fit in the camshaft hole.

8 The crankshaft and camshafts are now locked in position, preventing unnecessary rotation.

8-valve models

9 Rotate the crankshaft pulley until the timing hole in the camshaft sprocket is aligned with its corresponding hole in the cylinder head. Note that the hole is aligned when the sprocket hole is in the 8 o'clock position, when viewed from the right-hand end of the engine.

10 On early models, having a semi-automatic timing belt tensioner, a 10 mm diameter bolt (or a drill of suitable size) will be required to lock the crankshaft pulley in position.

11 On later models, which have a manually-adjusted timing belt tensioner the pulley can be locked in position with an 8 mm diameter bolt or drill. The special Peugeot locking pin is actually 10 mm in diameter, with only its end stepped down to 8 mm to locate in the cylinder block. To simulate this, wrap insulation tape around the outer end of the bolt/drill, to build it up until it is a snug fit in the pulley hole.

12 With the camshaft sprocket holes correctly positioned, insert the required bolt or drill through the timing hole in the crankshaft pulley, and locate it in the corresponding hole in the end of the cylinder block. Note that it may be necessary to rotate the crankshaft slightly, to get the holes to align.

13 With the crankshaft pulley locked in position, insert the appropriate bolt or drill through the timing hole in the camshaft sprocket and locate it in the cylinder head **(see illustration)**.

14 The crankshaft and camshaft are now locked in position, preventing rotation.

5 Crankshaft pulley (XU engine) - removal and refitting

Removal

1 Remove the auxiliary drivebelt (Section 1).

16-valve models

2 Undo the four pulley retaining bolts and remove the pulley from the end of the crankshaft, noting which way around it is fitted. If the pulley locating roll pin is a loose fit, remove it and store it with the pulley for safe-keeping. If necessary, the pulley can be prevented from rotating as described in paragraph 3.

8-valve models

3 To prevent crankshaft turning whilst the pulley retaining bolt is being slackened, select 4th gear and have an assistant apply the brakes firmly. *Do not* attempt to lock the pulley by inserting a bolt/drill through the pulley timing hole.

4 Unscrew the retaining bolt and washer, then slide the pulley off the end of the crankshaft. If the pulley locating roll pin or Woodruff key (as applicable) is a loose fit, remove it and store it with the pulley for safe-keeping.

Refitting

16-valve models

5 Ensure that the locating roll pin is in position in the crankshaft. Offer up the pulley,

6.1a Undo the two retaining bolts (arrowed) . . .

6.1b . . . and remove the upper timing belt cover

6.2 Free the wiring loom from its retaining clip . . .

ensuring that it is the correct way round. Locate the pulley on the roll pin, then refit the retaining bolts and tighten them to the specified torque. If necessary, prevent the pulley from rotating as described in paragraph 3.

6 Refit and tension the auxiliary drivebelt as described in Section 1.

8-valve models

7 Ensure that the Woodruff key is correctly located in its crankshaft groove, or that the roll pin is in position (as applicable). Refit the pulley to the end of the crankshaft, aligning its locating groove or hole with the Woodruff key or pin.

8 Thoroughly clean the threads of the pulley retaining bolt, then apply a coat of locking compound to the bolt threads.

9 Refit the crankshaft pulley retaining bolt and washer. Tighten the bolt to the specified torque, preventing the crankshaft from turning using the method employed on removal.

10 Refit and tension the auxiliary drivebelt as described in Section 1.

---

6 Timing belt covers (TU engine) - removal and refitting

Removal

Upper cover

1 Slacken and remove the two retaining bolts (one at the front and one at the rear), and remove the upper timing cover from the cylinder head **(see illustrations)**.

Centre cover

2 Remove the upper cover as described in paragraph 1, then free the wiring from its clips on the centre cover **(see illustration)**.

3 Slacken and remove the three retaining bolts (one at the rear of the cover, beneath the engine mounting plate, and two directly above the crankshaft pulley), and manoeuvre the centre cover out from the engine compartment **(see illustration)**.

Lower cover

4 Remove the auxiliary drivebelt as described in Section 1.

5 Remove the upper and centre covers as described in paragraphs 1 to 3.

6 Undo the three crankshaft pulley retaining bolts and remove the pulley, noting which way round it is fitted **(see illustrations)**.

7 Slacken and remove the single retaining bolt, and slide the lower cover off the end of the crankshaft **(see illustration)**.

Refitting

Upper cover

8 Refit the cover, ensuring it is correctly located with the centre cover, and tighten its retaining bolts.

Centre cover

9 Manoeuvre the centre cover back into position, ensuring it is correctly located with the lower cover, and tighten its retaining bolts.

10 Clip the wiring loom into its retaining clips on the front of the centre cover, then refit the upper cover as described in paragraph 8.

Lower cover

11 Locate the lower cover over the timing belt sprocket, and tighten its retaining bolt.

12 Fit the pulley to the end of the crankshaft, ensuring it is fitted the correct way round, and tighten its retaining bolts to the specified torque.

13 Refit the centre and upper covers as described above, then refit and tension the auxiliary drivebelt as described in Section 1.

6.3 . . . then undo the three bolts (locations arrowed) and remove the centre belt cover

6.6a Undo the three retaining bolts (arrowed) . . .

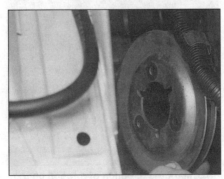

6.6b . . . and remove the crankshaft pulley

6.7 Undo the retaining bolt and remove the lower timing belt cover

13A

7 Timing belt covers (XU engine) - removal and refitting

Note: *The introduction of a manually-adjusted timing belt tensioner pulley is 1992.*

1580 cc and 1905 cc 8-valve models

Upper cover

1 Release the retaining clips, and free the fuel hoses from the top of the cover.
2 Undo the two cover retaining bolts (situated at the base of the cover), and remove the cover from the engine compartment.

Centre cover - models with a semi-automatic timing belt tensioner

3 Slacken and remove the four cover retaining nuts and bolts (two directly below the mounting bracket, and two at the base of the cover), then manoeuvre the cover upwards out of the engine compartment.

Centre cover - models with a manually-adjusted timing belt tensioner

4 Slacken and remove the two cover retaining bolts (located directly beneath the mounting bracket). Move the cover upwards to free it from the two locating pins situated at the base of the cover, and remove it from the engine compartment.

Lower cover

5 Remove the crankshaft pulley as described in Section 5.
6 Remove the centre cover as described above.
7 On early models, undo the three lower cover retaining bolts and remove the cover from the engine.
8 On later models, undo the two cover retaining bolts and remove the cover from the engine.

Lower (inner) cover - models with a semi-automatic timing belt tensioner

9 Remove the timing belt as described in Section 7.

7.24 Timing belt upper (outer) cover retaining clip (arrowed) - 1998 cc 16-valve models

10 Slacken and remove the remaining bolts, noting their correct fitted positions, and remove the cover from the end of the cylinder block.

1761 cc models

Upper cover

11 Proceed as described in paragraphs 1 and 2.

Centre cover

12 Proceed as described in paragraph 4.

Lower cover

13 Remove the crankshaft pulley as described in Section 5.
14 Remove the centre cover as described in paragraph 4.
15 Undo the two cover retaining bolts, and remove the cover from the engine.

1905 cc 16-valve models

Upper cover

16 Release the quick release clips from the timing belt cover.
17 Unscrew the upper cover securing screws and withdraw the cover.

Lower cover

18 Remove the crankshaft pulley as described in Section 5.
19 Unscrew the lower cover securing screws and withdraw the cover.

1998 cc 8-valve models

Upper cover

20 Release the retaining clip, and free the fuel hoses from the top of the timing belt cover.
21 Slacken and remove the two cover retaining bolts, then lift the upper cover upwards and out of the engine compartment.

Lower cover

22 Remove the crankshaft pulley as described in Section 5.
23 Slacken and remove the three retaining bolts, then remove the lower timing belt cover from the engine.

8.5 Mark the direction of rotation on the belt, if it is to be re-used

1998 cc 16-valve models

Upper (outer) cover

24 Undo the two upper retaining bolts securing the outer cover to the inner cover. Slide the cover retaining clip upwards to release it from its fasteners **(see illustration)**.
25 Ease the outer cover away from the engine. Lift it upwards, freeing it from its locating bolts at the base of the cover, and out of the engine compartment.

Lower cover

26 Remove the crankshaft pulley (Section 5).
27 Remove the upper (outer) cover as described above.
28 Slacken and remove the two upper cover lower locating bolts, along with their spacers. Undo the two lower cover retaining bolts, and remove the cover from the engine.

Upper (inner) cover

29 Remove the timing belt (see Section 9).
30 Remove both camshaft sprockets as described in Section 11.
31 Undo the six bolts securing the cover to the side of the cylinder head, and remove the cover from the engine.

Refitting

32 Refitting is a reversal of the relevant removal procedure, ensuring each cover section is correctly located, and the cover nuts and/or bolts are correctly tightened.

8 Timing belt (TU engine) - removal and refitting

Note: *Peugeot specify the use of a special electronic tool (SEEM C.TRONIC type 105 or 105.5 belt tensioning measuring tool) to correctly set the timing belt tension.*

Removal

1 Disconnect the battery negative terminal.
2 Align the engine assembly/valve timing holes as described in Section 3, and lock both the camshaft sprocket and the flywheel in position. *Do not* attempt to rotate the engine whilst the locking tools are in position.
3 Remove the timing belt centre and lower covers as described in Section 6.
4 Loosen the timing belt tensioner pulley retaining nut. Pivot the pulley in a clockwise direction, using a square-section key fitted to the hole in the pulley hub, then retighten the retaining nut.
5 If the timing belt is to be re-used, use white paint or similar to mark the direction of rotation on the belt (if markings do not already exist) **(see illustration)**. Slip the belt off the sprockets.
6 If signs of oil contamination are found, trace the source of the oil leak, and rectify it. Wash down the engine timing belt area and all related components, to remove all traces of oil.

Refitting

7 Prior to refitting, thoroughly clean the timing belt sprockets. Check that the tensioner pulley rotates freely, without any sign of roughness. If necessary, renew the tensioner pulley as described in Section 10. Make sure that the locking tools are still in place, as described in Section 3.

8 Manoeuvre the timing belt into position, ensuring the arrows on the belt are pointing in the direction of rotation (clockwise, when viewed from the right-hand end of the engine).

9 Do not twist the timing belt sharply while refitting it. Fit the belt over the crankshaft and camshaft sprockets. Make sure that the front run of the belt is taut - ie, ensure that any slack is on the tensioner pulley side of the belt. Fit the belt over the coolant pump sprocket and tensioner pulley. Ensure that the belt teeth are seated centrally in the sprockets.

10 Loosen the tensioner pulley retaining nut. Pivot the pulley anti-clockwise to remove all free play from the timing belt, then retighten the nut.

11 Fit the special belt tensioning measuring equipment to the front run of the timing belt, approximately midway between the camshaft and crankshaft sprockets. Position the tensioner pulley so that the belt is tensioned to a setting of 45 units, then retighten its retaining nut.

12 Remove the locking tools from the camshaft sprocket and flywheel, and remove the measuring tool from the belt.

13 Using a suitable socket and extension bar on the crankshaft sprocket bolt, rotate the crankshaft through four complete rotations in a clockwise direction (viewed from the right-hand end of the engine). *Do not* at any time rotate the crankshaft anti-clockwise.

14 Slacken the tensioner pulley retaining nut, and refit the measuring tool to the belt. If a new belt is being fitted, tension it to a setting of 40 units. If an old belt is being re-used,

tighten it to a setting of 36 units. **Note:** *Peugeot state that a belt becomes old after 1 hour's use.* With the belt correctly tensioned, tighten the pulley retaining nut to the specified torque.

15 Remove the measuring tool from the belt, then rotate the crankshaft through another two complete rotations in a clockwise direction, so that both the camshaft sprocket and flywheel timing holes are realigned. *Do not* at any time rotate the crankshaft anti-clockwise. Fit the measuring tool to the belt, and check the belt tension. A new belt should give a reading of 51 ± 3 units; an old belt should be 45 ± 3 units.

16 If the belt tension is incorrect, repeat the procedures in paragraphs 14 and 15.

17 With the belt tension correctly set, refit the timing belt covers as described in Section 6, and reconnect the battery negative terminal.

9 Timing belt (XU engine) - removal and refitting

Note: *Peugeot specify the use of a special electronic tool (SEEM C.TRONIC belt tensioning measuring tool) to correctly set the timing belt tension on models with a manually-adjusted timing belt tensioner pulley (from 1992).*

Removal

Models with a semi-automatic timing belt tensioner

1 Disconnect the battery negative terminal.

2 Align the engine assembly/valve timing holes as described in Section 4, and lock the camshaft sprocket and crankshaft pulley in position. *Do not* attempt to rotate the engine whilst the pins are in position.

3 Remove the centre and lower timing belt covers as described in Section 7.

4 Slacken (but do not remove) the two nuts

securing the tensioner assembly to the end of the cylinder block (see illustration). Loosen the tensioner cam spindle locknut, located on the rear of cylinder block flange.

5 Using a suitable open-ended spanner on the square-section end of the tensioner cam spindle, rotate the cam until the tensioner spring is fully compressed and the belt tension is relieved (see illustration). Hold the cam in this position, and tighten the locknut.

6 If required for improved access to the timing belt, remove the right-hand engine mounting bracket as follows: Place a jack beneath the engine, with a block of wood on the jack head. Raise the jack until it is supporting the weight of the engine.

7 Slacken and remove the three nuts securing the engine/transmission right-hand mounting bracket to the engine bracket. Remove the single nut securing the bracket to the mounting rubber, and lift off the bracket. Undo the three bolts securing the engine bracket to the end of the cylinder head/block, and remove the bracket.

8 If the timing belt is to be re-used, use white paint or chalk to mark the direction of rotation on the belt (if markings do not already exist), then slip the belt off the sprockets. Note that the crankshaft must not be rotated whilst the belt is removed.

9 If signs of oil contamination are found, trace the source of the oil leak and rectify it. Wash down the engine timing belt area and all related components, to remove all traces of oil.

8-valve models with a manually-adjusted timing belt tensioner

10 Disconnect the battery negative terminal.

11 Align the engine assembly/valve timing holes as described in Section 4, and lock the camshaft sprocket and crankshaft pulley in position. *Do not* attempt to rotate the engine whilst the pins are in position.

12 Remove the centre and/or lower timing belt cover(s) - see Section 7 (as applicable).

9.4 On early 1580 cc and 1905 cc models, slacken the tensioner assembly retaining nuts . . .

9.5 . . . and the spindle locknut, then release the belt tension by turning the tensioner cam spindle

13A

13 Loosen the timing belt tensioner pulley retaining bolt. Pivot the pulley in a clockwise direction, using a suitable square-section key fitted to the hole in the pulley hub, then securely retighten the retaining bolt.

14 On 1580 cc, 1761 cc and 1905 cc models, dismantle the engine right-hand mounting as described above in paragraphs 6 and 7.

15 On all models, remove and inspect the timing belt (see paragraphs 8 and 9).

1905 cc 16-valve models

16 Disconnect the battery negative terminal.

17 Align the engine assembly/valve timing holes as described in Section 4, and lock the camshaft sprockets and crankshaft pulley in position. *Do not* attempt to rotate the engine whilst the pins are in position.

18 Remove the timing belt lower cover as described in Section 7.

19 Loosen the timing belt front and rear tensioner pulley retaining bolts. Pivot the front pulley in a clockwise direction, using a suitable square-section key fitted to the hole in the pulley hub, then securely retighten the retaining bolt. Similarly pivot the rear pulley in an anti-clockwise direction and retighten the retaining bolt.

20 Check that the camshaft sprocket and crankshaft locking pins are still in position, then remove and inspect the timing belt as described in paragraphs 8 and 9.

1998 cc 16-valve models

21 Disconnect the battery negative terminal.

22 Align the engine assembly/valve timing holes as described in Section 4, and lock the camshaft sprockets and crankshaft pulley in position. *Do not* attempt to rotate the engine whilst the pins are in position.

23 Remove the timing belt lower cover as described in Section 7.

24 Loosen the timing belt rear tensioner pulley retaining bolt. Pivot the pulley in a clockwise direction, using a suitable square-section key fitted to the hole in the pulley hub, then retighten the bolt **(see illustration)**.

25 Loosen the two front tensioner assembly retaining bolts. Move the tensioner pulley away from the belt, using the same square-section key on the pulley backplate.

26 Check that the camshaft sprocket and crankshaft locking pins are still in position, then remove and inspect the timing belt as described in paragraphs 8 and 9.

Refitting

27 Before refitting, thoroughly clean the timing belt sprockets. Check that the tensioner pulley rotates freely, without any sign of roughness. If necessary, renew the tensioner pulley as described in Section 11.

28 Ensure that the camshaft sprocket locking pin is still in position. Temporarily refit the crankshaft pulley, and insert the locking pin through the pulley timing hole to ensure that the crankshaft is still correctly positioned.

Models with a semi-automatic timing belt tensioner

29 Remove the crankshaft pulley. Manoeuvre the timing belt into position, ensuring that any arrows on the belt are pointing in the direction of rotation (clockwise when viewed from the right-hand end of the engine).

30 Do not twist the timing belt sharply while refitting it. Fit the belt over the crankshaft and camshaft sprockets. Ensure that the belt front run is taut - ie, any slack should be on the tensioner pulley side of the belt. Fit the belt over the water pump sprocket and tensioner pulley. Ensure that the belt teeth are seated centrally in the sprockets.

31 Slacken the tensioner cam spindle locknut, and check that the tensioner pulley is forced against the timing belt by spring pressure.

32 Refit the crankshaft pulley, tightening its retaining bolt by hand only.

33 Rotate the crankshaft through at least two complete rotations in a clockwise direction (viewed from the right-hand end of the engine). Realign the camshaft and crankshaft engine assembly/valve timing holes (see Section 4). *Do not* at any time rotate the crankshaft anti-clockwise. Both camshaft and crankshaft timing holes should be aligned so that the locking pins can be easily inserted. This indicates that the valve timing is correct.

34 If the timing holes are not correctly positioned, release the tensioner assembly as described in paragraph 5, and disengage the belt from the camshaft sprocket. Rotate the camshaft and crankshaft slightly as required until both locking pins are in position. Relocate the timing belt on the camshaft sprocket. Ensure that the belt front run is taut - ie, that any slack is on the tensioner pulley side of the belt. Slacken the tensioner locknut, then remove the locking pins and repeat the procedure in paragraph 33.

35 Once both timing holes are correctly aligned, tighten the two tensioner assembly retaining nuts to the specified torque. Tighten the tensioner cam spindle locknut.

36 With the belt correctly installed and tensioned, where removed, refit the engine bracket to the side of the cylinder head/block, and securely tighten its retaining bolts. Refit the right-hand mounting bracket, and tighten its retaining nuts to the specified torque. The jack can then be removed from underneath the engine.

37 Remove the crankshaft pulley, then refit the timing belt covers (refer to Section 7).

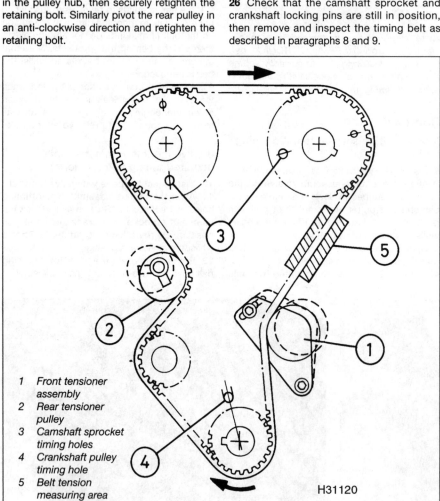

1　Front tensioner assembly
2　Rear tensioner pulley
3　Camshaft sprocket timing holes
4　Crankshaft pulley timing hole
5　Belt tension measuring area (using Peugeot special tool)

H31120

9.24 Timing belt arrangement - 1998 cc 16-valve models

38 Install the crankshaft pulley (Section 5), and reconnect the battery negative terminal.

Models with a manually-adjusted timing belt tensioner

Note: *Peugeot specify the use of a special electronic tool (SEEM C. TRONIC belt tension measuring tool) to correctly set the timing belt tension.*

39 Install the timing belt as described above in paragraphs 27 to 30.

40 Loosen the tensioner pulley retaining bolt. Using the square-section key, pivot the pulley anti-clockwise to remove all free play from the timing belt.

41 Fit the special belt tension measuring equipment to the front run of the timing belt. The tensioner roller should be adjusted so that the initial belt tension is 16 ± 2 units on 1998 cc models, and 30 ± 2 units on all other models.

42 Tighten the pulley retaining bolt to the specified torque. Refit the crankshaft pulley again, tightening its bolt by hand only.

43 Carry out the operations described in paragraph 33 (and, where necessary, paragraph 34, ignoring the information about the tensioner) to ensure both timing holes are correctly aligned and the valve timing is correct.

44 The final belt tension on the front run of the belt on all models should be 44 ± 2 units. Readjust the tensioner pulley position as required, then retighten the retaining bolt to the specified torque. Rotate the crankshaft through a further two rotations clockwise, and recheck the tension. Repeat this procedure as necessary until the correct tension reading is obtained after rotating the crankshaft.

45 With the belt tension correctly set, where removed, refit the engine bracket to the side of the cylinder head/block, and securely tighten its retaining bolts. Refit the right-hand engine mounting bracket, and tighten its retaining nuts to the specified torque. The jack can then be removed from underneath the engine.

46 On all models, remove the crankshaft pulley, then refit the timing belt cover(s) as described in Section 7.

47 Refit the crankshaft pulley (Section 5), and reconnect the battery negative terminal.

1905 cc 16-valve models

Note: *Peugeot specify the use of a special electronic tool (SEEM belt tension measuring tool) to correctly set the timing belt tension.*

48 Ensure that the camshaft and crankshaft sprocket locking pins are still in position. Slacken both tensioner mounting bolts so that they are free to pivot easily.

49 Manoeuvre the timing belt into position, ensuring that any arrows on the belt are pointing in the direction of rotation (clockwise when viewed from the right-hand end of the engine). Fit the timing belt in the sequence given in **(see illustration).**

50 Note that there may be timing marks on the belt, in the form of yellow lines, to ensure it

is correctly positioned on both camshaft sprockets and the crankshaft sprocket. The two single-line timing marks should be aligned with the timing dot (directly opposite the sprocket timing hole) on each camshaft sprocket. The double-line timing mark should be aligned with the crankshaft sprocket, where it will be directly opposite the sprocket Woodruff key slot. Peugeot state that the use of these timing marks is optional, but they are useful in helping to ensure that the valve timing is correctly set at the first attempt.

51 With the three locking pins in position, move both the front and rear tensioner pulleys towards the timing belt until both pulleys are contacting the belt. Securely tighten the retaining bolts.

52 Fit the special belt tension measuring equipment to the front run of the timing belt, between the front tensioner and the camshaft sprocket. Move the front tensioner pulley anti-clockwise so that the belt is tensioned to a setting of 19 units, then tighten the retaining bolt to the specified torque setting.

53 Slacken the rear tensioner pulley retaining bolt. Using the square-section key, pivot the pulley clockwise until the belt tension on the front run is 21 units. Hold the tensioner in position, and tighten its retaining bolt to the specified torque setting.

54 Remove the locking pins from the camshaft and crankshaft sprockets and, where fitted, the tensioning measuring device from the belt.

55 Rotate the crankshaft through at least two complete rotations in a clockwise direction (viewed from the right-hand end of the engine). Realign the camshaft and crankshaft engine assembly/valve timing holes (see Section 4). Do not at any time rotate the crankshaft anti-clockwise. Both camshaft timing holes and the crankshaft timing hole should be correctly positioned so that the locking pins can be easily inserted, indicating that the valve timing is correct.

56 If the timing holes are not correctly positioned, repeat the tensioning procedure.

57 Once the valve timing is correctly set, remove the locking pins and recheck the belt tension.

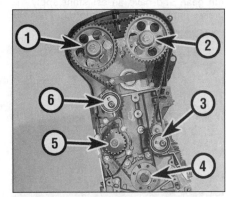

9.49 Fit the timing belt in the sequence given - 1905 cc 16-valve engines

58 The final belt tension on the front run of the belt, between the camshaft sprocket and tensioner pulley, should be 45 ± 5 units. Repeat the procedure as necessary, until the correct tension reading is obtained after the crankshaft has been rotated.

59 Once the belt tension is correctly set, refit the timing belt covers as described in Section 7. Refit the crankshaft pulley as described in Section 5, and reconnect the battery negative terminal.

1998 cc 16-valve models

Note: *Peugeot specify the use of a special electronic tool (SEEM belt tension measuring tool) to correctly set the timing belt tension.*

60 Ensure that the camshaft and crankshaft sprocket locking pins are still in position. Slacken the tensioner mounting bolts so that they are free to pivot easily.

61 Manoeuvre the timing belt into position, ensuring that any arrows on the belt are pointing in the direction of rotation (clockwise when viewed from the right-hand end of the engine).

62 Note that there are also timing marks on the belt, in the form of yellow lines, to ensure it is correctly positioned on both camshaft sprockets and the crankshaft sprocket. The two single-line timing marks should be aligned with the timing dot (directly opposite the sprocket timing hole) on each camshaft sprocket. The double-line timing mark should be aligned with the crankshaft sprocket, where it will be directly opposite the sprocket Woodruff key slot. Peugeot state that the use of these timing marks is optional, but they are useful in helping to ensure that the valve timing is correctly set at the first attempt.

63 With the three locking pins in position, move both the front and rear tensioner pulleys towards the timing belt until both pulleys are contacting the belt. Securely tighten the rear tensioner retaining bolt.

64 Fit the special belt tension measuring equipment to the front run of the timing belt, between the front tensioner and the camshaft sprocket. Move the tensioner pulley backplate so that the belt is initially over-tensioned to a setting of 45 units, then back the tensioner off until the belt tension is 22 ± 2 units. Hold the backplate in this position, and tighten both the tensioner pulley retaining bolts to the specified torque.

65 Slacken the rear tensioner pulley retaining bolt. Using the square-section key, pivot the pulley anti-clockwise until all free play is removed from the belt. Set the tensioner pulley so that the belt tension on the front run is 32 ± 2 units. Hold the tensioner in position, and tighten its retaining bolt to the specified torque setting.

66 Remove the locking pins from the camshaft and crankshaft sprockets and, where fitted, the tensioning measuring device from the belt.

67 Rotate the crankshaft through at least two complete rotations in a clockwise direction (viewed from the right-hand end of the engine). Realign the camshaft and crankshaft engine assembly/valve timing holes (see Section 4). Do not at any time rotate the crankshaft anti-clockwise. Both camshaft timing holes and the crankshaft timing hole should be correctly positioned so that the locking pins can be easily inserted, indicating that the valve timing is correct.

68 If the timing holes are not correctly positioned, slacken the tensioner assembly retaining bolts, and disengage the belt from the camshaft sprockets. Rotate the camshafts and crankshaft slightly as required until all locking pins are in position, then relocate the timing belt on the camshaft sprocket. Ensure that the belt top run and front run are taut - ie, ensure that any slack is on the rear tensioner pulley and water pump side of the belt. Repeat the tensioning procedure until the valve timing is correct.

69 Once the valve timing is correctly set, remove the locking pins and recheck the belt tension.

70 The final belt tension on the front run of the belt, between the camshaft sprocket and tensioner pulley, should be 53 ± 2 units. Readjust the rear tensioner pulley position as required, then retighten the retaining bolt to the specified torque. Rotate the crankshaft through a further two rotations clockwise, and recheck the tension. Repeat this procedure as necessary, until the correct tension reading is obtained after the crankshaft has been rotated.

81 Once the belt tension is correctly set, refit the timing belt covers (see Section 7). Refit the crankshaft pulley as described in Section 5, and reconnect the battery negative terminal.

10 Timing belt tensioner and sprockets (TU engine) - removal and refitting

Note: *This Section describes the removal and refitting of the components concerned as individual operations. If more than one of them is to be removed at the same time, start by removing the timing belt as described in Section 8; remove the actual component as described below, ignoring the preliminary dismantling steps.*

Removal

1 Disconnect the battery negative terminal.

2 Position the engine assembly/valve timing holes as described in Section 3, and lock both the camshaft sprocket and flywheel in position. *Do not* attempt to rotate the engine whilst the pins are in position.

Camshaft sprocket

3 Remove the centre timing belt cover as described in Section 6.

4 Loosen the timing belt tensioner pulley retaining nut. Rotate the pulley in a clockwise direction, using a suitable square-section key fitted to the hole in the pulley hub, then retighten the retaining nut.

5 Disengage the timing belt from the sprocket, and move the belt clear, taking care not to bend or twist it sharply. Remove the locking pin from the camshaft sprocket.

6 Slacken the camshaft sprocket retaining bolt and remove it, along with its washer. To prevent the camshaft rotating as the bolt is slackened, a sprocket-holding tool will be required. In the absence of the special Peugeot tool, an acceptable substitute can be fabricated as follows. Use two lengths of steel strip (one long, the other short), and three nuts and bolts; one nut and bolt forms the pivot of a forked tool, with the remaining two nuts and bolts at the tips of the 'forks' to engage with the sprocket spokes **(see illustration)**. *Do not* attempt to use the sprocket locking pin to prevent the sprocket from rotating whilst the bolt is slackened.

7 With the retaining bolt removed, slide the sprocket off the end of the camshaft. If the locating peg is a loose fit in the rear of the sprocket, remove it for safe-keeping. Examine the camshaft oil seal for signs of oil leakage and, if necessary, renew it.

Crankshaft sprocket

8 Remove the centre and lower timing belt covers as described in Section 6.

9 Remove the timing belt from the sprockets as described in Section 8.

10 To prevent crankshaft rotation whilst the sprocket retaining bolt is slackened, select 4th gear, and have an assistant apply the brakes firmly. *Do not* be tempted to use the

10.6 Using a home-made tool to hold the camshaft sprocket stationary whilst the retaining bolt is tightened (shown with cylinder head removed)

flywheel locking pin to prevent the crankshaft from rotating; temporarily remove the locking pin from the rear of the flywheel prior to slackening the pulley bolt, then refit it once the bolt has been slackened. *Do not* allow the crankshaft to turn more than a few degrees while loosening the bolt otherwise the pistons may touch the valves.

11 Unscrew the retaining bolt and washer, then slide the sprocket off the end of the crankshaft **(see illustrations)**. Refit the locating pin to the rear of the timing hole in the rear of the flywheel.

12 If the Woodruff key is a loose fit in the crankshaft, remove it and store it with the sprocket for safe-keeping. If necessary, also slide the flanged spacer off the end of the crankshaft **(see illustration)**. Examine the crankshaft oil seal for signs of oil leakage and, if necessary, renew it (refer to Section 14).

Tensioner pulley

13 Remove the centre timing belt cover as described in Section 5.

14 Slacken and remove the timing belt tensioner pulley retaining nut, and slide the pulley off its mounting stud. Examine the mounting stud for signs of damage and, if necessary, renew it.

Refitting

15 Clean the sprockets thoroughly, and renew any that show signs of wear, damage or cracks.

10.11a Remove the crankshaft sprocket retaining bolt . . .

10.11b . . . then slide off the sprocket

10.12 Remove the flanged spacer if necessary

16 Clean the tensioner assembly, but do not use any strong solvent which may enter the pulley bearing. Check that the pulley rotates freely about its hub, with no sign of stiffness or free play. Renew the tensioner pulley if there is any doubt about its condition, or if there are any obvious signs of wear or damage.

Camshaft sprocket

17 Refit the locating peg (where removed) to the rear of the sprocket, then locate the sprocket on the end of the camshaft. Ensure that the locating peg is correctly engaged with the cutout in the camshaft end.

18 Refit the sprocket retaining bolt and washer. Tighten the bolt to the specified torque, whilst retaining the sprocket with the tool used on removal.

19 Realign the timing hole in the camshaft sprocket (see Section 3) with the corresponding hole in the cylinder head, and refit the locking pin.

20 Refit the timing belt to the camshaft sprocket. Ensure that the front run of the belt is taut - ie, ensure that any slack is on the tensioner pulley side of the belt. Do not twist the belt sharply while refitting it, and ensure that the belt teeth are seated centrally in the sprockets.

21 Loosen the tensioner pulley retaining nut. Rotate the pulley anti-clockwise to remove all free play from the timing belt, then retighten the nut.

22 Tension the belt as described in Section 6.

23 Refit the timing belt covers as described in Section 6.

Crankshaft sprocket

24 Where removed, locate the Woodruff key in the crankshaft end, then slide on the flanged spacer, aligning its slot with the Woodruff key.

25 Align the crankshaft sprocket slot with the Woodruff key, and slide it onto the end of the crankshaft.

26 Temporarily remove the locking pin from the rear of the flywheel, then refit the crankshaft sprocket retaining bolt and washer. Tighten the bolt to the specified torque, whilst preventing crankshaft rotation using the method employed on removal. Refit the locking pin to the rear of the flywheel.

27 Relocate the timing belt on the sprockets. Ensure that the front run of the belt is taut - ie, ensure that any slack is on the tensioner pulley side of the belt. Do not twist the belt sharply while refitting it, and ensure that the belt teeth are seated centrally in the sprockets.

28 Loosen the tensioner pulley retaining nut. Rotate the pulley anti-clockwise to remove all free play from the timing belt, then retighten the nut.

29 Tension the belt as described in Section 6.

30 Refit the timing belt covers as described in Section 6.

Tensioner pulley

31 Refit the tensioner pulley to its mounting stud, and fit the retaining nut.

32 Ensure that the front run of the belt is taut - ie, ensure that any slack is on the pulley side of the belt. Check that the belt is centrally located on all its sprockets. Rotate the pulley anti-clockwise to remove all free play from the timing belt, then tighten the pulley retaining nut securely.

33 Tension the belt as described in Section 6.

34 Refit the timing belt covers as described in Section 6.

---

11 Timing belt tensioner and sprockets (XU engine) - removal and refitting

Note: *This Section describes the removal and refitting of the components concerned as individual operations - if more than one is to be removed at the same time, start by removing the timing belt as described in Section 9; remove the actual component as described below, ignoring the preliminary dismantling steps.*

Removal

1 Disconnect the battery negative lead.

2 Align the engine assembly/valve timing holes as described in Section 4, locking the camshaft sprocket(s) and the crankshaft pulley in position, and proceed as described under the relevant sub-heading. *Do not attempt to rotate the engine whilst the pins are in position.*

Camshaft sprocket - models with a semi-automatic timing belt tensioner

3 Remove the centre timing belt cover as described in Section 7.

4 Slacken (but do not remove) the two nuts securing the tensioner assembly to the end of the cylinder block. Loosen the tensioner cam spindle locknut, located on the rear of cylinder block flange.

5 Using a suitable open-ended spanner on the square-section end of the tensioner cam spindle, rotate the cam until the tensioner spring is fully compressed and the belt tension is relieved. Hold the cam in this position, and securely tighten the locknut.

6 Remove the locking pin from the camshaft sprocket. Disengage the timing belt from the sprocket and position it clear, taking care not to bend or twist the belt sharply.

7 Slacken the camshaft sprocket retaining bolt and remove it, along with its washer. To prevent the camshaft rotating as the bolt is slackened, a sprocket holding tool will be required. In the absence of the special Peugeot tool, an acceptable substitute can be fabricated from two lengths of steel strip (one long, the other short) and three nuts and bolts, as follows. One nut and bolt forms the pivot of a forked tool, with the remaining two nuts and

bolts at the tips of the 'forks' to engage with the sprocket spokes **(see illustration 10.6).** *Do not* attempt to use the sprocket locking pin to prevent the sprocket from rotating whilst the bolt is slackened.

8 With the retaining bolt removed, slide the sprocket off the end of the camshaft. If the locating peg is a loose fit in the rear of the sprocket, remove it for safe-keeping. Examine the camshaft oil seal for signs of oil leakage and, if necessary, renew it.

Camshaft sprocket - 8-valve models with a manually-adjusted timing belt tensioner

9 On all except 1998 cc models, remove the centre timing belt cover as described in Section 7.

10 Loosen the timing belt tensioner pulley retaining bolt. Rotate the pulley in a clockwise direction, using a suitable square-section key fitted to the hole in the pulley hub, then retighten the retaining bolt.

11 Remove the camshaft sprocket as described above in paragraphs 6 to 8.

Camshaft sprocket(s) - 1905 cc 16-valve models

12 With the timing covers removed, loosen the timing belt front and rear tensioner pulley retaining bolts. Pivot the front pulley in a clockwise direction, using a suitable square-section key fitted to the hole in the pulley hub, then securely retighten the retaining bolt. Similarly pivot the rear pulley in an anti-clockwise direction and retighten the bolt.

13 Remove the camshaft sprocket retaining bolt as described in paragraphs 6 and 7.

14 Slide the sprocket off the end of the camshaft. If the Woodruff key is a loose fit in the camshaft, remove it and store it with the sprocket for safe-keeping. Examine the camshaft oil seal for signs of oil leakage and, if necessary, renew it.

Camshaft sprocket(s) - 1998 cc 16-valve models

15 Loosen the timing belt rear tensioner pulley retaining bolt. Pivot the pulley in a clockwise direction, using a suitable square-section key fitted to the hole in the pulley hub, then securely retighten the retaining bolt.

16 Loosen the two front tensioner assembly retaining bolts. Move the tensioner pulley away from the belt, using the same square-section key on the pulley backplate.

17 Remove the camshaft sprocket retaining bolt as described in paragraphs 6 and 7.

18 Slide the sprocket off the end of the camshaft. If the Woodruff key is a loose fit in the camshaft, remove it and store it with the sprocket for safe-keeping. Examine the camshaft oil seal for signs of oil leakage and, if necessary, renew it.

Crankshaft sprocket - 8-valve models

19 Remove the centre and/or lower timing belt cover(s) (as applicable) as described in Section 7.

20 On models with a semi-automatic timing belt tensioner, release the timing belt tensioner as described above in paragraphs 4 and 5.

21 On later models with a manually-adjusted timing belt tensioner, release the timing belt tensioner as described in paragraph 10.

22 Disengage the timing belt from the crankshaft sprocket, and slide the sprocket off the end of the crankshaft. Remove the Woodruff key from the crankshaft, and store it with the sprocket for safe-keeping. Where necessary, also slide the flanged spacer (where fitted) off the end of the crankshaft.

23 Examine the crankshaft oil seal for signs of oil leakage and, if necessary, renew it.

Crankshaft sprocket - 16-valve models

24 Remove the lower timing belt cover as described in Section 7.

25 Release the timing belt tensioners as described above in paragraphs 12 or 15 and 16 (as applicable). Disengage the timing belt from the crankshaft sprocket, and remove the locking pin.

26 To prevent the crankshaft turning whilst the sprocket retaining bolt is being slackened, select 4th gear, and have an assistant apply the brakes firmly. *Do not* be tempted to use the locking pin to prevent the crankshaft from rotating.

27 Unscrew the retaining bolt and washer, then slide the sprocket off the end of the crankshaft. If the Woodruff key is a loose fit in the crankshaft, remove it and store it with the sprocket for safe-keeping.

28 Where necessary, slide the flanged spacer (where fitted) off the crankshaft.

29 Examine the crankshaft oil seal for signs of oil leakage and, if necessary, renew it.

Tensioner assembly - models with a semi-automatic belt tensioner

30 Remove the centre timing belt cover as described in Section 7.

31 Slacken and remove the two nuts and washers securing the tensioner assembly to the end of the cylinder block. Carefully ease the spring cover off its studs, taking care not to allow the spring to fly out as the cover is withdrawn. Remove the spring and cover from the engine **(see illustration)**.

32 Slacken and remove the tensioner cam spindle locknut and washer, located on the rear of cylinder block flange, and withdraw the cam spindle.

33 The tensioner pulley and backplate assembly can then be manoeuvred out from behind the timing belt.

Tensioner pulley - 8-valve models with a manually-adjusted belt tensioner

34 On all except 1998 cc models, remove the centre timing belt cover as described in Section 7.

35 Slacken and remove the timing belt tensioner pulley retaining bolt, and slide the pulley off its mounting stud. Examine the mounting stud for signs of damage and if necessary, renew it.

Tensioner pulleys - 1905 cc 16-valve models

36 The front and rear tensioner pulleys are removed as described above.

Tensioner pulleys - 1998 cc 16-valve models

37 The rear tensioner pulley is removed as described above.

38 To remove the front tensioner pulley, slacken and remove the two bolts securing the pulley backplate to the cylinder block, and remove the assembly from the engine.

Refitting

39 Clean the camshaft/crankshaft sprockets thoroughly, and renew any that show signs of wear, damage or cracks.

40 Clean the tensioner assembly, but do not use any strong solvent which may enter the pulley bearing. Check that the pulley rotates freely on the backplate, with no sign of stiffness or free play. Renew the assembly if there is any doubt about its condition, or if there are any obvious signs of wear or damage.

41 On models with a semi-automatic belt tensioner, the tensioner spring should also be carefully checked, as its condition is critical for the correct tensioning of the timing belt. The only way to check the spring tension is to compare it with a new one; if there is any doubt as to its condition, the spring should be renewed.

Camshaft sprocket - models with a semi-automatic timing belt tensioner

42 Refit the locating peg (where removed) to the rear of the sprocket. Locate the sprocket on the end of the camshaft, ensuring that the locating peg is correctly engaged with the cutout in the camshaft end.

43 Refit the sprocket retaining bolt and washer, and tighten it to the specified torque. Retain the sprocket with the tool used on removal.

44 Realign the hole in the camshaft sprocket

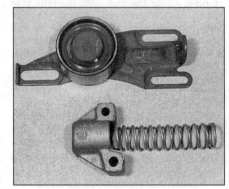

11.31 Timing belt tensioner assembly components - early 1580 cc and 1905 cc 8-valve models

with the corresponding hole in the cylinder head, and refit the locking pin. Check that the crankshaft pulley locking pin is still in position.

45 Refit the timing belt to the camshaft sprocket. Ensure that the front run of the belt is taut - ie, that any slack is on the tensioner pulley side of the belt. Do not twist the belt sharply while refitting it, and ensure that the belt teeth are seated centrally in the sprockets.

46 Release the tensioner cam spindle locknut, and check that the tensioner pulley is forced against the timing belt under spring pressure.

47 Tension the timing belt (see Section 9).

48 With the belt correctly tensioned, and the tensioner retaining nuts and locknut tightened to the specified torque setting (where given), refit the timing belt covers as described in Section 7. Reconnect the battery on completion.

Camshaft sprocket - models with a manually-adjusted timing belt tensioner

49 Refit the camshaft sprocket as described above.

50 With the timing belt correctly engaged on the sprockets, tension the belt as described in Section 9.

51 Once the belt is correctly tensioned, refit the timing belt covers (see Section 7).

Camshaft sprocket(s) - 16-valve models

52 Refit the Woodruff key to its slot in the camshaft end. Slide on the sprocket, aligning its slot with the Woodruff key.

53 Refit the sprocket retaining bolt and washer. Tighten the bolt to the specified torque, whilst retaining the sprocket with the tool used on removal.

54 Realign the hole in the camshaft sprocket with the corresponding hole in the cylinder head, and refit the locking pin.

55 Relocate the timing belt on the camshaft sprocket(s), and tension the timing belt as described in Section 9.

56 Once the belt is correctly tensioned, refit the timing belt cover (Section 7).

Crankshaft sprocket - 8-valve models

57 Slide on the flanged spacer (where fitted), and refit the Woodruff key to its slot in the crankshaft end.

58 Slide on the crankshaft sprocket, aligning its slot with the Woodruff key.

59 Ensure that the camshaft sprocket locking pin is still in position. Temporarily refit the crankshaft pulley, and insert the locking pin through the pulley timing hole, to ensure that the crankshaft is still correctly positioned.

60 Remove the crankshaft pulley. Engage the timing belt with the crankshaft sprocket. Ensure that the belt front run is taut - ie, that any slack is on the tensioner pulley side of the belt. Fit the belt over the water pump sprocket and tensioner pulley. Do not twist the belt sharply while refitting it, and ensure that the belt teeth are seated centrally in the sprockets.

61 On models with a semi-automatic timing belt tensioner, release the tensioner cam spindle locknut, checking that the tensioner pulley is forced against the timing belt under spring pressure. Tension the timing belt as described in Section 9.

62 On models with a manually-adjusted timing belt tensioner pulley, tension the timing belt as described in Section 9.

63 On all models, remove the crankshaft pulley, then refit the timing belt cover(s) as described in Section 7.

64 Refit the crankshaft pulley (Section 5), and reconnect the battery negative terminal.

Crankshaft sprocket - 16-valve models

65 Slide on the flanged spacer (where fitted), and refit the Woodruff key to its slot in the crankshaft end.

66 Slide on the crankshaft sprocket, aligning its slot with the Woodruff key.

67 Thoroughly clean the threads of the sprocket retaining bolt, then apply a coat of locking compound to the threads of the bolt.

68 Refit the crankshaft sprocket retaining bolt and washer. Tighten the bolt to the specified torque, whilst preventing crankshaft rotation using the method employed on removal.

69 Refit the locking pin to the crankshaft sprocket, and check that both the camshaft sprocket locking pins are still in position.

70 Relocate the timing belt on the crankshaft sprocket, and tension the timing belt as described in Section 9.

71 Once the belt is correctly tensioned, refit the timing belt cover (see Section 7).

Tensioner assembly - 8-valve models with a semi-automatic timing belt tensioner

72 Manoeuvre the tensioner pulley and backplate assembly into position behind the timing belt, and locate it on the mounting studs.

73 Insert the tensioner cam spindle through the backplate from the front of the block, and refit its washer and locknut, tightening it by hand only at this stage.

74 Fit the spring to the inside of the spring cover. Compress the spring, and slide the spring cover onto the two mounting studs, ensuring that the spring end is correctly located behind the backplate tang.

75 Refit the tensioner mounting nuts and washers, tightening them by hand only. Check that the tensioner is forced against the timing belt by spring pressure, and is free to move smoothly and easily.

76 Ensure that the front run of the belt is taut - ie, that any slack is on the pulley side of the belt. Check that the belt is centrally located on all its sprockets, then release the tensioner assembly and allow it to tension the belt.

77 Tension the timing belt, as described in Section 9.

78 With the belt correctly tensioned, and the tensioner retaining nuts and locknut tightened to the specified torque setting (where given), refit the timing belt covers as described in Section 7. Reconnect the battery on completion.

Tensioner pulley - 8-valve models with a manually-adjusted timing belt tensioner

79 Refit the tensioner pulley to its mounting stud, and fit the retaining bolt.

80 Ensure that the front run of the belt is taut - ie, that any slack is on the pulley side of the belt. Check that the belt is centrally located on all its sprockets. Rotate the pulley anti-clockwise to remove all free play from the timing belt, and securely tighten the pulley retaining nut.

81 Tension the belt (see Section 9).

82 Once the belt is correctly tensioned, refit the timing belt covers as described in Section 7.

Tensioner pulleys - 1905 cc 16-valve models

83 Refit the tensioner pulleys to their studs, and fit the retaining bolts. Tighten the bolts finger-tight only, so that both tensioners are free to pivot.

84 Tension the timing belt (see Section 9).

85 Once the belt is correctly tensioned, refit the timing belt cover (see Section 7).

Tensioner pulleys - 1998 cc 16-valve models

86 Refit the rear tensioner pulley to its mounting stud, and fit the retaining bolt. Align the front pulley backplate with its holes, and refit both its retaining bolts. Tighten all retaining bolts finger-tight only, so that both tensioners are free to pivot.

87 Tension the timing belt (see Section 9).

88 Once the belt is correctly tensioned, refit the timing belt cover (see Section 7).

13A

Notes

Chapter 13B
Peugeot 405 diesel 1988 to 1996

Contents

Specifications

Timing belt renewal interval . . . . Every 36 000 miles (60 000 km)

Note: *Although the normal interval for timing belt renewal is 72 000 miles (120 000 km), it is strongly recommended that the interval is halved on vehicles which are subjected to intensive use, ie, mainly short journeys or a lot of stop-start driving. The actual belt renewal interval is therefore very much up to the individual owner. That being said, it is highly recommended to err on the side of safety, and renew the belt at this earlier interval, bearing in mind the drastic consequences resulting from belt failure.*

Torque wrench settings	Nm	lbf ft
Brake vacuum pump drive pulley bolt	35	26
Camshaft sprocket bolt	45	33
Crankshaft pulley bolt:		
Stage 1	40	30
Stage 2	Tighten through a further 60°	
Cylinder head cover bolts	10	7
Engine/transmission left-hand mounting:		
Centre nut	70	52
Mounting bracket-to-body bolts	45	33
Mounting rubber-to-bracket nuts (all except 1.9 litre turbo engines) . .	20	15
Mounting stud	50	37
Mounting stud bracket bolts (1.9 litre turbo engines)	60	44
Engine/transmission rear mounting:		
Mounting assembly-to-block bolts	45	33
Mounting link-to-mounting bolt	50	37
Mounting link-to-subframe bolt	85	63
Engine/transmission right-hand mounting:		
Curved retaining plate bolts	20	15
Engine (tensioner assembly) bracket bolts	18	13
Mounting bracket retaining nuts	45	33
Fuel injection pump sprocket nut	50	37
Fuel injection pump sprocket puller retaining screws	10	7
Roadwheel bolts	86	63
Timing belt cover bolts	8	6
Timing belt tensioner adjustment bolt	18	13
Timing belt tensioner pivot nut	18	13

13B

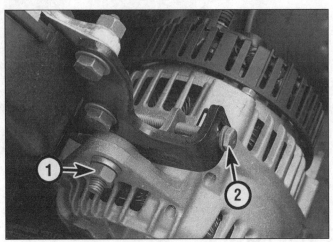

1.5 Alternator upper mounting nut (1) and adjuster bolt (2) - models without power steering or air conditioning

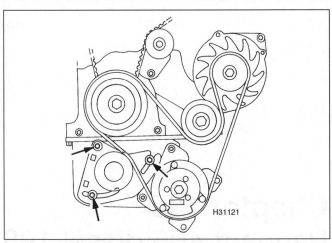

1.13 Tensioner pulley bracket securing bolts (arrowed) - early models with air conditioning, but no power steering

1 Auxiliary drivebelt - removal, refitting and adjustment

1 Apply the handbrake, then jack up the front of the vehicle and support it on axle stands. Remove the right-hand front roadwheel.
2 From underneath the front of the car, prise out the retaining clips, and remove the screws (where applicable), then remove the plastic cover from the wheel arch to gain access to the crankshaft pulley bolt.

Models without power steering or air conditioning

Removal

3 Disconnect the battery negative lead.
4 Slacken both the alternator upper and lower mounting nuts/bolts (as applicable).
5 Back off the adjuster bolt to relieve the tension in the drivebelt, then slip the drivebelt from the pulleys (see illustration).

Refitting and adjustment

6 Fit the belt around the pulleys, and take up the slack in the belt by tightening the adjuster bolt.
7 The belt should be tensioned so that, under

firm thumb pressure, there is approximately 5.0 mm of free movement at the mid-point between the pulleys.
8 To adjust, with the upper mounting nut just holding the alternator firm, and the adjuster bolt loosened, turn the adjuster bolt until the correct tension is achieved, then tighten the upper mounting nut.
9 Rotate the crankshaft a couple of times, then re-check the belt tension, and if necessary re-adjust.
10 Reconnect the battery negative lead.
11 Refit the plastic cover to the wheelarch, then refit the roadwheel and lower the vehicle to the ground.

Early models with air conditioning, but not power steering

Removal

12 Disconnect the battery negative lead.
13 Slacken the three bolts securing the tensioner pulley bracket, and turn the tensioner pulley until there is sufficient slack for the drivebelt to be removed from the pulleys (see illustration).

Refitting and adjustment

14 Fit the drivebelt around the pulleys, ensuring that the ribs on the belt are engaged

with the grooves in the pulleys, and that the drivebelt is correctly routed.
15 The belt should be tensioned so that, under firm thumb pressure, there is approximately 5.0 mm of free movement at the mid-point between the pulleys on the longest belt run.
16 To adjust the tension, with the tensioner pulley bracket bolts slackened, rotate the tensioner pulley assembly until the correct tension is achieved. Once the belt is correctly tensioned, tighten the pulley bracket securing bolts.
17 Proceed as described in paragraphs 9 to 11.

Early models with power steering, but not air conditioning

Removal

18 Disconnect the battery negative lead.
19 Slacken the two lockscrews securing the tensioner roller assembly (see illustration).
20 Turn the tensioner pulley adjuster bolt to move the tensioner pulley away from the drivebelt until there is sufficient slack for the drivebelt to be removed from the pulleys (see illustration).

Refitting and adjustment

21 Fit the drivebelt around the pulleys in the following order.
a) Power steering pump/air conditioning compressor.
b) Crankshaft.
c) Alternator.
d) Tensioner pulley.
22 Ensure that the ribs on the belt are correctly engaged with the grooves in the pulleys, and that the drivebelt is correctly routed. Take all the slack out of the belt by turning the tensioner pulley adjuster bolt.
23 The belt should be tensioned so that, under firm thumb pressure, there is approximately 5.0 mm of free movement at the mid-point between the pulleys on the longest belt run.

1.19 Slacken the two tensioner roller retaining screws (arrowed) . . .

1.20 . . . then turn the tensioner roller adjuster bolt to release the belt tensioner

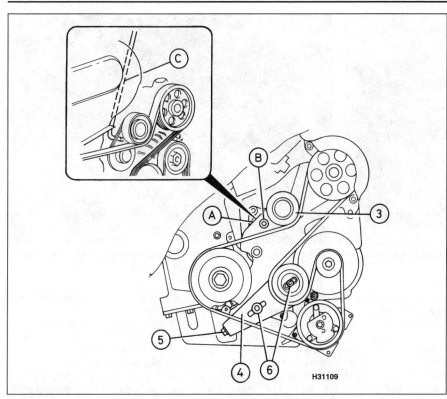

1.29 Auxiliary drivebelt arrangement on models with power steering and air conditioning

3   *Automatic tensioner pulley*
4   *Manual tensioner pulley*
5   *Adjuster screw*
6   *Lockscrews*

A and B
      Holes in tensioner pulley arm and bracket
C   Tensioner pulley locking rod

24 To adjust the tension, with the tensioner pulley assembly retaining screws slackened, rotate the adjuster bolt until the correct tension is achieved. Once the belt is correctly tensioned, tighten the pulley assembly retaining screws.

25 Proceed as described in paragraphs 9 to 11.

Later models with power steering or air conditioning

26 Proceed as described in paragraphs 18 to 25 for early models with power steering but no air conditioning.

Later models with power steering and air conditioning

Removal

27 Disconnect the battery negative lead.

28 Where applicable, remove the upper securing screw from the power steering pump pulley shield. Push the shield to one side, to allow access to the drivebelt.

29 Slacken the two lockscrews securing the manual tensioner pulley assembly **(see illustration)**.

30 Turn the manual tensioner pulley adjuster bolt to move the tensioner pulley until the holes in the automatic tensioner pulley bracket and the power steering pump bracket are aligned.

31 Lock the automatic tensioner pulley in position by inserting a suitable rod (such as a twist drill) through the holes in the automatic tensioner pulley arm and the bracket.

32 Slacken the manual tensioner pulley adjuster screw until the drivebelt can be removed from the pulleys.

Refitting and adjustment

33 Fit the drivebelt around the pulleys in the following order.
a) Power steering pump.
b) Automatic tensioner pulley.
c) Crankshaft.
d) Air conditioning compressor.
e) Alternator.
f) Manual tensioner pulley.

34 Ensure that the ribs on the belt are correctly engaged with the grooves in the pulleys, and that the drivebelt is correctly routed.

35 Tension the drivebelt by turning the manual tensioner pulley adjuster screw until the rod (see paragraph 31) begins to slide.

36 Remove the rod from the holes in the automatic tensioner pulley arm and the bracket.

37 Tighten the two lockscrews securing the manual tensioner pulley.

38 Rotate the crankshaft a couple of times, then re-check the belt tension, and if necessary re-adjust.

39 Where applicable, move the power steering pump pulley shield back into position, and refit the upper securing screw.

40 Reconnect the battery negative lead.

41 Refit the plastic cover to the wheel arch, then refit the roadwheel and lower the vehicle to the ground.

2 Brake vacuum pump drivebelt (early models) - removal and refitting

Removal

1 Slacken the pump adjuster bolt, pivot bolt and the adjuster strap lower mounting nut, then unhook the belt from the pump pulley and remove it from the engine.

Refitting and tensioning

2 Locate the new drivebelt over the camshaft drive pulley and the pump pulley.

3 Using a torque wrench, apply a torque of 5 Nm (4 lbf ft) to the adjuster nut **(see illustration)**. Maintain this torque, and tighten the bolts in the order shown (1, 2, 3, 4). Re-check the drivebelt tension, and if necessary re-adjust.

3 Engine assembly/valve timing holes - general information and usage

Note: *Do not attempt to rotate the engine whilst the crankshaft/camshaft/injection pump are locked in position. If the engine is to be left in this state for a long period of time, it is a good idea to place suitable warning notices inside the vehicle, and in the engine compartment. This will reduce the possibility of the engine being accidentally cranked on the starter motor, which is likely to cause damage with the locking pins in place.*

Note: *Three 8.0 mm diameter bolts and one*

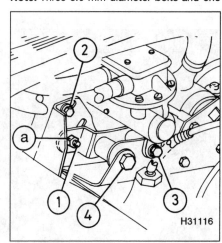

2.3 Tighten the brake vacuum pump pivot and adjuster bolts in the order shown

a Adjuster nut

13B

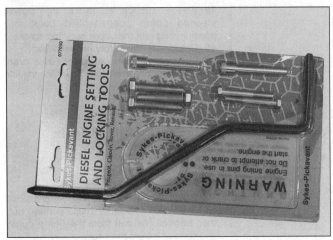

3.4a Suitable tools available for locking engine in position

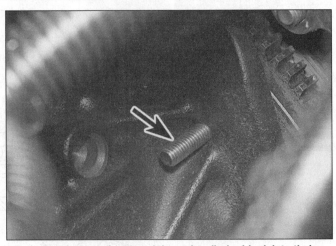

3.4b Rod (arrowed) inserted through cylinder block into timing hole in flywheel

8.0 mm diameter rod or drill will be required for this operation.

1 On all models, timing holes are drilled in the camshaft sprocket, injection pump sprocket and flywheel. The holes are used to align the crankshaft, camshaft and injection pump, and to prevent the possibility of the valves contacting the pistons when refitting the cylinder head, or when refitting the timing belt. When the holes are aligned with their corresponding holes in the cylinder head and cylinder block (as appropriate), suitable diameter bolts/pins can be inserted to lock both the camshaft, injection pump and crankshaft in position, preventing them from rotating unnecessarily. Proceed as follows. **Note:** *With the timing holes aligned, No 4 cylinder is at TDC on its compression stroke.*

2 Remove the upper timing belt covers as described in Section 6.

3 The crankshaft must now be turned until the three bolt holes in the camshaft and injection pump sprockets (one hole in the camshaft sprocket, two holes in the injection pump sprocket) are aligned with the corresponding holes in the engine front plate. The crankshaft can be turned by using a socket on the pulley bolt. To gain access to the pulley bolt, from underneath the front of the car, prise out the retaining clips and remove the screws (as applicable), then withdraw the plastic cover from the right-hand wing valance (access is easier with the car jacked up and supported on axle stands, with the roadwheel removed. Where necessary, unclip the coolant hoses from the bracket, to improve access further. The crankshaft can then be turned using a suitable socket and extension bar fitted to the pulley bolt. Note that the crankshaft must always be turned in a clockwise direction (viewed from the right-hand side of the vehicle).

4 Insert an 8 mm diameter rod or drill through the hole in the left-hand flange of the cylinder block by the starter motor; if necessary, carefully turn the crankshaft either way until the rod enters the timing hole in the flywheel **(see illustrations)**.

5 Insert three 8 mm bolts through the holes in the camshaft and fuel injection pump sprockets, and screw them into the engine finger-tight **(see illustrations)**.

6 The crankshaft, camshaft and injection pump are now locked in position, preventing unnecessary rotation.

4 Cylinder head cover - removal and refitting

Removal

1 Remove the intercooler (turbo models) or the air distribution housing (non-turbo models with a D9B engine) as described in Section 11 or 12.

2 Disconnect the breather hose from the front of the camshaft cover and, where

3.5a Bolt (arrowed) inserted through timing hole in camshaft sprocket

3.5b Bolts (arrowed) inserted through timing holes in injection pump sprocket

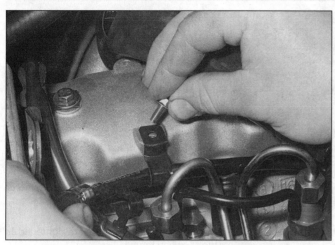

4.3 Removing the fuel hose bracket

4.4 Remove the bolts and washers . . .

necessary, remove the inlet duct from the inlet manifold.

3 Where applicable, unscrew the securing bolt and remove the fuel hose bracket from the right-hand end of the cylinder head cover **(see illustration)**.

4 Note the locations of any brackets secured by the three cylinder head cover retaining bolts, then unscrew the bolts. Recover the metal and fibre washers under each bolt **(see illustration)**.

5 Carefully move any hoses clear of the cylinder head cover.

6 Lift off the cover, and recover the rubber seal **(see illustration)**.

Refitting

7 Refitting is a reversal of removal, bearing in mind the following points:

a) *Refit any brackets in their original positions noted before removal.*
b) *Where applicable, refit the intercooler or the air distribution housing.*

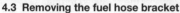

5 Crankshaft pulley -
   removal and refitting

Note: *It is advisable to use a new pulley retaining bolt on refitting.*

Removal

1 Remove the auxiliary drivebelt as described in Section 1.

2 To prevent crankshaft turning whilst the pulley retaining bolt is being slackened, select top gear and have an assistant apply the brakes firmly. **Note:** *If the engine is in the car and it proves impossible to hold on the brakes, remove the starter motor and use the locking tool shown to retain the flywheel* **(see illustration)**. *Do not* attempt to lock the pulley by inserting a bolt/drill through the timing hole. If the locking pin is in position, temporarily remove it prior to slackening the pulley bolt, then refit it once the bolt has been slackened.

3 Unscrew the retaining bolt and washer, then slide the pulley off the end of the crankshaft. If the pulley locating roll pin or Woodruff key (as applicable) is a loose fit, remove it and store it with the pulley for safe-keeping. If the pulley is a tight fit, it can be drawn off the crankshaft using a suitable puller.

Refitting

4 Ensure that the Woodruff key is correctly located in its crankshaft groove, or that the roll pin is in position (as applicable). Refit the pulley to the end of the crankshaft, aligning its locating groove or hole with the Woodruff key or pin.

5 Note: *Although not strictly necessary, it is recommended that the retaining bolt is renewed whenever it is disturbed, due to its tightening sequence (see Specifications at the start of this Chapter).* Thoroughly clean the threads of the pulley retaining bolt, then apply a coat of locking compound to the bolt

4.6 . . . and lift off the cylinder head cover

5.2 Notched tool (arrowed) positioned on ring gear teeth to lock flywheel

13B

6.3 Removing the upper front timing belt cover - early models

6.5 Removing the upper rear timing belt cover - early models

6.9 Lower timing belt cover securing bolts (arrowed)

threads. Peugeot recommend the use of Loctite (available from your Peugeot dealer); in the absence of this, any good-quality locking compound may be used.

6 Refit the crankshaft pulley retaining bolt and washer. Tighten the bolt to the specified torque, preventing the crankshaft from turning using the method employed on removal. Once the bolt has been tightened to the Stage 1 setting, angle-tighten it through the specified Stage 2 angle, using a socket and extension bar. It is recommended that an angle-measuring gauge is used during this stage of the tightening, to ensure accuracy. If a gauge is not available, use a dab of white paint to make alignment marks between the bolt and pulley prior to tightening; the marks can then be used to check that the bolt has been rotated sufficiently during tightening.

7 Refit and tension the auxiliary drivebelt as described in Section 1.

6 Timing belt covers - removal and refitting

Removal

Upper front cover - early models

1 If procedures are to be carried out which involve removal of the timing belt, remove the right-hand engine mounting-to-body bracket as described in Section 9. This will greatly improve access. Where applicable, remove the air trunking from top of the cover.

2 Release the upper spring clip from the cover.

3 Release the lower securing lug using a screwdriver, then lift the cover upwards from the engine (see illustration).

Upper rear cover - early models

4 Remove the upper front cover as described previously.

5 Release the two securing clips, manipulate the cover over the studs on the front of the engine, then withdraw the cover upwards (see illustration). Clearance is limited, and if desired, access can be improved by removing the engine mounting bracket (see Section 9).

Upper front cover - later models

6 Where applicable, remove the air trunking from the top of the cover, then slacken and remove the retaining screw and nut, and remove the cover from the engine.

Upper rear cover - later models

7 Remove the front cover as described in paragraph 6, then undo the retaining bolts and remove the rear cover from the engine.

Lower cover - early models

8 Remove the crankshaft pulley (Section 5).

9 Unscrew the two securing bolts and remove the cover (see illustration).

Lower cover - later models

10 Remove the crankshaft pulley (Section 5).

11 Remove both upper covers as described previously.

12 Slacken and remove the retaining nuts and bolts, and remove the lower cover.

Refitting

13 Refitting is a reversal of the relevant removal procedure, ensuring that each cover section is correctly located, and that the cover

retaining nuts and/or bolts are tightened to the specified torque.

7 Timing belt - removal and refitting

Removal

1 Align the engine assembly/valve timing holes as described in Section 3, and lock the camshaft sprocket, injection pump sprocket and flywheel in position. Do not attempt to rotate the engine whilst the pins are in position.

2 Remove the crankshaft pulley (Section 5).

3 Remove the right-hand engine mounting-to-body bracket as described in Section 9.

4 Loosen the timing belt tensioner pivot nut and adjustment bolt, then turn the tensioner bracket anti-clockwise to release the tension. Retighten the adjustment bolt to hold the tensioner in the released position. If available, use a 10 mm square drive extension in the hole provided to turn the tensioner bracket against the spring tension (see illustration).

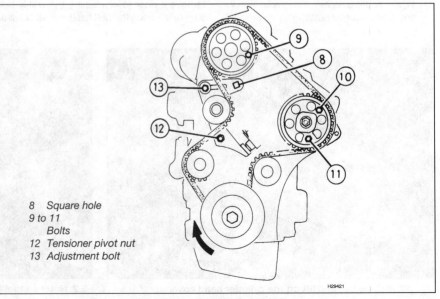

8   Square hole
9 to 11
    Bolts
12 Tensioner pivot nut
13 Adjustment bolt

7.4 Removing the timing belt

7.5a Mark the timing belt with an arrow to indicate its running direction

7.5b Removing the timing belt

5 Mark the timing belt with an arrow to indicate its running direction, if it is to be re-used. Remove the belt from the sprockets **(see illustrations)**.

Refitting

6 If signs of oil contamination are found, trace the source of the oil leak and rectify it. Wash down the engine timing belt area and all related components, to remove all traces of oil. Check that the tensioner and idler pulley rotates freely, without any sign of roughness. If necessary, renew as described in Sections 9 and 10 (as applicable).

7 Commence refitting by ensuring the 8 mm bolts are still fitted to the camshaft and fuel injection pump sprockets, and that the rod/drill is positioned in the timing hole in the flywheel.

8 Locate the timing belt on the crankshaft sprocket, making sure that, where applicable, the direction of rotation arrow is facing the correct way.

9 Engage the timing belt with the crankshaft sprocket, hold it in position, then feed the belt over the remaining sprockets in the following order:

a) *Idler roller.*
b) *Fuel injection pump.*
c) *Camshaft.*
d) *Tensioner roller.*
e) *Coolant pump.*

10 Be careful not to kink or twist the belt. To ensure correct engagement, locate only a half-width on the injection pump sprocket before feeding the timing belt onto the camshaft sprocket, keeping the belt taut and fully engaged with the crankshaft sprocket. Locate the timing belt fully onto the sprockets **(see illustration)**.

11 Unscrew and remove the bolts from the camshaft and fuel injection pump sprockets, and remove the rod/drill from the timing hole in the flywheel.

12 With the pivot nut loose, slacken the tensioner adjustment bolt while holding the bracket against the spring tension. Slowly release the bracket until the roller presses against the timing belt. Retighten the adjustment bolt and the pivot nut.

13 Rotate the crankshaft through two complete turns in the normal running direction (clockwise). Do not rotate the crankshaft backwards, as the timing belt must be kept tight between the crankshaft, fuel injection pump and camshaft sprockets.

14 Loosen the tensioner adjustment bolt and the pivot nut to allow the tensioner spring to push the roller against the timing belt, then tighten both the adjustment bolt and pivot nut to the specified torque.

15 Check that the timing holes are all correctly positioned by reinserting the sprocket locking bolts and the rod/drill in the flywheel timing hole - see Section 3. If the timing holes are not correctly positioned, the timing belt has been incorrectly fitted (possibly one tooth out on one of the sprockets) - in this case, repeat the refitting procedure from the beginning.

16 Refit the upper timing belt covers as described in Section 6, but do not lower the vehicle to the ground until the engine mounting-to-body bracket has been refitted.

17 Refit the right-hand engine mounting-to-body bracket, with reference to Section 9.

18 Refit the crankshaft pulley (see Section 5).

8 Timing belt sprockets -
removal and refitting

Camshaft sprocket

Removal

1 Remove the upper timing belt covers as described in Section 6.

2 The camshaft sprocket bolt must now be **loosened**. The camshaft must be prevented from turning as the sprocket bolt is unscrewed; this can be achieved in one of two ways, as follows **(see illustrations)**. Do not

7.10 Locate the timing belt on the sprockets as described in text

8.2a Using a home-made tool to prevent the camshaft sprocket from turning

8.2b Holding camshaft using a spanner on the lug between Nos 3 and 4 lobes

13B

8.7 Withdrawing the camshaft sprocket

8.16 Withdrawing the crankshaft sprocket

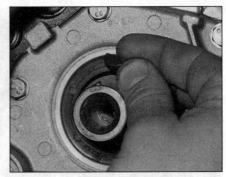

8.17 Removing the Woodruff key from the end of the crankshaft

remove the camshaft sprocket bolt at this stage.

a) *Make up a tool similar to that shown, and use it to hold the sprocket stationary by means of the holes in the sprocket.*

b) *Remove the cylinder head cover as described in Section 4. Prevent the camshaft from turning by holding it with a suitable spanner on the lug between Nos 3 and 4 camshaft lobes.*

3 Align the engine assembly/valve timing holes (see Section 3), and lock the camshaft sprocket, injection pump sprocket and flywheel in position. *Do not* attempt to rotate the engine whilst the pins are in position.

4 Loosen the timing belt tensioner pivot nut and adjustment bolt, then turn the tensioner bracket anti-clockwise to release the tension, and retighten the adjustment bolt to hold the tensioner in the released position. If available, use a 10 mm square drive extension in the hole provided to turn the tensioner bracket against the spring tension.

5 Remove the camshaft sprocket retaining bolt and washer.

6 Unscrew and remove the locking bolt from the camshaft sprocket.

7 With the retaining bolt removed, slide the sprocket off the end of the camshaft **(see illustration)**. Recover the Woodruff key if it is loose. Examine the camshaft oil seal for signs of oil leakage and, if necessary, renew it.

Refitting

8 Where applicable, refit the Woodruff key to the end of the camshaft, then refit the

camshaft sprocket. Note that the sprocket will only fit one way round (with the protruding centre boss against the camshaft), as the end of the camshaft is tapered.

9 Refit the sprocket retaining bolt and washer. Tighten the bolt to the specified torque, preventing the camshaft from turning using one of the methods described in paragraph 2.

10 Where applicable, refit the cylinder head cover as described in Section 4.

11 Align the holes in the camshaft sprocket and the engine front plate, and refit the 8 mm bolt to lock the camshaft in position.

12 Fit the timing belt around the fuel injection pump sprocket (where applicable) and the camshaft sprocket, and tension the timing belt as described in Section 7.

13 Refit the upper timing belt covers as described in Section 6.

Crankshaft sprocket

Removal

14 Remove the crankshaft pulley (Section 5).

15 Proceed as described in paragraphs 1, 3 and 4.

16 Disengage the timing belt from the crankshaft sprocket, and slide the sprocket off the end of the crankshaft **(see illustration)**.

17 Remove the Woodruff key from the crankshaft, and store it with the sprocket for safe-keeping **(see illustration)**.

18 Examine the crankshaft oil seal for signs of oil leakage and, if necessary, renew it.

Refitting

19 Refit the Woodruff key to the end of the crankshaft, then refit the crankshaft sprocket (with the flange nearest the cylinder block).

20 Fit the timing belt around the crankshaft sprocket, and tension the timing belt as described in Section 7.

21 Refit the crankshaft pulley (see Section 5).

Fuel injection pump sprocket

Removal

22 Proceed as described in paragraphs 1, 3 and 4.

23 Make alignment marks on the fuel injection pump sprocket and the timing belt, to ensure that the sprocket and timing belt are correctly aligned on refitting.

24 Remove the 8 mm bolts securing the fuel injection pump sprocket in the TDC position.

25 On certain models, the sprocket may be fitted with a built-in puller, which consists of a plate bolted to the sprocket. The plate contains a captive nut (the sprocket securing nut), which is screwed onto the fuel injection pump shaft. On models without the built-in puller, a suitable puller can be made up using a short length of bar, and two M7 bolts screwed into the holes provided in the sprocket.

26 The fuel injection pump shaft must be prevented from turning as the sprocket nut is unscrewed, and this can be achieved using a tool similar to that shown **(see illustration)**. Use the tool to hold the sprocket stationary by means of the holes in the sprocket.

27 On models with a built-in puller, unscrew the sprocket securing nut until the sprocket is freed from the taper on the pump shaft, then withdraw the sprocket. Recover the Woodruff key from the end of the pump shaft if it is loose. If desired, the puller assembly can be removed from the sprocket by removing the two securing screws and washers.

28 On models not fitted with a built-in puller, partially unscrew the sprocket securing nut, then fit the improvised puller, and tighten the two bolts (forcing the bar against the sprocket nut), until the sprocket is freed from the taper on the pump shaft **(see illustration)**. Withdraw the sprocket, and recover the

8.26 Using a home-made tool to prevent fuel injection pump sprocket from turning

8.28 Home-made puller fitted to fuel injection pump sprocket

9.5 Lifting a rubber buffer from the engine mounting

9.6 Removing the engine mounting-to-body bracket

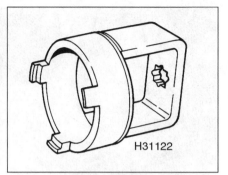

9.7a Peugeot special tool for removing and refitting right-hand engine mounting

Woodruff key from the end of the pump shaft if it is loose. Remove the puller from the sprocket.

Refitting

29 Where applicable, refit the Woodruff key to the pump shaft, ensuring that it is correctly located in its groove.

30 Where applicable, if the built-in puller assembly has been removed from the sprocket, refit it, and tighten the two securing screws to the specified torque, ensuring that the washers are in place.

31 Refit the sprocket, then tighten the securing nut to the specified torque, preventing the pump shaft from turning as during removal.

32 Make sure that the 8 mm bolts are fitted to the camshaft and fuel injection pump sprockets, and that the rod/drill is positioned in the flywheel timing hole.

33 Fit the timing belt around the fuel injection pump sprocket, ensuring that the marks made on the belt and sprocket before removal are aligned.

34 Tension the timing belt as described in Section 7.

35 Refit the upper timing belt covers as described in Section 6.

Coolant pump sprocket

36 The coolant pump sprocket is integral with the pump, and cannot be removed.

9 Timing belt tensioner - removal and refitting

General

1 The timing belt tensioner is operated by a spring and plunger housed in the right-hand engine mounting bracket, which is bolted to the end face of the engine. The engine mounting is attached to the mounting on the body via the engine mounting-to-body bracket.

Right-hand engine mounting-to-body bracket

Removal

2 Before removing the bracket, the engine must be supported, preferably using a suitable hoist and lifting tackle attached to the lifting bracket at the right-hand end of the engine. Alternatively, the engine can be supported using a trolley jack and interposed block of wood beneath the sump, in which case, be prepared for the engine to tilt backwards when the bracket is removed.

3 Release the retaining clips, and position all the relevant hoses and cables clear of the engine mounting assembly and suspension top mounting.

4 Where applicable, unscrew the two retaining bolts, and remove the plate from the

top of the mounting damper bolted to the body above the mounting.

5 Where applicable, unscrew the securing nut, then lift out (or unscrew) the rubber buffer to expose the engine mounting bracket-to-body securing nut **(see illustration)**.

6 Unscrew the three nuts securing the bracket to the engine mounting, and the single nut securing the bracket to the body, then lift off the bracket **(see illustration)**.

7 To remove the rubber mounting, first lift off the buffer bracket, where applicable, then unscrew the mounting from the body. **Note:** *On certain models, if the mounting is to be removed, a special tool is needed to unscrew it from the wing panel, and for refitting and tightening* **(see illustrations)**.

Refitting

8 Refitting is a reversal of removal. Tighten the retaining nuts and bolts (where applicable) to the specified torque.

Timing belt tensioner and right-hand engine mounting bracket

Note: *A suitable tool will be required to retain the timing belt tensioner plunger during this operation.*

Removal

9 Remove the engine mounting-to-body bracket as described previously, and remove the auxiliary drivebelt (see Section 1).

9.7b Improvised special tool for removing engine mounting

9.7c Using the tool . . .

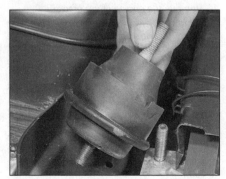

9.7d . . . to unscrew the engine mounting

13B

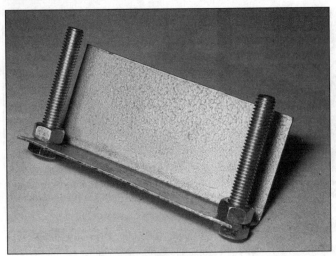

9.15 Fabricated tool for holding tensioner plunger in engine mounting bracket

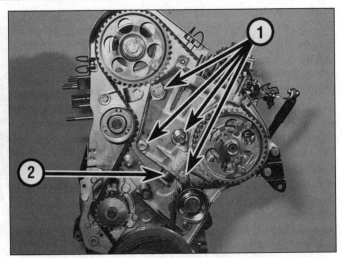

9.16a View of timing belt end of engine

1   Engine mounting bracket retaining bolts
2   Timing belt tensioner plunger

9.16b Tool in place to hold tensioner plunger in engine mounting bracket - timing belt removed for clarity

10 On models where the right-hand engine lifting bracket is attached to the right-hand engine mounting bracket, proceed as follows.
a) *If not already done, support the engine with a trolley jack and interposed block of wood beneath the sump.*
b) *Disconnect the hoist and lifting tackle supporting the engine from the right-hand lifting bracket.*
c) *Unscrew the two retaining bolts and remove the engine lifting bracket.*

11 Align the engine assembly/valve timing holes as described in Section 3, and lock the camshaft sprocket, injection pump sprocket and flywheel in position. *Do not* rotate the engine whilst the pins are in position.

12 Loosen the timing belt tensioner pivot nut and adjustment bolt, then turn the tensioner bracket anti-clockwise until the adjustment bolt is in the middle of the slot, and retighten the adjustment bolt. If available, use a 10 mm square drive extension in the hole provided to turn the tensioner bracket against the spring tension.

13 Mark the timing belt with an arrow to indicate its running direction, if it is to

be re-used. Remove the belt from the sprockets.

14 A tool must now be obtained in order to hold the tensioner plunger in the engine mounting bracket.

15 The Peugeot tool is designed to slide in the two lower bolt holes of the mounting bracket. It should be straightforward to fabricate a similar tool out of sheet metal, and using 10 mm bolts and nuts instead of metal dowel rods **(see illustration)**.

16 Unscrew the two lower engine mounting bracket bolts, then fit the special tool **(see illustrations)**. Grease the inner surface of the tool, to prevent any damage to the end of the tensioner plunger. Unscrew the pivot nut and adjustment bolt, and withdraw the tensioner assembly.

17 Remove the two remaining engine mounting bracket bolts, and withdraw the bracket.

18 Compress the tensioner plunger into the engine mounting bracket, remove the special tool, then withdraw the plunger and spring.

Refitting

19 Refitting is a reversal of removal, bearing in mind the following points:
a) *Tighten all fixings to the specified torque.*
b) *Refit and tension the timing belt as described in Section 7.*
c) *Refit and tighten the auxiliary drivebelt as described in Section 1.*

10 Timing belt idler roller - removal and refitting

Removal

1 Remove the auxiliary drivebelt as described in Section 1.

2 Align the engine assembly/valve timing holes as described in Section 3, and lock the camshaft sprocket, injection pump sprocket and flywheel in position. *Do not* attempt to rotate the engine whilst the pins are in position.

3 Loosen the timing belt tensioner pivot nut and adjustment bolt, then turn the tensioner bracket anti-clockwise to release the tension, and retighten the adjustment bolt to hold the tensioner in the released position. If available, use a 10 mm square drive extension in the hole provided to turn the tensioner bracket against the spring tension.

4 Unscrew the two bolts and the stud securing the idler roller assembly to the cylinder block, noting that the upper bolt also secures the engine mounting bracket.

5 Slightly loosen the remaining four engine mounting bolts, noting that the uppermost bolt is on the inside face of the engine front plate, and also secures the engine lifting bracket. Slide out the idler roller assembly.

Refitting

6 Refitting is a reversal of removal, bearing in mind the following points:
a) *Tighten all fixings to the specified torque.*
b) *Tension the timing belt as described in Section 7.*
c) *Refit and tension the auxiliary drivebelt as described in Section 1.*

11 Intercooler - removal and refitting

Removal

1 Lift the rubber surround/seal from the top of the intercooler.

2 Disconnect the air inlet tubing from the

11.2 Disconnect the air inlet tubing (arrowed)

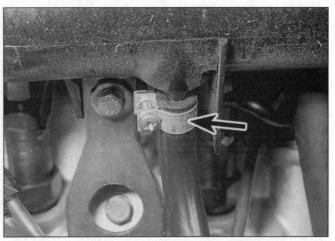

11.3 Disconnect the small hose (arrowed) from the front edge of the intercooler

right-hand end of the intercooler **(see illustration)**.

3 Disconnect the small hose from the front edge of the intercooler **(see illustration)**.

4 Where applicable, disconnect the two hoses from the valve clipped to the left-hand end of the intercooler **(see illustration)**.

5 Unscrew the two or three (as applicable) front intercooler bolts **(see illustration)**.

6 Unscrew the two or three (as applicable) rear intercooler bolts **(see illustration)**.

7 Lift the intercooler from the engine, and recover the sealing ring from the manifold joint if it is loose **(see illustrations)**.

Refitting

8 Before refitting, check that the intercooler fins are clear, and if necessary remove any debris using a soft brush. Check the manifold sealing ring, and renew if necessary.

9 Refitting is a reversal of removal.

11.4 Disconnect the two hoses from the valve at the left-hand end of the intercooler

11.5 Unscrewing a front intercooler securing bolt

11.6 Rear intercooler securing bolts (arrowed)

11.7a Lift the intercooler from the engine . . .

11.7b . . . and recover the sealing ring

13B

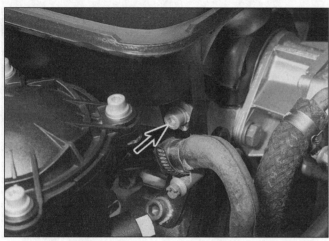

12.2 Front air distribution housing securing bolt (arrowed)

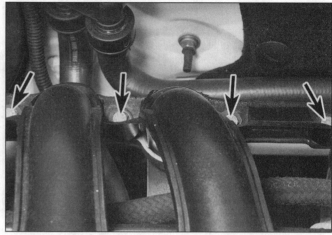

12.3 Air distribution housing-to-inlet manifold bolts (arrowed)

12 Air distribution housing (non-turbo models with D9B engine) - removal and refitting

Removal

1 Disconnect the air hose and the crankcase breather hose from the front of the air distribution housing.

2 Unscrew the two bolts securing the housing to the front mounting brackets **(see illustration)**. Recover the spacer plates.

3 Unscrew the four bolts securing the housing to the inlet manifold. Recover the washers **(see illustration)**.

4 Lift the housing from the inlet manifold, and recover the seals.

Refitting

5 Refitting is a reversal of removal, but examine the condition of the seals and renew if necessary.

Chapter 14A
Peugeot 406 petrol 1996 to 1997

Contents

Specifications

Timing belt renewal interval . . . .   Every 36 000 miles (60 000 km)

Note: *Although the normal interval for timing belt renewal is 72 000 miles (120 000 km), it is strongly recommended that the interval is halved on vehicles which are subjected to intensive use, ie, mainly short journeys or a lot of stop-start driving. The actual belt renewal interval is therefore very much up to the individual owner. That being said, it is highly recommended to err on the side of safety, and renew the belt at this earlier interval, bearing in mind the drastic consequences resulting from belt failure.*

Torque wrench settings	Nm	lbf ft
Auxiliary drivebelt tensioner assembly retaining bolts:		
Models with air conditioning	20	15
Models without air conditioning:		
1.6 and 1.8 litre engines	30	22
2.0 litre engines	20	15
Roadwheel bolts	90	66
1.6 litre engines		
Camshaft sprocket retaining bolt	35	26
Crankshaft pulley retaining bolt	120	89
Engine/transmission left-hand mounting:		
Centre nut	65	48
Mounting bracket-to-body	30	22
Mounting stud bracket-to-transmission	60	44
Mounting stud-to-transmission	60	44
Rubber mounting-to-bracket bolts	30	22
Engine/transmission right-hand mounting:		
Bracket-to-engine bolts	45	33
Mounting bracket retaining nuts	45	33
Rubber mounting-to-body nut	40	30
Upper engine movement limiter bolts	50	37
Timing belt cover bolts	8	6
Timing belt tensioner pulley bolt	20	15

14

Torque wrench settings (continued)

	Nm	lbf ft
1.8 and 2.0 litre engines		
Camshaft sprocket hub-to-camshaft retaining bolts	75	55
Camshaft sprocket-to-hub retaining bolts	10	7
Crankshaft pulley retaining bolt	120	89
Engine/transmission left-hand mounting:		
Centre nut	65	48
Mounting bracket-to-body	30	22
Mounting stud bracket-to-transmission	60	44
Mounting stud-to-transmission	60	44
Rubber mounting-to-bracket bolts	30	22
Engine/transmission right-hand mounting:		
1.8 litre engines:		
Mounting bracket-to-engine bolts	60	44
Mounting bracket-to-engine nuts	45	33
Mounting bracket-to-rubber mounting nut	45	33
Rubber mounting-to-body nut	40	30
Upper engine movement limiter bolts	50	37
2.0 litre engines:		
Mounting bracket-to-engine nuts/bolts	80	59
Mounting bracket-to-rubber mounting nut	45	33
Rubber mounting-to-body nut	40	30
Upper engine movement limiter bolts	50	37
Timing belt cover bolts	8	6
Timing belt tensioner pulley bolt	20	15

---

1 Auxiliary drivebelt - removal, refitting and adjustment

Note: *Depending on model and equipment fitted, access to the auxiliary drivebelt can be extremely limited. Where necessary, greater working clearance can be gained by removing the fuel injection/ignition electronic control unit (ECU) and its mounting box (Section 8).*

1 Apply the handbrake, then jack up the front of the car and support it on axle stands. Remove the right-hand front roadwheel.

2 Release the screws and clips and remove the wheelarch liner from under the right-hand front wing for access to the crankshaft pulley bolt. Where fitted, also remove the splash guard from under the front of the engine.

Models without air conditioning
Removal
3 Disconnect the battery negative lead.
4 Slacken the two bolts securing the tensioning pulley assembly to the engine **(see illustrations)**.

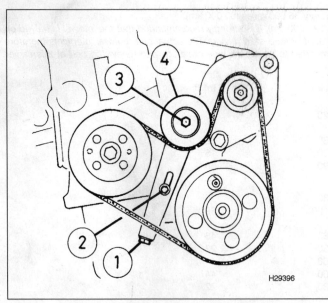

1.4a Auxiliary drivebelt adjustment details (1.6 and 1.8 litre models without air conditioning)
1 Adjuster bolt
2 Tensioning pulley assembly lower securing bolt
3 Tensioning pulley assembly upper retaining bolt
4 Tensioning pulley

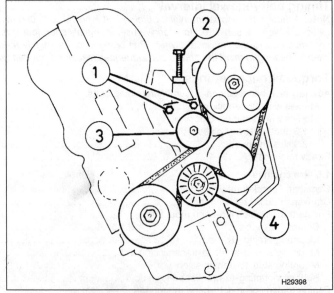

1.4b Auxiliary drivebelt adjustment details (2.0 litre models without air conditioning)
1 Tensioning pulley assembly securing bolts
2 Adjuster bolt
3 Tensioning pulley
4 Idler pulley

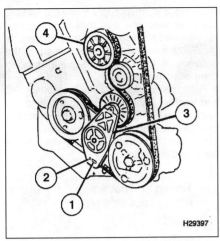

1.13 Auxiliary drivebelt adjustment details (models with air conditioning)

1 Tensioner arm square-section end
2 Setting hole (for 4.0 mm Allen key)
3 Tensioner arm
4 Idler pulley

5 Rotate the adjuster bolt to move the tensioner pulley away from the drivebelt until there is sufficient slack for the drivebelt to be removed from the pulleys.

Refitting

6 Fit the drivebelt around the pulleys in the following order:

a) Power steering pump.
b) Crankshaft.
c) Alternator.
d) Idler pulley (2.0 litre models).
e) Tensioner pulley.

7 Ensure that the ribs on the belt are correctly engaged with the grooves in the pulleys, and that the drivebelt is correctly routed. Take all the slack out of the belt by turning the tensioner pulley adjuster bolt. Tension the belt as follows.

Adjustment

8 The belt should be tensioned so that, under firm thumb pressure, there is about 5.0 mm of free movement at the mid-point between the pulleys on the longest belt run.

2.6 8 mm diameter drill inserted through the crankshaft pulley timing hole

9 To adjust the tension, with the two tensioner pulley assembly retaining bolts slackened, rotate the adjuster bolt until the correct tension is achieved. Once the belt is correctly tensioned, rotate the crankshaft four complete revolutions in the normal direction of rotation and recheck the tension.

10 When the belt is correctly tensioned, tighten the tensioner pulley assembly retaining bolts to the specified torque, then reconnect the battery negative lead.

11 Refit the wheelarch liner and, where fitted, the engine splash guard. Refit the roadwheel, and lower the car to the ground.

Models with air conditioning

Removal

12 Disconnect the battery negative lead.

13 Move the tensioner pulley away from the drivebelt, using a ratchet handle or extension bar with the same size square-section end as the hole in the base of the automatic tensioner arm **(see illustration)**. Once the tensioner is released, retain it in the released position by inserting a 4.0 mm Allen key in the hole provided. Disengage the drivebelt from all the pulleys, noting its correct routing. Remove the drivebelt from the engine, noting that in some cases, it may be necessary to slacken the automatic tensioner mounting bolts to disengage the belt from behind the tensioner pulley.

Refitting and adjustment

14 Fit the drivebelt around the pulleys in the following order:

a) Automatic tensioner pulley.
b) Crankshaft.
c) Air conditioning compressor.
d) Power steering pump.
e) Idler pulley
f) Alternator.

15 Where necessary, securely tighten the automatic tensioner mounting bolts to the specified torque.

16 Ensure that the ribs on the belt are correctly engaged with the grooves in the pulleys. Take the load off the tensioner arm and remove the Allen key. Release the tensioner

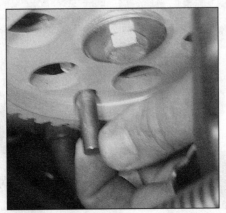

2.7 9.5 mm diameter drill inserted through the camshaft pulley timing hole

arm; the tensioner is spring-loaded, removing the need to manually adjust the belt tension.

17 Reconnect the battery negative lead.

18 Refit the wheelarch liner and, where fitted, the engine splash guard. Refit the roadwheel, and lower the vehicle to the ground.

---

2 Engine assembly/valve timing holes - general information and usage

Note: *Do not attempt to rotate the engine whilst the crankshaft/camshaft are locked in position. If the engine is to be left in this state for a long period of time, it is a good idea to place suitable warning notices inside the vehicle, and in the engine compartment. This will reduce the possibility of the engine being accidentally cranked on the starter motor, which is likely to cause damage with the locking pins in place.*

1 On all models, timing holes are drilled in the camshaft sprocket(s) and crankshaft pulley. The holes are used to align the crankshaft and camshaft, to prevent the possibility of the valves contacting the pistons when refitting the timing belt. When the holes are aligned with their corresponding holes in the cylinder head and cylinder block (as appropriate), suitable diameter pins can be inserted to lock both the camshaft and crankshaft in position. Proceed as follows:

2 Remove the timing belt upper cover with reference to Section 4.

3 Jack up the front of the car and support it on axle stands. Remove the right-hand front roadwheel.

4 From underneath the front of the car, unscrew the bolts and prise out the clips securing the plastic cover to the inner wing valance. Remove the cover to gain access to the crankshaft pulley bolt. The crankshaft can then be turned using a suitable socket and extension bar fitted to the pulley bolt. Note that the crankshaft must always be turned in a clockwise direction (viewed from the right-hand side of vehicle).

1.6 litre models

5 Rotate the crankshaft pulley until the timing hole in the camshaft sprocket is aligned with its corresponding hole in the cylinder head. Note that the holes are aligned when the sprocket hole is in the 8 o'clock position, when viewed from the right-hand end of the engine.

6 With the camshaft sprocket timing hole correctly positioned, insert an 8 mm diameter bolt or drill through the timing hole (8 mm diameter) in the crankshaft pulley, and locate it in the corresponding hole in the end of the cylinder block **(see illustration)**. Note that it may be necessary to rotate the crankshaft slightly, to get the holes to align.

7 Once the crankshaft pulley is locked in position, insert a 9.5 mm diameter bolt or drill through the camshaft sprocket hole and locate it in the cylinder head **(see illustration)**.

14

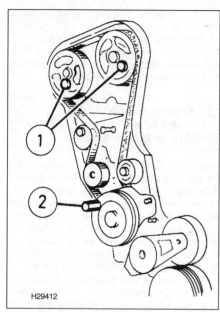

2.11 Camshaft sprocket timing holes (1) and crankshaft pulley timing hole (2) locked with suitable timing pins - 1.8 and 2.0 litre models

8 The crankshaft and camshaft are now locked in position, preventing rotation.

1.8 and 2.0 litre models

9 Rotate the crankshaft pulley until the timing holes in both camshafts are aligned with their corresponding holes in the cylinder head. The holes are aligned when the inlet camshaft sprocket hole is in approximately the 5 o'clock position and the exhaust camshaft sprocket hole is in approximately the 7 o'clock position, when viewed from the right-hand end of the engine.

10 With the camshaft sprocket holes correctly positioned, insert a 6 mm diameter bolt or drill through the timing hole in the crankshaft pulley, and locate it in the corresponding hole in the end of the engine.

Note that the hole size may vary according to the type of pulley fitted and auxiliary drivebelt arrangement. If the bolt or drill is not a snug fit, try a larger size until a good fit is achieved in both the pulley and cylinder block.

11 With the crankshaft locked in position, insert a suitable bolt or drill through the timing hole in each camshaft sprocket and locate it in the cylinder head (see illustration).

12 The crankshaft and camshafts are now locked in position, preventing rotation.

3 Crankshaft pulley - removal and refitting

Removal

1 Remove the auxiliary drivebelt (Section 1).

2 To prevent the crankshaft turning whilst the pulley retaining bolt is being slackened, select 4th gear and have an assistant apply the brakes firmly. *Do not* attempt to lock the pulley by inserting a bolt/drill through the timing hole. If the locking pin is in position, temporarily remove it prior to slackening the pulley bolt, then refit it once the bolt has been slackened.

3 Unscrew the retaining bolt and washer, then slide the pulley off the end of the crankshaft (see illustrations). If the pulley locating roll pin or Woodruff key (as applicable) is a loose fit, remove it and store it with the pulley for safe-keeping. If the pulley is a tight fit, it can be drawn off the crankshaft using a suitable puller.

Refitting

4 Ensure that the Woodruff key is correctly located in its crankshaft groove, or that the roll pin is in position (as applicable). Refit the pulley to the end of the crankshaft, aligning its locating groove or hole with the Woodruff key or pin.

5 Thoroughly clean the threads of the pulley

retaining bolt, then apply a coat of locking compound to the bolt threads. Peugeot recommend the use of Loctite Frenetanche (available from your Peugeot dealer); in the absence of this, any good-quality locking compound may be used.

6 Refit the crankshaft pulley retaining bolt and washer. Tighten the bolt to the specified torque, preventing the crankshaft from turning using the method employed on removal.

7 Refit and tension the auxiliary drivebelt as described in Section 1.

4 Timing belt covers - removal and refitting

Removal - 1.6 litre models

Upper cover

1 Release the retaining clips, and free the fuel hoses from the top of the cover.

2 Undo the two cover retaining bolts (situated at the base of the cover), and remove the cover from the engine compartment.

Centre cover

3 Slacken and remove the two cover retaining bolts (located directly beneath the mounting bracket). Move the cover upwards to free it from the two locating pins situated at the base of the cover, and remove it from the engine compartment.

Lower cover

4 Remove the crankshaft pulley as described in Section 3.

5 Remove the centre cover as described in paragraph 3.

6 Undo the two cover retaining bolts, and remove the cover from the engine. Note that on some models it may be necessary to unbolt the auxiliary drivebelt tensioner assembly and remove it from the engine in order to allow the cover to be removed.

3.3a Removing the crankshaft pulley retaining bolt

3.3b Removing the crankshaft pulley from the end of the crankshaft

Removal - 1.8 and 2.0 litre models

Upper (outer) cover

7 Undo the upper and lower retaining bolts securing the outer cover to the inner cover. Slide the cover retaining clip upwards to release it from its fasteners.

8 Ease the outer cover upwards and away from the engine, freeing it from its lower locations.

Lower cover

9 Remove the crankshaft pulley as described in Section 3.

10 Remove the upper (outer) cover as described above.

11 Slacken and remove the three retaining bolts, then remove the lower timing belt cover from the engine. Note that on some models it may be necessary to unbolt the auxiliary drivebelt tensioner assembly and remove it from the engine in order to allow the cover to be removed.

Upper (inner) cover

12 Remove the timing belt as described in Section 5.

13 Remove both camshaft sprockets as described in Section 6.

14 Remove the bolts securing the cover to the side of the cylinder head, and remove the cover from the engine.

Refitting - all models

15 Refitting is a reversal of the relevant removal procedure, ensuring that each cover section is correctly located, and that the cover retaining bolts are securely tightened to the specified torque.

---

5 Timing belt - removal and refitting

Note: *Peugeot specify the use of a special electronic tool (SEEM C105.5) to correctly set the timing belt tension.*

Removal

1.6 litre models

1 Disconnect the battery negative terminal.

2 Jack up the front of the vehicle and support it on axle stands. Remove the right-hand front wheel.

3 Prise out the clips and unbolt the inner splash guard.

4 Remove the auxiliary drivebelt as described in Section 1. Also unbolt and remove the auxiliary drivebelt tensioner.

5 Unbolt and remove the upper timing belt cover as described in Section 4.

6 Align the engine assembly/valve timing holes as described in Section 2, and lock the camshaft sprocket and crankshaft pulley in position. *Do not* attempt to rotate the engine whilst the pins are in position.

7 Remove the crankshaft pulley (Section 3).

8 Remove the centre and lower timing belt covers as described in Section 4.

9 Loosen the timing belt tensioner pulley retaining bolt. Pivot the pulley in a clockwise direction, using a suitable square-section key fitted to the hole in the pulley hub, then securely retighten the retaining bolt.

10 If the timing belt is to be re-used, use white paint or chalk to mark the direction of rotation on the belt (if markings do not already exist), then slip the belt off the sprockets. Note that the crankshaft must not be rotated whilst the belt is removed.

11 If signs of oil contamination are found, trace the source of the oil leak and rectify it. Wash down the engine timing belt area and all related components, to remove all traces of oil.

1.8 and 2.0 litre models

12 Disconnect the battery negative terminal.

13 Align the engine assembly/valve timing holes as described in Section 2, and lock the camshaft sprockets and crankshaft pulley in position. *Do not* attempt to rotate the engine whilst the pins are in position.

14 Remove the timing belt upper (outer) and lower covers as described in Section 4.

15 Move the engine wiring harness clear of the working area as necessary. This will entail the disconnection of certain connectors, and the removal of the harness from various cable clips and supports. Label any disconnected wiring and components as an aid to refitting.

16 Support the engine on a jack and remove the right-hand engine mounting components as described in Section 7.

17 Loosen the timing belt rear tensioner pulley retaining bolt and pivot the pulley in a clockwise direction, using a suitable square-section key fitted to the hole in the pulley hub, then retighten the retaining bolt.

18 Check that the camshaft sprocket locking pins are still in position, then remove and inspect the belt as described in paragraphs 10 and 11.

Refitting

1.6 litre models

19 Before refitting, thoroughly clean the timing belt sprockets. Check that the tensioner pulley rotates freely, without any sign of roughness. If necessary, renew the tensioner pulley as described in Section 6.

20 Ensure that the camshaft sprocket locking pin is still in position. Temporarily refit the crankshaft pulley, and insert the locking pin through the pulley timing hole to ensure that the crankshaft is still correctly positioned.

21 Remove the crankshaft pulley. Manoeuvre the timing belt into position, ensuring that any arrows on the belt are pointing in the direction of rotation (clockwise when viewed from the right-hand end of the engine).

22 Do not twist the timing belt sharply while refitting it. Fit the belt over the crankshaft and camshaft sprockets. Ensure that the belt front

run is taut - ie, any slack should be on the tensioner pulley side of the belt. Fit the belt over the water pump sprocket and tensioner pulley. Ensure that the belt teeth are seated centrally in the sprockets.

23 Temporarily refit the crankshaft pulley at this stage and tighten the bolt moderately, then refit the locking pin. **Note:** *The timing belt is tensioned with the timing covers removed, then the pulley is removed to fit the covers and finally refitted.*

24 Loosen the tensioner pulley retaining bolt. Using the square-section key, pivot the pulley anti-clockwise to remove all free play from the timing belt.

25 Fit the special belt tension measuring equipment to the front run of the timing belt. The tensioner roller should be adjusted so that the initial belt tension is 30 ± 2 units.

26 Remove the locking pins, then rotate the crankshaft through two complete rotations in a clockwise direction (viewed from the right-hand end of the engine). Realign the camshaft and crankshaft engine assembly/valve timing holes (see Section 2). *Do not* at any time rotate the crankshaft anti-clockwise. Both camshaft and crankshaft timing holes should be aligned so that the locking pins can be easily inserted. This indicates that the valve timing is correct. If all is well, remove the pins.

27 If the timing holes are not correctly positioned, repeat the fitting procedure so far.

28 Rotate the crankshaft two more turns without turning it backwards, then refit the camshaft locking pin, then check that the final belt tension on the taut front run of the belt is 44 ± 2 units. If not, repeat the complete fitting procedure.

29 With the belt tension correctly set, remove the camshaft locking pin, then remove the crankshaft pulley and refit the timing cover(s).

30 Refit the crankshaft pulley but this time apply locking fluid to the threads of the bolt before inserting it. Tighten the bolt to the specified torque and refer to Section 3 if necessary.

31 Refit the auxiliary drivebelt tensioner then refit and tension the drivebelt with reference to Section 1.

32 Refit the inner splash guard and front right-hand wheel, then lower the vehicle to the ground.

33 Reconnect the battery negative terminal.

1.8 and 2.0 litre models

34 Before refitting, thoroughly clean the timing belt sprockets. Check that the tensioner pulley rotates freely, without any sign of roughness. If necessary, renew the tensioner pulley as described in Section 6.

35 Ensure that the camshaft sprocket locking pin is still in position. Temporarily refit the crankshaft pulley, and insert the locking pin through the pulley timing hole to ensure that the crankshaft is still correctly positioned.

36 Remove the crankshaft pulley. Manoeuvre the timing belt into position on the crankshaft sprocket, ensuring that any arrows on the belt

14

are pointing in the direction of rotation (clockwise when viewed from the right-hand end of the engine).

37 Refit the timing belt lower cover and the crankshaft pulley (Sections 4 and 3).

38 Refit the locking pin to the crankshaft pulley.

39 Without removing the locking pins, slacken the camshaft sprocket retaining bolts (three on each sprocket). Check that both sprockets are free to turn within the limits of their elongated bolt holes.

40 Tighten the camshaft sprocket retaining bolts finger tight, then slacken them all by one sixth of a turn.

41 Turn each sprocket clockwise to the ends of their retaining bolt slots.

42 With the timing belt engaged with the crankshaft sprocket, keep it tight on its right-hand run and engage it with the front idler pulley then up and into engagement with the inlet camshaft sprocket.

43 Keeping the belt tight and rotating the inlet camshaft sprocket anti-clockwise as necessary, feed the belt over the exhaust camshaft sprocket, taking care not to let the belt jump a tooth on the crankshaft sprocket as it is being fitted.

44 While still keeping the belt tight, feed it over the rear tensioner pulley and finally around the coolant pump.

45 Fit the special belt tension measuring equipment to the front run of the timing belt. The tensioner pulley should be adjusted by turning it anti-clockwise to give a belt pre-tensioning setting of 45 units. Hold the tensioner pulley in this position and tighten the retaining bolt to the specified torque.

46 Remove one retaining bolt from each camshaft sprocket and check that the sprockets are not at the end of their retaining bolt slots. If they are, repeat the refitting operation. If all is satisfactory, refit the two removed bolts, and tighten the sprocket retaining bolts to the specified torque.

47 Remove the locking pins, then rotate the crankshaft through two complete rotations in a clockwise direction (viewed from the right-hand end of the engine). Realign the crankshaft engine assembly/valve timing hole and refit the locking pin to the crankshaft pulley.

48 Slacken the camshaft sprocket retaining bolts, retighten them finger tight, then slacken them all by one sixth of a turn.

49 Refit the camshaft sprocket locking pins, then slacken the tensioner pulley retaining bolt once more. Refit the belt tension measuring equipment to the front run of the belt and turn the tensioner pulley to give an initial setting of 26 units on the tensioning gauge. Hold the tensioner pulley in this position and tighten the retaining bolt to the specified torque.

50 Retighten the sprocket retaining bolts to the specified torque.

51 Remove the locking pins, then rotate the crankshaft once again through two complete rotations in a clockwise direction. Realign the crankshaft engine assembly/valve timing hole and refit the locking pin to the crankshaft pulley.

52 Slacken the camshaft sprocket retaining bolts, retighten them finger tight, then slacken them all by one sixth of a turn.

53 Refit the camshaft sprocket locking pins, then slacken the tensioner pulley retaining bolt once more. Refit the belt tension measuring equipment to the front run of the belt and turn the tensioner pulley to give a final setting of between 32 and 40 units on the tensioning gauge. Hold the tensioner pulley in this position and tighten the retaining bolt to the specified torque.

54 Retighten the sprocket retaining bolts to the specified torque.

55 Once the belt tension has been correctly set, refit the right-hand engine mounting components as described in Section 7, and reconnect all the disconnected engine wiring.

56 Refit the timing belt upper (outer) and lower covers as described in Section 4, and reconnect the battery negative terminal.

---

6 Timing belt tensioner and sprockets - removal and refitting

Note: *This Section describes the removal and refitting of the components concerned as individual operations - if more than one is to be removed at the same time, start by removing the timing belt as described in Section 5; remove the actual component as described below, ignoring the preliminary dismantling steps.*

Removal

1 Disconnect the battery negative terminal.

2 Align the engine assembly/valve timing holes as described in Section 2, locking the camshaft sprocket(s) and the crankshaft pulley in position, and proceed as described under the relevant sub-heading. *Do not attempt to rotate the engine whilst the pins are in position.*

Camshaft sprocket - 1.6 litre models

3 Remove the upper timing belt cover as described in Section 4.

4 Loosen the timing belt tensioner pulley retaining bolt. Rotate the pulley in a clockwise direction, using a suitable square-section key fitted to the hole in the pulley hub, then retighten the retaining bolt.

5 Remove the locking pin from the camshaft sprocket. Disengage the timing belt from the sprocket and position it clear, taking care not to bend or twist the belt sharply.

6 Slacken the camshaft sprocket retaining bolt and remove it, along with its washer. To prevent the camshaft rotating as the bolt is slackened, a sprocket holding tool will be required. In the absence of the special Peugeot tool, an acceptable substitute can be fabricated at home **(see illustration)**. *Do*

attempt to use the sprocket locking pin to prevent the sprocket from rotating whilst the bolt is slackened.

7 With the retaining bolt removed, slide the sprocket off the end of the camshaft. If the locating peg is a loose fit in the rear of the sprocket, remove it for safe-keeping. Examine the camshaft oil seal for signs of oil leakage and, if necessary, renew it.

Camshaft sprockets - 1.8 and 2.0 litre models

8 Remove the timing belt upper (outer) and lower covers as described in Section 4.

9 Move the engine wiring harness clear of the working area as necessary. This will entail the disconnection of certain connectors, and the removal of the harness from various cable clips and supports. Label any disconnected wiring and components as an aid to refitting.

10 Support the engine on a jack and remove the right-hand engine mounting components as described in Section 7.

11 Loosen the timing belt rear tensioner pulley retaining bolt and pivot the pulley in a clockwise direction, using a suitable square-section key fitted to the hole in the pulley hub, then retighten the retaining bolt.

12 Check that the camshaft sprocket locking pins are still in position, then disengage the timing belt from the camshaft sprockets and position it clear, taking care not to bend or twist the belt sharply.

13 If the sprockets are to be removed without their hubs, undo the three retaining bolts and remove the relevant sprocket. Suitably mark the sprockets 'inlet' and/or 'exhaust' as they are removed.

14 If both the sprockets and the hubs are to be removed, remove the sprocket locking pins, then slacken the sprocket hub centre retaining bolt. To prevent the sprockets rotating as the bolt is slackened, a sprocket holding tool will be required. In the absence of the special Peugeot tool, an acceptable substitute can be fabricated at home **(see illustration 6.6)**. *Do not* attempt to use the

6.6 Using a home-made tool to retain the camshaft sprocket whilst the sprocket retaining bolt is loosened

sprocket locking pin to prevent the sprocket from rotating whilst the bolt is slackened.

15 Undo the three retaining bolts and remove the relevant sprocket. Remove the previously slackened hub retaining bolt and withdraw the hub from the end of the camshaft. Note that the hubs are marked for identification with a single digit on their front face. On 1.8 litre models, the inlet hub is marked 1 and the exhaust hub is marked 2. On 2.0 litre models the inlet hub is marked 3 and the exhaust hub is marked 4.

Crankshaft sprocket - 1.6 litre models

16 Remove the upper, centre and/or lower timing belt cover(s) (as applicable) as described in Section 4.

17 Loosen the timing belt tensioner pulley retaining bolt. Rotate the pulley in a clockwise direction, using a suitable square-section key fitted to the hole in the pulley hub, then retighten the retaining bolt.

18 Disengage the timing belt from the crankshaft sprocket, and slide the sprocket off the end of the crankshaft. Remove the Woodruff key from the crankshaft, and store it with the sprocket for safe-keeping. Where necessary, also slide the spacer (where fitted) off the end of the crankshaft.

19 Examine the crankshaft oil seal for signs of oil leakage and, if necessary, renew it.

Crankshaft sprocket - 1.8 and 2.0 litre models

20 Remove the timing belt upper (outer) and lower covers as described in Section 4.

21 Move the engine wiring harness clear of the working area as necessary. This will entail the disconnection of certain connectors, and the removal of the harness from various cable clips and supports. Label any disconnected wiring and components as an aid to refitting.

22 Support the engine on a jack and remove the right-hand engine mounting components as described in Section 7.

23 Loosen the timing belt rear tensioner pulley retaining bolt and pivot the pulley in a clockwise direction, using a suitable square-section key fitted to the hole in the pulley hub, then retighten the retaining bolt.

24 Check that the camshaft sprocket locking pins are still in position, then disengage the timing belt from the crankshaft sprocket and slide the sprocket off the end of the crankshaft. Remove the Woodruff key from the crankshaft, and store it with the sprocket for safe-keeping.

25 Examine the crankshaft oil seal for signs of oil leakage and, if necessary, renew it.

Tensioner pulley - 1.6 litre models

26 Remove the upper and, where necessary, the centre timing belt covers as described in Section 4.

27 Slacken and remove the timing belt tensioner pulley retaining bolt, and slide the pulley off its mounting stud. Examine the mounting stud for signs of damage and if necessary, renew it.

Tensioner and idler pulleys - 1.8 and 2.0 litre models

28 Remove the timing belt upper (outer) and lower covers as described in Section 4.

29 Move the engine wiring harness clear of the working area as necessary. This will entail the disconnection of certain connectors, and the removal of the harness from various cable clips and supports. Label any disconnected wiring and components as an aid to refitting.

30 Support the engine on a jack and remove the right-hand engine mounting components as described in Section 7.

31 Loosen the timing belt rear tensioner pulley retaining bolt and pivot the pulley in a clockwise direction, using a suitable square-section key fitted to the hole in the pulley hub, then retighten the retaining bolt.

32 Check that the camshaft sprocket locking pins are still in position, then disengage the timing belt from the camshaft sprockets and position it clear, taking care not to bend or twist the belt sharply.

33 Undo the tensioner and idler pulley retaining bolts and remove them from the engine.

Refitting

34 Clean the camshaft/crankshaft sprockets thoroughly, and renew any that show signs of wear, damage or cracks.

35 Clean the tensioner/idler pulleys but do not use any strong solvent which may enter the pulley bearings. Check that the pulleys rotate freely, with no sign of stiffness or free play. Renew them if there is any doubt about their condition, or if there are any obvious signs of wear or damage.

Camshaft sprocket - 1.6 litre models

36 Refit the locating peg (where removed) to the rear of the sprocket. Locate the sprocket on the end of the camshaft, ensuring that the locating peg is correctly engaged with the cut-out in the camshaft end.

37 Refit the sprocket retaining bolt and washer, and tighten it to the specified torque. Retain the sprocket with the tool used on removal.

38 Realign the hole in the camshaft sprocket with the corresponding hole in the cylinder head, and refit the locking pin. Check that the crankshaft pulley locking pin is still in position.

39 Refit the timing belt to the camshaft sprocket. Ensure that the front run of the belt is taut - ie, that any slack is on the tensioner pulley side of the belt. Do not twist the belt sharply while refitting it, and ensure that the belt teeth are seated centrally in the sprockets.

40 With the timing belt correctly engaged on the sprockets, tension the belt as described in Section 5.

41 Once the belt is correctly tensioned, refit the timing belt covers (see Section 4).

Camshaft sprockets - 1.8 and 2.0 litre models

42 If both the sprockets and the hubs have been removed, engage the sprocket hub with the camshaft. Ensure that the correct hub is fitted to the relevant camshaft by observing the hub identification markings described in paragraph 15.

43 Refit the sprocket hub retaining bolt and washer, and tighten it to the specified torque. Temporarily refit the sprockets to allow the hub to be held stationary with the tool as the bolt is tightened.

44 Turn the hub so that the locking pin can be engaged.

45 If the sprockets have been removed, leaving the hubs in place, position the sprocket on its hub and refit the bolts finger tight only at this stage. Ensure that the correct sprocket is fitted to the relevant camshaft according to the identification made on removal.

46 Relocate and tension the timing belt as described in Section 5.

Crankshaft sprocket - 1.6 litre models

47 Slide the spacer (where fitted) into position, taking great care not to damage the crankshaft oil seal, and refit the Woodruff key to its slot in the crankshaft end.

48 Slide on the crankshaft sprocket, aligning its slot with the Woodruff key.

49 Ensure that the camshaft sprocket locking pin is still in position. Temporarily refit the crankshaft pulley, and insert the locking pin through the pulley timing hole, to ensure that the crankshaft is still correctly positioned.

50 Remove the crankshaft pulley. Engage the timing belt with the crankshaft sprocket. Ensure that the belt front run is taut - ie, that any slack is on the tensioner pulley side of the belt. Fit the belt over the water pump sprocket and tensioner pulley. Do not twist the belt sharply while refitting it, and ensure that the belt teeth are seated centrally in the sprockets.

51 Tension the timing belt as described in Section 5.

52 Remove the crankshaft pulley, then refit the timing belt cover(s) as described in Section 4.

53 Refit the crankshaft pulley as described in Section 3, and reconnect the battery negative terminal.

Crankshaft sprocket - 1.8 and 2.0 litre models

54 Refit the Woodruff key to its slot in the crankshaft end.

55 Slide on the crankshaft sprocket, aligning its slot with the Woodruff key.

56 Relocate and tension the timing belt as described in Section 5.

Tensioner pulley - 1.6 litre models

57 Refit the tensioner pulley to its mounting stud, and fit the retaining bolt.

58 Ensure that the front run of the belt is taut - ie, that any slack is on the pulley side of the

14

belt. Check that the belt is centrally located on all its sprockets. Rotate the pulley anti-clockwise to remove all free play from the timing belt, and securely tighten the pulley retaining nut.

59 Tension the belt as described in Section 5.

60 Once the belt is correctly tensioned, refit the timing belt covers as described in Section 4.

Tensioner and idler pulleys - 1.8 and 2.0 litre models

61 Refit the tensioner and idler pulleys and secure with the retaining bolts.

62 Relocate and tension the timing belt as described in Section 5.

7 Engine right-hand mounting (1.8 and 2.0 litre models) - removal and refitting

1 Disconnect the battery negative terminal. Release all the relevant hoses and wiring from their retaining clips. Place the hoses/wiring clear of the mounting so that the removal procedure is not hindered.

2 Place a jack beneath the engine, with a block of wood on the jack head. Raise the jack until it is supporting the weight of the engine.

3 Slacken and remove the two nuts and two bolts securing the right-hand engine/transmission mounting bracket to the engine. Remove the single nut securing the bracket to the mounting rubber.

4 Undo the bolt securing the upper engine movement limiter to the right-hand mounting bracket, and the four bolts securing the movement limiter mounting bracket to the body. Lift away the right-hand mounting bracket and the movement limiter assembly.

5 Lift the rubber buffer plate off the mounting rubber stud, then unscrew the mounting rubber from the body and remove it from the vehicle. If necessary, the mounting bracket can be unbolted and removed from the front of the cylinder block.

6 On reassembly, screw the mounting rubber into the vehicle body, and tighten it securely. Refit the mounting bracket to the front of the cylinder head, and securely tighten its retaining bolts.

7 Refit the engine movement limiter assembly to the engine mounting bracket and to the body and tighten the bolts to the specified torque.

8 Refit the rubber buffer plate to the mounting rubber stud, and install the mounting bracket.

9 Tighten the mounting bracket retaining nuts to the specified torque setting. Remove the jack from underneath the engine and reconnect the battery.

8 Electronic Control Unit (ECU) - removal and refitting

1 The ECU is located in a plastic box which is mounted on the right-hand front wheelarch.

2 Ensure that the ignition is switched off then lift off the ECU module box lid. On automatic transmission models there will be two ECUs in the box; the fuel injection/ignition ECU is the unit nearest to the engine.

3 Release the wiring connector by lifting the locking lever on top of the connector upwards. Lift the connector at the rear, disengage the tag at the front and carefully withdraw the connector from the ECU pins.

4 Lift the ECU upwards and remove it from its location.

5 Refitting is a reversal of removal.

Chapter 14B
Peugeot 406 diesel 1996 to 1997

Contents

Specifications

Timing belt renewal interval . . . . Every 36 000 miles (60 000 km)

Note: *Although the normal interval for timing belt renewal is 72 000 miles (120 000 km), it is strongly recommended that the interval is halved on vehicles which are subjected to intensive use, ie, mainly short journeys or a lot of stop-start driving. The actual belt renewal interval is therefore very much up to the individual owner. That being said, it is highly recommended to err on the side of safety, and renew the belt at this earlier interval, bearing in mind the drastic consequences resulting from belt failure.*

Torque wrench settings	Nm	lbf ft
Auxiliary drivebelt tensioner pulley assembly retaining bolts:		
Models without air conditioning	22	16
Auxiliary drivebelt tensioner pulley retaining bolt:		
Models with air conditioning	50	37
Roadwheel bolts	90	66
1.9 litre engines		
Camshaft sprocket bolt	45	33
Crankshaft pulley bolt:		
Stage 1	40	30
Stage 2	Tighten through a further 51°	
Engine/transmission left-hand mounting:		
Centre nut	65	48
Mounting bracket-to-body	30	22
Mounting stud-to-transmission	60	44
Rubber mounting-to-bracket bolts	30	22
Engine/transmission right-hand mounting:		
Mounting bracket-to-engine nuts	45	33
Mounting bracket-to-rubber mounting nut	45	33
Rubber mounting-to-body nut	40	30
Upper engine movement limiter bolts	50	37
Fuel injection pump sprocket nut	50	37
Fuel injection pump sprocket puller retaining screws	10	7
Timing belt cover bolts	8	6
Timing belt tensioner adjustment bolt	20	15
Timing belt tensioner pivot nut	20	15

14

Torque wrench settings (continued)

	Nm	lbf ft
2.1 litre engines		
Camshaft sprocket bolt	50	37
Crankshaft pulley bolt:		
Stage 1	40	30
Stage 2	Tighten through a further 60°	
Engine/transmission left-hand mounting:		
Centre nut	65	48
Mounting bracket-to-body	30	22
Mounting stud-to-transmission	60	44
Rubber mounting-to-bracket bolts	30	22
Engine/transmission right-hand mounting:		
Mounting bracket-to-engine nuts	45	33
Mounting bracket-to-rubber mounting nut	45	33
Rubber mounting-to-body nut	40	30
Upper engine movement limiter bolts	50	37
Fuel injection pump sprocket nut	50	37
Fuel injection pump sprocket puller retaining screws	10	7
Timing belt cover bolts	8	6
Timing belt idler pulley	37	27
Timing belt tensioner nut/bolt	10	7

1 Auxiliary drivebelt - removal, refitting and adjustment

Note: *Depending on model and equipment fitted, access to the auxiliary drivebelt can be extremely limited. Where necessary, greater working clearance can be gained by removing the diesel injection electronic control unit (ECU) and its mounting box as described in Section 11.*

Note: *If working on the 2.1 litre model, the help of an assistant will also be beneficial.*

1 Apply the handbrake, then jack up the front of the car and support it on axle stands. Remove the right-hand front roadwheel.

2 Release the screws and clips and remove the wheelarch liner from under the right-hand front wing for access to the crankshaft pulley bolt. Where fitted, also remove the splash guard from under the front of the engine.

Models without air conditioning

Removal

3 Disconnect the battery negative lead.

4 Slacken the two bolts securing the tensioning pulley assembly to the engine **(see illustration)**.

1.4 Auxiliary drivebelt adjustment details (models without air conditioning)

1 *Adjuster bolt*
2 *Tensioning pulley assembly lower securing bolt*
3 *Tensioning pulley assembly upper retaining bolt*
4 *Tensioning pulley*

5 Rotate the adjuster bolt to move the tensioner pulley away from the drivebelt until there is sufficient slack for the drivebelt to be removed from the pulleys.

Refitting

6 Fit the drivebelt around the pulleys in the following order:
a) *Power steering pump.*
b) *Crankshaft.*
c) *Alternator.*
d) *Tensioner pulley.*

7 Ensure that the ribs on the belt are correctly engaged with the grooves in the pulleys, and that the drivebelt is correctly routed. Take all the slack out of the belt by turning the tensioner pulley adjuster bolt. Tension the belt as follows.

Adjustment

8 The belt should be tensioned so that, under firm thumb pressure, there is approximately 5.0 mm of free movement at the mid-point between the pulleys on the longest belt run.

9 To adjust the tension, with the two tensioner pulley assembly retaining bolts slackened, rotate the adjuster bolt until the correct tension is achieved. Once the belt is correctly tensioned, rotate the crankshaft four complete revolutions in the normal direction of rotation and recheck the tension.

10 When the belt is correctly tensioned, tighten the tensioner pulley assembly retaining bolts to the specified torque, then reconnect the battery negative lead.

11 Refit the wheelarch liner and, where fitted, the engine splash guard. Refit the roadwheel, and lower the vehicle to the ground.

Models with air conditioning

Removal

12 Disconnect the battery negative lead.

13 Working under the wheelarch, slacken the

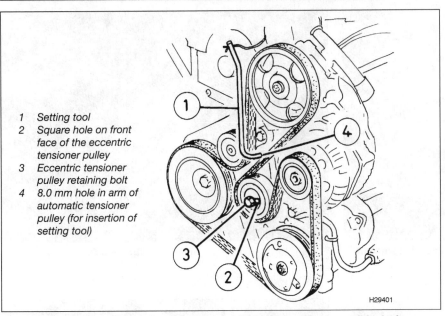

1 Setting tool
2 Square hole on front face of the eccentric tensioner pulley
3 Eccentric tensioner pulley retaining bolt
4 8.0 mm hole in arm of automatic tensioner pulley (for insertion of setting tool)

1.13 Auxiliary drivebelt adjustment details (models with air conditioning)

retaining bolt located in the centre of the eccentric tensioner pulley **(see illustration)**.

14 Insert a cranked, 7.0 mm square section bar (a quarter inch square drive socket bar for example) into the square hole on the front face of the eccentric tensioner pulley.

15 Using the bar, turn the eccentric tensioner pulley until the hole in the arm of the automatic tensioner pulley is aligned with the hole in the mounting bracket behind. When the holes are aligned, slide a suitable setting tool (a bolt, or cranked length of bar of approximately 8.0 mm diameter) through the hole in the arm and into the mounting bracket.

16 With the automatic tensioner pulley locked, turn the eccentric tensioner pulley until the drivebelt tension is released sufficiently to enable the belt to be removed.

Refitting and adjustment

17 Fit the drivebelt around the pulleys in the following order:

a) Air conditioning compressor.
b) Crankshaft.
c) Automatic tensioner pulley.
d) Power steering pump.
e) Alternator.
f) Eccentric tensioner pulley.

18 Ensure that the ribs on the belt are correctly engaged with the grooves in the pulleys.

18 Turn the eccentric tensioner pulley to apply tension to the drivebelt, until the load is released from the setting bolt. Without altering the position of the eccentric tensioner pulley, tighten its retaining bolt to the specified torque.

20 Remove the setting bolt from the automatic tensioner arm, then rotate the crankshaft four complete revolutions in the normal direction of rotation.

21 Check that the holes in the automatic

adjuster arm and the mounting bracket are still aligned by re-inserting the setting bolt. If the bolt will not slide in easily, repeat the tensioning procedure from paragraph 19 onward.

22 On completion, reconnect the battery negative lead, refit the wheelarch liner and, where fitted, the engine splash guard. Refit the roadwheel, and lower the vehicle to the ground.

2 Engine assembly/valve timing holes - general information and usage

Note: *Do not attempt to rotate the engine whilst the crankshaft/camshaft/injection pump are locked in position. If the engine is to be left in this state for a long period of time, it is a good idea to place suitable warning notices inside the vehicle, and in the engine compartment. This will reduce the possibility of the engine being accidentally cranked on*

the starter motor, which is likely to cause damage with the locking pins in place.

1 On all models, timing holes are drilled in the camshaft sprocket, injection pump sprocket and flywheel. The holes are used to align the crankshaft, camshaft and injection pump and to prevent the possibility of the valves contacting the pistons when refitting the timing belt. When the holes are aligned with their corresponding holes in the cylinder head and cylinder block (as appropriate), suitable diameter bolts/pins can be inserted to lock both the camshaft, injection pump and crankshaft in position, preventing them from rotating unnecessarily. Proceed as follows.

Note: *With the timing holes aligned, No 4 cylinder is at TDC on its compression stroke.*

2 Remove the upper timing belt covers as described in Section 5.

3 The crankshaft must now be turned until the bolt holes in the camshaft and injection pump sprockets (one hole in the camshaft sprocket, one or two holes in the injection pump sprocket) are aligned with the corresponding holes in the engine front plate. The crankshaft can be turned by using a socket on the pulley bolt. To gain access to the pulley bolt, from underneath the front of the car, prise out the retaining clips and remove the screws, then withdraw the plastic wheelarch liner from the wing valance, to gain access to the crankshaft pulley bolt. Where necessary, unclip the coolant hoses from the bracket, to improve access further. The crankshaft can then be turned using a suitable socket and extension bar fitted to the pulley bolt. Note that the crankshaft must always be turned in a clockwise direction (viewed from the right-hand side of the vehicle).

4 Insert an 8 mm diameter rod or drill through the hole in the left-hand flange of the cylinder block by the starter motor; if necessary, carefully turn the crankshaft either way until the rod enters the timing hole in the flywheel/driveplate **(see illustrations)**. On 2.1 litre models, access is very restricted, and it may be easier to remove the starter motor to be able to locate the hole.

5 Insert one 8 mm bolt through the hole in the camshaft sprocket, and two (1.9 litre models)

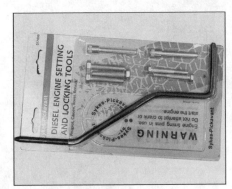

2.4a Suitable tools available for locking engine in position

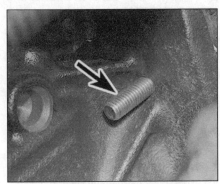

2.4b Rod (arrowed) inserted through cylinder block into timing hole in flywheel/driveplate

14

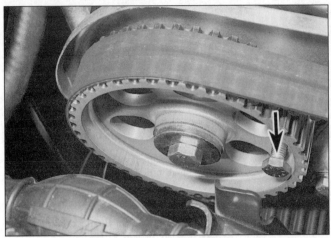

2.5a Bolt (arrowed) inserted through timing hole in camshaft sprocket on 1.9 litre models . . .

2.5b . . . and on 2.1 litre models

2.5c Two bolts (arrowed) inserted through timing holes in fuel injection pump sprocket on 1.9 litre models . . .

2.5d . . . and single bolt inserted through the pump sprocket on 2.1 litre models

or one (2.1 litre models) bolt(s) through the fuel injection pump sprocket, and screw them into the engine finger-tight **(see illustrations)**.
6 The crankshaft, camshaft and injection pump are now locked in position, preventing unnecessary rotation.

3 Cylinder head cover -
removal and refitting

Removal - 1.9 litre models

1 Disconnect the breather hose from the front of the cylinder head cover and remove the air cleaner inlet ducts as necessary for access.
2 Unscrew the securing bolt and remove the fuel hose bracket from the right-hand end of the cylinder head cover **(see illustration)**.
3 Disconnect the vacuum hose from the fast idle control diaphragm unit, then undo the two bolts and move the unit to one side.

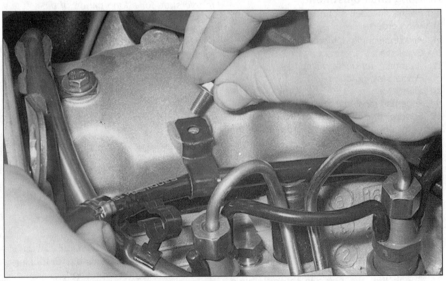

3.2 Removing the fuel hose bracket from the cylinder head cover

3.4 Remove the cylinder head cover retaining bolts and washers

3.12 Lifting off the cylinder head cover on 2.1 litre models

4 Note the locations of any brackets secured by the three cylinder head cover retaining bolts, then unscrew the bolts. Recover the metal and fibre washers under each bolt **(see illustration)**.
5 Carefully move any hoses clear of the cylinder head cover.
6 Lift off the cover, and recover the rubber seal.

Removal - 2.1 litre models

7 Remove the timing belt upper cover as described in Section 5.
8 Remove the inlet manifold upper part as described in Section 12
9 Disconnect the breather hose from the front of the cylinder head cover.
10 Note the locations of any brackets secured by the cylinder head cover retaining bolts, then unscrew the eleven bolts in a progressive spiral sequence.
11 Carefully move any hoses clear of the cylinder head cover.
12 Lift off the cover, and recover the rubber seal **(see illustration)**.

Refitting - all models

13 Refitting is a reversal of removal, bearing in mind the following points:
a) *Refit any brackets in their original positions noted before removal.*
b) *Refit the inlet manifold (2.1 litre models) and air inlet ducts described in Chapter 4B.*

4   Crankshaft pulley - removal and refitting

Note: *Although not strictly necessary, due to its tightening sequence, it is recommended that the retaining bolt is renewed whenever it is disturbed.*

Removal

1 Remove the auxiliary drivebelt (Section 1).
2 To prevent the crankshaft turning whilst the pulley retaining bolt is being slackened, select 4th gear and have an assistant apply the brakes firmly. *Do not* attempt to lock the pulley by inserting a bolt/drill through the timing hole. If the locking pin is in position, temporarily remove it prior to slackening the pulley bolt, then refit it once the bolt has been slackened.
3 Unscrew the retaining bolt and washer, then slide the pulley off the end of the crankshaft **(see illustrations)**. If the pulley locating roll pin or Woodruff key (as applicable) is a loose fit, remove it and store it with the pulley for safe-keeping. If the pulley is a tight fit, it can be drawn off the crankshaft using a suitable puller.

Refitting

4 Ensure that the Woodruff key is correctly located in its crankshaft groove, or that the roll pin is in position (as applicable). Refit the pulley to the end of the crankshaft, aligning its locating groove or hole with the Woodruff key or pin.
5 Thoroughly clean the threads of the pulley retaining bolt, then apply a coat of locking

4.3a Removing the crankshaft pulley retaining bolt

4.3b Removing the crankshaft pulley from the end of the crankshaft

14

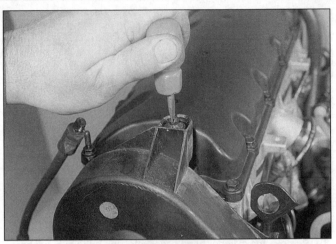

5.6 Undo the single retaining bolt (arrowed), located in the centre of the upper cover on 2.1 litre models

5.7 On 2.1 litre models, turn the fastener clockwise to release the cover locking peg

compound to the bolt threads. Peugeot recommend the use of Loctite Frenetanche (available from your Peugeot dealer); in the absence of this, any good-quality locking compound may be used.

6 Refit the crankshaft pulley retaining bolt and washer. Tighten the bolt to the specified torque, preventing the crankshaft from turning using the method employed on removal, then tighten through the specified angle.

7 Refit and tension the auxiliary drivebelt as described in Section 1.

5 Timing belt covers - removal and refitting

Removal - 1.9 litre models

Upper front cover

1 Slacken and remove the retaining screw and nut, and remove the cover from the engine.

Upper rear cover

2 Remove the front cover as described previously, then undo the retaining bolts and remove the rear cover from the engine.

Lower cover

3 Remove the crankshaft pulley as described in Section 4.

4 Remove both upper covers as described previously.

5 Slacken and remove the retaining nuts and bolts, and remove the lower cover.

Removal - 2.1 litre models

Upper cover

6 Undo the single retaining bolt, located in the centre of the cover **(see illustration)**.

7 Turn the upper fastener a quarter of a turn clockwise to release the locking peg **(see illustration)**.

8 Manipulate the cover up and off the front of the engine.

Centre cover

9 Remove the auxiliary drivebelt as described in Section 1.

10 Undo the two bolts and remove the centre cover from the front of the injection pump **(see illustration)**.

Lower cover

11 Remove the crankshaft pulley as described in Section 4.

12 Remove the right-hand engine mounting assembly as described in Section 10.

13 Remove both upper covers as described previously.

14 Slacken and remove the retaining bolts, and remove the lower cover **(see illustration)**.

Refitting - all models

15 Refitting is a reversal of the relevant removal procedure, ensuring that each cover section is correctly located, and that the cover retaining nuts and/or bolts are tightened to the specified torque.

5.10 Removing the centre cover from the front of the injection pump on 2.1 litre models

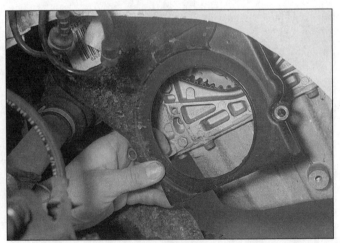

5.14 Removing the lower timing belt cover on 2.1 litre models

6 Timing belt -
removal and refitting

Removal - 1.9 litre models

1 Align the engine assembly/valve timing holes as described in Section 2, and lock the camshaft sprocket, injection pump sprocket and flywheel in position. *Do not* attempt to rotate the engine whilst the pins are in position. Disconnect the battery negative terminal.

2 Remove the remaining timing belt covers as described in Section 5.

3 Remove the right-hand engine mounting and mounting bracket as described in Section 8, then loosen the timing belt tensioner pivot nut and adjustment bolt, then turn the tensioner bracket anti-clockwise to release the tension. Retighten the adjustment bolt to hold the tensioner in the released position. If available, use a 10 mm square drive extension in the hole provided to turn the tensioner bracket against the spring tension **(see illustration)**.

4 Mark the timing belt with an arrow to indicate its running direction, if it is to be re-used. Remove the belt from the sprockets.

Removal - 2.1 litre models

5 Align the engine assembly/valve timing holes as described in Section 2, and lock the camshaft sprocket, injection pump sprocket and flywheel in position. *Do not* attempt to rotate the engine whilst the pins are in position. Disconnect the battery negative terminal.

6 Remove the remaining timing belt covers as described in Section 5.

7 Slacken the timing belt tensioner pulley retaining nut, situated just to the left of the engine mounting carrier bracket.

8 Using a 5 mm Allen key inserted through the hole in the engine mounting carrier bracket, slacken the timing belt tensioner locking bolt **(see illustration)**.

9 Using a 10 mm socket or box spanner inserted through the same hole, retract the tensioner by turning its shaft clockwise to the extent of its travel **(see illustrations)**.

10 Mark the timing belt with an arrow to indicate its running direction, if it is to be re-used. Remove the belt from the sprockets **(see illustration)**.

Refitting and tensioning

11 If signs of oil contamination are found, trace the source of the oil leak and rectify it. Wash down the engine timing belt area and all related components, to remove all traces of oil.

12 Check that the tensioner and idler pulley rotate freely, without any sign of roughness. If necessary, renew as described in Sections 8 and 9 (as applicable).

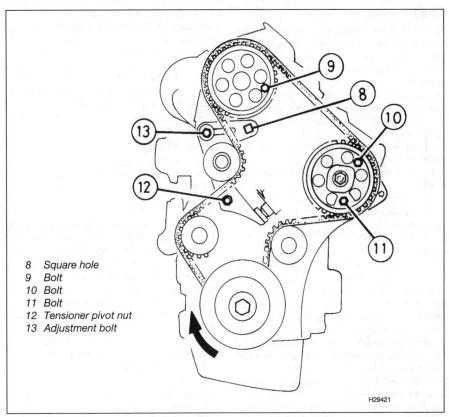

8 Square hole
9 Bolt
10 Bolt
11 Bolt
12 Tensioner pivot nut
13 Adjustment bolt

6.3 Removing the timing belt - 1.9 litre models

6.8 On 2.1 litre models, slacken the timing belt tensioner locking bolt using a 5 mm Allen key

6.9a Timing belt tensioner pulley retaining nut (A) and locking bolt (B) on 2.1 litre models

6.9b Timing belt tensioner arrangement on 2.1 litre models showing tensioner 10 mm shaft (arrowed)

6.10 Removing the timing belt

14

1.9 litre models

13 Commence refitting by ensuring that the 8 mm bolts are still fitted to the camshaft and fuel injection pump sprockets, and that the rod/drill is positioned in the timing hole in the flywheel.

14 Locate the timing belt on the crankshaft sprocket, making sure that, where applicable, the direction of rotation arrow is facing the correct way.

15 Engage the timing belt with the crankshaft sprocket, hold it in position, then feed the belt over the remaining sprockets in the following order:

a) Idler roller.
b) Fuel injection pump.
c) Camshaft.
d) Tensioner roller.
e) Coolant pump.

16 Be careful not to kink or twist the belt. To ensure correct engagement, locate only a half-width on the injection pump sprocket before feeding the timing belt onto the camshaft sprocket, keeping the belt taut and fully engaged with the crankshaft sprocket. Locate the timing belt fully onto the sprockets.

17 Unscrew and remove the bolts from the camshaft and fuel injection pump sprockets and remove the rod/drill from the timing hole in the flywheel.

18 With the pivot nut loose, slacken the tensioner adjustment bolt while holding the bracket against the spring tension. Slowly release the bracket until the roller presses against the timing belt. Retighten the adjustment bolt and the pivot nut.

19 Rotate the crankshaft through two complete turns in the normal running direction (clockwise). **Do not** rotate the crankshaft backwards, as the timing belt must be kept tight between the crankshaft, fuel injection pump and camshaft sprockets.

20 Loosen the tensioner adjustment bolt and the pivot nut to allow the tensioner spring to push the roller against the timing belt, then tighten both the adjustment bolt and pivot nut to the specified torque.

21 Check that the timing holes are all correctly positioned by reinserting the sprocket locking bolts and the rod/drill in the flywheel timing hole, as described in Section 2. If the timing holes are not correctly positioned, the timing belt has been incorrectly fitted (possibly one tooth out on one of the sprockets) - in this case, repeat the refitting procedure from the beginning.

22 The remaining refitting procedure is a reversal of removal.

2.1 litre models

23 Commence refitting by ensuring that the 8 mm bolts are still fitted to the camshaft and fuel injection pump sprockets, and that the rod/drill is positioned in the timing hole in the flywheel.

24 Ensure that the timing belt tensioner is still retracted, then tighten the tensioner pulley retaining nut. Using the 10 mm socket or box spanner, release the tensioner by turning it anti-clockwise to the extent of its travel.

25 Locate the timing belt on the crankshaft sprocket, making sure that, where applicable, the direction of rotation arrow is facing the correct way.

26 Engage the timing belt with the crankshaft sprocket, hold it in position, then feed the belt over the remaining sprockets in the following order:

a) Idler roller.
b) Fuel injection pump.
c) Camshaft.
d) Coolant pump.
e) Tensioner roller.

27 Be careful not to kink or twist the belt. To ensure correct engagement, locate only a half-width on the injection pump sprocket before feeding the timing belt onto the camshaft sprocket, keeping the belt taut and fully engaged with the crankshaft sprocket. Locate the timing belt fully onto the sprockets.

28 Slacken the tensioner pulley retaining nut to allow the tensioner to tension the belt.

29 Unscrew and remove the bolts from the camshaft and fuel injection pump sprockets and remove the rod/drill from the timing hole in the flywheel.

30 Rotate the crankshaft through two complete turns in the normal running direction (clockwise). **Do not** rotate the crankshaft backwards, as the timing belt must be kept tight between the crankshaft, fuel injection pump and camshaft sprockets.

31 Slacken the tensioner pulley retaining nut, then rotate the crankshaft through a further two complete turns in the normal running direction, stopping at the timing setting position.

32 Slacken the tensioner pulley retaining nut one turn to allow the tensioner to finally tension the belt. Tighten tensioner pulley retaining nut and the timing belt tensioner locking bolt to the specified torque.

33 Check that the timing holes are all correctly positioned by reinserting the sprocket locking bolts and the rod/drill in the flywheel timing hole, as described in Section 2. If the timing holes are not correctly positioned, the timing belt has been incorrectly fitted (possibly one tooth out on one of the sprockets) - in this case, repeat the refitting procedure from the beginning.

34 The remaining refitting procedure is a reversal of removal.

7 Timing belt sprockets - removal and refitting

Camshaft sprocket

Removal

1 Remove the timing belt (see Section 6).

2 Slacken the camshaft sprocket retaining bolt and remove it, along with its washer. To prevent the camshaft rotating as the bolt is slackened, a sprocket holding tool will be required **(see illustration)**. *Do not* attempt to use the sprocket locking pin to prevent the sprocket from rotating whilst the bolt is slackened. Alternatively, on 1.9 litre models, remove the cylinder head cover as described in Section 3. Prevent the camshaft from turning by holding it with a suitable spanner on the lug between Nos 3 and 4 camshaft lobes **(see illustration)**.

7.2a A sprocket holding tool can be made from two lengths of steel strip bolted together to form a forked end. Bend the ends of the strip through 90° to form the fork 'prongs'

7.2b Holding the camshaft using a spanner on the lug between Nos 3 and 4 lobes

7.5 Withdrawing the camshaft sprocket

7.13 Withdrawing the crankshaft sprocket

3 Remove the camshaft sprocket retaining bolt and washer.

4 Unscrew and remove the locking bolt from the camshaft sprocket.

5 With the retaining bolt removed, slide the sprocket off the end of the camshaft **(see illustration)**. Recover the Woodruff key from the end of the camshaft if it is loose. Examine the camshaft oil seal for signs of oil leakage and, if necessary, renew it.

Refitting

6 Refit the Woodruff key to the end of the camshaft, then refit the camshaft sprocket. Note that the sprocket will only fit one way round (with the protruding centre boss against the camshaft), as the end of the camshaft is tapered.

7 Refit the sprocket retaining bolt and washer. Tighten the bolt to the specified torque, preventing the camshaft from turning as during removal.

8 Where applicable, refit the cylinder head cover as described in Section 3.

9 Align the holes in the camshaft sprocket and the engine front plate, and refit the 8 mm bolt to lock the camshaft in position.

10 Refit it the timing belt as described in Section 6.

11 Refit the timing belt covers as described in Section 5.

Crankshaft sprocket

Removal

12 Remove the timing belt (see Section 6).

13 Slide the sprocket off the end of the crankshaft **(see illustration)**.

14 Remove the Woodruff key from the crankshaft, and store it with the sprocket for safe-keeping **(see illustration)**.

15 Examine the crankshaft oil seal for signs of oil leakage and, if necessary, renew it.

Refitting

16 Refit the Woodruff key to the end of the crankshaft, then refit the crankshaft sprocket (with the flange nearest the cylinder block).

17 Refit the timing belt as described in Section 6.

Fuel injection pump sprocket

Removal

18 Remove the timing belt as described in Section 6.

19 Remove the 8 mm bolt(s) securing the fuel injection pump sprocket in the TDC position.

20 On certain models, the sprocket may be fitted with a built-in puller, which consists of a plate bolted to the sprocket. The plate contains a captive nut (the sprocket securing nut), which is screwed onto the fuel injection pump shaft. On models not fitted with the built-in puller, a suitable puller can be made up using a short length of bar, and two M7 bolts screwed into the holes provided in the sprocket.

21 The fuel injection pump shaft must be prevented from turning as the sprocket nut is unscrewed, and this can be achieved using a tool similar to that shown **(see illustration)**. Use the tool to hold the sprocket stationary by means of the holes in the sprocket.

22 On models with a built-in puller, unscrew

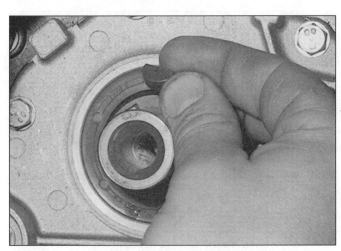

7.14 Removing the Woodruff key from the end of the crankshaft

7.21 Using a home-made tool to prevent the fuel injection pump sprocket turning

14

7.23 Home-made puller fitted to fuel injection pump sprocket

the sprocket securing nut until the sprocket is freed from the taper on the pump shaft, then withdraw the sprocket. Recover the Woodruff key from the end of the pump shaft if it is loose. If desired, the puller assembly can be removed from the sprocket by removing the two securing screws and washers.

23 On models not fitted with a built-in puller, partially unscrew the sprocket securing nut, then fit the improvised puller, and tighten the two bolts (forcing the bar against the sprocket nut), until the sprocket is freed from the taper on the pump shaft **(see illustration)**. Withdraw the sprocket and recover the Woodruff key from the end of the pump shaft if it is loose. Remove the puller from the sprocket.

Refitting

24 Refit the Woodruff key to the pump shaft, ensuring that it is correctly located in its groove.
25 Where applicable, if the built-in puller assembly has been removed from the sprocket, refit it, and tighten the two securing screws securely ensuring that the washers are in place.
26 Refit the sprocket, then tighten the securing nut to the specified torque, preventing the pump shaft from turning as during removal.

27 Make sure that the 8 mm bolts are fitted to the camshaft and fuel injection pump sprockets, and that the rod/drill is positioned in the flywheel timing hole.
28 Fit the timing belt around the fuel injection pump sprocket, ensuring that the marks made on the belt and sprocket before removal are aligned.
29 Tension the timing belt as described in Section 6.
30 Refit the upper timing belt covers as described in Section 5.

Coolant pump sprocket

31 The coolant pump sprocket is integral with the pump, and cannot be removed.

8 Timing belt tensioner (1.9 litre models) - removal and refitting

Note: A suitable tool will be required to retain the timing belt tensioner plunger during this operation.

1 The timing belt tensioner is operated by a spring and plunger housed in the right-hand engine mounting bracket, which is bolted to the end face of the engine. The engine mounting is attached to the mounting on the body via the engine mounting-to-body bracket.

Removal

2 Before removing the engine mounting-to-body bracket, the engine must be supported, preferably using a suitable hoist and lifting tackle attached to the lifting bracket at the right-hand end of the engine. Alternatively, the engine can be supported using a trolley jack and interposed block of wood beneath the sump. In which case, be prepared for the engine to tilt backwards when the bracket is removed.
3 Release the retaining clips and position all the relevant hoses and cables clear of the engine mounting assembly and suspension top mounting.

4 Unscrew the three nuts securing the bracket to the engine mounting, and the single nut securing the bracket to the body, then lift off the bracket.
5 Remove the auxiliary drivebelt as described in Section 1.
6 If not already done, support the engine with a trolley jack and interposed block of wood beneath the sump.
7 Where applicable, disconnect the hoist and lifting tackle supporting the engine from the right-hand lifting bracket (this is necessary because the lifting bracket is attached to the engine mounting bracket, and must be removed).
8 Unscrew the two retaining bolts and remove the engine lifting bracket.
9 Align the engine assembly/valve timing holes as described in Section 2, and lock the camshaft sprocket, injection pump sprocket and flywheel in position. *Do not* attempt to rotate the engine whilst the pins are in position.
10 Loosen the timing belt tensioner pivot nut and adjustment bolt, then turn the tensioner bracket anti-clockwise until the adjustment bolt is in the middle of the slot, and retighten the adjustment bolt. If available, use a 10 mm square drive extension in the hole provided to turn the tensioner bracket against the spring tension.
11 Mark the timing belt with an arrow to indicate its running direction, if it is to be re-used. Remove the belt from the sprockets.
12 A tool must now be used to hold the tensioner plunger in the engine mounting bracket.
13 The Peugeot tool is designed to slide in the two lower bolt holes of the mounting bracket. It should be straightforward to fabricate a similar tool out of sheet metal, and using 10 mm bolts and nuts instead of metal dowel rods **(see illustration)**.
14 Unscrew the two lower engine mounting bracket bolts, then fit the special tool. Grease the inner surface of the tool, to prevent any damage to the end of the tensioner plunger **(see illustrations)**. Unscrew the pivot nut and

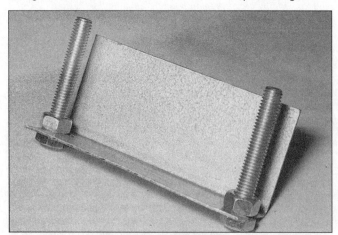

8.13 Fabricated tool for holding tensioner plunger in engine mounting bracket

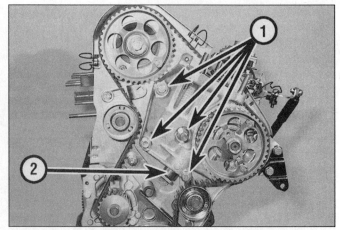

8.14a View of timing belt end of engine
1 Engine mounting bracket retaining bolts
2 Timing belt tensioner plunger

8.14b Tool in place to hold tensioner plunger in engine mounting bracket - timing belt removed for clarity

11.2 Lift off the ECU module box lid for access to the ECU wiring connector (arrowed)

adjustment bolt, and withdraw the tensioner assembly.

15 Remove the two remaining engine mounting bracket bolts, and withdraw the bracket.

16 Compress the tensioner plunger into the engine mounting bracket, remove the special tool, then withdraw the plunger and spring.

Refitting

17 Refitting is a reversal of removal, bearing in mind the following points:
a) *Tighten all fixings to the specified torque.*
b) *Refit and tension the timing belt as described in Section 6.*
c) *Refit and tighten the auxiliary drivebelt as described in Section 1.*

---

9 Timing belt idler roller - removal and refitting

Removal - 1.9 litre models

1 Remove the auxiliary drivebelt as described in Section 1.

2 Align the engine assembly/valve timing holes as described in Section 2, and lock the camshaft sprocket, injection pump sprocket and flywheel in position. *Do not* attempt to rotate the engine whilst the pins are in position.

3 Loosen the timing belt tensioner pivot nut and adjustment bolt, then turn the tensioner bracket anti-clockwise to release the tension, and retighten the adjustment bolt to hold the tensioner in the released position. If available, use a 10 mm square drive extension in the hole provided to turn the tensioner bracket against spring pressure.

4 Unscrew the two bolts and the stud securing the idler roller assembly to the cylinder block, noting that the upper bolt also secures the engine mounting bracket.

5 Slightly loosen the remaining four engine mounting bolts, noting that the uppermost

bolt is on the inside face of the engine front plate, and also secures the engine lifting bracket. Slide out the idler roller assembly.

Removal - 2.1 litre models

6 Remove the timing belt as described in Section 6.

7 Unscrew the idler roller centre bolt and remove it from the engine.

Refitting - all models

8 Refitting is a reversal of removal, bearing in mind the following points:
a) *Tighten all fixings to the specified torque.*
b) *Refit and/or tension the timing belt as described in Section 6.*
c) *Refit and tension the auxiliary drivebelt as described in Section 1.*

---

10 Engine right-hand mounting (2.1 litre models) - removal and refitting

Note: *Removal and refitting of the right-hand mounting on 1.9 litre models is described in Section 8 as part of the timing belt tensioner procedure.*

1 Disconnect the battery negative terminal. Release all the relevant hoses and wiring from their retaining clips. Place the hoses/wiring clear of the mounting so that the removal procedure is not hindered.

2 Place a jack beneath the engine, with a block of wood on the jack head. Raise the jack until it is supporting the weight of the engine.

3 Slacken and remove the two nuts and two bolts securing the right-hand engine/transmission mounting bracket to the engine. Remove the single nut securing the bracket to the mounting rubber.

4 Undo the bolt securing the upper engine movement limiter to the right-hand mounting bracket, and the four bolts securing the movement limiter mounting bracket to the

body. Lift away the right-hand mounting bracket and the movement limiter assembly.

5 Lift the rubber buffer plate off the mounting rubber stud, then unscrew the mounting rubber from the body and remove it from the vehicle. If necessary, the mounting bracket can be unbolted and removed from the front of the cylinder block.

6 On reassembly, screw the mounting rubber into the vehicle body, and tighten it securely. Refit the mounting bracket to the front of the cylinder head, and securely tighten its retaining bolts.

7 Refit the engine movement limiter assembly to the engine mounting bracket and to the body and tighten the bolts to the specified torque.

8 Refit the rubber buffer plate to the mounting rubber stud, and install the mounting bracket.

9 Tighten the mounting bracket retaining nuts to the specified torque setting. Remove the jack from underneath the engine and reconnect the battery.

---

11 Electronic Control Unit (ECU) - removal and refitting

Note: *The ECU is fragile. Take care not to drop it or subject it to any other kind of impact, and do not subject it to extremes of temperature, or allow it to get wet.*

1.9 litre models

1 The ECU is located in a plastic box which is mounted on the right-hand front wheel arch.

2 Lift off the ECU module box lid **(see illustration)**.

3 Release the wiring connector by lifting the locking lever on top of the connector upwards. Lift the connector at the rear, disengage the tag at the front and carefully withdraw the connector from the ECU pins.

4 Lift the ECU upwards and remove it from its location.

14

11.9a On the Lucas EPIC system ECU, lift the locking lever upwards . . .

11.9b . . . and disconnect the wiring connector

5 If necessary, the ECU module box can now be removed by undoing the internal and external retaining bolts.

6 Refitting is a reversal of removal.

2.1 litre models

7 The ECU is located in a plastic box which is mounted on the right-hand front wheel arch.

8 Lift off the ECU module box lid.

9 Release the wiring connector by lifting the locking lever on top of the connector upwards. Lift the connector at the rear, disengage the tag at the front and carefully withdraw the connector from the ECU pins (see illustrations)

10 Lift the ECU upwards and remove it from its location (see illustration).

11 To remove the ECU module box, turn the injection pump wiring connector on the top of the box clockwise, disengage the retaining lug using a screwdriver, then turn the connector anti-clockwise and lift off (see illustrations).

12 Undo the two screws securing the wiring connector base to the module box and lift off the connector base (see illustration).

13 Undo the internal and external retaining bolts and remove the module box (see illustrations).

14 Refitting is a reversal of removal.

11.10 Lift the ECU upwards and remove it from the module box

11.11a Turn the injection pump wiring connector clockwise, disengage the retaining lug using a screwdriver . . .

11.11b . . . then turn the connector anti-clockwise and lift off

11.12 Undo the two base retaining screws and lift off the connector base

11.13a Undo the internal and external retaining bolts . . .

11.13b . . . and remove the module box

12.1 Slacken the retaining clip and disconnect the air intake duct from the inlet manifold upper part

12.2 Remove the clip securing the flexible portion of the EGR pipe to the manifold

12 Inlet manifold upper part (2.1 litre models) - removal and refitting

Removal

1 Slacken the retaining clip and disconnect the air intake duct from the manifold upper part **(see illustration)**.

2 Remove the clip securing the flexible portion of the EGR pipe to the manifold. If the original crimped clip is still in place, cut it off; new clips are supplied by Peugeot parts stockists with a screw clamp fixing **(see illustration)**. If a screw clamp type clip is fitted, undo the screw and manipulate the clip off the pipe.

3 Undo the four retaining bolts and lift off the manifold upper part. Recover the four rubber connecting tubes from the lower part **(see illustrations)**.

Refitting

4 Refitting is a reversal of removal, bearing in mind the following points.

a) Renew the four rubber connecting tubes as a set if any one shows signs of deterioration.

b) Tighten all fixings to the specified torques, where applicable.

c) Secure the EGR pipe with a new screw clamp type clip, if a crimped type was initially fitted **(see illustration)**.

12.3a Undo the four retaining bolts (arrowed) . . .

12.3b . . . lift off the manifold upper part . . .

12.3c . . . and recover the four rubber connecting tubes

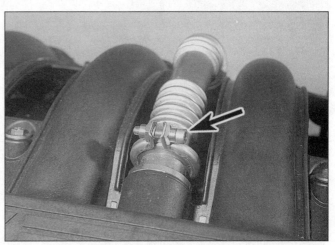

12.4 Secure the EGR pipe with a screw clamp type clip (arrowed) when refitting

14

Notes

Chapter 15
Peugeot 505 petrol 1979 to 1989

Contents

Specifications

Timing belt renewal interval .... Every 36 000 miles (60 000 km) or 3 years - whichever comes first

Engine codes

1995 cc .... ZEJK
2165 cc .... ZDJ L

Torque wrench settings	Nm	lbf ft
Alternator mounting bolt	45	33
Crankshaft pulley bolt:		
ZEJ	80	59
ZDJ	130	96
Spark plug:		
With sealing washer	22	16
Taper-seat	15 to 20	11 to 15
Thermostat housing cover	15	11
Timing belt tensioner	25	18
Timing gear sprockets	50	37

15

1.2 Removing the drivebelt (fan removed for clarity)

2.10 Removing the crankshaft pulley

2.11 Removing the timing belt cover

1 Auxiliary drivebelt - removal, refitting and adjustment

1 Loosen the alternator adjustment and pivot bolts, and swivel the alternator towards the engine.

2 Slip the drivebelt from the alternator, water pump, and crankshaft pulleys, and remove it over the fan **(see illustration)**.

3 Refitting the drivebelt is a reversal of removal, but adjust the belt tension as follows. Pivot the alternator so that the belt deflection, under firm thumb pressure at a point midway between the pulleys, is approximately 12.5 mm. Do not overtension, as this may damage the alternator bearings. Tighten the alternator adjustment and pivot bolts on completion. After a nominal mileage has been covered, check the tension of the drivebelt again.

2 Timing belt - removal and refitting

Removal

1 Drain the coolant, and remove the radiator, auxiliary drivebelt and fan.

2 On models fitted with power steering, remove the pump drivebelt (Section 5)

3 On models fitted with air conditioning, remove the compressor drivebelt.

4 Disconnect the battery negative lead.

5 Remove the spark plugs.

6 Remove the thermostat housing (Section 4) and the additional air valve.

7 Remove the alternator (Section 6).

8 On manual gearbox models, have an assistant engage top gear and depress the brake pedal. Unscrew and remove the crankshaft pulley bolt.

9 On automatic transmission models, remove the TDC sensor plate on the front of the transmission, and have an assistant lock the starter ring gear with a wide-bladed screwdriver. Unscrew and remove the crankshaft pulley bolt.

10 Remove the pulley from the front of the crankshaft sprocket **(see illustration)**.

11 Remove the timing belt cover(s) **(see illustration)**.

12 Refit the pulley bolt, then turn the engine clockwise until the timing mark on the camshaft sprocket is between the 10 and 11 o'clock position (ie, 45° from horizontal position). This is not in fact the No 1 TDC position, although No 1 piston is half way up its compression stroke. Where the camshaft sprocket has a square hole in it, check its position **(see illustration)**.

13 Loosen the tensioner retaining nut and bolt.

14 Insert a screwdriver in the side of the

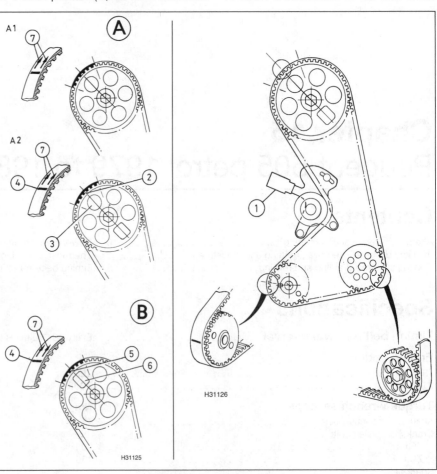

H31126

H31125

2.12 Timing belt chart

A ZEJ engine	2 Timing mark on sprocket (ZEJ)	5 Timing mark on sprocket (ZDJ)
B ZDJ engine	3 Circular aperture (ZEJ)	6 Square aperture
1 Tensioner	4 Timing mark on belt	7 Rotation direction arrows

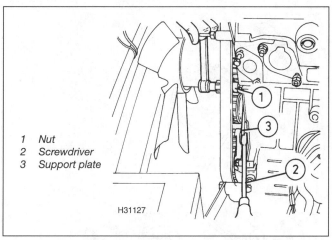

1 Nut
2 Screwdriver
3 Support plate

H31127

2.14 Retracting the tensioner support plate

2.16a Removing the timing belt tensioner roller . . .

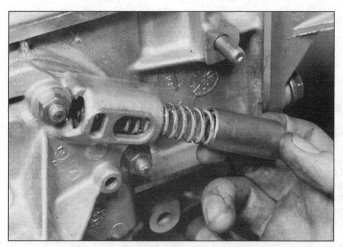

2.16b . . . followed by the spring and plunger

2.17 Tensioner roller locked in its retracted position

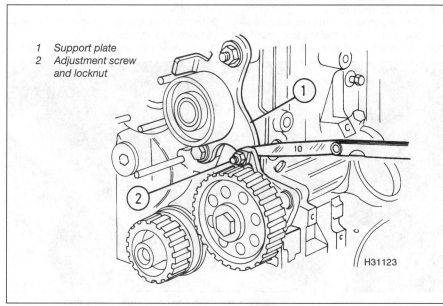

1 Support plate
2 Adjustment screw
  and locknut

H31123

2.18 Checking the support plate clearance

tensioner support plate, lever the plate against the spring tension, then tighten the nut to retain the plate **(see illustration)**.

15 Remove the timing belt. Note that the timing belt must not be flattened to less than a 60 mm diameter arc, otherwise it may be damaged.

16 If necessary, the tensioner roller may be removed by unscrewing the nut and bolt, and the spring and plunger extracted from the water pump housing **(see illustrations)**.

Refitting

17 Refit the tensioner roller, together with its spring and plunger. Lock the support plate in its retracted position **(see illustration)**.

18 Using a feeler blade, check that the clearance between the support plate and the intermediate sprocket housing bolt is between 0.1 and 0.15 mm **(see illustration)**. If necessary, loosen the nut, remove the bolt, apply locking fluid to its threads, then refit and adjust. Tighten the locking nut.

19 Offer the timing belt to the sprockets, with the directional arrows pointing clockwise.

15

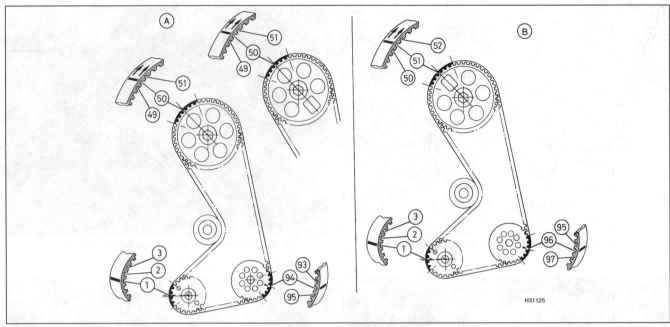

2.19 Timing belt marking diagram

A *ZEJ engine (116 teeth, white markings)*   B *ZDJ engine (118 teeth, yellow markings)*

Besides the arrows, there should be three marks on the timing belt, which should align with the timing marks on the camshaft, intermediate shaft, and crankshaft sprockets when the belt is fitted. If the belt has no such marks, make some **(see illustration)**.

20 Centralise the belt on the sprockets, and recheck that the timing marks are aligned.

21 Loosen the tensioner nut, and allow the spring to tension the timing belt. Tighten the tensioner retaining nut and bolt **(see illustration)**.

22 Refit the timing belt cover(s).

23 Check that the locating pins are fitted **(see illustration)**, then fit the crankshaft pulley against the sprocket.

24 Clean the threads of the crankshaft pulley bolt, then apply a little locking fluid, insert the bolt, and tighten it to the specified torque **(see illustration)**. Lock the crankshaft with reference to paragraphs 8 or 9.

25 Refit all the removed components with reference to the appropriate Sections, and reconnect the battery negative lead.

3 Cooling system - draining and refilling

Draining

1 Position the heater temperature control on full heat.

2 Unclip the expansion bottle, and pour its contents into a container.

3 Suspend the expansion bottle from a

2.21 Tightening the tensioner nut and bolt

2.23 Crankshaft pulley locating pins (arrowed)

2.24 Tightening the crankshaft pulley bolt

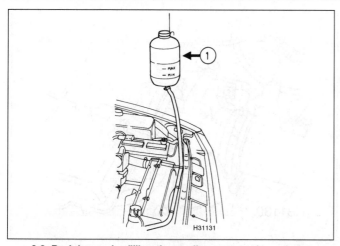

3.3 Draining and refilling the cooling system through the expansion bottle (1)

3.4 Removing the radiator drain plug

convenient point on the bonnet, as high as the connecting hose will allow **(see illustration)**.
4 Place a suitable container beneath the left-hand side of the radiator, then unscrew the drain plug and drain the coolant **(see illustration)**.

5 Drain the cylinder block by removing the plug located on the right-hand rear (carburettor engines), or left-hand front (fuel injection engines), of the block **(see illustrations)**.
6 Disconnect the wiring from the coolant level

sender on the radiator. Unscrew the cap, and withdraw the sender from the radiator **(see illustrations)**.

Refilling

7 Refit the hoses and plugs as necessary.

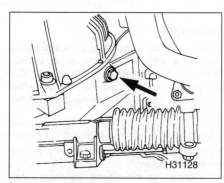

3.5a Cylinder block drain plug location on carburettor engines

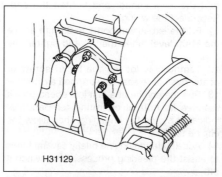

3.5b Cylinder block drain plug location on the fuel injection engines

3.6a Disconnect the level sender wire . . .

3.6b . . . unscrew the cap . . .

3.6c . . . and withdraw the sender

3.8a Coolant bleed screw (arrowed) on carburettor engines

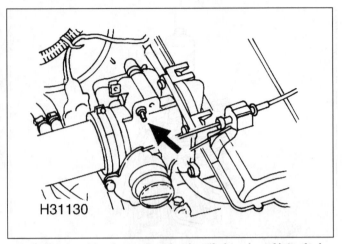

3.8b Coolant bleed screw on the throttle housing of later fuel injection engines

3.12 Filling the radiator with coolant

8 To refill the system, first loosen the bleed screw (if fitted). This will be located either on the uppermost coolant hose on carburettor engines **(see illustration)**, or on the throttle housing on later fuel injection engines **(see illustration)**. On carburettor engines without a bleed screw, disconnect the coolant hose from the carburettor automatic choke housing.

9 Fill the radiator with fresh coolant **(see illustration)**, and tighten the bleed screw, or refit the hose, when the coolant emerges in a continuous stream, free of bubbles.

10 Pour coolant into the expansion bottle until the radiator overflows, then immediately refit the level sender and tighten the cap. Reconnect the wiring.

11 Fill the expansion bottle to 25 mm above the MAXI level mark, then fit and tighten the cap.

12 Temporarily loosen the bleed screw or heater hose to release any trapped air.

13 Run the engine at a fast idle speed until it reaches its normal operating temperature, indicated by the fan engaging, then allow the engine to idle.

14 Accelerate the engine briefly several times to assist the bleeding process, then switch it off.

15 Refit the expansion bottle, beside the radiator.

16 Allow the engine to cool completely.

17 Check that the coolant is up to the MAXI level mark, and top up if necessary.

4 Thermostat housing - removal and refitting

Removal

1 The thermostat housing on carburettor engines is integral with the water pump, located on the front of the cylinder head. On fuel injection engines, it is separate from the water pump, on the front left-hand side of the cylinder head.

2 Drain the cooling system as described in Section 3.

3 Disconnect the radiator top hose from the thermostat housing.

4 Unscrew and remove the two thermostat housing cover bolts, and remove the cover **(see illustrations)**. This may need to be

4.4a Unscrew the bolts . . .

4.4b . . . and remove the thermostat housing cover (carburettor engine)

5.1a Loosen the power steering pump tension bolt . . .

5.1b . . . and disconnect the drivebelt

tapped lightly with a wooden or plastic-faced mallet to free it.

Refitting

5 Clean the mating surfaces, then fit the cover and tighten the bolts.
6 Reconnect the radiator top hose. and refill the system as described in Section 3.

---

5 Power steering pump drivebelt - removal and refitting

1 Loosen the tension adjustment bolt, push the pump towards the engine, and disconnect the drivebelt from the pulley **(see illustrations)**. Note that, on some models, it is necessary to unbolt the pulley from the pump.
2 Refitting is a reversal of removal, but tension the drivebelt as follows. Adjust the pump so that the deflection of the belt, under firm thumb pressure, midway between the pulleys, is approximately 12.5 mm do not over-tension.

---

6 Alternator - removal and refitting

Removal

1 Disconnect the battery negative lead.
2 Loosen the pivot and adjustment bolts, swivel the alternator towards the engine, then remove the drivebelt from the pulley.
3 Unscrew the nut and disconnect the main

cable from its terminal. Also disconnect the warning lamp wire **(see illustration)**
4 Remove the adjustment bolt and spacer. If necessary, the adjustment link may be unbolted from the cylinder head or block as applicable **(see illustrations)**.

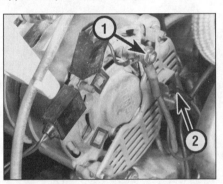

6.3 Alternator main cable (1) and warning lamp wire (2)

6.4b Alternator adjustment link removal

5 Remove the pivot bolt, and lift the alternator from the engine **(see illustration)**.

Refitting

6 Refitting is a reversal of removal, but tension the drivebelt as described in Section 1.

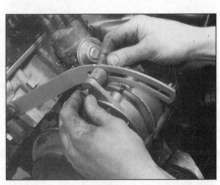

6.4a Removing the alternator adjustment bolt and spacer

6.5 Removing the alternator pivot bolt

15

Notes

Whenever servicing, repair or overhaul work is carried out on the car or its components, observe the following procedures and instructions. This will assist in carrying out the operation efficiently and to a professional standard of workmanship.

Joint mating faces and gaskets

When separating components at their mating faces, never insert screwdrivers or similar implements into the joint between the faces in order to prise them apart. This can cause severe damage which results in oil leaks, coolant leaks, etc upon reassembly. Separation is usually achieved by tapping along the joint with a soft-faced hammer in order to break the seal. However, note that this method may not be suitable where dowels are used for component location.

Where a gasket is used between the mating faces of two components, a new one must be fitted on reassembly; fit it dry unless otherwise stated in the repair procedure. Make sure that the mating faces are clean and dry, with all traces of old gasket removed. When cleaning a joint face, use a tool which is unlikely to score or damage the face, and remove any burrs or nicks with an oilstone or fine file.

Make sure that tapped holes are cleaned with a pipe cleaner, and keep them free of jointing compound, if this is being used, unless specifically instructed otherwise.

Ensure that all orifices, channels or pipes are clear, and blow through them, preferably using compressed air.

Oil seals

Oil seals can be removed by levering them out with a wide flat-bladed screwdriver or similar implement. Alternatively, a number of self-tapping screws may be screwed into the seal, and these used as a purchase for pliers or some similar device in order to pull the seal free.

Whenever an oil seal is removed from its working location, either individually or as part of an assembly, it should be renewed.

The very fine sealing lip of the seal is easily damaged, and will not seal if the surface it contacts is not completely clean and free from scratches, nicks or grooves. If the original sealing surface of the component cannot be restored, and the manufacturer has not made provision for slight relocation of the seal relative to the sealing surface, the component should be renewed.

Protect the lips of the seal from any surface which may damage them in the course of fitting. Use tape or a conical sleeve where possible. Lubricate the seal lips with oil before fitting and, on dual-lipped seals, fill the space between the lips with grease.

Unless otherwise stated, oil seals must be fitted with their sealing lips toward the lubricant to be sealed.

Use a tubular drift or block of wood of the appropriate size to install the seal and, if the seal housing is shouldered, drive the seal down to the shoulder. If the seal housing is unshouldered, the seal should be fitted with its face flush with the housing top face (unless otherwise instructed).

Screw threads and fastenings

Seized nuts, bolts and screws are quite a common occurrence where corrosion has set in, and the use of penetrating oil or releasing fluid will often overcome this problem if the offending item is soaked for a while before attempting to release it. The use of an impact driver may also provide a means of releasing such stubborn fastening devices, when used in conjunction with the appropriate screwdriver bit or socket. If none of these methods works, it may be necessary to resort to the careful application of heat, or the use of a hacksaw or nut splitter device.

Studs are usually removed by locking two nuts together on the threaded part, and then using a spanner on the lower nut to unscrew the stud. Studs or bolts which have broken off below the surface of the component in which they are mounted can sometimes be removed using a stud extractor. Always ensure that a blind tapped hole is completely free from oil, grease, water or other fluid before installing the bolt or stud. Failure to do this could cause the housing to crack due to the hydraulic action of the bolt or stud as it is screwed in.

When tightening a castellated nut to accept a split pin, tighten the nut to the specified torque, where applicable, and then tighten further to the next split pin hole. Never slacken the nut to align the split pin hole, unless stated in the repair procedure.

When checking or retightening a nut or bolt to a specified torque setting, slacken the nut or bolt by a quarter of a turn, and then retighten to the specified setting. However, this should not be attempted where angular tightening has been used.

For some screw fastenings, notably cylinder head bolts or nuts, torque wrench settings are no longer specified for the latter stages of tightening, "angle-tightening" being called up instead. Typically, a fairly low torque wrench setting will be applied to the bolts/nuts in the correct sequence, followed by one or more stages of tightening through specified angles.

Locknuts, locktabs and washers

Any fastening which will rotate against a component or housing during tightening should always have a washer between it and the relevant component or housing.

Spring or split washers should always be renewed when they are used to lock a critical component such as a big-end bearing retaining bolt or nut. Locktabs which are folded over to retain a nut or bolt should always be renewed.

Self-locking nuts can be re-used in non-critical areas, providing resistance can be felt when the locking portion passes over the bolt or stud thread. However, it should be noted that self-locking stiffnuts tend to lose their effectiveness after long periods of use, and should then be renewed as a matter of course.

Split pins must always be replaced with new ones of the correct size for the hole.

When thread-locking compound is found on the threads of a fastener which is to be re-used, it should be cleaned off with a wire brush and solvent, and fresh compound applied on reassembly.

Special tools

Some repair procedures in this manual entail the use of special tools such as a press, two or three-legged pullers, spring compressors, etc. Wherever possible, suitable readily-available alternatives to the manufacturer's special tools are described, and are shown in use. In some instances, where no alternative is possible, it has been necessary to resort to the use of a manufacturer's tool, and this has been done for reasons of safety as well as the efficient completion of the repair operation. Unless you are highly-skilled and have a thorough understanding of the procedures described, never attempt to bypass the use of any special tool when the procedure described specifies its use. Not only is there a very great risk of personal injury, but expensive damage could be caused to the components involved.

Environmental considerations

When disposing of used engine oil, brake fluid, antifreeze, etc, give due consideration to any detrimental environmental effects. Do not, for instance, pour any of the above liquids down drains into the general sewage system, or onto the ground to soak away. Many local council refuse tips provide a facility for waste oil disposal, as do some garages. If none of these facilities are available, consult your local Environmental Health Department, or the National Rivers Authority, for further advice.

With the universal tightening-up of legislation regarding the emission of environmentally-harmful substances from motor vehicles, most vehicles have tamperproof devices fitted to the main adjustment points of the fuel system. These devices are primarily designed to prevent unqualified persons from adjusting the fuel/air mixture, with the chance of a consequent increase in toxic emissions. If such devices are found during servicing or overhaul, they should, wherever possible, be renewed or refitted in accordance with the manufacturer's requirements or current legislation.

OIL CARE · FOLLOW THE CODE · OIL BANK LINE **0800 66 33 66**

Note: It is antisocial and illegal to dump oil down the drain. To find the location of your local oil recycling bank, call this number free.

Introduction

A selection of good tools is a fundamental requirement for anyone contemplating the maintenance and repair of a motor vehicle. For the owner who does not possess any, their purchase will prove a considerable expense, offsetting some of the savings made by doing-it-yourself. However, provided that the tools purchased meet the relevant national safety standards and are of good quality, they will last for many years and prove an extremely worthwhile investment.

To help the average owner to decide which tools are needed to carry out the various tasks detailed in this manual, we have compiled three lists of tools under the following headings: *Maintenance and minor repair, Repair and overhaul,* and *Special.* Newcomers to practical mechanics should start off with the *Maintenance and minor repair* tool kit, and confine themselves to the simpler jobs around the vehicle. Then, as confidence and experience grow, more difficult tasks can be undertaken, with extra tools being purchased as, and when, they are needed. In this way, a *Maintenance and minor repair* tool kit can be built up into a *Repair and overhaul* tool kit over a considerable period of time, without any major cash outlays. The experienced do-it-yourselfer will have a tool kit good enough for most repair and overhaul procedures, and will add tools from the *Special* category when it is felt that the expense is justified by the amount of use to which these tools will be put.

Maintenance and minor repair tool kit

The tools given in this list should be considered as a minimum requirement if routine maintenance, servicing and minor repair operations are to be undertaken. We recommend the purchase of combination spanners (ring one end, open-ended the other); although more expensive than open-ended ones, they do give the advantages of both types of spanner.

☐ *Combination spanners:*
    Metric - 8 to 19 mm inclusive
☐ *Adjustable spanner - 35 mm jaw (approx.)*
☐ *Spark plug spanner (with rubber insert) - petrol models*
☐ *Spark plug gap adjustment tool - petrol models*
☐ *Set of feeler gauges*
☐ *Brake bleed nipple spanner*
☐ *Screwdrivers:*
    Flat blade - 100 mm long x 6 mm dia
    Cross blade - 100 mm long x 6 mm dia
    Torx - various sizes (not all vehicles)
☐ *Combination pliers*
☐ *Hacksaw (junior)*
☐ *Tyre pump*
☐ *Tyre pressure gauge*
☐ *Oil can*
☐ *Oil filter removal tool*
☐ *Fine emery cloth*
☐ *Wire brush (small)*
☐ *Funnel (medium size)*
☐ *Sump drain plug key (not all vehicles)*

Repair and overhaul tool kit

These tools are virtually essential for anyone undertaking any major repairs to a motor vehicle, and are additional to those given in the *Maintenance and minor repair* list. Included in this list is a comprehensive set of sockets. Although these are expensive, they will be found invaluable as they are so versatile - particularly if various drives are included in the set. We recommend the half-inch square-drive type, as this can be used with most proprietary torque wrenches.

The tools in this list will sometimes need to be supplemented by tools from the *Special* list:

☐ *Sockets (or box spanners) to cover range in previous list (including Torx sockets)*
☐ *Reversible ratchet drive (for use with sockets)*
☐ *Extension piece, 250 mm (for use with sockets)*
☐ *Universal joint (for use with sockets)*
☐ *Flexible handle or "breaker bar" (for use with sockets)*
☐ *Torque wrench (for use with sockets)*
☐ *Self-locking grips*
☐ *Ball pein hammer*
☐ *Soft-faced mallet (plastic or rubber)*
☐ *Screwdrivers:*
    Flat blade - long & sturdy, short (chubby), and narrow (electrician's) types
    Cross blade – long & sturdy, and short (chubby) types
☐ *Pliers:*
    Long-nosed
    Side cutters (electrician's)
    Circlip (internal and external)
☐ *Cold chisel - 25 mm*
☐ *Scriber*
☐ *Scraper*
☐ *Centre-punch*
☐ *Pin punch*
☐ *Hacksaw*
☐ *Brake hose clamp*
☐ *Brake/clutch bleeding kit*
☐ *Selection of twist drills*
☐ *Steel rule/straight-edge*
☐ *Allen keys (inc. splined/Torx type)*
☐ *Selection of files*
☐ *Wire brush*
☐ *Axle stands*
☐ *Jack (strong trolley or hydraulic type)*
☐ *Light with extension lead*
☐ *Universal electrical multi-meter*

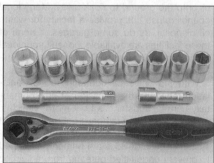

Sockets and reversible ratchet drive

Brake bleeding kit

Torx key, socket and bit

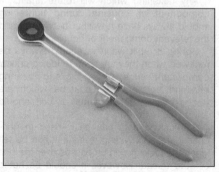

Hose clamp

Angular-tightening gauge

Special tools

The tools in this list are those which are not used regularly, are expensive to buy, or which need to be used in accordance with their manufacturers' instructions. Unless relatively difficult mechanical jobs are undertaken frequently, it will not be economic to buy many of these tools. Where this is the case, you could consider clubbing together with friends (or joining a motorists' club) to make a joint purchase, or borrowing the tools against a deposit from a local garage or tool hire specialist. It is worth noting that many of the larger DIY superstores now carry a large range of special tools for hire at modest rates.

The following list contains only those tools and instruments freely available to the public, and not those special tools produced by the vehicle manufacturer specifically for its dealer network. You will find occasional references to these manufacturers' special tools in the text of this manual. Generally, an alternative method of doing the job without the vehicle manufacturers' special tool is given. However, sometimes there is no alternative to using them. Where this is the case and the relevant tool cannot be bought or borrowed, you will have to entrust the work to a dealer.

- ☐ Angular-tightening gauge
- ☐ Valve spring compressor
- ☐ Valve grinding tool
- ☐ Piston ring compressor
- ☐ Piston ring removal/installation tool
- ☐ Cylinder bore hone
- ☐ Balljoint separator
- ☐ Coil spring compressors (where applicable)
- ☐ Two/three-legged hub and bearing puller
- ☐ Impact screwdriver
- ☐ Micrometer and/or vernier calipers
- ☐ Dial gauge
- ☐ Stroboscopic timing light
- ☐ Dwell angle meter/tachometer
- ☐ Fault code reader
- ☐ Cylinder compression gauge
- ☐ Hand-operated vacuum pump and gauge
- ☐ Clutch plate alignment set
- ☐ Brake shoe steady spring cup removal tool
- ☐ Bush and bearing removal/installation set
- ☐ Stud extractors
- ☐ Tap and die set
- ☐ Lifting tackle
- ☐ Trolley jack

Buying tools

Reputable motor accessory shops and superstores often offer excellent quality tools at discount prices, so it pays to shop around.

Remember, you don't have to buy the most expensive items on the shelf, but it is always advisable to steer clear of the very cheap tools. Beware of 'bargains' offered on market stalls or at car boot sales. There are plenty of good tools around at reasonable prices, but always aim to purchase items which meet the relevant national safety standards. If in doubt, ask the proprietor or manager of the shop for advice before making a purchase.

Care and maintenance of tools

Having purchased a reasonable tool kit, it is necessary to keep the tools in a clean and serviceable condition. After use, always wipe off any dirt, grease and metal particles using a clean, dry cloth, before putting the tools away. Never leave them lying around after they have been used. A simple tool rack on the garage or workshop wall for items such as screwdrivers and pliers is a good idea. Store all normal spanners and sockets in a metal box. Any measuring instruments, gauges, meters, etc, must be carefully stored where they cannot be damaged or become rusty.

Take a little care when tools are used. Hammer heads inevitably become marked, and screwdrivers lose the keen edge on their blades from time to time. A little timely attention with emery cloth or a file will soon restore items like this to a good finish.

Working facilities

Not to be forgotten when discussing tools is the workshop itself. If anything more than routine maintenance is to be carried out, a suitable working area becomes essential.

It is appreciated that many an owner-mechanic is forced by circumstances to remove an engine or similar item without the benefit of a garage or workshop. Having done this, any repairs should always be done under the cover of a roof.

Wherever possible, any dismantling should be done on a clean, flat workbench or table at a suitable working height.

Any workbench needs a vice; one with a jaw opening of 100 mm is suitable for most jobs. As mentioned previously, some clean dry storage space is also required for tools, as well as for any lubricants, cleaning fluids, touch-up paints etc, which become necessary.

Another item which may be required, and which has a much more general usage, is an electric drill with a chuck capacity of at least 8 mm. This, together with a good range of twist drills, is virtually essential for fitting accessories.

Last, but not least, always keep a supply of old newspapers and clean, lint-free rags available, and try to keep any working area as clean as possible.

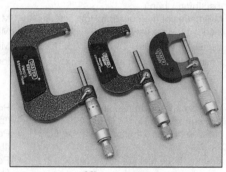

Micrometers

Dial test indicator ("dial gauge")

Strap wrench

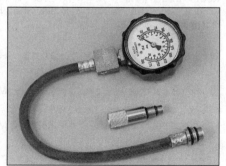

Compression tester

Fault code reader

Conversion Factors

Length (distance)

Inches (in)	x 25.4	= Millimetres (mm)	x 0.0394	= Inches (in)	
Feet (ft)	x 0.305	= Metres (m)	x 3.281	= Feet (ft)	
Miles	x 1.609	= Kilometres (km)	x 0.621	= Miles	

Volume (capacity)

Cubic inches (cu in; in³)	x 16.387	= Cubic centimetres (cc; cm³)	x 0.061	= Cubic inches (cu in; in³)	
Imperial pints (Imp pt)	x 0.568	= Litres (l)	x 1.76	= Imperial pints (Imp pt)	
Imperial quarts (Imp qt)	x 1.137	= Litres (l)	x 0.88	= Imperial quarts (Imp qt)	
Imperial quarts (Imp qt)	x 1.201	= US quarts (US qt)	x 0.833	= Imperial quarts (Imp qt)	
US quarts (US qt)	x 0.946	= Litres (l)	x 1.057	= US quarts (US qt)	
Imperial gallons (Imp gal)	x 4.546	= Litres (l)	x 0.22	= Imperial gallons (Imp gal)	
Imperial gallons (Imp gal)	x 1.201	= US gallons (US gal)	x 0.833	= Imperial gallons (Imp gal)	
US gallons (US gal)	x 3.785	= Litres (l)	x 0.264	= US gallons (US gal)	

Mass (weight)

Ounces (oz)	x 28.35	= Grams (g)	x 0.035	= Ounces (oz)
Pounds (lb)	x 0.454	= Kilograms (kg)	x 2.205	= Pounds (lb)

Force

Ounces-force (ozf; oz)	x 0.278	= Newtons (N)	x 3.6	= Ounces-force (ozf; oz)
Pounds-force (lbf; lb)	x 4.448	= Newtons (N)	x 0.225	= Pounds-force (lbf; lb)
Newtons (N)	x 0.1	= Kilograms-force (kgf; kg)	x 9.81	= Newtons (N)

Pressure

Pounds-force per square inch (psi; lbf/in²; lb/in²)	x 0.070	= Kilograms-force per square centimetre (kgf/cm²; kg/cm²)	x 14.223	= Pounds-force per square inch (psi; lbf/in²; lb/in²)
Pounds-force per square inch (psi; lbf/in²; lb/in²)	x 0.068	= Atmospheres (atm)	x 14.696	= Pounds-force per square inch (psi; lbf/in²; lb/in²)
Pounds-force per square inch (psi; lbf/in²; lb/in²)	x 0.069	= Bars	x 14.5	= Pounds-force per square inch (psi; lbf/in²; lb/in²)
Pounds-force per square inch (psi; lbf/in²; lb/in²)	x 6.895	= Kilopascals (kPa)	x 0.145	= Pounds-force per square inch (psi; lbf/in²; lb/in²)
Kilopascals (kPa)	x 0.01	= Kilograms-force per square centimetre (kgf/cm²; kg/cm²)	x 98.1	= Kilopascals (kPa)
Millibar (mbar)	x 100	= Pascals (Pa)	x 0.01	= Millibar (mbar)
Millibar (mbar)	x 0.0145	= Pounds-force per square inch (psi; lbf/in²; lb/in²)	x 68.947	= Millibar (mbar)
Millibar (mbar)	x 0.75	= Millimetres of mercury (mmHg)	x 1.333	= Millibar (mbar)
Millibar (mbar)	x 0.401	= Inches of water (inH₂O)	x 2.491	= Millibar (mbar)
Millimetres of mercury (mmHg)	x 0.535	= Inches of water (inH₂O)	x 1.868	= Millimetres of mercury (mmHg)
Inches of water (inH₂O)	x 0.036	= Pounds-force per square inch (psi; lbf/in²; lb/in²)	x 27.68	= Inches of water (inH₂O)

Torque (moment of force)

Pounds-force inches (lbf in; lb in)	x 1.152	= Kilograms-force centimetre (kgf cm; kg cm)	x 0.868	= Pounds-force inches (lbf in; lb in)
Pounds-force inches (lbf in; lb in)	x 0.113	= Newton metres (Nm)	x 8.85	= Pounds-force inches (lbf in; lb in)
Pounds-force inches (lbf in; lb in)	x 0.083	= Pounds-force feet (lbf ft; lb ft)	x 12	= Pounds-force inches (lbf in; lb in)
Pounds-force feet (lbf ft; lb ft)	x 0.138	= Kilograms-force metres (kgf m; kg m)	x 7.233	= Pounds-force feet (lbf ft; lb ft)
Pounds-force feet (lbf ft; lb ft)	x 1.356	= Newton metres (Nm)	x 0.738	= Pounds-force feet (lbf ft; lb ft)
Newton metres (Nm)	x 0.102	= Kilograms-force metres (kgf m; kg m)	x 9.804	= Newton metres (Nm)

Power

Horsepower (hp)	x 745.7	= Watts (W)	x 0.0013	= Horsepower (hp)

Velocity (speed)

Miles per hour (miles/hr; mph)	x 1.609	= Kilometres per hour (km/hr; kph)	x 0.621	= Miles per hour (miles/hr; mph)

Fuel consumption*

Miles per gallon (mpg)	x 0.354	= Kilometres per litre (km/l)	x 2.825	= Miles per gallon (mpg)

Temperature

Degrees Fahrenheit = (°C x 1.8) + 32   Degrees Celsius (Degrees Centigrade; °C) = (°F - 32) x 0.56

It is common practice to convert from miles per gallon (mpg) to litres/100 kilometres (l/100km), where mpg x l/100 km = 282

A

ABS (Anti-lock brake system) A system, usually electronically controlled, that senses incipient wheel lockup during braking and relieves hydraulic pressure at wheels that are about to skid.

Air bag An inflatable bag hidden in the steering wheel (driver's side) or the dash or glovebox (passenger side). In a head-on collision, the bags inflate, preventing the driver and front passenger from being thrown forward into the steering wheel or windscreen.

Air cleaner A metal or plastic housing, containing a filter element, which removes dust and dirt from the air being drawn into the engine.

Air filter element The actual filter in an air cleaner system, usually manufactured from pleated paper and requiring renewal at regular intervals.

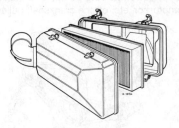

Air filter

Allen key A hexagonal wrench which fits into a recessed hexagonal hole.

Alligator clip A long-nosed spring-loaded metal clip with meshing teeth. Used to make temporary electrical connections.

Alternator A component in the electrical system which converts mechanical energy from a drivebelt into electrical energy to charge the battery and to operate the starting system, ignition system and electrical accessories.

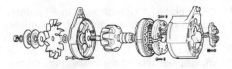

Alternator (exploded view)

Ampere (amp) A unit of measurement for the flow of electric current. One amp is the amount of current produced by one volt acting through a resistance of one ohm.

Anaerobic sealer A substance used to prevent bolts and screws from loosening. Anaerobic means that it does not require oxygen for activation. The Loctite brand is widely used.

Antifreeze A substance (usually ethylene glycol) mixed with water, and added to a vehicle's cooling system, to prevent freezing of the coolant in winter. Antifreeze also contains chemicals to inhibit corrosion and the formation of rust and other deposits that would tend to clog the radiator and coolant passages and reduce cooling efficiency.

Anti-seize compound A coating that reduces the risk of seizing on fasteners that are subjected to high temperatures, such as exhaust manifold bolts and nuts.

Anti-seize compound

Asbestos A natural fibrous mineral with great heat resistance, commonly used in the composition of brake friction materials. Asbestos is a health hazard and the dust created by brake systems should never be inhaled or ingested.

Axle A shaft on which a wheel revolves, or which revolves with a wheel. Also, a solid beam that connects the two wheels at one end of the vehicle. An axle which also transmits power to the wheels is known as a live axle.

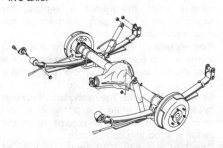

Axle assembly

Axleshaft A single rotating shaft, on either side of the differential, which delivers power from the final drive assembly to the drive wheels. Also called a driveshaft or a halfshaft.

B

Ball bearing An anti-friction bearing consisting of a hardened inner and outer race with hardened steel balls between two races.

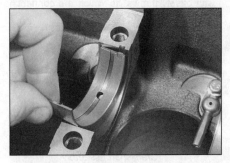

Bearing

Bearing The curved surface on a shaft or in a bore, or the part assembled into either, that permits relative motion between them with minimum wear and friction.

Big-end bearing The bearing in the end of the connecting rod that's attached to the crankshaft.

Bleed nipple A valve on a brake wheel cylinder, caliper or other hydraulic component that is opened to purge the hydraulic system of air. Also called a bleed screw.

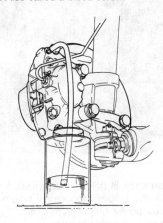

Brake bleeding

Brake bleeding Procedure for removing air from lines of a hydraulic brake system.

Brake disc The component of a disc brake that rotates with the wheels.

Brake drum The component of a drum brake that rotates with the wheels.

Brake linings The friction material which contacts the brake disc or drum to retard the vehicle's speed. The linings are bonded or riveted to the brake pads or shoes.

Brake pads The replaceable friction pads that pinch the brake disc when the brakes are applied. Brake pads consist of a friction material bonded or riveted to a rigid backing plate.

Brake shoe The crescent-shaped carrier to which the brake linings are mounted and which forces the lining against the rotating drum during braking.

Braking systems For more information on braking systems, consult the *Haynes Automotive Brake Manual*.

Breaker bar A long socket wrench handle providing greater leverage.

Bulkhead The insulated partition between the engine and the passenger compartment.

C

Caliper The non-rotating part of a disc-brake assembly that straddles the disc and carries the brake pads. The caliper also contains the hydraulic components that cause the pads to pinch the disc when the brakes are applied. A caliper is also a measuring tool that can be set to measure inside or outside dimensions of an object.

Camshaft A rotating shaft on which a series of cam lobes operate the valve mechanisms. The camshaft may be driven by gears, by sprockets and chain or by sprockets and a belt.

Canister A container in an evaporative emission control system; contains activated charcoal granules to trap vapours from the fuel system.

Canister

Carburettor A device which mixes fuel with air in the proper proportions to provide a desired power output from a spark ignition internal combustion engine.

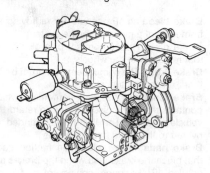

Carburettor

Castellated Resembling the parapets along the top of a castle wall. For example, a castellated balljoint stud nut.

Castellated nut

Castor In wheel alignment, the backward or forward tilt of the steering axis. Castor is positive when the steering axis is inclined rearward at the top.

Catalytic converter A silencer-like device in the exhaust system which converts certain pollutants in the exhaust gases into less harmful substances.

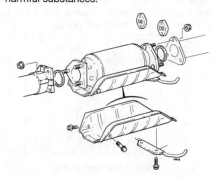

Catalytic converter

Circlip A ring-shaped clip used to prevent endwise movement of cylindrical parts and shafts. An internal circlip is installed in a groove in a housing; an external circlip fits into a groove on the outside of a cylindrical piece such as a shaft.

Clearance The amount of space between two parts. For example, between a piston and a cylinder, between a bearing and a journal, etc.

Coil spring A spiral of elastic steel found in various sizes throughout a vehicle, for example as a springing medium in the suspension and in the valve train.

Compression Reduction in volume, and increase in pressure and temperature, of a gas, caused by squeezing it into a smaller space.

Compression ratio The relationship between cylinder volume when the piston is at top dead centre and cylinder volume when the piston is at bottom dead centre.

Constant velocity (CV) joint A type of universal joint that cancels out vibrations caused by driving power being transmitted through an angle.

Core plug A disc or cup-shaped metal device inserted in a hole in a casting through which core was removed when the casting was formed. Also known as a freeze plug or expansion plug.

Crankcase The lower part of the engine block in which the crankshaft rotates.

Crankshaft The main rotating member, or shaft, running the length of the crankcase, with offset "throws" to which the connecting rods are attached.

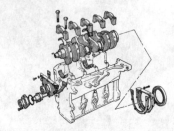

Crankshaft assembly

Crocodile clip See Alligator clip

D

Diagnostic code Code numbers obtained by accessing the diagnostic mode of an engine management computer. This code can be used to determine the area in the system where a malfunction may be located.

Disc brake A brake design incorporating a rotating disc onto which brake pads are squeezed. The resulting friction converts the energy of a moving vehicle into heat.

Double-overhead cam (DOHC) An engine that uses two overhead camshafts, usually one for the intake valves and one for the exhaust valves.

Drivebelt(s) The belt(s) used to drive accessories such as the alternator, water pump, power steering pump, air conditioning compressor, etc. off the crankshaft pulley.

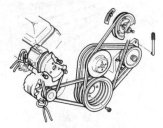

Accessory drivebelts

Driveshaft Any shaft used to transmit motion. Commonly used when referring to the axleshafts on a front wheel drive vehicle.

Driveshaft

Drum brake A type of brake using a drum-shaped metal cylinder attached to the inner surface of the wheel. When the brake pedal is pressed, curved brake shoes with friction linings press against the inside of the drum to slow or stop the vehicle.

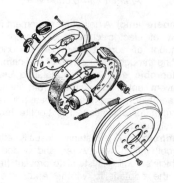

Drum brake assembly

E

EGR valve A valve used to introduce exhaust gases into the intake air stream.

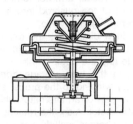

EGR valve

Electronic control unit (ECU) A computer which controls (for instance) ignition and fuel injection systems, or an anti-lock braking system. For more information refer to the *Haynes Automotive Electrical and Electronic Systems Manual*.

Electronic Fuel Injection (EFI) A computer controlled fuel system that distributes fuel through an injector located in each intake port of the engine.

Emergency brake A braking system, independent of the main hydraulic system, that can be used to slow or stop the vehicle if the primary brakes fail, or to hold the vehicle stationary even though the brake pedal isn't depressed. It usually consists of a hand lever that actuates either front or rear brakes mechanically through a series of cables and linkages. Also known as a handbrake or parking brake.

Endfloat The amount of lengthwise movement between two parts. As applied to a crankshaft, the distance that the crankshaft can move forward and back in the cylinder block.

Engine management system (EMS) A computer controlled system which manages the fuel injection and the ignition systems in an integrated fashion.

Exhaust manifold A part with several passages through which exhaust gases leave the engine combustion chambers and enter the exhaust pipe.

Exhaust manifold

F

Fan clutch A viscous (fluid) drive coupling device which permits variable engine fan speeds in relation to engine speeds.

Feeler blade A thin strip or blade of hardened steel, ground to an exact thickness, used to check or measure clearances between parts.

Feeler blade

Firing order The order in which the engine cylinders fire, or deliver their power strokes, beginning with the number one cylinder.

Flywheel A heavy spinning wheel in which energy is absorbed and stored by means of momentum. On cars, the flywheel is attached to the crankshaft to smooth out firing impulses.

Free play The amount of travel before any action takes place. The "looseness" in a linkage, or an assembly of parts, between the initial application of force and actual movement. For example, the distance the brake pedal moves before the pistons in the master cylinder are actuated.

Fuse An electrical device which protects a circuit against accidental overload. The typical fuse contains a soft piece of metal which is calibrated to melt at a predetermined current flow (expressed as amps) and break the circuit.

Fusible link A circuit protection device consisting of a conductor surrounded by heat-resistant insulation. The conductor is smaller than the wire it protects, so it acts as the weakest link in the circuit. Unlike a blown fuse, a failed fusible link must frequently be cut from the wire for replacement.

G

Gap The distance the spark must travel in jumping from the centre electrode to the side

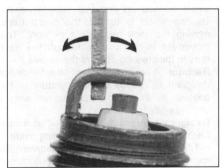

Adjusting spark plug gap

electrode in a spark plug. Also refers to the spacing between the points in a contact breaker assembly in a conventional points-type ignition, or to the distance between the reluctor or rotor and the pickup coil in an electronic ignition.

Gasket Any thin, soft material - usually cork, cardboard, asbestos or soft metal - installed between two metal surfaces to ensure a good seal. For instance, the cylinder head gasket seals the joint between the block and the cylinder head.

Gasket

Gauge An instrument panel display used to monitor engine conditions. A gauge with a movable pointer on a dial or a fixed scale is an analogue gauge. A gauge with a numerical readout is called a digital gauge.

H

Halfshaft A rotating shaft that transmits power from the final drive unit to a drive wheel, usually when referring to a live rear axle.

Harmonic balancer A device designed to reduce torsion or twisting vibration in the crankshaft. May be incorporated in the crankshaft pulley. Also known as a vibration damper.

Hone An abrasive tool for correcting small irregularities or differences in diameter in an engine cylinder, brake cylinder, etc.

Hydraulic tappet A tappet that utilises hydraulic pressure from the engine's lubrication system to maintain zero clearance (constant contact with both camshaft and valve stem). Automatically adjusts to variation in valve stem length. Hydraulic tappets also reduce valve noise.

I

Ignition timing The moment at which the spark plug fires, usually expressed in the number of crankshaft degrees before the piston reaches the top of its stroke.

Inlet manifold A tube or housing with passages through which flows the air-fuel mixture (carburettor vehicles and vehicles with throttle body injection) or air only (port fuel-injected vehicles) to the port openings in the cylinder head.

J

Jump start Starting the engine of a vehicle with a discharged or weak battery by attaching jump leads from the weak battery to a charged or helper battery.

L

Load Sensing Proportioning Valve (LSPV) A brake hydraulic system control valve that works like a proportioning valve, but also takes into consideration the amount of weight carried by the rear axle.

Locknut A nut used to lock an adjustment nut, or other threaded component, in place. For example, a locknut is employed to keep the adjusting nut on the rocker arm in position.

Lockwasher A form of washer designed to prevent an attaching nut from working loose.

M

MacPherson strut A type of front suspension system devised by Earle MacPherson at Ford of England. In its original form, a simple lateral link with the anti-roll bar creates the lower control arm. A long strut - an integral coil spring and shock absorber - is mounted between the body and the steering knuckle. Many modern so-called MacPherson strut systems use a conventional lower A-arm and don't rely on the anti-roll bar for location.

Multimeter An electrical test instrument with the capability to measure voltage, current and resistance.

N

NOx Oxides of Nitrogen. A common toxic pollutant emitted by petrol and diesel engines at higher temperatures.

O

Ohm The unit of electrical resistance. One volt applied to a resistance of one ohm will produce a current of one amp.

Ohmmeter An instrument for measuring electrical resistance.

O-ring A type of sealing ring made of a special rubber-like material; in use, the O-ring is compressed into a groove to provide the sealing action.

O-ring

Overhead cam (ohc) engine An engine with the camshaft(s) located on top of the cylinder head(s).

Overhead valve (ohv) engine An engine with the valves located in the cylinder head, but with the camshaft located in the engine block.

Oxygen sensor A device installed in the engine exhaust manifold, which senses the oxygen content in the exhaust and converts this information into an electric current. Also called a Lambda sensor.

P

Phillips screw A type of screw head having a cross instead of a slot for a corresponding type of screwdriver.

Plastigage A thin strip of plastic thread, available in different sizes, used for measuring clearances. For example, a strip of Plastigage is laid across a bearing journal. The parts are assembled and dismantled; the width of the crushed strip indicates the clearance between journal and bearing.

Plastigage

Propeller shaft The long hollow tube with universal joints at both ends that carries power from the transmission to the differential on front-engined rear wheel drive vehicles.

Proportioning valve A hydraulic control valve which limits the amount of pressure to the rear brakes during panic stops to prevent wheel lock-up.

R

Rack-and-pinion steering A steering system with a pinion gear on the end of the steering shaft that mates with a rack (think of a geared wheel opened up and laid flat). When the steering wheel is turned, the pinion turns, moving the rack to the left or right. This movement is transmitted through the track rods to the steering arms at the wheels.

Radiator A liquid-to-air heat transfer device designed to reduce the temperature of the coolant in an internal combustion engine cooling system.

Refrigerant Any substance used as a heat transfer agent in an air-conditioning system. R-12 has been the principle refrigerant for many years; recently, however, manufacturers have begun using R-134a, a non-CFC substance that is considered less harmful to

the ozone in the upper atmosphere.

Rocker arm A lever arm that rocks on a shaft or pivots on a stud. In an overhead valve engine, the rocker arm converts the upward movement of the pushrod into a downward movement to open a valve.

Rotor In a distributor, the rotating device inside the cap that connects the centre electrode and the outer terminals as it turns, distributing the high voltage from the coil secondary winding to the proper spark plug. Also, that part of an alternator which rotates inside the stator. Also, the rotating assembly of a turbocharger, including the compressor wheel, shaft and turbine wheel.

Runout The amount of wobble (in-and-out movement) of a gear or wheel as it's rotated. The amount a shaft rotates "out-of-true." The out-of-round condition of a rotating part.

S

Sealant A liquid or paste used to prevent leakage at a joint. Sometimes used in conjunction with a gasket.

Sealed beam lamp An older headlight design which integrates the reflector, lens and filaments into a hermetically-sealed one-piece unit. When a filament burns out or the lens cracks, the entire unit is simply replaced.

Serpentine drivebelt A single, long, wide accessory drivebelt that's used on some newer vehicles to drive all the accessories, instead of a series of smaller, shorter belts. Serpentine drivebelts are usually tensioned by an automatic tensioner.

Serpentine drivebelt

Shim Thin spacer, commonly used to adjust the clearance or relative positions between two parts. For example, shims inserted into or under bucket tappets control valve clearances. Clearance is adjusted by changing the thickness of the shim.

Slide hammer A special puller that screws into or hooks onto a component such as a shaft or bearing; a heavy sliding handle on the shaft bottoms against the end of the shaft to knock the component free.

Sprocket A tooth or projection on the periphery of a wheel, shaped to engage with a chain or drivebelt. Commonly used to refer to the sprocket wheel itself.

Starter inhibitor switch On vehicles with an

automatic transmission, a switch that prevents starting if the vehicle is not in Neutral or Park.

Strut See MacPherson strut.

T

Tappet A cylindrical component which transmits motion from the cam to the valve stem, either directly or via a pushrod and rocker arm. Also called a cam follower.

Thermostat A heat-controlled valve that regulates the flow of coolant between the cylinder block and the radiator, so maintaining optimum engine operating temperature. A thermostat is also used in some air cleaners in which the temperature is regulated.

Thrust bearing The bearing in the clutch assembly that is moved in to the release levers by clutch pedal action to disengage the clutch. Also referred to as a release bearing.

Timing belt A toothed belt which drives the camshaft. Serious engine damage may result if it breaks in service.

Timing chain A chain which drives the camshaft.

Toe-in The amount the front wheels are closer together at the front than at the rear. On rear wheel drive vehicles, a slight amount of toe-in is usually specified to keep the front wheels running parallel on the road by offsetting other forces that tend to spread the wheels apart.

Toe-out The amount the front wheels are closer together at the rear than at the front. On front wheel drive vehicles, a slight amount of toe-out is usually specified.

Tools For full information on choosing and using tools, refer to the *Haynes Automotive Tools Manual.*

Tracer A stripe of a second colour applied to a wire insulator to distinguish that wire from another one with the same colour insulator.

Tune-up A process of accurate and careful adjustments and parts replacement to obtain the best possible engine performance.

Turbocharger A centrifugal device, driven by exhaust gases, that pressurises the intake air. Normally used to increase the power output from a given engine displacement, but can also be used primarily to reduce exhaust emissions (as on VW's "Umwelt" Diesel engine).

U

Universal joint or U-joint A double-pivoted connection for transmitting power from a driving to a driven shaft through an angle. A U-joint consists of two Y-shaped yokes and a cross-shaped member called the spider.

V

Valve A device through which the flow of liquid, gas, vacuum, or loose material in bulk may be started, stopped, or regulated by a movable part that opens, shuts, or partially obstructs one or more ports or passageways. A valve is also the movable part of such a device.

Valve clearance The clearance between the valve tip (the end of the valve stem) and the rocker arm or tappet. The valve clearance is measured when the valve is closed.

Vernier caliper A precision measuring instrument that measures inside and outside dimensions. Not quite as accurate as a micrometer, but more convenient.

Viscosity The thickness of a liquid or its resistance to flow.

Volt A unit for expressing electrical "pressure" in a circuit. One volt that will produce a current of one ampere through a resistance of one ohm.

W

Welding Various processes used to join metal items by heating the areas to be joined to a molten state and fusing them together. For more information refer to the *Haynes Automotive Welding Manual.*

Wiring diagram A drawing portraying the components and wires in a vehicle's electrical system, using standardised symbols. For more information refer to the *Haynes Automotive Electrical and Electronic Systems Manual.*

Haynes Manuals – The Complete List

Title	Book No.
ALFA ROMEO	
Alfa Romeo Alfasud/Sprint (74 - 88)	0292
Alfa Romeo Alfetta (73 - 87)	0531
AUDI	
Audi 80 (72 - Feb 79)	0207
Audi 80, 90 (79 - Oct 86) & Coupe (81 - Nov 88)	0605
Audi 80, 90 (Oct 86 - 90) & Coupe (Nov 88 - 90)	1491
Audi 100 (Oct 82 - 90) & 200 (Feb 84 - Oct 89)	0907
Audi 100 & A6 Petrol & Diesel (May 91 - May 97)	3504
AUSTIN	
Austin/MG/Rover Maestro 1.3 & 1.6 (83 - 95)	0922
Austin/MG Metro (80 - May 90)	0718
Austin/Rover Montego 1.3 & 1.6 (84 - 94)	1066
Austin/MG/Rover Montego 2.0 (84 - 95)	1067
Mini (59 - 69)	0527
Mini (69 - Oct 96)	0646
Austin/Rover 2.0 litre Diesel Engine (86 - 93)	1857
BEDFORD	
Bedford CF (69 - 87)	0163
Bedford/Vauxhall Rascal & Suzuki Supercarry (86 - Oct 94)	3015
BMW	
BMW 316, 320 & 320i (4-cyl) (75 - Feb 83)	0276
BMW 320, 320i, 323i & 325i (6-cyl) (Oct 77 - Sept 87)	0815
BMW 3-Series (Apr 91 - 96)	3210
BMW 3- & 5-Series (sohc) (81 - 91)	1948
BMW 520i & 525e (Oct 81 - June 88)	1560
BMW 525, 528 & 528i (73 - Sept 81)	0632
CITROEN	
Citroën 2CV, Ami & Dyane (67 - 90)	0196
Citroën AX Petrol & Diesel (87 - 97)	3014
Citroën BX (83 - 94)	0908
Citroën C15 Van Petrol & Diesel (89 - Oct 98)	3509
Citroën CX (75 - 88)	0528
Citroën Saxo Petrol & Diesel (96 - 98)	3506
Citroën Visa (79 - 88)	0620
Citroën Xantia Petrol & Diesel (93 - 98)	3082
Citroën XM Petrol & Diesel (89 - 98)	3451
Citroën ZX Diesel (91 - 93)	1922
Citroën ZX Petrol (91 - 94)	1881
Citroën 1.7 & 1.9 litre Diesel Engine (84 - 96)	1379
COLT	
Colt/Mitsubishi 1200, 1250 & 1400 (79 - May 84)	0600
FIAT	
Fiat 126 (73 - 87)	0305
Fiat 127 (71 - 83)	0193
Fiat 500 (57 - 73)	0090
Fiat Cinquecento (93 - 98)	3501
Fiat Panda (81 - 95)	0793
Fiat Punto Petrol & Diesel (94 - 99)	3251
Fiat Regata (84 - 88)	1167
Fiat Tipo (88 - 91)	1625
Fiat Uno (83 - 95)	0923
Fiat X1/9 (74 - 89)	0273

Title	Book No.
FORD	
Ford Capri II (& III) 1.6 & 2.0 (74 - 87)	0283
Ford Capri II (& III) 2.8 & 3.0 (74 - 87)	1309
Ford Cortina Mk IV (& V) 1.6 & 2.0 (76 - 83)	0343
Ford Escort (75 - Aug 80)	0280
Ford Escort (Sept 80 - Sept 90)	0686
Ford Escort & Orion (Sept 90 - 97)	1737
Ford Escort Mk II Mexico, RS 1600 & RS 2000 (75 - 80)	0735
Ford Fiesta (76 - Aug 83)	0334
Ford Fiesta (Aug 83 - Feb 89)	1030
Ford Fiesta (Feb 89 - Oct 95)	1595
Ford Fiesta Petrol & Diesel (Oct 95 - 97)	3397
Ford Granada (Sept 77 - Feb 85)	0481
Ford Granada & Scorpio (Mar 85 - 94)	1245
Ford Ka (96 - 99)	3570
Ford Mondeo Petrol (93 - 99)	1923
Ford Mondeo Diesel (93 - 96)	3465
Ford Orion (83 - Sept 90)	1009
Ford Sierra 4 cyl. (82 - 93)	0903
Ford Sierra V6 (82 - 91)	0904
Ford Transit Petrol (Mk 2) (78 - Jan 86)	0719
Ford Transit Petrol (Mk 3) (Feb 86 - 89)	1468
Ford Transit Diesel (Feb 86 - 99)	3019
Ford 1.6 & 1.8 litre Diesel Engine (84 - 96)	1172
Ford 2.1, 2.3 & 2.5 litre Diesel Engine (77 - 90)	1606
FREIGHT ROVER	
Freight Rover Sherpa (74 - 87)	0463
HILLMAN	
Hillman Avenger (70 - 82)	0037
HONDA	
Honda Accord (76 - Feb 84)	0351
Honda Accord (Feb 84 - Oct 85)	1177
Honda Civic (Feb 84 - Oct 87)	1226
Honda Civic (Nov 91 - 96)	3199
HYUNDAI	
Hyundai Pony (85 - 94)	3398
JAGUAR	
Jaguar E Type (61 - 72)	0140
Jaguar MkI & II, 240 & 340 (55 - 69)	0098
Jaguar XJ6, XJ & Sovereign; Daimler Sovereign (68 - Oct 86)	0242
Jaguar XJ6 & Sovereign (Oct 86 - Sept 94)	3261
Jaguar XJ12, XJS & Sovereign; Daimler Double Six (72 - 88)	0478
JEEP	
Jeep Cherokee Petrol (93 - 96)	1943
LADA	
Lada 1200, 1300, 1500 & 1600 (74 - 91)	0413
Lada Samara (87 - 91)	1610
LAND ROVER	
Land Rover 90, 110 & Defender Diesel (83 - 95)	3017
Land Rover Discovery Diesel (89 - 95)	3016
Land Rover Series IIA & III Diesel (58 - 85)	0529
Land Rover Series II, IIA & III Petrol (58 - 85)	0314
MAZDA	
Mazda 323 (Mar 81 - Oct 89)	1608
Mazda 323 (Oct 89 - 98)	3455

Title	Book No.
Mazda 626 (May 83 - Sept 87)	0929
Mazda B-1600, B-1800 & B-2000 Pick-up (72 - 88)	0267
MERCEDES-BENZ	
Mercedes-Benz 190, 190E & 190D Petrol & Diesel (83 - 93)	3450
Mercedes-Benz 200, 240, 300 Diesel (Oct 76 - 85)	1114
Mercedes-Benz 250 & 280 (68 - 72)	0346
Mercedes-Benz 250 & 280 (123 Series) (Oct 76 - 84)	0677
Mercedes-Benz 124 Series (85 - Aug 93)	3253
MG	
MGB (62 - 80)	0111
MG Midget & AH Sprite (58 - 80)	0265
MITSUBISHI	
Mitsubishi Shogun & L200 Pick-Ups (83 - 94)	1944
MORRIS	
Morris Ital 1.3 (80 - 84)	0705
Morris Minor 1000 (56 - 71)	0024
NISSAN	
Nissan Bluebird (May 84 - Mar 86)	1223
Nissan Bluebird (Mar 86 - 90)	1473
Nissan Cherry (Sept 82 - 86)	1031
Nissan Micra (83 - Jan 93)	0931
Nissan Micra (93 - 99)	3254
Nissan Primera (90 - Oct 96)	1851
Nissan Stanza (82 - 86)	0824
Nissan Sunny (May 82 - Oct 86)	0895
Nissan Sunny (Oct 86 - Mar 91)	1378
Nissan Sunny (Apr 91 - 95)	3219
OPEL	
Opel Ascona & Manta (B Series) (Sept 75 - 88)	0316
Opel Ascona (81 - 88) (Not available in UK see Vauxhall Cavalier 0812)	3215
Opel Astra (Oct 91 - Feb 98) (Not available in UK see Vauxhall Astra 1832)	3156
Opel Calibra (90 - 98) see Vauxhall/Opel Calibra Book No. 3502	
Opel Corsa (83 - Mar 93) (Not available in UK see Vauxhall Nova 0909)	3160
Opel Corsa (Mar 93 - 97) (Not available in UK see Vauxhall Corsa 1985)	3159
Opel Frontera Petrol & Diesel (91 - 98) see Vauxhall/Opel Frontera Book No. 3454	
Opel Kadett (Nov 79 - Oct 84)	0634
Opel Kadett (Oct 84 - Oct 91) (Not available in UK see Vauxhall Astra & Belmont 1136)	3196
Opel Omega & Senator (86 - 94) (Not available in UK see Vauxhall Carlton & Senator 1469)	3157
Opel Omega (94 - 99) (See Vauxhall/Opel Omega Book No. 3510)	
Opel Rekord (Feb 78 - Oct 86)	0543
Opel Vectra (Oct 88 - Oct 95) (Not available in UK see Vauxhall Cavalier 1570)	3158
Opel Vectra Petrol & Diesel (95 - 98) (Not available in UK see Vauxhall Vectra 3396)	3523

Title	Book No.
PEUGEOT	
Peugeot 106 Petrol & Diesel (91 - 98)	1882
Peugeot 205 (83 - 95)	0932
Peugeot 305 (78 - 89)	0538
Peugeot 306 Petrol & Diesel (93 - 99)	3073
Peugeot 309 (86 - 93)	1266
Peugeot 405 Petrol (88 - 96)	1559
Peugeot 405 Diesel (88 - 96)	3198
Peugeot 406 Petrol & Diesel (96 - 97)	3394
Peugeot 505 (79 - 89)	0762
Peugeot 1.7/1.8 & 1.9 litre Diesel Engine (82 - 96)	0950
Peugeot 2.0, 2.1, 2.3 & 2.5 litre Diesel Engines (74 - 90)	1607
PORSCHE	
Porsche 911 (65 - 85)	0264
Porsche 924 & 924 Turbo (76 - 85)	0397
PROTON	
Proton (89 - 97)	3255
RANGE ROVER	
Range Rover V8 (70 - Oct 92)	0606
RELIANT	
Reliant Robin & Kitten (73 - 83)	0436
RENAULT	
Renault 5 (Feb 85 - 96)	1219
Renault 9 & 11 (82 - 89)	0822
Renault 18 (79 - 86)	0598
Renault 19 Petrol (89 - 94)	1646
Renault 19 Diesel (89 - 95)	1946
Renault 21 (86 - 94)	1397
Renault 25 (84 - 92)	1228
Renault Clio Petrol (91 - May 98)	1853
Renault Clio Diesel (91 - June 96)	3031
Renault Espace Petrol & Diesel (85 - 96)	3197
Renault Laguna Petrol & Diesel (94 - 96)	3252
Renault Mégane & Scénic Petrol & Diesel (96 - 98)	3395
ROVER	
Rover 213 & 216 (84 - 89)	1116
Rover 214 & 414 (89 - 96)	1689
Rover 216 & 416 (89 - 96)	1830
Rover 211, 214, 216, 218 & 220 Petrol & Diesel (Dec 95 - 98)	3399
Rover 414, 416 & 420 Petrol & Diesel (May 95 - 98)	3453
Rover 618, 620 & 623 (93 - 97)	3257
Rover 820, 825 & 827 (86 - 95)	1380
Rover 3500 (76 - 87)	0365
Rover Metro, 111 & 114 (May 90 - 96)	1711
SAAB	
Saab 90, 99 & 900 (79 - Oct 93)	0765
Saab 900 (Oct 93 - 98)	3512
Saab 9000 (4-cyl) (85 - 95)	1686
SEAT	
Seat Ibiza & Cordoba Petrol & Diesel (Oct 93 - 99)	3571
Seat Ibiza & Malaga (85 - 92)	1609

Title	Book No.
SKODA	
Skoda Estelle (77 - 89)	0604
Skoda Favorit (89 - 96)	1801
Skoda Felicia Petrol & Diesel (95 - 99)	3505
SUBARU	
Subaru 1600 & 1800 (Nov 79 - 90)	0995
SUZUKI	
Suzuki SJ Series, Samurai & Vitara (4-cyl) (82 - 97)	1942
Suzuki Supercarry (86 - Oct 94)	3015
TALBOT	
Talbot Alpine, Solara, Minx & Rapier (75 - 86)	0337
Talbot Horizon (78 - 86)	0473
Talbot Samba (82 - 86)	0823
TOYOTA	
Toyota Carina E (May 92 - 97)	3256
Toyota Corolla (Sept 83 - Sept 87)	1024
Toyota Corolla (80 - 85)	0683
Toyota Corolla (Sept 87 - Aug 92)	1683
Toyota Corolla (Aug 92 - 97)	3259
Toyota Hi-Ace & Hi-Lux (69 - Oct 83)	0304
TRIUMPH	
Triumph Acclaim (81 - 84)	0792
Triumph GT6 & Vitesse (62 - 74)	0112
Triumph Spitfire (62 - 81)	0113
Triumph Stag (70 - 78)	0441
Triumph TR7 (75 - 82)	0322
VAUXHALL	
Vauxhall Astra (80 - Oct 84)	0635
Vauxhall Astra & Belmont (Oct 84 - Oct 91)	1136
Vauxhall Astra (Oct 91 - Feb 98)	1832
Vauxhall/Opel Calibra (90 - 98)	3502
Vauxhall Carlton (Oct 78 - Oct 86)	0480
Vauxhall Carlton & Senator (Nov 86 - 94)	1469
Vauxhall Cavalier 1600, 1900 & 2000 (75 - July 81)	0315
Vauxhall Cavalier (81 - Oct 88)	0812
Vauxhall Cavalier (Oct 88 - 95)	1570
Vauxhall Chevette (75 - 84)	0285
Vauxhall Corsa (Mar 93 - 97)	1985
Vauxhall/Opel Frontera Petrol & Diesel (91 - Sept 98)	3454
Vauxhall Nova (83 - 93)	0909
Vauxhall/Opel Omega (94 - 99)	3510
Vauxhall Vectra Petrol & Diesel (95 - 98)	3396
Vauxhall/Opel 1.5, 1.6 & 1.7 litre Diesel Engine (82 - 96)	1222
VOLKSWAGEN	
VW Beetle 1200 (54 - 77)	0036
VW Beetle 1300 & 1500 (65 - 75)	0039
VW Beetle 1302 & 1302S (70 - 72)	0110
VW Beetle 1303, 1303S & GT (72 - 75)	0159
VW Golf & Jetta Mk 1 1.1 & 1.3 (74 - 84)	0716
VW Golf, Jetta & Scirocco Mk 1 1.5, 1.6 & 1.8 (74 - 84)	0726
VW Golf & Jetta Mk 1 Diesel (78 - 84)	0451
VW Golf & Jetta Mk 2 (Mar 84 - Feb 92)	1081

Title	Book No.
VW Golf & Vento Petrol & Diesel (Feb 92 - 96)	3097
VW LT vans & light trucks (76 - 87)	0637
VW Passat & Santana (Sept 81 - May 88)	0814
VW Passat Petrol & Diesel (May 88 - 96)	3498
VW Polo & Derby (76 - Jan 82)	0335
VW Polo (82 - Oct 90)	0813
VW Polo (Nov 90 - Aug 94)	3245
VW Polo Hatchback Petrol & Diesel (94 - 98)	3500
VW Scirocco (82 - 90)	1224
VW Transporter 1600 (68 - 79)	0082
VW Transporter 1700, 1800 & 2000 (72 - 79)	0226
VW Transporter (air-cooled) (79 - 82)	0638
VW Transporter (water-cooled) (82 - 90)	3452
VOLVO	
Volvo 142, 144 & 145 (66 - 74)	0129
Volvo 240 Series (74 - 93)	0270
Volvo 262, 264 & 260/265 (75 - 85)	0400
Volvo 340, 343, 345 & 360 (76 - 91)	0715
Volvo 440, 460 & 480 (87 - 97)	1691
Volvo 740 & 760 (82 - 91)	1258
Volvo 850 (92 - 96)	3260
Volvo 940 (90 - 96)	3249
Volvo S40 & V40 (96 - 99)	3569
Volvo S70, C70 & V70 (96 - 99)	3573
YUGO/ZASTAVA	
Yugo/Zastava (81 - 90)	1453
AUTOMOTIVE TECHBOOKS	
Automotive Brake Manual	3050
Automotive Carburettor Manual	3288
Automotive Diagnostic Fault Codes Manual	3472
Automotive Diesel Engine Service Guide	3286
Automotive Disc Brake Manual	3542
Automotive Electrical and Electronic Systems Manual	3049
Automotive Engine Management and Fuel Injection Systems Manual	3344
Automotive Gearbox Overhaul Manual	3473
Automotive Service Summaries Manual	3475
Automotive Timing Belt Manual - Ford	3474
Automotive Timing Belts Manual - Austin/Rover	3549
Automotive Timing Belts Manual - Peugeot/Citroën	3568
Automotive Timing Belt Manual - Vauxhall/Opel	3577
Automotive Welding Manual	3053
In-Car Entertainment Manual (3rd Edition)	3363
OTHER TITLES	
Automotive Fuel Injection Systems	9755
Car Bodywork Repair Manual (2nd Edition)	9864
Caravan Manual (2nd Edition)	9894
Motorcaravan Manual, The	L7322
Small Engine Repair Manual	1755
SU Carburettors	0299
Weber Carburettors (to 79)	0393

CL08.09/99

Preserving Our Motoring Heritage

< The Model J Duesenberg Derham Tourster. Only eight of these magnificent cars were ever built – this is the only example to be found outside the United States of America

Almost every car you've ever loved, loathed or desired is gathered under one roof at the Haynes Motor Museum. Over 300 immaculately presented cars and motorbikes represent every aspect of our motoring heritage, from elegant reminders of bygone days, such as the superb Model J Duesenberg to curiosities like the bug-eyed BMW Isetta. There are also many old friends and flames. Perhaps you remember the 1959 Ford Popular that you did your courting in? The magnificent 'Red Collection' is a spectacle of classic sports cars including AC, Alfa Romeo, Austin Healey, Ferrari, Lamborghini, Maserati, MG, Riley, Porsche and Triumph.

A Perfect Day Out

Each and every vehicle at the Haynes Motor Museum has played its part in the history and culture of Motoring. Today, they make a wonderful spectacle and a great day out for all the family. Bring the kids, bring Mum and Dad, but above all bring your camera to capture those golden memories for ever. You will also find an impressive array of motoring memorabilia, a comfortable 70 seat video cinema and one of the most extensive transport book shops in Britain. The Pit Stop Cafe serves everything from a cup of tea to wholesome, home-made meals or, if you prefer, you can enjoy the large picnic area nestled in the beautiful rural surroundings of Somerset.

John Haynes O.B.E., > Founder and Chairman of the museum at the wheel of a Haynes Light 12.

< Graham Hill's Lola Cosworth Formula 1 car next to a 1934 Riley Sports.

The Museum is situated on the A359 Yeovil to Frome road at Sparkford, just off the A303 in Somerset. It is about 40 miles south of Bristol, and 25 minutes drive from the M5 intersection at Taunton.
Open 9.30am - 5.30pm (10.00am - 4.00pm Winter) 7 days a week, *except Christmas Day, Boxing Day and New Years Day*
Special rates available for schools, coach parties and outings Charitable Trust No. 292048